GENRE, MYTH, AND CONVENTION
IN THE FRENCH CINEMA, 1929–1939

GENRE, MYTH, AND CONVENTION IN THE

French Cinema

1929–1939

COLIN CRISP

INDIANA
University Press

This book is a publication of

Indiana University Press
601 North Morton Street
Bloomington, IN 47404-3797 USA

http://iupress.indiana.edu

Telephone orders   800-842-6796
Fax orders   812-855-7931
Orders by e-mail   iuporder@indiana.edu

The paper used in this publication meets the minimum
requirements of American National Standard for Information
Sciences—Permanence of Paper for Printed Library Materials,
ANSI Z39.48-1984.

Manufactured in the United States of America

Library of Congress Cataloging-in-Publication Data

Crisp, C. G.
  Genre, myth, and convention in the French cinema, 1929–1939 / Colin
Crisp.
    p. cm.
A viewer's guide [to 200 or so films]: p.
Filmography, 1929–1939: p.
Includes bibliographical references (p.) and index.
  ISBN 0-253-34072-1 (alk. paper) — ISBN 0-253-21516-1 (pbk. : alk.
paper)
  1. Motion pictures—France—History. 2. Film genres—France. I.
Title.
  PN1993.5.F7 C785 2002
  791.43'0944—dc21

                                    2002001184

1 2 3 4 5 07 06 05 04 03 02

For Jane (again)

CONTENTS

ACKNOWLEDGMENTS

I would like to thank Griffith University for the period of leave and the initial funding which allowed me to undertake this disconcertingly large project, and the Australian Research Council for the subsequent funding which allowed me to complete it. An earlier version of chapter 8 was given as a paper at the Film and History Conference in Canberra in 1995, while some aspects of chapter 9 were covered at a conference, "Cinema of the Occupation," at Rutgers University in November 1996.

I am also grateful to the Bibliothèque de l'Arsenal and the BiFi in Paris for the use of their resources, and most particularly to the IDHEC library out of which the BiFi evolved: it had a card index system which, confronted by computerized equivalents, I remember with nostalgic affection and not a little longing.

INTRODUCTION

Most books which deal with the classic French cinema avoid or minimize the topic of genre and focus on individual films or on directors. There have been study guides to *Les Enfants du paradis, Le Jour se lève, nous la liberté,* and *La Règle du jeu.* Avant-Scène Cinéma has reprinted the scenarios of dozens of films, from *Pepe le Moko* to *Les Visiteurs du soir, Le Ciel est à vous, Les Dernières Vacances, Toni, Le Corbeau, L'Opéra de quat'sous, Le Passage du Rhin, Monsieur Ripois, La Grande Illusion,* and *Jeux interdits.* But however well these texts may be introduced, the focus on a single film precludes any adequate explanation of the form and content of the work, let alone the fact that it should have emerged from a production system which stifled so many others at birth.

Likewise, the focus on directors such as Renoir, Carné, Grémillon, Clouzot, Duvivier, and Vigo, which has motivated the production of many other books on the classic French cinema, can never aspire to any very convincing explanatory power, since to regard the director (or, for that matter, such scriptwriters as Prévert, Aurenche, Bost, Spaak, Sigurd, and Jeanson) as the point of origin of such films is to ignore the vast cultural repertoire on which they were drawing, and the often intense political and industrial constraints on their ability to draw freely on that repertoire, not to mention the various types of formal or informal "training" that they had had, which led them to draw on one rather than another sector of the available repertoire.

Finally, the ideological orientation of many researchers has led them to focus on the dramatic conditions experienced by the French cinema during the war years, analyzing the extent to which the films produced then were or were not politically correct, and this in turn has led to a focus, within the thirties, on those fascinating but largely anomalous films that can be more or less directly related to the Popular Front. The idea that the period from 1930 to 1945 formed a block, and that the cinema of Vichy was already present in the popular cinema of 1935, has been put forward by a number of critics[1] and is explicit in the title of Garçon's book *De Blum à Pétain.*[2] Yet even if one extends this "pre-Vichy" cinema to include all the films generally categorized as "poetic realist," as Geneviève Sellier has rightly pointed out, one is talking about "an insignificant proportion of the production of the time, and hardly one representative of the tastes of the movie-going public."[3]

Most studies of the cinematic scene are happy to ignore these problems, since they take as their point of departure a canonic and very limited range of films and a mythic commitment to individual creativity, or at least they are targeted at a readership which has learned to take these as its point of departure. The present study focuses neither on "the great directors" nor on "the great social and political movements." Rather, it constitutes one stage of an attempt to provide a more adequate explanatory model for the existence and nature of a national cinema, based on the triple concepts of social system, industrial system, and textual system. My previous book in the series, *The Classic French Cinema 1930–1960*,[4] looked at the industrial structure and mode of production of the French cinema during those three decades in the light of social, political, and economic conditions—looked, that is, at the industrial system in the light of the socio-economic system. The present volume, and its successor dealing with the period 1940–60, aims to outline the textual system which the filmmakers of the time drew on and, in turn, constructed in the course of their filmmaking activities. By "textual system," I mean simply the sum total of the three thousand or so films produced in France and/or regarded by French audiences as French films between 1930 and 1960, considered as one single global text, with overlapping and recurrent narratives, recurrent yet evolving characters and settings, established yet developing technical practices, and arising from all these a recognizably distinct array of thematic material.

In one very important respect, a detailed study of that textual system will forever be impossible, since a large number of the films produced during the thirty-year period have disappeared, and many of the rest are difficult or impossible to access. This problem is particularly acute in dealing with the decade of the thirties, for which period Raymond Borde estimated that some 70 percent of films had disappeared. My own research would tend to suggest that no more than 10 percent are currently available from the early thirties, but over 30 percent and perhaps as many as 40 percent after 1934. There may be a significantly greater number hidden away in various archives, since in a 1986 afterword Jeancolas mentions a survey undertaken by the seven principal French archives which suggested that an astonishing 76 percent of 1930s French feature films still existed, and perhaps even 80 percent.[5] Nevertheless, the great bulk of these are not available to researchers.

Despite this lack of primary material, which constitutes a major obstacle, the films that are available provide a sufficient body of work for generalizations concerning recurrent story lines, characters, technical effects, motifs, and themes to have statistical validity, especially when supplemented by contemporary plot summaries and reviews of the missing films.

It is on this basis that the present study aims to analyze the textual web of interrelated material constituted by the thirteen hundred films produced in the thirties.

To describe the textual system of the classic French cinema as a "system" is already to imply a significant level of conventionality within it. Indeed, many elements within the films, at the level of plot, character, iconography, and technical practices, were in some sense well known to the filmmakers and spectators of the time, and whenever they appeared within a given film they were felt to have a significance broader than their simple visual presence. Tramp figures appeared so frequently in plots in which bourgeois households were disrupted that they came to stand for the subversion of established social rules, for freedom, and even for anarchy. Orphans, or twins, or street singers, or aviators could not be introduced into a plot without arousing quite precise expectations, deriving from the numerous previous occasions on which the audience half-remembered seeing analogous figures in analogous situations. Such "agreed meanings" also clustered around settings such as tall, isolated apartment buildings, casinos and nightclubs, remote peasant communities, *guinguettes* (open-air restaurants) on the banks of the Marne, and outposts of empire. At some level, viewers recognized the significance of tilted frames, rapid editing, low-key lighting, and the various forms of background music, and they recognized them because those forms had been recurrently used with quite specific meanings in a number of films.

It was inevitable that some degree of conventionality should exist within the classic French cinema, if only because it borrowed so heavily, especially in the early days, from neighboring textual systems in which generic conventions had a long and often elaborately articulated history—conventions deriving from operetta, vaudeville, boulevard comedy, romantic and historical novels, melodrama, and the popular song, for example. Where these generic forms were borrowed wholesale, and particularly where theatrical and other texts were simply or largely transposed into film, the resultant classic cinema could itself be said to have a solid generic base. Yet it is widely recognized that at no time did the French cinema approach the level of formulaic conventionality manifested by Hollywood or, for that matter, other large-scale film industries. Although, on occasion, it transposed existing genres, it evolved relatively few of its own, and those few proved relatively unstable and short-lived. It was not that the French cinema "escaped" conventionality, but rather that such conventional elements as developed within it seldom coalesced into the *recurrent arrays of related conventions* that are necessary for a genre to begin to exist in the minds of filmmakers and spectators.

The reasons for this state of affairs were outlined in *The Classic French Cinema 1930–1960*.[6] The principal cause was the fragmented production system that characterized the industry of the time. Consisting of a multitude of mostly transitory and under-funded production firms, few of which owned their own means of production and none of which maintained a stable of stars or a corps of technical personnel on long-term contract, the classic cinema was ill adapted to replicate successes. By the time a film had proved to be a hit with the public, the production company might no longer exist, and even if it did it would inevitably have to begin almost from zero in its attempt to replicate that success, with a new writer, new technicians, and a new set of actors and actresses. Moreover, the production of French films from conception to screening took a longer time than in the U.S., so it was seldom less than a year before the producers could know whether the project was to be successful, and thus whether it might be worth replicating.

A closely related problem was the relative lack of a star system in France. The high degree of industrial organization needed to fabricate and sustain the mythic stereotypes essential to the very existence of such a system simply did not exist in France. Lacking an institutionalized publicity machine to feed the public the necessary "information" about a given actor, lacking the established channels through which the public could then express its admiration, lacking a secretariat to respond to the resultant "fan mail," lacking the stable of accommodating scenarists who might be instructed to develop a series of convergent scenarios for a given actor, and, indeed, unable to call on an actor at will, the production system had no way of responding promptly to an audience's enthusiasm for a given role or performance. The French film industry was frozen in an artisanal mode of production, whereas it is arguable that a full-fledged industrial capitalism such as existed in Hollywood is necessary to support the merchandising of actors central to a star system, and a fortiori to support the development of a genre system.

Yet if the generic framework of French cinema was relatively undeveloped, it was nevertheless quite common for production companies to appeal to generic labels in the marketing of their films, and even more common for industry publications such as *Cinéopse, La Cinématographie Française,* and *Le Film Français* to categorize the respective year's production according to those widely understood generic labels. Little study of these labels has been undertaken; yet they are important as an indication of the ways in which the industry conceptualized its product. Moreover, a breakdown of the changing proportions of texts categorized under the various generic labels can provide a first indication of the way in which the textual system was evolving over the decades in question.

Critics and commentators also referred to these generic categories when writing about films, though very few of them manifested any respect for films that could be seen to conform too readily to generic formulas. The chapter on genres (chapter 7) undertakes to survey all such books and articles written during the classic period, in order to identify the generic labels which critics recognized as relevant to the French cinema of the day and to summarize the views they expressed both about specific genres and about the concept of genre as a critical tool. Aspects of this survey cover the entire thirty-year period of the classic cinema, from 1930 to 1960, in order to better recognize patterns and trends, but it focuses more specifically on the thirties when discussing the genres that critics and commentators saw as typical of that decade.

A second way to arrive at an understanding of the textual system from outside the textual system itself is to look at the discourses surrounding the actors and actresses of the day. How were the leading actors of the day discussed, described, and categorized in popular film magazines? As an initial broad generalization, because the acting fraternity in the thirties moved freely between the cinema and the theater, it usually brought to its cinematic activities a range of pre-established categories within which it felt at home. These categories, or *emplois*—young lead, ingénue, servant, and so on—were all the more readily accepted into the cinema as they corresponded to the casting of the theatrical productions which for several years dominated the talkies. Gradually, however, the influence of theatrical categories waned, the recurrent social roles which they served to characterize began to dissolve, and ready-made categorizations fell into disrepute under the influence of the myth of the psychological, self-determined individual.[7]

Nevertheless, it is demonstrably the case that mythic character types continued to exist and to evolve throughout the thirties. The evidence lies in the articles published in fan magazines, such as gossip columns, film reviews, snippets of information about the stars' activities, and occasional more extended accounts of the life of a particular actor. Articles such as these construct the actors and actresses in clearly differentiated ways over the years, reflecting, for the most part in a totally unselfconscious way, the larger preoccupations of the time and the related forms of fantasized identity that spectators wished to see attributed to their screen heroes and heroines. These various discourses woven around actors provide, then, a further indication of the forms of characterization that one might expect to find in the textual system of the day, and the way those forms of characterization might evolve. For the discourses, of course, are not stable. To take an extreme instance, a radically different set of fantasies gets woven around the emergent stars of the fifties from the more established *emplois* and traditional social roles that were regularly attributed to their equivalents in the early thirties. The later set are more oriented toward the new audiences of the fifties, and particularly toward a younger generation that is more financially independent and more inclined to define itself against its parents, encouraged by an emergent neo-capitalism toward a "revolutionary" morale of sensual self-gratification that would constitute the young as appropriate citizens of the coming consumer society. As a first step toward charting the evolution of these discourses over the whole thirty-year period, chapter 8 looks at the principal discourses surrounding stars in the thirties.

A third way of charting the evolution of the textual system is to identify the most popular films of each year, and thus to chart the evolution of popular taste as expressed through entries and box-office success. The crucial questions are: "Which films were most popular, which textual elements recurred most frequently in them, and what satisfactions were those elements providing for the audiences?" The first step in the process of identifying the most popular films of the classic period has been taken for us by contemporary researchers in the Centre National de la Cinématographie, who from 1948 on published data that were reproduced in industry journals such as *La Cinématographie Française* and *Le Film Français* concerning entries and earnings for first-release films in Paris and the provinces. Unfortunately, no equivalent data exist for the years prior to 1948, because various vested interests saw to it that they remained confidential, so the results arrived at in the present volume relating specifically to the thirties are the product of a relentless scanning of the weekly film programs of Paris, supplemented by some less reliable indicators of box-office success which appeared in more discursive and subjective form or in unsystematic local and regional surveys. One might be justified in asking whether data based primarily on Paris box-office figures are really the most reliable indicator of a film's national popularity, since (where they exist) data concerning the long-term nationwide success of a given film often modify or radically contradict any conclusions one might be tempted to draw on the basis of Parisian data. These factors are discussed at the end of the chapter on box-office success in the thirties (chapter 9).

All such ancillary institutional data external to the textual system which help us to track the evolution of that system must be secondary to an analysis of the system itself. The chapters dealing with external indicators are to be found in the second part of the present book, while part 1 looks at the textual system itself. Together, the two parts aim to provide an understanding of the extent to which genre, stereotype, and convention were present, and were recognized as being present, in the classic French cinema of the thirties. They thus provide an indication of the communal repertoire of characters, stories, and settings on which filmmakers were drawing at any given moment. The reasons for undertaking such a study are many, but two predominate. First, a knowledge of the repertoire on which films were drawing can contribute to a demystification of production, by rendering a little more translucent the process of "creativity" that went into the composition of each film. This process is commonly mythologized, within the romantic approach to literature, music, painting, and, more recently, filmmaking, as an essentially incomprehensible and even magical process, originating in a special talent of the "author" (composer, writer, painter, director) that is commonly called genius. Often regarded as innate and intuitive, this talent is seen as expressing itself spontaneously in the production of works of art.

A more matter-of-fact approach to the process of textual composition has recently seen the production of works of art in any medium as, at least in part, the product of a perfectly rational and comprehensible process of selection and assemblage, according to practices which allow for endless recombinations and modifications of given material. The "inventiveness" of the creative artist, that is, can be seen as subordinate to, and even dependent on, the conventional forms and practices of the day, in the use of which the artist is formally or informally trained. Even the ways of breaking the rules and conventions of the day are part of those conventions. In this sense, an awareness of the overall repertoire of settings, characters, and stories available at the time can render less singular the appearance of any one of them in a specific film. The aviator in *La Règle du jeu* thus becomes a textual commonplace, as do the fairground in *Quai des brumes* and the climactic siege in *Le Jour se lève*. To contextualize thus the process of production is not to reduce all films to a similar level of banality. There are always degrees of "inventiveness" among filmmakers—that is, a greater or lesser degree of skill in the manipulation of the material drawn from the filmic and other repertoires. Simply, the source of the material itself, and the procedures for manipulating it, can more readily be identified, as can the forms of "training" in these processes of selection and organization that the filmmakers have experienced.

A second reason for examining the evolution of the textual system is to achieve a better understanding not of production but of consumption. That subset of the global textual system which consists of each year's most popular films and of those containing the most frequently recurring conventions can stand in for the relatively weak genre system as a guide to the mythic aspirations of audiences. The connection between myth and genre has often been invoked. In the case of the Western, to take just one well-known example, Will Wright's book *Sixguns and Society* argues the case for any genre providing its audience with satisfactions analogous to those that the folktale provided in earlier days.[8] But whereas the folktale, designed for a relatively static feudal society, did not need to evolve noticeably over the centuries, the Western (like other contemporary genres) was designed for a society undergoing constant change. The needs of its citizens were themselves evolving, so the various fictional genres embodied in its cultural artifacts needed to evolve in order to accommodate those needs. Hence Wright's periodization of the Western according to the way it catered to the needs of the thirties, the forties, or the fifties.

But Wright, like Propp[9] in the case of the folktale, could readily isolate the recurrent structural elements of the genre in question, or at least that of the most popular Western films. When one works within a textual system resistant to the development of genres, it is the most widespread conventions and the most popular films, however diverse their apparent generic allegiance, that must constitute the primary evidence of mythic status. It is, therefore, narratives, characters, and settings which recur and evolve across the whole subsystem, and technical practices that become standardized and gradually change over the years which will provide the most useful information. Hence the decision to treat the textual system as a whole, and more particularly the subset of the textual system constituted by its most popular films, in the same way as other critics have approached more well-established and widely recognized genres.

It is, then, with a number of significant reservations but an even stronger belief in the worth of the task that I have set out to describe the repertoire of the first decade of the French classic cinema, both in itself and as seen from the vantage point of ancillary textual systems such as fan magazines, industry journals, and critical commentary. My aim is to chronicle the evolution of that repertoire, and thus to clarify aspects of the production and consumption of the films of the day. It could well be argued that the textual web thus described is arbitrarily limited to French films and commentary, when in fact any web of the sort defined here extends seamlessly across adjacent fictional media and adjacent national film systems. In particular, it could be argued that in order to identify what was mythic for the audiences of the day it would be desirable to analyze all the films that entered the French market during the thirties, particularly American films, since French audiences often rated them as highly as they did indigenous productions. This is a perfectly valid observation, but to implement such a course of action would have more than doubled the already onerous work required for the present study. For the moment, French production alone will form the object of analysis.

Despite this limitation, the approach can prove profitable. As an instance of the sort of new light that it might shed on an apparently well-known film, the following observations attempt to situate the opening scene of *La Règle du jeu* within the textual web of the classic French cinema by noting certain elements of the repertoire which it mobilizes. It should be said, first of all, that the film is based on elements of a more extended textual web, as Renoir was happy to acknowledge, since he borrowed the underlying narrative pattern from Alfred de Musset's *Les Caprices de Marianne*. The elements common to the two texts can be listed quite readily. There is a triangular relationship in which a dignitary's wife is importuned, unsuccessfully, by an ardent romantic lover. The lover's friend (in both cases named Octave) is willing to act as go-between, but his pleading on his friend's behalf makes it only too apparent that he also is fascinated by the dignitary's wife. That wife's commitment to her husband is undone by the husband's own inadvertence, with the result that she is willing to reconsider the importunate lover, or Octave, or indeed anyone. Her capricious behavior thus presents Octave with the possibility of a romantic liaison, but he nobly renounces it, sending his friend to the rendezvous in his guise. The friend is killed by the husband's underling.

Although this general schema is borrowed from de Musset, there are many other textual elements in the film which can be related to films or genres of the decade. This is particularly apparent in the opening scene, in which Jurieux, the aviator, is seen returning from a record-breaking flight to the acclamation of the people, only to undermine the celebratory nature of the occasion by allowing his personal disappointments to intrude on the reception. There are six points that I would like to make relating to intertextual conventions operating at this moment.

1. At a very general level, we can say that many films of the period opened or closed with such a scene, involving the **dramatic contrast between public celebration and private despair.** Some instances are well known—the ending of *Hôtel du Nord* (38.50) in which the character played by Jouvet, recognizing that his hope of escape with Renée to a better life "over there" is doomed, allows himself to be killed by a rival gangster—as it happens, amidst the general conviviality of Bastille Day—or the ending of *Les Enfants du paradis* (1943) in which Garance leaves Baptiste forever, carried away by the rejoicing carnival throng against which Baptiste struggles in vain. Similar incidents involving an ironic contrast between public conviviality and private grief abound in films of the day. In *La Bête humaine* (38.12), Lantier's private tragedy is played out against a background of suave orchestral music emanating from the nearby ballroom. In *Paradis perdu* (39.69) the lovers part and die during a grand gala. In *La Duchesse de Langeais* (1941) Rontriveau despairingly searches for the duchess amidst the Mardi Gras celebrations. In *Au bonheur des dames* (1943) the distraught Baudu is crushed beneath the hooves of a delivery van's horses while inside the department store the employees are enjoying their annual ball. Similar ironic scenes occur in *La Petite Lise* (30.66), *La Chienne* (31.31), *Macadam* (1946), *Lumière d'été* (1942), *Sortilèges* (1944), and many others, both before and after *La Règle du jeu*.

   It would be futile to try to identify a single origin for such a common rhetorical figure of the time, which, aside from its general dramatic power, often (though not always) served to represent the people as a source of vitality—the only true source—but at the same time as individually doomed to a joyless destiny.

2. More specifically, this scene mobilizes a particular form of celebratory occasion—**the arrival of the popular hero.** This was another common element of the popular mythology of the thirties and forties. Standard codings of such an event include darkness, a chaos of half-glimpsed shapes, a continuous din of excited acclamation, surging throngs, news-hounds with flashbulbs, the desperate attempts of a thin line of policemen to contain the exuberance of the people, emotion outflanking law and order, and, quite commonly, a final act of violence that disrupts the occasion and undercuts the celebration.

In *Le Ciel est à vous* (1943), an aviatrix returns from setting a long-distance record: night, a crowd seething across the air field, glimpses of a shadowy plane, reporters surging forward, police unable to cope. . . . Yet, largely because of wartime restrictions on the production of morbid and debilitating films, *Le Ciel est à vous* seems bland alongside *La Règle du jeu,* lacking the bitter counterpoise of a private tragedy. In *Le Bonheur* (35.12), however, this too is present: Clara Stuart, the popular film star, arrives at the St. Lazare station; it is night, clouds of smoke, shafts of light, a surging throng of fans, the flashes of reporters' cameras; then, in the fictional version at the end, if not in the "real" events earlier, the sudden glimpse of a gun, a shot, and the film star collapses.

In a slightly different register, the people's hero in *De Mayerling à Sarajevo* (39.21) is the archduke, represented here as someone who has been able to out-maneuver the politicians and work for the good of the people. He arrives by train, and the platform is crowded with supporters: shouts, banners, a thin line of police, a shot, the archduke collapses.

The representation of such moments, of course, is not limited to the films of the day. The arrival of Maurice Chevalier from the U.S. is reported in fan magazines of the day in similar terms. He is "the object of indescribable emotion; the crowd massed behind the barricades jostles the forces of order and rushes forward to greet their idol and express their joy. . . . Emerging finally from this popular delirium, [Chevalier] is machine-gunned unremittingly by the flashbulbs of the reporters and cameramen."[10]

Louise Brooks's arrival the previous year to star in *Prix de beauté* (30.69) had been reported in similar terms in *Ciné Miroir*: "On the platform, crowded with a mass of people, [were] journalists, photographers, women bearing masses of flowers; if there had been policemen there, it would have seemed like the arrival of a monarch; feverishly the army of journalists and photographers charges along the platform, looking for her face [. . .]. Finally, there she is! Flowers rain down, photographers crowd around, flashbulbs explode."[11] The same magazine records an earlier visit by Chevalier, this time by ship: "Surging forward, the reporters crowd onto the monster's flanks, rush across the salon and up the stairs, to cluster triumphantly around their prodigal son: cries of joy, acclamations, unbridled emotion."[12]

If I cite these magazines and "real life" popular heroes, it is not at all with a view to validating *La Règle du jeu* as an authentic record of contemporary existence, but, on the contrary, because these fan magazines themselves constitute a textual system, closely related to the cinema's own textual system, catering to the same audience and the same needs. The elements of reality recounted time after time in them, such as the arrival of the popular hero, are as mythic as the elements (often the same elements) recurring in films of the day. It is self-evident that not all realities are recounted this insistently in any textual system, but only those elements in which readers can recognize aspects of their fantasy life, elements which render their social situation comprehensible and/or tolerable, and elements which can be used to construct or reaffirm their social identity.

3. More specifically still, what we have here is **the aviator as popular hero.** At the time, this was something of a commonplace. World War I had seen the flying ace come to prominence for his reputed courage, gallantry, and daredevil aerial acrobatics. The extension of this technology to civil aviation in the twenties had led to a rage for setting long-distance and speed records across oceans and across deserts. The importance of aviation as the contemporary archetype of technological progress ensured it a place in popular mythology. Writing in 1931 of the scripts commonly received by production companies for evaluation, one commentator singles out those involving "an almost lyrical taste for science, modern inventions, progress . . . the ship that sets sail, the airplane that crosses continents, the car that roars past, the locomotive that burns up the track—the public recognizes the grandeur of all that."[13]

St. Exupéry had articulated all this most effectively for more sophisticated audiences in *Courrier-Sud* (1929), *Vol de nuit* (1931), *Terre des hommes* (1939), and *Pilote de guerre* (1942): the aviator as modern knight, his horse and armor a plane and a leather flight jacket, pitting himself against the forces of nature—sandstorm, darkness, distance—isolated in the heavens high above humanity, but committed to the task of welding scattered communities into a single human family. This romantic adventurer, one of the principal figures of the man of action of the period, promoted not only by St. Exupéry but by Montherlant, Hemingway, and Malraux, had already been called upon by Renoir in *La Grande Illusion* (37.54), in which Gabin's Maréchal is a crashed pilot. Of course, Renoir himself was an aviator in World War I, crashing his plane and trailing a game leg around for the rest of his life, but this would have no significance for the present purpose had the aviator not already been established as a mythic figure, embodying popular fantasies and aspirations.

Like Renoir, but more spectacularly, Roland Toutain, who plays Jurieux, was an aviator noted for his daredevil exploits. The role of Jurieux, therefore, is picking up on discourses surrounding Toutain in fan magazines of the previous ten years, capitalizing on public knowledge about his exploits and his reckless personality.

This discourse was woven not only around Toutain, but around any star whose biography could be stretched to accommodate it—Murat, a pilot in World War I, André Roanne, "a flying ace," or Marie Bell, who owned her own plane and was reported to have made various attempts at long-distance records.

For the next twenty years, the aviator was to be one of the most common figures to appear in fan magazines (see chapter 8). In fact, in representing his popular hero as an aviator Renoir was picking up on a standard mythic figure of the thirties, who had already figured in such films as *Sous le casque de cuir* (31.126); *Brevet 95–75* (34.18); *Anne-Marie* (36.6), scripted by St. Exupéry; *Courrier sud* (36.28, from the St. Exupéry novel); *Avion de minuit* (38.7); and a host of reverential documentaries such as Pathé's *Les Routes aériennes* (1938) and *Les Acrobaties aériennes*. Subsequently, the aviator was to continue his career not only in *Le Ciel est à vous,* but in *Ceux du ciel* (1940), *Mermoz* (1942), *Retour de flamme* (1942), *Les Ailes blanches* (1942), *Aux yeux du souvenir* (1948), *Le Paradis des pilotes perdus* (1948), *Au grand balcon* (1949), which like *Courrier-Sud* recounts the exploits of the Aéropostale, Mermoz, and Didier Daurat, and *Dakota 308* (1950–51) in which Toutain again plays the pilot. So we can safely say that from 1930 to 1950 the figure of the aviator had a widely recognized role in French films. Looking back at the changes wrought to Louwyck's novel *Retour de flamme* between 1929, when it was published, and its screen production in 1942, Garçon notes the new focus on aviation, specifically, as the field of human endeavor foregrounded by the plot. Totally absent from the novel, it is the backbone of the 1942 film: "Between these two dates, a shock was felt that brought aviation to the forefront of contemporary concerns."[14] By 1950, however, advances in technology had been such as to deprive the aviator of the mythic status which they had previously helped to bestow on him. Now, he was no longer an aviator, but simply a pilot. This "banalization" of the role of aviator is apparent in the way it becomes available to "ordinary people" such as the housewife in *Le*

Ciel est à vous, or, more relevantly, its immediate predecessor, *Sur le plancher des vaches* (39.85), which was contemporary with Renoir's film and which cast Noël-Noël as an ordinary Frenchman who is privileged to gain access to the mythic status of aviator.

4. In terms of technical coding, the oppositions exploited in the opening scenes of *La Règle du jeu* are equally recognizable. It would be futile to detail the innumerable films in which different locales embodying the contrasting concepts of order and disorder were represented through the use of such **contrasting technical practices**. The influence of the expressionists on any representation of disorder in the early sound cinema has been more than adequately chronicled. The first five years of French sound film are full of underworld locations inhabited by what the French called apaches and their molls, attracting post-expressionist technical practices. The "street," notorious in German films of the twenties, was almost as common in French films of the early thirties, and its representation as a place of danger normally involved nighttime lighting, with looming shadows and odd camera angles and framings. Subsequently, the development of "poetic realism" focused attention on the signifying function of sets and lighting as a means to characterize threat, anguish, and despair.

   Pepe le Moko (36.99) provides an example of the use of these already conventionalized technical practices in its opening sequence. The opposing locations of police station and Kasbah attract, respectively, interior and exterior settings, open and constrained spaces, uniformly lit or mysterious, involving slow editing and fast, level camera and highly variable angles. Cumulatively, these contrasted technical practices serve to construct, respectively, a coherent site inhabited by the forces of law and order, and a bewildering site into which those forces are unable to penetrate. The analogy with *La Règle du jeu*, in which airfield and chateau are characterized, respectively, as places of disorienting confusion and of utmost clarity by analogous techniques—rapid camera movement contrasting with static observation, shadowy nighttime shapes contrasting with orderly interiors, a confused babble of voices contrasting with posed speech—is quite striking. Again this is not to say that Renoir was in any sense imitating Duvivier, which would be to personalize and particularize the relationship, but simply to note that it would have been normal and even conventional to consider opening a film with contrasting locations which established the conflict to be worked out in the narrative, and subsequently to mobilize available technical resources so as to characterize those locations in sharply opposed ways.

5. To return to a more general level, it would not be hard to show that this particular variant of the popular hero is often represented in the period

1929–39 as **a doomed figure,** coming into conflict with material forces too powerful to allow his continued existence. In *L'Argent* (36.8), it is the power of capital in the form of the banking establishment, rather than the rules of the social game; but in one way or another the forces of order, of a ritualized frozen and outdated social structure, or of a heartless political or economic materialism conspire to undermine the ideals of the romantic hero or even to bring about his death.

This general formulation of the situation is helpful in reminding us of the analogies between *La Règle du jeu* and other contemporary mythic representations of the outsider figure hounded by an implacable destiny, played, as often as not, by Jean Gabin. Rather than distorting *La Règle du jeu* in order to tout it as a prophetic film foreshadowing World War II (as if a prophet were needed to foresee that in 1939), we should see it as arising, like many films of the preceding decade, out of a climate of despair and disillusion generated by the depression and by the failure of the Popular Front. In killing off Jurieux, Renoir is better seen as recapitulating a well-known textual strategy involving the death of romantic ideals than as prophesying some violent future reality.

6. Finally, and still on a very general level, we should not forget that this initial scene of the film, as Renoir himself later acknowledged, presents us with **an outsider figure irrupting into a rigidly controlled and self-satisfied order.** The role of the outsider, of course, is to show up the hollowness of the said social order, to expose it to ridicule, to subvert and disrupt its routines and assumptions. It is not really surprising, under these circumstances, that he often suffers for his presumption.

But again we can note that this is far from an original narrative opening. Renoir had himself used it a few years earlier in *Boudu sauvé des eaux* (32.25, from a popular play by René Fauchois), just as Dostoevsky had routinely used a "holy fool" or "idiot," and just as, in the years preceding *La Règle du jeu,* such films as *La Terre qui meurt* (36.127) had used the marshlander Jean to show up the farmers' world, and *Cavalcade d'amour* (39.11) had used that old favorite, the troupe of traveling players, to call into question the values of a feudal world.

It is a strategy that has a long history in French literature: Montesquieu's Persians and Voltaire's extra-galactic creatures had a similar function, as had the Chinese visitors in Malraux's *La Tentation de l'Occident* (1926) and the multiple sets of outsiders developed by the surrealist Morand—Asians visiting London, Americans visiting Spain, and Turks visiting Norway—not to mention Camus's *L'Étranger* (1942). Always, the outsider's fundamental function is to denaturalize the ideology of the visited society, to distance the reader or viewer from the mores of that society, and thus to call into question the rules of the social game.[15]

So, rather than exclaiming over the creative genius displayed by Renoir in the opening scenes of *La Règle du jeu,* we might rather admire the way in which, in the process of composing the film, he and his associates drew on a number of very general elements, but also on a number of very precise elements, made available to him at the time by the current repertoires of the cinema and surrounding media. Our admiration for the film and for the filmmakers' achievements will be no less, but our understanding of the process of filmmaking and of the place of this specific film within the intertextual web of thirties cinema will be enormously increased. Moreover, if we do not proceed thus we are liable to be misled, by the disappearance of so many films contemporary with this one and by the canonic elevation of Renoir to the status of artist, into believing that his "genius" and "originality" extended far further than they did. He was, in fact, drawing on the repertoire provided to him by his own and previous ages, in this and other media, and was being judged by his audiences according as they recognized and appreciated what he was doing with that material. Rather than appealing to transcendent aesthetic criteria considered appropriate to works of art, this study aims to identify the criteria by which audiences of the day were judging Renoir and other filmmakers of the decade via generic patterns, contemporary commentaries, and box-office returns. It is worth noting that, despite the notorious and perhaps not entirely spontaneous protests of the audiences of the time, who were reputedly disconcerted by its mixture of modes, *La Règle du jeu* was far from unsuccessful by box-office criteria. It was bidding fair when the war interrupted its exclusive release to rate among the top third of films in a very successful year. Wherever relevant, the various chapters of this study, particularly those in part 1 dealing with the different types of filmic conventions, will return to this film in order to identify further elements of the contemporary repertoire which Renoir and his collaborators mobilized when transposing de Musset's play.

Of course, several other critics have explored a similar line of inquiry over the last few decades, or have focused on related aspects of the thirties cinema, not least Ginette Vincendeau, who has traced the Gabin myth through its main manifestations and has set the cinema of the Popular Front within a broader context of contemporary production;[16] Michèle Lagny, whose group undertook an extremely ambitious semiotic and structuralist exploration of typical generic patterns in the colonial and war genres, among others;[17] and Noël Burch and Geneviève Sellier, whose study of the distinctly odd array of gender relations developed in many wartime films traces the origin of these relations back to the cinema of the thirties.[18] Jeancolas took a more institutional approach in *15 ans d'années 30,* which is based, as its title suggests, on the proposition that the cinema of the war years forms a single block with that of the late thirties, and that the ideology of Vichy is already present in the cinema of 1935.[19] François Garçon took this observation a stage further in *De Blum à Pétain,* published the following year, proposing that the films of this period demonstrated French society of the time to have been, as Marc Ferro notes in the introduction, "ready, even predisposed in advance, so to speak, to adopt the Vichy program."[20] This emphasis on socio-political, or at least ideological, aspects of late-thirties cinema was at the heart of Geneviève Guillaume-Grimaud's work, which was also limited largely to the better-known political films of the time, despite the fact that these would have been almost unknown to contemporary audiences.[21]

It was perhaps the Cahiers de la Cinémathèque de Toulouse that first began the exploration continued here of the hidden bulk of thirties production when it published its 1977 volume *Le cinéma du sam'di soir.* To this was soon added Raymond Chirat's *Cinéma des années 30.*[22] While it would be impossible (and indeed undesirable) to ignore the achievements of these critics, in the present study I attempt to limit my focus to the views expressed by critics and commentators writing at the time the films appeared on such matters as genre, convention, stereotype, and myth, together with the views expressed by the spectators of the time on these same matters through the box office. The study is therefore at once more ambitious, in trying to take account of the total filmic and critical output of the thirties free from any subsequent critical interpretation, and also, necessarily (and as a result of this very ambition), somewhat less profound in its exploration of any one given set of conventions and stereotypes that it brings to the surface. Inevitably, however, it provides both supplementary evidence relating to the above-mentioned critics' commentaries and new evidence for further commentators to work on.

Part One

THIRTEEN HUNDRED FILMS

[W]hat is re-presented in representation is not directly reality itself but other representations. The analysis of images always needs to see how any given instance is embedded in a network of other instances.
—Richard Dyer, *The Matter of Images* (1993)

When you come to think about it, everything is an adaptation of something else. . . . Certain scenarios that are supposedly original in fact resemble any one of a thousand novels or ten thousand plays.
—Coissac (1929)

ONE

Identity: Reflecting on the Self

I n Part One of this study, we explore the thirteen hundred films produced during the thirties in order to see what mythic identities were embodied in them. The investigation has been organized as follows: the present chapter deals with films which explicitly foreground questions of identity in a thematic way, while subsequent chapters explore the different sub-types of identity, beginning with the most broad and communal forms (what it means to be human, to be French, to be male or female, to be middle class or working class, to be a parent or a child) and moving toward the more specific and personal (what it means to be a teenager, to be sensual or self-disciplined, to be a doctor, lawyer, engineer, or aviator, to be a success or failure, to be an intellectual). Inevitably, not all such identities are relevant to the films of the thirties, and we deal only with the mythic identities which recur sufficiently often to suggest that they were of importance to the filmmakers and audiences of the day. Part 1 closes as it opens, with a topic that provides an overview of these identities: "what it means to be an artist." In films which represent the nature of art and the artist, a certain reflexivity often incites the filmmakers to discuss the function of the films that they are producing and the relationship that those films establish between them and their public. In so doing, they occasionally debate, overtly or metaphorically, the role of the cinema as myth, and of the filmmaker as mythmaker.

1.1 TYPICAL IDENTITY NARRATIVES

A number of well-known films of the classic period will immediately spring to mind as dealing with the question of identity. In *Le Grand Jeu* (33.62), the protagonist tries for most of the film to decide whether the barmaid whom he meets in an Algerian village is the same person as the society woman who had been the cause of his disgrace. His ambivalence is echoed by the spectator's, since the two characters are played by the same actress, but another actress's voice is substituted for hers in one of the roles. The film also raises the question of identity in relation to all foreign legion films, in which a common theme is the abandonment of the protagonist's old and tainted identity in favor of a new start in a new environment. Who is Pierre's friend Nicholas? Does Mme Blanche know? Why is his photo in the newspaper that Pierre discovers in his belongings? We will never know, because "he has earned the right to be silent about his past." In a somewhat similar way, in *Hôtel du Nord* (38.50), the character played by Jouvet, in an attempt to put rival criminals off his track, has totally transformed his personality, becoming the antithesis of the person they had known. Other Carné films of the classic period were to explore questions of identity in no less overt a fashion. In *Les Visiteurs du soir,* the inhabitants of the chateau are faced with the task of recognizing as envoys of the devil the all-too-charming guests whom they take in. Their task is further complicated by the fact that one of the devil's ploys has been to send a female envoy in the guise of a male. In addition, at one point the devil exploits his ability to assume the appearance of one of his less conscientious envoys, in an attempt (alas, ineffectual) to corrupt the heroine. In *Les Enfants du paradis,* Jericho the second-hand-clothes seller, in his role as provider of costumes to the troupe, is effectively a seller of identities, which makes it all the more ironic that, much to his outrage, his own identity should be "stolen" by Baptiste for use in one of the mimes. That mime is watched by Frédéric, now a famous actor who, like many famous persons, prefers to conceal his identity when among the public. And, just after the mime, Garance encounters Lacenaire, who does not at first react to her greeting because he has assumed so many names and identities over time that he tends to lose track of them. As he remarks, insolently, to the Count's supercilious inquiry as to who he is, asking people "who they are" verges on the impertinent.

In *Le Crime de Monsieur Lange* (35.27), the evil Batala, who is believed to have died in a train accident, conceals his survival by appropriating the clothes and identity of a priest and reappears in a publishing community that is now thriving as a result of Lange's exploitation of his fantasized Arizona Jim persona. Even in *La Règle du jeu* (39.78), the climactic "accident" has the gamekeeper shooting Jurieux under the impression that he is shooting Octave, who has just lent Jurieux his coat. And of course, here as elsewhere, this standard narrative mechanism of farce—the loan or exchange of clothes, names, or identities, leading to "comic" incidents involving mistaken identity—conceals more serious questions about the nature of the poachers/rabbits that the gamekeeper is employed to eliminate.

Indeed, wherever one looks in the classic cinema, the question of identity looms large. Over 25 percent of plot summaries reveal identity to be central to the films of the thirties, and on closer analysis the proportion increases still further: of those I have viewed, another 30 percent mobilize one or more of the tropes listed in this chapter. One reason for the theme's pervasive influence is that it is closely associated with the notion of "acting," and thus with the notions of roles and sincerity. Characters who are accustomed to spinning a line in their role, say, of lover—for instance, in *Gueule d'amour* (37.57)—have inordinate difficulty in convincing the person they love that *this* time they are being sincere. Identity is also associated with the theme of free will and determination, as instanced most memorably in overt Jekyll and Hyde stories such as *Le Testament du Dr Cordelier* and many more oblique films involving split identities, or in *La Bête humaine* (38.12), in which a genetic fatality, momentarily dominated, proves in moments of stress impossible to control. In a number of interesting films, the question of identity is foregrounded via some narrative pretext such as illness, a road accident, or a wartime injury which results in memory loss, and a consequent quest to (re)discover who one really is.

If certain common thematic preoccupations tend to foreground questions of identity and the nature of the self, so do many generic formulas of the classic period, which was no doubt a principal cause of the popularity of those genres. Of course, most murder mysteries involve an investigation to determine the identity of the criminal, which is a far from trivial task since it involves discerning indexes of concealed guilt that are often obscure, and thus of discriminating between the guilty and the innocent in a world in which no one is entirely one or the other. The task is rendered appropriately difficult in that criminals tend to hide behind a public facade of respectability, and police officers tend to operate under cover. As Fleury remarks to the girl who is being used as bait to catch the murderer in *Pièges* (39.71), she seems to turn up in a number of places in an amazing array of different roles. Nobody is what he or she seems, but if there is one consistent factor in the genre it is a determined cynicism concerning the appearance of respectability.

Likewise, certain traditional mechanisms of melodrama—babies abandoned, stolen, substituted, or swapped at birth, or identical twins, or orphans—are also a means of articulating anxieties about identity, since they involve the relative importance of nature and of nurture in the development of the personality. But it is the comic genres that most frequently deploy narrative mechanisms foregrounding identity, relying for their effect on such procedures as mistaken identities, assumed identities, aristocrats pretending to be servants or swapping roles with their servants with amorous intent, people with the same name or appearance as one another, and people who have constructed a false or fictional identity for themselves, perhaps subsequently being trapped into living up to it. Finally, though they were never common in the French classic cinema, horror films, with their literal transfigurations of the self into something other, splitting of the self into doubles, and selling of the self to the devil, make explicit what is often only implicit in less generic films. But wherever they occur, be it within genre conventions or in "authored" films, the thematics of identity call into question easy assumptions about the self and its relationship to society, gender, class, and nation, if only often to replace them by equally facile assumptions.

As a general principle, there are four categories of narrative dealing with identity:

- Those in which characters actively conceal their identity for interested motives.
- Those in which characters involuntarily become someone or something else.
- Those in which characters are mistaken for someone else, thus getting drawn willy-nilly into a world of confused identities.
- Those in which characters construct fantasized identities, whether for themselves or as totally independent characters.

In the first category, the protagonist has agency and is thus in control of the situation to some degree, at least at first. Criminals may adopt the facade of a respectable identity, a famous personage may travel incognito, two individuals may exchange identities, or characters may disguise themselves as someone else, whether by way of masks, disguises, or disciplined transformations of their personality. The second category—of involuntary transformations—includes the horror transformations into werewolf, vampire, or other monster, Dr. Jekylls into Mr. Hydes, and the eugenic determination of a suppressed aspect of one's personality, but also those involuntary transformations due to memory loss or other traumatic event.

Of the first two categories, the former (in which X poses as Y) is by far the more common. Almost as common, however, is the third category, in which one character is mistaken for another. In the extreme, this type of story may be linked with the second category, as when doubles or, even more clearly, identical twins "doom" the protagonist to be forever defending himself or herself against imputations arising from the other's activities. In both cases, the confusion can become a narrative pretext for suggesting that, in some oblique way, X is not incorrectly mistaken for Y—there are indeed important aspects of Y in X. Finally, in the fourth category, blowhards and braggarts often find themselves trapped into living out the fictional identities that they have created around themselves, and the compulsive storyteller may find his or her self diffused among a number of equally fanciful invented selves. The resultant split or multiple personality is sometimes presented as psychotic (not infrequently when it is embodied in Le Vigan), and at other times as triumphant, as in the case of the chameleon trickster who cannot be pinned down. Almost as common, especially in "poetic" films, are fictional entities invented by characters as supports for their own identities. In the more banal instances, these personae may be invented relatives who serve as scapegoats for the protagonist's escapades, or they may verge on fairy folk, figuring the protagonist's fantasized escape from an intolerable reality. There is always a strong element of wish fulfillment associated with these fictions, especially in the case of fantasized doubles who dare to indulge the desires which the protagonist is physically, morally, or psychologically unable to explore. At the other end of the spectrum, genetic or, more commonly, social determination often takes the form of a set of mechanical creatures—clockwork dolls, puppets, robotic chess players, or simply mechanical musical devices—which bear witness to the relentless fatality impending over the characters.

Before considering any further the thematic implications of these questions of identity, we should acknowledge that they are articulated by a number of readily recognizable narrative mechanisms which have inherently pleasurable effects. This at once links the present topic to a number of others, and helps to explain why such topics were commonplace. As a narrative ploy, for instance, abandoned, stolen, or swapped babies lead to enigma narratives driven by such questions as "Who am I?" "Is she who she thinks she is?" "Whose son am I?" "By whom was he abandoned, and why?" Enigma mechanisms, in turn, lend themselves to a form of detective narrative in which the protagonist seeks out clues to help solve the mystery. An analogous set of enigmas can be generated by memory loss, as the recovering patient gradually pieces together clues to his or her earlier existence.

Such narratives normally place the spectators in a position of ignorance analogous to the protagonist's and allow them to explore and resolve the enigma along with the protagonist. Much of the pleasure is generated by curiosity progressively satisfied and by related identification mechanisms. Other texts, however, prefer the surprise effect of a series of stunning and unexpected revelations, more typical of melodrama than of the detective story: a character discovers to her astonishment, and to ours, that she is the daughter of a countess stolen at birth, that the man with whom she has fallen in love is the son of her boss, or is a crook/police officer in disguise, or that the elderly man whom she is resigned to marrying is in fact the father of the man she loves. Or we discover that the man with whom the queen has fallen in love is a revolutionary bent on overthrowing her; or that the heir to the throne whom the tramp resembles and has replaced has turned up again, so the tramp can return to his happy-go-lucky life.

Perhaps more common than mechanisms dependent on mutual ignorance are those which place the audience in a position of privileged knowledge: we know, though the characters don't, that she is not a common working girl but a countess/film-star/rich industrialist's daughter in disguise, and that he is not a "mere" mechanic but a famous composer/millionaire/baron, or the czar himself. We know, though she doesn't, that he is only pretending to be a crook/happily married man/assassin, because he knows that's what turns her on. We know, as the American tourists or slumming aristocrats don't, that these are only actors putting on a show of being thugs and whores to give the visitors a thrill. We know, as everyone else doesn't, that he is a famous tenor/politician/film star traveling incognito, that his young wife has gone to the ball not with an elegant male admirer but "merely" with her female cousin dressed as such, that the wife's supposed lover is in fact "merely" her father, and the husband's supposed mistress is "merely" his mother. In particular, we know that these supposed women are in fact unemployed men dressed as women to get a job in a female orchestra, or tramps dressed as women to get into the reception for a free meal, or a young admirer dressed as a maid-in-waiting to get into the duchess's bedchamber. It is at least partly from our superior knowledge that we derive pleasure, as we watch other, less knowledgeable creatures fall into ridiculous traps of their own devising.

When we share with the protagonist a knowledge about his or her identity that others refuse to accept, the result is often a drama in which the spectator's principal pleasure is in seeing wrongs righted: mistaken for a criminal because of some fortuitous similarity of name/appearance/voice, the protagonist finally proves himself innocent; disbelieved and reviled by the community, the famous tenor finally proves his identity by bursting into song; having nobly taken the blame for the legitimate son, the adopted son finally clears his name; having been despised and manipulated, the humble teacher turns the tables and proves himself an improbable master of manipulation.

In a more comic mode, the satisfaction of seeing the con man get his comeuppance produced numerous narratives in which the female secretary is passed off as the wife, until the wife herself unexpectedly returns; in which the waiter claims to be a prince, until the prince himself turns up; in which the nephew pretends to be his aunt, until the real aunt turns up; or in which the bandit adopts the identity and residence of an upright bourgeois, until the bourgeois unexpectedly returns home. These pleasures interact with the comic confusions arising from having two husbands, two wives, two aunts, two bankers, or two princes, whose entrances and exits intersect balletically.

Finally, an analogous form of audience satisfaction arises from seeing braggarts or hypocrites caught out in their own fantastic claims for themselves and having to try to live up to the mythic qualities and roles (aviator, explorer, racing driver, Tour de France cyclist) which they have appropriated. These satisfactions are compounded when the characters prove grotesquely inadequate to the task—the lover passed off as a singing teacher proves to have a far from exemplary voice, the tramp passed off as an interpreter and the window-dresser passed off as an American business colleague prove to have surprising linguistic inadequacies. The pleasure is almost as great when, against all odds, the comic inadequate finally, through the intervention of fate, wins the car race or the Tour de France.

An essential mechanism of these confusions of identity or assumed identities is that they involve extremes of one sort or another—extremes of wealth and position are exchanged for or disguised as extremes of poverty, as are extremes of class (noble and menial) or gender (vamp and soldier). The tramp has the same name as a millionaire, or is the double of a wealthy banker, the parish priest finds himself in military uniform, while on a desert isle the baron and the ship's stoker exchange roles. Sometimes, these diametric opposites are exploited purely for comic effect, but often there is a suggestion that a fundamental identity exists between, for example, the respectable mother and the chorus girl, or that what the prissy author is lacking is precisely the common touch which the new persona provides. But even to describe such narrative mechanisms and the pleasures they offer is to indicate the wealth of thematic material which they articulate, and which offers more specific pleasures of a mythic or ideological nature. This thematic material lies principally in the field of personal identity, social identity (class, career and wealth, status), and gender, though it also less directly brings into play racial and national stereotypes. These matters will be dealt with at greater length in their respective chapters, but recognizing the way in which they emerge from this central preoccupation with identity serves as a preliminary indication of their relative importance.

1.2 CLASS AND GENDER IN IDENTITY NARRATIVES

From the fairy tale, many thirties comedies inherit a wish-fulfillment happy ending whereby the loved one turns out to be someone of great wealth or high social status, often of the nobility. A rich countess may pretend to be a working girl (29.1), or a princess may travel incognito as a woman of the people (30.36); an exiled queen may hide her identity (30.55), a princess and an officer may pose, respectively, as a manicurist and a grocer's assistant, or the rich Lord Kingdale may pretend to be the poor Biscotte in order to accompany pretty Solange on a trip to the Côte d'Azur (31.98; see also 33.20). In all of these, the main function of this plot element is to set up a final delightful revelation for the protagonist who thought he or she was in love with a mere commoner. An archetypal example of this narrative pattern is provided by *Le Congrès s'amuse* (31.38). Christel, the humble working girl, accidentally becomes involved with a passing celebrity when the bouquet she hurls is thought to be a bomb. The relationship between the celebrity and Christel develops rapidly, until to her astonishment she discovers she is involved in a relationship with the czar of Russia himself. This allows for a standard revelation of male magnificence, which is from time to time throughout the film contrasted with her waif-like wonderment.

Identities are further "amusingly" confused by the fact that the czar has a stand-in, also played by Garat, to perform certain duties, and Christel is represented as not responding to the sexual chemistry of the stand-in in the least. Moreover, the czar mixes incognito with "the people" in order to conduct his affair with Christel. If only they realized who it was (!). Czars in particular are disposed to dream of wandering freely among their people, incognito (38.56); sometimes, for a brief moment, a czar can even become a simple lover out strolling with his girl.

Such poses and disguises suggest a residual fascination with and admiration for the aristocracy; yet this admiration is really common only in the sentimental comedy of the early thirties, or in the melodrama of substituted babies of the same years, in which an orphan is revealed—say, by a birthmark—to be the countess's daughter (32.50) or the duke's daughter (35.84) or the pasha's son (30s16). Instances from the late thirties are rare, though in *Mayerling* (36.77), the man she loves and believes to be a commoner turns out to be the archduke, while in *Place de la Concorde* (38.79) the chauffeur turns out to be a duke. Another way in which this fascination with a title is expressed is in narratives in which the poor and insignificant pose as counts or princes, seeing this as the most likely way to impress—a waiter passes himself off as a prince (33.69), a street singer as a baron (30.78), an elevator attendant who has won the lottery as a count (34.30), and a car saleswoman as a countess, to impress a mechanic (33.139), while a young Arab girl is passed off as a princess (35.92), and an actor pretends to be a prince (34.81; cf. 33.30).

The thirties fairytale does not rely solely on aristocratic titles, however; a millionaire or famous artist (film star, tenor, diva, even composer) will serve the same function, as will a bishop's son (30.75). Given the social context, it is not surprising that extremes of wealth should acquire intense significance. The fact that counts, countesses, millionaires, and film stars so often adopt the guise of, or exchange roles with, their secretary or accountant is no doubt due to the convenient proximity of characters holding those lowly positions, but it would also seem that the mythic roles of millionaire, film star, or famous singer were felt to be so powerful that no one could be expected to evaluate objectively the "person" behind them, so, as in legend, such mythic creatures tactfully veil their divinity behind a more human role before approaching any targeted mortal. In effect, they feel the need to test the sincerity of a potential relationship, given the near certainty that it would otherwise be tainted by the targeted mortal's desire for wealth or fame. Thus, a young millionaire hides behind a job as a barman (33.106) or swaps identities with his secretary to test the sincerity of the woman he has met (31.107), a millionaire and his servant involuntarily exchange roles (34.22), a rich American poses as his own secretary (35.60), a wealthy man takes the position of secretary to the woman he feels he could love (31.94), the man loved by the blind shepherdess turns out to be an American millionaire travelling incognito (37.92), and, in a slightly different register, a wealthy woman hides her wealth and becomes governess to the girl whom she feels needs looking after (37.66). From 1933 on, musicians adopt the same practice—a famous composer gets the job of servant to the woman he loves (33.126), a famous singer disguises himself as a gondolier (33.28), while others find true love by posing as humble working men (34.67; 38.58). Once assured of the sincerity of their lowborn or poor lover's affection, of course, they can cast off their disguise and complacently reveal to their dazzled partner their true identity.

Narratives such as these, which allow the revelation of great wealth or renown as a reward for true love, are paralleled by fantasies in which humble people are taken or pass, at least momentarily, for people of transcendent wealth or artistic ability. A clerk who has been unable to bank the day's takings (33.145) or who is the victim of a practical joke published in a newspaper (34.27) is taken for a millionaire; a taxi driver's daughter is mistaken for a millionaire's daughter (36.95); two fishermen pass themselves off as wealthy businessmen to win their girls, who in turn are pretending to be film stars (38.109). In some of these narratives, there is an implied critique of the wealth and status so ardently sought or so haphazardly acquired, but even narratives which seem to decry these mythic roles are often pandering to them obliquely: though a millionaire, he retains his humble day job as a waiter while living it up in the evening (30.65), or pretends to be his own secretary, to get a bit of peace and quiet (31.87), or adopts the identity of his accountant to go on a spree (36.137; 38.67). Renowned artists are likewise given to renouncing the hurly-burly of publicity and fame for "the simple life," perhaps leaving a double behind to take care of the shop (35.58).

It is noticeable that the role of millionaire in these fairytale scenarios is curiously devoid of commercial context. There is seldom any sense that the wealthy have actually earned their wealth by financial or industrial activities. Indeed, as we will see, involvement in commercial activity was more likely, in the thirties, to have extremely negative connotations, with bankers, financiers, and industrialists suffering the most consistently unfavorable representation. In this sense, the millionaire of early-thirties fairytales is close to the aristocrat in that he or she inherits a largely decontextualized and dehistoricized status. The same is true of "the boss" with whom the secretary or typist, in true "Mills and Boon" fashion, establishes an unwitting relationship while on holiday (31.42; 31.47).

There are, however, several recurrent narrative patterns which more seriously call into question the fairytale status of millionaires and princes. Frequently, having tasted the suspect pleasures of such positions due to a confusion of identity, the protagonist will ultimately reject them, returning to the simple life of ordinary working-class existence, or perhaps to that other mythic extreme of thirties existence, the open road. The elevator attendant who has won the lottery takes great pleasure in showing up the hypocrisy of the wealthy, to whom he has hitherto been invisible but who now court him assiduously; ultimately, though, sick of their unctuous ways, he opts to marry the humble seamstress who has been true to him (34.30). In Renoir's film, if not in the original play (32.25), Boudu, having tasted the delights of middle-class existence, opts to abandon it for a life on the open road, just as Charlot had done innumerable times in the twenties. In *Rothchild* (33.113), a tramp of that name exploits the fact in order to taste the life of high finance, only to return to the road at the end. Perhaps the most entertaining version of this theme is *Un soir de bombe* (35.117), in which a happy-go-lucky tramp, rendered amnesiac by an accident, is mistaken for a banker who has decamped under threat of blackmail. The tramp is installed in the banker's residence and proceeds to live it up for once in his life. He and his mate soon get bored with this existence, however, and hit the road again—though not before seeing the banker consigned to a lunatic asylum. Money and propriety combine to make life intolerable for the free spirits of the thirties—all you need is the open road and a good mate to stand by you. *À nous la liberté* (31.1) proposed a similar message very early in the decade.

The stand-in narrative, in which a commoner replaces a prominent public figure, is also often mobilized to call into question the qualities of the original incumbent, since the stand-in, with no training and often drawn from humble social position solely on the basis of resemblance, proves infinitely more competent as president, banker, government negotiator, or prince (34.97), often taking over the incumbent's wife or mistress as well as his position. A music-hall singer doubles for a banker, fooling the minister and even the banker's own wife (35.48); a street cleaner doubles for the president, to the people's evident satisfaction (34.77); a fairground girl doubles for the baroness, to the baron's evident pleasure (34.4). The number of such films appearing in 1934 is astonishing, and all that appear before or after are less striking. Many derive from the "understudy" narrative, in which the sickness of a leading actor, or singer, or jockey (etc.) provides the opportunity for the stand-in to succeed (e.g., 36.75; 30.67), or, less commonly, and later in the decade, to fail dismally, as in *La Fin du jour* (38.37). For instance, an actress abandons her role and is replaced by her stand-in both in the play and in her husband's affections (35.36). The classic instance is *Le Roi bis* (32.123), in which the king doesn't feel up to his public role and hires a detective to find a double to substitute for him. The humble street-seller who moves in becomes the lover of the queen, whom he also, incidentally, imagines to be a double. Six years later, yet another humble Parisian shop owner stands in for a debauched prince (38.110). It is worth mentioning for their relevance to this theme the two "role reversal" films of the thirties, in which a person in authority and a menial wrecked on a desert island (33.29) or conscripted into the military (35.29) find their hierarchical status reversed. In the first of these, *Charlemagne,* a stoker orders a baron around until they are rescued and traditional patterns re-established. The implication that working-class people had superior practical survival skills in demanding situations proved immensely popular with the public of 1933, especially outside Paris.

The picture of authority as impotent, debauched, and incompetent which emerges from such identity narratives is reinforced by the parallel set of stand-in narratives which show it as corrupt and self-interested, seeking to avoid responsibility and to shift the blame for its misdemeanors onto the poor and needy. Such narratives are common from 1932 to 1937. All involve doubles who agree to take the blame for a rich and powerful man's incompetence or criminality. A stepson takes the blame for the real son's botched medical work (32.27); a worker agrees to take the blame for a rich man in exchange for his son's education (34.78); a tailor substitutes for a banker when gangsters threaten (35.49); a down-and-outer is induced to double for another scheming banker (37.35); a fashion designer employs a down-and-outer to do time for him (36.98); another down-and-outer is induced to take responsibility for an insurance fraud (36.76).

These latter narratives introduce the scheming upper-middle class, which was to play such a large part in thirties cinema. Many films imply an identity between successful businessman and crook. This may be done jovially, as in *À nous la liberté* (31.1); with a curious ambivalence, as in *Ces messieurs de la Santé* (33.23); or, with different connotations, melodramatically, as in *Les Misérables* (33.92). In all of these, escaped or released criminals become rich and powerful figures in the community. An equally fascinating film, *Carrefour* (38.16), based on amnesia, has the identity of a respectable bourgeois called into question insofar as he may well be a former crook who has unwittingly assumed the personality of a dead hero. Throughout the film, an ambivalence reigns in which respectable present and possible criminal past are intertwined. A more explicit representation of this theme was to occur in a very common narrative pattern of the forties, which sees public benefactors gradually stripped of their facade of respectability, to be revealed as the head of criminal gangs. *L'Étrange Monsieur Victor* (37.40) is probably the best-known precursor of these.

A variant which glamorized the criminal was the gentleman-crook narrative, in which a suave and elegant man, often a count or a baron (32.5; 32.97), sometimes a (self-styled) English lord (30.34), turns out to be the notorious master thief. Of the many elusive master criminals of 1932 who could pose as high-society gentlemen, Fantômas is no doubt the best known (32.59; cf 32.7). *Le Roman d'un tricheur* (36.115) contains an echo of this narrative pattern. It was so common that lovers often posed as gentleman thieves, or as equally romantic apaches, in order to seduce the women they loved (30.39; 31.86; 39.75). In *Jim la Houlette* (35.62), one of the multiple identity changes involves the novelist's male secretary posing as the notorious bandit Jim la Houlette in order to impress the novelist's wife. An odd inversion of this theme has Garat as a gentleman thief abandoning his criminal activities and posing as a respectable wealthy man in order to seduce the woman he loves, accepting that his fantasy will end when his money runs out. The surviving copy has no trace of the up-beat ending outlined by Chirat: the girl seems to have committed suicide when he abandons her, and we leave Garat in the rain, plodding glumly through a bleak Paris night (38.2).

It was particularly common for the respectable facade and double identity concealing criminality to involve legal personnel, who are hiding their nefarious behavior behind the uniform of a police inspector or the robes of a lawyer. *Le Procureur Hallers* (30.70) introduced this theme into the French sound cinema, presenting a lawyer by day, a thief and pimp by night, while others reveal the criminal to be posing as a police inspector (30.59; 39.88) or a private detective (37.11). One of the many delights of *Drôle de drame* is the way in which it plays with this established narrative pattern (37.37). Allied to such stories are those in which judges rant at the misdemeanors of the accused, only to discover that the latter are closer to them than they could ever have imagined—a brother, perhaps (34.14), or a son (36.27). It is, however, feminism, rather than the law, that is being mocked when the aspiring female lawyer's proposed husband, whom she has rejected without ever meeting him, poses as a criminal in order to acquire her as his defense lawyer and gradually initiates her into the supposed ways of the underworld. Her chambers are rapidly transformed into a den of vice, and she herself into a pseudo-apache in sweater and cloth cap, with a cigarette dangling from the corner of her mouth (36.136). The effect, nevertheless, is to poke sly fun at the law as an institution.

The critique of class often took the form of the "borrowed plumage" narrative, in which it becomes apparent that all that separates class from class is access to appropriate clothes (or cars, or houses, etc.). Once a worker or tramp is appropriately clothed, he proves perfectly capable of carrying off the role of businessman, banker, or noble with at least the same aplomb and competence as a "true" member of the superior class. For this reason, several films revolve around clothes shops. In *Chacun sa chance* (30.18), Gabin, as a shop clerk, has the task of dressing the dummies in the shop window. When an eccentric baron inadvertently borrows some of his clothes, he in turn borrows an elegant suit off the dummy and leaves his own on it, much to the fastidious shop owner's horror. Gabin's love interest, a sweet-seller at the theater, is given the star's elegant attire, so that when she and Gabin first meet both are dressed in borrowed finery, with inevitable misunderstandings about their relative statuses in society. Indeed, much of the narrative depends on exchanges of clothing between rich and poor, which result in the former being jailed as criminals and the latter being welcomed into high-society venues and given limitless credit. *Le Million* (31.84) presents a second-hand-clothes dealer, Le père la Tulipe, whose buying and selling of old clothes for actors foreshadows that of Jericho in *Les Enfants du paradis,* and underlines the relevance of clothes to the "performance" of an identity.

The assumption or loss of any formally recognized uniform, such as a military uniform in innumerable vaudevilles, or a clergyman's clothes, proved a popular narrative mechanism (32.30). In 1935, both Jules Berry in *Le Crime de Monsieur Lange* and Fernandel in *Jim la Houlette* assume the outfit of a sleeping or dead clergyman to escape arrest, the latter being trapped into having to fulfill his clerical duties in a new parish, with easily imaginable consequences, while the former acquires an appropriately misleading disguise for a seedy businessman on the run (35.27; 35.62). In fact, of course, the effect here is to extend the connotations of disrepute and complicity in right-wing corruption to the general category of clergymen. The same could be said of *Sans famille* (34.92), in which a pickpocket disguises himself as a clergyman to win the trust of some simple folk. As he himself says, somewhat wryly, "If you can't trust a clergyman, who can you trust?" The general message of such films was that all such costumes are part of a gigantic confidence trick: only their clothes distinguish the lunatic or the escaped criminal from the priest, the count, or the financier. As the baron says to Pepel in *Les Bas-Fonds* (36.15), voicing a commonplace of the period, "Life is one long series of costume changes." Identities are roles and, given the appropriate accessories, anyone can act the role of prince or of clergyman—often more competently than the prince or the clergyman can.

The lowly can also be trained in the roles of the respectable and the noble of the land. It is not just costume, but manner, accent, taste, and social convention that make the difference between the privileged and the underprivileged, and these, too, can be assumed—indeed, are nothing but learned behaviors. Hence the importance of Pygmalion stories, which see an urchin or waif "trained" in the ways of respectability so effectively that her new identity deceives even the most refined arbiters of taste. In *Cette vieille canaille* (33.26), the elderly doctor has the fairground waif whom he has rescued and to whom he has become ambivalently attached trained in the ways of his own world, notably through history lessons and the acquisition of appropriate cultural knowledge. In *La Rosière des halles* (35.98), the author hastily trains the market girl in the ways of elegant society in order to take her out to a high-class restaurant, though in this case much of the fun is derived from the catastrophic failure of his overly hasty training.

Perhaps the nicest example of the Pygmalion theme has Aouina, a happy-go-lucky, tomboyish waif from North Africa, "civilized," again by an author, into the elegant Princesse Tam-Tam. Aside from much false laughter, this involves not just clothes and manicures but music lessons, dancing lessons, and the acquisition of academic knowledge such as mathematics. Essentially, however, in this film civilization itself is defined as the ability to deceive and lie with conviction, and Aouina remains savage at heart (i.e., sincere, genuine), as she demonstrates by her ultimate return to her humble origins (35.92).

In terms of class, the other main direction toward which identity narratives point is the shame involved in occupying humble positions—a shame which drives people to conceal large parts of their lives from those around them, and even from their own families. The best known of these "shame" narratives is *Le Chasseur de chez Maxim's,* twice filmed in the thirties (32.32; 39.13). In some respects, it resembles the famous German shame narrative of the twenties, *Die Letzte Mann,* if only because of the porter's role, and it recurs, thinly disguised, in 1935 (35.127). More understandably, several narratives depend for their effect on the desire of protagonists to conceal their "shameful" profession of good-time girl (38.30; 38.69) or dancer (37.25)

A large proportion of the films mentioned so far involve instances of adultery, whether real, planned, or suspected. In fact, the most common narrative motivation for concealing identity was to suppress knowledge of adultery, to attempt to put oneself in a position to commit adultery, or to test the validity of one's suspicions of adultery. Alongside adultery, there is a recurrent preoccupation with the legitimacy of offspring. Both children who have never known, or who have come to doubt, the identity of their fathers and exchanged, abandoned, or substituted babies are incited to ask the question "Who am I?" "What are my origins?" "Where do I belong?" In this sense, the family—particularly the middle-class family—is centrally concerned in a high proportion of identity narratives, and the health of that institution is significantly called into question. Perhaps the most astonishing instance of this is to be seen in the blithely unselfconscious racism of *Le Blanc et le noir* (30.13), in which a respectable middle-class woman's black newborn baby, conceived during a petulant fling on a particularly dark night, is (naturally) hidden from her by those attending the birth and swapped for a baby of a more acceptable color (!).

A number of identity narratives hover between the public and the private spheres in that they involve respectable, often married, men or women who, tempted (perhaps extramaritally) come to lead a double life. In public terms, such narratives present the two lives as, respectively, family life and adulterous life, while in private terms individuals are represented as having a double personality, as being torn between the superego and the id. In this, they are variants of the lawyer-criminal, the gentleman-thief, or indeed the queen who falls for a revolutionary, insofar as they all involve a tension between two personae, constituted, respectively, of self-discipline and self-indulgence, observance and rejection of prevailing social constraints and conventions. Often the working class is figured as the id. It and the criminal class are seen as classic sites of unconstrained morals, where there is freedom to transgress social conventions, and a number of thirties films tell of lawyers or other professionals transformed and revitalized by contact with the amoral life-force of the working class (e.g., 39.17). In effect, they are discovering a hitherto unsuspected aspect (working class, underworld) of their own personality. In other films, people bound by social convention (middle class, wives and husbands, members of the aristocracy) "become" members of the working class in order to experience genuine emotion, genuine passion (31.7; 31.108; 31.124). But quite often the split personality is overtly Freudian, as when the wife turns out to be a (former) midinette or good-time girl (32.47) whom the husband had perhaps had an affair with years earlier in Indochina (38.69), or when the wife is torn between respectability and passion (32.85) and leaves her husband for three days of passion with a scoundrel (32.29), or doubles as a tart to deceive her husband (33.124), or transforms herself into a seductive coquette to retain her husband (31.91).

The classic instance of this double identity is *Sans lendemain* (39.80), in which Babs, the good-time girl and queen of La Sirène nightclub, struggles to reassume her motherly identity as Eveline because her son has returned unexpectedly from his boarding school and a former admirer has turned up who is not aware of her descent in the world. She hastily constructs a semblance of respectability around herself, using borrowed money, but is worried by the credibility of her act—is it convincing? Indeed, which is the real her? Can Babs ever really become Eveline again? Finally, on the point of success, she opts out, preferring suicide to living a lie for the rest of her life. Yet, as so often in such stories, this film suggests that women are inherently duplicitous—at once Eveline and Babs, mother and whore. A similar message emerges from a similar film, *Le Drame de Shanghai* (38.27), in which Kay is at once a singer trapped in a sleazy Shanghai nightclub existence and the mother of a young daughter, Vera, who returns to Shanghai from boarding school. The interconnection between the two roles is explicit: Kay has accepted the former in order to be able appropriately to fulfill the duties of the latter. Shucking off her persona as queen of Shanghai's nightlife, she attempts to reassume a credible persona as respectable parent, but her past catches up with her and she is murdered saving Vera. As in the previous film, the sensual, degraded nightclub self dooms any long-term maternal relationship. In a sense, Kay's former lover, played by Jouvet, is in the same boat—once a sensitive, caring person, he too has been toughened by life, and an analogous double self is attributed to him. As is usual in such cases, however, it is violence, rather than sexuality, which defines the second male self, and it is, moreover, not his drama which is central to the narrative. Some texts do present a man's duality as central, as when a prudish man inherits a bawdy club and discovers a repressed part of his own personality (33.64), but when this happens there is none of the distraught intensity that accrues around the female version of such dramas.

In the instances listed above, the Freudian split is figured as two sides of a single personality, but often, without any change in significance, it is figured in two different characters. For instance, a husband may find himself faced with a choice between his wife and a seductive woman of loose morals whom he meets on a train (36.100); or between two Widow Martins, one who keeps a respectable boarding house, the other a brothel (32.21); or between two identical women, one a society woman, the other a good-time girl, who may just conceivably be the same person (33.62). Equally, he may meet a woman strangely resembling his wife, who turns out to be her illegitimate half-sister (35.102). A prudish man may have a twin brother who is a scoundrel and whom he has to try to rehabilitate (39.15), or may invent a fictional twin brother who does all the things he himself dare not do (33.128; 38.85). In many cases of this sort, the two aspects of the single human personality are allocated to twins or doubles, or to legitimate and illegitimate siblings, or are represented in parallel or sequential lives—but always with the same opposed characteristics, equivalent either to the ego and the id or to the superego and the id.

It was normal to raise such fraught topics within the genre of the farce, where nobody, surely, could take it seriously. There is a certain appropriateness in this stratagem, given Freud's discussion of the connection between jokes and the unconscious. A splendid example, which incorporates both "doubled" personalities and a sequential transformation, is *Drôle de drame* (37.37). Molyneux, the respected and highly proper author, is also Félix Chapelle, the writer of gruesome detective stories that sell like hotcakes. His cousin the bishop also leads a double life—the height of propriety by day but demonstrating regrettably lascivious tastes by night. Both run into trouble trying to keep the two parts of their lives separate. As Molyneux says, "A double life is no life at all." Suspected of murdering his wife, Molyneux is forced to flee, and, as Félix Chapelle, he is commissioned to write sensational articles on himself. Meanwhile, the bishop, in an effort to recover incriminating evidence, disguises himself in a fetching kilt. The faint flavor of transvestism introduced by this disguise is underlined by policemen dressing up as old ladies in order to trap Kramp, the dreaded butcher of butchers. Kramp has been transformed into a criminal by Félix's gruesome genre tales, and is out to get revenge. In the course of his quest, Kramp meets up unawares with Mme Molyneux and falls desperately in

love with her. Faced with his (naked) ardor, she is spontaneously transformed from a harridan who detests soppy things such as flowers into a
girlish creature known as "Daisy." This hilarious series of identity switches
and disguises, then, can all be traced back to the contrast between respectable facades (as wife, bishop, policeman, moralistic author, etc.) and a
fascination with the forbidden (transvestism and violence, music hall and
murder).

Roughly the same set of Freudian oppositions, proposed in the same
farcical tone, structures *Mam'zelle Nitouche* (31.77), in which the two principal sets are a convent and a music hall. Célestin, the convent organist, is
also Floridor, a closet music-hall composer, and one of his female choristers
becomes a covert star in his show, allowing for much climbing over convent
walls and hasty switches between salacious and religious singing, saucy actress and convent girl. The lieutenant, who is engaged to Denise, the convent girl (whom for narrative convenience he has not yet met), falls for the
saucy actress at the music hall and breaks off his engagement to her other
persona. Incidentally, in the tradition of the military vaudeville to which
this film is distantly related, Denise is "rescued" disguised as a soldier, thus
once again introducing transvestism into the Freudian array of themes.

Related to these Freudian narratives, and straddling the same boundary
between the public and the private, are those narratives involving a sexual
relationship which turns out, once the identities of those involved are clarified, to have incestuous implications. These will be dealt with more fully in
chapter 4, but they can be foreshadowed here since the narratives often depend on people having or assuming false identities. In relatively few cases
are incestuous relationships dealt with openly. It is not often in these films
(though it occasionally is elsewhere, as in *Le Simoun* [33.116]) a question of
actual father-daughter, mother-son, or brother-sister relationships, but
rather of quasi-incestuous relationships between foster parents or foster sisters, people who are believed (wrongly) to be sisters or fathers, or lovers
whom one is obliged by circumstances to pass off as siblings or offspring.
Thus a count passes off the woman found in his bed as his sister (32.90); a
sister falls for the man she believes (wrongly) to be her brother (32.138); or
a fan passes herself off as a male star's foster sister in order to gain access to
her idol (39.59). To con beauty-parlor customers, a girl pretends to be her
lover's mother, wonderfully rejuvenated (32.126); caught in her rooms with
a young student, a woman passes him off as the son she had at the age of
twelve (!) (32.63). In a classic instance, the Oedipal young pilot finds to his
horror that he has become the lover of his fatherly boss's wife (35.42).
Again, a husband suspects an old banker of being his wife's lover, but the
man she has been visiting turns out "merely" to be her father (33.79); a man
about to marry is informed (wrongly, as it turns out) by the bride-to-be's
mother that his fiancée is his own daughter (34.29); a rich banker pretends

to be his own accountant, so has to pass his mistress off as his daughter (38.67); or a woman learns that the man she loves is her own foster father (39.92). Clearly, all such "pretext" narratives invoke mistaken identity in order to talk of prohibited forms of sexuality. They are extremely common throughout the decade.

An analogous fantasy involves women who marry for a second time, only to find that their first husband, whom they believed dead, is, in fact, still alive. Several films explore the protocols appropriate to such a bigamous situation: where lies the fault, and who should give ground in the ambivalent set of relationships consequent on the discovery? Some represent the first husband as a sinister villain (30.62), while others blame the woman for an over-hasty remarriage; in the extreme, the first husband triumphs and manipulates the situation to his advantage (33s3). What they all have in common is that they serve as pretexts for fantasized bigamy, in which the legal husband or wife is conveniently, if temporarily, sidelined.

A similar point can be made about the numerous transgender roles that find characters "obliged," by circumstances beyond their control, to conceal their identity beneath the clothing and appearance of the opposite sex. These roles are particularly common in the comedies of the early thirties, especially in military vaudevilles, in which women are frequently introduced into the barracks in military uniform (31.77; 33.55; 33.145; 36.132), or soldiers are dressed as women (38.62) or blunder around a girls' school pretending to be schoolmistresses (37.116). A fascination with the opposition between femaleness and the more aggressive aspects of maleness, as evidenced in the soldier, is paralleled with a delight in undermining the latter. At least two films take the woman's potential military role more seriously, having her join the legion as a Zouave in order to follow her love (34.98), or in order to fight alongside her fellowmen on the barricades (33.92). More simply farcical are those tales in which young men dress up as sexless old women. The film based on *Charley's Aunt* is the classic case (35.76), but not the only one (33.124). Indeed, *Un de la Canebière* (38.109) reproduces a number of the plot elements of *La Marraine de Charley,* including the wealthy aunt impersonated to lend credibility to a financial scam. The remaining half-dozen cases include two instances in which a pair of tramps/unemployed musicians dress as female musicians to get into a reception or into a female orchestra (31.79; 35.45), and the story of a granddaughter who, by mistake, sends her grandfather a photo of herself dressed as a man and is obliged thereafter to live out the male role in his company (32.61). While the tone of these films is generally comic, there are well-known moments in *L'Atalante* (34.9) when Père Jules models the dress for his boss's wife, and in *La Grande Illusion* (37.54), during the amateur theatricals in the prison camp, in which the transvestite and gay implications of such gender changes are foregrounded with disconcerting power.

The nearest these films come to dealing explicitly with same-sex relationships is when the woman goes to the ball with her female cousin dressed as a man (31.65), and presumably in *Sapho* (34.93), which I have not been able to view or to find an adequately detailed account of. In the case of *Un de la Canebière* (38.109), a simple "pretext" narrative has Margot making amorous advances to Aunt Clarisse, knowing full well that Pénible has dressed as Aunt Clarisse to con his creditors, only to discover that this is the real Aunt Clarisse (who is, of course, suitably outraged by Margot's advances). A mannishly dressed woman—a countess dressed for the hunt—can be sufficiently credible as a potential lover that the boyfriend bursts into his girlfriend's room in a jealous rage (31.135). The most complicated instance of cross-gender impersonation that I know of comes from a plot summary for an apparently vanished film in which a female impersonator falls ill, whereupon an unemployed woman takes over his act, pretending to be a man pretending to be a woman (33.60). Then there is the traditional tale of the young man who dresses as a woman to be admitted to the duchess's retinue. The new "serving girl" finds peculiar favor with the duchess (32.65). The frequency of such narratives, the explicit nature of certain titles (*La Femme en homme, Sapho, Georges et Georgette*), and the lengths to which the films go to inject new variations into a widely recognized set of conventions all attest to the intense fascination exercised by the idea of transvestism.

At the level of the individual personality, certain character types are the focus of attention in identity narratives. One is the chameleon trickster figure whose fictions about himself, constantly changing, weave a web of deceit which he is unable to control. While there are not many instances of this figure, of which the best-known example is Valentine in *Le Jour se lève* (39.48), they embody a broader distrust of the intellectual life, of people who are too clever by half and cannot be trusted. A woman plays an analogous role in *Naples au baiser du feu* (37.80), while the criminal professor in *Alibi* (37.6) who is a master of many disguises is recognizably related. From 1937 on, such trickster figures come to the fore in opposition to the simple worker, but also in parallel to the rise of spy thrillers and the fear of infiltrators. With such characters, one never knows where one stands.

Occasionally, the worker, in his quick-witted persona from the early thirties, could himself be the trickster figure. This was the case with *Le Roi des resquilleurs* (30.78), the plot of which is worth summarizing briefly because of its relevance and because of the immense popularity of the film. Its basic premise is the widely used ploy, described earlier, of a street singer who passes himself off as a baron in order to impress a pretty girl. The need to squire her to various elegant events while avoiding the outlay of nonexistent cash constitutes an on-going narrative joke. His trickster characteristics are further in demand when he needs to get into the beauty parlor where she works. He pretends to be a plumber, bursting in on various women in a state of undress, then has to disguise himself in discarded female clothes, at the risk of being subjected to breast enhancement and depilatory treatment. His final rendezvous with her is at a rugby match, which he can enter only by dressing in team colors. Taken for the new team member, he rather lets the side down until an accidental injection of horse-dope triggers fantastic feats of physical prowess, and he is carried off by his teammates in triumph, having been instrumental in his side winning the game. Multiple transformations of persona have allowed him to enter elite circles and to cross both class and gender barriers, finally winning the day and, if not the girl, then at least her stepmother.

In his rugby exploits he is not unlike the many blowhards and braggarts who claim attributes that they do not have and are caught in the web of their own deceit. Such characters are interesting as much for the mythic nature of the attributes to which they (falsely) lay claim—aviator (31.13), race-car driver (32s2; 34.102), incomparable athlete (32.11), Tour de France cyclist (33.108), and African explorer (34.99). A solitary example later in the decade has Fernandel trapped by his big mouth into the role of adventurer and record-breaker, trying to circle the globe in one hundred days with no more than five sous to sustain him (39.16). Like the King of Con Men in his rugby match, Fernandel's character accidentally wins his race, just as the feckless fool trapped in a knight's armor, careering all over the field on his drugged horse, accidentally wins the tournament (35.1). The mythic roles to which these characters aspire join the aristocrat, the millionaire, the artist, the clown, the crook or convict, the good-time girl, and the tramp as emblematic figures of the thirties, in terms of which the class and family dramas so central to the decade were played out.

1.3 IDENTITY AND DESTINY

A final theme raised by the identity narrative under consideration is that of free will: of what importance is human intentionality, and to what extent are human agents masters of their own destiny? Of course, in all narratives there are vast gaps in logic which speak of determinants far more powerful than the apparently motivated decisions made by the characters, but here we are interested only in certain specific ways in which such forces manifest themselves in identity narratives. On the one hand, a number of films speak of the power of the human agent totally to transform his or her personality, at will. Puny intellectuals transform themselves from timid teachers into something—anything—more admirable (31.14; 32.134; 33.109; 36.129), men or women in love totally transform themselves to become the object of desire of their loved one, or crooks totally transform their personality so as to be unrecognizable to police or to vengeful rivals. In the extreme, Judge Hallers defeats "the criminal in himself" apparently by sheer force of will (30.70), as if Dr. Jekyll had defeated Mr. Hyde.

On the other hand, people are commonly portrayed as trapped in a life which they have not chosen and cannot escape. Many identity films at least imply one or the other of these, and some of them introduce episodes which make it explicit. On occasion, destiny is even embodied in a narrative agent whose role is to monitor or hunt down the protagonist, ultimately intervening to ensure the predestined end. In *Les Misérables* (33.92), Javert can be read as an embodiment of Jean Valjean's criminal past, hounding him implacably until he has expiated his guilt, and so, of course, can the judge in *Crime et châtiment* (35.28). Indeed, more generally, this is one aspect of the crime genre that made it so popular both with the general public and with ambitious authors. A more portentous death figure hounds the child in *Le Roi des aulnes* (30.77), finally claiming him as his own, while the cynical Lord Oswill provides a distinctly more grotesque but no less effective counterpart in *L'Homme à l'Hispano* (33.65), and for much of *La Bandera* (35.6) the bounty-hunter played by Le Vigan fulfills a similar function. These are as nothing, however, compared to the embodiments of death and destiny that were subsequently to frequent the films of the occupation.

Destiny is not always represented in such negative terms, however. An obscure and generally benevolent destiny, for instance, may be shown as guiding the affections of lovers who, having rejected out of hand the marriage proposed by their parents, fall for a stranger who turns out to be none other than the intended bride or husband (31.77; 33.93; 36.136; 37.73; 38.1). Indeed, nearly all of the sixty-nine films of the decade in which people discover to their astonishment, that X is none other than Y speak of such a destiny, conceived as a sort of chess player meticulously moving the pieces on the narrative board to bring about, through apparent coincidence and despite the intentions of the participants, the predestined end. Moreover, within a fictional context, all of the many instances in which protagonists win at lotteries or at gambling, or inherit unexpected fortunes, imply that a benign or malign destiny has singled them out for its "personal" attention. Likewise, the "accidental" encounters which so often trigger crucial narrative episodes are never in this fictional context the result of pure chance or of coincidence, but rather provide an opportunity for destiny to confirm that the protagonists whom the narrative has apparently elected at random to introduce us to do indeed figure among the elect. We might note, for instance, that if a young man is knocked over by a car it will prove to have been driven by an attractive young woman who is "meant for" him (33.40), and if an unhappily married man traveling alone in the mountains runs out of gas and is forced to spend the night in a remote hotel, he will find there the attractive childhood friend whom he has always really loved and who has also run out of gas (35.41). Such events are so common as to barely register as coincidences when viewing a film, and they are particularly common in the early thirties (e.g., 31.14; 31.62; 31.79; 31.142; 32.149; 34.27).

Cars are not the only form of transportation mobilized to this effect. For some reason, no doubt related to the disruption in daily routines occasioned by any long journey, but also to the mythic exhilaration associated in this decade with train journeys, a large proportion of such encounters take place on trains, and almost as many on ocean liners. The titles of a number of thirties films promise as much—*Les Surprises du sleeping* (33.121), *Compartiment de dames seules* (34.29), *Un train dans la nuit* (34.107), *Train de plaisir* (35.114), *La Petite Dame du wagon-lit* (36.100), and so on. Melodramas, of course, are notorious for the presence of coincidences that imply an arbitrary and apparently malevolent destiny, which, once the characters' fortitude has been sufficiently tested, intervenes just as arbitrarily in its more benign guise. Narratives such as those of *Les Deux Orphelines* (32.50) are riddled with a series of calamitous misfortunes, which are finally resolved by a contrary series of benign eventualities. In general, one could say that destiny is generically predisposed: a fundamentally benign destiny presides over comedies, while its malign counterpart presides over dramas, and particularly over tragic dramas. In the latter genres, it is given to a sort of malicious irony, ensuring that just as events seem to be turning out well and the characters are managing to take control of their existence, a "totally unforeseeable" (yet oddly appropriate) tragedy will strike them down. Just as Henriette recognizes that the poor blind beggar singing in the street below is her long-lost sister, the police burst in and arrest her (32.50). Just as Fritz summons up the determination to break with the baroness, his mistress, in order to devote himself to his pure young love, the baron discovers the key to his quarters among the baroness's possessions (33.76). Just when the relief column appears and Pierre seems saved, a stray enemy bullet strikes him down (35.6). Just when André and Françoise's idyll seems assured, L'Africain returns to reveal his secret and André flees, missing Françoise by seconds (37.87). Just as Franck and Cora arrive at long last at an understanding and seem destined for happiness, they run into a truck and she dies (39.23). Of course, it is arguable that in many, if not all, of these cases it is "the past sins of the characters" which are finding them out, but this is just to say that a sadistic destiny presides over such narratives to ensure that their sins will indeed find them out, and will do so just as they thought they had left their past behind them.

Occasionally, these malevolent interventions of destiny are given a degree of narrative foregrounding by being presented as the working out of predictions and prophecies. The Tarot laid out by Madame Blanche in *Le Grand Jeu* (33.62) is just the best known of such incidents. Christ, of course, is free to foretell his own betrayal and death (35.53), but numerous less qualified imitators in the form of fortune-tellers and sorcerers serve the same narrative function, predicting the death both of kings (38.87) and of underlings (31.32). Prophetic tramps are not believed by the foolish (36.62), and husbands or lovers have good reason to be apprehensive when importunate females propose to read their dear one's hand. Florence reads Hélène Maury's in *L'Équipage* (35.42), predicting that she is unlikely to be happy with the man she loves, and the fortune-teller reads Rose's in *Sarati le terrible* (37.103), foretelling the importance of another man. However central as narrative mechanisms these "predictions" may be, serving to fore-shadow certain possibilities and to arouse expectations (which may not, of course, always be fulfilled [37.80] and which lend themselves to parody [32.24]), they also serve to construct the idea of an apparently extra-textual but in fact all-too-textual destiny, whose decisions are irrevocable and whose pleasure it is to mock the petty plans of (textual) humankind. Some similar implication is present where an overt repetition or circularity serves to imply that abstract formal patterns imposed by "the nature of things" guide and determine the characters' fate, rather than any intentionality on their part. Many of the best-known films of the decade are structured around such formal procedures, notably *La Petite Lise* (30.66), *Sous les toits de Paris* (30.84), *Le Bonheur* (35.12), *Toni* (35.110), and *Trois valses* (38.107).

Although destiny, in its many manifestations, presides over the out-come of a large number, perhaps even a majority, of the films of the thir-ties, it usually intervenes anonymously and sporadically, infiltrating through occasional interstices of the narrative chain. Nevertheless, there are certain films which, like *Procureur Hallers,* take as their thematic center the task of exploring the extent to which individuals can assume their own destiny and determine their own identity. One of these, *L'Homme de nulle part* (36.54), is perhaps unique in representing the act of divesting oneself of one's self as an exhilarating and liberating experience. Based, like L'Her-bier's silent film, on Pirandello's *Feu Mathias Pascal,* it relates the story of a man who comes by chance to be thought by his family and acquaintances to have died. Immediately, he sees the opportunity to abandon his former identity as a means of escaping the debilitating pettiness and grayness of an unchosen existence, and as an essential first step in the process of con-structing a self for which he can assume responsibility. The narrative thus constitutes a sort of extended existentialist metaphor in which the protag-onist learns to define the person he is to be. In one sense, the film suggests that identity is superficial, as in the case of clothes and appearances—a mere matter of plausibility and the appropriate documentation—but in another sense, it suggests that what we normally take for a personality is the dead weight of an involuntary past into which we have been unwillingly socialized, and which must be shrugged off so that we can begin to construct a more authentic personality from zero. There is a certain irony, however, in having this growth toward self-possession triggered by a lottery win toward which the protagonist has been guided by a kind of personified destiny.

While it has a narrative that is the reverse of that of *L'Homme de nulle part*, *Le Grand Jeu* (33.62) can also be read as a sort of relativistic morality play. Guilty of an unspecified sin, Pierre has been banished from the world of effortless pleasure that he had always taken for granted. Recapitulating the biblical story, this "fall from grace" leaves him abandoned in a bleak and desolate world—the foreign legion—where, through a woman who resembles his former lover Florence, who has lost her memory and may even be Florence, he seems at times to recapture glimpses of his pre-lapsarian paradisiacal existence. What he has to learn, and has in fact learned at the end, is that in this world there are no certainties and there is no going back. There are no Platonic true images, only inadequate simulacra. In resigning himself to an existence in "this world," Pierre is resigning himself to the human condition and learning to accept the inevitability of his own mortality, as foreshadowed in that of his friend and alter ego, Nicholas. His doom has been spelled out in the cards long before, as it so often was in thirties films.

Perhaps the most interesting of the surviving films to focus primarily on identity is *Carrefour* (38.16), which, in a sense, combines both of the above narratives—a fall from grace and a process of self-definition from zero. In addition, it involves a police investigation which parallels the progressive investigation by the protagonist of his own self. Roger de Vétheuil believes he is a returned serviceman distinguished in combat for his bravery, and a wealthy businessman with a happy family. When he is blackmailed by someone who claims to have proof that he is someone quite other—a bad lad called Jean Pelletier with a criminal record and a regrettable way with women—he calls in the police. Yet little by little, as evidence accumulates, he becomes less and less certain of his own identity, and more and more convinced that the world of wealthy self-possession to which he has been accustomed was a fraud, an illusion which he can never recover. As he investigates his past, he gets involved in a violent underworld which seems all too familiar, and risks (re-)becoming the criminal and murderer who he probably once was. He comes to accept that the war trauma which caused him to lose his memory has unwittingly provided the equivalent of Mathias Pascal's pretext for divesting himself of his former life—it has allowed him unwittingly to exchange identities with the dead de Vétheuil and to construct from zero a self which, as Jean Pelletier, he could never have hoped to know, and which indeed even Roger de Vétheuil might never have been able to construct. He has become the good and honorable man who Jean Pelletier might conceivably have been, if born into different social circumstances. His wife, the police, and his former mistress all seem to accept this, the latter sacrificing herself to protect his right to continue to live (probably fraudulently) as Roger de Vétheuil.

Destiny, then, may be implicit or explicit, embodied or disembodied, accepted or struggled against. It may be some distant, implacable force determining the course of human existence, or it may be something much more concrete—socio-political or socio-economic conditions which, to a greater or lesser extent, determine the direction of the characters' lives. On occasion, it may be genetic and hereditary, as in *La Bête humaine,* where Gabin's compulsion to kill is beyond his control, and in the less well-known *Pièges* (39.71), in which the character played by Pierre Renoir is driven by an analogous compulsion and a similar sexual trigger. In most cases, these operations of destiny are represented as implacable and irreversible. A favorite metaphor for this, or any, form of fatality which reduced the intentions of the protagonists to insignificance was the mechanical doll, the clockwork human, the robot deprived of soul and of will, which does what it has to do.

The idea that contemporary industrial capitalism constituted a form of enslavement of the masses, depriving them not just of their liberty but of their very humanity, had been present in various expressionist films, not least *Metropolis*. *Tumultes* (31.134) takes up this idea briefly in the opening scenes, as does *À nous la liberté* (31.1) more systematically but more jocularly. Factories become prisons manned by zombies without will or soul. Ruled by clocks, slaves to the machines they serve, regimented and manipulated by others or by the system, workers turn into mere automata. In *À nous la liberté,* technological progress comes out quite well in the end, releasing the workers, who have been given control of the factory, so that they can become re-humanized by nature and leisure—fishing, dancing, and playing games with one another—but later films which use the metaphor of automata are not so benign in outlook. Of course, all of René Clair's characters are in some sense automata—mere ciphers, or chess pieces, scornfully moved about on his narrative board, subject to the musical rhythms he imposes and to relentless formalist patterns of repetition and variation. They have no more substance in *Quatorze juillet* (32.116), for instance, than do the multiplicity of other objects that circulate, meet, and part, to fall in the end into their predestined slots. So it is not surprising to find, at the most dramatic point in the narrative, a player piano ritually patterning the scene in which Jean is apparently enmeshed in an inevitable descent into the underworld, and to find it "accidentally" triggered during the struggle between him and his erstwhile criminal colleagues. The triggering of a pianola was to figure, of course, at the climactic moment in an even more famous film, *Pepe le Moko* (36.99), when Régis is cornered and begging for his life. The hectic music that accompanies his execution may seem to be at odds with the somber nature of the scene, yet it is oddly apt as a metaphor for the relentless working out of his traitor's destiny.

Something of this atmosphere of implacable inevitability carries over into any scene with mechanical-piano accompaniment, such as that in Ophüls's *Liebelei* (33.76), in which the characters are again effectively puppets caught up in and acting out an age-old narrative ritual that can end only in their deaths. Even the recurrent return of a musical motif on a gramophone can have such an effect, as in *La nuit du carrefour* (32.97). Yet the presence of mechanical toys, and especially of mechanized humans, foregrounds the theme of a relentless fatality more effectively, and was often used during the decade. Such toys appear in both *La Nuit du carrefour* and *L'Atalante* (34.9). When Juliette explores Père Jules's cabin she discovers amidst the baroque clutter that he has accumulated various mechanical toys, including an animated conductor figure. Later, helpless and drifting in Paris, she comes across a fairground attraction involving mechanical people, dancing as she had danced earlier. With due allowance for the difference in genre, such toys serve a similar purpose in *Éducation de prince* (38.29). As it happens, the prince's girlfriend lives, as had Père Jules, on a canal-boat, where her father keeps an array of mechanical dolls (a clown, a dancing bear, a doll, etc). Her father warns the prince about the tendency of human beings to manipulate one another, as, indeed, his mother the queen and her ally the industrialist are trying to manipulate him at that very minute in order to enrich themselves.

The most complex use of this metaphor occurs in *Le Joueur d'échecs* (38.54), which opens in an automated forge where Baron von Kempelen is at work constructing automata. His quarters are crowded with shrouded figures that can be set in motion by chain-pulls, making for one of the most stunning sets of the decade. The baron is the protector, at Catherine the Great's court, of the Polish patriots/revolutionaries struggling for freedom from Russian rule, and various of the automata are constructed to represent the main protagonists, with interesting implications for the historical inevitability of the political outcome, but also leading to fascinating scenes in which characters dance with their automated doubles. In supporting the Poles, the baron is carrying out the posthumous wishes of a countess, and apart from this executive role he, like his automata, has abandoned all humanity. Pitied by the others for living exclusively amid characters lacking all human warmth, he protests that this is the essence of their virtue—life's "vitality" is nothing but a weakness. He is working on an automated army, the army of the future, which will eliminate life with ruthless efficiency. But his prime ambition is to create a mechanized chess player which will be able to defeat all human opponents because it will not be subject to their irrational impulses. When the leading Polish patriot is wounded and must hide, the baron trains him to live inside the automated chess player. But the chess piece ends up as a gift for Catherine, who has penetrated the ruse and plays with the baron's fears for the Polish patriot inside it. There is a hallucinatory scene in which the Russian army commander casually "slaughters" various automata, hanging as from a gallows the one that is the double of the baron, and setting the automated army in motion as he has just set his own army in motion against the Poles. When in Catherine's presence the chess player is finally "executed," it is the baron himself who staggers forth from it, having sacrificed himself to save the Polish leader, and a final series of images shows the baron's body lying disarticulated in the snow, like an automaton; the Russian army commander is also dead, surrounded by the lethal automated army he has set in motion.

The automata are therefore used throughout the narrative to keep in play the themes of doubles; of pawns, puppets, and puppet-master; of the ruthless inhumanity of modern warfare; and of politics and narrative itself as complicated chess games—not to mention the themes of history, of destiny, and of the definition of life—what it means to be human. This, the decade's summative statement about the possible uses of mechanized humans in fictional narrative, provides a useful context for the mechanical dolls in *La Règle du jeu* (39.78). There, the implication right from the beginning, when they appear in the marquis's quarters as his favorite collectors' items, is that they stand for the formally regulated world of the old order, where all knew their place in the scheme of things, as they knew their proper relationships one to another. If human beings are not free, it is because sociological conditioning has so regulated their behavior as to severely limit the possibilities open to them. Such a world runs like clockwork, and the film proposes reasons, despite its shortcomings, for which that world should not be despised. Such a rigorously regulated behavior suppresses the "rabbit" in us all, that natural complex of instinct and desire which finds its expression in the various forms of poaching that are manifested both outside and inside the chateau. Gamekeepers are needed to maintain the rules of the social game. The marquis and Schumacher are the formal representatives of this formal order, and the hunt scene in which they and their sort mechanically and ruthlessly eliminate anything animal within range of their guns foreshadows the final gunning down of that other animal/ poacher, Jurieux. His predestined end is foreshadowed in ways that would have been perfectly familiar to audiences of the day—the discussion between him and Octave during the hunt in which they fear being mistaken for rabbits, Schumacher's threat to take a potshot at anyone "poaching" Lisette, and not least the danse macabre of the amateur theatricals. Moreover, the mechanism by which destiny achieves its end might well have seemed quite banal in its day—first, an ironic scene in which, "just as he is on the point of giving up his mistress," the marquis is glimpsed kissing her by his wife, and second, not one but two exchanges of clothing, which lead to two cases of mistaken identity. These mechanisms duly prove fatal. But the end is far from random: Jurieux, after all, given all he has come to stand for, is the "natural" antagonist of Schumacher the gamekeeper, delegated by his betters to keep animals and poachers in check.

One of the less conventional aspects of the mechanical toys in this film is their use to represent the compulsive *instinctual* behavior of certain of the characters. As he is telephoning his mistress, the marquis winds up a mechanical doll and sets it going; as Marceau is romping around the kitchen table with Lisette, he does the same. It is not only social regulation that determines behavior, but fundamental human instincts, and the automata come to embrace both sides of the opposition established in the opening scenes. Unfortunately for the old order, the rules of their social game are ceasing to be effective. The machinery is ceasing to function, or taking on a life of its own, as when the pianola keys take it upon themselves to play the dance of death, to Charlotte's bemusement, or when the giant mechanical organ, the pride of the marquis's collection, jams and emits a horrible cacophony during the "hunt" inside the chateau.

Throughout the film, these mechanical toys and dolls and the mechanical musical devices which impersonally regulate the activities of the protagonists combine with a number of other powerful metaphoric devices to comment both on the characters and on their actions, and to foretell and shape the necessary end of a society whose ideological conviction and self-confidence have failed. Renoir himself, both a dancing bear in and the "conductor" of this social drama, is obliged to acknowledge his inability to conceive a means of controlling the forces unleashed by this failure. Mechanical humans may be abhorrent, but animal humans are no less dangerous, and they are equally ruthless.

TWO

Nation and Race: French and Not-French—Stereotypes and Myths

2.1 NATIONAL AND RACIAL STEREOTYPES

Of all the major determinants of social identity in films of the thirties, perhaps that which was least often insisted upon in identity narratives was the protagonist's nation of origin. This in itself is significant, suggesting that national allegiance was considered something so simple and fundamental as to be unproblematic. A more detailed study of films of the thirties set outside France and/or foregrounding a non-French protagonist only serves to confirm this assumption: the vast majority of these films manipulate national stereotypes which are considered to be unproblematic and to have an inherent comic or dramatic potential. Nevertheless, it is of interest to note what those stereotypes were, and which were most commonly mobilized. More generally, it is interesting to note with which areas of the globe the French of the thirties considered themselves most closely engaged, and in what way; or, rather, which areas had gained a significance in some way connected with their own existence and needs. First, we look briefly at the principal stereotypes represented in the films, then at the various functions which these stereotypes served. Table 2.1 lists the principal nations, regions, and ethnic groups featured in thirties French films and indicates the number of films in which they were foregrounded.

The two most common nationalities are Americans and Russians. Of these, Americans dominate the years 1930–33 (particularly 1931, when at least fourteen films feature them prominently), while Russians dominate the years 1935–38. In 1934, Gypsies suddenly appear in at least three films and Hungarians in another four, while neither of these groupings occur to any significant extent for most of the rest of the decade. British characters appear sporadically at the beginning of the decade and again toward 1936, characters from the Austro-Hungarian empire (particularly Vienna) figure occasionally but regularly each year, while Italians appear rarely, and only in the middle of the decade. It is surprising to see how seldom and how innocuously Germans figure, even after the ascension of Hitler.

Table 2.1   Nations, Regions, and Ethnic Groups in French Films of the Thirties

Year	1930	1931	1932	1933	1934	1935	1936	1937	1938	1939	Total
Nation or race											
United States	7	14	6	6	0	2	4	5	3	2	49
Russia	2	4	0	4	2	6	6	11	9	3	47
North Africa	1	5	2	3	2	4	5	7	4	2	35
United Kingdom	4	5	1	3	3	6	6	3	1	2	34
Orient	3	1	0	3	2	0	1	8	3	2	23
Spain	5	3	2	2	0	1	1	1	0	1	16
Austria	3	1	1	2	1	1	3	1	0	3	16
Fantasy	0	1	2	2	2	1	2	0	3	0	13
Germany	0	3	1	1	1	2	2	1	0	2	13
Jewish	3	2	0	2	0	3	0	1	0	1	12
Hungary	0	0	1	1	4	3	1	0	1	1	12
Gypsy	0	0	3	0	3	1	0	1	0	0	8
Italy	0	0	0	2	0	3	0	1	1	0	7
Other	1	4	2	3	3	1	5	6	3	5	33
Total	29	43	21	34	23	34	36	46	28	24	318

It is also surprising to see how seldom most of the colonial territories administered by France or in which France had an interest figure in the films. The only recurrent site is North Africa, primarily Algeria, which figures as the prime locus of colonial rule, missionary zeal, and exile. Few of the films presenting Asia or Asians deal with France's colonies in Southeast Asia, though several refer to their concessional access to China and Mongolia. Five films deal with Lebanon or Syria, while five deal with Egypt or the Sudan, but the number of films focusing on South America outnumber all these spheres of French interest put together. In six films, Canada or Canadians are central to the plot, with primary reference to Quebec, and of the five South Pacific films, three feature French Polynesia. In addition to Russia, the French clearly felt a residual relationship with other Slav or Latin countries of Eastern Europe, such as Poland and Romania.

These numbers are not large, especially in the context of an output of some thirteen hundred films. If one takes the minimum figure of three hundred films in which foreign nations or nationals are central (in fact, a viewing of all of the films of the period, if that were possible, would undoubtedly reveal numerous other foreign figures and settings, though mostly of a secondary nature), the presence of Americans, Russians, and Viennese is sufficiently frequent in the more successful films to be significant, along with the colonial theme worked out in North African films. Because most of the rest (and, indeed, most of these) deal in stereotypes, it is sufficient as a first step simply to outline these stereotypes briefly in order to reconstruct a representation of the world as it figured in the imagination of thirties French filmmakers and their audiences.

It is perhaps significant that, among neighboring countries, neither Belgians nor Italians appear at all frequently, and when they do there is little consistency in the characterization. The Spanish, however, are very clearly typed. Spanish womanhood is represented almost exclusively by the passionate singer/dancer swirling her skirts and clicking her castanets in the local bar (five films). She is the focus of attention of all classes of Spanish male—noble, bullfighter, fisherman, and bandit—and of any Frenchman so rash as to venture south of the border (36.73). Her passion is matched only by her religion, as when a novice is kidnapped from a nunnery (30.20). It goes without saying that all Spaniards are highly emotional and unstable, to the point of being dangerous. Indeed, the violence of their emotions leads to their frequently being cast in the role of bandits, white slavers, or terrorists. At the very least, they will be engaged in violent family vendettas (35.4). The introduction of a Spanish character in a French film invariably signals the onset of seduction, violence, and death.

In Vienna, on the other hand, the calendar is constantly set at the Belle Époque of the Austro-Hungarian empire. Noblewomen are forever flirting with dashing officers, to the chagrin of their husbands, who are distracted by courtly intrigue. The life of Johann Strauss is told and retold (33.63; 36.141; 39s1). Elegant balls, at which the orchestra's repertoire seems limited to the waltz, presage a duel at dawn, and fine points of honor lead to suicide. Courtly intrigue and affectation become fossilized, inhibiting all true feeling and spontaneity, perhaps leading to the death of Archduke Rudolph (36.77), while liberal-democratic ideals threaten the end for the old order, leading to the death of Archduke Ferdinand at Sarajevo (38.108; 39.21). Insofar as it participates in this imperial elegance, Hungary, too, has its share of officers, noble families, balls, and operettas, but there is an underside to the representation of Hungary that did not exist in the case of Austria: it borders on Turkey, not to mention Transylvania, and is peopled, at least in part, by a motley crowd of cardsharps, bandits, Gypsies, and fortune-tellers. Superstition and instability are a recurrent motif, and vampires lurk in neighboring shadows (31.146).

At the fringes of Europe, the representation of the Other in national terms tends to give way to representation in racial terms. This is all the more true the farther one departs from known territories. Arabs are not distinguished in national terms, and East Asia tends to be peopled by an undifferentiated Oriental race, as the Pacific is by Polynesians. Some twenty-one films are set on the coastal fringe of Southeast Asia, and despite the fact that the races and nationalities involved range from Indian to Malaysian, Chinese, Japanese, and Mongolian, there is a certain coherence in their representation. A key feature holding them together as a group is the presence of Sessue Hayakawa and Valéry Inkijinoff in the role of "the swarthy Oriental." Hayakawa may turn up as a Mongolian prince, a Chinese gang boss/banker, or a Japanese spy, and Inkijinoff as a Malaysian, a Chinese sect hitman or bandit, a Mongolian maître d'hôtel, or a Japanese captain (reprising in the latter case the role played by Hayakawa in the silent period). For the most part, these Orientals are sinister figures, involved in the most various forms of trafficking. They are also figures of power, sexually predatory and fascinating to the European female. The Orient itself, in its more Chinese manifestation, is not unlike the Kasbah in being represented as a labyrinth of narrow streets, steep and cluttered, seething with a diverse humanity, where street stalls impede progress and alien eyes form implacable judgments. Concealed doorways lead to feverish gambling dens or the cool, spacious, but no less sinister domain of the master, whose suave and impassive exterior conceals a destructive lust. Prerevolutionary political intrigue generates tales of communist activists, gun running, triad generals with private armies, and Europeans either caught up helplessly in the resultant chaos or attempting to profiteer from it (37.75; 38.27). A surprising number of these "exotic" films feature British territories—India, Singapore, and particularly Malaya—but then, the disorienting effect on the self-possessed European of such an Oriental experience holds as true for the English as for the

French, and for the French of the thirties there was an even more radical opposition between the Englishman and the Oriental than between the Frenchman and the Oriental.

Indeed, the representation of Britishness in French films emphasized precisely those stilted, stuffy, unworldly (or, at best, reserved) characteristics most likely to be distressed by "Oriental" scenes of excess and emotional violence. This cold, haughty, distant, self-possessed temperament attributed by the French to the English is often figured as aristocratic distance. Most English characters in the period up to 1935 are noble males—lords, or sons of lords, who may act the fairytale Prince Charming role. Equally often, however, they get involved with foreigners drawn from one of the "passionate" nations. If male, they triumph, at the cost of the foreigner, who may sacrifice herself for love of him; if female, they are fascinated by the forbidden, but also terrified of it. In the middle of the decade, three dramatic films propose relationships between an English lord and a lowborn Frenchwoman, such as a chanteuse, with consequent anxieties about misalliances (35.125; 36.44; 37.122).

When the English are at home, however, they are engaged primarily in murder mysteries of various kinds or in spy dramas. The former, drawn mainly from English plays and novels in which Scotland Yard figures prominently, are largely confined to the first half of the decade, especially 1930–33 (*Drôle de drame* [37.37] comes late in the series). The latter constitute part of the shift of focus toward international politics in the second half of the decade (35.100; 36.35; 36.119; 38.43) and toward the alliance against Germany, culminating in *Entente cordiale* (39.33), which overtly (if in a historical setting) promotes the necessity for the English–French political alliance to be maintained in the face of conspiratorial forces.

Of all the countries commonly represented in French thirties films, Russia is the one with which the French appear to feel the closest affinity. Many Russians were working in the French film industry in the twenties and, although their industrial presence was not as prominent in the thirties, Russian production companies, such as Albatros and Ermolieff, were undoubtedly influential in mounting a number of films dealing with Russia. It is nevertheless true that German, American, and French companies produced as many of these films as did Russian companies, which suggests that audiences were assumed by production companies of all nationalities to have a predisposition toward Russia, its history, and its culture. This is further suggested by a number of routine narratives that are set in Russia with no apparent thematic justification, or that substitute Russian protagonists for French ones: Russia was simply an alternative to France, with the added exoticism of distance (37.124; 38.27). Certain of these "Russian" films are analogous to the Viennese ones that deal with the old order, the aristocracy, the military, debts of honor, duels, and emperors dallying with charming peasant girls. Such narratives could be set in any Eastern European country with the appropriate traditions (33.118; 35.30; 35.124; 39.7). There are, however, four characteristically "Russian" categories of film produced in the thirties—stories involving Russian immigrants in France, stories involving revolution, stories evoking a colorful episode in Russian imperial history, and stories based on the somber novels for which Russian literature had become recognized.

The Russian immigrant population in France appears regularly throughout the decade (at least ten films). Sometimes, a Russian political or family drama spills over into Paris, which is seen as the natural refuge for any Russian forced into exile (33.73; 35.112). In general, life in France for these exiles is seen as stressful, often involving persecution (37.55); it is natural that obtaining a valid French passport should become an important preoccupation, perhaps even in the comic mode, leading a Russian princess in exile to offer herself to a Parisian taxi driver (38.81). On the whole, however, Russians are seen as having the spirit and culture necessary to make their way in Parisian academic and artistic life (31.9; 38.52). Montmartre seems to be largely populated by artistic Russians, and the portrait that emerges is overwhelmingly sympathetic.

It is understandable that these Russians should have wished to emigrate to France, or indeed to *anywhere,* given the representation of Russian history, politics, and society that emerges from adjacent films. Russian history is represented as involving a succession of despots, Machiavellian machinations, and attempted assassinations, in which Empress Catherine and Rasputin figure prominently. Russian history seen from below is equally, if differently, debilitating. Adaptations such as *Crime et châtiment* (35.28), *Les Frères Karamazov* (31.60), *Les Bas-Fonds* (36.15), and *La Sonate de Kreutzer* (37.83) saw to that. The "underworld" in which people live is characterized by prostitutes, extortionate money-lenders, thieves, and assassins, and their life is one of misery, degradation, humiliation, sin, and depravity, except when lightened by the spiritual purity of some flower-like young woman. Only one film tries to bring together the squalor and the majesty of imperial Russia, *La Tragédie impériale* (37.113), in which Harry Baur embodies a magnificently riotous yet charismatic Rasputin.

The Russian revolution thus comes to seem inevitable, and a series of films deal with plots to overthrow or assassinate one or another of the autocratic czars. Any attempt by well-meaning advisors or consorts to mitigate the harshness of imperial rule is ruthlessly curtailed by interested courtiers, as when Katia tries to induce the czar to introduce democratic reforms, only to see him assassinated on the eve of their wedding (38.56). Several films set in the period 1916–18 involve disturbances leading up to the successful revolution of 1918. Frequently, French nationals are drawn into such revolutionary machinations out of sympathy or by accident. The immigrant population in France is itself occasionally involved, plotting the overthrow of the recently established communist régime (39.60) or reluctantly acknowledging its legitimacy (35.112). It is clear that the Russian immigrant population consists essentially of the entire Russian aristocracy in exile, and is thus essentially antipathetic to the revolution. Yet, if only because of a general analogy with the French revolution, the French cinema is well disposed toward the idea of a popular revolution. The solution identified by a surprising number of films is to focus on Polish attempts to revolt against the Russian oppressor. Certain films deal with later, unspecified attempts to liberate a country, probably Poland, from the ruthless Russians—espionage narratives at the frontier of Poslavie, for instance (31.101), or on an unspecified Russian border (36.10). Such revolutionary narratives increase in number in the late thirties, and their titles are often significant (*Le Rebelle, Le Patriote*). Russian Cossacks besiege Poland (36.125), Russia is metonymized as a citadel from which imprisoned Poles struggle to escape (37.26), or sympathizers within Russian court circles strive to help Polish rebels escape the clutches of Empress Catherine (38.54).

The representation of Russia, then, is complex to the point of being schizophrenic. Russian aristocrats are ruthless and authoritarian, except when they have emigrated to France and become artists, students, and taxi drivers. Revolution and liberation are essential Russian phenomena, except when they are characteristic of Poles revolting *against* Russian oppression. Despite this ambivalence, one thing is clear about Russian history, politics, and society: it essentially came to an end in 1918, and nothing of any importance (to France) happened thereafter. Two isolated adventure films, one set in Manchuria in 1928 (33.10), which has a group of political refugees fleeing the Russians and caught up in a local civil war, and the other set in China at around the same time, which has similar refugees caught up in the troubles in Shanghai (38.27), only serve to emphasize this absence by their isolation and their Asian setting.

While the French could always recognize one or another aspect of their existence or their history in the Russian experience, the fascination that they felt for America arose primarily from its very otherness. While that otherness was in part due to the longstanding antagonism between Anglo-Saxon and Gallic cultures, the antagonism is tempered in the thirties by a reluctant admiration for the Americans' apparently effortless wealth and for the narrative ease, industrial dominance, and unrivaled glamour of the American cinema. The latter, in particular, can stand as a metonym for the love-hate relationship that is common to much of the representation of America in the thirties.

More films feature the United States and Americans than any other nationality. In part, this is because of the American intervention in French cinema in the early sound period (though the same cannot be said of Germany, which intervened almost as aggressively, if more tactfully). Well over two thirds of the films featuring Americans were made in the period 1930–33, and nearly half of those (fourteen in the period 1930–32) were multiple-language versions with an American master version, often drawing on a prior American novel or play. Thus, they are a product of the incipient cultural colonialism which the French saw the American cinema as threatening. Nearly all of them, whether made by American or French filmmakers, are romantic comedies, and a surprising number deal with romantic relationships between an American male and a French female, or, less commonly, the reverse. Throughout the decade, and again whether made by American or French filmmakers, the nature of the starkly contrasting national temperaments embodied in these "partnerships" is consistent.

If we are to believe these films, there are two qualities that America has to offer the French—wealth and fame/glamour. There are three qualities that France has to offer the American—tradition, an artistic/cultural ambience, and warmth/humanity/sensuality. Typical narrative lines might involve:

- A ruined French aristocrat who, to earn the right to marry a rich American girl, accepts an offer to go and work in her father's factory. He is too successful, becoming so Americanized that she no longer recognizes the light-hearted Frenchman she had fallen for; he must backtrack and demonstrate his Frenchness by abducting her romantically (30.42).

- A young American woman travelling in France with a jealous older husband makes herself up as an old woman to reassure him, but a French lad sees her without her wig, falls for her, and courts her; happily, under the influence of France (notably champagne and vivacious girls), the husband has acquired tolerance and humanity (32.103).

- A young American businessman, fed up with the hurly-burly of his business life, inherits a tumbledown chateau in Normandy and, while visiting it, learns the pleasures of lazing around doing nothing in the agreeable company of an attractive Frenchwoman (38.97).

- An American banker buys a French chateau out from under the very nose of the local countess; his wife and daughter come to take possession of it and are both successfully romanced by local Frenchmen—an aviator and the countess's son; the aviator marries his American girl, while the banker proves remarkably tolerant of his wife's "flirtation," offering the young count a job in his business (33.1)

Rich widows and divorcees and millionaire businessmen are the stock American characters of the genre, frequently providing a naive fairytale ending, while uncles or sons return from America with the know-how to serve their French family's fading commercial fortunes (30.56); the lure of Hollywood and stardom, nonetheless, is no less intense. From 1932 on, young French women and men alike are fascinated by the possibility of marrying a star, or of being discovered and whisked off to stardom (32.142; 33.90; 37.97). French self-respect requires from time to time, however, that this glamour and wealth be seen as mere tinsel, a frivolous illusion (33.101), and the American cinema becomes the butt of satire (37.104). At least four narratives have French men or women, particularly aristocrats, fascinated or tempted by the wealth and glamour of an American relationship, only to realize the superior, if humbler, virtues of their original French admirer (30.57; 31.36; 31.96; 32.35)! In the other direction, timid young Americans are sent to Paris to learn about life (31.13) because sensuality is, as everyone knows, alien to them (31.100); the French nightclub, the midinette or chanteuse, and the thrill of visiting some (perhaps hastily contrived) atmospheric dive (30s5) is what attracts them. If male, they buy up French chateaux; if female, they are seduced by handsome French musicians, or even by Michel Simon (38.18). Culture, tradition, sensuality, and joie de vivre are thus effortlessly acquired, in return for wealth and business know-how.

The abrupt cessation of these stories in 1933 is followed by a sparser series of analogous stories from 1935 to 1938. These are now interspersed, however, with quite different narratives, as when a Hollywood star's assassination in Paris provides a sensational pretext for a police drama (37.114), or when an American diplomat caught up in the Munich crisis neglects and thus loses his French actress wife (39.77).

2.2 THE FUNCTIONS SERVED BY NATIONAL STEREOTYPES

There is some minor interest simply in noting and describing the half-dozen national stereotypes which figure most prominently in the French mythology of the thirties, but, as the instance of America and Americans makes abundantly clear, the prime interest in such a study must reside in recognizing the underlying function that they served for the French themselves. French filmmakers selected and mobilized, and French audiences appreciated and approved through the box office, those foreign stereotypes which provided them with some form of mythic satisfaction as they contemplated what they as French men and women were, or were not, or would like to be, or must never be. More particularly, these national stereotypes serve the following six functions:

- They recognize/regret the end of an era, and in so doing, they embody a nostalgia for the supposedly simpler world of the past.
- They seek to speak, under cover of "foreignness," of erotic excesses which cannot be figured as a legitimate part of any society, even French society.

- They serve to define the inherent virtues of Frenchness and to promote the French nation as the highest embodiment of civilization, as evidenced, say, in its beneficent actions beyond its borders.

- They speak of an apprehension about the political disruptions of the contemporary world and of the need to prepare for war, or, more generally (but obliquely), of the inadequacy of contemporary political and economic structures.

- They propose an international coterie of cultured aesthetes to which the French belong by right, and whose existence is intrinsically more valuable than is that of the political and financial swindlers with whom the audience is all too familiar, and in so doing, such films place the French filmmaking fraternity implicitly in a relationship of comradeship with these foreign geniuses.

- They debate, through stateless people such as Jews, Gypsies, and immigrants, the adequacy of the contemporary nation-state, and possible internal threats to it.

These functions seldom correlate neatly with specific foreign countries or peoples. As we have seen, the exotic as erotic might be represented by the Chinese, the Malayan, or the Spanish, while the civilizing mission of the French might be evidenced in any "backward" region—not just Algeria, Tunisia, and Morocco, but also Syria, China, and Manchuria.

Certain of these functions are worth exploring more fully. Overt critiques of political authority tend to be confined fairly exclusively to fantasy kingdoms invented specifically for this allegorical purpose. Although René Clair's Casinario is perhaps the best known (34.35), numerous other fanciful kingdoms surround it, with names such as Cerdagne, Polestrie, Silistrie, Donogoo, Vodénie, Tryphème, Chimérie, and Slopoldavie. The most common narrative pattern structuring these allegories is the "substitute king" pattern, in which the king or prince of the fantasy realm proves inadequate in some way and has to be replaced by a humble citizen whose fortuitous resemblance to the monarch predestines him for the position. This humble citizen is, surprisingly, often found on the streets of Paris—as when, for instance, a Parisian street vendor replaces Fernando XXIII of Chimérie (32.123), a record seller replaces the Slav prince of Polestrie (37.81), or a lowly Parisian storekeeper replaces the prince of Vodénie (38.110). An analogous narrative has the young king of Silistrie introduced as a Parisian student, and relieved to be able to remain so when a republican revolution sweeps his country and deprives him of his throne (38.29).

In nearly all these cases, the political and financial establishment is pitted against true love, and the public sphere is seen as inherently inimical to the private. Perhaps more important, authorities of all sorts are seen as inadequate clowns, if not insane fascists, and any hope for the state lies with the humble man in the street, whose resourcefulness is a match for any challenge and whose value system is infinitely preferable to that of the established authorities. Le père Lampion, for instance, is a gutter-sweeper who effortlessly replaces the president of the assembly of his country, with benevolent effects that are widely appreciated by the populace (34.77). Not surprisingly, such allegorical critiques fall mainly within the years 1932–34.

The variant from later in the decade, *Éducation de prince* (38.29), provides an instructive instance of these fantasy-kingdom allegories. A prologue in the comic mode establishes the fact that a revolution, in which one authoritarian general has replaced another, has taken place in the banana republic of Silistrie, and that the French businessman Chautard is anxious to install a puppet monarch in the cash-strapped state so that he can exploit its potential oil wealth. But the prince, who is the obvious choice, is studying in Paris and not anxious to return to Silistrie. He prefers to paint watercolors and read poetry, and has been confronting the police on the Paris streets with his left-wing student mates. The palace conspiracy funded by the French magnate overrules his objections and, after a final few hours of freedom in which he discovers nature (camping, fishing, tranquillity), he is installed as king.

Essentially, to this point, the main purpose of the plot has been to represent all forms of authority and wealth as pompous, pretentious, arrogant, brutal, grasping, and self-interested, and to contrast them with the gaiety, simplicity, sincerity, and wisdom of the young and those of modest means in Paris. The prince's affectionate relationship with a French fellow student is, of course, threatened by the devious conspiracies of the powerful, and his girlfriend's father provides a contrast between those who manipulate the people and those who feel sympathy and understanding for them. A standard fairytale ending allows the student to be king of Silistrie while preserving his values and his love for his French girlfriend, but the political orientation of the film has long been established as communitarian and profoundly distrustful of business and politics, separately or in alliance.

Alongside these allegorical critiques are a very few attempts to speculate about the form of an ideal society. *Donogoo* (36.36), from the script of which Romains subsequently fashioned a novel, postulates "an imaginary town, invented by a geographer, which subsequently comes into existence as a real community where all desires are given free rein." Both this and (even more improbably) *Les Aventures du roi Pausole* (33.12) were produced by German companies—UFA and Tobis, respectively. The latter is more of a sexual fantasy, involving the voluptuary King of Tryphème, whose idyllic annual round requires that he service his 366 queens in succession. It is odd to find a German company agreeing to release such a technically incompetent film, with an incoherent narrative and no justification except titillation.

In the "real" world, contemporary political strife of a contentious nature is always distanced by being set "out there" in China or Mongolia, or at least in Spain. Malraux's attempt in *Espoir* (39s6) to introduce a realistic representation of fascist aggression and republican response is well known, but it was not released until 1945. Given the relative lack of restraint shown by the cinema in its representation of sexual matters, and the relative ineffectiveness of any formal censorship, it is quite striking how rare is the presence in films of the 1930s of any concrete reference to the ideological conflicts that were tearing apart contemporary Europe. The prerevolutionary struggles in China receive a little more attention, notably in Pabst's *Le Drame de Shanghaï* (38.27), which devotes a good deal of space to constructing a sympathetic portrait of Tchang, a communist agitator who is attempting to politicize and mobilize the workers of Shanghai. The private story of a Russian family's attempt to escape from the strife-torn city intersects with the Black Serpent's nefarious nationalist plots to assassinate Tchang and defuse the revolutionary potential of his activities. The final scenes of the workers' uprising incorporate a Potemkin-like sequence in which the workers appeal (successfully) to the Black Serpent's militia: "Don't fire on your brothers! Let's join forces!"

If contemporary political processes were seldom dealt with overtly, neither was the erotic. In France, as in America, thirties films tended to externalize erotic desire, projecting it onto exotic characters of a swarthy disposition, whose dark skin served as a metaphor for the evil passions seething within. The dark seductress may be a Spaniard, a Hungarian, or an East Asian; She is frequently a Gypsy as well. Passionate, tempestuous, given to excesses of jealousy and revenge, she can lead the civilized European (i.e., the white man) to betray his birth and give free rein to instincts better left repressed. This may lead to actual or attempted murder—drowning in the Camargue (34.89), murder by her father "according to the inexorable law of the Gypsy" (32.69), hara-kiri, self-immolation, or entombment (37.110). Alternatively, this "dark side" may be tamed by Christian marriage to a Hungarian noble (35.8) or other Eastern European officer (35.66).

It is a common narrative pattern for a wellborn lady to have to choose between a handsome Gypsy and an army officer (34.20). Sensuality could be contrasted with propriety, passion with frigidity, and intensity with discipline as the moral poles between which such exotic dramas were acted out. Gambling, with its connotations of risk and intensity, is often associated with sensuality as a central element of the fascination of the exotic. Whether in Macao or Mongolia, Hayakawa's roles explore these connotations. In *Forfaiture* (37.48), as a Mongolian prince, he presses his attentions on a French engineer's wife, using her gambling debts to entrap her. Once she is in his power, he brands her with a hot iron. The balance of fascination and revulsion which he arouses is nicely constructed, and Francen as her husband, in his recurrent role as the honorable but rather unimaginative French professional, accepts her protestations that she may have been foolish but was never unfaithful.

Race and sexuality link the exotic and the erotic again in *La Dame de Malacca* (37.30), though this time the sensuality of the Orient is most emphatically triumphant. Here, the white woman is trapped in a loveless marriage to a stuffy doctor (English, of course), whose milieu is defined by bridge and the necessity to flatter those in authority in the interest of advancing his career. Dreaming of romance and the jungle, whose combined forces might subvert the propriety and convention of respectable English society, she meets on a ship Prince Selim (not Hayakawa or Inkijinoff this time, but a heavily made-up Richard-Willm). The usual storm, which disrupts the Englishmen's card game, but which she finds exhilarating, facilitates her acquaintance with the prince. We find out that he had been to England to study but could never get close to the English because of their distance and formality, and because he had "dark blood." "The heart speaks more truly," she says.

Once in Malaya, and despite her husband's warning that all natives are thieves, she finds herself in sympathy with the life of the Malayans. The identification between Malaya and sensuality is made clear in such scenes as that in which Selim is showing her the exotic flower which blooms for a few hours of a single night. As they speculate about the possibility of their own relationship blooming, a brief, almost subjective image is presented of several bare-breasted native women flashing past. It is clear, however, that Malaya represents for her not just release and sensuality, but something more violent—or, rather, that conventions broken and sensuality unleashed can be not just exhilarating but destructive, if taken to excess. The Malaya to which she escapes is a place of seedy bars, cockfights, drunken sailors, and loose women. Sexuality is closely allied to chaos and nearly leads to her own death; she must learn to navigate between the extremes of formality and sensuality, both of which are represented as intolerable in their pure state. The prince marries her and engineers her rehabilitation, such that she can lord it over the desiccated expatriate Englishwomen who have come to stand as the principal representatives of propriety. In sum, as effectively as any film of the decade, *La Dame de Malacca* demonstrates the function of the exotic as erotic, aligning the dark-skinned and the foreign with the heart, liberty and sensuality, against rules, conventions, and calculation, but also with the risk of chaos and death, against security and belonging. It is fascinating but frightening—necessary, but needing to be skillfully negotiated if one is to survive, let alone benefit.

As well as linking sexuality to darkness of skin, the exotic genre commonly linked it to the "primitive" and barbarous, which could be represented as dangerous, violent, and evil, or as a welcome escape from the re-strictive conventions of the hyper-civilized. Gauguin's South Seas produced tales such as that of a French man and an English woman, both pilots en-gaged in a record attempt, who crash separately on the same desert island. Free from family expectations and national stereotypes, they establish an easy relationship, but once rescued they are quickly reminded of the force of convention (37.7). This is a readily recognizable sort of tale, in which a nat-ural catastrophe fortuitously results in the disruption of conventional pro-prieties and lets the heart speak, or lets innate talent come to the fore at last. In a slightly more deliberate vein, a stoker, disgusted by the social hierarchy and inequalities that he has witnessed on board ship, deserts to a South Sea island and sets up house with a native woman. Rescued, he realizes all that he is losing and plunges overboard to swim back to his island (30.15).

If the exotic is often erotic, and sometimes a form of purification, for-eignness is almost as often interpretable in a quite different way—as a fasci-nation with "high culture." The importance of art and the artist is a large topic that will be dealt with more fully later. Here, we may note that while a large number of exotic creatures are wild and passionate singers or dancers, many others are cultured artists or musicians, gazing soulfully into the mid-dle distance as their fingers (tactfully hidden by the frame of the piano) per-form improbable and apparently effortless feats of virtuosity. The spiri-tuality of the aesthetic is seldom questioned in these films, which typically focus on the life and loves of some real or fictional foreign artist. One of the few relatively consistent characteristics of the Italian is as a romantic cul-tural figure—most obviously in a film about Pergolesi (32.8), but also as a singing gondolier or a romantic tenor. The same is true of Vienna, where a series of films focusing on the lives of artists culminates in Gance's ponder-ous and pretentious life of Beethoven (36.135), which likens his sufferings to the martyrdom of Christ.

Such films about foreign artists complement the numerous parallel films dealing with the lives of French artists, such as Gance's almost equally atrocious but very popular film on the composer Charpentier (39.49). As in the case of American films, in which the French tended to emerge as sensi-tive and cultured aesthetes, all of these films about artists directly or indi-rectly cast the French in a favorable light as cosmopolitans with an inherent appreciation of things cultural. This is very obvious in the case of Chopin, who is, after all, an honorary Frenchman (34.25). More reflexively, as many studies of French film criticism have shown, French filmmakers seem from the beginning to have categorized their own activity as art, subject to the same romantic myths as painting, music, or literature, and the celebration of great artistic achievements of other nations was an indirect way of in-serting themselves into this ahistorical and transnational company of mas-ter artists.

But for thirties filmmakers and their audiences, the French have other, more practical and material virtues, and these are concretely displayed in their activities in colonial territories. The engineer is a key figure in many of these narratives—a dynamic professional devoted to transforming the primitive societies he finds into productive communities with an industrial infrastructure and a modern communications network. In the thirties, the activities of these engineers range from railway construction to oilfield development, and they may even conceive of building floating islands in the mid-Atlantic to serve as airports (32.72), or tunneling under the Atlantic from Europe to America (!) (33.134). The more extravagant feats come from the early thirties and verge on science fiction, while the more prosaic feats of civil engineering date from 1936 and take place mostly, but not exclusively, in East Asian countries where French trading concessions gave France a commercial and political foothold. French engineers are constructing or maintaining railways across China and Mongolia (37.90; 37.48), or even Ethiopia (33.116), but are thwarted in their fundamentally humanitarian mission by the jealous feuding and short-sighted self-interest of local tribes or bandits and hampered by their wives' descent into melancholy and madness. Indeed, in these exotic tales the "male engineer" is seen as an appropriate contrasting role to that of the erotically aroused wife or foreign vamp spy, since such a contrast recycles standard gender oppositions concerning reason and instinct, the public and the private, the reliable and the treacherous. In romantic comedies, this led to several films in which the hero was nominally qualified as an engineer, without actually having to engage in any engineering activities. It was simply the case (at least from 1933 on, since earlier examples tended to represent engineers as gullible and easily conned) that engineering was seen as an appropriately dynamic career for a hero. The one interesting exception is St. Exupéry's scenario for *Anne-Marie* (36.6), which proposes a female engineer in civil aviation around whom no fewer than five adoring pilots cluster and who undertakes a daring record attempt in the course of which a sixth pilot saves and wins her.

Because there are so many more of them, the films set in Algeria, Morocco, Tunisia, and other French regions in North and West Africa provide a more complex picture of Frenchness in action overseas. In this context, the focus on civil engineering which predominates in other French spheres of interest can be seen as simply one stage in a grand narrative about the establishment and consolidation of Empire. This narrative is constructed piece by piece by the films of the decade and establishes the essential elements of the relationship between the Frenchman and the Arab. It consists of five main stages:

- *Exploration* of " virgin" territory.
- *Pacification:* the military suppression of rebels and bandits.

- *Missionary work:* colonizers and missionaries establishing outposts of French society and culture, and demonstrating the superior spiritual values thus made available to the colonized.
- *Civilization:* engineering works (railroads, oil wells, dams, roads) to make the newly settled land habitable.
- *Integration:* the development of a complex love-hate relationship between the colonials and metropolitan France in which North Africa is the same but different.

Alongside this public story of national expansion, there are three typical "private" narratives that intersect with, or find fruitful ground in, the colonial narrative:

- *The foreign legion story,* in which individuals, fleeing shame or the law, join the foreign legion and are redeemed, often at the cost of their lives.
- *The inter-racial story,* in which relationships of friendship, respect, and love develop between representatives of the colonial power and the indigenous population.
- *The Freudian drama,* in which (as in other exotic countries) forbidden or repressed desires are worked out under cover of an exotic otherwhere.

The public story expounded in the grand narrative is similar in general form to the conquest of the west as outlined in the Western genre, with its pioneers, settlers, railroads, combats with Indians, and ultimate transformation of a wilderness into a garden. Indeed, Raoul Walsh's *Big Trail* is the American master version of *La Piste des géants,* in which a caravan of French settlers duplicates in the French-settled southern regions of what is now the United States the standard pioneer/settler narrative of the central-western states. In Africa, analogous narratives tell of Brazza's exploration of the Congo and establishment of Brazzaville (39.6), and of de Foucauld's venture into Morocco disguised as a Jew in preparation for subsequent French expeditions and appropriations, and his later venture into the southern Sahara as a missionary (36.7). One of the most popular elements of the narrative is pacification of the newly explored regions. The legionnaires, though themselves outcasts, rejects, and criminals, are led by noble officers who have a visionary approach to France's civilizing mission and always have the betterment of the locals at heart. In Africa, it is largely the legion that is shown undertaking, in the most arduous fashion and under the oppressive heat of a desert sun, the manual aspects of the engineering feats which will transform that desert into a fertile land (39.44). In this aim, however, they are hampered by the greed of marauding bandits; by the incomprehension of the local tribespeople, who, when not engaged in fratricidal wars, join in resisting all attempts at civilization; and by the treacherous behavior of foreign and even French gunrunners who arm the local tribespeople. If the arms dealer is male, he commits suicide, leaving his wife to come to terms with the heroic French officer (38.8); if female, she falls for the heroic French officer herself, but it can never be, and true to his duty he blows up her yacht with her in it (37.45).

The standard heroics of the small band of brothers overcoming hordes of indigenous tribespeople forms a climax to many of these films. It is common for the protagonist, if not of the whole detachment, to die tragically, with the officer perhaps reduced to blowing up the besieged outpost to prevent the capture and torture of his few remaining men (36.111), though their resistance to that point is represented as beyond all expectations: theirs is a glorious death (35.6; 38.38).

The foreign legion story that intersects here is well known: wanted for murder (35.6), fleeing scandal (33.62; 39.15), having broken with the family (34.82), or simply because of some unnamable but unspecified shame (five films), the son/brother/husband/lover flees to the legion. There, in the company of others of his kind, he learns a form of rough brotherhood, combined with grudging respect for the officers who drive their men hard, but drive themselves even harder. Memories of the woman who was the cause of their disgrace, or glimpses of someone who might even be her (33.62), or her actual arrival (38.78), or even, in one case, finding her now married to his captain (31.120) complicate the process of rehabilitation and redemption; but in the climactic battle the exile proves himself a man, and either dies gloriously for a cause greater than his own personal existence, or, renouncing definitively any personal happiness, re-enlists in what has become the only life worth living (36.134).

The best known and easily the most popular of these foreign legion films is *La Bandera* (35.6). It is exceptional in that it is set in the Spanish foreign legion rather than the French, but otherwise it follows classic lines. Gabin, as Pierre, in one of the roles which established him as a star and which served to define his screen persona, has blood on his hands and no money. Forced to join the legion, he experiences all the standard induction procedures—mates and rivals, drink and cards, bars and billiard halls, girls and horseplay, the native woman with whom he establishes a more enduring relationship, backbreaking work, and the gradual approach of combat with the indigenous Arabs, which will end with his heroic death defending a remote outpost against impossible odds. An added interest in the film is the slimy presence of le Vigan as Lucas, who may or may not be a police officer but who, a little like Javert in *Les Misérables,* slyly pursues Pierre until the final climactic siege when, alone with Pierre facing the alien hordes, he develops a respect for the man he has sought to betray and is himself transformed by the experience.

Unlike exploration and pacification, colonization and civilization are not, for the most part, represented heroically in North African stories. Colonials are most commonly found in the seedy bars and bistros of remote outposts, surrounded by the debilitating signs of their decline into native ways of life. On the other hand, the spiritual values that France had to offer the African continent are most effectively propounded in *L'Appel du silence* (36.7), which, with *La Bandera,* was the most successful of all North African films, and one moreover which had been sponsored by the Catholic church and funded by public subscription. A conventional recounting of "the life of a great man," *L'Appel du silence* relates the life of Charles de Foucauld first as a military man, then as a missionary. It thus combines the pacification story with the humanization story, and pivots around a central scene in which Charles, having explored and pacified much of Algeria, Tunisia, and Morocco, is finding inadequate the material mastery provided to him by French arms, industry, and science, and is looking for some higher cause. In a church in the desert, Christ's face appears to him, accompanied by a portentous clash of orchestral sound; he burns his past and abandons his former self and the world to take on the silence of the monk and of the desert. Numerous parallels with Christ's life should have reassured the Tuareg that his quest has divine approval, but, instead, when he is betrayed by his own Judas, they slaughter him and his congregation. Altogether, the film manages to represent both the material and the spiritual forms of civilization that France was bestowing on the natives, while leaving no doubt that the latter are the more profound and enduring.

In this spirit of universal brotherhood, numerous films tell of amicable or intimate relationships developing between the French and their Arab "brothers." This may happen in the army, as for example when a young French officer loves a Moroccan girl who momentarily believes that the French are responsible for her parents' death and intends to kill the officer. Of course, the real assassins are ultimately unmasked (37.86). A classic, if trashy, example of this situation is to be found in *Baroud* (31.18), which has survived in its British version. The French captain in the foreign legion is a close friend of the Arab pasha's son, but falls for and courts the pasha's daughter unawares. Since he is an infidel, this means dishonor for the Arab family, and his friend is distraught at the thought of having to kill him. But just then, dissident rebel tribesmen attack the loyal pasha's fortress and the two friends are reunited in defense of it. Naturally, a French relief column arrives just in time. The brotherhood of the French and of "sensible" Arabs is reaffirmed.

French civilians are just as liable as are their legionnaire compatriots to strike up such brotherly relationships—between, for instance, a young colonial and the Caïd's niece (35.15), between a Tuareg and the French girl whom a young colonial saves in the desert (31.46), or between a young medical couple and their indigenous patients, leading them to adopt the daughter of a local rebel engaged in yet another fratricidal war (34.48). Friendship, respect, compassion, affection between peoples of different races—all are possible in the more humanitarian order being created by the French, but they are in tension with the tendency in these films to see North Africa in the same light as other exotic locations—intrinsically other, and therefore a suitable field on which to act out the unleashing of Freudian repression. A common pattern, perhaps best known from *Pepe le Moko* (36.99), is to set up a triangle in which the male protagonist has to choose between a French and an indigenous woman. In this opposition, the French woman is coquettish and calculating, the indigenous woman passionate but also compassionate, and true to the death. This pattern also appears in Loti's *Roman d'un spahi,* filmed earlier the same year (36.114). More generally, French women in Africa are sexually destructive, often in perverse ways. Re-enacting their roles from *L'Équipage* (35.42), Vanel and Aumont are manager and assistant in a remote colonial outpost. The manager's wife, who has destroyed him and driven him to Algeria, turns up at the remote agency that he runs, and seduces and destroys his "son" before being killed by marauding bandits (38.95). In an analogous story, Vanel is again the paternal partner in a foreign legion friendship when his younger colleague gets involved with his wife (38.57). In yet another film of this sort, Gabin and Aumont act out the Oedipal triangle (37.72).

It is not only father/son partnerships that evoke Freud. In *Sarati le terrible,* Raimu is the patriarchal master of the Algerian dockyards, obsessed by an incestuous love for his niece (37.103). Even more explicitly, in *Le Simoun,* a colonial whose wife dies summons to Algeria the daughter he has never known, and faced with her resemblance to his beloved wife gradually becomes sexually obsessed with her. The hot desert wind of the title is present on the night that he declares his incestuous passion (33.116).

At the end of the grand narrative of colonization, then, French North Africa is the principal element of an empire which itself, with the approach of war, is represented in many documentaries as a string of pearls manifesting France's high destiny among nations. *Courrier d'Asie* (39s5) brings a light admixture of fiction to this documentary tradition, as an average Frenchman proceeds on a tourist voyage around the world from one French sphere of interest to another, beginning in Marseille and touching down in Tunis, Alexandria, and Beirut en route to Hanoi. But if these territories are seen as intrinsically French, they are still other—the same as us, but different—and this ambivalence allows both for humanitarian gestures of solidarity and brotherhood and for mutual recognition of difference. Attitudes and values cannot be transplanted without modification. Some French men and women find the adaptation impossible, as when a colonial brings his girlfriend—a musical star—to Algeria, only to have her retreat to France and her theatrical life (37.74).

But some North Africans find adaptation to France impossible, too, usually because of its overly materialist preoccupations. This allows for a critique of contemporary French values from a spiritual standpoint, as when a young Tunisian woman brought to Paris to study finds the worldly life of the capital intolerable (35.92), or when de Foucauld arouses the natives' interest in France and asks the authorities to show them the cathedrals and places of worship, only to have them shown the rush and bustle of industrial progress. They return disillusioned (36.7). The former of these, *Princesse Tam-Tam,* constitutes a particularly forceful rejection of the supposed advantages of Western civilization. Not only does Josephine Baker give the Tunisian character a vitality and humanity notably lacking in the Europeans, but the one Westerner who appreciates her, Max, is played by Albert Préjean, intentionally or not, as a giggling, supercilious idiot whose appreciation is valueless. Disillusioned by him and by the culture he represents, which is equated with affectation, lies, and deceit, she returns to Tunisia to marry one of her own. The final scene is one of the great moments of thirties cinema: as she and her indigenous husband play with their cherubic child in an idyllic Tunisian landscape, their ass comes upon a copy of Max's latest book, based on his relationship with Tam-Tam; it is called *Civilization.* The ass curls its tongue appreciatively around the title page, gathers it up into its mouth, and, in a close-up, munches meditatively on it and on all it stands for.

Two fascinating films set themselves the task of representing this ambivalent relationship—*Pepe le Moko* (36.99) and *La Maison du Maltais* (38.60). The former is famous for its characterization of the Kasbah as both a refuge and a trap for the hero. He can reign supreme there, respected and loved, free to do anything he wishes—except leave it. Technical codes characterize the Kasbah as a place of chaos and instability, the lawless enclave of a country in which the lawless find refuge, but it is also a place of true affection, in which Pepe has his family and friends. Yet no one who has seen the film will forget the nostalgic longing for Paris that emerges most powerfully from the brief song sung by Fréhel about La Place Blanche. Pepe's indigenous mistress and, later, Slimane the police spy both mock his inability to return to the one place where he might feel at home, and Gaby, with whom he has exchanged reminiscences about Paris, and notably about La Place Blanche, comes to represent the home of which he dreams. With her, he says, he feels as if he's back in Paris. The representation of the colony as exile is finally confirmed by the notorious dockside grill through which the doomed Pepe watches the steamer departing, as Gaby returns home alone (well, not quite alone). North Africa portrayed thus as a place of exile is well known from several surviving films—*La Bandera,* in which Pierre reminisces about the streets of Paris to which he can never return because of his crime, and *Sarati le terrible,* in which Gilbert, likewise exiled by a crime which he has gone there to forget, carries on about the home he will never see again. The same pattern occurs in *Maria de la nuit* (36.73), in which a young French man exiled for a crime that he has not committed has to choose between a Spanish chanteuse and a French woman who can open the way to his return home, and again in *Le Danube bleu* (39.20), though in this case the unjust exile is not from France.

But the theme of exile from France is nowhere near as common as the theme of France as itself a place of exile from some imagined haven—"là-bas"—where the protagonist might feel at home. For narrative purposes, this imaginary land may be located in South America or, less commonly, on other continents, but its main function is to reflect unfavorably on the conditions of the daily life of the protagonist(s) in France. On the surface, it might seem as if the themes of exile from France and exile in France are inherently incompatible, but the common representation of the protagonists' daily existence as an intolerable burden excluding all possibility of social integration or personal fulfillment is common to both. This places them closer to the theme of class and society, which will be discussed in chapter 3.

A film that deals with the contrasting representations of Paris and North Africa in a more complex and balanced way is *La Maison du Maltais.* Greta is a good-time girl working in a nightclub in Sfax. Consumed by tuberculosis, she reminisces about the fields and streams of her childhood home in provincial France. To this point, the film seems to be seeing Tunisia simply as a place of exile. Her friend Safia, however, complicates this representation, as she has had an affair with Mattéo the Maltese but, wrongly believing him dead, leaves for France with an honorable French officer who offers her refuge. Later, when Mattéo travels to Paris in cahoots with a North African gang, Safia is faced with an impossible choice between on the one hand the sophisticated elegance of her comfortable Paris life, which has hardened her and led her to think of Mattéo in suspicious mercenary terms of blackmail and buying off, and on the other hand the impoverished and harsh North African world which is that of criminality but also of true passion, sincerity, poetry, and dreams. Her decision is preempted by Mattéo the poet and gangster, who recognizes that he must withdraw from her life for her sake (and for that of their child, who has been adopted by the French officer) and commits suicide.

Alongside these political narratives dealing with colonization, settlement, and exile, we find an equal number of narratives dealing with international conflict. Together, the two genres, like the Western and war genres in America, provide the most overt forms of national self-definition. There are three categories of narrative concerning international conflict—the relatively rare war stories, most of which relate to World War I; the more common spy dramas, also centering on World War I but overlapping into the interwar years; and the romantic and family dramas in which national conflict provides an often incidental crisis in a fundamentally private narrative. A related category of film explores postwar internationalist and pacifist themes consequent on the horrors of World War I. Cumulatively, these films constituted about 4 percent of the output of the decade, and were concentrated primarily (though not exclusively) in the years 1935–39. In the twenties there had been very few films dealing with World War I until 1927–28, when a small group of influential films appeared, two of which were completely refilmed in sound versions—*Verdun, visions d'histoire,* which became *Verdun, souvenirs d'histoire* (31.147), and *L'Équipage* (35.42). Gance's 1919 film *J'accuse* was also remade by the director in a sound version (37.64). Of the dozen films of this genre produced up to 1934, most are not set in France but deal with wartime conflicts on the margins of the Austro-Hungarian empire—in Poland, Russia, North Italy, Romania, Austria, or Serbia—though two of the most effective of those set in France appear amidst a sudden burst of six films in 1931—*Verdun* itself, and *Croix de bois* (31.45). From 1935 on, however, the output increases and the focus is almost exclusively on the French experience of World War I.

Romantic or family dramas in which the war figures incidentally are of less interest here, though their number testifies to the extent to which the recent experience of war was fundamental to the identity of families of the thirties, to the point of forming an almost inevitable episode in any film dealing with the evolution of family relationships. Typical episodes inserted briefly in such family dramas are the departure, a brief montage of trench warfare, a stretcher, a hospital, nurses, the recovery and return to find that all has changed back home (36.115; 39.69). Believed dead, perhaps blinded, the soldier finds that his romantic expectations have come to nothing, or misunderstandings and losses have occurred that can only be put right much later (37.46; 38.49).

It is the spy dramas which are most clearly formulaic, invariably underpinning a narrative of political espionage with a sexual narrative of seduction that puts to the test the national allegiance of at least one of the spies. In most cases, the male spy is French, and his allegiance is tested by a seductive German woman who is either actively involved in counter-espionage or unwittingly being used by the military. Usually these spies are foreign, as in *Mademoiselle Docteur* (36.69), which is based on the exploits of Anne-Marie Lesser and which is unusual in that it is told in large part from the point of view of German spies and spymasters trying, with some degree of success, to deceive and defeat the French. Mlle Docteur is sent on a mission to Greece to penetrate French military and diplomatic circles but becomes romantically involved with a handsome French officer, which inhibits her normal ruthless efficiency. The usual confusion of spies and counter-spies, turncoats and traitors, intrigue, disguise, and deception constructs the moral ambivalence of this world, which is echoed in a number of technical codes (lighting, camerawork). Mlle Docteur steals crucial documents and gets messages through the lines, but in the climactic German air attack she is chased and gunned down by none other than the French officer with whom she has been romantically involved. As in the earlier instance involving a female arms dealer, in any conflict between love and duty the French officer is true to his calling, sacrificing the private to the demands of the public.

In all these films, the most emblematic character is the beautiful female spy. Closely related to the vamp, and often played by the same actresses, she commonly serves the standard Western function of presenting temptation by the female as inimical to male honor and duty, though that opposition is all the starker when "male duty" involves a threat to the nation. Women are associated with the enemy, and are thus inherently treacherous, but are capable on occasion of redemption through sexual submission to the male. Several of these narratives take place in Alsace, Belgium, and northern Europe, where borders and allegiances are less clearly demarcated. Thus a German spy's beautiful wife saves a French officer and they fall in love; fortuitously, her husband is unmasked and dies (31.138); a French deserter is accepted into German counter-espionage and subsequently unmasked as a French spy, but is saved by a beautiful German spy, who betrays her country for him (33.87); a French spy succeeds in obtaining the plans for a new German airplane engine, so the Germans send their most beautiful spy to seduce and kill him, but the two fall in love and she sacrifices her life to save him (35.31); a beautiful German spy is fomenting rebellion among the Ethiopians, but she falls for a French official and dies with him in the resulting cataclysm (33.147). Whichever of the warring countries is the setting, a local supply of seductive females is available for such purposes. In Russia, one lures the hero into gambling debts and suspicion of treachery (34.70). In Romania, one is sent to identify and kill a traitor in an air squadron; having succeeded, she marries the French officer who had aided her (31.126).

Fortunately for France, it, too, had a good supply of Mata Haris. When German spies steal the formula for a new gas, a French female spy is sent after it; like her foreign counterparts, she falls for one of those she is spying on (the son of the German general) and is thus faced with a conflict between love and duty, but in the resulting moral struggle, duty inevitably wins out over desire (36.68). The following year, the beautiful Alsatian Marthe Richard's "real-life" adventures were recounted; she gets herself hired by the Germans and wins the trust—and more—of the head of German espionage, who finally discovers the truth and commits suicide in de-

54 | THIRTEEN HUNDRED FILMS

spair (37.70). Many of these spy stories involve confrontations between the French Deuxième Bureau (manned almost exclusively, it would seem, by Capitaine Benoît) and German counterintelligence (35.31; 36.53; 38.15; 39.27).

Aside from stealing documents, plans, and formulas, the espionage missions may be aimed at establishing intelligence networks (37.107) or opening secret routes through enemy lines (37.88). In a typical example, in occupied northern France, German counterintelligence is trying to suppress a transit route. The Deuxième Bureau is aided in its attempts to keep the route open by the local populace, by the fact that the French officer in charge has an identical twin who is the local abbot, by an Alsatian French spy among the German ranks, and by a beautiful local woman who successfully attracts and dupes the German high commander. With twin spiritual and military powers, and with sexuality on its side as well, the Deuxième Bureau cannot lose, and the film ends with a montage of victory parades, the *Marseillaise,* and the Arc de Triomphe.

It is characteristic of these formulaic spy stories, however, that the Germans are not portrayed at all badly. There is something of the knightly tradition of the chivalrous duel about the clash of national interests as portrayed in these films. The Germans are worthy adversaries and men of honor (or at least the officers are), capable of dying nobly (31.138). Moreover, any simplistic national oppositions such as those outlined in *Marthe Richard* are undermined by the extraordinary presence of von Stroheim as the German officer who falls for the title character. His suicide, in which he injects poison, strips off his rank, and sits at the piano to play a funereal piece, steals the film and makes the French heroine's victory appear squalid. "I believed we were participating in a grand adventure," he murmurs, "but she was just a petty spy like the others." Likewise, in *Deuxième Bureau contre Kommandantur,* the arrival of a German officer midway through the film to try to pierce the French codes and deceptions swings the plot from a spy story to a mystery thriller in which, for much of the rest of the film, we adopt the detecting German's point of view. The audience tends to identify with the investigator, and indeed the French victors ultimately acknowledge his virtues and salute him: out of respect, they allow him to live (39.27).

Of course, several of these films were German co-productions, and several others were directed by Germans. Nevertheless, the absence of any rancor in the portrayal of "the enemy" is significant. This same absence of rancor is apparent in the few more straightforward war stories of the decade. Combined with a lack of heroics and a reluctance to single out individuals as protagonists for the audience to identify with, this makes all these films somewhat akin to the humanist pacifist films which were markedly more common than simple war stories. Thus, *Croix de bois* (31.45) follows a squad of enlisted men as they form a unit, are initiated into battle, form bonds of comradeship, spend brief days of leave behind the front, then return to the front to die. The anonymous horror of the experience, re-created with mind-numbing authenticity, makes this film more a comment on the horror of war and "the pity of it all" than a celebration of national heroism. An hour's screen time of suffering, slaughter, and stolid endurance, unrelieved by narrative advancement, underlines the senseless, shapeless chaos of the experience, while the briefer but parallel shots of German soldiers enduring the same experience undermine any residual potential for national self-righteousness. (Incidentally, the narrative concerning induction into a military unit, noted above as underlying *Croix de bois,* is in part strikingly similar to that, often unstated, which underlies the host of military vaudevilles being produced at that time, though these deal with the same material in a vastly different way.)

Similar observations about the connotations associated with Germanness can be made of *Verdun,* which is distinguished by the anti-psychological orientation of the characterization and the general theme of respect for the enemy in a time of senseless collective suffering. Thus, these supposed war films are not far from *La Grande Illusion* (37.54), in which von Stroheim again brings an improbable humanity to "the enemy," or the peacetime *Alerte en Méditerranée* (38.4), in which English, French, and German navies collaborate to stymie a band of pirates who have stolen poison gas and in which the German captain dies saving a ship of French passengers. The more overtly internationalist films produced during the decade suggest both a professional respect for and a closer understanding between officers of different nations than between classes of the same nation, since the former recognize a common code of honor and share a knowledge of the same clubs and social circles—may, indeed, share common family bonds. The men in *Alerte* harbor residual patriotic prejudices, which the officers "rise above," while the French officers and men in *La Grande Illusion* are fighting for quite different Frances—on the one hand, Fouquets and Maxims, on the other, one's mates in the corner bar. "We have nothing in common," as Maréchal says to Boieldieu, whereas the transnational sympathy of "the people" resembles that of the cows they tend, who "care nothing for nationalities." Reconciliation is still the theme in 1938 (*Paix sur le Rhin,* 38.72), when two brothers return to their family home in Alsace at war's end, one having fought for the French, the other for the Germans. Initial awkwardness gives way to a realization that national and racial antagonisms are baseless and must be overcome.

A particularly fascinating film with an internationalist theme is *Le Tunnel* (33.134), which has survived, at least, in its 1935 English version. The project to build a tunnel under the Atlantic is explicitly presented to its financial backers as a way of uniting nations and continents and ensuring peace, which perhaps explains their reluctance to fund it. One consequence will be a reduction of armaments, to the fury of a fiendish arms manufacturer, who in the British version is French. Happily, his machinations are confounded. The nobility of these internationalist ideals is somewhat qualified by a speech late in the film in which the American president makes it clear that the unity and peace that are envisioned are targeted primarily at making the "Western confederation" (somewhat corresponding to the present-day NATO) strong enough to confront the Eastern confederation, which has been threatening world peace. It is not so much civilization which is at stake as "our" civilization.

Most outspoken of all the internationalist films is Gance's *J'accuse,* in which the ghosts of the dead of the Great War are summoned to prevent any recurrence (37.64). But numerous other films of the decade echo this disillusion consequent on the horrors of an earlier conflict (34.24; 35.5), or on family tensions generated by that conflict which can be resolved only in the next generation (37.16; 37.46; 38.49; 39.7). The same disillusion runs through *Le Temps des cerises* (37.109), in which young workers who have fought heroically in the war find themselves no better off twenty years later—indeed, exploited by the idle rich, their internationalist ideals and class bitterness speak of a refusal in future to fight for France as they know it. This film was, of course, made to promote the Communist Party's policies with regard to the aged, and was never commercially released.

Outside all reference to the war, other films carry the same message of reconciliation. Best known is Pabst's *Tragédie de la mine,* in which, after an explosion in the French mine, German workers come to the aid of their French colleagues, only to see the mine tunnel connecting the two countries closed off again once the crisis is over (31.131). But other internationalist themes involve a music competition destined to improve harmony (so to speak!) and understanding between nations (30.19), the foundation of a Universal Republic in the face of a threatened comet strike on Earth (30.38), and *La Kermesse héroïque* (35.67) in which the women's policy of providing plenty of food, wine, and sex proves effective in cementing international relations. It is not going too far to say that the overwhelming proportion of films that deal overtly with international relations are in favor of reconciliation and brotherhood, while the overwhelming proportion of films that deal with Germany represent Germans in a generally sympathetic and fraternal light. Although several films foreground xenophobic attitudes among the French, they do so disapprovingly, except in the case of Guitry's *Remontons les Champs-Elysées* (38.87), which not only manifests a profound distrust of the English, but characterizes the Germans by the tramp of fascist jackboots. The immediate reference is to the Franco-Prussian war, but it is nevertheless a little ironic in the light of Guitry's subsequent wartime behavior. In fact, this film makes clear the extent to which he despised not just other nations but 90 percent of his own compatriots.

Even as World War II approaches and films begin reporting on military preparations at the frontier (38s3), the anti-German mutterings of a group of schoolteachers ("Ach, foreigners . . . can't stand them" [38.25]) are condemned and proved unjustified. Admittedly, it is again von Stroheim who is the object of them, and the extent to which his presence as the personification of Germany in thirties films "distorted" French representations of that country is hard to estimate. Finally, L'Herbier's *Entente cordiale* (39.33) promoting Anglo-French solidarity by way of the Francophile Prince of Wales, later Edward VII, as the source of victory in World War I, and unambiguously foreshadowing the need for a similar alliance in 1939, proclaims in a postscript that it is "dedicated to all those who work for peace."

2.3 PARIS AND THE PROVINCES

If the representation by thirties films of overseas territories and of war tells us much about the hopes, fears, and beliefs of the French in that decade, so does their representation of France itself. To some extent, all the rest of this study deals with that topic, but as a form of introduction, it is useful to identify the geographical, historical, and cultural aspects of France which figure in these films—its internal topography, so to speak—and to ask to what degree it is seen as a coherent nation and to what extent a fragmented one, and to the degree that it is fragmented how the various fragments are characterized. Clearly, most of France and most of French history figure scarcely at all in films of this or any period.

A set of preliminary generalizations about French history in thirties cinema would have to begin by acknowledging the minimal place that it occupied. Costume dramas were not common as a genre—even in the immediate prewar years, when a (relatively small) number were noted for their technical skill, lavish sets, and popularity—and very few of them established any recognizable connection with actual historical events. When they did, it was primarily with the Napoleonic emperors of the nineteenth century, though a few films dealt with the revolution or the last days of Louis XVI. Effectively, French history was all but suppressed, and the past became little more than a convenient setting for fantasized dramas. While large numbers of films were set in the period 1870–1914, few made any attempt to represent actual historical events or figures. At best, the French cinema constructed an impressionistic portrait of the forms of everyday existence at two or three points in the preceding 150 years.

Specific historical references tend to cluster in the period 1750–1830, from Louis XV and Madame de Pompadour (30.90; 33.21) through Louis XVI and Marie Antoinette (29s1) and the revolution itself—*Danton* (32.48), *La Marseillaise* (37.69), and the chaotic period which followed the revolution (35.106; 39.89)—to Napoleon (31.73; 33.35; 34.46), including

Gance's sonorized film (35s3), and l'Aiglon (31.3; 33.3). The focus, not surprisingly, is on the few archetypal figures who can be represented as standing for all that is most glorious in the French character. Several films use narrative devices to underline the importance of this past to the present, such as Guitry's *Les Perles de la couronne* (37.89), in which the necklace links a series of historical events, or the brave revolutionary drummer's drumsticks in *Trois tambours,* which stir the courage of successive generations of the oppressed (39.89), or the soldier from Napoleon's Russian campaign who falls into a cataleptic trance and is revived a hundred and seventy years later (34.46). The best known of these devices linking the past to the present is the professor in Guitry's *Remontons les Champs-Élysées* (38.87), whose self-sufficiency is almost the equal of Guitry's own, and who recounts the history of the Champs-Élysées in order to link up three hundred years of French history. To a greater or lesser extent, all those mentioned so far hark back to the era of the revolution and of Napoleon's campaigns, when the French national spirit is represented as having manifested itself most forcefully in the commitment to high moral and spiritual values. It is in the light of such films that we can begin to understand Duvivier's odd film *Untel père et fils,* which was made in 1940 but not released until after the war, and which traces the strength of the humble French man in the street from generation to generation.

Although a range of narrative techniques converge to serve a single function in these films, it would be foolish to ignore the political battle lines drawn up by these "history lessons," as right-wing reverence for position, authority, and tradition vie with left-wing revolutionary fervor to decide which version of French history will become canonical. While there is scarcely enough material to justify statistical conclusions, it is fairly clear that a certain romanticized patriotism and national self-glorification combines with Guitry's portentous nonsense to give the right-wing version a marked dominance over left-wing "views from below," such as *La Marseillaise* and *Untel père et fils* (and, of course, the only two films of the decade to deal concretely with the contemporary French political situation—*La Vie est à nous* [36s2] and *Le Temps des cerises* [37.109]—but they were not commercialized fiction films). Wherever audience reaction can be measured, the right-wing view proves to have been markedly more popular.

A similar set of preliminary geographical generalizations would note that Paris is so insistently present as almost to coincide with the notion of France itself, but Paris in these films is confined mainly to two named locations—Montmartre and the Left Bank, characterized, respectively, by artistic life (36.75) and by student life (39.75)—though a usually unspecified working-class suburbia, sometimes identified as Belleville, is also very often represented. Outside Paris, the only region of France to appear at all commonly is the Midi, both for its quaint Provençal character and for its more glamorous Côte d'Azur/Riviera/Monte Carlo associations. The center and southwest are almost totally absent as, more surprisingly, is Alsace-Lorraine, until 1939 (39.57), though, as noted, the north is occasionally the focus of international anxieties related to heroics in World War I. Le Havre appears in *Quai des brumes,* of course, and occasionally elsewhere as the departure point for transatlantic crossings, and Brittany appears more often, mainly as a stark coastline on which austere fishing villages are to be found (33.102; 34.46; 38.44). It is dominated by the ocean: sea breezes are capable of restoring consumptive urban children to health, but the cult of the sea can also bring the threat of death (32.121).

But by far the most common region to appear in thirties films is the Midi, Provence. The number of films whose titles appeal directly to audience knowledge of the south is sufficient indication that it was considered a highly marketable region— *Côte d'Azur, Justin de Marseille, Un coup de mistral, Paris-Camargue, Au soleil de Marseille, Les Filles du Rhône, Titin des Martigues, Un soir à Marseille, Un de la Canebière, Marseille mes amours.* One concrete reason for this intense presence was, of course, the existence of a small-scale film production industry in Marseille— notably the energetic Roger Richebé—supplemented very soon by the films of Pagnol, funded by the success of *Marius—Fanny, Angèle, Cigalon, César, Regain, Le Schpountz,* and *La Femme du boulanger,* not to mention *Merlusse* and *Topaze* or Pagnol's contribution to *Toni.* But aspects of southern France were already consecrated in French literature, and several novels or plays were filmed in the thirties based on these— *Tartarin de Tarascon, Mireille,* and the Maurin books. Cumulatively from these and many other films of the thirties, a relatively coherent picture of the south emerges: it is characterized by the sun, a more relaxed and leisurely lifestyle, not to mention an accent and a vocabulary which lend color and humor to any narrative. Southerners are more volatile and voluble than northerners, lacking any neurosis or repression. Their emotions are never far from the surface: they are expansive, quick to take offense, but quick to forgive and forget. Less defensively individualistic than northerners, they have an easy set of social and familial relationships, constantly threatened by their volatile explosive personalities, but always triumphant. These characteristics lend themselves particularly well to two genres, the comedy and the melodrama.

But although a certain coherence is apparent, there are several distinct sub-territories within the Midi, each with its own distinctive markers. The Côte d'Azur is the first to appear, dominating the early thirties and continuing more sporadically throughout the decade. As might be expected, it foregrounds the leisurely tourist lifestyle, but pushed in the direction of glamour, elegance, and excitement. Attractive women recline on St. Tropez beaches, seeking romance (35.96). Secretaries get a chance to play the grande dame and seduce their bosses (31.42). Behind the Promenade des

Anglais, elegant hotels and palaces provide a stylish setting for boulevard comedies (31.141; 32.14; 32.111; 38.69), as they do for convalescing royalty (33.104). The convalescing lion-tamer, however, who desperately needs a stay in an alpine sanatorium, is bullied by his selfish and pleasure-seeking woman into a holiday on the Riviera which proves the death of him (35.109). It is the universal holiday destination. When, in *Paris-Méditerranée,* a romantic musical comedy, a secretary sets off on holiday with a millionaire mistakenly believing him to be a poor salesman who has won his posh car in a lottery, they will naturally voyage south, and the various lines of action will converge on the Grand Hotel in Cannes. Fortunes are won and lost, with the usual narrative consequences, at Monte Carlo (31.25) or Juan les Pins (32.86). Attracted by all this wealth, crooks seek to prey on the gamblers (35.63). And consecrating this early thirties generic pattern, Guitry, in his one really magnificent film, *Le Roman d'un tricheur* (36.115), has his philosophical con artist work as an elevator attendant in a casino, get involved with a countess, and team up with a female thief to cheat the casino and break the bank, only to be shamed into honesty, whereupon he loses all he has gained. Consistently hilarious, the film assembles, works through, and transfigures the scattering of conventions that had been developing over the previous five years (and indeed somewhat before).

Farther west, in Marseille, the atmosphere, characters, and plot lines are very different. Occupying a place in the local scene somewhat similar to that of Paris for the whole of France, Marseille is represented as a complex city dominated by its Vieux Port, its bars, and its underworld. No film set there can resist a loving pan over the port and the transporter bridge, and the characters who live in the latter's shadow share the vitality of Parisian working-class con artists (38.109). For Marius, of course, the sailing ships leaving the port open onto the unimaginably exotic world "out there," the lure of which is too strong to confine him in his father's bar and Fanny's arms (31.81; 32.58; 36.21), leading to a standard melodrama concerning an illegitimate son and the discovery of paternity. But bars, docks, and crime recur repeatedly (33.11; 34.96). As is frequently the case in the early thirties, there is no clear dividing line between honorable working-class men and women and the criminal fauna who haunt bars, run prostitution rackets, and smuggle drugs. Not only are the latter often regarded with sympathy and understanding, they even become folk heroes to the people among whom they work, who have as little liking for the law as they do.

Prefiguring in some ways Pepe le Moko, Justin de Marseille (34.53) is an amiable small-time gang leader and drug smuggler working the Vieux Port area, with its nightclubs, brothels, and bars, now confronted by Italian interlopers whom he finally dispatches. His gang, which is run as a family affair, protects the weak and maintains a form of order in what would otherwise be a cutthroat quarter. Justin himself treats women roughly, but they love him for it and reproach their pimps at any hint of treachery. He has an understanding with the local police and arranges for them to clean up the dregs of the rival gang after he has disposed of the chief. At the end of the film, he is casually strolling through "his" Marseille, showing his new woman the world over which he rules. In a similar vein, an amiable white slaver who packs indigent girls off to the brothels of South America is well regarded by his fellow citizens, though his activities are less well tolerated by the local police and he is finally put away (37.49).

In its introductory segment, *Justin de Marseille* overtly likens the city to Chicago. This is not, however, the only Marseille: elsewhere, local sportsmen are obsessed with soccer, perhaps ultimately making good in the big-time sporting world of the capital (37.12; 37.102), while the Vieux Port fisherfolk engage in frivolous romantic adventures, apparently unaware of the colorful underworld operating among them (37.106; 38.109).

Even farther west again, from Martigues to Les Saintes-Maries de la Mer, another set of characters act out more somber plots in the distinctively flat and marshy setting of the Camargue. A certain Western flavor enters these stories, if only because of the analogy between *gardian* and cowboy, though horses and bulls replace the cattle of the Western genre. However, the treacherous swampy ground of the region introduces a distinctive gothic element into the range-riding narratives, and the bullfighting for which the Camargue bulls are being prepared allows for macho heroics and stories of pride, honor, and shame. Violent emotions, notably jealousy, are the norm, often generated by rivalry between a simple local girl and a vamp, perhaps from the city (35.87; 36.90) and very likely involved with criminals (36.116). In a more realistic mode, *Toni* replays this triangular drama (35.110). The well-known treachery of womankind is metaphorically and even metonymically associated with the treachery of swamp and marsh.

If the coast is characterized by three different atmospheres, the extensive interior, with its bleached massifs, olive vegetation, and sparse villages, which constitutes "the true Provence," is characterized by a single atmosphere, most closely associated with the films which Pagnol set there over the years. Essentially, this consists of innocent charm, exuberant fantasy, and gentle humor. The villagers may be eccentric, they may allow their imagination to run away with them (34.99), they may engage in feuds with rival villages (36.51) or with one another (33s5), but they are basically simple and lovable (35.20; 38.38) unless the corruption of city life intrudes, as it does so memorably in *Angèle* (34.5).

The harsh, bleached landscape reduces existence to certain basic elements, and in the Pagnol films from the late thirties on, those elements are accorded a quasi-religious significance, which contrasts with the dismissive attitude toward formal religion. "Bread," "water," and "soil" are what matter, and *La Femme du boulanger* (38.34) returns them to a more authentic and pagan ritual, in which the sensuality of the flesh also plays an important role. *Regain* (37.100) represents a high point in this consecration of the basic prerequisites of social existence. In its celebration of the regeneration of an abandoned community through the mythologization of water, earth, seed, the plow (here passed on from generation to generation), the founding couple, and the produce of these—wheat and a child—the film foreshadows the conservative values ("the soil," "work," "tradition") promoted a few years later by the Vichy régime. Moreover, in its distrust of machinery and of "progress," with the exploitation of human labor that attends them, and its even deeper distrust of all forms of law, authority, and broader social organization or regulation ("In general, the clothes you wear for taking orders are no use for working in"), it embodies very forcefully the right-wing anarchism that was one of the most powerful undercurrents of French political and cultural life in the first half of the twentieth century.

Of the four sub-territories, this interior of Provence was the last to appear, taking over in the mid-thirties from the fading myth of the Côte d'Azur and Monte Carlo. The mythic Marseille dockyard and street life were largely exhausted by the end of the decade, and its bars, with their attendant meridional characters, were losing their savor. A film from the end of the decade has some of those characters reflecting on the decline of their mythic existence and forming a club to attempt to restore to the community its lost joie de vivre (39.18). The myth of the Camargue was to be perpetuated, however, into the forties, while the connotations associated with the parched interior are still as potent as ever.

Although, in mythic terms, the south was by far the most fully realized region of France in the thirties, certain aspects of that representation were shared with all other provincial regions, establishing a very general representation of provincial life and character, as opposed to Parisian life and character. This antinomy between city and countryside, which was the dominant structural opposition of perhaps 6 percent of films made during the thirties, is not, of course, peculiar to the thirties or to France. Ever since the rise of the bourgeois urban community (and much earlier in other forms—indeed, ever since the rise of urban existence), a consistent pattern of contrasts has structured cultural representations of agricultural life and urban marketplace life. These structural oppositions were enthusiastically recycled throughout the thirties in France. Essentially, they involve a contrast between, on the one hand, the agricultural past, with its residual feudal institutions, a continuing respect for local aristocracies, an attachment to the land, and a conservative view of family and gender patterns, and, on the other, a commercial and industrial future which is constantly evolving and in which all social institutions and personal relationships are being renegotiated. This opposition does not contain any inherent value judgment, each side being open to either positive or negative evaluation. The calm certainties of the past can be represented as either reassuring or boring, while the dynamic flux of the city can be represented as either dangerously destructive or exhilarating. One of the more interesting measures of the ideological orientation of a culture is the extent to which it will opt for the feudal past or the urban future. While a number of French films of the thirties are relatively neutral in their stance, merely exploiting the opposition for its known effectiveness, it is nevertheless apparent that in those films which deal explicitly with this opposition the provinces benefit from a markedly more favorable representation than does Paris.

Of course, Paris is not the only representative of the urban thirties in French cinema of the decade. The same opposition is worked out in films dealing with Canada, Morocco, and Hungary, while within France the agricultural versus the urban may be played out regionally in terms of Nantes, Marseille, or any other regional capital. Nevertheless, the myth foregrounds Paris as the archetypal urban agglomeration, in which all these antinomies are pushed to the limit. If the representation of Paris and of the future is far from favorable in this decade, it is due largely to two factors, both associated with class relationships. Paris is seen as the site of conflict between the working class and the haute bourgeoisie, and both of these classes are inextricably involved with criminality. On the one hand, in a cultural tradition inherited from the nineteenth century and more immediately from the apache of the 1920s, the working class is seen as harboring or as merging into the criminal underworld of the city. On the other hand, as a result of the inheritance of embezzlement scandals culminating in the great depression, members of the haute bourgeoisie are seen as greedy, corrupt, incompetent, and hypocritical, considering themselves above the law.

These factors will be explored in more depth in the next chapter; for the moment it suffices to note that when they are taken in conjunction with the tendency to link unbridled sexuality with the night life, students, and artists of Paris, the city is far more often in the thirties seen as a site of sexual license and criminality than of freedom and social justice. This is not so apparent till 1932, but thereafter the proportion of negative representations is about three to one. In addition, and largely as a consequence, as the decade wears on the city comes to be seen as the site of various forces tending to undermine commonly held values, and more specifically as the site of an individualism which is destructive to any sense of community. The provinces, on the other hand, benefit from association with nature's healing powers, which constitutes the decade's principal myth of nature (though not its only one). A visit to the provinces can thus provide a necessary purificatory experience for the jaded or corrupted urban individual—it is a source of salvation, or at least of healing.

Not surprisingly, this geographic opposition gives rise to a recurrent narrative trajectory: most commonly, provincials visit Paris and are horrified by what they see; if not irremediably corrupted, they return to their provincial village sadder but wiser. Thus, in melodramas innumerable innocent provincial girls are attracted to Paris only to be seduced and abandoned by callous Parisians (e.g., 32.74; 35.98). This narrative normally results in an illegitimate child and, sometimes, a descent into prostitution. This, in turn, brings them into contact with pimps and thugs, police raids, brutality, and other sordid aspects of the all-too-familiar Parisian underworld (32.87; 35.34). The Parisian locations most cited as triggering this downfall are nightclubs, though night life of any sort at all is considered dangerous. Actresses are particularly common agents of degradation, though all artistic and student life is considered intrinsically impure. A provincial girl's period in Paris studying will almost inevitably lead, through involvement in one of these milieus, to prostitution, drugs, and (at least attempted) suicide (e.g., 36.19). Parisians are sophisticated, fast-talking confidence artists, all too capable of conning the gullible provincial. Provincial men who go to Paris seeking their sister are likely to find that she has been corrupted by the big city (36.130); after rescuing or attempting to rescue her, they return gratefully to Arles or Brittany. If they fall for a Parisian woman, perhaps not realizing that she comes from Paris, she is sure to turn out to have a shady sexual past which renders her unsuitable (34.93; 36.31). Even the threat of a visit to Paris by a provincial fiancé ("to learn the ways of the world") is enough to win him his modest country girl, and it may become necessary for a fatherly provincial figure to travel to Paris in order to put his wayward young relative on the right track (35.16)—a nephew, in this case, who was about to desert in favor of an actress the girl he had seduced and made pregnant. Indeed, these narratives frequently end with a return to the country, where modesty, fidelity, community, and affection ultimately provide the necessary purgative process.

Occasionally, rather than a return trajectory of this sort, a man is torn between a wife in the provinces and a mistress in Paris (37.87), or vice versa (33.54). Occasionally, the conflict is triggered by the visit of a Parisian to the provinces, which causes a scandal or, at least, reveals an irreconcilable incompatibility between the two sets of values. Typically, a model marries into a provincial family and, try as she might to please her provincial in-laws, she cannot ever be other than an intruder (30.93), or an actress finds herself lodging with a provincial judge (38.80) of the strictest morality. In these stories, the provincial family is invariably stern, austere, and disapproving, while the Parisian is at least provocative and often ruthless, such as the actress in *Paris-Camargue* who is out to wring everything possible from the provincial heir (35.87). Alternatively, the provincial is something of a simpleton, naive to the point of gullibility, like Molière's *Monsieur de Pour-*

ceaugnac (32.93), and easily conned by the fast-talking sophisticated trick-sters of the capital. Thus, a provincial whose quaint ways have been paro-died by a Parisian comedian goes to Paris and is made fun of by the comedian's circle (36.86). Thus, a provincial, lured into standing for parlia-ment by a volatile Parisian actress, comes to realize the callousness and hol-lowness of the city, and returns to the country (38.33). Thus a naive but lovable provincial girl implicated involuntarily in the comic sexual com-plexities of a middle-class Parisian household will fall back in relief on her working-class aspirant from the adjacent marketplace, the nearest Paris can offer to sincere affection (35.98). Often, of course—indeed, usually—the gullibility of the provincial simpleton is found to conceal a superior wisdom which sees him or her safely through all trials. In Pagnol's treatment of this theme, *Le Schpountz* (37.104), the innocent and gullible provincial harbors dreams of becoming an actor, and a passing Parisian film company sees in him the ideal butt of their jokes. Mocked and manipulated, dressed grotes-quely for comic roles in what he had been led to believe were serious dra-mas, he finally comes to realize that these Parisian filmmakers, whom he had thought his friends, are, in fact, heartless, arrogant, and cynical. Other com-mon themes of the thirties intersect with this one to allow the provincial to triumph and return as a prodigal son to his modest family home, the virtues of which he has now learned appreciate, but the general narrative trajec-tory is exemplary, as is the association between modern media, Paris, and corruption.

At the beginning of the decade, in *Le Rosier de Madame Husson* (31.118), the cinema is already foregrounded as prime agent of immorality and licen-tiousness in the provincial town—indeed, Monsieur Husson reputedly fled Madame's rigid morality for the traditional Parisian actress, ending up in the cinema with her. Likewise, at the end of the decade we find a Paris radio station "discovering" the authentic charm of a provincial family, and ex-ploiting it to detrimental effect (39.37). As the agent of contact between city and country, the media were seen as emblematic of the social mobility that was to disrupt age-old traditional structures and corrupt the innocence of country ways. In *Le Schpountz,* this factor is exacerbated by the Ameri-canized ways of the production team, which identifies Paris not only with national forms of degradation but with international threats to national in-tegrity.

Paris is not always represented so negatively, however. If the provincials have so often to go through a learning experience involving disillusion, it is precisely because the illusion exists as a powerful reality in the first place: Paris has a special fascination for a younger generation of provincials who are apparently beginning to find the constraints of rural existence intolera-ble, and to whom the media have been whispering of more exciting possi-bilities. Two Paris districts hold a particular attraction—the Left Bank/

Montparnasse and Montmartre/Pigalle—though it is quite astonishing to note how relatively infrequently even these two neighborhoods figure in films of the decade. They are respectively, of course, the retreats of students and of artists, though the distinction is not very clear. Only two films refer to the Left Bank in their titles—*Rive gauche* (31.115), which tells of a model's love for a composer, her momentary distraction by a wealthy banker, and her ultimate recognition that the Bohemian life of Montparnasse holds superior attractions, and *Quartier latin* (39.75), dealing with the romantic dramas of a female student's life. The area clearly had not acquired its full mythic status at this point, though it must be said that the young as a category had not done so either. Pigalle/Montmartre figures incidentally as the site of innumerable nightclub scenes in films of the decade, but the only films in which it seems to be central are the Tino Rossi vehicle *Marinella* (36.75) and Gance's film on the life of Charpentier (39.49). The latter constitutes a classic evocation of the mythic Montmartre of painters, poets, and musicians, living and loving in charming little flats clustered on the slopes of the butte, where it always seems to be springtime.

Both Parisian districts are therefore capable of contributing elements of glamour and fascination to the portrait of Paris, though there is also an undercurrent of sleaze, at least at the foot of the butte. The provinces, however, can be much worse. If the protagonist in *Angèle* is, in many respects, a conventional product of the times—the seeds of corruption sown by a vile urban seducer, the illegitimate child, the city, prostitution and degradation—nevertheless the severity of her treatment when she is brought back to the country shows the rigid provincial morality in an unusually harsh, and potentially sadistic, light. Films that take this further present life in the provinces as a stuffy, boring existence, by contrast with which the city seems to promise limitless freedom and independence. As the two songs in *Il est charmant* (31.68) note, "There's no laughter in Riom" ("On ne rit pas à Riom"), so "Let's talk rather of Paris" ("En parlant un peu de Paris"). About half a dozen films overtly mock the hidebound morality of provincial life, beginning with *Le Rosier de Madame Husson* and continuing with *La Dame de chez Maxim's* (32.47), in which a lively Parisian girl startles provincial society, and *La Route heureuse* (35.99), in which a Parisian marries into a provincial family only to find it insufferably claustrophobic; she would leave it forever, were it not that she discovers she is pregnant. These few films link up with the "local making good in the big city" narrative (34.31; 39.88) to provide the few relatively positive images of Paris as a dynamic and fascinating environment, though even here (as in *Le Schpountz*) disillusion is possible (37.102). Disillusion is also the result in that better-known film from this genre, *L'Atalante,* in which the young wife's intoxication with Parisian night life would have led her to follow the same path as Angèle and dozens of others were it not for Père Jules (34.9).

A few films go to the extreme of representing the provincial world as not just an outdated and rather quaint relic of the past, but as dying or already dead. The agricultural economy on which it is based is seen as exhausted, the land infertile, and provincial social structures are disintegrating; survival requires that the younger generation move to the city. The first French color film, *La Terre qui meurt* (36.127), took this line. Although ideologically wedded to the land, to patriarchal structures, and to the age-old rituals of agricultural life, the film acknowledges that the children are justified in leaving the dying earth and their dead mother for the qualified but real pleasures of an urban industrial existence. Nevertheless, the film ends with a new couple forming to undertake the regeneration of the land, and a final title announces "Thus, despite everything, the soil of France will become fertile again, through the love and work of its children"—a lesson not far from that of *Regain* in the following year or of Vichy a few years later.

But if *La Terre qui meurt* captures something of the ambivalence of the period toward this antinomy of Paris and the provinces, city and country, there is no doubt where its heart lies—close to nature and the eternal cycle of the seasons. Most commonly, when a thirties film with an urban setting allows its characters a visit to the country, it is figured as a moment of idyllic transcendence, when the routines of daily existence and the struggle for a crust can be momentarily forgotten. In *Retour au paradis,* a doctor quite literally explores the health-giving qualities of a stay in the country for a diverse group of urban dwellers (35.94), and in numerous films Parisians, wearied by the strains of their city life, find on a country holiday romance and happiness which proves lasting (e.g., 38.58). For the working and lower-middle classes, the Sunday in the country and the *guinguette* (open-air restaurant) on the banks of the Marne constitute the equivalent of such vacations in many late-thirties films, not least *Partie de campagne* (36s1). In *Le Temps des cerises,* the workers experience a moment of pure pleasure during an illegal fishing party on the boss's property (37.109). But instances of this effect abound in the decade: numerous films provide idyllic moments close to nature, such as that in which the young Poil de Carotte bathes naked in the stream, "rehearses" his wedding to Mathilde in the fields, and processes accompanied by the farm animals (32.109). A particularly interesting variant is found in *Faubourg-Montmartre* (31.55) when Ginette momentarily escapes the working-class squalor, prostitution, and drugs represented as typical of Paris and reaches a southern country village. Idyllic farmyard scenes and strolls along country lanes are contrasted with subjective memories of nightmarish city streets. But an abrupt change of gears presents a quite different view of this country village: misled as to the nature of the visitors' relationship, the villagers turn against them and exorcise them in a charivari which resembles a medieval witches' Sabbath, with fires at night, wild dancing, weird carnival masks, and effigies on gallows. The countryside—"la France profonde"—suddenly becomes a favored site for the forces of superstition and unreason, and "nature" something dark and primeval rather than idyllic and harmonious. Anomalous in the films of the thirties, as far as I know, this episode recalls the expressionism of the twenties and the rural gothic that was to appear in wartime films.

In sum, then, France's principal internal frontier as constructed by the textual field of thirties films is between Paris and the provinces, while its principal external frontier is between France and certain key countries—the United States, Britain, Russia, and, to a lesser extent, Spain, the inhabitants of all of which are contrasted with those of France in fairly stereotyped ways. As the psychological distance from France grows, it is races rather than nations that are stereotyped, notably Asians. Cutting across these categories, and potentially the more threatening precisely because they do not fit, are Jews and Gypsies. Jews do not appear as frequently as might be expected in French films of this decade, given the long-standing anti-Semitism of a large proportion of the French populace, particularly on the right, but also given their presence in the literature on which so many of these films were based, and the contemporary foregrounding of that stereotype as a result of the racial policies promoted by the Nazis. I have been able to identify only thirteen films produced between 1929 and 1939 in which the presence of a Jew is thematically foregrounded, though more extensive viewing, were it possible, would certainly have identified others. The image of the Jew that emerges from these films is by no means as negative as one might expect. Indeed, the majority of the instances are emphatically positive, representing Jewishness by way of attractive young women named Esther or Rachel, or embodying them in solid, substantial, well-liked French actors.

The prevailing stereotype of Jews at the time was not due directly to the Jewish religion, of course, however much the original cause for stigmatizing Jews may have been their supposed implication in the murder of Christ. Rather, its basis was their particular cunning in the financial arena. Undoubtedly, a good deal of envy underlay this representation of Jews as usurious. It resulted in a stereotype which involved sly and shifty characters with wispy gray beards, hooked noses, rimless spectacles, a tendency to hunch their shoulders and wring their hands, and an unwillingness to spend their vast wealth on their own persons or their surroundings, which are therefore smelly, dingy, and dilapidated. The sense of difference generated by this image is only exacerbated by the occasional appurtenances and symbols of an "alien" religion, and by the odd Hebrew phrase.

The literal mobilization of this image was, however, extremely rare in the thirties. It is clearly present in *Le Gendre de Monsieur Poirier* (33.59): when Gaston's creditors arrive to demand their due, they turn out all to have Jewish names—Isaac, Cohen, Salomon—and manifest a greedy desire to lay their hands on anything movable. Fortunately, Monsieur Poirier knows how to deal with usurious Jews. This representation of Jewishness is also present in Grémillon's early film *La Petite Lise* (30.66), from a scenario by Charles Spaak, in which the Jewish pawnbroker is accidentally killed in a robbery planned by the desperate Lise and her pimp, but there is no suggestion that the murder is either justified or "understandable." Indeed, several of the Jews who appear in these movies are or have been murdered, but their status is always as victim, occasionally of anti-Semitic prejudice. A café proprietor suffers agonies of guilt at having killed a Jew fifteen years before, dreams he has been discovered, wakes, and drops dead (31.72). The Jewish ghetto in a little Galician town is being looted, and our sympathies are with the Jews, who suffer nobly under these indignities (30.31). Again, the Jews in the Prague ghetto are being victimized and put their faith in the golem, who is finally roused to destroy their persecutors (35.52). Admittedly, this successor to the German expressionist cinema of the twenties associates Jews with alchemical knowledge and strange rites, but no more so than everyone else in the film; and it gives them all the stirring lines ("Revolt is the birthright of the slave!") and a plucky young girl (called Rachel, of course) to lead their revolt.

Elsewhere, an attractive young Jewish woman is presented as a suitable mate for an Austrian officer and gentleman, until her own people disapprove (30.31). Several films relate romantic tales involving young Jewish couples, not least the Lévy series. The four films that constitute this light-hearted series construct a Jewish family saga focusing on two (middle-aged male) Jewish immigrants to America, their families, and their business operations there and, later, in Paris (30.48; 31.63; 35.81; 36.74). These films, especially the first, were immensely popular, as was *Le Juif polonais* (31.72), and there is nothing to suggest in the surviving plot summaries that there were significant negative connotations attached to the representation of Jewishness in them, except insofar as a certain comic quaintness attaches to any stereotype of that sort. Louis Bélières, who figured in over thirty other films in that decade, many of them profoundly nationalistic, and Charles Lamy, who often played a French aristocrat, acted the two lead roles in the series, while Marie Glory and André Burgère, who played lead roles throughout the thirties, played the young couple in the first. It is hard to see any mobilization of anti-Semitic feeling in all this. Moreover, that glorious paean to French nationalism, *L'Appel du silence*, was happy to remind viewers in an extended sequence that Charles de Foucauld had disguised himself as a Jewish businessman to gain entry to Morocco (36.7).

It is true, however, that nearly all films in which Jews appear show them as involved in finance and banking, or at least in prosperous affairs. The well-known biography of the Frankfurt Rothschilds had led to an expectation, exploited to comic effect in *Rothchild* (33.113), that the whole point of a male Jewish character in any film would be his financial adroitness. Given the suspicion in which finance was held at this time, what is surprising is the extent to which Jews escape any condemnation for their part in it. The enigmatic film *Ces messieurs de la Santé* (33.23) is of interest here: the escaped criminal and resurgent banker, Tafard, played by Raimu, is a Greek, but he takes a Jew as his financial assistant to deal with the day-to-day aspects of his financial wizardry. The latter conforms to the stereotype in being weaselly-looking and sycophantic. As they triumph over the world of French capitalism, they draw on the help of a Jewish bank (called Moïse et Salomon, after the characters in the Lévy films?). Yet despite his visually suspect appearance, the Jewish assistant, like his master, profits enormously from their gleeful, if dubious, financial deals and ends up wealthy and vindicated. Indeed, his boss adopts a Jewish pseudonym once he escapes from jail in order to put the police off his tracks.

This brief account of the representation of Jewishness in thirties French films establishes an interesting framework for the two notable films in which Jews appear later in the decade, *La Grande Illusion* (37.54) and *La Règle du jeu* (39.78). Both use Dalio in the role, and he had not only played a Jew before, in *Le Golem*, but was himself Jewish (his real name was Israel Moshe Blauschild). In *La Grande Illusion*, he is, like most of his predecessors, from a banking family, the Rosenthals, and can afford regular food parcels, which he shares with his fellow captives, as he shares the basket of theatrical costumes. He is quickly on good terms with "the men" and the particular mate of Maréchal (Gabin), with whom he escapes. Interestingly, we are told that his sort of person spells the end of the aristocracy, whose chateaux they have bought up and taken over. It is therefore somewhat ironic, or perhaps singularly appropriate, that an aristocrat should sacrifice himself to ensure Maréchal and Rosenthal's escape. Although the representation of Jewishness was predominantly positive throughout the decade, this film constitutes a high point, and a deliberate statement of principle, given that Rosenthal was a late addition to the script, replacing another "marginal"— a dignified Negro intellectual who was originally to have escaped with Maréchal.

In *La Règle du jeu*, the Jew (again of the Rosenthal family) has not just displaced the aristocrat from the chateau, but has himself become an aristocrat in it. When one of the servants voices the expected anti-Semitic sentiments concerning Frankfurt yids (*"métèques"*), the cook counterattacks with a peculiarly moving defense of the marquis's sensitivity, his "true" aristocracy, the more effective for being exemplified in something as humble as the correct preparation of a potato salad. Not least important is the express contrast between, on the one hand, the Jewish marquis's "taste" and fitness for the role and, on the other, certain French aristocrats' unfitness. Of course, the fact of having a Jew as a marquis is itself in line with the omnipresence in the film of an element of "outsiderness" even in those who seem most to belong. After all, his wife, Christine, is not French but Austrian, which was by no means a neutral observation in the context of the day, since it both ties in with musicality (all Austrians were inherently musical) and explains her inability to treat her husband's adultery as the conventions of French society (and the boulevard genre) expect. For her it is an alien tradition. Moreover, we are reminded that the most vigorous of all defenders of the social rules, Schumacher himself, has a Germanic name and is probably of Alsatian origin, judging by the vicious fate that he imagines would have befallen certain poachers and fornicators if they had been caught in that frontier territory. It is interesting to see Germans and Jews aligned in this film in the common role of outsiders. Nevertheless, the incongruity of having a Jewish actor play a French aristocrat would have been seen as provocative, and would have registered all the more strongly with audiences of the day in that Dalio had for several years tended to be typecast as a degenerate, a cowardly sadist, and a hysterical traitor.

THREE

Class: Authority, Oppression, and the Dream of Escape

3.1 THE REPRESENTATION OF AUTHORITY

It was inevitable that one of the principal categorizations arising from an analysis of thirties French films would be class. Capitalism was experiencing a crisis, and two radical alternative forms of social organization existed to further call into question the iniquitous class system that it had generated. Innumerable studies have been devoted, in whole or in part, to a discussion either of class relations in the thirties or of the representation of class relations in the films of that decade. Particular attention has been paid to the films of the Popular Front and the slightly broader category of "poetic realism." It should be noted, however, that those studies have been confined mainly to about a dozen films produced in the years 1935–39—a very small segment of the output of the French cinema. In attempting to cast a broader net, the analysis that follows will ignore those previous studies and identify patterns of class representation with an origin earlier in the decade. These patterns are unlikely to contradict in any radical way the accepted data about poetic realism and the Popular Front, but they may serve to put them in a broader textual context, where it is more normal to relate them directly to an extra-textual socio-political context.

It seems easiest to begin with the bourgeoisie rather than the working class, because the representation of the bourgeoisie was more consistent and coherent. Enough was said about the nobility in chapter 1, where the acquisition of an aristocratic alliance was seen to serve in textual terms as little more than a fairytale reward in romantic comedies of the first half of the decade. Occasional recurrences of this function are apparent right up to 1938 (e.g., 38.79), but the representation of nobility is otherwise confined to historical (costume) dramas, where it seems no less remote from reality (e.g., 38.56). In those films, the nobility serves to provide visual spectacle by staging ceremonial events involving elegance, grace, glitter, and a certain statuesque solemnity. All matters of political import are settled by gaudily caparisoned men sitting around tables liberally scattered with chalices, and all matters involving personal relationships are settled in the course of stately balls and duels. Often, these personal matters are of a conflictual or tragic nature, thus serving to oppose the public spectacle of the ball and private tragedy. For instance, the disguised hero is captured at a ball (34.17), or learns at a ball that his hopes of settling his gambling debts have been thwarted and he must kill himself (34.70); or again it is at a ball that the fiendish Russians come to suspect that the Polish patriot is hidden inside the chess-playing automaton and decide to have it destroyed (38.54). Perhaps the only films seriously to retain an overt reverence for feudal hierarchies are Guitry's *Les Perles de la couronne* (37.89) and *Remontons les Champs-Élysées* (38.87), in which the most trivial, boring (and no doubt fictitious) anecdotes about monarchs and courtiers are presumed to have an intrinsic interest, only the aristocratic are considered able to experience the higher and finer emotions, revolutionaries are decried as slavering sadists, and "the people" are seen as being intrinsically unreliable, if not treacherous, because motivated exclusively by unthinking envy. A few other films, notably *La Grande Illusion*, *La Règle du jeu*, and *L'Homme de nulle part* (37.54; 39.78; 36.54) "chronicle" the end of the feudal order with a certain comic regret for a time when people knew their place and their betters had style, or dignity, or a sense of social responsibility which is being lost either because of the rise of the materialistic bourgeoisie or because of the spread of a drab mass democracy.

By contrast with the declining nobility, almost the only occasions when the bourgeoisie is represented favorably are those in which it either replaces or is contrasted with that nobility. In the former, "the boss" replaces "the count" in romantic comedies. Here, we are not really dealing with industrialists or businessmen as men of finance, but rather with "the boss" as a good catch. In these "Mills and Boon" romances, typified by the *Dactylo* films, the humble secretary wins the boss's heart while vacationing on the Riviera (31.47); the barmaid, romanced by a rich young industrialist to put pressure on his family, proves so fascinating that he finally abducts her (31.125); the young woman ruined by a banker becomes his chauffeur on a bet, but their antagonism turns to true love, and, having won her bet, she tears up his check (32.41). Occasionally, especially from 1933 onward, a problematic aspect of these secretary-boss romances is introduced by the boss experiencing financial problems consequent on the crash, as in the second *Dactylo* film (34.32), in which the secretary's boss (now her husband) is ruined. Aside from such romantic comedies, the well-off middle-class male is seen to advantage only when contrasted with a nobility whose scandalous and dissolute ways he funds with a good-natured and ultimately benevolent tolerance (33.59). *Le Maître de forges*, with its transfer of the qualities of nobility and sensitivity to the bourgeoisie and its poeticization of the dynamism of heavy industry, was remade in 1933 (33.80). This dynamism is also admired in *Chotard and Cie* (32.34), which may begin by satirizing the materialistic Chotard and contrasting him with the playful and indulgent approach to business of his son-in-law the poet, but ends with a ringing assertion of the poetry and creativity inherent in mercantile dynamism. Both films were produced in the early thirties, when it was still not uncommon to celebrate the entrepreneurial ability of a bourgeoisie not dependent on inherited wealth and power but able at will to start again from zero and re-create an empire (33.96). It was in 1933 that Pagnol filmed *Le Gendre de Monsieur Poirier,* in which the impoverished aristocratic snob has married an industrialist's daughter for mutual advantage, but also with mutual scorn. The daughter truly loves him, however, and as in *Le Maître de forges,* but with a gender reversal, he comes to appreciate her qualities and is reborn as an honorable and self-respecting individual. This occasional fascination with the entrepreneurial drive and uprightness of the middle classes does not entirely disappear with the crash: in *L'Argent* (36.8), the ruined banker refuses to be defeated and mounts a new industrial project involving the exploitation of radium, and in *La Maison d'en face* the sacked banker/administrator takes over the brothel opposite and makes such a financial success of it that he is able to take over the direction of another bank (36.71).

The majority of the films mentioned here were based on plays or novels of an earlier period. Nevertheless, the crash (which hit France in 1932) and the scandals which accompanied it significantly clarified the representation of the bourgeoisie, big business, and finance. A key transition film, fascinating for the ambivalence of its representation, is *Ces messieurs de la Santé* (33.23). At one level, it, too, is an account of a dynamic financier who, escaping from a prison where he has been wrongly incarcerated, starts from nothing and builds a powerful business empire. At times, the film expresses a sort of guilty delight in the way his cunning, his ability to think on his feet, and his knowledge of the levers of finance, power, and human weakness allow him to rise and rise, finally to regain his rightful place in control of a firm. Moreover, everyone else also ultimately benefits from his rise. Yet he has been imprisoned for corruption, and it is not until near the end that there is any indication that this imprisonment might not have been justified: until then, what we see is an escaped embezzler conning and manipulating others, as we suspect he had done before to earn his prison sentence, working at best on the margins of the law and at worst in disregard of it. For most of its length, that is, the film could be read as an exposé of the methods of a corrupt financier. He is simply an amoral money-making machine—that is how he gets his kicks, and we are led to believe that there is a natural hierarchy in which quick-witted con artists will always be able to manipulate the system to come out on top.

To complicate the representation, he explicitly represents "modern" business methods: he takes over a backward family firm, uses aggressive and deceptive publicity, thinks big, and seeks to inspire confidence without justification. He is of Greek extraction and works with Jews, including a Jewish bank, since they understand this sort of business practice. He falsifies mineral assays and engages in international arms trafficking, which is all "just doing business." Yet, ultimately, he is exonerated by the courts and makes everyone richer and happier. So powerful is he that his final coup is to confess that he's the escaped embezzler so that the stock exchange, which had come to depend on his high-flying deals, will collapse, and he can buy up for a song everything he doesn't already own—an ending used by another film in the same year (33.113).

It is, then, an extraordinarily ambivalent film. All the "little people" support and love him, call him "an honest person in his way," name their children after him, or want to marry him, and the ending constructs him as the savior of these little people, innocent of all past accusations. Yet, most of the film has constructed him, convincingly, as quite the opposite. At the end, the police apologize to him, pointing out how careful they have to be these days, "with so many corrupt businessmen about."

Of course, the negative representation of financiers did not derive specifically from the crash. We are reminded by thirties films that Christ drove the moneylenders from the temple (35.53), and that usurers were a standard feature of nineteenth-century melodramas (36.41). But whereas this past history has much to do with French attitudes toward Jewishness, the banker of the thirties is condemned for quite other reasons. Not only does he value money and property above human relations, but he is blamed for professional incompetence and for using his financial power to exploit others, notably workers and women. He is despicable for his desire to pull the wool over other people's eyes, and thus is closer to a con man than to the traditional representation of the Jew. Numerous films represent him as having ties with the underworld. Above all, he is morally tainted. Typical adjectives describing the thirties banker are "seedy" and "crooked." This is such a standard character type in thirties films that frequently the banker/financier/industrialist doesn't have to *do* anything to earn the label "corrupt"; it is simply assumed that any banker will be so, as an inevitable consequence of his station or social role: to be involved with money is ipso facto to be corrupt. When the fat boss in *La Rue sans joie* (38.93), who has been making unwanted sexual advances to his secretary, is handcuffed and led off by the police, there is no real diegetic explanation—an off-hand remark suggests that not for the first time he has been fiddling the books, and the implication is that he is "like all his kind." His employees end up on the street, and his secretary seems for a while to have no alternative but the nearby brothel.

By this time, the representation of businessmen who manipulate the market has become unequivocally negative. In *Le Tunnel* (33.134), made in the same year as *Ces messieurs de la Santé,* a greedy financier planning a coup very similar to Tafard's—flooding the market with his shares to create panic, intending in the resultant crash to buy up all the remaining shares—fares far less well. His plan is looked on no longer as a cunning wheeze, but as typically criminal behavior. Betrayed by a colleague, the financier poisons him out of spite. Thereafter, respectable financiers, when subjected to investigation, will inevitably be found to have conned investors into investing in nonexistent oil deposits (33.111) or to have made their money by poisoning orchards so that they could buy up the good land cheap (38.73), or to have profited from gun-running, the responsibility for which they now hypocritically try to assign to the ship's captain (37.75). In the comic mode, they will sell their wife or daughter for a quick profit (36.113; 38.103), even if it means disposing of an inconvenient son-in-law first (30.80). In *Le Comte Obligado* (34.30), the greedy industrialists are perfectly willing to condone their wives' relations with the wealthy count in anticipation of a little investment in their super-phosphate scam, but are somewhat mortified to discover that he is their former elevator attendant. So it is not surprising that by the late thirties, in a film exploring "behind the facade" of the respectable world, one of the principal targets is a corrupt financier (39.25). In police dramas of the day, a banker was either "one of the usual suspects" (33.85), or the victim whom everyone would have had good reason to kill (38.14). More generally, to be of the middle class, to be well off, was to be corrupt. If the depression foregrounded the representation of class, it also polarized it, so that the whole middle class lived under the shadow of its more extreme representatives and their shady deals.

This polarization resulted, at the other extreme, in a mythologization of the tramp figure, seen as totally disengaged from the world of money and thus free of any moral taint. The tramp figure already had a considerable cinematic history, notably in the Chaplin films, which established him as a figure of innocence and purity, but in opposing him so consistently to the banker/financier, thirties French films make of his conscious rejection of the capitalist world a noble and heroic act. Tramps are often seen participating in the mythic natural world, where simplicity and directness are figured by a life of lying in the sun, fishing, and lazing away the days unhampered by social convention or economic constraints. The final image of the protagonist definitively abandoning these constraints—indeed, often abandoning a world of considerable financial ease—in order to hit the open road is a standard ending to thirties films. This image is gently mocked at the end of *Les Bas-Fonds* (36.15) with a slow iris out on the departing tramp figures, but this mockery is itself testimony to the stereotypical nature of the image. The ending of *À nous la liberté* is a precursor, though in this case it is technological advances introduced by the industrialist himself that have freed the workers to play skittles and go fishing, and that have freed the industrialist himself to hit the road; more typical is *Boudu* (32.25), in which, having subverted the fraught middle-class household, won the lottery, and married, Boudu abandons his respectability and financial security, floating away down the stream to poverty and to freedom. The final images establish the community of the open road as the locus of true happiness.

Of course, this theme is not specific to the world of thirties tramps, since it picks up on the well-known saying that money can't bring happiness. If you are wealthy, any apparent happiness is a momentary delusion. You will soon find that your wife has been unfaithful and your supposed daughter is not your own (30.27). However, thirties French films take that saying a step further: only by rejecting money can you find true happiness (32.102). In this tradition, a tramp becomes a banker and trumps his financial rivals, only to reject it all and hit the road again (33.113); rather than claim the reward for a valuable necklace, the tramp gives it away to a young woman who's been kind to him and hits the road again (36.45); a tramp resembles a financier, doubles for him, and takes over, only to renounce the financial life and hit the road again (35.117). In the latter case, the financier's life is represented as having been plagued by intolerable anxieties, and now he is being blackmailed as well (and of course cheated on by his wife—how could any woman be faithful to a banker), whereas the tramp's existence, on the contrary, before he is mistaken for the banker, has been idyllic, strolling the streets with his mate, singing and playing a horribly out-of-tune violin. The opposition between bankers and tramps rapidly becomes conventional, with the one regularly becoming the other, and reverting (34.7); when tramps inherit fortunes or win lotteries, they readily renounce the illusory promise of happiness that their apparent good fortune has provided (32.17).

Circus folk are frequently represented as sharing this footloose and fancy-free life, and images of them hitting the road overlap with those of tramps (39.4). More generally, artists of all sorts are represented as opposed to the conventions of the bourgeois world, and thus able to move easily back and forth between art and the road. In a classic instance, a Corsican singer is a financier's rival for a young woman whom he follows to Paris. While the financier proposes marriage and sets off with both the woman and (literally) a shipload of gold, the singer is "reduced" to sleeping under the bridges of Paris with a group of tramps. They offer him a glimpse of true community and human warmth and show a spontaneous appreciation of his music. "We have nothing but the evening breeze, the rays of the moon," he sings, and they sing back, "We may be totally lacking in worldly wealth, but we have a more valuable treasure" (36.11).

But if singers, musicians, poets, and circus folk were as commonly contrasted with bankers as were tramps, it was for a slightly different purpose: tramps rejected money in favor of liberty, whereas artists rejected money in favor of love. It was generally accepted that the wealthy had no access to either of these. Thus, a model leaves her composer friend to marry a banker, but she can't forget her Montparnasse past and returns to a life of poverty, art, and true love (31.115); the fat businessman has lecherous designs on the young singer and tries to shut down the theater in which she and her singer boyfriend are putting on a show (worse still, turn it into a movie theater), but they dispose of him in a humiliating way and triumph together. To a large extent, this opposition between banker and artist calls on standard knowledge of the incompatibility of art and commerce, of more interest to the representation of art than of class; like the tramp, however, the artist is the focus of identification in such stories, and his or her values are thus promoted as superior (34.31).

Represented as they so often were—fat, greasy, or overly suave and slick-talking, insincere and exploitative—it stood to reason that financiers could not attract sincere affection, so the theme of money being incompatible with true love evolved into a whole sub-genre of films in which someone in a position of wealth agonizes over the sentiments of the woman (or man) whom they love. Can they be sincere, or is it just the attraction of money (35.95)? Many films assert this danger to be real, with the suitor seeking nothing but mercenary advantage from a marriage (30.86; 32.73; 33.1; 33.13; 36.13; 36.63). Inherited wealth, industrial wealth, or a lottery win brings suspect adulation. It is all too easy for a woman to be seduced by a gleaming Hispano (33.65). It thus becomes conventional belief that rich people can find sincere affection only by disguising their wealth (31.87; 31.107; 33.20; 33.106), pretending to be barmen, chauffeurs, secretaries, accountants, or to have been ruined/robbed of their wealth (35.103). Alternatively, the rich woman's poor suitor backs off for fear of being thought mercenary (35.125). *Sept hommes . . . une femme* (36.121) combines both of these: a rich widow is loved by a poor childhood friend who dares not declare his love since he has nothing to offer her (well, if one excludes his title). She collects around her numerous society figures who aspire to her hand and her fortune, but when she pretends to have lost the latter they all prove unworthy by backing off. Her childhood friend is about to declare his love for her at last when she reveals to him that it was all a trick—she is still rich—so once again he retires gracefully. Of course, all comes right in the end, but the opposition of sincerity and wealth is archetypal. The heart is more important than the wallet, as film after film proclaimed (34.30; 36.121; etc). The experience of wealth is enough to disgust or bore any honorable man or woman, and innumerable such worthies reject rich

Parisian or American merchants for the humble working man or woman whom they have always loved (31.35; 31.111; 32.128; 39.39).

This world of mercantile insincerity is the world of schemers and slick talkers out of which Prévert's Batala arises (35.27). It is a world in which dishonesty is the fastest route to social success and respectability, as Pagnol's Topaze learns to his advantage in a film remade by Pagnol himself four years after its first production, though, interestingly, the remake did not enjoy the enormous popularity of the original (32.134; 36.129). It is a world in which politicians can be bought and sold and criminality is assumed to be endemic in the establishment. Respectability invariably hides double dealing, as in *L'Étrange Monsieur Victor,* in which Victor turns out to be a fence and murderer (37.40). Press barons turn out to be arms traffickers and blackmailers (38.14), and a banker (admittedly Oriental) is secretly running a gambling den next door to his bank (39.51).

So, while many of these films, written and directed in the tradition of the individualist psychodrama, focus on specific individuals who turn out to be morally corrupt, there is often, if not always, an implicit critique of the system as a whole, of which the banker and the industrial baron are emblematic figureheads. On occasion, this critique of capitalism becomes overt. This is particularly true in 1934, not just because the depression, which hit France in 1932, seemed to point to the economic failure of capitalism, but because of several specific financial scandals in that year. Nevertheless, examples of overt criticism can be found throughout the decade. Characteristics of the system which come in for criticism are its tendency to exploit and enslave, its tendency to favor organizational efficiency over humanity, and its bureaucratic tendency toward red tape. The inherent conflict of class interests is seen as breeding distrust, injustice, and violence. In the extreme, capitalism is seen simply as one of many hierarchical systems that perpetuate privilege and constrain the human imagination.

Anarchic rejection of all authority sometimes borrows from surrealist or, more commonly, from expressionist techniques and themes. Mad doctors on the Caligari model are still to be found in France in the thirties, and still in charge of mental asylums (30s7). Occasionally, the Germanic influence is direct, as in Dreyer's *Vampyr,* also with its mad doctor (31.146), while Lang has a lineage of mad doctors spreading death and destruction in society (33.123). Even in 1934, an expressionist story is made in which an alchemist transmutes lead into gold for the benefit of industrialists (34.74), while the following year Duvivier retells the tale of the golem, the weird clay monster fashioned by the Jews in the Prague ghetto, which comes to life to destroy their oppressors (35.52). In general, tales of insane authority and anguished oppression tend to be set far afield, in Mongolia, Russia, or the Pacific, or in unspecified allegorical lands where the oppressed rise up to crush ruthless dictators (32.104; 33.150; 36.87; 38.99). Clair's mad financier/dictator in *Le Dernier Milliardaire* falls into this same category (34.35). As in the original German expressionist movement, however, the very existence of such films, however abstract, speaks of a social distress and distrust of existing governance.

More specific criticisms of a more clearly characterized capitalist society can be found throughout the thirties, from Clair's *À nous la liberté* (31.1) to *Quai des brumes* (38.84). As is well known, the former focuses on the dehumanizing and alienating effects of assembly-line practices, and constitutes a critique of recent American developments. Produced in the same year, *Tumultes* (31.134) also begins with a scene which implies that the prison régime and workers' daily routines on the assembly line are indistinguishable. In the same year, *Pour un sou d'amour* (31.107) is fundamentally a romance based on a rich man and his poor mate swapping identities to test the sincerity of women's affection, but at one point the capitalist system is overtly blamed for the disappearance of any true human feeling from the modern world. Whether in the comic or the earthy realist mode, this characterization of the bourgeoisie as lacking in humanity, warmth, or feeling is consistent throughout the thirties. In a startling comic pastiche of the capitalist system, Fernandel, in *Ernest le rebelle* (38.32), is shanghaied to work on a South American plantation where the workers are treated as slaves overseen by ruthless managers and exploited by international capitalists.

The harsh conditions generated for the bulk of the population by capitalism were the constant theme of a series of "realist" films, most of them set in Paris. These tended to mix a more or less heavy dose of traditional melodrama with vivid location shooting that evoked the poor quarters, the slums, the depressed margins of Paris—the "zone." In these repulsive surroundings, living hand to mouth, often unemployed, never far from crime or suicide, the poor are represented as hopelessly condemned to a life of corruption, exploitation, and drudgery. From *La Petite Lise* (30.66) through *Faubourg Montmartre* (31.55), *La Rue sans nom* (33.114), and *Jeunesse* (34.52) to *Le Temps des cerises* (37.109), *Les Musiciens du ciel* (39.59), and *Quartier sans soleil* (39.76), squalid slums and condemned buildings speak of a suffering which is seen as an inevitable part of contemporary capitalism. The more melodramatic of these films opted to dramatize this suffering through the hardships of a pure young woman alone in a big city, surrounded by corruption, trapped or tricked into prostitution, tempted by suicide, sometimes saved at the last minute by the love of a fellow sufferer (32.50; 33.92; 34.52; 34.92; 36.19; 38.94). The same story appears transposed to Japan (37.124). Extensive poverty is the mark of a system which breeds malice and viciousness in the worst, shame and humiliation in the best, insanity and death in far too many.

In the trial scene at the end of *La Rue sans joie* (38.93), in which Jeanne is wrongly accused of murder because her poverty has pressured her into situations that look bad for her, her journalist friend develops a passionate indictment of society in her defense, blaming the prevailing economic system, which has forced many girls into prostitution. His harangue is greeted by applause in court. In *Ménilmontant* (36.78), the system has created gross inequalities, poverty, and suffering, but the rich are either blithely ignorant of this or arrogant and self-serving. When the poor try to help themselves and actually improve conditions for their children, the rich and powerful take over and hog the limelight. The lot of the poor is to be beasts of burden (literally, in the case of Arsule in *Regain* [37.100]). The rich regard them with distaste, hate flowers, birds, and "love" (36.27), and will do anything to prevent their sons from marrying across the class divide.

The bourgeoisie, who are represented as responsible for all this suffering and degradation, or who are blamed for preferring to ignore it, for profiting from it, and for doing nothing to rectify it, are inherently unlovely physically, an expressionist ugliness standing as a metaphor for their moral ugliness (34.31; 36.99). Greed is often represented as their driving force, making money their sole obsession, and human relations suffer as a result. Families collapse (30.28), lovers are parted, hard-working people are ruined. The corrupt banker becomes a routine mechanism for setting the narrative machine in motion (30.21; 32.23; 32.41; 32.128; 36.132; 37.11; 37.35). As Pagnol proposes in *Topaze,* this world is one in which the dishonest flourish. In an even more cynical film, *La Banque Némo* (34.13), an arriviste banker dabbles in shady deals but, protected by friends in high places, enjoys the fruits of his criminal activities. Nothing can stop the rich and powerful, it seems, except the masked marvel Judex, who kidnaps a banker to punish him for ruining so many humble people and induces him to repent his evil ways (33.73), or the master of disguise Arsène Lupin, who disrupts a rich financier's murderous activities (37.11). The rich have police and politicians in their pocket, and to ruin them requires the fantasized ingenuity of a masked vigilante, a lone avenger.

As the official administrators of a system whose effects were almost universally represented as degrading, bureaucrats might have been expected to come in for severe criticism. Instead, throughout the thirties, public servants are seen as ridiculous—comical figures, pompous, inefficient, dull, and pedantic, mindlessly implementing regulations which have long ceased to be meaningful. This image of the bureaucrat has a long history, and the principal instances of it in the thirties are drawn from plays of an earlier decade—*L'École des contribuables* (34.37), from a play by Verneuil and Berr, and *Messieurs les Ronds-de-Cuir* (36.80), based on characters by Courteline. In the former, the taxation department is the butt of an ongoing joke involving a school which teaches taxpayers systematically to fiddle their returns and which is taken over by the department itself to train its own staff. The latter, also in the comic mode, is altogether more comprehensive and classic in its ridicule: it is set in a government department manned by public servants who delight in thwarting their clientele by means of red tape, laziness, and procrastination. Dossiers pass from office to office, absenteeism is the norm, and the staff are eccentric to a man; they even transform their department into a rehearsal room for the Folies. A song whose theme is "It's not easy to do nothing" sums up their attitude. An ingenuous title at the beginning advises the audience that just as Courteline was not ridiculing the army in *Le Train de 8h47* and *Les Gaietés de l'escadron,* so he was not ridiculing the public service here—"after all, he was in the army and the public service himself."

In the dozen or so other films of the decade in which they figure prominently, bureaucrats are consistently represented thus—sometimes eccentric, lively, crazy, sometimes dull, fat, pedantic, but always inefficient, unconcerned by either their own duties or their clients' needs. A principal purpose of such films is not to criticize the system but to contrast the regimentation and regulation for which it stands with a freer, happier life based on gaiety and good humor (31.103; 34.16) or a sensuality unconstrained by the pettiness of social or moral strictures (33.12). That said, one of the most brilliant films of the decade was based on precisely such a bureaucrat. The protagonist of *Monsieur Coccinelle* (38.66) is a civil servant in the Bureau of Statistics. His daily routines are hilariously satirized, and all the standard red-tape jokes are reinvigorated. A file of doomed men trudges through his office as through the cityscapes of *Metropolis,* accompanied by funereal music. His home life (at Béton-sur-Seine!) is even worse, and he dreams of breaking out and becoming dictator of the world—like all wimps, as his wife says. His aunt's apparently unjustified belief in life as a fantasy endlessly rich with possibilities provides a useful contrast to his resignation. Her (supposed) death brightens for a moment his drear existence, but outraging the social order she comes to life again and heads off into the sunset with her lover, leaving M. Coccinelle thinking glumly, "Tomorrow, the office again."

3.2 THE WORKING CLASS AND CRIMINALITY

On the whole, then, the social and economic structures of the day do not fare well in thirties cinema. This is scarcely surprising in view of the prevailing economic climate. It is interesting, however, to note the various remedies which are put forward to solve this crisis. Where the problem is seen as one of corrupt individuals, the solution is often a legal one, though the legal institutions of the day are commonly seen as neither independent nor powerful enough to contain the spread of corruption. Occasionally, however, members of the middle classes are offered a form of revitalization in the course of which they rediscover a belief in life and humanity. This may come from romantic contact with a vivacious woman (31.38; 31.43; 31.103; 34.44), but its true source is outside the realm of official sociality. In the classic *Dame de chez Maxim's* (32.47), for instance, it is specifically a good-time girl who undermines the austere principles of Petypon and disrupts the rigid morality of provincial circles. The revitalizing women are always women of the people or marginals from the world of the night, and this marginality is the source of the vitality with which they can afford to be so prodigal. The working class and its marginal associates have not been stultified by the social and moral conventions which surround middle-class life, and a dip into this hitherto unknown world of seething spontaneity can work wonders for the pomposity of the arrogant rich—indeed, even of the aristocracy (31.38). Such an immersion can provide not just a delicious thrill of adventure, but occasionally a total transformation of the middle-class self. Perhaps the most vivid instance of this is *Circonstances atténuantes* (39.17), in which a judge (improbably played by Michel Simon) is stranded by a car accident in a working-class suburb late at night; at first distastefully, then more and more enthusiastically, he is forced into contact with a convivial working-class community. The bar/hotel in which he and his wife stay is called Les Bons Vivants, and under its influence the judge rapidly loosens up and learns to appreciate the simple joys of working-class humanity (notably as represented by Arletty).

As was often the case, the working-class community into which the judge is received is involved in various marginal and even criminal activities, and he effectively becomes the leader of an amiable gang, learning quite explicitly the joys of infringing on the legal regulations which he had previously worked to uphold. Admittedly, he cheats a little, organizing robberies involving his own petty cash, a motor-scooter that he has surreptitiously purchased, and the tacky furniture from his own home that he has always hated, but it is all in the interest of the new-found camaraderie with his "mates" the criminals. In a somewhat similar way, and in the same year, *Fric-Frac* (39.39) figures a conflict between the moral rectitude of middle-class convention and the working class in its marginal/criminal guise, when a jeweler's assistant, destined for a life of stultifying rectitude in his employer's shop and his employer's daughter's bed, accidentally discovers the warmth, affection, humor, humanity, and community of the working class (again in the form of Arletty but with Michel Simon now more at home as one of the marginals). When he is caught up and caught out in their less-than-legal activities, his newfound friends stick by him. They may be thieves, but many respectable people would not have done as much, he notes. The message of the film is that there is no such thing as respectable people; they're all thieves, but these people don't try to hide it—they are open and honest about it. If the jeweler's assistant emerges from the "underworld" at the end of the film to marry the jeweler's daughter after all, it is with a totally different slant on the world, not least because she, too, has experienced the vivifying effect of the marginal. It was normal, then, for the revitalization of the bourgeoisie to involve at least a metaphoric criminality, and for the agent to be a worker, a marginal, or a social outcast. Boudu is following in this tradition when he acts as catalyst for the revitalization of the bourgeois family that takes him in (32.25). Stuffy, self-opinionated stars are awakened by the rough passion of an apache (31.97); the pompous author who is so immersed in literature that he can't remember enough about love to write a convincing love scene has to be plunged into the world of working-class language and feeling in order to regain his humanity (35.98); in *Dédé* (34.34), a lawyer becomes humanized by contact with shop-girls and criminals, while the respectable businessman's wife fantasizes about an affair with young Dédé, and ends up doing an erotic Arabian dance to escape arrest.

Indeed, the identification between the working class and the milieu of criminal activities is underlined throughout the thirties. "The people," that seething mass of humanity that inhabits the working-class quarters, is a turbulent sea in which the shady elements swim with ease—or, rather, criminality is an insalubrious current in this social ocean. Some revel in it, others do their best to avoid it, but, diffused and diluted, it seeps into every home, and the working classes are shown as moving back and forth easily and, for the most part, unselfconsciously between salubrious and insalubrious waters. The effect is to make of criminality a metaphor for the disenfranchised status of the working classes, obliged as they are from time to time to acknowledge their powerlessness and alienation.

In this respect, criminality functions very differently depending on the class in which it was situated. In the middle classes, it acts consistently as a metaphor for the moral and social corruption that exists behind a facade of respectability, foregrounding the hypocrisy of the dominant class, and is therefore condemned. In the working classes, it is seldom condemned, often tolerated, sometimes celebrated. This situation is slightly confused by constant interaction between criminality as it attaches to these two social classes and criminality as it attaches to women as an "inescapable" aspect of their gender, but this aspect of criminality, which has an even longer history, is dealt with in a later chapter.

Insofar as the working classes can be characterized by their association with crime, they manifest four types of criminality—the picturesque apache, the squalid social realist, the sentimental, and the poetic realist. The first three are more apparent in the early thirties, while the last supersedes them and, in some senses, gathers them into a more powerful dramatic representation of the oppressed worker in the latter half of the decade. The gangster version of working-class life, a hangover from earlier decades, was already largely exhausted in 1930. The apache himself was, of course, a colorful figure, inhabiting sordid bars and dingy apartments and warehouses; decked out picturesquely in striped shirt, tall and violent, he was nonetheless the object of servile fascination for his women, whom he treated roughly but who loved him for it. Often a pimp, he lived off his women's earnings, and prostitution was an inherent part of the underworld activities in which he was involved.

Pabst's version of *The Beggar's Opera*, called *L'Opéra de quat'sous* (30.61), draws on this tradition, as does *La Chienne* (31.31), various early Gabin films set in the "milieu" (31.34; 31.36; 31.97), and some with Charles Boyer (31.134; 34.55). Often, in this colorful and stylized world, it is quite difficult to distinguish workers and workers' unions from criminals and criminal gangs, so interchangeable are the representations (34.34). Even workers' cooperatives, for instance, which are idealized in *Le Crime de M. Lange* (35.27), can often seem rather like criminal organizations, and vice versa. In Siodmak's *Tumultes* (31.134), the "Coopérative des amis dans le malheur" seems to be a Mafia-like ring of ex-convicts planning their next coup, while in *Dédé* the striking unionists resemble nothing so much as thugs as they run riot through the shoe shop. (34.34).

But that the figure of the apache is already on its way out in the early thirties is signaled by a number of films which actually "perform" it. In the course of one of the nightclub or variety acts which form an essential element of the structure of many thirties films, for instance, singers, dancers, or actors may act out typical scenes from the milieu involving principally the apache and his moll (34.31); or perhaps a couple of Americans being shown a faked version of Paris nightclub life may happen upon a poor unfortunate girl being maltreated by an apache (30s5), not realizing it is all an act; or, as in *Paris la nuit,* a French countess may be treated to the same exotic spectacle (30.63).

A more sordid connection between the working class and the underworld is set up in realist melodramas about slum life in Paris. Here, the connection is social: a certain inevitability attends the slide of vulnerable working-class men and women into criminal activities. With no other resources to call upon, and the constant need of money for rent or to feed the family, survival requires extreme measures. These are true "street" films, in which malice, lust, and the will to survive drive desperate people to commit theft, rape, and murder. Such films aim to arouse pity for the plight of working-class women forced into prostitution (33.41) or resigned to virtual rape (33.114), or for that of oppressed but basically decent workers who are induced to join in a hit on some rich apartment and whose past peccadilloes catch up with them, or who are betrayed to the police just when they seemed to be making a go of it (33.114; 39.76). The titles of such films are indicative of their mood and theme—*Dans les rues, La Rue sans joie, La Rue sans nom, Quartier sans soleil, Faubourg-Montmartre*—though some, such as *Ménilmontant,* have a more up-beat element. *Les Bas-Fonds* (36.15) and *Crime et châtiment* (35.28) share something of this mood and theme, though the gross artificiality of the sets works against the former, and the motivation of the latter is philosophical/religious rather than social.

Alongside this linked representation of the criminal and the worker there arose a more sentimental representation of "the little people of Paris" —their struggles, their loves, their moments of despair and moments of hope. The origins of this strand are generally attributed to Clair's films, notably *Sous les toits de Paris* (30.84) and, to a lesser extent, *Quatorze juillet* (32.116), though it has not attained the level of affection and sentimentality in these films that it was to acquire elsewhere. Clair's ruthlessly clinical portrait of the "little people" operating on the margins of legality and taking kickbacks from petty thieves, and who feel that it's perfectly reasonable to rob the rich and cheat their friends, is in fact far less sympathetic than is usually acknowledged. Moreover, the air of unreality in Clair's films is heightened by Meerson's magnificent but highly stylized sets. The actor in *Sous les toits de Paris*—Albert Préjean—went on to make a number of films in which his character works on the margins of the law—passing himself off as the son of a rich man to make a killing (32.138), flogging to the gullible public phony ways of transmuting metal into gold (34.73), conning gamblers in a casino (38.51), or playing a petty thief who cons victims in bars (34.96)—and occasionally goes to prison for it (33.127). Essentially, however, he lacks any dramatic weight. These characters are amiable, good-natured, full of a bumptious joie de vivre. The streets and bars that they inhabit have none of the squalor or despair of true street movies. Around the corner there is always an attractive affectionate working-class woman who will win Préjean back to honest ways, or collect him at the prison door, or head off to America with him (34.73). Préjean is better cast in *Princesse Tam-Tam* as the middle-class author whose "civilizing" program strikes Aouina as intolerably phony; one night, she plays hooky and plunges into the world of the common people, who know how to enjoy themselves and who have something of her own simple openness and genuineness (35.92).

Out of these three forms of worker/criminal of the early thirties grew the doomed outcast of the late-thirties poetic realist film, fashioned largely by Prévert and often embodied in Gabin. Basically, it took the social realism and tragic compassion from the second form, blending it with the picturesque stylization of the first and the sympathetic individualized protagonist of the third. Tourneur's *Justin de Marseille,* one of the few of these films to be set outside Paris, already brings certain of the relevant elements together (34.53)—the underworld boss with a good heart who runs a tight ship and for whom the little people of "his" city feel a real affection—an unofficial but more reliable and benign form of governance than the official forces of order, a folk hero of the sort Gabin later embodied in *Pepe le Moko* (36.99). Combined with the simple worker protagonist of *Le Crime de Monsieur Lange,* this generated the figure of the outcast, deserter, and justified murderer of the late-thirties heroes played by Gabin, by which time the dying hopes of the Popular Front had added the tragic sense of inevitable failure already present in some street films (38.84; 39.48).

Throughout the decade, alongside this running metaphor of criminality and disenfranchisement, the worker is characterized by other metaphors which serve to reinforce or to counterbalance this criminality: his being an orphan, his ability to sing, his appreciation of flowers and nature. The figure of the orphan can seem omnipresent in films of the thirties. In at least thirty-four films, the fact of being an orphan is foregrounded, with a marked increase in frequency toward the end of the decade. It is best known from *Le Jour se lève* (39.48), in which both François and Françoise are orphans, their names implying that it is the archetypal status of the French people of the day. Other well-known instances are *Hôtel du Nord* (38.50), in which much is made both of the Spanish refugee children orphaned by the Spanish Civil War and of the orphan-like status of the doomed lovers, and *Quai des brumes,* in which Nelly is effectively an orphan in the care of her "guardian," Zabel. Both she and Jean are "alone in the world." So are Jean and Eva in *L'Escale* (35.43), which is why they get along so well. He is a solitary man, a northerner who has never been able to make friends easily, and she is an orphan, "with no place to call home, and no one to wait up for her." It's not surprising that she has fallen in with criminals, and will do so again despite her desire to prove worthy of Jean. *Les Deux Orphelines* (32.50) provides another example, in which the significance of the orphan (compounded here by blindness) is foregrounded.

Because the orphan has no "home," no sense of belonging, no community, he or she is vulnerable to victimization by the "criminal" class—namely, the rich and powerful. While a minority of thirties orphans exemplify this class-based vulnerability and alienation, however, most of them belong with stories of "adopted sons and daughters," where they focus attention on dysfunctional families and sexuality rather than on class. They will thus be discussed in a later chapter. For the present purpose, what is most important about orphans is their marginality, which makes of them victims unable to escape the hypocritical strictures of a tight-fisted bourgeois morality. One recourse available to them is to adopt the strategy of the tramp and take to the road. Indeed, orphans acquire significance as representatives of a sort of inverse society, footloose and unencumbered by conventional morality, as witness the high proportion who are taken in by circus or theater folk in the late thirties (31.39; 34.115; 35.105; 38.111; 39.4; 39.92). Nevertheless, some of them serve to focus on the social causes of criminality among the under-privileged and disenfranchised (38.83), and thus to fill out the critique of a society which constructs its own criminals. The proposition that society constructed its own criminals was the theme of a number of films in the period 1937–39, notably those structured around reformatories. In these films, the poor are forced into crime by an unjust society, and it is rehabilitation, rather than punishment, that is required (37.95; 38.83). This becomes most explicit at the end of *La Tradition de minuit* (39.88), an interesting murder mystery in which a former criminal who has found love and who dreams of going straight bemoans the social determinants which have led to his criminal ways and which have ensured that he will never be able to escape the destiny of the poor.

Against this background of anomie, disenfranchisement, and metaphoric criminality, the poor are regularly portrayed as having access to simple joys that their richer compatriots might envy. For one thing, despite being characterized as outside official society, they are frequently—indeed, normally—represented as belonging to a (anti-) community which has more validity than that of the rich, because it is a community of the heart. When the rich are represented, it is as isolated monsters or as oppressive and self-interested families. It is rare to find poor or working-class individuals represented as isolated figures, or even as families. They are usually seen in groups of two or three "mates," and most often as members of an extensive network of supportive friends who come to their aid when the need arises. The exception is in melodramas, in which isolation and its attendant vulnerability are an essential element of the generic mechanism. Elsewhere, they share in a sense of belonging which is superficially at odds with their marginal status. To some extent, this is a product of number and situation: they are vastly more numerous than the wealthy, they live in populous quarters where the nature of the housing does not allow the degree of privacy available to the rich. Consequently, they live in public, on the street. Their life is characterized by a number of popular sites such as the bar-restaurant and the dance-hall, which appear so frequently that they constitute the standard backdrop to crucial narrative developments in films featuring the working class. Their life, then, is by definition communal: they cannot help but know a great deal about the lives and fortunes of those around them, and their involvement in one another's activities is therefore of a far greater intensity than is that of the rich.

The sporting arena is of particular interest as a communal site. It ties in with the popularity of the *sportif* (sporty type) in the thirties, with its emphasis on physical prowess, but it also allows for representation of the masses as emotional, full of exuberance and vitality. The names of many thirties films illustrate this tendency—*Princes de la cravache* (30.67), *Les As du turf* (32.10), *Rivaux de la piste* (32.119), *Direct au cœur* (32.51), *Prince des Six Jours* (33.108), *Chouchou poids plume* (32.35), *Une femme au volant*

(33.141), *Toboggan* (34.100), *Les Deux Favoris* (36.32), *Les Rois du sport* (37.102), *Champions de France* (38.19), *Pour le maillot jaune* (39.73). Clearly, producers saw a title which announced a sporting theme as a desirable form of promotion for their film. A great number of films involve a visit to a racetrack or a stadium as a crucial episode in the narrative. Invariably, these visits provide an opportunity for convivial interaction and a sense of adventure, but also for greater interaction with petty criminals (pickpockets, con men), and for the notorious gambling incidents which are pivotal narrative mechanisms in so many of these films. The immensely popular *Théodore and Cie* (33.124) begins at a racetrack, where two mates bet all their money on a horse and think they've won, only to find that they had registered the wrong number. The crowds, the tips, the race, and the comic drama all construct the mates as amiable types who would rather live by their wits than work, but who are suddenly desperately short of funds.

Another such film, *Les Cinq Sous de Lavarède* (39.16), ends in a bicycle race: obliged to circle the world in one hundred days, Lavarède finally finds himself on a stolen bicycle caught up in the final leg of the Tour de France, which, of course, he wins. The comic bumbling and/or amiable hero can always attain fame and win the girl's heart by some accidental sporting achievement. In fact, then as now, one of the few ways for a man of the people to achieve fame and wealth was to excel in some sport. In all but two films of the thirties, sporting accomplishments are seen as inherently and unquestionably desirable and admirable. There are at least twenty instances of protagonists who take up sports to impress a woman, who pretend to be sporting types to win a woman, or who win a woman as the "natural" consequence of winning a sports championship. The two exceptions to this general rule are films in which *sportifs* are considered superficial when compared to an artist (32.144) or to a doctor (38.119). In a number of related films, the sporting hero is compensated for losing a crucial fight or race by the love of an understanding woman. Occasionally, it is the distraction and/or physical debility caused by love of a woman which is represented as the cause of the loss (31.139; 32.51). The notion that sexual activity can "sap vital fluids" and that abstinence breeds aggression and success were common currency in the early thirties.

By far the greatest number of films featuring these sporting protagonists appear in the first half of the thirties—some thirty out of a total of forty-five. Horse and bicycle races were among the most common sports, and the most consistently foregrounded throughout the decade. Boxing was common, but only in the first half of the decade, while the more "refined" sports of tennis, golf, and rowing appear more in the second half. A general trend from the boisterous and intensely physical toward the refined and skillful is apparent. By the end of the decade, the *sportif* as hero could be satirized in the Fernandel films *Les Cinq Sous de Lavarède* and *Raphaël le tatoué* (39.16; 38.85); in the latter, not only are the various racing-driver heroes of the decade mocked, but also the futuristic aerodynamic shape of their cars.

The core of the working-class affection for sporting events is to be found in the early Bouboule films of 1930–31, *Le Roi des resquilleurs* (30.78) and *La Bande à Bouboule* (31.17), and possibly, though to a lesser extent, in *Le Roi du cirage* (31.116), *Bouboule 1er roi nègre* (33.19), and *Prince Bouboule* (38.81), in all of which Georges Milton played the immensely popular ebullient working-class rogue who is never far from a boxing match, a cycling race, a rugby match, or a race track. In fact, *Le Roi des resquilleurs* can be thought of as a series of six acts or sequences, four of which focus centrally on mass sporting events—the races, a boxing match, a bicycle race, and a rugby match—into all of which Bouboule has to wangle his way without paying. He and his mate are street singers, and one of the other two sequences is set on Montmartre, where they stroll the streets with a band, singing and selling their songs.

The contradiction is only apparent between the sporting man's physicality and the tendency of working-class protagonists to burst into song at the slightest provocation. A crucial aspect of the "community" formed by these poorer protagonists is their appreciation of a good song, and the two instruments that best characterize their relationship to music are the accordion and the harmonica. The middle classes never sing. They may sell pianos or rent out theaters (34.31), but their interest in art or music could never be other than mercenary, and is usually malicious. It is "the people," with their lively or sentimental songs, whose characteristic vitality and affectivity is best captured in music. This is what music shares with sporting arenas. In the grimmest realist drama, the disappointed protagonist can still wander into a bar and sing a melancholy love song to the accompaniment of an accordion (33.114). In a more positive mood, any moment of popular celebration will be marked by the appearance of an accordion and a sentimental song or dance (39.23). In *Circonstances atténuantes* (39.17), the appearance of an accordion and the singing of "the people" (who had at first seemed so sinister) in the bar is the key event that causes the middle-class couple to revise their view of the bar-hotel where they have been stranded, and to begin to see the people's existence as marked by an enviable joie de vivre. Even in a spy story, the street accordionist is a key link in the resistance chain (39.27). And, of course, *Les Musiciens du ciel* (39.59) makes of the accordion something close to an instrument of salvation: when the Salvation Army girl plays it, the con artist who is pretending to be blind reluctantly begins to acquire a certain humanity. Indeed, it is the ugly, destitute old man, who truly is blind, who teaches him to play the accordion and thus "heals his soul." Spiritual health and humanity are bound up in music, particularly the music of the accordion, and it is only the poor who have access to it.

There is a distinct increase in the number of films featuring street singers in the course of the thirties, with a sort of musical apotheosis toward 1939. Even in 1934, however, the central characters can be street singers—mates, one accompanying the other on an accordion (34.26). Later, Fernandel plays an entertainer on a cruise liner, accompanying himself on the accordion (38.32). As with sport, there was a pragmatic connection here. In the thirties, as today, music was one of the few avenues to fame and fortune for the oppressed. But, as represented in the films of the day, it becomes much more than that: it is compensation for suffering, the way to celebrate humble joys, and the expression of an otherwise inexpressible humanity that has elsewhere been destroyed by a ruthlessly mercenary society.

Most instances of street singers in thirties films accord with this set of conventions: the singer, a working-class man himself, promoting the songs of the day, focus of a sizable group of fellow workers who beat time and join in as they get to know the words, or buy a copy of the sheet music and sing along in pairs and groups, participating in one of the more recognizable public ceremonies of working-class communal life. Among them, there are usually some better-off people, the natural and proper prey of the pickpockets with whom these street people are half in league. The archetypal (and perhaps the earliest) instance is *Sous les toits de Paris* (30.84), where the protagonist is himself the street singer, and his sessions on the street structure the narrative.

The role of street singer was more often a walk-on character role than a principal role (34.26), but it rapidly became established as a focus of popular sentiment and good nature. A slightly more jaundiced instance from later in the thirties (37.2) has the distraught heroine caught up in the bustle and noise of a fairground, almost tempted by the sentimentality of a street singer and his accordion accompaniment into believing in the sincerity of a friend's sexual intentions, until the reality of hotel rooms rented by the hour supervenes. This is a rare instance in which the myths of popular sentimentality and sincerity and of romantic love, for all of which the street singer and the accordion stood guarantee, are presented as a seductive but basically fraudulent illusion.

Although music is a prime signifier of the solidarity and humanity of the working class, it is far more often associated with the male than the female. For the working-class woman, however, a number of key images recurred to indicate her parallel accession to a form of transcendence. Principal among these were the occupations of florist and laundress. The connotations of nature, innocence, growth, and blossoming associated with these activities combined to endow women with a quasi-religious status. The best-known florist is probably Françoise in *Le Jour se lève* (39.48) who in the opening sequence arrives at the sand-blasting factory where François works with her (soon wilting) bouquet in her hand, and whose greenhouse is an oasis of fertility and hope in a depressing slum landscape. Earlier in the decade, Anna in *Quatorze juillet* (32.116) had also been a florist, and her handcart of flowers had already guaranteed her a privileged ideological status. In *Drôle de drame* (37.37), Madame Molyneux can't stand trees or flowers, which give her hay fever (and no doubt recall her husband's passion for mimosa)—until, that is, Kramp the slaughterer of butchers, offers her a posy, whereupon she becomes disconcertingly girlish and decides that they are all right. Indeed, she becomes known to Kramp as "Daisy." These are only the best known of a large number of working-class men and women whose relationships are authenticated by association with flowers. Perhaps the first had been the protagonist in *Jean de la Lune* (31.70), whose occupation is an outward and visible sign of his good heart and humble status. Thereafter, female flower sellers prove irresistible to cabaret singers (32.101) and to the sons of magistrates (36.27), whose middle-class fathers, of course, can't abide flowers or the sentimental virtues that they symbolize. Such plots constitute a pale reflection of the myth of nature, as it is represented in a cinema centrally preoccupied with urban lifestyles, but it is crucial that it should be the poor who are illuminated by this myth, not the rich.

Another form that the nature myth takes is the predilection of the workers for the *guinguette* on the banks of the Marne. Of course, this phenomenon functions as a sign of the worker's desire for escape from the grinding oppression of workday routine—a form of escape both more mild and more realizable than other fantasized forms of escape—but it is significant that such an escape should be from the urban industrial domain to that of nature. *Une partie de campagne* (36s1) is a relic of an age when it was the lower-middle classes who were beginning to appreciate such an escape, but *La Belle Équipe* (36.17) enthrones the *guinguette* as a mythic goal of specifically working-class dreams. Its significance is most apparent in realist dramas such as *Jeunesse* (34.52) because of the violence of the contrast between workday routines and the fantasized escape, but it can equally well turn up in a musical as the logical place for a Sunday outing for lovers (36.75). It is at a *guinguette* that Michel Simon and Arletty begin to teach the jeweler's daughter and the jeweler's assistant the joyous ways of the people in *Fric-Frac* (39.39). While the best-known instances of *guinguettes* come from late in the decade, there is a classic example in *Cœur de Lilas* (31.34), in which the undercover policeman, André, in his professional, then personal, pursuit of Cœur de Lilas, moves through numerous typically working-class locales, such as the bar-restaurant and the dance-hall. He ends up at a *guinguette* on the banks of the Marne, where he learns to his dismay that she did indeed commit the crime that he is investigating.

If the florist connotes an alternative to and an escape from urban working-class routines, the laundress represents some sort of absolution for the worker's daily implication in industrial sin. The socio-economic oppression which the middle classes inflict on workers is here often—indeed, normally—paralleled by sexual oppression, and laundresses are particularly subject to sexual harassment from the arrogant rich. Valentine in *Le Crime de Monsieur Lange* (35.27) is a particularly well-known example, and her self-absolution particularly striking. Her colleague Estelle's absolution, if more difficult, is no less complete, but an earlier film, which has apparently been lost, had brought together a number of these threads: a humble shoe-repairer who "cultivates a single pitiful flower in a jam jar," falls for a laundress "whose virtue is under intense pressure" from a slick seducer (32.100). Inevitably, the mild shoe-repairer wins out.

In the same year, Duvivier's *Poil de Carotte* (32.109) presented the unhappy boy of the title with a new serving-maid whose principal activity is the family laundry. The washing scrubbed and hung on the line foreshadows his concomitant glimpse of happiness; later, he joins the young Mathilde, with her crown of flowers, in an idyllic pastoral "wedding ceremony." Such films established the routines for many later films. Zouzou becomes a laundress (34.115), but it is her fellow laundress (named Claire!) with whom Zouzou's "brother" falls in love. In the next couple of years, a number of laundresses characterize the working class (35.13), including one who is an orphan (35.13), another who starts up a restaurant (35.20), another whose role is to "purify" a brothel (35.18), and yet another whose even more ambitious task is to purify an unhappy middle-class household (36.117)—but then, she has St. Theresa on her side. All of these are resolutely positive figures. The last to appear is the only negative one: in *Entrée des artistes* (38.31), the laundry where Isabelle works is a signifier of ignoble commerce rather than of purification. What is more, it is overtly opposed to Art, and what could hope to win out against Art in a thirties film, especially when Jouvet is the prosecutor.

The "social roles" of florist and laundress, commonly available to the working-class female, contrast interestingly with the equivalent role very commonly assumed by the working-class male—taxi driver/chauffeur. Several important protagonists of the thirties are taxi drivers, while many others have mates or helpers who are so. To a certain extent, the recurrence of taxis in these movies is due to their narrative convenience. The actions of a narrative helper in transporting the protagonist across Paris or from one level of reality to another (39s3) are facilitated by a job as taxi driver. In this sense, the taxi is the rather pedestrian (so to speak!) equivalent of the magic carpet or of the genie from a bottle granting improbable wishes. Yet its archetypal significance as a marker of working-class characteristics is guaranteed by the fact that Bouboule himself, no less, is a taxi driver (even if he does get his taxi stolen while at the races [31.17]). Several films foregrounding class in a parodic way use taxi drivers or chauffeurs as the working-class component of an incongruous match, as when a lawyer pretends to be a chauffeur to get at a hidden treasure (30.91) or a Russian princess propositions a taxi driver to obtain French citizenship (38.81). The chauffeur may, in a "Mills and Boon" revelation, turn out to be a duke (38.79), or he may pretend to be his aristocratic boss in order to rent out the chateau (35.119). In all cases, the role of taxi driver is included specifically to contrast with that of the elegant and the aristocratic. Harry Baur, playing the heroine's father in *Paris,* is a taxi driver who becomes convinced that his daughter, who has aspirations above her station, is ashamed of her father's working-class background (36.95). If further proof were needed, one need only look to *Gardez le sourire* (33.57), in which the struggling working-class couple, after many trials, finally realize their dreams by purchasing a taxi.

This acts as a reminder that the role of taxi driver is a marker not just of the character's working-class station, but of his particularly prestigious role as a working-class man who has made good. It is one way in which the poor could have access to the toys of the rich. It was thus a signifier of technical sophistication and of relative autonomy. Taxi drivers, or occasionally mechanics, were people who understood how modern machinery worked and/or could control it. This gave them a mobility prohibited to most of their mates, and was thus in some ways the working-class equivalent of the aviator figure, whose mythic significance was then at its height. Indeed, several taxi drivers/chauffeurs become involved with, or even (in the comic mode) themselves become aviators. The taxi driver may simply blunder into flying by accident (37.17), or he may use his technical skills to learn to fly in order to impress the aviatrix he adores (33.18). He may indeed be an ex–war pilot down on his luck who, through the accident of a handbag left in his taxi, gets a job in films as an aviator, and marries the star (37.5).

But probably the best-known taxi driver is Jean in René Clair's *Quatorze juillet* (32.116). As in the case of street singers and florists, it is René Clair who recognizes the mythic significance of the taxi and who serves to bring it into sharper focus as a narrative tool available to subsequent filmmakers. The climactic moment, when the estranged lovers "meet" in an accident involving his taxi and her flower cart, brings together a number of key components of the decade's filmic repertoire, not least the game-like public debate in the middle of the street as his and her defenders manifest the affective volatility and humanity of the people and their love of public spectacle. In addition, the incident serves to remind us that it is not by accident that the male role involves a machine, while the female role involves a natural organism. It is clearly yet one more metamorphosis of the opposition between nature and sociality, instinct and reason, stasis and dynamism that has long dogged Western representations of gender.

Certain connotations of technological sophistication, dynamism, mobility, and autonomy shared by planes, trains, and cars extended to the canal boat. It is already clear in *L'Atalante* (34.9) that the master of a canal boat could be distinguished as a working man who has made good without having forsaken his class roots. Master of his own relatively autonomous world, freed from the humiliating stasis of industrial routines, he is privileged not to need the fantasized forms of escape which beset other workers. At the same time he is not, or is not represented as, implicated in the world of commerce in the same way as the manager of a small urban enterprise. Workers who had made good as singers might well return to their roots on a canal boat and marry the owner's daughter (33.8)—though, as in *L'Atalante*, life aboard holds less interest for the wife, who is constantly tempted by dreams of an existence more intense than the tranquil mobility of the canal (32.20). On the other hand, wayward women might well find their match in the quiet authority of a canal-boat captain (32.40). The romance of the waterways did not survive the early thirties, though the canal-side streets of Paris retained a picturesque quality in later films (36.27), best remembered from *Hôtel du Nord* (38.50).

3.3 DREAMS OF ESCAPE

In contrast to these relatively rare representations of the working man as transfigured by contact with a transcendent reality or as calmly in control of a relatively autonomous (and mobile) world, the more common representation of his life is as a trap from which he can only dream of escaping. The limiting nature of this trap is all the more cruel in that, as the preceding account indicates, the worker is commonly represented as vital, dynamic, affectionate, considerate, and with a limitless but unrealized potential.

Some of the films in which this trap/escape theme figures have become widely known. In *Hôtel du Nord,* most of the characters have sought or are seeking escape from an intolerable reality, though the form taken by that escape varies considerably—the immigrant child has sought escape in France, but the French, in turn, are seeking it elsewhere—the young couple in a suicide pact, and the ex-gangster Paolo/Robert in a life as a new person, "Monsieur Edmond." Most strikingly, Monsieur Edmond glimpses the possibility of a more hopeful future in a new land with the aptly named Renée. But Renée realizes her error, and Monsieur Edmond allows the ship to sail for Port Saïd without him, accepting at the end what the young couple had believed at the beginning—that the only attainable form of escape is to be found in death.

Late-thirties films are notoriously marked by the tragic inability of protagonists such as Monsieur Edmond to escape from the trap of social reality. Often, the metaphoric identity of social reality as a prison from which the worker/criminal must necessarily seek escape is foregrounded by the plot. Chéri-Bibi in his prison in Guyana (37.22), Nelly (and indeed the center's director) in the rehabilitation center (37.95), and at another level the boarding-school trio at St. Agil (38.25) all dream of escape to a better future from their institutional captivity. *Quai des brumes* (38.84) is the best-known instance of the worker/criminal, in this case a deserter, seeking to escape to a new life in a new land—in this case Venezuela. Again, however, the crucial final scenes are set on the dockside, and the ship sails without Jean. Clearly, these port settings are important insofar as they mediate between the social reality of France and a fantasized better life—they mediate, that is, between the here and the elsewhere, France and a promised land "over there." Adults are less likely to reach that promised land than the younger generation: Babs ensures that her son will "escape" to Canada, even if she herself never can (39.80), while Kay likewise ensures that her daughter escapes the chaotic political scene in Shanghai, though she herself is doomed not to do so, mortally stabbed but carried helplessly along in the crush of demonstrating workers and foreigners attempting to board the last boat leaving the stricken city (38.27). Docksides, then, are useful in that they evoke the seamier aspects of industrial reality in conjunction with ships and sailors whose comings and goings speak of other, more exotic possibilities. It would have been interesting to compare the apparently lost film *Le Récif de corail* (38.86) with these films in that, as in *Quai des brumes*, Gabin and Morgan embody a romantic couple on the run—this time in the South Seas—seeking to reach the Great Barrier Reef, which has come to signify for them the transcendence of past sufferings, the plenitude of a definitive escape.

Although all these films date from the late thirties, all the recurrent elements of the drama had been established long before. Marius, after all, had from his dockside bar mythologized the tall clipper ships that sail for Brazil and Madagascar. The bar-keeping routine which represents his tie to a frustrating social reality is nowhere near as onerous as that figured later in the decade, and his dream is an older one—the "call of the sea"—yet the obsession which drives him to explore new worlds has something in common with later "escapes" (31.81). Perhaps closer to the later films and dating from the same year was another lost film, *Partir* (31.99), in which a criminal on the run joins a circus and embarks with the troupe for a life in a new land, only to find, at sea off Colombo, that escape is impossible except in the form of suicide.

Among some fifty other films which echo these themes, it is inevitably the more naturalistic ones that construct the most convincing argument for the necessity to escape. In *La Rue sans nom* (33.114), Méhoul tells the dying child of a destitute family stories of far-off lands that he's visited and promises that someday he'll take him there, knowing that he never will. In *Jeunesse* (34.52), the unemployed poor speak wistfully of leaving for the colonies to build a better life, and rather surprisingly one of them—the father of the illegitimate child—later proves to have done so. In *Le Crime de Monsieur Lange* (35.27), Lange's fantastic tales of Arizona Jim are explicitly a form of escape to a place in the sun where injustices are righted and the downtrodden defended by a mythic avenger. America (or the Americas, since Brazil, Venezuela, Mexico, and, of course, French Canada figure prominently) is the most common of these fantasized lands. Toni talks of taking Josefa with him to a new life under new skies (35.110); Liliom has dreamed of heading off to America to start a new life over there (as Lang, the director, was doing at that very moment, with the help of the fee for this film) (34.55); in a very clumsily inserted episode, the couple in *Pour un sou d'amour* (31.107) sing of escape to a new life in a new land, to the accompaniment of a montage of coastal and ocean shots; Jacques in *La Belle Équipe* (36.17) realizes his dream of a new life in Canada; the protagonist of *L'Homme de nulle part* is heading for America until he meets the tramps and assumes the identity of one of them (36.54); the young boy in *Les Disparus de St. Agil* (38.25) is thought to have fled to America as he had always talked of doing; and Eva twice has to watch from shore the departing liner on which Jean is lieutenant (35.43). The impatient Viviane in *Métropolitain,* who wants it all now, sees a ticket to America as central to the realization of her dream (38.63), while Françoise in *Le Jour se lève* (39.48) has postcards of the south, of the Riviera, and of mimosa pinned up in her room—Valentine had seduced her with just such images—but also with talk of America. Other protagonists have Egypt (30.82) or Pondicherry (37.95) as their goal; or, more commonly, they simply repeat the vague mythic phrases "partir," "ailleurs," "là-bas," "une nouvelle vie," "Ah qu'il serait beau de partir, très loin" ("setting sail," "another world," "over there," "a new life," "Ah, how wonderful it would be to go far, far away") (39.88). A reference to this motif had become almost obligatory in films of the second half of the decade.

Three films are worth mentioning in a little more detail, since they provide interesting metaphors for this omnipresent theme—*La Tendre Ennemie* (35.109), *La Route enchantée* (38.92), and *Monsieur Coccinelle* (38.66). In the first, the daughter loves an aviator and dreams of setting off with him "far, far away, to a new life" but is prevented by her family, who wish her to marry sensibly. A chorus of ghosts who are monitoring the family's activities because they were involved in an analogous situation with the mother finally ensures that the younger generation is able to do what the older generation was not. The mother had loved a sailor and dreamed the same romantic dream, but had been prevented from leaving with him by her own mother; now she recognizes the need to end the cycle and lets the daughter follow her heart. In the second, a musical comedy, Jacques, played by Trénet, is a composer whose dream is of a treasure hidden in a chateau, to which an "enchanted road" leads. His music is effectively both the pointer to this happier world and the means by which he reaches it. Moreover, his father is an astronomer, and Jacques and his brother spend their evenings gazing through his telescope at other worlds, where, in imagination at least, it is possible to believe that people lead finer lives. Jacques hits the road as a vagabond troubadour and, since this is a musical comedy, finds his chateau. Unsurprisingly, the countess who lives in it has a charming daughter. In the last of the three films, the bureaucratic M. Coccinelle sees no possibility of escape from his drear life and doesn't take seriously his aunt's lifelong conviction that existence is inherently rich with fantasy. Her own existence would seem to prove the contrary, since as a young girl she had fallen for a magician, the Great Illusio, but had been parted from him by the family. Ever since, she has kept watch at her window, awaiting his return. She is, of course, ultimately justified when he arrives in grandeur, calms the angry populace with a shower of magical gold, and whisks the aunt off to a new life in unimaginable lands.

A number of films, including *Le Grand Jeu* (33.62) and *Pepe le Moko* (36.99), enact a variation of this theme of contemporary France as a trap from which one dreams of escaping. In them, the protagonist actually *is* overseas, usually in North Africa, and dreams of return from his exile to a France which is the fantasized promised land. Pepe's Kasbah is at once refuge and trap. As a criminal on the run, he has realized "the impossible dream" of the oppressed French worker/criminal, only to find that "over there" is as much a trap as was the land he fled. Although there are certain inversions in this sort of narrative, the climactic dockside scene in which the steamer sails without him, as it does in *Le Grand Jeu* without Pierre, remind us of the continuities.

Occasionally in these North African exile films, however, the dream, implicitly, and sometimes explicitly, is of escape back to a French childhood figured as a paradise lost. It is not to a better future in a new land that the oppressed wish to escape, but rather to a nostalgic past in the old country. Gilbert, on the run in Algiers from a violent episode, remembers his only true happiness as being associated with the Breton countryside of his past. He came to North Africa to forget and to be forgotten, but he dreams of "going home" (37.103). In *La Maison du Maltais,* it is again nostalgic dreams of childhood in the French countryside that the exile feels most strongly (38.60). More commonly, "home" for these exiles means Paris, and specifically the working-class suburbs of the Pigalle area. Fernand and his mates reminisce about La Place Blanche even as his son is thinking of enlisting to get away from it all (37.53). Deep in the South American jungle, the escaped convicts reminisce about Paris and particularly about La Place Blanche, where it's always Sunday (37.22), while for Pepe, La Place Blanche is the symbolic locus of his encounter with Gaby, and (along with America) the focus of Tania's reminiscences in the unbearably poignant song she sings for him (36.99). Of course, one reason for the metonymic selection of La Place Blanche to bear this metaphoric weight is the paradoxical combination of whiteness and working-class slum; but its relationship to the mythic role of the laundress reminds us that it has not just a passive and ironic role but an active purgative role in raising the lost past to a level of paradoxical purity never again attainable.

In most of these more "realistic" films, escape can seem possible only by leaving France or, if that proves impossible, then in death, yet a large number of films, both realist and escapist, use the simple narrative mechanism of a lottery win, a gambling win, or an inheritance as a means of fantasizing about escape from the poverty trap. It is very rare, however, for this abrupt and unearned wealth to prove an unqualified benefit. Very often, indeed, it proves precisely the contrary, and the implicit moral relates to the corrupting nature of all money. As the humble must learn, it is because they are poor that they are morally superior to the beneficiaries of the system.

While lotteries, inheritances, and gambling wins, not to mention the finding of lost valuables, all serve certain common purposes linked to an abrupt crisis in the economic status of a large proportion of the population, there are important distinctions in the way they function within a narrative. Lottery wins tend to be totally unexpected, most notably by the owner of the ticket, who has often forgotten he bought it and has trouble locating it. In *Le Million*, the narrative is devoted almost exclusively to this pursuit of a lost ticket (31.84). If the problem of locating a lost ticket can have a certain suspense value, the win itself is a total surprise. It usually occurs in the opening sequence, triggering narrative problems or possibilities, as when the mates in *La Belle Équipe* explore ways to use their unexpected winnings (36.17), but it can occasionally come at the end of the narrative, calling an abrupt halt to it (34.30). In 1931 and 1932, however, it was gambling wins which had been more likely to call an abrupt halt to the narrative, by solving financial problems and allowing the hero to marry the heroine (31.116; 32.6; 32.10; 32.86; 32.149). Unexpected inheritances had served a similar purpose (31.88; 31.137). Guitry tended to rely heavily on one or another of these mechanisms, as did boulevard comedy in general, because they provided narrative motivation without the obligation to develop characterization. In *Bonne Chance* (35.13), the characters' relationship is "lucky," proving that they are meant for one another: he wins a lottery, which triggers the narrative machine, and in the final scene he wins at gambling, thus ensuring a happy ending. Likewise, the narrative of *Le Comte Obligado* (34.30) is triggered by an inheritance, and a happy end is ensured by a lottery win. Both of the most popular comedies of the early thirties open with a gambling scene—in *Le Roi des resquilleurs* (30.78) Bouboule backs the wrong horse by mistake, and it wins; in *Théodore et Cie* (33.124), on the contrary, Théodore backs the wrong horse by mistake, and it loses (while the right one wins).

Gambling tended, however, to be used more commonly for its suspense value. The need for money was established in an introductory segment, then the gambling scene, often involving fluctuating fortunes, could be expanded and repeated for dramatic purposes. Such scenes commonly developed an intensity which the other mechanisms lacked, which made them of particular value in realistic dramas. Inheritances, on the other hand, were more common in comedies of the picaresque or vaudeville genres, leading to comic consequences from which Fernandel, Bach, and Rellys had great difficulty extricating themselves. Of particular delight to filmmakers and audiences alike were problematic inheritances, which came with conditions attached. At least seventeen of these were produced in the thirties. Most commonly, the condition attached to the inheritance was marriage: the protagonist will inherit only if he marries in a particular way, perhaps before he comes of age (i.e., tomorrow: 34.20), perhaps within a year (33.78; 36.107). Usually, he must marry someone not known, or at least not loved (33.84)—love will, of course, follow—perhaps a widow (31.112) or someone socially below him (34.106; 38.62). Slight variants involve the need to conceal a second marriage (33.44) or a twin (36.66). Occasionally, the condition is more exotic, requiring the potential heir to undertake tasks for which he is radically unfitted—a prude to manage a nightclub (33.64), an ineffectual blowhard to undertake a round-the-world adventure on five sous (39.16), a timid man to become a pilot (39.61) or a lion-tamer in a circus (38.26). The idea that inheriting money involves some sort of curse is often directed more at the thematics of the family than of class, and it is most explicitly thematized in a horror film involving an inherited Stradivarius that is cursed by its maker (35.107). More generally, however, all contact with unearned money is seen in this tradition as corrupting, since it allies the acquirer of such wealth with the corrupt middle classes of society.

The characters who are most at risk of such corruption are, of course, the poor and humble. At a time when the depression was demonstrating all too clearly the desirability of financial stability, those who had never known it or who had known and lost it are represented as initially rejoicing— naively, as it turns out—in their sudden acquisition of wealth. Typical protagonists in such narratives are waiters, tramps, elevator attendants, dishwashers, postmen, aging soldiers or teachers, valets, and laundresses. *La Belle Équipe* adds to the list a travelling salesman, an unemployed worker, and an illegal immigrant (36.17). In the early thirties, the feckless young party-goer could fulfill this function, but from 1932 onward it is more "deserving" categories of the poor who benefit.

One standard problem to which the inheritance exposes the heir is false friends. From being a disregarded and marginalized member of society, the heir rapidly becomes a social success with milling throngs of parasites and admiring women. The theme of sincerity, so common in many genres during this decade, again comes to the fore, together with the heir's inflated sense of self-importance. Hypocrisy and self-delusion are finally defeated either by the revelation that the protagonist has not after all inherited, or by his decision to renounce the inheritance and return to a simpler and thus purer life. In either case, it is with relief that he finds himself no longer encumbered with money and able to marry the humble (and thus sincere) working girl who has been true to him all along (seventeen films in all). In one such film, having finally managed to get rid of his inherited wealth, the protagonist learns in despair that he has won the lottery (34.30).

Inevitably, it is in gambling scenes that the curse of monetary success is most often apparent. The focus of such wins is the casino or the nightclub, both normally characterized as sites of violence and chaos. Those who live after dark have something to hide; their values are the reverse of those who live by day. Indeed, the gambling den often represents the dark side of the capitalist system. This may be explicit, as in *Macao* (39.51), in which the banker passes through a secret door to the gambling den which he and his gang of thugs run on the side, but it is often at least implicit: in *Le Dernier Milliardaire* (34.35), the capitalist is called in to set Casinario back on an even keel. To citizens of the mid-thirties, there could seem to be as little difference between the stock exchange and a casino as between a banker and a Mafia boss. Owners of nightclubs are invariably sinister, and to fall into their hands is to be blackmailed into behaving in a way quite foreign to one's normal personality. Pretty women fall into the hands of wealthy seducers (31.27; 37.48), honorable soldiers fall into the hands of entrepreneurs out to ruin them (34.70), and directors of institutes gamble away their funds (39.87). At the very least, the gamblers (and often their friends) are forced onto the street or into prison (seven films). An atypical Guitry film has the sentimental idyll between rich woman and gentleman crook terminate in a final gambling fling in Biarritz which fails, leading to separation and perhaps death (38.2). Undoubtedly the best known of these films that focus on a casino is *Pension Mimosas* (34.76), in which the craving for wealth and for that moment of intensity and uncertainty at the gambling table is most explicitly aligned with unhealthy passions that destroy the family. For dramatic effect, those caught up in such corrupt maneuvers are often contrasted with young women of ineffable purity who survive the underworld of finance unscathed (36.62; 39.51; etc.).

Roulette and baccarat are by far the most favored forms of gambling, though horse racing figured more commonly in the early thirties—seven out of the sixteen films identified as using these mechanisms to 1935 involve horse racing (31.57; 32.10; 32.149; 33.41; 33.124; 35.5; 36.2), but none of the nineteen thereafter. This fall from favor must have been to do partly with the recognition that horse racing is too public, ebullient, and open-air a sport to generate the desired intensity, whereas the casino, with its dramatic lighting, hushed atmosphere, and prevalence of close-ups proved much more appropriate. It might be more accurate to say that the connotations of gambling change significantly from 1935 on. But whatever the nature of the gamble—indeed, whatever the nature of the mechanism for endowing the protagonists with unearned wealth, or for depriving them of it, a strong sense of destiny is thereby introduced into these films. The scenarios strive to suggest that the outcome of the lottery, inheritance, or gamble involves a certain sense of rightness, even inevitability, which speaks of the hand of the gods.

Although the two principal forms of escape fantasized by the thirties French cinema explore geography and the uncertain benevolence of the gods, there is, of course, a third option which is relatively little explored, but which is in a sense the obvious and logical one: the socio-political transformation of the conditions of daily existence by local or global political action, or by revolutionary action. Some of the films which explore this option are well known—*La Marseillaise* (37.69) and *Le Crime de Monsieur Lange* (35.27), not to mention the political-campaign films *La Vie est à nous* (36s2) and *Le Temps des cerises* (37.109), which insist that "things must change." This can give the impression that the political option was strongly represented and had broad audience recognition and support. Statistically, however, it was not and did not. The few films which chose to explore these dimensions, including all of the above, were more or less unsuccessful in box-office terms—when, that is, they even managed to reach the movie theaters.

Of the thirty or so films that deal with radical social or political transformations of, or alternatives to, the existing system, most—especially those from the early thirties—apply routine romantic formulas to dramas which take place in safely imaginary countries. Bandit chiefs subvert the tyrannical régime of Ferdinand of Naples (30.41), queens fall unwittingly for revolutionaries (30.55), or female revolutionaries momentarily influence the life of fellow travelers at the frontiers of imaginary countries (31.101). Sympathy is invariably on the side of the revolutionary, who proves, though lowly, to be a heroic and even noble individual (31.121). When present, the French are invariably on the side of these heroic individuals. But if the revolutions do not take place in an imaginary country such as Cucaracha (38.32), they take place in a distant and often culturally remote region—

Turkey (39.34), the South Seas (36.87), or Tibet (38.99)—and the revolution is aimed at subverting not a socio-economic régime recognizably similar to that of France, let alone Western capitalism, but rather some autocratic, intolerant dictatorship that could not conceivably attract legitimate support. At best, Russian revolutionaries are supported in their attempt to overthrow the czarist régime, or Polish revolutionaries are engaged in a similar, if earlier, enterprise (36.123; 37.26; 38.54; 39.60); and one apparently lost film features a league of resistance ("Pax"), represented by a female revolutionary, struggling against a European dictatorship (32.104).

The remaining fifteen or so films can be divided into those which see innovative workers displace incompetent bosses, cooperatives displace hierarchical systems, and revolutions transform the whole of society. Among these are the very few films of the decade which actually mention the depression explicitly (e.g., 36.85). Early in the decade, such themes tend to be treated in a comic or lighthearted way, but later the tone is more somber. Indeed, up until 1934, no film can be said to have treated the material seriously. *À nous la liberté* (31.1) represents the capitalist system as inhuman, mechanistic, deadening, but all it takes is a reminder from a former cellmate and the successful entrepreneur hands his factory over to the workers and returns to the congenial fecklessness of the vagabond. Moreover, it is his industrial advances based on automation and mass production, which had initially caused the problems, which finally are represented as solving them, allowing the workers to devote their time to more leisurely activities—"freedom," defined in terms of fishing, boating, dancing, and the open road. Even less programmatic is *Les Aventures du roi Pausole* (33.12), in which Pausole's 366 wives initiate a revolution against the black-suited functionaries who bureaucratically maintain his sensual régime. And *Cognasse* (32.39) proposes a cynical right-wing thesis: the apostle of socialism, once he finds himself in charge of the factory, renounces all his principles and runs it as ruthlessly as any capitalist. In the same vein, a later film has the photograph of a husband smacking his wife promoted first as a revolutionary image— the revolt of the downtrodden—then as a reactionary image—the counter-attack of the forces of order (37.44).

The first of the more thoughtful films to deal with political change is *Si j'étais le patron* (34.97), in which an inventive worker develops a muffler that will revolutionize motoring, but is thwarted by vested interests and unimaginative management. He is promoted to boss by a new board member, an eccentric enlightened investor who sees the need for such creative individuals if his investment in the firm is to be saved. There is a certain analogy with the eccentric and absent-minded Mounier in *Lange*, who blithely and uncomprehendingly agrees to having a workers' cooperative replace Batala (35.27). Descended from the harebrained eccentric millionaires of tradition, these dei ex machina can scarcely be considered a useful contribution to revolutionary thought, but they were surprisingly tenacious in left-wing films: *Hercule* (37.59) provides a variant in the gullible young inheritor of a newspaper, whose naivete is ruthlessly exploited by a cynical manager, until he recognizes what's going on, turns the tables, and hands the newspaper over to a workers' cooperative. The idea of a cooperative had, of course, been central to *Lange:* no longer were hierarchical inequalities to be the norm, but rather a comradely version of mateship translated into (necessarily small-scale) industrial production. Roughly the same mateship/cooperative is the focus of *La Belle Équipe* (36.17), which is more ambivalent about the possibility of such practices bringing about effective social change or improving the lot of the workers, since it had alternative endings in which the cooperative based on mateship either triumphed or failed.

To sum up, if the informal socialism of mateship was supported throughout the thirties, the slightly more formal version of it involved in a cooperative was less widely promoted or accepted, and the direct presentation of socialist principles within a political film promoting radical social change was extremely rare. The only two films to tackle the contemporary political situation in France overtly and systematically are *Le Temps des cerises* and *La Vie est à nous*. The former (37.109) is an earnest but clumsy attempt to present the Communist Party's policies toward the aged in a partially fictional form; it is hard to see it convincing any but the already converted. The latter (36s2), on the contrary, is a brilliant and constantly fascinating technical tour de force, employing dramatic segments, documentary material, and a wide array of propaganda techniques. The vicious portrayal of bloated boardroom plutocrats gambling in the casino and grumbling about the workers' demands even as they prepare to sack them could hardly be exceeded in cruelty, unless it is in the following scene, which shows them gunning down silhouettes of workers in a clay-pigeon shoot. But of course, this film was never screened commercially. Indeed, it would seem that the industrial "common sense" of the time decreed that no film could succeed if it foregrounded a contentious political or social message. Toward the end of the thirties, the very notion of class as an organizing principle is called into question, not least by Renoir. One only has to compare *La Grande Illusion* (37.54) with *La Règle du jeu* (39.78) to recognize the shift that has taken place. The former explicitly asserts that class is more important than nation as a social determinant. The officer class of the French and German armies have a similar upbringing and experience, not to mention mutual acquaintances, which bind them in a common appreciation of mutually held values, while the officers and the men within the French army share no such common bond. For the officers, Paris means Fouquet's and Maxim's, whereas for the men it means the bistro on the corner. Boieldieu still says "vous" to his wife, while Maréchal says "tu" to everyone. As Maréchal notoriously says to Boieldieu, "Everything separates us." Taking this a step further, *La Marseillaise* (37.69) has the men of opposing armies rush to embrace one another on hearing word that the conflict is over, only to have the Royalist guard open fire on them.

Yet one year later, opting for an analogous hierarchical situation, *La Règle du jeu* asserts precisely the opposite: despite the radical disparities in their social standings, it is the similarities between the representatives of different classes which are the most profound. In very general terms, this film is based on the conventions of boulevard comedy, and of the many surviving boulevard comedies that the French cinema had produced or, more commonly, transcribed in the thirties it is most recognizably allied to Guitry's *Désiré* (37.34) and Mirande's *Sept hommes . . . une femme* (36.121). This genre provided a set of rigidly class-bound conventions: set in high society, it figured two categories of character—first, the central characters, who were rich, occupied powerful positions in society, and were often aristocratic, and second, their servants. These two categories of character allowed for a number of lighthearted interactions and parallels between events and relationships upstairs and down, and particularly for complicities between master and servant, mistress and maid, whose relationships were often more intimate and more sincere than the chronically frail marriage relationships. What might seem an extraordinary series of curious complicities in *La Règle du jeu* between characters at opposite poles of the diagram—between Christine and Lisette, of course, but also between Jurieux and Marceau, between the marquis and Jurieux, who discovers an unexpected sympathy for the rules just when Christine wants him to forget them, and finally even between Marceau and Schumacher—is therefore merely an adaptation of generic norms. Likewise, when the film brings the marquis and Marceau together, partly on the amusing pretext that both want the rabbits killed, and Marceau is somewhat more efficient at it than is Schumacher, there may well be underneath this superficial similarity the trace of a deeper one—the marquis is as much an outsider, indeed as much a poacher, as is Marceau—but there is also a standard play with generic norms. It is not possible to ignore the similarities between these antics and those that structure Guitry's earlier film, in which conversations and meals are also intercut with or paralleled by those below-stairs. The bedtime rituals in *Désiré* likewise evoke those at La Colinière, and the cook's husband, a policeman, plays a role analogous to Schumacher's. In particular, the central episode, where the characters depart for a moment of respite in the country, is reminiscent of the parallel scenes in Renoir's film. Of course, such trips into nature were a part of the standard repertory, and occasionally they proved as here anything but restful. In the Mirande film, for instance (36.121), when the widow invites her suitors to her country house for a hunt, the expedition proves distinctly uncomfortable for them, since it is the moment when they are tested and found wanting. A hunt is again the centerpiece of the film, highly edited, but somewhat briefer than in Renoir's film; it leads to the countess being surprised in a half-embrace with one of the suitors, and ends with a round of boisterous bedtime rituals in the tiled corridors of the chateau.

This film, too, exploits a series of below-stairs scenes that echo and comment on those above-stairs. Nevertheless, the numerous scenes in *La Règle du jeu* showing those above-stairs and those below-stairs conspiring together or helping one another out have a distinctly different effect from others in the boulevard comedy genre, in which class is irrevocable and fundamental, since here it serves rather to minimize the significance of social stratification and to imply that all the most important problems are common to humanity as a whole. Effectively, class has ceased to be the principal determining factor in Renoir's films, which are in the process of moving toward a more humanist, or indeed pantheist, thematics.

FOUR

Gender and the Family: The Formation and Dissolution of the Couple

---

4.1 WHAT ARE MEN AND WOMEN LIKE?

The formation and dissolution of the couple, covering the fields of gender, sexuality, and the family, ranks with class as one of the two major thematic fields of the day. It has been explored more fully than the others in part 1 by commentators interested in the social construction and textual representation of gender and in the implicitly incestuous relationships proposed by many films of the day. Nevertheless, it is well to chronicle the extent of these and related topics in the films of the thirties, if only to provide the broader context for the films dealt with by those commentators.

Films that foreground one or another aspect of this broad thematic field comprise between 38 percent and 61 percent of the films in each year of the decade, beginning at the lower end, hitting a peak in 1936, and falling back steadily to 44 percent by 1939. For convenience, we can distinguish films that focus on gender and gender relations from films that deal with marriage and the family, though in practice there is inevitably a high degree of overlap. The former constitute on average 20 percent of each year's output, with a maximum of 27 to 30 percent in 1933, 1936, and 1938, while the latter constitute on average 24 percent of each year's output, with a high of 32 percent in 1936. Cumulatively, 1936, with 61 percent, and 1937, with 50 percent, are the years most marked by this theme. As well as these films which foreground the thematics of the couple, nearly all films of the time (as is normal in Western culture) incorporate at least a secondary theme relating to couple formation, regardless of their primary thematics. There must be fewer than thirty which do not do so in any way, notably the more political films, which minimize narrative and/or individualist characterization.

The best way to approach this broad topic is by considering what, according to the films, men and women are like. The representation of gender has been the subject of theoretical debate for some years, and much of what one finds in thirties French films falls readily within conventional categories recognizable from the production of other media, other cultures, and other ages. Inevitably, the representation is skewed: as a global text, at least till late in the decade, French films manifest no doubt as to what men are like and spend relatively little time on articulating or developing those assumptions. The otherness of woman is, however, an endless source of mystery, fascination, and fear. The representation of men, moreover, is largely a function of métier, and thus of class—they are defined by their role in society and, as a result, the cinema's class preferences designate certain forms of maleness which are represented not so much as inherent as socially determined. Men may be bankers or factory workers or taxi drivers (etc.), and their function in the plot is colored by that social role—indeed, generated by it. Lacking for the most part any such clear social determination, women are seen as primarily determined by an essential femaleness.

A crucial aspect of that femaleness is the female body—women are primarily physical creatures, defined in large part by their surface appearances. This is exemplified most obviously in the large numbers of women who trade in their bodies. Films of the decade take for granted the presence in the social background of women earning their living by displaying their bodies in cabarets, nightclubs, and casinos, selling themselves in these venues and, more formally, in brothels, or exploiting their bodies to prey on the rich and corrupt. Sometimes, the good-time girls and prostitutes are not represented in predatory or malevolent ways—the long-standing cliché of the prostitute with the heart of gold appears throughout the decade. Occasionally, the sensual aspects of the role are even regarded as vivifying, as when young men, even young husbands, are "cured" of their inhibitions through the ministrations of a "loose woman" (e.g., 35.101; 36.143). Often, of course, this good-hearted prostitute is called upon to sacrifice herself to save the hero. Perhaps the most fascinating and enigmatic of these is Michèle in *Carrefour* (38.16), whose sacrifice saves the amnesiac de Vétheuil from discovering that he may be the gang boss Pelletier. Dostoevsky's dramas *Les Frères Karamazoff* (31.60) and *Crime et châtiment* (35.28) present similar prostitutes with good hearts, capable of self-sacrifice and, indeed, of regeneration through love. Even here, however, it is in the nature of woman to be a prostitute, and thus to need regeneration. In other cases, women who have previously been respectable are subsequently found to have descended to the level of good-time girls and prostitutes or, in another context, geishas (37.124; 38.27; 39.80). Respectable men may selflessly try to save such women from their baser selves, but with little hope of success!

Twin sisters were often used to pose the double nature of women, seemingly pure but inwardly corrupt, as in *Faubourg Montmartre* (31.55; 36.15). In the extreme, one sister is a vampire and bares her teeth at the other (31.146). The corruption of woman was often partially socially motivated by the theme of urbanization, as we saw earlier, with Parisian corruption gripping the women in contrast to the provincial honor of a landed brother (36.130). Nearly all films involving the underworld, from *L'Opéra de quat'-sous* on, involved a theme of female prostitution, while the pressure of poverty which forces a woman into prostitution was a common theme of melodrama (e.g., 36.19; 39.80). Perhaps the grimmest and most unsympathetic representation of prostitution is that in Renoir's *La Chienne,* in which the prostitute systematically cons and deceives the naive Maurice until, discovering the truth, he kills her and allows her pimp to take the blame.

This enormous proliferation of women-seen-in-terms-of-flesh, together with an uncertainty as to how to represent that fleshliness, speaks of both a fascination and a fundamental ambivalence. One film deals with this theme overtly: *Le Puritain* (37.96) has Jean-Louis Barrault as a man of rigid morals who stabs a prostitute to death in a fit of righteous rage, only gradually to recognize that his act was motivated as much by his attraction to her and by jealousy as by moral outrage. Madness ensues—a madness that indicts the whole cinema of the time, which is implicitly recognizing that it is itself "mad" in its construction of women in the terms outlined here.

A parallel strand in the representation of women focuses likewise on their physicality as fundamental, but approaches it through contemporary mechanisms for perfecting and glorifying the female body—beauty institutes, beauty parlors, beauty parades, models, and stars. Contemporary attitudes toward beauty salons are articulated with unselfconscious clarity in the extraordinarily popular film *Le Roi des resquilleurs* (30.78): the incident in which the two likable rogues manage to introduce themselves into the beauty salon where their girlfriends work is no more than a narrative pretext for salacious scenes involving almost-naked women. It is not just that women are the object of such fantasies, but that they are represented as offering themselves willingly as such. Yet attitudes toward this physicality are necessarily ambivalent: constructed as desirable to men, it is nevertheless more often condemned as inadequate by comparison with a range of moral values based on simplicity, humility, sincerity, and spirituality. On the positive side, a humble working-class girl (inevitably a florist) is rejected by her man in favor of a star, but wins a beauty competition and herself becomes a star, thus winning back her man (32.101); and an ugly girl manipulated by crooks has cosmetic surgery, which transforms her both physically and morally—she proceeds to save the family she had been planted to rob. Beauty and glamour can, then, on rare occasions solve problems (33.67). More often, however, cosmetic surgery creates moral dilemmas (36.138), and winning beauty competitions implicates honorable women in sordid situations (37.92). As the director of a beauty institute and nudist center discovers, the cousin whom he had initially found ugly can be more appealing than the perfect bodies he has been promoting (30.9). In the extreme, beauty institutes and fashion houses are indistinguishable from brothels, as in *La Rue sans joie* (38.93), where Fréhel manages both and where the catwalk is no more than a slightly arty pretext for the display of the female body. Fashion houses, catwalks, and designers were a standard object of comic mockery for the gender perversions seen as inherent in them (34.30).

The morality arising from this is most effectively articulated in *Prix de beauté* (30.69), largely written and (surely) partially directed by René Clair. Lucienne enters a beauty competition, partly in the hope of escaping the squalor and ugliness of working-class life. Having won it, however, she has her head turned by the attentions of counts and Indian princes and is torn between the glamorous international lifestyle opening up before her and her former fiancé, the typesetter André. Reluctantly, she resigns herself to a married life of ironing and making do, in a constricted flat in a working-class neighborhood (accompanied by the inevitable metaphor of a caged bird). The Indian prince discovers her address and urges her to leave André. She does so, and is offered a generous contract to star in films (a contract which André, "as chance would have it," is given to typeset). Humiliated and outraged, he follows her to the projection room where the rushes for her film are being screened and shoots her dead, while her image continues to sing "their song" on the giant screen overhead. Women are often thus torn between a humble marriage and promotion of the physicality which is associated with beauty contests and stars, and if they cede (and how could they not, the thirties cinema asks), the results are always disastrous and often, as here, fatal.

The idea that heads—especially female heads—can be turned by a glamorous lifestyle which is incompatible with the simple sincerity of morally more admirable people is one that we have met before. Heads may be turned by Hollywood, but true love awaits back in France. Heads may be turned by the glamorous lifestyle of Paris, when true feeling resides in the provinces. Heads may be turned by the glamour of wealth, when true feeling resides with the working classes. Models are as subject to such understandable delusions as are beauty-contest winners and stars—indeed, the three categories are largely interchangeable in the cinema of the thirties. The opposition between glamour and sincerity is acted out over and again, with a Parisian model and her boyfriend's provincial family (30.93), an haute couture model who has to learn that her mechanic boyfriend is worth more than the elegant twits who court her (31.69), a star who renounces her dream of Hollywood for her French window-washer (32.142), another star who can't bring herself to reject an engagement even to attend her own honeymoon (32.154), and yet another who renounces her glamorous lifestyle because her astronomer boyfriend is shocked by it (37.25). One star is so besotted by the limelight that she ignores her soldier boyfriend's plea to join him in a colonial life in Algeria (37.74). The allocation of roles is remarkably consistent: the humble, honest working-class man, the woman who has loved him but who becomes a star/beauty queen/fashion model, and her seduction, sometimes temporary, sometimes permanent, by a glamorous lifestyle and the various associated benefits—the adulation of the masses, say, or the importunings of an aristocrat. A worker may fall for a star and win her with the help of his friends (36.94), but more typical is the humble blood donor whose blood saves a star—in recognition, she tries to incorporate him into her show, but unsuccessfully; he returns wryly to his humble life (36.55).

The conclusion is fairly obvious: women are creatures of impulse, easily led; all body, with no more than a semblance of moral rigor, they are happy to abandon commitments if one of these mythic roles offers itself. The ambivalence of the males witnessing this is nicely caught in that fine film *Le Bonheur* (35.12), in which the anarchist first attempts to assassinate the star because she represents all he despises, only to fall in love with her and try—but fail—to live out with her the mythic euphoria that the notion of "star" seems to offer.

But it is not just the falsity and (self-)delusion that these females flaunt which disconcerts men. Unquestionably, their principal crime against mankind [*sic*] is to aspire to a form of power which is rightly the male's prerogative. Feminist critics have discussed the extent to which Marlene Dietrich, for example, was subject to the male gaze, objectified by it, or, on the contrary, was the puppet-mistress, mesmerizing and manipulating the male viewer with her performance. The rage so often inspired by these "physical" women of thirties French films suggests the latter—they are simply the most successful and powerful of that extensive array of women whom the decade's films enjoyed condemning for their unnatural craving to dominate men. It is not only the anarchist of *Le Bonheur* who wants to murder them. Film stars are the perfect victims in murder mysteries (32.143; 37.114) because, for a variety of partially Freudian reasons, every man might well want to murder them. Extreme instances of this female who embodies all male desires but uses the power it gives her to dominate or destroy the male are the queen bees, Antinéa of *L'Atlantide* (32.12) and Marguerite of *La Tour de Nesle* (37.112). The latter takes a different lover every night, only to have him executed at dawn. The former, whose lethal feminine grace is externalized in her pet leopard, and whose majesty is manifest in the giant sculpted head that we come across in her underworld lair, is the queen/goddess of a secret desert civilization. When two French explorers are captured and taken to her domain, they discover others of their race, besotted by their adoration for Antinéa, rendered desperate by the casual unconcern with which she uses and abandons them, drugging themselves with opium and on the verge of death. When one of the explorers resists her, putting male friendship above love for her, she has his pal kill him. Nothing must call into question the dominance of the female principle. Basically, this Atlantis (which it is rather odd to find buried so deep in the desert) stands for any imaginary land in which traditional gender values are reversed. To the male travelers, it is a frightening yet obsessively fascinating world.

At the opposite extreme from the sheer physical ruthlessness of these women, but sharing with them an equivalent castrating power, are the cold authoritarian matriarchs who ruthlessly pursue their ends, manipulating all those around them, not least their menfolk, whom they despise for their feebleness. Catherine of Russia is sometimes represented thus, but any number of thirties films evoked lesser matriarchs, closer to home and more recognizable, coldly imposing their will on the community or on the family. Madame Husson, of *Le Rosier de Mme Husson* (31.118), is one such— guardian of the town's morals, embodiment of ruthless propriety. She is easily mocked, but she has many equally authoritarian, irascible, ruthless, or ambitious sisters, bullying their husbands and sons, driving them at times to suicide or to murder. Poil de Carotte's mother is one such (32.109); playing yet another, Françoise Rosay drives her son to suicide and her daughter-in-law to a convent (35.73). Strong female actresses such as Rosay reveled in such roles, while in boulevard comedies, Marguerite Moreno or Elvire Popescu often played less sinister equivalents (33.115; 37.42; 39.5). Gabrielle Dorziat provided a less strong portrait of the same category of woman in *Mollenard* (37.75): not only does she reject the swashbuckling husband's crudeness as unacceptable, but she sneers triumphantly as she humiliates him in the name of righteousness. "I am a monster, perhaps," he agrees, "but it is because of you and your world." Such overbearing women are summed up in *La Route enchantée* (38.92), in which the operetta that Jacques is composing transposes his mother into the wicked witch. Titles such as *Ma femme, homme d'affaires* (32.77), *Ma tante, dictateur* (39.50), and the ironic *Le Sexe faible* (33.115) are symptomatic of the distrust which such women incur. At the lower end, these shrews and bigots shade into the village gossips who appear in so many films of the decade. Occasionally, they are "taught a well-deserved lesson," as when the pushy wife, anxious to acquire the Légion d'Honneur for her husband, pushes him to be kind to the Beaux Arts director's wife, with predictable results (39.5). Another, having driven her husband into his secretary's arms, returns repentant only to find that she has to share his favors. When the village gossips force him to choose, he chooses the secretary (39.56).

The misogyny that runs through these films is rarely voiced explicitly, and frequently the confirmed bachelors who do voice it (32.22; 33.6) do so only so that their subsequent discovery of romance will be all the more dramatically satisfying, but a degree of real hatred and fear lies behind the recurrent images of ruthless female power. It is most consistently voiced in the "comedies" that Sacha Guitry designed to manifest his own masterful personality. Any female who may pose a threat to his status is put in the wrong or in a state of inferiority or ignorance. Her subsequent humiliation may not always be so severe as when one of them has her black male baby exchanged for a white female baby without her knowledge (30.13), but there will always be some patronizing decision made for her by men who understand all too well her feeble nature and can see better than she can what is best for her. In *Le Nouveau Testament* (36.91), the initial sequence, in which the doctor becomes aware that his wife is having an affair with the son of a friend, guarantees him thereafter superior knowledge, which he exploits ruthlessly to humiliate the wife (as if she deserved it more than he himself, given that he has fathered an illegitimate daughter whom he playfully passes off as his mistress).

This Guitry-esque conspiracy among men to patronize and humiliate women is mitigated only in those of his films in which he plays an elderly gentleman enjoying a relationship with a younger "daughter," where age and wealth ensure a certain "superiority." In *Mon père avait raison* (36.83), the moral of male superiority is articulated more explicitly than ever, but the possible disadvantages of such an attitude are finally acknowledged: brought up generation after generation by successive fathers to despise women, to see family and female companionship as an illusion, and to exploit women merely for sensual pleasure, the males of the family perpetuate an almost genetic misogyny, which is finally undone when the current male heir comes to see that marriage may have a role in his life (providing, of course, that the woman can subdue her baser instincts). The passing on of male "wisdom" here proves useless, however true the men's judgment of women may be; men must simply resign themselves to enduring the tribulations caused by women.

The fear of women implicit in this misogyny is equally apparent in another representation of the female common to Western culture—female sexuality as beyond the pale of civilized society and frequently aligned with criminality. This theme is implicit in the insistent presence of the prostitutes, good-time girls, and madams discussed above. Female sexuality may often be flaunted or offered for sale in bars, nightclubs, and brothels, but it is present less overtly in the recurrent association between desirable females and the underworld. Sometimes the female is the villain's daughter (as in Bond movies, decades later), but even when there is no direct territorial battle for her of this somewhat Oedipal sort, she is seen from the beginning as contaminated and in need of purification by the hero.

Cumulatively, this sort of representation of femaleness is unquestionably present in some two hundred of the thirteen hundred films of the decade, and probably many more, given the number which I have not been able to view. Because of its omnipresence, the examples cited below are drawn primarily from films still available, some of which are widely known.

Among the "taints" attached to the notion of femaleness, perhaps the mildest is simply that of being, at the moment when the protagonist encounters her, aligned with his enemy, the villain, or with other unsavory characters. In *Les Nuits moscovites,* Natacha is engaged to the tyrannical merchant Pierre as a result of her family's financial indebtedness, as Captain Ignatieff discovers to his dismay when he meets and falls for her (34.70). More commonly, women's association with evil is voluntary, implicating them in the values of their protectors. Thus, when Pepe meets Gaby she is the kept woman of a bloated capitalist, and if her final departure with that same capitalist is due to a misunderstanding fostered by the police chief, it is nevertheless not entirely unwilling; the life he offers more than compensates for any duties required (36.99). As Madeleine, Mireille Balin plays a similar role in *Gueule d'amour* (37.57), again risking compromising her status with her protector for Lucien, a character again played by Gabin. But even more clearly than in *Pepe le Moko,* a simple life of true love in a cramped flat is here identified as not enough for a woman whose life has been lived in casinos, mansions, and Deauville villas. She has no intention of permanently sacrificing the good life for a passing fancy, however seductive. In this film, moreover, the convention of the femme fatale who divides two mates is explicitly foregrounded: Madeleine turns up later as the fiancée of Lucien's friend, René, and, in the grip of one of those outbursts of uncontrollable fury that were to become a trademark, Lucien/Gabin strangles her. Of course, in a sense, Lucien is only experiencing poetic justice, since he is presented at the beginning as a glamour boy and lady-killer, yet the alignment of the female with high life, wealth, self-interest, and the scornful manipulation of men is much more forcefully constructed by the film than is any male counterpart. The latter is a mere game, the former a matter of life and death. To put it another way, the notional viewer of this and similar texts is male, and he may fantasize about such games but cannot accept an equivalent female player within his fantasies.

In the same tradition, Elsa in *Baccara* (35.5) is the kept woman of the seedy banker Gouldine, in whose frauds she risks being implicated. The war hero Leclerc has to win her over to the values of the heart, aided somewhat by the hasty disappearance of the embezzling banker. In a different genre, René Clair's early sound films had firmly situated the female as unreliably associated with criminality. Pola in *Sous les toits de Paris* (30.84) is as ready to take up with the thuggish Fred and his gang as she is to bestow her favors on Albert and Louis—incidentally generating a divisive quarrel between the two buddies; in *Quatorze juillet* (32.116) the same Pola is in cahoots with a gang of pickpockets and robbers, drawing Jean into criminal ways, until chance redirects him toward Anna, the flower girl. Pola Illery, who plays these roles, also played Finocle's daughter Noâ in the sordidly realistic *Rue sans nom.* In this film, she is again the daughter and associate of gangsters, and if Cruseo the American is left with her at the end, the audience's interpretation of this is somewhat colored by the clumsy coupling they have witnessed her engaging in with the other gangster's raffish son on the kitchen table (33.114).

Polish and Russian women (Pola, Sandra, Natacha) are particularly likely to have their sexuality linked with criminality. In part, this is an assertion that females are effectively a foreign race, "alien"—that female sexuality is "other." Sandra in *Au nom de la loi* is Polish, and is mixed up in drug smuggling for an Oriental gang. The honorable young policeman, André, falls for her even as he is investigating her. Seduced from his principles to the point of helping her escape back to Poland, he is prevented from succeeding by his chief, leading to Sandra's poignant suicide (31.11).

If "criminal" females tended to be East European and blonde in the early thirties, they became more sultry and lethal in the mid-thirties, leading to the recurrent image of the female spy who appeared in so many films of the last half of the decade. As we saw in chapter 2, females make perfect spies because of their "innate" talent for deception and betrayal, their delight in manipulating over-confident males, and their callous disregard for any death and destruction that they might bring about. The female spy's powers of deception allow her to con even the French military hero despite her (inevitable!) attraction to him, and to "escape," perhaps to her death, under cover of the German bombing of Salonica that she has arranged (36.69). But sultry spies were not necessarily foreign: the French also had their female super-spy in *Marthe Richard* (37.70), who likewise has an ambivalent sexual relationship with the German officer (played by von Stroheim) whom she dupes and drives to a magnificent suicide as he watches the climactic bombing of his base.

These representations from 1937 of the supremely deceptive and destructive power of woman had been made possible by a number of more domestic tales of deception and destruction in the years 1934–37, when passionate dark-haired women began to dominate the cinematic scene. In *Toni* (35.110), Josefa assumes this role, though the documentary realism of that film does not allow for the generation of a pathological intensity within the relationship in the way that later psychodramas were to do. Nor do the stagy sets of *L'Escale* (35.43), though in that film the implication of the adored woman in the devious activities of the underworld is spelled out explicitly, as is the "innate" weakness which leads women to abandon themselves to sensual enjoyment even when they realize that it is not in their long-term interest. In *Naples au baiser du feu* (37.80), Lolita arrives in Naples on the run, having stowed away on a ship (from the United States? from Argentina? Which of her stories is one to believe?) and takes delight in exercising her sultry powers over the naive musician Mario and his friend Michel, driving a wedge between them and displacing the innocent girlfriend Assumta. Leaving Assumta waiting at the church, Mario engages in a passionate affair with Lolita, who unfortunately turns out not to be able to resist exercising her powers over every other available man as well. Finally "unmasked" for the treacherous creature she is, she is cast out and the two mates are friends once more. Viviane Romance, who (as she so often did) played the vamp in this Tino Rossi musical drama, had played the Assumta role in another one the previous year—*Au son des guitares* (36.11), in which the besotted singer and his mate leave Corsica to follow a dark foreigner to Marseille and thence to Paris. Like the Mireille Balin vamps, this one is too interested in the good life that financiers can provide, however fraudulent they may be, to devote herself to a humble Corsican singer, but in a moment of altruism she says that she will not destroy him—love is not for her, he should go back to his Corsican girl and forget her.

Such musical dramas are the pale, sentimentalized shadows of dramas such as *Le Dernier Tournant* (39.23), a powerful version of *The Postman Always Rings Twice,* in which Cora enlists the aid of a vagabond to do away with her husband. Again, a key relationship is the strange (and strangely persistent) friendship between the vagabond and the husband, which the vamp's sensuality and treacherous passion must destroy. Another, better-known instance of Viviane Romance in this vamp role is as the wife of Charles (Vanel) in *La Belle Équipe* (36.17), tempting Jean (Gabin) into acts that will—at least in the filmmakers' preferred version—definitively destroy their bond of friendship and, indeed, destroy the entire (male) cooperative venture. Ginette Leclerc plays a more earthy version as the vamp (not surprisingly named Viviane) in *Métropolitain* (38.63). When the dock worker, Pierre, witnesses from the overhead métro what seems to be a murder, he gets involved with her and her sinister associate, the magician Zoltini. It is a relationship that clearly foreshadows that of the female lead and the sinister dog trainer played by Jules Berry in *Le Jour se lève* (39.48). For Pierre, meeting Viviane opens doors onto a world of deadly intensity where nothing is what it seems; such women can drive a man to any extreme. A little to our surprise, at the end of the film the magician kills her in reality, as he had seemed to kill her in the opening sequence, allowing Pierre to return to his wife. But, of course, his attitude toward his wife has now been significantly transformed. The lesson of all these films is not that there are two kinds of women—on the one hand quiet wives, innocent country girls, and on the other femmes fatales who draw men into a vortex of intensity—but that woman is double: female sexuality is inherently destructive, and only by resisting, subduing, or constraining it within the bonds of domesticity and marriage can it be made tolerable to a civilized society.

This double nature of women leads to the creation of a number of female characters whose official maternal persona is undermined by the revelation of a sensual darker side to their personality, manifested, for instance, in a job as a chanteuse or good-time girl in a nightclub, for which they show a talent unsuspected by their husbands, friends, and children (38.27; 39.80). This "taint" inherent in female sexuality can easily prove the death of the woman, however honorable a mother she may be. It will certainly lead to her being categorized as outside the bounds of civilized society, fit only to live among brutes and thugs, and will doom any attempt that she may make to better herself (31.34; 35.43).

This tradition of male suspicion and distrust of female sexuality pro- poses a rather unusual context for the Michèle Morgan personality which emerges from films of the late thirties. Like the Naples stowaway men- tioned above, the Morgan persona is a mystery which every male character is irresistibly induced to try to solve. She is the "mysterious stranger," a po- eticized and kindlier version of female "otherness" represented elsewhere and earlier as foreign, treacherous, deadly, solipsistic. In the Michèle Mor- gan films, the "mystery of female sexuality" still needs to be investigated, but it is a gentler mystery than in its other representations—no less fasci- nating, and ultimately no less deadly, but lacking the calculation, self-inter- est, and ruthlessness that had earlier been seen as intrinsic to it. In this version, it is no longer male friendships that the female threatens, but the family. In *Gribouille* (37.55), she is still a foreigner, a Russian immigrant called Nathalie, and still implicated obliquely in criminality, since it is at her trial that we actually meet her, but her quiet and rather abstracted air al- ready foreshadows her performance in *Orage* (37.87) and *Quai des brumes* (38.84). Rather than a passionate intensity, it is an intense inwardness that draws the juror father and his son to her and threatens to disrupt the family as she comes between husband and wife, father and son. We never do find out basic facts about her past or the extent of her guilt.

In subsequent films, this mystery deepens further; in *Remorques,* she is a waif, born out of the violence of a metaphoric storm, which she brings with her into the hero's life, and which destroys the family (39.79). And in *Quai des brumes* she is the "ward" of Michel Simon's twisted Zabel. Both in *Gribouille,* where at the trial she is said to have had many previous lovers, and in *Orage,* where the number of her previous affairs is left open, there is an implication of amorality, of sexual license, of sensual self-indulgence which is at odds with the contained surfaces of the persona that her perfor- mance constructs, and it is this paradox which is so fascinating: what storms seethe beneath the still surface, what has she experienced with the twisted and violent men with whom she has consorted? A final "softening" effect on the persona that she presents is her own awareness of the destruc- tive effect she produces, and her despair at the unhappiness that spreads out from her every attempt to seek happiness. The one seems to be incompati- ble with the other: like the good-hearted prostitute, she may have to com- mit suicide to free her man from the destructiveness that she generates, or at least she may try to send him away; certainly, she does not embody the malevolent, implacable, and ultimately destructive will of some instinctual female force that her predecessors so frequently embodied.

The double nature of women outlined so far has the "inevitable" consequence of rendering them inherently duplicitous, treacherous. When men betray one another, it is usually represented as a matter of great psychological consequence: they experience anguish, remorse, and regret because they are not being true to a unitary self (33.114). Most often, the nature of their treachery is having an affair with their friend's woman or wife. In such cases, the treachery occurs only after a considerable struggle, and the viewer is positioned to understand and sympathize with that anguish. Such dramas are often played out on a noble level, involving honor, integrity, and renunciation. Often, the setting is military. In *L'Équipage* (35.42) and *Le Roman de Werther* (38.91), the act of falling in love with a friend's woman is "excused" because the protagonist is unaware of the relationship. In neither case does the woman, typically deceptive, tell about her other relationship. In the latter film, when Werther finally learns the truth, he commits suicide, of course. In *L'Équipage,* when Jean learns that the woman he loves is his partner's wife, he is distraught: "But your husband and I are more than brothers, we're a team." The rest of the film is organized around his attempts to cope with his distress, and with Hélène's duplicity. The film's conclusion is that the only way out for him is to die nobly on a dangerous mission. In *Légions d'honneur* (38.57), when the hero falls for his comrade's wife, he renounces her and accepts dishonor rather than betray a friend.

This high-minded nobility so "typical" of the male is not, alas, evident in the case of female treachery, which is represented, instead, as the natural consequence of being a woman. When the treachery is sexual, it is because women—whether vamp or coquette—are changeable, fickle, and cannot help trying to seduce any man who comes along. Instances of such betrayal are numerous in films of the thirties (e.g., 34.100; 35.14; 36.114; 38.48), but in the first half of the decade they tend to have more serious consequences, involving the imprisonment or death of the man betrayed. Betrayed by a woman, Roger la Honte is accused of a crime committed by his enemy and imprisoned for life with hard labor (32.122), though he subsequently escapes to exact vengeance. Jealousy leads the smuggler's mistress and the banker's mistress to betray them to the police (34.56; 36.8), though the latter is waiting at the prison gate on the banker's release. Perhaps the best known of these betrayals is that of Pepe le Moko by Inès, which results in his capture and suicide (36.99), but an equally telling betrayal is that of Ralph by his woman in *Tumultes* (31.134). During Ralph's stay in prison, Ania has set up house with Gustave; when Ralph is released and duly kills Gustave, she sets up house with Ralph's mate, Willy, and betrays Ralph to the fatherly commissioner, which much offends Willy's finely honed male sense of propriety. Ralph, in turn, stabs Willy, only to have Ania sprawl over the prostrate Willy and call him "my love." These cumulative sexual and legal betrayals sicken Ralph to the point where he turns to the commissioner and says, "It's enough to make you want to be back in jail. What are human beings made of, I ask you?" Male protagonists may be criminals, but they have high standards and finer feelings. The women they encounter and on whom they come to depend have no such scruples, until the arrival of Michèle Morgan in the late thirties.

This account is a little lopsided insofar as a male equivalent of the heartless deceiver did exist—what might be called the lady-killer. The figures of the lady-killer are not deceptive, however—they do not pretend to be anything except cavalier figures, enjoying the admiration of women and passing from flower to flower. Moreover, especially in the first half of the decade, they often feature in lighthearted romps rather than psychological dramas. They are clearly male fantasy figures, briefly living out a life of multiple uncomplicated conquests before acquiring "wisdom" and recognizing the virtues of the quiet country girl who was their first love (32.9; 32.84; 33.75). The "disavowal" of these fantasized lady-killers is evident in *Cavalier Lafleur* (34.23), in which the protagonist has the same name as the lady-killer and has to cope with the undeserved reputation and consequences of his namesake's actions. Insofar as this figure survives into the second half of the decade, it is in a form closer to the female deceiver—a tragic figure who receives the punishment due to such actions. Gabin's embodiment of him at the beginning of *Gueule d'amour* has already been mentioned, and in Gance's *Voleur de femmes* he comes to a different, if no less somber, end—the traditional "charming young thing" whom the lady-killer was accustomed to fall back on at the end of his suave conquests is here all too well aware of his past and refuses him; he has to flee and later finds her married and happy. Out of spite, he tries to ruin the husband but fails and is left desolate (37.123). Finally, another handsome young lady-killer enters a typical community of thirties apartment dwellers and sows discord and distress; only with his departure can any semblance of harmony return and the young woman whom he has seduced and abandoned be taken in by the honest young worker (39.84).

4.2 INCESTUOUS IMPLICATIONS

If many of these representations of men, women, and the relationships between them seem all too familiar—seem, in fact, the sort of representations that might be considered typical of Western patriarchal culture—there are some, nevertheless, which are so distinctive as to be quite astonishing, even shocking. Perhaps the most striking of these is the recurrent representation of a sexual relationship, real or potential, between an aging man and a young woman who is, who may be, or who could be his daughter. At least eighty films were made during the thirties exploring such a relationship. They are spread evenly over the decade, though they are slightly more numerous in the first five years, with maximums of ten to thirteen films (about 8 percent of production) in 1931, 1933, and 1937. Often, the relationship is between a twenty-year-old girl and a fifty- or sixty-year-old man, though elsewhere the age difference may be not much more than twenty years. What is crucial is that these films all treat the age difference, however great or small, as the central narrative problem.

An interesting, if perhaps predictable, shift occurs in the social status of the "old" man in the course of the decade. Early on, in line with the predominance of boulevard comedies in the years 1930–33, the older man is often a count (31.104), baron (30.17; 30.39; 31s8), duke (30.57), or colonel (33.98). Parallel to these social roles, however, are others which categorize the older man as belonging to one of the "desiccated" professions—antiquary (32.63), philatelist (31.129; 32s5), notary (32.95), or public servant (31.103). These characters often serve the same narrative function as the dry-as-dust professors in zany American comedies of the thirties, who are clearly destined to be revitalized by a dynamic younger woman or to transform themselves into more dynamic characters in order to rescue that younger woman. In France, these characters become particularly common in the middle of the decade, when, after a slow start, no fewer than eight films feature older male professors who become besotted with one of their students. To some extent, this can be attributed to the scriptwriters' defensive preference for intellectuals as protagonists—and particularly for intellectuals who win the attractive young heroine. In this sense, it represents a mild form of reflexivity, such as is more apparent in the decade's almost unqualified enthusiasm for artists (see chapter 6). A third category of older men predominate in the later years of the decade, namely "bosses"—magnates and industrialists, bankers, or simply employers. Except for one ambiguous instance earlier in the decade (33.6), eight of the nine identified bosses appear in the years 1937–39.

There are three interesting lines of textual inquiry to follow up if we are to understand the significance of these relationships between older men and younger women. One is implicit in the social roles of the older men and involves the nature of the social relationship between certain of them and the young woman with whom they establish or desire to establish a relationship. In the case of professors, it is almost invariably a female student who attracts their attention (seven instances), though occasionally "professor" stands simply for crusty old man (31.8), and "student" stands simply for independent-minded young woman (31.9). In the case of bosses, the relationship is sometimes with an employee, as when the boss ultimately prefers his young secretary to his wife (39.56), or with a male employee's sister (38.118), though in that case it is much more normal for the role simply to stand for "a position of power," signifying a man who is used to getting his way (37.103) or who has a social standing that renders him vulnerable to blackmail (38.83). Certainly, a factor common to all these narratives is an unequal power relationship between male and female, since the traditional gender inequalities are exacerbated by differences in social standing and influence, and by the ability of bosses or professors (and, indeed, counts, colonels, and captains) to determine the future of the young women whom they come to desire.

Regardless of the specific social positions attributed to the older man and the younger woman, there is good reason to see the fascination exercised over the decade by these discrepant relationships as a fascination with incest. In some sense, most, if not all, of them are speaking of a fascination with father-daughter relationships. It is amusing to see the knots into which the films tie themselves in order to deny this incestuous relationship, while at the same time evoking it as a possibility. Often, the relationship is that of father to *adopted* daughter. The older man has rescued a young girl who had been done wrong and made pregnant and, as time passed, he has begun to be attracted to her for less compassionate reasons. Thus, a philatelist takes in a pregnant girl (31.129), or a professor his abandoned and pregnant student (36.52). Of course, there is the well-known instance of Panisse taking in Fanny in similar circumstances (32.58). Circus films abound with foundling stories that have the same effect: a lion-tamer has brought up a foundling girl for whom he develops other affections (35.105); two clowns have brought up the daughter of a dead trapeze artist (39.92), and they end up like the old clown in *Les Saltimbanques,* who had fallen for the young dancer (30s14). But an aging picador can do the same (32.106), as can Lagardère in *Le Bossu* (34.17), a middle-aged man who has rescued Aurore, the daughter of his slain comrade, Philippe de Nevers, and brought her up in secrecy. Aurore is a mere babe in swaddling clothes when he carries her off to safety, only to marry her twenty years later. Again, *Dernière Jeunesse* (39.24) relates the story of a colonist who rescues a young woman from poverty only to fall for her; when he realizes that her affections lie elsewhere, he strangles her. The female categories of actress and circus girl recur in the role of "attractive but available young women" (e.g., 33.26; 37.97).

At other times, it is not an adopted daughter but a daughter-in-law who attracts the attention of the father figure: a father may fall for the son's girlfriend (31.104), an actress whom he has forbidden his son to marry and whom he meets without realizing who she is; or the baron may visit his prospective son-in-law, only to find that son-in-law's very attractive mistress in residence (31s8); or the son's mistress (a seamstress, of course) offers her friend, another young seamstress, to his father (36.83). In the extreme, the father may try to marry his daughter off to some young man with an attractive mistress whom he can appropriate (37.15). The strained efforts of such narratives to disguise the father-daughter relationship show even further in the tale of a widower who marries his former son-in-law's former wife (33.120). Appropriately entitled *Les Surprises du divorce,* the film parallels this story with that of the son-in-law, who had divorced in order to escape an oppressive mother-in-law and now finds that his ex-wife is his mother-in-law, and the mother-in-law whom he had sought to escape is now (if I have understood aright) his mother-in-law's mother-in-law.

Quite common is the introduction of an uncle/niece relationship, as when an uncle tries to help his niece and her husband, who is neglecting her, only to get too involved (35.104), as well-intentioned older men are all too inclined to in this decade (36.5), though ultimately they usually come to realize the error of their ways, stand aside, and reunite the young couple. Again, there is a contorted version of this narrative, in which an uncle due to meet his niece sends his (male) secretary in his place. The niece has also sent a substitute—her young friend; the uncle comes to fall for his supposed niece, only to find out to his relief that there is no family bond after all (35.60). But by far the most intense of the surviving films featuring these uncle/niece stories is *Sarati le terrible* (37.103). Sarati, played by Harry Baur, is a powerful dock boss in Algiers who has brought up his niece as his own daughter since childhood. He is intensely possessive and jealous of any young rival. For a while his niece/daughter seems to respond to his insistent physical advances, until, in a moment of revulsion, she rushes out. Sarati pursues her, tells her that he has loved her since birth and wants to marry her. When she marries someone else, Sarati gets drunk at the wedding and screams that his niece has been stolen from him; after a night of progressively more drunken raging, he storms up to the marriage bedchamber where she is languorously half asleep, opens his clasp knife, and stabs . . . himself.

Still closer to home are stories of young women who need to marry urgently for some formal reason, and therefore contract a *mariage blanc* (marriage in name only) with an older man (37.67), perhaps a godfather (33.78). Or a girl must acquire a father if she is to marry the man she loves; she does so, only to get involved in a relationship with the pseudo-father which ends up in an engagement. At this point, she finds out—just in time, and to everyone's surprise, of course—that the pseudo-father whom she is about to marry is in fact her real father, and thus (of course!) out of bounds (33.49). Such father-daughter relationships are very common in the sort of boulevard comedy in which Guitry specialized. As Guitry aged and his leading ladies (often played by his own current wife) got younger, the contrast in age was often foregrounded thematically. In *Le Nouveau Testament* (36.91), to get revenge on his wife he engages a young secretary and proceeds to play with his wife's doubts as to whether she is his daughter or his

mistress, or indeed both. In *Bonne Chance* (35.13), he is an artist who wins
the lottery and proposes a trip with a young laundress as "brother and sister." In the course of the trip he admires an older man and a younger
woman dining together in a restaurant, dismissing young couples as without interest. Their trip together (to the Riviera) is so successful that they
begin to feel they are playing with fire, because of which (or despite which)
he proposes to adopt her as his daughter. Very soon, however, their relationship becomes a sexual one, and the marriage ceremony that she had organized with a younger man is appropriated for their own use. Their
relationship, then, has passed from brother and sister to father and daughter to man and mistress, and finally to man and wife.

Many of the titles of these films deliberately evoke such titillating relationships: *Mon gosse de père, Le Fils de l'autre, Le Fils improvisé, Ève cherche
un père, Les Surprises du divorce, Mademoiselle Josette ma femme, Mademoiselle ma mère.* But, after all the narrative circumlocutions that they engage
in, it is quite a relief to find two films overtly dealing with father/daughter
affections of a forbidden kind. In both cases, widowers are taken back
twenty years to their early married life by the sudden reappearance of a
daughter who resembles the wife they loved. In *La Nuit de décembre* (39.64),
the musician protagonist falls for such a young woman, not realizing that
she is actually his own daughter; when he discovers the truth, he steps aside,
seeking consolation in his music. In *Le Simoun* as in *Sarati le terrible,* however, the colonist (such things are more thinkable "over there," where isolation preys on the mind and the wild desert wind of the title can evoke the
primitive passions of a more barbaric time and place) summons to his side
the daughter he has not known since childhood and, in full knowledge of
their relationship, tries to induce her to substitute for her dead mother
(33.116). She flees, distraught. Alongside these two films we should remember *La Bête humaine,* in which it is in part the implication that the "godfather" whom Roubaud's wife has been visiting rather too often is in fact her
father that triggers the determination to murder him.

The weight of evidence in these films—both the quantity of them and
the intensity of several of those that survive—leaves no room to doubt the
source of the fascination. It is clear, however, that agency in initiating the
relationships most often lies with the older male "partner," as one would expect given the power relationships. There is little sign of the younger female
actively seeking an older man, though when circumstances match her up
with one she is often represented as finding that it is just what she had un-
consciously been needing.

Unfortunately for the older man, these narratives do not often turn out
so positively. Indeed, the third major feature of interest is the rivalry that
frequently develops between the older man and one or more younger rivals.
Again, one can read this rivalry in Oedipal terms as being between the old

man and his offspring for control of the women of the "herd." The young rival may take many different forms: a dashing lieutenant, a neighbor, a picador/circus performer, or an assistant to the older professor or doctor. It is rare to present the young couple formed by this rivalry as committed in an uncomplicated way to one another, but threatened by a sinister older man. One of the few couples of this sort appears in *Mireille* (33.91), in which they have to cope with a jealous guardian. In *Fanny* and *César,* Marius and Fanny have established a relationship in a previous film which complicates the rivalry between younger and older man. Again, in Feyder's *Les Gens du voyage,* the lion-tamer's son has an affair with the circus owner's daughter, and is accused by the owner of an Oedipal desire to wrest the circus from his control (37.53). Throughout this subplot, the viewer is positioned with the young couple. A similar Oedipal struggle for control occurs in *L'Embuscade* (39.29), in which the militant worker inciting his mates to strike finds out, to his surprise, that he is the boss's (step-) son. More commonly, however, such films position the viewer with, or closer to, the older man for whom the young rival is a threat, or at least they present the relationship between old man and younger woman as an established fact. Quite often this established fact is an "unbalanced" marriage, and the problem proposed by the film is the young wife's adultery with a "son" (30.87; 31.8; 31.24). Such narratives are more common at the beginning of the decade, though *La Femme du boulanger* (38.34) is a well-known example from later on.

In most of these (often quasi-incestuous) situations, the "son" is presented as unaware of the existing relationship between his father figure and the woman he has come to love, so not really guilty, even of simple disloyalty. The student at a naval school where his father is a professor falls unawares for the woman to whom his father is engaged (36.105). The woman whom Frantz has met and fallen in love with turns out to be his commandant's mistress. How could he have known (37.71)? As mentioned earlier, in the extremely popular *L'Équipage* (35.42) a young aviator falls for an attractive young woman whom he later discovers, to his horror, to be the wife of his much-admired captain. Similarly, a young wife on a cruise has an affair with a young man who turns out to be her husband's son by an earlier marriage (31.58; see also 31.104 and 31.122). Just as frequently, however, the rivalry between father and son for the young woman is overt—she is the son's mistress, whom the father appropriates (31s8), or the father's forthcoming mistress, whom the son appropriates (33.47), or the father's wife in a *mariage blanc* for whom the son falls (37.67). In *Toine* (32.133), the father unmasks a woman who has already caused his ruin and is about to cause his son's. In *Boissière* (37.16), the son comes upon the woman who has been the father's mistress and has ruined him but discovers a strange fascination for her. Such overt rivalry between father and son for the same woman, or elaboration of a situation in which father and son have the same mistress, was a stock in trade of thirties films: two lion-tamers, father and son, both have Rosita as their mistress (30.92); Dmitri Karamazoff falls for the woman who is already his father's mistress (31.60). Occasionally, as when the father/daughter relationship is disguised as uncle/niece, the father/son relationship is softened into uncle/nephew (30.17; 38.68; 39.9).

These overtly Oedipal relationships seldom end with the literal death of the father. By far the preferred ending, throughout the decade, is for the father to "come to his senses," to realize that his day is past and that he must step aside in favor of young love. He may have thoughts of suicide, may even try it (39.9), but is more likely simply to retire into a solitary old age, consoled, if not by his music, then by some childhood friend who he now realizes will make a more fitting partner (38.68). As in *Gribouille* (37.55), however, the Oedipal conflict is often presented as threatening to tear the family apart before it is finally resolved, usually in favor of the young couple. The old man's final decision to step aside is usually characterized as the proper moral ending to such a tale, and indeed the proper Oedipal ending, if somewhat diluted, involving the victory of the son and of "young love." It occurs in roughly three-fifths of the narratives that have a clear resolution. At times the stepping aside of the older man takes dramatic forms, as when the old lion-tamer allows himself, in his despair, to be eaten by his lion (35.105) or the old picador allows himself to be torn apart by a bull (32.106).

A more modest but better-known instance of Oedipal rivalry occurs in *Le Gendre de Monsieur Poirier* (33.59), in which Poirier has married his daughter off to a feckless aristocrat, whom he despises, in the desire to acquire a title. When the marriage seems to collapse, his delight edges toward the suspect, since he takes his daughter on his knee and kisses and cuddles her—she is "all his" once again. His hopes are foiled, however, by a reconciliation between daughter and son-in-law. The overt rivalry between father and son-in-law was a stock situation to draw on in boulevard comedies, though it was seldom so explicit as in the extremely popular drama *La Ronde des heures* (30.80), in which the wealthy father openly despises the aspiring young singer whom his daughter has married and tries (for money reasons) to replace him with one of his own friends. In *Louise* (39.49), the eponymous heroine's father is outraged by his daughter's relationship with the composer Charpentier—another artist, alas. At the sight of them together he has some sort of indefinable fit, takes to his bed, and begins to pine away. Emotional pressure forces her to return to the family, where, while her mother looks on suspiciously, Louise's father takes her on his lap and sings to her. He tries to prevent her from returning to her now successful composer with cries of "What about me?!" Finally, overwrought, sickly, and furious with jealousy, he collapses and curses Paris and the world at large for depriving him of what he loves most.

If the threat is to an existing family relationship, it might, on the contrary, be the young man who "steps aside," perhaps dying in the process. Such narratives appear in the remaining two-fifths of the films—those in which the existence of a relationship, often with a wide discrepancy in age, is considered viable or even desirable. The austere public servant benefits from his shaking up at the hands of a young woman and marries her (31.103); the old professor, shaken by his young wife's adultery, is touched by her tender care during his consequent illness, and they come to accept their real affection for one another (30.87); the philatelist realizes in time that he is not paying enough attention to his young wife and sends her young admirers packing (32s5); the provincial notary's young wife engages in a flirtation with a count who turns out to be a crook, so she is delighted to be saved from his clutches by her husband's legal expertise (32.95); transformed by a visit to Paris, the dry-as-dust provincial teacher is suddenly wildly attractive to the student who has made his life a misery (33.109). Like Lagardère and Pagnol's baker, many old men find that, problematic though they may be, such relationships are at least viable, and may indeed be the most fulfilling. In the extreme, when one aging lover tries to step aside in favor of his "son," the girl he loves comes to *her* senses and pursues him (37.10).

So common were these narratives in the thirties that certain middle-aged male actors risked being typecast in the role of "the older man." Alcover, Gabrio, Vanel, Pierre Renoir, Guitry, and Murat all tried their hand at it, while Francen played it at least five times, but several of the key embodiments of it went to Harry Baur and Raimu. Baur was (among others) an old lighthouse keeper whose young wife is seduced first by his assistant, then by an escaped convict (31.24), and most notably the ferocious Sarati (37.103). In *Cette vieille canaille*, he plays an aging surgeon who rescues a young circus waif who has been in a fight and takes her home. A curiously ambivalent relationship develops between them. While his jealousy of other men is always explicit, the nearest the film comes to asserting that his attraction to her has been consummated is when his young fairground rival rounds on him and says, "She was my mistress before she was yours." Ultimately she chooses the younger man, the circus, and a life on the road, but the surgeon maintains the upper hand by operating on the younger man when he falls from the flies, thus altruistically saving his life (33.26). Raimu played this sort of role even more often than Baur: he was (among others) the austere public servant (31.103), the juror who is responsible for freeing the young woman whom he then takes into his household (37.55), the village baker who lets his fire go out when his young wife deserts him (38.34), the colonist who saves then strangles an impoverished young woman (39.24), and M. Brotonneau, who triumphs over his wife and opts for a permanent relationship with his young secretary (39.56). Inevitably, there is a less clearly defined list of actors for the other roles in this narrative set, since the young woman and (where present) her younger lover could be played by any young leading man and woman. To list the most common actresses—Darfeuil, Chantal, Field, and Gaël, with occasional help from Florelle, Annabella, Romance, St. Cyr, Darrieux, and Morgan—is not very revealing. This is even truer of the actors who played the male role, a list in which Roanne, Aumont, and Gil figure twice.

These eighty or more films are closely related to numerous others, also implicitly Freudian, where the assistant/employee steals the boss's/headmaster's wife/woman, but in which there is not always so dramatic an age gap between the two males (e.g., 35.62; 36.50; 37.72). Alongside these, we find some twenty which explore the reverse situation—an intense and at least implicitly incestuous relationship between mother and son. These are spread fairly evenly across the decade, though there is a cluster of five in 1934. Several of them overlap with others already mentioned insofar as the rivalry between "father" and "son" is occasionally for an older woman (36.50). Sometimes, surviving accounts make it difficult to identify the nature of the relationship, if only because the age difference is not made clear. In most cases, however, it is clear that, with genders interchanged, the plots parallel the more common plots involving older men. Some plots leave implicit the mother/son relationship, developing fantasies about older women who prove irresistibly attractive to, or are irresistibly attracted to, younger men. These older women are most commonly allocated a status which "explains" their somewhat unconventional relationship(s). They are singers or actresses (31.124; 34.6), or at least they have the mixed blood of a Creole (30.30). They fall for young men their son's age, and perhaps abandon their husband (36.91; 37.68), only (of course) to realize the error of their ways. In *Fauteuil 47* (37.42), Françoise Rosay plays an actress worshiped by a young playwright admirer, who, but for an exchange of seats with a baron, would have become her lover. Later, there is a scene typical of such films, in which, at cross purposes, she sounds him out as a worthy match for her daughter while he believes he's to become her own lover. There is an implicit rivalry throughout between daughter and mother in which the mother is always the stronger, though the young man never realizes his desires. One who does is Gérard in *Le Rosaire* (34.91), in which an older woman nobly renounces a young lover only to have him go blind (!). She nurses him incognito, and when he discovers that his "nurse" is his former love, "he opens his arms to her."

Just as often, the mother–son relationship is figured in terms of an aunt–nephew relationship, as when a retired singer begins a relationship with her niece's boyfriend (34.6) or a nephew accepts blame for an aunt's thefts because he is madly in love with her (33s7). Alternatively it may be figured in terms of a pseudo-son, as when the antiquary's mistress is discovered with a young man and hastily invents a story in which he is a son to whom she gave birth at a piteously young age (32.63), or when an actress and her son-in-law experience an illicit attraction (37.42), or when the older mistress and her young love start a beauty parlor, using as their advertising ploy the amazing rejuvenating effects of their products on his "mother" (i.e., his mistress) (32.126). Some of these have the wonderfully contorted narratives that were found in the films with older men, as in *Compartiment de dames seules* (34.29), which Chirat summarizes as follows: "On the day of his marriage, Robert confesses to his father-in-law that twenty years previously he had improperly exploited the opportunity of finding himself alone with a lady in a train compartment. His mother-in-law overhears, and convinces her husband that it was *her* in the train, so her daughter is actually her son-in-law's daughter." He has made love to the mother and married his own daughter. Her claims, of course, are ultimately disproved. A similarly contorted narrative has Arlette's mother convincing her *filleul de guerre* (her "son" acquired via the adopt-a-soldier program) that he is Arlette's father. When Arlette grows up, he marries her for pragmatic reasons ("to save her from ruin") presumably in a *mariage blanc*, and inevitably begins to fall in love with her. Again, she turns out not to be his daughter, but again the relationship is with both mother and daughter—his own daughter. Occasionally, the relationship (actual or at least implicit) is between a son and his actual mother. Certainly, it is common to find mothers moved by a passion for their sons which is rather more than maternal. When a Breton sailor falls for an outsider to their village and leaves mother and fiancée for her, his jealous mother murders the seductress (38.44).

Few of the relationships involving an older woman are benign. Most involve intense anxiety and a jealous rivalry which culminates in violence or in the melancholy self-effacement which characterizes so many of this decade's films. Perhaps the best-known of the surviving films with this narrative form are Carné's *Jenny* (36.62) and Feyder's *Pension Mimosas* (34.76). In the former, Françoise Rosay plays the middle-aged owner-manager of a nightclub with a doubtful reputation. Her relationship with the young Lucien is disrupted when her pure young daughter, Danielle, turns up and learns with dismay of her mother's occupation but is not above attempting to convert Lucien to the path of righteousness. Confronted with the rivalry of her daughter, Jenny first tries to have Lucien disposed of, then considers suicide, but finally reconciles herself to her loss and devotes herself once again to her nightclub, "the gayest place in town." Lucien fluctuates, then, between being Jenny's lover (and therefore Danielle's "father") and Danielle's lover (and therefore Jenny's "son"). The mother/daughter rivalry ends in victory for the younger generation and the retirement of the older. In *Pension Mimosas*, Rosay again plays the obsessive mother—Louise, this time—managing not a nightclub but a guest-house. Her stepson, Pierre, becomes the object of an obsessive devotion on her part, which leads her to worry about his doubtful morals and criminal associates, but even more about the young casino worker, Nelly, with whom he is living. Torn with jealousy, alternately raging at Pierre and rocking him in her arms like a baby, Louise becomes "more than a mother" to him, as Nelly complains. The narrative has Louise trying more and more desperately to save her stepson from his own feckless behavior, ultimately ending up at his bedside cradling his dying body in her arms and kissing him passionately. The film is astonishingly explicit in its representation of an older woman's passion for a younger man who is, at least in effect, her son.

This plethora of incestuous or quasi-incestuous narratives, supplemented by a smaller number that play with incestuous brother–sister relationships (34.115; 38.107), amounting to at least 8 percent of the total output of the decade, often produces neurotic images that would have delighted Freud himself. The young lover's "blindness" mentioned above is one such, but impotence figuring as blindness or as paralysis occurs in numerous films of the decade (34.87; 36.65; 37.75; 37.100; 38.49). "Criminals" seize and abduct the wife on her wedding night (30s11), and fiendish seducers die of snakebite (35.54). The protagonist of *Lac aux dames,* after dallying with a naked Elvire Popescu, suffers a textually obscure wound to the arm which festers for the rest of the film. He also rolls in a heap of grain with Simone Simon, who buries him in it as she buried her dolls in it when she was a child (34.54)! This underlay of Freudian imagery and incident comes to the surface again in a narrative about a young couple leaving for their honeymoon on a train, but interrupted in their lovemaking by the ticket inspector. The timid young man is rendered impotent by this interruption and seeks the counsel of his father, who advises a night with a woman of easy virtue. Unfortunately, the father becomes interested in the same courtesan (36.143). The film is entitled *Vous n'avez rien à déclarer*!

The impression that Freud's ideas were becoming broadly accepted, or at least widely recognized, at this time and that filmmakers could assume some familiarity with them on the part of their audiences is proven not only by the omnipresence of related themes but by the number of films in which his name or his theories are explicitly mentioned. A brief indication of a few of these will bear out this claim. Although it doesn't mention Freud himself, a film made in 1937 seems to expect the audience to recognize key references. Jacqueline has broken fourteen engagements and finally, to spite her father, marries, somewhat at random, an elderly balding gentleman, who, as she remarks pointedly, "is the same age as you, Father." She refuses him entry to her bedroom, however, and when she meets his son by an earlier marriage rapidly becomes emotionally entangled. In the middle of a (rather drunken) embrace she and the stepson discuss how they got to this point. He likens himself to Oedipus, her to Phaedra. When the stepson finally realizes that his "parents'" marriage has been unconsummated, he abducts his "mother." They leave a message for his father signed "your two children" (37.67).

In *Noix de coco* (38.69), we learn early on that there is some sort of furtive relationship between Antoine and his stepmother which she is trying to get him to acknowledge. This is the film in which the father comes to realize that his (second) wife is the floozy with whom he had a fling in Saigon years ago. Antoine admits to loving his stepmother and indeed to having written her several love letters, and wryly acknowledges the Freudian nature of their relationship. His sister is cheating on her husband with a dentist who regularly sneaks into her bedroom, leading Antoine to remark that she, too, seems to have her Freudian tendencies. The network of relationships is even more complex than this, however, and when the mother finally can't stand it any longer and leaves home, the father throws up his hands in despair and rushes after her, exclaiming, "What a family!" The closing shots are of his catching the train on which she is leaving, which, like so many other trains, proceeds to plunge into a tunnel.

Noix de coco was the filmed version of an Achard boulevard comedy. In 1937, Guitry had also filmed one of his boulevard comedies, *Désiré* (37.34). Guitry himself plays the eponymous butler who, as it turns out, has developed an overwhelming erotic desire for the lady of each of the houses in which he has served, and they for him. This displaced mother fixation is played out yet again in the present instance, in which both he and the mistress of the house experience erotic dreams about one another. Horrified, she rushes out to buy *The Interpretation of Dreams,* only to find when she comes to read it that the butler has got in before her and cut out the erotic section. She has been reading it in bed; laying it aside to sleep, she doesn't notice that it rests on the bell that summons the butler. . . .

4.3 OTHER DYSFUNCTIONAL MIDDLE-CLASS FAMILIES

When this obsessive fascination with sexuality and incest is related to the extensive debate about sexuality conducted under the heading of vamps, criminality, doubles, half-castes and other interracial liaisons, the cinema of the thirties can easily seem like the extended nightmare of a sick society. It is useful to bear this background static in mind when considering the widespread but more "normal" aspects of dysfunctional family relationships to be found in these films. They include the absence of either father or mother from the family—especially the latter—the problematic nature of maleness within the patriarchal family, the commonness of orphan figures, and especially the presence of vulnerable young women who are seduced then abandoned to look after their illegitimate children. Admittedly, a number of these phenomena are readily recognizable as conventions of the melodrama, but it is precisely the recurrent presence and popularity of the conventions of the melodrama and the boulevard comedy that need to be explained. They interlock with more "realistic" representations of bourgeois family life as deadening or as frightening, often concealing beneath a suave surface secret shame and guilt.

Perhaps a good place to begin consideration of this topic is with families which are dysfunctional because of the absence of one or both parents, since this is both a commonplace in films of the period and a frequent "explanation" for the protagonist's problems. At least thirty-five films make a point of the fact that the protagonist is an orphan and/or a foundling. In the later years of the decade, this trope developed, particularly in Prévert's hands, into a signifier of a dysfunctional socio-economic system from which the orphan is alienated, but it had existed (and continued to coexist) as the signifier of a dysfunctional family environment. The fact that nearly all such orphaned children are girls is sufficient indication of the sentimentalism that came to surround their struggle to survive. The details of their grand narrative are too well known to need much elaboration. Their parents die when they are young, or at least are believed to have died; unable to fend for themselves, they fall prey to unscrupulous exploitation of various kinds, often of a sexual nature. Seduced and abandoned, they are forced into prostitution. Perhaps there are two foundling sisters, and one must look after the other, cost what it may (32.50; 36.48). At the height of their suffering, they are saved by the kindly intervention of a savior figure—early on, a doctor (32.50; 33.86); later on, one or, preferably, two amiable older men (34.115; 35.91; 35.105; 39.92) with quaint names—le père Mélé, le père Ballot, le père Exquis, le père la Frite. If he is young enough, the savior—if not, his son—will fall for the piteous but pure creature (31.39; 37.73). In the early years of the decade, the orphan commonly discovers late in the narrative that her mother or father is still alive after all and, reunited with her or him, she can face the future with confidence. This was in the half of the decade when cynicism about the family had not yet set in and it was still conceivable that the orphan might *want* to be reunited with the family. By 1932, however, Poil de Carotte is already regretting the fact that he is *not* an orphan, and by the last half of the decade, films about orphans are becoming more reflexive, ironizing about the orphaned state. *Le Roman d'un tricheur,* of course, has the protagonist satisfactorily orphaned precisely because (as a punishment) he is forbidden by his family from eating the mushrooms that kill the rest of them (36.115). In *Abus de confiance* (37.2), the female protagonist, who is orphaned at the beginning of the film, systematically exploits the sentiment attached to that state and the consequent search for a father. In *Battement de cœur,* orphans are proposed as ideal pupils in a school for thieves (39.2). On the side of socio-economic orphans, the nearest to this wry commentary on the orphaned state is *Le*

Jour se lève (39.48), in which the significantly named François and Françoise discuss their common fate, which by then has practically become the archetypal state for a French man or woman.

Quite apart from their insistent presence in this melodramatic tradition, however, vulnerable young women who were seduced, abandoned, and left with an illegitimate child were a particular preoccupation of the decade. A film often claimed to be the very first "French" sound film—*Les Trois Masques* (29s3)—has a Corsican girl, seduced and pregnant, avenged by her two brothers. Thereafter, at least fifty films focus on the problem of illegitimacy. About thirty of these—melodramatic in their sentimentality—deal with the problems of the mother (and occasionally others) at the time of the illegitimate child's birth. The rest deal with the consequences of the illegitimate birth twenty years later, often taking the form of a revenge narrative in which the illegitimate child, now a young man, comes into conflict with his father and seeks to punish him and/or claim his rightful heritage (e.g., 30.33; 36.21; 37.122; 39.29). An interesting variation has a number of illegitimate sons of the same English lord ganging up to test their father to see if he is worthy of them (30.64). Often, such father–illegitimate son relationships are figured in terms of criminality—either the father is a criminal, whose return generates social tensions, or the son is a criminal, whose return generates guilty recognition (by the father) of his own "criminal" behavior in begetting the son. For even more contrast, two of these latter films have the father as a judge trying a young man who, as he finally comes to realize, is his own illegitimate son (34.14; 36.27). In a sense, a sociological explanation of the son's criminality is provided by the absence of any fatherly guidance in childhood, but in poetic terms "criminality" stands as a metaphor for the son's illegitimate extra-social status and the father's "criminal" behavior. In the surviving example, Bernard's *Le Coupable,* the father comes to recognize and proclaim publicly to the jury that it is not his son who is the criminal, but himself; he had taken a wrong turn in life, accepting paternal pressure to enter law when his real interest had always been in music. He has wasted thirty-three years, but the encounter with his son has brought him to his senses.

Two crucial patterns are apparent here—one a set of opposed metaphors, the other a set of opposed representations of masculinity. Both are jointly present throughout the decade, but particularly in the years 1935–39. Cumulatively, they introduce a debate about masculinity which may be peculiar to the French cinema of the day. If the representations of femaleness in that cinema are often forceful, they are nevertheless relatively conventional and add little to Western civilization's repertoire of mostly pejorative judgments regarding women and their sexuality. It is, however, fascinating to find masculinity being regarded as equally problematic and the patriarchy itself being reflected upon critically.

The two primary representations of masculinity in *Le Coupable* might be characterized schematically as the gentle and the authoritarian. Music and the law stand in for these opposing values. The father, Jérôme, had expected to make a career in the former but is pushed by his own father into the latter. He falls for Thérèse, who is (perhaps inevitably) an assistant in a flower shop. His own father, he says, hates flowers, birds, and love, as he had despised the proposed musical career of his son. Their affair leaves Thérèse pregnant, and he is prevented from putting things right by the war and conscription. She marries her cousin, the jingoistic Édouard, who trains her and Jérôme's son in military ways, and Thérèse's death removes the "maternal" values that might have saved him. Graduating from institutional care to criminality, the son comes before Jérôme, now a judge, who recognizes his own guilt and pleads for the man whom he now realizes is his own son. The consequent reconciliation is a common narrative ending for such films, re-creating the harmonious family environment which had been disrupted by the initial illegitimacy. The father gives up the law, and the son devotes himself to agriculture, since all he has ever really loved is flowers, fields, and animals. "For generations," says Jérôme, "we Lécuyers have been magistrates from father to son. Now we will try to be men." True masculinity lies not in aggressive activities or in successful public careers, but in feeling, sensitivity, caring—in the values of the heart, which spontaneously come to the fore on contact with nature and are often expressed through artistic activity.

Of course, the nature imagery apparent in this film was to echo through the poetic realist films of the following years, and its associated artistic values were no less positively represented throughout the decade, as chapter 6 will show. But the focus on "what it means to be a man" is a topic that needs further exploration here, since it determines the narrative form of many family dramas of the thirties. Fatherhood and the patriarchy are the problematic source of many of the disruptions in films exploring the family late in this decade (and, indeed, throughout the following one). In most cases, the disruption is caused by the traditional masculine drive toward domination, which is represented as breeding a toughness, if not a brutality, that renders the male insensitive to the needs of others. An early instance is embodied in Duvivier's 1932 remake of his silent film *Poil de Carotte* (32.109), but in that case the insensitivity of the boy's father is caused primarily by a retreat from his wife's shrewish ways. That the resultant withdrawal and insensitivity to his son's needs should bring the boy close to suicide is, however, typical of such narratives. Essentially, it is an account of the breakdown in the relationship between father and son, of the last-minute recognition by the father of the "tragic" outcome of such a breakdown, and of his consequent return to the ways of the heart (as opposed, say, to the ways of the law, of property, or of moral rectitude). In general, unlike German films of the time, French films of the thirties were not at all preoccupied with the young (i.e., those younger than eighteen, by which time they might be played by a *jeune premier* in a standard dramatic or romantic role). The one partial exception is this example of intergenerational misunderstanding focusing on the breakdown of family relationships. Several siblings of Poil de Carotte's felt themselves neglected and abandoned by their father in the course of the decade (e.g., 33.119; 38.18). Many others suffered from tyrannical and authoritarian fathers—at least two more of them judges (32.64; 39.74) and one a bishop (30.75). One does not dare to tell his father that he has married (32.64), another that he has a son (39.74). Often such men are driven, as was Poil de Carotte, by the father's unfeeling attitude to attempt suicide, with the usual effect of softening and humanizing the father in extremis and thus effecting a reconciliation. Of the many such narratives, only the first (30.75) has a tragic outcome, the reconciliation coming too late to save the son's unsuitable love (she is a foundling and thus, of course, not a worthy match for him), who collapses and dies as she emerges from church on their wedding day. More typical is *Le Tunnel* (33.134), in which the engineer learns that his own estranged son is working on the transatlantic tunnel which he is constructing. When it is in danger of collapsing, he risks his life to save his son and fellow workers, and there are the usual touching scenes of reconciliation.

Parallel to such tales of brutal, violent, or simply inhumanly rigorous fathers who must learn to be "true" fathers, the thirties produced a number of stories of brutal and violent husbands. As in *Toni* (35.110), a standard pattern is for the wife to be driven to desperate lengths to escape the daily persecution of these beasts, often leading to murder (34.36; 37.4). If the husband is not killed by his wife, he is killed by her mother (38.96), or by men moved by her situation (37.43), or else he meets an appropriately violent end, which releases the unfortunate woman. One dies of congestion in a moment of jealous passion, shooting what turns out to be only the hero's reflection in a mirror (35.123); another dies in a trident duel (!) (37.47). Raimu's Sarati le terrible, who dies by his own violent hand, is a classic instance, combining the jealous rage of a pseudo-husband with the ruthlessness of an authoritarian pseudo-father. Finally, in Pagnol's well-known film *Angèle* (34.5), Angèle's father, overcome with shame at his daughter's giving birth to an illegitimate child, retreats into an inhuman and destructive attitude, which extends to sequestering his daughter and her baby in the dark cellar of the family house. This inhuman attitude, atypical in a meridional, is inspired by traditional proprieties which are here represented as destructive. It is ultimately qualified by the more compassionate attitude of the younger generation of males, notably in the form of Albin.

A classic instance of such an "unfeeling father" is that portrayed by Michel Simon in *La Chaleur du sein* (38.18). It is the more striking in that

his remoteness from his son Gilbert is contrasted with the close affection between Gilbert and his three successive step-mothers, all of whom prefer him
to his Egyptologist father. His problem is generalized when a friend visits
him in hospital, where he is recuperating from an attempted suicide. Gilbert tells him that he misses his real mother, and the friend tells him that his
own real parents had always squabbled. It had been a passionate and violent
household, and his father had finally killed his mother then committed suicide. "There must be lots of us in this sort of situation," he says. "How difficult family life has become." That Gilbert's problems and those of all these
other families are primarily due to the fathers becomes apparent when the
Egyptologist returns home, is accused of parental inadequacies, and finally
admits that he ought to have been more interested in the present and the future than in the past. There follow the expected scenes of father–son reconciliation. The next time the father goes on a trip he will take Gilbert with
him, and the film ends on Gilbert's exclamation "Papa, I've wanted to get to
know you all my life." Cumulatively, these narratives about callous and unfeeling males whose lack of human warmth and compassion proves destructive to the family constitute an ongoing inquiry into the validity of
traditional male values. They are, to some extent, balanced by films which
advocate the firm masculine hand as a necessary and proper corrective to the
moral laxness of contemporary life, but these latter are fewer in number and
were not nearly as popular as those which evoke masculine authoritarianism
only to call it into question. Russians and Asians provided stock instances of
brutal and ruthless husbands, though they tend to figure problematic male
sexuality rather than problematic fatherhood.

Given the marked anxiety which these films manifest concerning relations between husband and wife, father and son, and father and daughter,
it would seem logical to expect that the means by which marriage relationships are established would also be the subject of considerable attention. It
is true that a very large number of films focus on the topic, but they are
primarily romantic comedies which do not explore the topic as a problem
requiring solution. Nevertheless, the narrative patterns which regularly
structure these reflections on marriage clearly embody common understandings of the nature of that institution and, in their turn, no doubt affected the expectations of audiences commonly exposed to them. Two of
these narrative patterns are quite striking, and both were not only common
but popular. They might be termed the "arranged marriage" and the "predestined marriage."

The arranged marriage involves a son or daughter who is pressured by
his or her mother and/or father into a loveless marriage out of worldly considerations, most commonly rank and money. The son, often of fallen aristocracy, is to marry a rich heiress/duchess to restore the family fortunes,
or the daughter is to marry a duke/baron/financier/banker. The standard

opposition that arises is between these worldly calculations and the spontaneous impulses of the heart. Naturally, the latter are more positively represented and ultimately prevail. The arranged marriage usually founders, and
true love wins out. Very often, this results in a match which is "socially im-
proper" as it involves an alliance with a social inferior—an actress rather
than the intended heiress (31.104; 34.83), a secretary rather than the aristocrat for whom she was intended (36.26), the foreman's daughter rather
than the rival industrialist's daughter who would have united their business
empires (36.39; 36.74). Normally, a marginal family member—grandmother, aunt, or uncle—proves more understanding, and intervenes to ensure that true love prevails.

Among the better known of these narratives condemning arranged
marriages are *Le Malade imaginaire* (34s2) and *Mayerling* (36.77). They
frequently provide an opportunity to mobilize archetypal figures already
discussed—the banker/financier, the brutal husband (e.g., 37.4), the fascinating Oriental (e.g., 37.30). Only four out of thirty-five such stories identified have a less than happy ending. In those, love itself proves deceptive,
and the girl resigns herself to the loveless arranged marriage (35.47), or misunderstandings lead to the lover marrying someone else (36.97; 36.140).
Yamilé sous les cèdres is particularly interesting in introducing a religious
conflict into this narrative: the Maronite Christian girl rejects the young
man whom her family has destined for her in favor of a Muslim youth,
with whom she elopes. Caught, she refuses to repent and accepts death at
her family's hands (39.93).

Even the few melancholic or tragic narratives in this group nevertheless
mostly defend the values of the heart as superior to calculation, wealth,
family, or religion. As a whole, the group overlaps with those constituting
the second narrative class, films which imply obliquely that forced or accidental associations resulting in marriage may exemplify the working out of
a mysterious destiny which understands the human heart better even than
those directly involved. In this narrative category, two young people are
brought together involuntarily—occasionally by an arranged marriage, but
more frequently by some "accident." The situation is given piquancy by
their refusal to accept their fate: instant antagonisms delay their recognition
that they are meant for one another; filial disobedience leads them to reject
the intended spouse, only to find that it is the very person they had independently come to love; tricked into seduction or marriage, they are outraged at such devious behavior, and only reluctantly come to acknowledge
that true love has displaced calculation. The arranged marriage with a convent girl is extremely inconvenient when the lieutenant falls for a saucy actress, but of course she turns out to be one and the same person (31.77).
The arranged marriage between M Poirier's daughter and the aristocrat is a
bore for that aristocrat, until he begins to realize that she is worthy of his

love (33.59). A benevolent providence has overseen these improbable unions, after all.

Such piquant narratives are often the pretext for introducing mildly salacious situations: wrongly believed to be a couple, the young man and woman are urged, resisting, into the same bedroom (32.19); in a last fling before an arranged marriage, he finds he has ended up locked in a bedroom with his friend's fiancée (31.88); visiting a former servant, the impoverished aristocratic woman is offered the bed of the absent count, who, of course, returns unexpectedly (32.90); for commercial reasons, a man offers his wife to her former husband, only to find that they have taken the proposal further than he intended (33.44). The *mariage blanc* was a particular favorite situation in such narratives, as at least ten films exploited it: childhood friends marry largely to outrage their parents; going their separate ways, they are accidentally reunited in the bedroom of a remote alpine hotel (35.40); or a reporter "marries" the accused girl to save her, only to find he is really coming to love her (36.46); or misunderstandings lead two people who each love someone else into a *mariage blanc*, but the honeymoon night undermines their chaste intentions (33.38). Arlette accepts a *mariage blanc* to the man she believes is her father to save them from financial ruin (34.8). In one of the more dramatic of these narratives, the well-known *Maître de forges,* the amorous industrialist finds he has been trapped unawares in a *mariage blanc*, because his wife is still in love with a despicable aristocrat. Gradually, she comes to see the worth of her husband, and the fake marriage becomes a genuine marriage (33.80).

The fatality which oversees these accidental or involuntary marriages can take many forms. Particular favorites were the car breaking down (36.106) or an encounter in a train, though a bet (35.7) or a joint lottery win (35.13) could suffice. Equally, the gloom of a movie theater could trick a man into embracing one woman, believing her to be another (35.82). It is interesting, however, that so many of these "fated" relationships should begin as commercial and exploitative relationships, only to develop a depth of unexpected sincerity. Of the many that turn out thus, *Baccara* (35.5) is typical: the returned war hero, short of cash, agrees to marry (for a price) to save the woman from becoming involved in the crash of a fraudulent banker who has been keeping her, only to develop a genuine desire to win her love. Such transformations of the commercial into the sincere are particularly common in the immediate prewar years, when individuals paid to marry or to pretend to be married rapidly develop sincere feelings for their wife or husband (e.g., 37.1; 37.23; 37.118).

In *Cavalcade d'amour* (39.11), Jean Anouilh scripted for Raymond Bernard a veritable compendium of such narratives. The film is in three episodes, set in three different ages, and involving three different generations of the same family. The first two episodes exploit the "arranged marriage" plot, in which an aristocrat's son or daughter, who is due to marry lovelessly for pragmatic purposes, falls for someone below himself or herself in station—a travelling player, their intended's seamstress—with tragic consequences for the latter. The third episode exploits something closer to the "predestined marriage" plot. Two young people, intended for one another by their parents, discuss the earlier incidents and wish they had been free to choose one another rather than being matched by their parents for grossly pragmatic purposes—namely, to ally finance with aristocratic birth. Their alliance can be joyfully consummated only when her father loses his money in a crash—though in an epilogue he recoups it with interest and wonders how to break the bad news to the children. Like many late-thirties plots, this one shows a reflexive awareness of the patterns that had been set up in the course of the decade and a conscious foregrounding of them, often with variations and often to ironic effect.

One of the most important of these patterns was the set of characteristic gender relationships established by the boulevard comedy, which saw marriage not just as dysfunctional but as a mere game to be played out between cynical exploiters of both sexes. Casual sexual dalliance is central to the plot of such comedies. The faithful wife is a figure of fun, who serves as a challenge to young rakes and suave men-about-town. The husband caught in adultery, others caught or nearly caught as they hide behind curtains or bushes, and doors opening and shutting hastily to allow nervous lovers or enraged husbands to escape or to burst in, just in time or just too late—these were the stock in trade of the genre; they figure prominently in many thirties films, and notably in *La Règle du jeu*. Christine, like her acknowledged model Marianne, but also like the countess in *Sept hommes . . . une femme* (36.121), has been a faithful wife, resisting all attempts at seduction until she learns of her husband's indiscretions, whereupon she abandons herself to the rules of a new generic game—a typically French game, as Octave notes, which as a foreigner she had at first found alien. Her husband has been playing it for years with Geneviève, and even his sudden determination to renounce her and be worthy of his wife is a typically flippant treatment of gender relations. In *Sept hommes*, the countess, on learning of her late husband's adultery, had shattered his bust (!) and set out to entertain her seven suitors. On learning of her husband's adultery, Christine dallies with only three such suitors. The effect in both films, however, is to put a fascinating woman at the center of a network of desire, with each male maneuvering for her favors. The same set of relationships surrounds Lisette downstairs, with Octave linking the two sets, devoted to Christine (who bears a tenuous relationship to many incestuous heroines in being Octave's "sister") but skittishly affectionate toward Lisette.

The riotous chases, dissemblings, and discoveries that result from these capricious relationships, together with the commentaries upon them by those involved, constitute a comprehensive meditation on the generic patterns relating to family, marriage, and sexuality provided by the boulevard comedy. The conditions or possibility of love and of friendship between the sexes, the desirability or possibility of fidelity and of adultery, of trust and of betrayal, of passion, of rules, and of happiness, are all explored in ways reminiscent of the conventions underlying the film's generic predecessors, and yet sufficiently reflexive and self-aware as to constitute a commentary upon them. If there is one thing, however, which an audience acquainted with these conventions might not have expected, it is the abrupt death of the aviator at the end. However well prepared in earlier scenes, it had few precursors in the decade, and none of the films which incorporated such an ending were successful with audiences.

FIVE

Education, the Media, and the Law: The Training of a Citizen

5.1 CRIMINALS AND INVESTIGATORS

This discussion of the family has led to a consideration of the ways in which the young were socialized, often problematically and with disastrous effect, into contemporary French society. The present chapter is the first of two to be devoted to a discussion of the ways in which a number of more or less formal institutions for the socialization of the citizen—ideological apparatuses, and in some cases ideological *state* apparatuses—were represented in the French cinema of the thirties. These institutions—education, the church, and the law, together with the no less powerful, if less formalized, institutions of the media, entertainment, and art—have in common the function of ideological regulation. Among their main, if sometimes unofficial, tasks, they are expected to train citizens in the social and moral values considered normal and desirable within a society, to monitor their performance within this ideological framework, to judge and punish those found wanting, and on occasion to rehabilitate or "save" them.

Of all these ideological apparatuses, the law is the most frequently represented in the French cinema of the thirties, as is apparent from the widespread recognition accorded the murder mystery throughout that decade. The status of the criminal investigation as the contemporary form of a fundamental narrative type has been widely debated in recent decades. But in addition to this, some of the reasons for the contemporary popularity of this thematic have been noted earlier: criminality acted as a metaphor both for the corruption represented as endemic among the rich and the powerful, and for the disenfranchised and marginal status of the worker. In both cases, it thus stood for the injustices at the heart of the social system. It also acted as a metaphor for female sexuality, represented as being beyond the pale. It is not surprising, then, to find that at least 317 films (i.e., about 24 percent) deal explicitly with illegal activities and the attempts of the legal system, or of people acting on behalf of it, to bring "criminals" of one sort or another to justice.

Nor is it surprising that in a large majority of those films in which "the law" has connotations that are primarily sociological, it is not viewed favorably. The point of view adopted by the narration is often that of the outsider, the rough diamond, the folk hero, the tough with a heart of gold, and there is sympathy for the criminal; or else the law is seen as corrupt and in collusion with the rich and powerful. The law, that is, is at best an ass and at worst the embodiment of some malevolent and implacable fatality. Early in the decade, it may be seen as amiably corrupt and in the pay of the crooks, as in *L'Opéra de quat'sous* (30.61); later, it is seen as merely incompetent. In the extreme, master criminals hold their own "anti-trials," mirror images of official trials, but more likely to bring about truth and ensure justice. In *Jim la Houlette*, we are introduced to two interconnected narratives, both comic, the one involving the establishment conning, preying upon, trying, and ultimately condemning to death a humble and talented young man (played by Fernandel), the other involving an anti-establishment run by a gentleman thief which rights these wrongs and prosecutes the persecutors in an anti-trial which is the embodiment of "true" justice (35.62).

It would be inaccurate, however, to see the decade's films as proposing any single monolithic representation of the law and its activities. To some extent, this is because there are so many different categories of "lawmen," ranging from law students through aspiring young lawyers (three of whom are female) and solicitors to attorneys-general, judges, and chief justices. Generally, the younger and the less implicated in "the system" they are the more sympathetic and affectionate the representation. Once they become powerful authority figures, they are frequently subject to the same distrust accorded politicians, bankers, and entrepreneurs. Essentially, at that point in their careers, their only hope is to be (re)humanized by one of the recognized "marginal" agencies—attractive women, criminals, or the poor (or, preferably, a combination of all three). As a second generalization, the law in its younger and more romantic form is more common at the beginning of the decade, while the more austere and implacable magistrates appear in the latter half of the decade.

Thus, earlier in the decade, Garat could play the law student as romantic lead, railing at the boredom of cramming for exams, which he duly fails (31.68); Murat could play an unemployed young lawyer who gets caught up in a romantic adventure (30.91); and the lawyer played by Richard-Willm could be the love interest and savior of a successful singer (30.88). These were three of the principal young lead actors of the decade. Young lawyers of the type they embodied in these films frequently figured in boulevard comedies, where as professionals they provided an acceptable alternative to counts and dukes (e.g., 31.102). Gravey and Garat could reprise their young-lawyer roles in 1936 and 1938, but by this time they were dated (36.82; 38.35): the law was much more commonly embodied in a problematic older, paternalistic figure who has been dehumanized by his practice of the law.

The first such austere and tyrannical figure I have been able to identify appears (briefly) in *Cœur de Lilas* (31.34), in which a particularly nasty judge presides over the eponymous protagonist's trial, but another one appears the following year in a comic film (32.64), and aging comic lawyers are not uncommon in the years 1932–35 (see 34.47; 35.44). However, the tone becomes steadily more somber as the years pass. In the latter half of the decade, they are at best unwelcome figures, bearers of bad news, and at worst sinister, greedy, vulture-like creatures in the service of wealthy exploiters of the poor, particularly farmers (36.127). Lawyers' fees, for instance (admittedly in a comedy), ultimately reduce an inheritance of two hundred thousand francs to thirty thousand francs (34.30). It's not surprising that lawyers should be yet another category of humanity to prove irresistible to assassins (32.45; 32.75). Pride, arrogance, and unyielding self-righteousness are their prime characteristics (35.19; 39.74), and the narratives take delight in undermining this sanctimoniousness in ways already mentioned. Judges who have ranted against the lax morals of the age are forced to recognize their complicity with the accused (34.14; 36.27), while lawyers and magistrates imprisoned or forced by circumstances to meet those whom they regularly imprison are overwhelmed by their humanity and converted on the spot to the values of the heart (34.34; 39.17; 39.74).

Because it is represented so unsympathetically, the law is regularly contrasted with some preferable and more humane set of values. A characteristic example is *Il est charmant* (31.68), in which the delights of the Folies-Bergère prove infinitely more attractive for young law students. Youth, love, and life itself are intrinsically opposed to the law, as the young solicitor demonstrates by transforming the provincial legal office bought for him by his uncle into a cross between a nightclub and a brothel. As we shall see, to be a law student was to be irrevocably schizophrenic, since the connotations associated with the law were incompatible with those associated with being a French student. In the later years of the decade, when the debilitation caused by the law had reached tragic dimensions and Jouvet could play a disreputable lawyer with thugs to do his bidding, living off blackmail and racketeering (37.117), the law came to be contrasted with more weighty humanist values—the fine arts, classical music, and nature at its most refined and ennobling (36.27). By this time, the earlier representation of the law looks almost idyllic, and when Jouvet's crooked lawyer is momentarily softened by nostalgia for his less corrupt past, it will probably prove the end of him. This cynical attitude toward the law can be summed up by two films at the end of the decade, one a drama and one a comedy.

In the comedy (39.17), a magistrate falls in with some amiable, if slightly criminal, representatives of the people, and begins to rethink his view of them:

"Ah, 'the people'—we don't really understand them."
"That didn't stop you from passing judgment on them. In your time, you've passed judgment on a good number of them without understanding them."
"Indeed. If we understood people better, we'd create a more humane justice system."
"The word 'humane' coming out of your mouth! You must be really drunk."

In the drama, after a criminal investigation in an apartment building in which everyone in any position of power or authority, including the chief justice of the Court of Appeal, has been shown to be hiding some guilty secret, an epilogue has one of the tenants hold forth on his lack of respect for the law, then hand the loot over to the young "bank thief" who had initially confessed to stealing it in order to help a poor girl and her father (39.25).

As an aside, it is interesting to note three films involving female lawyers, appearing at the transition between lighthearted sentimental lawyers and somber-to-the-point-of-corrupt lawyers. In general, these three echo the transformation. The first seems to have been wholeheartedly feminist, since her husband is initially extremely upset by her career and turns to more "feminine" women, until he is taught his lesson and begs his wife to return to the bar, even becoming her secretary (34.57). The second is less favorable: Danielle Darrieux plays a female lawyer who refuses her family's arranged marriage only to find that the scoundrel she has saved and fallen in love with is none other than that same man, "planted" by her all-seeing family (36.136). She comes across as an amiable but gullible innocent whose humiliation is well deserved, though rather because she's a bumptious woman than because she's a lawyer. The last of the three is the most famous: Danielle Darrieux again plays a young and, this time, impoverished law student who, in desperate straits, foists herself on a family as the father's long-lost daughter. At once relieved by her newfound comfort and ashamed by the confidence trick she is playing on her "father," she uses her first appearance at the bar to plead the cause of underprivileged children who go wrong—her own cause, in effect. Moved by the plea, her "mother," who has long suspected the truth and has recently acquired proof of the law student's deceit, is reconciled to the role her "daughter" has come to play in their newly restored family (37.2).

This progressively more somber view of the workings of the justice system leads, not unnaturally, to a marked preoccupation with narratives involving miscarriages of justice. Thirty-eight of the films involving trial scenes focus on innocent people wrongly prosecuted, convicted, and imprisoned. A large number of these belong to the melodramatic traditions either of persecuted innocence or of the tension between love and duty. Should the lawyer break his professional code of secrecy and have the woman he loves sent to jail for murder, or allow her son to be wrongfully imprisoned (30.28)? Should the sister save her fiancé by telling the terrible truth about her brother (31.36)? Should the poor workman turn over the real killer or take the blame himself, in which case the killer has agreed to fund his son's education (34.78)? Numerous noble but misguided innocents allow themselves to be wrongfully accused and jailed to save a member of the family who is the real killer, or whom they believe to be the real killer (e.g., 30.66; 31.113; 32.27; 35.35). Most such plots allow for high-minded posturing in the melodramatic tradition, which takes particular pleasure in the wrongful persecution and imprisonment of the innocent (34.92), and the bulk of these films appear in the first half of the decade. In the years 1935-39, the two people allowing themselves to be jailed wrongly are, respectively, a reporter trying to get inside information (36.1) and a failure trying to get publicity (36.85), and their subsequent inability to prove their innocence is ironic rather than melodramatic.

Narratives of wrongful imprisonment often derive from the false testimony of a malicious enemy or a treacherous friend (notably that old favorite, the treacherous female). All but three of these narratives end well for the person wrongfully imprisoned (30.66; 33.112; 37.22), though rarely as a result of the effective functioning of the justice system, and the three that end grimly include two of the most powerful films of the decade—Grémillon's *La Petite Lise* and Mathot's *Chéri-Bibi*. When things end well, rather than the official legal system, it is various members of the family, notably the accused's son (34.78), daughter (32.45; 33.149; 35.35), or wife (35.122), who solve the mystery and identify the real criminal. Frequently, the accused or imprisoned man has to escape from prison in order to try to clear his own name. This narrative trope is well known from *The Count of Monte Cristo*, of which three film versions were to be made between 1942 and 1961, but the saga of Roger la Honte, on which another three films were to be based between 1945 and 1963, provides another instance (32.122). Often there is considerable emphasis on the innocent victim's period in jail, which lasts for only one year in Roger's case, but elsewhere lasts for five (38.113), seven (37.40), ten (31.23; 36.103), or even twenty years (34.80; 35.35; 37.22), and is often described in poignant detail. The penal colony in French Guyana is mythologized in two of these films as the obverse of civilization (30.66; 37.22). The narrative of *Chéri Bibi* is constructed along the lines of *Heart of Darkness*, with the prisoners' progressive exile first from Paris, then from France and Europe, to end up finally in the tangled fastnesses of the South American jungle.

Insofar as prison served as one of the principal metaphors for the oppression of the "little people," prisoners stood for the mass of ordinary people whose lives were iniquitously circumscribed by financial hardship. They were doomed by society, long before being condemned by it. Both *Tumultes* (31.134) and *À nous la liberté* (31.1) are explicit about the close relationship between jail and factory life under capitalism. Prison life is quite commonly represented as offering opportunities for mateship, altruistic gestures, communal support, and noble self-sacrifice found elsewhere in the society only among the working classes. Early sound films, notably the extremely popular *Big House* (30.12), favored the recognition of the condemned man's nobility by the authorities, who consequently commute the prisoner's sentence and release him. If, on the other hand, the prisoners are forced to escape in order to find the guilty man themselves, their vengeance often becomes more global, aimed not just at individuals but at the system as a whole or, Robin Hood–like, at the establishment. Indeed, Robin Hood figures are a popular fantasy throughout the decade, whether in the form of Fra Diavolo (30.41), Lopez the bandit (30.49), or Gaspard de Besse (a great admirer of Mandrin) (35.51). Judex was, however, the most renowned righter of wrongs and protector of those persecuted by authority, and Feuillade's 1917 film was remade by Champreux as *Judex 34* (33.73). Slightly more sophisticated, if less altruistic, the gentleman thief, who is fastidiously polite, very English, and never steals from pretty women, was also admired in the literature and the films of the decade. Jim la Houlette (35.62) and Monsieur Personne (36.84) inherit this role from the enigmatic Mr. Parkes (30.34) and less certainly from the Joker (30.46). Henri Garat was considered well suited to this role (38.2); as early as 1930, his character, though in reality merely a (boring, of course) man of letters, "acted out" the role of gentleman thief in order to win the woman he loved (30.39), just as Bretonneau's secretary, the true author of Bretonneau's novels, has to disguise himself as the suave international brigand Jim la Houlette in order to make himself attractive to Madame Bretonneau. Clearly, the tradition of the romantic criminal, generous and fascinating to women, was well established by the beginning of the decade and constituted yet another implicit critique of the law. A romantic aura clung to brilliant crooks such as Vidocq (38.116), and stories about them always emphasized the facility with which they triumphed over the bumbling lawmen.

A more "proper" view of the law and its tireless struggle against the forces of disorder can be found in those films adhering more closely to the conventions of the crime story. There are two extremes of this genre in the thirties—those in which master detectives battle master criminals whose infinite evil threatens the very foundations of society, here considered worth saving, and those in which the justice system, or its representatives, engages in combat with whole bands, groups, and gangs of thieves, thugs,

and miscreants. Between these two extremes, stolid, implacable police in-
spectors track down anonymous murderers. Perhaps the best known of
these is Simenon's Inspector Maigret, who led three murder investigations
in films of the thirties. Admittedly, the following decade was to see many
more of Simenon's novels made into films, but the three Maigret films
made during the war were all to feature Albert Préjean as a distinctly light-
weight and even frivolous Maigret. In the thirties, all three films to focus
on Maigret were produced in 1932, when Pierre Renoir (32.97), Abel Tarride (32.33), and Harry Baur (32.132) give Maigret a bulkier and more
somber presence. There is, however, no sensationalism in these plots of the
sort that would arise from the pitting of such a figure against a master
criminal. On the contrary, the sordid environment in which they conduct
their investigations, further depressed by nighttime settings and incessant
drizzle, implies that criminality is no more than the inevitable emanation
of a generalized social malaise.

Among master criminals, the sneering, arrogant Fantômas and his
nemesis, the brilliant police inspector Juve, were firm favorites. Much like
Holmes and Moriarty, the two were engaged in a lifelong duel in which the
law always triumphed, though, true to his name, Fantômas himself always
managed to elude Juve's clutches at the last moment (32.60). Numerous
other arch-villains inhabit the films of the first half of the decade (30.59;
30.62; 32.135), notably in the French version of Lang's *Le Testament du
docteur Mabuse* (33.123). This film acts as a reminder of the connection between sinister super-criminals who are masters of disguise and the para-
noiac anxieties of German expressionism. Certainly, films of this sub-genre
made in France borrowed heavily from the technical effects associated with
expressionism. Both settings and lighting are characteristic, with ruined cas-
tles, trapdoors, secret passages, and most of the action taking place at night.

Less-spectacular criminals engage in more routine forms of criminality—cheating at gambling (33.46; 36.1; 38.51), forgery (38.25; 39.59) and
no fewer than five insurance crimes. A quite different category is the crime
of passion, present throughout the decade, not least in Renoir's films—*La
Chienne* (31.31), *Toni* (35.110), and *La Bête humaine* (38.12)—and about
a dozen others, including, of course, the Carné-Gabin films, in which outbursts of passionate rage typically result in the killing of the woman's seedy
associates (38.84; 39.48). Normally, these films are constructed around triangular relationships in which the husband/lover kills a (sometimes wrongly) suspected rival; alternatively, in a fit of jealous rage he may kill the
woman he believes has betrayed him. A variant has the husband merely suspected of killing the rival, when in reality it is the wife who did so (33.149);
alternatively, the girl's father may murder his daughter's seducer/lover
(30.14; 32.69). It is rare for crimes of passion to be represented as occurring within respectable middle-class families. Animal passions are more

commonly conceived of as overwhelming the frailer national and social types inhabiting the Mediterranean regions—Spain and Italy, in particular—or the squalid underside of society, the poor and criminal classes. Passion may also overwhelm artists (33.149; 38.100), Gypsies (32.69), or circus folk (30.1), but not the middle classes—or, rather, tales of such jealous passion are distanced by being embodied in their more animal others, "out there."

Related to crimes of passion by their intensely personal nature and the frequent focus on sexual infidelity are crimes involving blackmail. Inevitably, a constant feature of such crimes is the presence in the blackmailed person's past of indiscretions, sexual liaisons, or, less commonly, violence and criminality. In the part of the narrative recounted in the present tense, the blackmailed person has to have achieved a significant social standing for the threatened revelation about this past (or this secret double life) to register as dangerous. He may be a politician (30.33; 36.9), a businessman (37.40; 38.16), a baron (30.18), or a count (34.115); she may be the wife of a colonel (33.98), a police chief (39.86), or another dignitary. Indeed, all wives are fair game for blackmailers, and there is a particular emphasis in the more dramatic films of this sort on the rather suspect pleasure that men experience through the power they gain by blackmailing women.

Blackmail obviously involves secret knowledge of a sort available to certain categories of people—former lovers, private detectives (38.60), lawyers (37.117), or press magnates who threaten to publish "or else" (32.134; 36.129; 38.14). They can be divided roughly into people who are already in positions of power and whose corrupt nature is shown by their willingness to use that power ruthlessly, and—perhaps more interesting—"little people" whose frustrations at life's injustices find expression in acts of blackmail in order to exercise a power that has always hitherto eluded them. In different registers, a mechanic may blackmail a count whose supposed exploits he himself has, in fact, performed (34.115), or the impoverished illegitimate son of a politician's early liaison may blackmail his father (30.33). In the comic mode, tales of blackmail often result in a turning of the tables, which sees the blackmailed blackmailing the blackmailer (32.134; 36.129), or two amiable blackmailers falling in love (36.96), while in the dramatic mode they often result in murder (37.40), suicide, or attempted suicide (33.98; 36.102; 37.60; 38.16; 38.46). In only two of the many films of this sort does blackmail ultimately lead to a confession which clears the air and reunites the couple.

One of the most interesting blackmail films is *Carrefour* (38.14), described earlier. In it, a slimy Jules Berry blackmails an honorable industrialist who has suffered amnesia during the war and just might once have been a criminal, who has since unwittingly assumed the identity of the (dead) industrialist. On his return from war, the industrialist's wife has accepted him

as her husband, "regardless of what he was before," but the evidence of former associates gradually raises doubts in his own mind. Having testified at
the trial that the amnesiac is indeed the industrialist in order to maintain
him in a state of dependency, the blackmailer presents him privately with
fairly conclusive evidence that he is not. The industrialist's son learns "the
truth" and attempts suicide; the industrialist himself tries to trap and murder the blackmailer during a pay-off; finally, he is saved by a nightclub girl
who may have known him in his possible criminal past, who shoots the
blackmailer and sacrifices herself for the man she (still?) loves. The real interest of the film lies in the protagonist's progressively more agitated investigation into his own past, and the consequent fluctuating superimposition
of the double identities—squalid criminal/honorable industrialist—which
is never entirely resolved either to the viewer's satisfaction or to the supposed industrialist's. The film also constructs a curiously ambivalent view
of "the family" as perilously based on truths better suppressed. The sacrifice
of a nightclub girl to save a wife and family is as interesting as the necessary
suppression of the criminal to save the industrialist. Blackmail had threatened to expose the foundations of the disreputable edifice of middle-class
respectability and of capitalist industrialism.

Nearly all the films mentioned so far involve "urban" crimes, represented as being generated by sociological or psychological causes (and, in
La Bête humaine, by genetic causes). A more exotic category of crime was
committed by bandits and brigands at sea, on the highway, or in gothic circumstances. Over twenty films deal with such bands of brigands, and one
of their favorite crimes was kidnapping. Early in the decade, bandits kid-
nap primarily women—an actress (30s10), a newly married wife (30s11),
the chieftain's daughter (30.71), a pretty woman held for ransom (who in
one case falls for her abductor) (34.108; 38.10). But later the kidnappings
are more often of men, and mainly for financial gain (34.18; 36.124;
37.94). More general acts of piracy clearly belong to the exotic genre of the
adventure story, as witness the locations—Canada, Morocco and Arabia,
Russia, the South Pacific, and China. If they occur in France, it could only
be in Brittany (37.60) or in the sufficiently distant past (34.21; 37.3).

These more exotic and adventurous acts of criminality mostly involve
gun running or drug smuggling, though three involve white slavery. South
American cabarets and brothels could not get enough French women down
on their luck (33.48; 36.23; 37.49). A constant trickle of smuggling films
produces a total of fourteen in the course of the decade, but nearly all of the
twelve gun-running films occur in the last years of the decade, as anxieties
about war and national territorial integrity become more acute. Frontiers
figure prominently in drug-smuggling films, primarily the Franco-Belgian
frontier, with customs officers, Inspector Maigret, or a pair of policewomen
finally getting the better of the villains. Cocaine is the principal threat, and

the Chinese are invariably behind attempts to bring it in, particularly in cases where it comes through ports. Drug smugglers are an evil lot, and they target women in particular: in *Escale* (35.43), they cynically undermine the last desperate attempts of a fallen woman to make a new life for herself, while in *Stupéfiants* (32.130) the hero's sister, a young actress, collapses into dependency at the hands of a drug ring masterminded by Peter Lorre, no less. At the end of the decade, Lavarède crosses the path of an opium baron in San Francisco (39.16), whose coffin proves an apt hiding place for drugs. Earlier, Justin had hidden cocaine smuggled from China to Marseille in a similar coffin (34.53) while, at the beginning of the decade, the most interesting of all drug-smuggling films, *Au nom de la loi,* had firmly established the coordinates for the sub-genre—cocaine, Chinese suppliers, and foreign adventurers, a spectacular police siege that exactly prefigures Gabin's in *Le Jour se lève,* and a sensuous vamp who turns the policeman planted to spy on them, is cornered, and commits suicide at the end. The European adventurers in East Asia recall Malraux a little, just as the sentiments expressed by the vamp prefigure in a way the theme of intoxication in *La Condition humaine:* she tempts the policeman with talk of freedom from moral constraints and praises cocaine as a way of forgetting the limitations of the human condition (31.11).

Arms smuggling is more likely to take place in French colonial territories, where it threatens the stability of empire. Rebels receive illicit arms with which to foment independence struggles, and noble French commanders strive to stifle the trade, even when their ship is sunk under them (36.89; 37.45; 38.8). In *Alerte en Méditerranée,* the arms smugglers imperil the world as we know it by accidentally triggering a gigantic cloud of poison gas which threatens to engulf the whole of southern Europe, and inimical navies are drawn nervously into a common plan to overcome the threat. In such cases, gun running is seen as a despicable and ignoble activity. Elsewhere, it can be almost respectable, since the protagonist himself—a North African poet—has been engaged in it (38.60), while the earliest film to mention it, *Ces messieurs de la Santé* (33.23), is, as mentioned earlier, notoriously hard to read: the escaped prisoner, a banker, in his rise to renewed commercial stardom, transforms the humble corset factory in which he gets a job as accountant into a giant multinational which subsequently proves, among its many astonishing activities, to be providing machine guns to foreign revolutionaries. Wherever there's money to be made, morality goes out the window; he's just "doing business," and the film is largely admiring of his inexhaustible talent and initiative. Gun smuggling appears in the film almost incidentally as one of the gleefully mentioned sidelines of his corset business.

The most outspoken "defense" of a gun runner can be found, however, in *Mollenard* (37.75). Mollenard is a captain in the service of the Société des Armements Militaires, and with their implicit accord he has been engaging in a sideline of gun running which has proved immensely profitable for them, as well as for him and his crew. Now they find it convenient to dump him. He is constructed as an independent-minded, disrespectful, no-nonsense man of the world who has earned the total respect of his crew. He is full of heart beneath a deliberately gruff exterior. By contrast, behind a facade of respectability, the firm he works for is hypocritical, greedy, cynical, and ruthless, and to make matters worse for him his wife and family represent all the worst aspects of middle-class propriety, prudery, and prissiness. If he is a monster, he says, it is because she and her world have made him one. Worn down, humiliated, and reduced almost to suicide by the combined malice of the company and his wife, he is reinstated by his crew in a quasi-piratical fashion and dies at their head, at sea. The critique of social and commercial respectability is incessant; and gun running in these circumstances comes to stand for a total disregard for official procedures and the establishment, for a brutal realism that contrasts with the firm's hypocrisy, and ultimately for a desire to circumvent and even subvert the existing social order.

Ranged against these malefactors of one sort or another, we find, aside from the official law-enforcement agencies, various unofficial representatives of the law. Two of them are worthy of specific mention—the private detective and the reporter. The private detective comes trailing residual aspects of his English origins, but in the thirties he is never given a serious cerebral mystery to unravel in the Sherlock Holmes tradition. All nine examples identified are comedies, intended as vehicles for Bach, Berry, Baroux, Fernandel, and Duvallès, or at least sentimental comedies in which Préjean or Roanne are the private detectives (30.46; 32s5; 37.1). Their standard task is the surveillance of a wife or mistress for a jealous husband or lover but, as the decade advances, their "investigations" become more and more parodic, more and more hysterical. In a hilarious sequence from *Mademoiselle, ma mère* (37.67), the stepson has a private detective trail his disturbingly attractive stepmother, who turns out to have been having a riotous time, while in *Arsène Lupin, detective* (37.11) Berry plays the gentleman thief who is running a slightly grotesque detective agency as a front for his nefarious activities. Its promotional campaign parodies both the current "excesses" of advertising and the detective agency as an institution. As a private detective investigating a murder, Arsène Lupin is on the best of terms with the police; unmasked as the notorious criminal, he still manages to escape in the company of a murderer's mistress.

Tricoche et Cacolet (38.103) is less parodic but even more frenetic. Fernandel and Duvallès at first seem to be those sports-mad "men of the people," knowing and inventive, familiar from many working-class films earlier in the decade. Revealed as private detectives, they become more like trickster figures, with an eye for the main chance, out to con the world and, if possible, one another. Their detective agency has a revolving bookcase hiding a wardrobe full of disguises, which they exploit with increasing rapidity, one or both appearing as an Arab, a fire chief, a valet and maidservant, a military officer in bearskin, and their client's mistress's mother and lawyer. While the rest of the cast seem to be trying to act out a routine boulevard comedy, the two private detectives subvert it with vaudeville and farce, finally combining to extort and enrich themselves (and run off with the mistress). This representation of the private detective couldn't be further from that of the British original or from that of the American cinema in the ensuing decade.

The reporter figure as an alternative investigator in criminal matters is interesting both in itself and as the most obvious representative of the mass media in films of the thirties. This character constituted the positive aspect of an institution which otherwise was regarded with marked suspicion throughout the decade. The negative connotations associated with the media had a double origin: press magnates, as members of the establishment, were assumed to be inherently criminal, as corrupt and duplicitous as all other persons in authority (38.14), while the media in general were seen as a principal instrument in the ideological enslavement of the gullible poor. The latter attitude was particularly prevalent in the first half of the decade, when the occasional film echoes Georges Altman's scathing indictment of all capitalist institutions, but particularly the media. In several films, the mass media are specifically blamed for cultivating a false glamour around the figure of the star. Humble working girls are seduced by dreams of fame to betray their origins and those that love them (30.69; 35.12) and are, in their turn, betrayed and destroyed. The anarchist in *Le Bonheur* is particularly incensed at the sentimentality of popular culture, which purveys cheap dreams of a fulfillment which people can never attain in real life but which prevent their ever calling into question the system which enslaves them. It is interesting to compare this process of mythologization, which panders to, even as it produces, "human folly," with Lange's overtly political and "healthy" fictions about Arizona Jim and his fight against the fascists (35.27). Lange's world also, of course, has been corrupted by the media boss, played by Berry. A fascinating Fernandel film which seems not to have survived has a naive provincial following in Lange's footsteps—inheriting a Parisian daily, discovering the duplicity of those running it, firing them, and handing management of the paper over to a workers' cooperative (37.59).

Yet, despite their recognition of the negative effects of the press as a capitalist institution, and of its need for reconstruction, the films of this decade cannot refrain at times from glamorizing it, even as they critique it, as one of the symbols of a technological age. Like the futurist theorists, with their reverence for all forms of modern dynamism, the filmmakers of this decade represent the machinery of the press in a way analogous to their representation of the railroads and airways, as vital, exhilarating, and urgent. The most obvious form that this takes is a transitional montage sequence which signals some newsworthy event in the narrative. Whenever a murder is committed, an arrest is made, a trial takes a sensational new twist, a train crashes, a singer triumphs, or an enemy warship is sunk, such a montage sequence is inserted, and I have identified about forty of them in surviving films. They rapidly became something of a cliché, acquiring a readily recognizable form which involved superimpositions and cross-dissolves linking some or all of the following: presses turning, editions rolling off the presses, headlines flashing past, paper boys cycling the streets, a flurry of newspaper stands, and crowds of eager buyers. As well as corresponding in their intrinsic vigor to the sensationalism of the revelations, such sequences gave a momentary dynamism to the narrative, causally connecting what was often a relatively private narrative to its wider public effects.

This mythologization of the production of the daily paper goes hand in hand with mythologization of the reporter. The hero of at least twenty films in the decade, the reporter is typically young, athletic, enterprising, inventive, perceptive, and persistent. Gaston Leroux's Rouletabille, especially as played by Roland Toutain, has all the youthful dynamism and athleticism which the myth requires. He refuses to be excluded from the scene of the crime, takes the investigation over from the police (who are usually corrupt or incompetent, anyway), assembles and interprets the relevant clues, presents them to an amazed gathering, and wins the commissioner's daughter (30.59; 30.62; 31.13). The charismatic nature of the reporter can be appreciated from the fact that Murat, Garat, Préjean, and Larquey all assumed the role at one time or another.

Normally, the young reporter as investigator, like the young law student, appeared in the standard murder mystery in the first half of the decade, displacing the police as locus of knowledge and power. Indeed, a crucial element in the reporter's role was his ability to outwit both the criminal and the police. Later on, however, it was in the more exotic genre of the adventure film that the reporter starred. His job and investigations might take him to all parts of the globe—to Hungary (31.13), to India (36.88), to Rio (36.23), or via the Orient Express (37.14) to China (38.27) and Macao (39.51). In these climes, he may have to deal with bandits, white slavers, enemy agents, or Oriental assassins rather than the standard French criminal, but his activities always serve to further the interests and repute of the French nation.

Nearly all reporters are young, French, and male. They are modern knights, and their task is most commonly to rescue attractive young females who are being persecuted by criminals or who have been wrongly charged with a crime (38.93). But a few are foreign, and two are female.

Any American reporter benefited from a distinctive prestige, as witness the readiness of the devious Mademoiselle Docteur to adopt the persona of an American reporter in order to further her sinister plots (36.69). The other woman reporter appears in a comic 1939 film in which the protagonist's girlfriend is obsessed with the mythic role of the reporter and seizes upon his race around the world against the clock to realize her dream of an international scoop (39.16). One other 1939 film that attests to the status of the reporter is *Macao, l'enfer du jeu* (39.51) in which Toutain reprises his role as the go-getting athletic journalist to rescue Jasmine from the squalid criminal activities of her father, the gang boss of Macao. The status of the reporter's role can be said to be mythic insofar as, although nominally investigating gun-running for a newspaper, Toutain is very much a freelance agent and has no direct contact with a newspaper at any stage of the story. It is therefore to some extent an arbitrary attribution. Of course, the notion of "investigation" allies the reporter to detectives and police and acts as a pretext to involve the character in any contemporary newsworthy event or activity. Both these latter films, particularly *Les Cinq Sous de Lavarède*, constitute further instances of the tendency of films produced late in the thirties to recognize, foreground, and comment on the mythic status of their own material.

5.2 CHILDHOOD, EDUCATION, AND THE REFORMATORY

On the whole, the media receive relatively little attention in the films of the thirties, and the same is true of education. Indeed, childhood as a whole is a thematic field that the thirties left relatively unexplored. Certain well-known exceptions will spring to mind—*Poil de Carotte* (32.109), *Ménilmontant* (36.78), *Les Disparus de St. Agil* (38.25), and a number of melodramas in which the suffering and deprivations of innocent children are recounted in poignant detail—yet even if one includes stories about students and about young people's growth to maturity, the proportion of films dealing even marginally with the young is remarkably small. By contrast with the war years, when nearly one in three films dealt with this category of character, the thirties dealt with it in only about one in twelve. After a total lack of interest in the initial years of sound film, when the level was nearer one in a hundred, between 1932 and 1939 there is a steady stream of about ten to twelve films a year that feature young people, though often fairly marginally, with peaks of interest in 1936 and 1938. Overall, one could justifiably talk of an irregular increase in the proportion of stories about childhood and education throughout the decade, followed by a wartime period in which they constitute one of the dominant preoccupations.

In general terms, the most common stories told about the young range from tales of their trials and tribulations in unhappy families, to their turning to crime and the need to re-educate or rehabilitate them, their life away from home in boarding schools and student digs, their sexual and romantic initiation, and various climactic experiences which occasion a growth to "maturity." They deal, that is, with the formal and informal socialization of the young, its inadequacies in the contemporary social order, and ways of remedying these inadequacies.

In certain films of the period, there is an implicit acceptance of the myth of childhood as a time of innocence and purity, which can only be corrupted by entry into social life. The life of adults undergoing severe trials can be totally transformed by the appearance of a child (33.39; 35.14), or it can be destroyed by the death of a child, seen as the ultimate cosmic injustice. Fathers can be driven mute and mad by it (32.152) or be appropriately chastened for their hubris (34.88). More commonly, the trials and tribulations of an unhappy childhood are exploited for their sentimental potential in melodramas. Children are abandoned or stolen, adopted by wandering singers (34.92), or maltreated by their supposed families (35.84); they endure penury and exploitation or are used as counters in domestic war games (36.34). Boys turn to crime and girls to prostitution, or at least are in danger of doing so, only to find ultimate salvation and happiness in new families or be restored to their true families. The titles of many of these films, notably those featuring two waifs, are sufficient indication of the most common representation of childhood of the time—*Sans famille* (34.92), *Les Deux Gamines* (36.33), *Les Deux Gosses* (36.34), *Jacques et Jacotte* (36.60), *Le Petit Chose* (38.76), *Un Gosse en or* (38.111), *L'Enfer des anges* (39.32), and *Jeunes Filles en détresse* (39.47). Josette, Lucette, Cosette, and Colette are favored names, the diminutives appealing to easy sentiment. The recurrent setting of Parisian working-class suburbs emphasizes the role of urbanization and its attendant social inequalities in the "cosmic" injustice affecting children of the decade, and this is frequently explicit in the narratives (e.g., 36.78; 36.112; 36.60; 39.63).

Occasionally, the education system is seen as contributing to this unhappy state of affairs; less often, it is seen as a means of combating it. The total number of films in which teachers and education are central is not sufficiently great to justify any generalizations, or indeed to justify seeing education as an important institution in the imaginary life of the decade. Most frequently, the label "professor" or "academician" is interchangeable with a number of other labels establishing the holder as having a position of authority which renders him at once suspect of corruption behind the scenes and prey to mockery and ridicule. Boulevard comedies used the austere or dry-as-dust professor as a point of comic orientation in their adulterous games (30.3; 32.60; 33.93; 37.21) or, in more dramatic mode, as an aging lover uncertain how to cope with a sensuous and/or adulterous young woman (30.87; 31.8; 37.10). Pagnol, of course, capitalized on the rather unworldly and gauche stereotype to engineer a more positive image for teachers in his *Topaze,* which, at least in its 1932 film version, was very popular. Sacked for not pandering to an aristocratic parent, Topaze is taken on as a front man by a corrupt businessman, but gradually comes to realize how he is being exploited and turns the tables on the businessman so effectively that he ends up complacently making money hand over fist through illegal operations. The teacher who began by inculcating precepts such as "Money doesn't buy happiness" and "Ill-gotten gains never benefited anyone" ends up explaining to his bewildered colleague that money is the force that governs the world (32.134). So successful was this film that not only was it remade (less successfully) by Pagnol himself in 1936 (36.129), but the general theme was imitated in 1933 in *Professeur Cupidon* (33.109). In that case, it was a trip to Paris which effected the worldly transformation of a foolish and gullible teacher.

Other, usually younger, teachers are positively represented in the late thirties, including another by Pagnol (35.79), but if they may occasionally triumph as individuals, the context of institutional life to which they are condemned is mostly represented as rigid, hierarchical, and antagonistic to human values. The Pensionnat Muche—the boarding school, where Topaze works—is ruled over in tyrannical and manipulative fashion by the director and his daughter. The Pensionnat of St. Agil is a place of distrust and sinister mysteries in which, in typical expressionist fashion, the director turns out to be in league with a gang of forgers. Both teachers and students dream of escape, the latter through secret clubs, writing fiction, or a Gabin-like transatlantic fugue to a new life "over there" (38.25). In fact, boarding schools are regularly seen as a form of exile from family life (30s17; 33.119) or a convenient depository for the children of broken families (39.47). For the female teacher in *La Dame de Malacca,* institutional life is so grim and forbidding that any alternative must be preferable, even marriage to an unloved and unlovely civil servant (37.30). Like many of these teachers, "trapped" in prison-like institutions (even von Stroheim), she feels an instinctive affection for and sympathy with the children (and, later, natives; and, no doubt, animals) because they are, like her, fellow victims of a harsh system. *Zéro de conduite* (33s8) is therefore not atypical in its representation of the school as a grotesquely oppressive institution, which strives to eliminate all humanity and joy from the lives of its charges. The film is distinct only for the use of surrealist techniques to represent the oppressive educational regime of the day, rather than the more commonly used expressionist techniques—for emphasizing, that is, a possible liberated future rather than a depressingly regulated present.

There is therefore little distinction in the films of the decade between the boarding school and the reformatory or prison into which children and adolescents are thrust when they inevitably go wrong. Indeed, there is little distinction between all these and the women's prisons and rehabilitation centers for adults that come to the fore in the latter half of the decade (e.g., 38.83). In a film that seems in some respects to have foreshadowed *Les 400 Coups,* a boy is sent to a reformatory for a minor crime and finds life there intolerable. He flees, and on the point of being recaptured tries to commit suicide (33.14). Other young people caught up in the justice system can be found in *Abus de confiance* (37.2), in which the young lawyer who knows herself to be as guilty as them hears people of her own age being tried for minor crimes—petty theft, vagrancy, occasional prostitution—and being sent off to a rehabilitation center. She pleads for one as for herself, noting that it is primarily social factors that have induced these crimes, not inherent evil. All have been brought up in poverty, one has a drunkard as a father, another has a mother who has run off with a plumber, and so on. All are "unfortunates" rather than criminals.

The idea that women, and young women in particular, were vulnerable to such social pressures and needed refuges and retreats where they could be safe from temptation was a theme of increasing interest in films in the second half of the decade. Whether on a lighthearted note (35.87) or a more somber one (36.24), films show women finding a moment of respite and communal support in "homes" and "refuges." When such protection is lacking, the films plead more and more insistently for the sociological origin of criminality to be taken into account. *Prisons de femmes* (38.83) makes a powerful appeal for compassion rather than rigor in the treatment of such women. Institutionalized for trying to escape from a brutish family who use her as a household slave and plan to sell her off in an undesirable marriage, Juliette is condemned to three years' hard labor. We witness her induction into prison routines, her experience of solitary confinement, and her friendship with other women whose tales are even more unjust than her own. Many years later, married respectably and even elegantly, she is threatened by a blackmailer, and her sorry past emerges. The message of the film is that the fault is not in her but in society, and her older husband, whose strict morality had been offended by her past conduct, must learn to be compassionate.

Among these films dealing with the socialization or rehabilitation of the young, there is one—*Prison sans barreaux* (37.95)—that is of particular interest in that it is structured around precisely this conflict of paradigms. On the one hand, there is the old order, which is harsh, doctrinaire, distrustful of the inmates, and imposes on them an unyielding routine; on the other, a more humane and understanding administration that works through consideration, trust, and even affection. Rather than being seen as rascals or criminals and inherently corrupt, the inmates are seen as "unfortunates," who should be ruled not through fear and brutality but through understanding and compassion. The terms in which the argument is put are somewhat similar to those outlined in St. Agil, and guarantee the ultimate victory of the more humane order. Interestingly, the arrival of the new, more humane order is consequent on the state assuming control of the rehabilitation center, and the final reminder of "liberté, égalité, fraternité" implies that the new order represents the natural extension of the rights of all citizens to inmates of prisons. A similar claim for French republicanism as being based on a more humanitarian order can be found the following year in *Éducation de prince* (38.29), in which the young prince of a fictional foreign land ("Sylvestrie") learns to appreciate the humane and considerate treatment accorded to French students, by contrast with the rigid and authoritarian structures which governed his upbringing at home.

In general, although the number of films is not large enough to justify any major thesis concerning paradigm changes, it is probably valid to see the progressive increase in films concerning youths, teachers, and education as a sign of a progressive dissatisfaction with schools, reformatories, and prisons based on rigid discipline, punishment, fear, and repression, and a recognition of the need to transform the system.

Within the old order, the well-being, and even salvation, of the young is seen as dependent on either the saintly devotion of altruistic individuals or the random patronage of the rich. A standard element in the melodramatic narrative of abandoned children was the good-hearted but impoverished individual who provided a momentary respite in their tribulations, and this spilled over into other genres as well, notably the social realist document. These acts of individual goodness in a morass of social evil might be committed by a neighbor (36.64), a seedy shopkeeper (35.91), a young man (39.31), or, more improbably, a lawyer (36.33). On occasion, it is someone officially charged with looking after children—a teacher (33.86), a policewoman (36.20), a man of religion (39.63), or a scout mistress (35s1)—but there is little sense at the best of times that the children's good fortune is anything other than an isolated event. Expelled from school, Babs's son is saved from the debilitating environment in which she now moves only by the chance encounter with a Canadian "uncle" (39.80). Any optimistic resolution that such films might have is due not to any systematic social action that would allow it to be generalized to most or all such cases, but rather to the standard narrative ploys of the decade: the chance encounter, the inheritance (35.91), the rich man's gratitude (36.64), or the aristocrat's benevolent gesture (38.47).

One film to explore these problems in a little more depth is *Ménil-montant* (36.78), which deals with poor children in a working-class Paris suburb. Their educational facilities are grossly inadequate, but the narrative solution to their woes is the finding of a valuable ring by two workers associated with the school. When they return it to its wealthy owner, she is overwhelmed by their honesty, their altruism, their unaffected charm, and their refusal of a reward. She is astonished to hear that there are poor kids not getting a proper education—if only she had known earlier. . . . She provides funds to build a residence designed especially for kids. But as the project evolves, it gets taken over by entrepreneurs and politicians, whose arrogance and self-importance threaten to subvert the whole project. The workers are no longer central to it, but have come to seem just obstructive squatters whose rough shacks are in the way of the development, and at the inauguration of the residence they are sidelined and forgotten. The ambivalence of the film is fundamental. The kids' problems are social, and class is at the root of their suffering; the workers manifest solidarity and integrity, whereas the rich and powerful are in general ruthless and self-seeking—as one character says, "How can you expect people who have everything to be human?" Yet the only solution is a random act of gratitude by one of the wealthy, who simply hadn't realized that the problem existed. Understandably, the workers are themselves ambivalent at the end, having lost their "squat" to the development they initiated. "Still, what matters is that the residence exists," says one, but the other is cynical about the future of any development run by the wealthy and by politicians for ends that are primarily self-promotional.

Although there were relatively few films dealing with children of primary- or high-school age, there are considerably more dealing with university students, art students, and young intellectuals. Indeed, one in three of the films of the decade dealing with young people has a university student as protagonist. This has little to do with the importance of university education or even student life, however, and more to do with what students are represented as having in common with artists, Gypsies, and circus folk—a freer attitude toward middle-class morality and a spontaneous joie de vivre. They combine this joyous gaiety and the irresponsibility of marginal folk with a degree of intellectual substance which, perhaps fortunately, they seldom have to demonstrate in the course of the narrative. They therefore make attractive romantic protagonists, are given to easy sexual relationships, and can prove to be unproblematic lovers and mistresses. They have a sense of fun which might lead them into "student pranks" of a licentious kind (34.71), but are basically good-natured and genuine. When these characteristics are combined with the well-documented moral laxity of the artist, those studying art, drama, or music have all these qualities to excess.

Consequently, although there are a number of films organized around such characters, few of them—only six in all—deal with student life as a milieu in its own right, and when they do so the focus is on the Latin Quarter, bars, shared rooms, sentimental rivalries, and jealousies little connected to the academic or social function of student life. The communal life typical of student days does lead, however, to communal affections. Male students tend to travel in threes, all of whom fall for the same woman

(31.68; 33.32; 36.131; 38.22). Both male and female students are attractive to older members of the opposite sex—sometimes, but not always, their teachers (31.9; 34.45; 36.52; 37.20). Perhaps most important, they are represented as not in the least interested in politics or in social movements of any sort. In this, they are quite unlike their Russian and Serb counterparts, who seduce generals to save their husbands from political persecution (30.72), plot to blow up trains (37.14), harbor then betray revolutionary friends (36.123), or, in the adaptation of *Crime et Châtiment* (35.28), engage in cat-and-mouse games with the police prosecutor and with God. The nearest a French student will get to philosophical, social, political, or other principled activity is a (very rare) protest demonstration, and even then it is less a political act than a protest against politics. Thus, foreign princes (in the student prince tradition) can demonstrate their humanity—that is, their basic antipathy to the formal and pompous public role for which they are destined—by engaging in public protests (38.29), or perhaps even being arrested by their own police (36.77). In sum, studenthood in France had little to do with any representation of the education system and more to do with the representation of a momentary glimpse of liberty between the oppression of childhood and the oppression of a working life.

5.3 THE SUPPRESSION AND RESURGENCE OF A SHAMEFUL PAST

Aside from the frivolous, even feckless gaiety of French student life, the period of adolescence as seen in the films of the thirties is not something to look back on with affection. Except in the few cases of exiles regretting their French childhood, nostalgia for an idyllic childhood is almost unknown in the thirteen hundred films that were made in these ten years. Two films tell distinctly fantastic stories of drugs that ensure eternal youth, but these are not motivated by nostalgia for an idyllic youth that might ideally be prolonged; rather, they are no more than pretexts for scabrous tales of sexual excess or pseudo-incest (32.107; 32.126). Far more common are the tales of a misspent youth or a shameful past which threatens to catch up with the protagonists in later life, and which has been or, if possible, has to be suppressed. Again, the number of films relating such stories increases dramatically in the second half of the decade, and the intensity of the anguish generated by this inconvenient past foreshadows the importance of this theme in wartime films. Effectively, childhood and early adulthood may in theory be a time of innocence, but social and sexual pressures inevitably lead to a corruption of that innocence and to forms of criminal or licentious behavior which expose the protagonists to blackmail or scandal in later life.

I have identified twenty-one films whose primary focus is the need to suppress the truth about one's youthful past. Most date from 1936 to 1939, and the increasing intensity of the distress that they embody can be measured by the increasing complexity of their narration, involving not just reminiscences and multiple flashbacks but, in the case of the most complex of them, a mix of past and pluperfect tenses and a personalized narrator who intervenes in and finally resolves the story (38.83). Most of the earlier stories, on the contrary, present in a straightforwardly linear fashion firstly the youthful indiscretions of the protagonist then the complications they cause in later life—a narrative form which doesn't lend itself so easily to the generation of that intense air of mystery, anxiety, and distress that was to characterize wartime embodiments of the theme. Indeed, the first of the films to propose a deprived and distressed childhood as the cause of later criminality has the reminiscences of an unhappy youth which explain the character's later criminality appended as a mere afterthought to the narration of that criminality: at his trial, his mother hopes to mitigate her son's involvement with a crime gang by invoking his fatherless state, which has exacerbated their poverty and the social pressures of working-class life (33.41). Similar last-minute sociological explanations lend a certain poignancy to the death of the murderer in *La Tradition de minuit* (39.88).

The more interesting films, however, are those which present youthful errors as central thematic material rather than last-minute afterthoughts. When this happens, there is a clear gender differentiation: male protagonists are haunted by criminal acts in their youth, while females are haunted by sexual indiscretions. Thus a male tennis champion can't shed his past association with a band of wastrels who have turned to robbery, is wounded while resisting their attempt to rob his mistress, and consequently loses his crucial tennis match (33.42); a male political leader is blackmailed over a theft he committed as a young man (36.9); and, despite redeeming himself in the colonies, the nephew of an industrialist cannot escape the youthful indiscretions which led to his exile (34.12). Such stories presuppose an anxiety about some fundamental violence underlying the male personality, which success in later life can never entirely redeem or cancel out.

As one might expect, this more public and aggressive orientation of the young male's past criminality contrasts with the more private and affective nature of the young female's past sexual misdemeanors, though "lady-killer" stories such as *Liebelei* (33.76), in which a rake's past affairs re-emerge to doom a present "true love," imply an anxiety about male sexual misdemeanors. Aside from these, *Le Coupable* (36.27) is the only film I have recorded in which a young man's past sexual behavior catches up on him in his later respectable life, when as a judge he is called upon to try his own illegitimate son. But this film is also narrated in linear fashion, setting out cause and effect in a way which does not allow the construction of an atmosphere of uncertainty, secrecy, and apprehension. And although at the end the judge beats his breast and proclaims his guilt for past sins, the spectator who has followed the chain of events as they happened has always been aware that it was not fundamentally his fault but that of the old grandfather, who, through his class prejudice and lies, had been responsible for the involuntary sexual betrayal by his son and the descent into criminality of his grandson. Happily, the grandfather ultimately dies of shock at the outcome of his actions.

But this film is exceptional—normally, it is women who turn out to have a shady past; or, rather, the negative connotations which seem always in Western culture of recent centuries to have attached to female sexuality are represented in these films as doubts about the purity of the woman chosen as wife—doubts which all too often, alas, turn out to be substantiated. This contrast between apparent purity and hidden perversity is all the more powerful when associated with the opposition between puritanical provincial male and sexually adventurous Parisian female. Thus, a young provincial man may meet an attractive girl at a masked ball and come to love her, only to discover that she has led a dissolute life in her youth. He leaves her, returns, forgives . . . but finally departs for America without her (34.93). Another provincial falls for a Parisian girl only to learn she has not been as pure as he thought. Though engaged, he refuses to marry her and returns to his country chateau with his sister, who has been more fortunate (36.31). Marie Bell, who played this role, also played the apparently prudish wife of Loulou (Raimu) who, as he eventually comes to realize, is none other than the chanteuse who was his mistress in Saigon many years ago (38.69). This film develops its sense of apprehension in a game-like way, having the happily married wife suddenly faced with the prospect of her palm being read by a friend of her husband's who claims to be able to uncover a person's hidden past. Not realizing that he is just a con artist demonstrating his favorite technique for getting to know women, she suffers a hysterical crisis which unlocks her husband's memories of their past encounter in Saigon. "Aargh! I slept with my wife!" exclaims the husband, for whom it has admittedly become an atypical experience, and he proceeds to become comically jealous of the idiot he was at that time.

Most films treat the suppressed and resurgent past more somberly. In that same year, in a film pointedly entitled *J'étais une aventurière*, Edwige Feuillère plays a respectable married woman whose shady past erupts when she is blackmailed by a former lover. She is forced to admit her past to her husband, who (as in the previous instance) magnanimously pardons her and helps her put the memory of her dissolute youth behind her (38.53). The respectable woman who turns out to have been a high-class tart in her youth was a standard character type in the late thirties. Nina Petrovna proves unable to escape her past and is reduced to suicide in despair (37.71), while in *Nitchevo* (36.89) Thérèse is now married to a commandant, but the hectic excesses of her youth emerge (again through the threats of a former lover). The outcome is more fortunate this time, again allowing an opportunity for male magnanimity to be manifested.

If these later films show an intensification of the theme of a dissolute youth it is because each one initially presents a "present tense" in which middle-class respectability and rectitude prevail. Into this apparently idyllic family life intrude progressive hints of the wife's more sordid and dissolute past, which she struggles desperately to keep secret from her unsuspecting husband. A classic instance is *Prisons de femmes* (38.83), in which Juliette has married a strictly moral industrialist without telling him of her past (and admittedly somewhat unjust) incarceration for attempted murder. Blackmail, confidants, incipient suspicions, and anxieties about "basing her whole life on a lie" construct an atmosphere of intense emotion which ends when her husband finally learns the awful truth and is coaxed into forgiveness: "At last the nightmare is over." This is the film in which multiple tenses and narrators are mobilized (ambitiously, but not always successfully) to engender an impression of nightmarish mental evasions.

Feyder's *Les Gens du voyage* (37.53), made the year before, is remarkable for being organized around no fewer than three stories of youthful indiscretions which threatened present happiness. Two of these focus on females whose sexual indiscretions manifest themselves in illegitimate offspring, and one on a male whose criminal past catches up with him despite his attempts to go straight. Madame Flora is an animal-tamer in a circus, and unmarried. Her son, Marcel, loves the boss's daughter, but his illegitimate origins are held against him by the boss, who tells Flora, "You don't even know who his father is." But she does, all too well, and so do we very soon: Fernand, who is on the run, takes refuge in the circus to see Flora and their son, and worms his way into the boss's good graces without, of course, revealing his criminal past. Meanwhile, the boss's daughter has been packed off to Paris, but too late to prevent a pregnancy. The gradual presentation of information about these three sets of youthful indiscretion, both to other characters and to the spectator, provides an effective narrative form. The result, however, is to construct adolescence as a time of reckless inconsequence, engendering secrets which threaten to undermine and destroy any hope of happiness in later life. Indeed, they do destroy it in Fernand's case, since he is shot by police as he flees across the rooftops and falls to his death.

The most effective of these films generate intensity through curiosity about the past which leads to an investigative narrative structure. The extreme instance of this is provided by *Carrefour* (38.14), described earlier, in which, in Freudian fashion, amnesia has suppressed an unacceptable past, and the protagonist is led to investigate his own past self. Such narratives make it apparent that it is not just the repressed indiscretions of youth that are in question, nor even simply gender stereotypes, but once again the question of bourgeois respectability seen as nothing but a hypocritical facade. It is a facade which crumbles easily, since such stories tend to involve patterns of repetition or circularity, as the respectable adult is gradually driven to repeat the criminal or sexual acts which he or she had tried to suppress. In *Carrefour*, the character played by Vanel finds himself contemplating the murder of his blackmailer, in order to suppress the implication that he was once a murderer. Even *La Fin du jour* (38.37) manifests this sort of repetitive narrative pattern, as St. Clair's rivalry with Marny over Juliette threatens to replicate the tragedy of his past seduction of Marny's "one true love." This largely unspoken past rivalry is only gradually revealed to the spectator, as its significance is only gradually revealed to St. Clair himself. Such self-knowledge is more than he can bear—his eyes glaze, and he moves toward suicide.

Two final instances of this suppression of youthful indiscretions are worth mentioning, again from the final years of the decade, and again organized into a narrative format which generates an atmosphere of anxiety—*Sans lendemain* (39.80) and *Le Drame de Shanghaï* (38.27). Initially, the first of these seems to be quite the contrary of a story about youthful indiscretions undermining present respectability, since it introduces us to a high-class tart, good-time girl, and risqué nightclub performer who meets her "one true love" of yesteryear and has to strive desperately to construct a respectable present for herself so as not to disillusion him. But we gradually come to understand that the reason she left him without explanation all those years ago was that even then she had had a shady past, as the wife of a criminal, which she had desperately sought to conceal from him. Narrated in linear fashion, there would be three successive suppressions of the past—her husband suppressed his criminality, which she finds out about too late; she in turn suppresses her marriage to the criminal, but cannot therefore marry her suitor and true love, and disappears mysteriously; and years later when she meets him again she suppresses all of this, together with the descent into seedy sexual encounters to which she has subsequently been reduced. Only the last of these is told in the present tense; the others are related in oblique references or in flashbacks. The result is a psychodrama in which this (and by implication any) woman's life is revealed as a series of deceits, and in which her facade of respectability in the present tense is represented as merely the latest of a series of hastily contrived paperings-over of an association with criminality and illicit sexuality. Like all women, she is two-faced—Eveline on the surface, but Babs underneath, and she has to pay for it with the loss of the man she loves, the loss of the son she adores, and ultimately the loss of her own life.

Le Drame de Shanghaï replicates this narrative form to the extent that it presents us with a mother who has been reduced to the life of a chanteuse/good-time girl in a nightclub because she needs the money to support her daughter, Vera, at boarding school. Vera feels this is no longer the mother of old, but doesn't realize why until she overhears the sardonic yet moving reminiscences of her mother and a man she comes to feel must be her father. Their mutual slide into degradation surfaces at last, and through the agency of photos which reveal to Vera a very different past from an even earlier age—her family's aristocratic ease and elegance in czarist Russia. As in so many of these stories, it is members of the older generation who have become morally or criminally corrupt, and when this corruption surfaces they must pay heavily, while the appalled younger generation is offered the possibility of that new start in a new land that proved inaccessible to their parent's generation—but with the older generation's awful example as a warning. This is also the import of *La Tendre Ennemie* (35.109), in which each of the ghosts recounts his role in the mother's life, gradually working back to the initial disaster which blighted her life and that of so many others. They then proceed to manipulate the living so as to ensure that the daughter doesn't make the same (deadly) mistakes as her mother and her mother's mother. This is just one of several such "generational" films in which the sins of one generation of a family are replicated in the next, destroying the happiness of successive sets of offspring until a final intervention breaks the cycle and opens up the possibility of future happiness. These were dealt with more fully in chapter 4.

In this reading, the "suppressed past" films of the last years of the decade construct adolescence as a time of tragic errors, when the unacceptable realities of male violence and female licentiousness (not to mention family tyranny) most readily find their regrettable expression. A mature adult may, in exceptional cases and through the magnanimity of stronger personalities, manage to transcend all this and put it behind him or her, though in all justice he or she should pay the supreme penalty for it, and often does. This set of propositions, which was to be taken to extremes during the war years, reinforces the decade's global view of childhood as a time of innocence tested and readily corrupted by social pressures, of education as inadequate to the needs of the young, of the boarding school as an institution analogous to and as ineffectual as the reformatories of the penal system, and of the law as flawed by innumerable miscarriages of justice. Lawyers, judges, teachers, and the police are, or soon become, corrupted by power and self-interest, just as were those most directly responsible for the trials of the working people of the decade—bankers, financiers, and bosses. Only in a few films of the final years of the decade are there signs of a paradigm change which might see the rigid inhumanities of these "ideological apparatuses" softened by compassion and understanding.

While it would be excessive to see any of the material in this chapter as central to the concerns of *La Règle du jeu,* it is interesting to hear such a sardonic view of contemporary social institutions being voiced by Octave at the point when Christine talks of her life having for three years been based on a lie. "Listen, Christine," he says, "that's a sign of the times too. This is an age when everyone lies—ads for drugs, the radio, the newspapers, the government, the cinema. . . . Not one of them tells the truth. . . . Why should you expect individuals to be any different?"

SIX

Art and Transcendence:
Spirituality and Reflexivity

6.1 ARTISTS AND THEIR LIVES

Several chapters have noted the tendency toward the end of the decade for filmmakers to become aware of the sets of conventions underlying the structure of their films and to comment, often ironically, on the meanings thus produced. Inevitably, this reflexivity was most apparent when the film was overtly reflecting on its own existence as a film and on the functions of those involved in its production. Since those involved—especially the scriptwriters and directors, but usually the entire technical team and the producer as well—commonly represented film as an art form and themselves as aesthetically motivated, it is not at all surprising that art and the artist should figure so prominently in films of the time. At least 297 out of some 1,300 films produced during the decade (about 23 percent), and probably many more, contain some representation of the artist as a foregrounded element. These 297 films are spread fairly evenly throughout the decade, at a rate of about 30 films each year, though there are peaks in 1931 and 1938, separated by a trough in 1934.

At one level, it is of interest to note what forms of artistic activity filmmakers saw as most worthy of representation. At another, it is more interesting to note what view of art and the artist is mobilized, regardless of the art form involved. With respect to the first of these, perhaps because cinema is a demotic art form, but also because of the favorable light in which "the people" were viewed throughout the decade, the types of artistic activity represented were spread very broadly across both middle-class forms of high art and working-class forms of popular culture. Throughout the decade, there was a tendency toward the more popular cultural forms, in a proportion of about three to two. In addition to the cinema itself, those popular forms included circus performers and occasional jazz musicians or orchestras, but by far the greatest number were popular singers and dancers. Anyone conversant with the cinema of the time will recall numerous instances of street singers, music-hall performers, and nightclub and cabaret acts. Radio appears several times as a popular medium, and television once (31.76).

Among the more classical arts, various forms of musical expression are the most frequently identified (56 films), followed by the theater (33), the visual arts (19), and literature (13). This relatively low number might seem surprising, given the literary background of so many of the scriptwriters, but compared to the performance arts the act of writing is inherently less cinematic. Indeed, in all these artistic activities, for that very reason, there is a tendency to focus on the performance aspect of creativity rather than on the conceptual—on actor and musician rather than on composer, playwright, or novelist. Composers, whether Beethoven or Trénet, had to be performers as well (or romantically linked to performers) to achieve a place in the cinematic pantheon. Writers are noticeably absent, and the cinema establishes early in the decade that they are a drab lot, unlikely to interest the public or the opposite sex in their own right, but needing to be disguised as a gentleman thief (30.39; 35.62) or to pretend to be assassinated if they are to inspire a romantic attachment (31.51). Dramatists are considered particularly risible, because of their inevitable lack of contact with "real life" (35.98), which leads them to produce grotesque works such as the "mutist" play in *Fauteuil 47* (37.42).

Although the act of painting could be seen as accumulating both creative and performative elements, there is a reasonable explanation for filmmakers' reluctance to tackle it: the absence of color for much of the period. When they do introduce a painter, thirties films carefully present him only while drawing, leaving his painterly skills to be extrapolated (35.13; 37.124), and even his drawing skills are suggested rather than demonstrated. Thus, it is the performative aspect of the musical and theatrical arts which is the principal focus of "art." For the same reasons, circuses, street singers, musicians, and dramatic acts are most common popular art forms.

Certain generalizations can be made about each of these popular forms of cultural activity, before we move on to a consideration of their common functions. Among the "low culture" forms, the circus had long been celebrated in France, and the thirties was perhaps the last decade in which this could be stated without qualification. In an age of sedentary populations, the circus travelling from town to town brought to each community a moment of exhilaration, adventure, and the extraordinary, though precisely because they were forever on the move, circus personnel shared that enviable but slightly suspect privilege of the Gypsy, a certain "shiftiness" which went with the open road. Their arrival brought excitement and intensity, and their departure inspired dreams of the great unknown, out there, into which they disappeared. But anything or anyone might disappear with them. In Germany, of course, circuses and fairgrounds had a quite different set of connotations deriving from their place in expressionist representation as a site of disorder, even chaos. To some extent, this built on a more general Western tradition of carnival, in which festivities associated with fairgrounds, processions, and masked celebrations allowed populations to participate in forms of expression that were normally illicit, broke with propriety, or totally inverted social norms and structures.

The circus of thirties French films draws on both these traditions. In general, films whose principal location is the circus are concentrated in the first half of the decade and benefit from a romantic representation. One pragmatic reason there are so many is that they allowed the narrative to present a number of circus acts, often by renowned performers, as an "incidental" background to the main narrative. Such films tend toward the episodic, or at least are organized around a series of performances often marginal to the central narrative. This is a circus of outsiders, constantly on the move, rejecting society and being rejected by it, sometimes momentarily tempted to settle down, but ultimately hitting the road again (39.4). In the final years of the decade, the circus or circus personnel are usually involved in an isolated narrative incident, in which they stand for some well-consecrated value—adventure, disorder, melancholy, and so on. Indeed, they tend toward the fairground more than the circus, and thus create apprehension more often than exhilaration. *Les Gens du voyage* (37.53) is the one full-scale circus story from the last half of the decade. It exploits the romance of a footloose life, the routines of erecting and dismantling the big top, the performances, and the back-stage conspiracies, but in keeping with the more somber mood of these later years it conceals a hotbed of sexuality and of painful memories from a suppressed past.

Three categories of circus personnel were favored by the thirties cinema—trapeze artists/acrobats, animal-tamers, and clowns. Each category had its recurrent qualities and narratives, though the principal division is between the dynamic, dangerous, and potentially lethal professions of trapeze artist and lion-tamer, and the "safe" but more emotionally unstable profession of clown. The former are a passionate and violent lot, harboring bitter grievances against one another and flying into jealous rages which often result in the death of their rival or partner (30.1; 30.92; 35.121). They allow one another "accidentally" to crash to the ground or be eaten by wild beasts, or at least they contemplate doing so. Typical of these stories is one already mentioned, in which an animal-tamer has brought up a young girl; as she grows up, he comes to love her and marries her; but she, alas, loves a trapeze artist and, in despair, the animal-tamer allows himself to be devoured by his beasts (35.105). There are another two such films in 1935: in *La Tendre Ennemie* (35.109) one of the ghosts was in his lifetime a lion-tamer, "Rodrigo le Vainqueur." The errant wife had fallen for him but selfishly ignored his medical condition, and when she insists that he live it up in the bright lights of the Côte d'Azur rather than retiring to the mountain sanatorium for the medical treatment he so urgently needs, he becomes so debilitated that his tigers kill him. In *Les Gens du voyage,* Françoise Rosay, in her role as female lion-tamer, is lucky to escape the same fate when mauled by her lions (37.53).

Clowns are a more melancholy and passive category of character. As is well known, their impassive masked faces conceal untold depths of feeling, but the unspoken admiration that they feel for some attractive female— usually a dancer or performer's assistant—counts for little beside the wealth of an aristocrat or the passion and drama of a trapeze artist or an animal-tamer. Sadly, the clown stands aside and returns to his task of spreading a joy which he himself can never experience (30s14; 31.66). In other narratives, a woman comes to appreciate the inherent nobility of the melancholy clown and learns to love him (32.79; 33.5; 35.21). One of the most popular films of the decade foregrounded clown figures: in *La Ronde des heures* (30.80), the melancholy singer who has lost his voice and abandoned his family develops a second career as half of a clown duo which proves immensely successful. Since he is working under an assumed name and is always heavily made up his real identity is unknown, and he is invited to perform at the second marriage of his own wife. Fortunately, his voice returns and his daughter recognizes him, with easily imaginable consequences. His wife, of course, has never ceased to love him, deep down. Clowns were the most sentimentalized of thirties characters.

Although there were different stereotypes among the circus characters, the general air of suspicion that surrounded circus performers of all sorts can best be appreciated from the number of times that they are roped in as suspects in some criminal investigation (31.49; 36.38; 37.121), proving guilty if they are acrobats, innocent if clowns. When they appear, the owners of these circuses, like theater managers (32.130) and all representatives of authority, are treated badly in thirties films, and will also prove to be guilty of whatever crime has been committed (39.4; 39.69). Their main interest, at least until Grémillon's *Les Gens du voyage,* is in power, money, or the graceful body of one of their young female employees. They are thus often at the origin of the narrative conflict, inspiring jealous hatred or melancholy resignation.

As the decade progresses and the focus shifts from narratives about circus life to those in which circuses and fairgrounds appear episodically, locations tend toward the urban and connotations more emphatically toward the negative. The fairground is now set up in an urban wasteland and has acquired a distinctly sinister array of sideshows—shooting alleys, fortune-tellers, grotesque waxworks, and reenacted assassinations. It is a raucous, bustling place, always visited at night by people driven to desperate measures. It is also a working-class location, and the criminal element so often associated with the working class in thirties films is here seen at its seediest and most sinister: Jacques, the ne'er-do-well apache brother in *Dans les rues* (33.41), frequents such a sideshow alley with its fence dealing in stolen goods; the young couple's hopes of a happy marriage in *Jeunesse* (34.52) are mocked even as they are articulated by a penny-a-throw ball knocking over a bride and groom; and the eponymous hero of *Liliom* (34.55) is a fairground barker, allied in some suspect way both with the female boss and with criminals. This film systematically builds up a contrast between the humble but drab prospects of a respectable but impoverished marriage and the intense, risky, but glamorous pleasures associated with sexuality, criminality, and the fairground. It is always night in fairgrounds, so bustling crowds, looming shadows, shafts of light, and frightening physical monstrosities make of it a place to avoid or escape. It is from a stall in such a fairground that the respectable Dr Vautier picks up the waif who has been injured in a squabble and for whom he will develop such an ambivalent affection (33.26).

In a quite different genre, but serving the same purpose, the fairground in *Mayerling* (36.77) is the place where, masked and seeking some form of escape from his stifling, loveless bourgeois marriage, amid the bustling nocturnal crowds, Archduke Rudolph finds and rescues Marie Vetsera. At the end of the decade, *La Tradition de minuit* (39.88) contains an analogous scene and, in *Abus de confiance* (37.2), it is a place of confusion where moral norms do not hold; here, the female protagonist is almost seduced but manages to resist. It is notable that in this environment even the street singer's mythic appeal is undercut, since the romantic love of which he sings turns out to be a seductive but delusory trap. Such films serve to provide a useful context for the weird fairground in *Quai des brumes* (38.84), where both love and the revenge that will lead to the death of love come to the fore.

Normally, of course, the street singer was a romantic, even revered, figure in thirties cinema. From 1930 on, when *Sous les toits de Paris* (30.84) established him as the archetypal working-class wise guy (*débrouillard*), the street singer benefited from broadly positive representation (31.59; 32.110). His ability to sing is at once a talent with broad popular appeal and an external signifier of the vitality which characterizes the working class in such films. The focus of a circle of appreciative people who join in choruses and buy the sheet music at the end, street singers are also a signifier of "community." One of the most negative representations of circus life is *Chansons de Paris*, which relates the exploitation of a young street singer and his accompanist friend—the former has to pretend to lose his voice to escape from the circus (34.26).

More generally, singers were common in thirties films because musical comedy and operetta were among the most prolific of genres of the decade, and many of those focused on the rise of a protagonist whose singing talent distinguished him as someone out of the ordinary, a worthy protagonist and natural object of romantic love. Nearly all the early-thirties stars had initially been singers. At the very least, the ability to carry a tune was an essential career requirement. Jean Gabin, Fernandel, Tino Rossi, and Maurice Chevalier all came from the music hall, as did Arletty, Josephine Baker, Garat, André Beaugé, and Florelle, and all could and did play the role of a singer. The films of the decade are scattered with somber moments in which Mistinguett, Edith Piaf, Fréhel, Damia, or Yvette Guibert comment on the action via a cabaret song. To sing was to be a folk hero at the time (as it still is). But rather than being, as it is now, a signifier of youthfulness and trendiness, it spoke of profound emotional integrity and intuitive access to the fundamental truths of existence.

Some of these female singers, notably Josephine Baker and Florelle, are accorded affectionate roles in which they attract audience sympathy and identification. Florelle's songs in *Faubourg Montmartre* (31.55) and *Le Crime de Monsieur Lange* (35.27) are cases in point. For the most part, however, female singers are implicated in negative aspects of society, such as crime, sexual misdemeanors, and suicide. Fréhel, for instance, is most likely to turn up as a gangster's moll or a brothel manager (36.99; 38.60; 38.93), and the nightclubs in which she and her colleagues sing will always be the sleazy haunt of criminals and of drug peddlers.

Indeed, as a gross generalization, there is a gender divide in singers, dancers, and actors/actresses: narratives organized around males are of the romantic-comedy genre, relating their professional and sentimental successes, while those organized around females are more somber dramas, relating not only their own downfall but the implication of other, worthier people in that downfall. To some extent, this was due to the gendered differentiation within popular song itself: the earthier type of song (*chanson réaliste*) was a female genre, and its proponents are integrated into "realistic" narratives of a doom-laden nature. It was also partly due to the standard gender representations of the age. The cabaret singer operated within an urban nighttime environment in which alcohol, sexuality, and popular enthusiasm spoke of instinctual forces unleashed. Such sites readily allow the chanteuse to overlap with the femme fatale (32.133; 38.18). She is regularly involved in ephemeral sexual relationships (31.106; 32.118), often trails illegitimate children behind her (34.44; 36.22; 36.44), and is a natural suspect in adultery, or in any criminal investigation (30.2), because (like all popular figures) she associates with criminals and lives on the fringes of their illicit activity (30.4; 36.112). Often she herself commits crimes such as blackmail (30.33; 36.12) or incites others to commit them (35.57), and, if not herself involved in assassinations, quite commonly drives others to murder third parties or to suicide. Even the more benign ones are trapped and compromised by their involvement in this nocturnal world (35.34) and, treated badly by life, will be found singing of their despair and abjection in the more squalid dives of Saigon, Singapore, or Shanghai (31.124; 38.27).

Although the theatrical actress could also be implicated in the seedier aspects of the performance industry, such as drug peddling (32.130), there is a slight distinction to be made between her and the chanteuse. While both participate in that well-known disposition of the female performer to be women of easy virtue, the actress has none of the singer's tendency toward the sleazy, the squalid, and the criminal. She is often, rather, a frivolous, superficial figure, mobilized more often in comedies than in dramas as an appropriate "professional" with whom a central figure can have, or can be discovered to be having, an adulterous affair. She is the pretty young thing whom the bourgeois husband has set up in a flat. While this might seem an unpromising role, it has its serious side. The actress serves to puncture the hypocritical facade of respectability with which authority figures seek to surround themselves. In the course of the thirties, at least twenty films featured actresses serving this function with respect to such authority figures as a colonel (32.18), a press magnate (37.97), a count (34.102), a prince (34.83), and a politician (31.43). More generally, boxers, directors, producers—anyone admired or respected by the public—might find themselves distracted by the naive charms of an actress. A fiancé (31.80) or a disapproving father may find himself in danger of reproducing his profligate son's improprieties (31.104), or a provincial gentleman may squander his fortune on a Parisian actress (35.87). In thus deflating the pretentious and the self-righteous, the actress shares, if in an attenuated form, that fundamental characteristic of all artists, the rejection of the social and moral conventions of the day. Somewhat less often, the (successful) actress figure can be mobilized in boulevard comedies as a member of the establishment who herself needs to be deflated and brought down to earth (37.42). In *Désiré*, it is a man of the people, namely the butler, who does this, by way of mutually satisfying erotic fantasies (37.34). Such actresses, now mistresses of a house, partake of the dubious status of star, and are treated with the same distrust.

The great bulk of these narratives appear in the first half of the decade, in filmed versions of the boulevard comedies and vaudevilles that thrived in those years. While the same is true of the chanteuse, she was able to survive and flourish even in the more somber and bitter narratives of the second half of the decade. But it is the male popular singer who most commonly assumes the responsibility for representing the naively sentimental view of art and the artist. One means that many filmmakers of the day adopt to liberate him from the dubious connotations of the nocturnal urban popular culture which taints his female counterpart is to attribute to him rural origins, or to remove him for key segments of the story to the countryside.

This was almost essential in the case of Tino Rossi, whose Corsican origins were so apparent in his accent, and whose narratives are as a consequence often set in southern locations. In his first starring role, he plays a Corsican; though he is seduced away from that island by a femme fatale, he is ever nostalgic for it—the essential simplicity of the country lad never deserts him (36.11). The following year, again as a singer, he tries to realize his dream of peace and happiness by the sea, only to be betrayed yet again by the feckless ways of a femme fatale (37.80); while a year later, again a fashionable singer, he flees the sycophantic city crowd to find peace in the countryside, this time discovering true love with a country girl whom he courts incognito (38.58).

In his thirties films, Trénet followed the same pattern. In his first film, he returns to the country chateau, now being run by his uncle as a boarding school for girls, and saves both uncle and institution with his songs (38.52). In the next, he again heads off into the country in search of the chateau he has dreamed of; when he finds it, it is (unsurprisingly) inhabited by an attractive young woman, whom he is able to marry on the basis of his singing successes (38.92). In short, a principal strategy for distinguishing the male singer as a romantic hero is to integrate him into the Paris/provinces and city/countryside oppositions which operate widely throughout the decade. Female singers were not allowed this privilege. Toward the end of the decade, however, three films present young female singers as deserving cases, but only on condition that they come to appreciate the strength, devotion, and support of the male who saves them from suicide, launches them on a career, and frees them from their shady associates (39.8; 39.50; 39.96).

In general, male singers favored by the decade's films participate in the same set of values, attributes, and narrative conventions as the dozens of classical singers and musicians who appear in the repertoire and, indeed, as any high-culture artist, writer, or actor. These derive from and, in turn, constitute the romantic myth of art and the artist as it has existed since the beginning of the nineteenth century. An essential element is the glorification of the artist as inhabited by an exceptional gift, which he has not had to acquire but with which he has been invested by fate. "Practice," "work," and "technique" are alien to this myth, let alone "training," which would call into question the originality of the output. His innate talent (or hers, though it usually is a male) leads the artist to create a quite distinctive and original output, which bursts on the astonished world with the force of revelation; though in the classical as opposed to the popular variant, it is often so remote from current conventions that it is not recognized, and years of unremitting struggle are necessary before the artist (of whatever persuasion) accedes to his rightful place in the pantheon.

Two fundamental cleavages divide the conceptual world of the artist: that between money and art, and that between convention and art. The two are, of course, related. Convention implies rules, regulations, the known, and the routine; the romantic myth of the artist sees art as unconstrained, limitlessly inventive, reaching out into the unknown. It has no pragmatic function, no "use," but is timeless in its forms, its values, and even its discoveries. Its most despised antagonist is the commercially minded bourgeois who cannot see beyond the possible monetary value of its products, or even worse, wishes to constrain it by dint of commissioning works, and thus determining by financial means the direction and form the work is to take.

These values and attitudes are usually incorporated into one of a very few standard narrative forms, of which the most common is "the artist's life." A series of possible tropes in this narrative involve humble beginnings, realization of a vocation, struggle against reaction and lack of understanding, a moment of revelation in which inexplicable talents are manifested, deception by women or patrons, rivalry and scorn from the established cliques, the rise to mastery, and final (often only posthumous) recognition: a new way of seeing and understanding the world has been imposed on a blinkered public. Within the context of a performance art, some of these narrative tropes can be incorporated into an account of "the mounting of a production," with its struggle to fund the production, betrayals and desertions by insufficiently motivated cast members, illnesses, and ultimate success, often achieved in the face of sentimental loss—but then, "the show must go on." An intersection between this and the previous narrative may be provided by the star falling ill on opening night and the understudy, or an unknown, being called on at the last minute. The understudy is, of course, a revelation, and a new star is born.

Since there are fewer instances of the latter narrative, it is easier to illustrate it with some degree of comprehensiveness. One of the very earliest sound movies embodies some of these narrative moves. *La Route est belle* (29.5) presents a struggling singer who rises to success when he is called on to replace the famous tenor at the last minute. *Paris Béguin* (31.97) uses as one of its narrative lines the stock relationship between bloated producer and actress, along with the rehearsals and (partial) performance of the show in which they are involved. Already it is clear in this film that one of the themes to be treated most affectionately by this genre will be the intricate interplay between life and art. The star reworks her role to fit her experience of the night before and, in so doing, foreshadows the tragic end; her man dies in her arms on the night of her triumph, but she still sings her heart out up there on stage, smiling through her tears. The show must go on. The role of art is at once to deny the importance of life and to capture the essence of life, transmuting it into something more meaningful, transcendental, eternal.

These themes, treated lightheartedly in the early years of the decade (e.g., 31.77), will be taken more and more seriously as the decade wears on. Among surviving films, those that deal with the mounting of a performance include *La Crise est finie* (34.31) (a provincial tour, with stand-in, rehearsals, egotistic star, the setting up of a rival company, finding a theater, financial problems, lecherous producers, more rehearsals, the opening night, and the consecration of a new star); *Zouzou* (34.115) (the musical to be staged, the petulance of the white star contrasted with the natural talent of the black laundress, the rehearsal, the star walks out, the laundress sings, "Who is that girl?" says the producer, and despite losing her man, she goes on to sing her heart out, grief transmuted into art); *Rigolboche* (36.112) (Mistinguett, on the run, tries out for a basement cabaret, is a great success, is taken up by the aristocracy, buys a theater to put on her own show, rehearsals, performance); and *Marinella* (36.75) (rehearsal, star sick, Tino Rossi is discovered and stands in for the star, all in the first ten minutes).

The shows themselves, insofar as audiences are privileged to witness them, are less than overwhelming. In particular, the choreography is disastrous—almost self-consciously so at times. On the other hand, the singing is often extremely moving, and toward the end of the decade a number of Negro musicians and singers join Josephine Baker to assert the supposedly intuitive feeling that blacks have for rhythm and melody (35.43). Princess Tam-Tam, unduly constrained by white middle-class society, seeks solace first among the working class ("real people, who know how to enjoy themselves"), then in a bar where a Negro jazz band is playing and a black singer is reminiscing nostalgically about the delights of his tropical home (35.92). Every nightclub seems to have its resident Negro saxophonist or pianist, its Negress singer (37.6; 38.16; 38.27; 38.63; 39.71). Their negritude accorded with the natural "untrained" intuitive values promoted by the myth, which prizes spontaneity and improvisation, and benefited from the positive connotations of the rural. The most convincing association between negritude and music is, however, the earliest—the Negro chanting, singing, and accompaniment to *La Petite Lise* (30.66), as is the most grotesque—the Negro tenor taken as a lover, sight unseen, by the petulant wife (30.13). Musically, the opening scenes of *La Petite Lise* are among the great moments of thirties film.

But it is not only black performers who participate in this myth. A number of films were made in which a band of aspiring musicians gets together, finds an appropriate performance site, and puts on a show (38.36); a talented singer is found (35.17); and crapulous producers, with reprehensibly mercenary motives, are thwarted (38.6). The "big band" itself, however, as the focus of a popular cult was not as significant an element in thirties films as it was to be in postwar films. Even Ray Ventura and his band, which provided the backing for nine films in the course of the decade (nearly always playing scores composed by Misraki), seldom featured in the diegesis. They do so only three times (36.130; 38.36; 39.87), twice constituting the focus of the narrative action. Of these films, *Tourbillon de Paris* provides a clear indication of the way this and other bands will feature in the following decade. A band is formed by a group of collegians, which immediately associates swing with the young and the trendy—indeed, there is an overt opposition between the swinging young and the conservatism of classical music, as represented by an older and uptight classical composer who marches his party out of the restaurant as an expression of disgust when the youngsters starts playing. Both the collegians and the audience subsequently ridicule the classical composer's pretentious opera, and the collegians begin an alternative performance in the stalls. The story is a classic one of a fight against the disapproval of established authorities, which, unsurprisingly, leads to popular success and an idyllic finale. The fact that both films in which the formation of a big band is central were made late in the decade, and that in general Ventura's appearances were clustered in the years 1936–39, identifies the point of origin of the swing/jazz cult that was to come to the fore between 1945 and 1955.

In general, the more popular cultural forms of whatever sort evoke and recycle the romantic myth of the artist only in an attenuated form. Its most forceful representation is to be found in biographical narratives relating "the life of the artist"—specifically, the lives of certain well-known artists. For the reasons noted above, these were almost entirely great musicians—indeed, great composer/performers. The thirties saw dramatized portraits of Pergolesi (32.8), Chopin (34.25), Beethoven (36.135), Charpentier (39.49), Schubert (39.82), and Strauss—the last both early and late in the decade (33.63; 39s1), and again in mid-decade in less explicit form (36.141). The combination of a popular figure whose waltzes evoked the elegance and the aristocracy of the Austro-Hungarian Empire was irresistible. Alongside these musicians, only Bartholdi, the sculptor of the Statue of Liberty, represents the other high arts (37.65).

Parallel to these biographical films of "real" artists, innumerable fictional analogues drawn from the whole range of high art forms embody elements of the same myth. Humble beginnings, poverty, and an early life of struggle and disappointment are crucial to this narrative. Typical of these is *Rigolboche* (36.112), in which Mistinguett plays a singer suspected of murder, pursued by the police, holing up in a poverty-stricken quarter of Paris, yearning for the son who doesn't know that she is his mother; and *Le Grand Refrain* (36.49), in which a talented composer begins in poverty and descends to total indigence, faced with the public's inability to appreciate the originality of his compositions. It went without saying that great art was incompatible with easy popular success, and especially with commercial rewards. The cleavage between great and false art, elitist and popular forms, indigence and profitability is represented as profound. Thus, alliances between artists and wealthy families are doomed, at least until the artist has suffered in some sufficiently abominable way in order to hone his sensitivities. Setting the tone for the decade, the bourgeois father of *La Ronde des heures* (30.80) disapproves totally of his talented singer son-in-law and wants to dispose of him so he can marry his daughter off again to an advantageously endowed friend. He therefore rejoices at the tenor's double pneumonia, loss of voice, and subsequent disappearance (he becomes a clown) and tries to talk his daughter into a divorce. When his daughter recognizes her husband's singing voice, he is invited to perform his clown act in the family home; he almost collapses, but rallies ("the show must go on"). The unmasking of a singer's identity by way of a casually overheard song was so standard as to become a cliché in this first decade of the talkie (31.77; 34.92; in a sense, 38.27), providing a fitting form of recognition to round off an artist's life.

A classic instance of the opposition between art and money occurs in *Chotard et Cie,* in which the poetic young actor is treated by his industrialist father-in-law as a hopelessly impractical ne'er-do-well until he receives the Prix Goncourt, and the official sanction which that prize connotes causes the father-in-law radically to review his preconceptions. But the artist is not to be won over so easily: a typically poetic disregard for money and "work" has the poet "playing" at his job of shop assistant and giving away the stock to passing kids (32.34). An even more feckless disregard for money gets a singer into trouble with the teaching profession because he refuses to charge the going rate for the lessons he gives. When he learns that his opera has been accepted for performance not on its merits but because it has been subsidized by a wealthy patron, he is in despair, as any true artist would be (32.16). The omnipresent distrust of producers and bankers in films featuring artists is thus merely an extreme manifestation of one of the recurrent characteristics both of the artist and of the thirties (and not only of the thirties, of course).

Although poverty and a life of material hardship are essential to this spiritual profession, other forms of suffering turn out to be equally effective in tempering the artistic talent. Beethoven's deafness provides an archetypal form of suffering and deprivation (36.135) but muteness or blindness would do just as well (31.71). Sentimental reverses compound Beethoven's suffering, and the malific role of women in the life of the artist cannot be overestimated. In the extreme, the artist is doomed to be misunderstood throughout his life, since fate reserves for him only posthumous fame. Several films play this out, notably Gance's Beethoven film, while others satirize it mildly by having the artist or his supporters feign his death/suicide (32.113; 36.49; 36.85). Only thus can he witness his own consecration as an artist.

More commonly, the artist is allowed to transcend his or her suffering in one way or another, transmuting it into great art. Usually, this involves some form of heroic sacrifice, on the part either of the artists or of the lovers who release them to their destiny. Constantia must sacrifice her own desires for Chopin's sake (34.25); both Juliette and Thérèse, in their different ways, are expected to sacrifice their existence to that of Beethoven (36.135), while Beethoven himself is characterized as a martyrized Christ; Zouzou, now a successful singer, must sacrifice her own desires for her "brother's" sake (34.115); the tenor who loses his voice and cannot support his family in the manner to which they have become accustomed must step aside and let them return to his wife's aristocratic and disapproving family (30.80); Pierre, the painter in *Paradis perdu,* must renounce his last chance at happiness for his daughter's sake (39.69); a female artist must renounce romantic happiness and reconcile herself to her loveless life by devoting herself to her art (38.11). Renunciation and tragedy systematically hound the aspiring artist—his daughter is drowned, he must renounce the pupil he is learning to love, he loses his voice, his sanity, and finally his life (32.152).

These psychodramas of renunciation are all the more melodramatic in that artists are represented as feeling everything so much more deeply than other men and women: their aesthetic sensitivities expose them to a crueler destiny. But they are half in love with death already, since it is taken for granted that their aspiration is toward the eternal. Cumulatively, this sensitivity and spirituality render them more worthy than others, and in the standard situation in which a woman is faced with a choice between an artist and a non-artist there can be little doubt where her favor will fall. She will, of course, prefer an artist to a banker (31.115), but, more impressively, she will prefer him to a sportsman (32.144). She will even prefer an artist to an officer and a prince (35.66) because, basically, the prince, like the sportsman and the banker, can offer only worldly position, material not spiritual sustenance, the physical and the transitory rather than the eternal. Indeed, the artist wins on all counts, since he or she is more passionate, more romantic. When women elope in thirties movies, it is with an artist. Pergolesi abducts Maria; Lixie, about to marry the director of the Opera, comes to her senses (or perhaps loses them) and elopes with her tenor lover (33.129); Louise defies her family to elope with a composer (though when her father falls ill, she sacrifices her happiness at least temporarily in the name of duty) (39.49). A similar opposition is in play in *Liebelei* (33.76), when Fritz sees through the artificiality of court life and abandons the baroness as soon as he meets Christine, whose father is conductor of the orchestra in which she plays the cello, and who therefore will be represented as bringing warmth, humanity, and a simple sincerity into his stale and superficial life.

The stereotype which emerges from the life and character of the artist has at its core the notion of a disorderly and unconventional life which makes the artist the archetypal marginal figure in polite society, living in a different world from other people. It renders him yet another typical perpetrator of a crime of passion (38.100)—or at least a likely suspect (33.149). It is also so widely and immediately recognizable that it is called upon with great regularity in light comedies of the boulevard and sentimental genres. Although the artist figure does not always come off so well in these genres, it would not be accurate to see them as satirizing that figure; rather, they are simply mobilizing it as a well-known element of the available repertoire. Nevertheless, it is true that they do not treat the artist as respectfully as do the more dramatic productions. A particularly common tendency in boulevard comedies is for artist figures to feature in situations of multiple or confused identity. They are chameleon figures who may turn out to be the Prince of Rumelia (33.69), an engineer, or an inventor (33.24), and they often circulate disguised or masked. The "unknown singer" was a stock figure: a musician might disguise himself as a student to re-enroll at the Con on a bet (38.1), or as a servant to test the sincerity of the woman he loves (34.67), or as a ghost to frighten heirs from a chateau (34.72), or even as a woman to enroll in a female orchestra (35.45). A singer might be mistaken for a banker, or for the Count of Mareno, or, in a much-loved story, for an empress, with tragic consequences (35.117; 32.151; 38.9). A crucial element of their identity is, therefore, to have a somewhat slippery identity— exuberant, passionate, volatile, marginal, ineffable. In films of the thirties, the artist is one of the forms adopted by the trickster figure.

6.2 FORMS OF REFLEXIVITY

The true apotheosis of this chameleon artist comes on those occasions when he (or, much less commonly, she) participates in theatrical dramas in which "acting" is a central preoccupation. Then it becomes apparent that the artist's great virtue is to understand all roles, all identities, all the various local manifestations of reality, because he draws his knowledge from sources outside time and space. Probably the most telling expression of this set of views can be found in Jouvet's speech in *Entrée des artistes* (38.51), but a number of scriptwriters and playwrights for whom the actor was God worked it into script after script—writers as diverse as Jeanson, Mirande, and, of course Guitry, but also in later years, Renoir, not to mention Prévert in *Les Enfants du paradis*. Few will forget the (over)emphatic and quasi-mystical expression of this point of view in Jouvet's master-class in *Entrée des artistes,* but those who have read his unspeakable treatise on the theater will be grateful that Jouvet himself was not scripting the film.

Insofar as it glorifies the young actor's moment of initiation into the realm of the sacred, *Entrée des artistes* is, however, only one of a number of thirties films which had focuses on the initiation of the young into theatrical life, and their gradual realization of the privilege and obligations that it bestows on them. *Coquecigrole* (31.39) seems to have been one of the first of these in the sound-film period, and all narratives involving "staging a performance" contained elements of it; yet there is no doubt that it reached full (im)maturity in 1938 and 1939. Guitry, always inclined toward self-glorification, promotes himself as puppet-master in *Remontons les Champs-Élysées* (38.87), manipulating the children in the audience as he manipulates his puppets; and the travelling players of *Cavalcade d'amour* (39.11) are mythologized as the lowest yet, paradoxically, the highest of citizens, the real aristocracy, the true royalty, alone capable of inspiring authentic love. *La Fin du jour* is another well-known film organized around this theme, though focusing on aging actors rather than young initiates (38.37).

In these and many other films, the principal message concerns the magical transformation that reality undergoes as it is elevated into dramatic action. Endless use is made of the interpenetration of life and theater, life and art. The one imitates yet embroiders on, varies, and transposes the other in constant interaction. The cliché "la vie, quel théâtre" takes on renewed meaning when murmured in *La Fin du jour.* At times, "reality" is represented as of little consequence except insofar as it can provide suitable material for dramatization, and the actors live fully only when on stage. Their fantasy life is more important to them than the raw material from which their imagination fashions it, since it involves that purposeful reorganization of reality which provides them with their identity and self-understanding, and which makes life worth living.

When one of Jouvet's students claims to have no confidence in herself, Jouvet retorts, "What does it matter, as long as you have confidence in the character you are acting . . . what matters is to put a little art in one's life, and life in one's art . . . nothing is false, what matters is to have faith . . . don't forget, it's only when the curtain rises that life begins . . . what matters is to have believed in one's role." Inevitably, the students find that their private lives are being taken over by their stage roles—that, indeed, their lives are no more than a series of roles, and that nothing any longer comes naturally, even the words of love, which sound to them now (as indeed to us) like a hackneyed script. In the limit, Cecilia's dying is no more than a well-acted role, which gets its due recognition in a round of applause.

Bernstein's play *Le Bonheur,* as filmed by Marcel L'Herbier (35.12), provides a particularly well-orchestrated presentation of such interactions be-

tween life and art: the early scenes, in which the star arrives by train, performs her sentimental song, and is shot by the anarchist, are reproduced as
part of a transposed drama which is rehearsed and reenacted by the star to
capitalize on popular accounts of the incident. The other "reenactment" of
the initial events in the trial scene is equally packed with such ironies, as the
star performs a convincing number to get the anarchist released, then performs it again in a more sincere version; and the anarchist's final departure
likewise involves accusations that her imploring him not to leave is a particularly effective scene, which might come after the station scene in her film.
Finally, he leaves the "real" star to better enjoy her recorded performances,
which will be all the convincing for her having known him. The film cuts
from her saying "Chéri" in their final farewell to her performing that same
farewell on screen, saying "Chéri" while he watches from the stalls.

The cinema of the thirties, newly conscious of recorded sound, was particularly fond of these ironic contrasts between the "real" and the "recorded." René Clair's script for *Prix de beauté* (30.69) ends with the beauty-
queen-become-star being murdered by her embittered husband during the
projection of the rushes of her film. Even as she gaily sings her song about
not being jealous up on the screen, her jealous husband is sidling in with his
revolver to shoot her, and as she collapses and dies in her seat her recorded
image sings naively on, the flickering of the projector illuminating oddly
the fatal tableau. At the end of *Trois Valses* (38.107), a similar situation is en-
gineered: the couple who are in love are required to act out a love scene, and
she (an established star) balks at "pretending" to love an actor who is, in her
view, merely an incompetent amateur. As in *Prix de beauté,* they are left
thoroughly immersed in a lovers' quarrel, while above them on a giant
screen her recorded image sings a sentimental song.

The more normal interplay of life and art had been a part of the cinematic repertoire since talkies began, if one is to judge by Vanel's role(s) in *La
Maison jaune de Rio* (30s10): a bandit aims to abduct the beautiful Anita;
by a happy coincidence he resembles her lover, who is an actor and about to
enact the bandit's life on stage. The bandit replaces him on stage, playing
himself. Vanel, of course, played both roles. Subsequently, actors delight in
simulating low-life situations to con the jaded aristocracy out for a thrill
(30.63); acted scenes are mistaken for real assassinations by passers-by
(38.63); or plays or operettas are mounted which directly or indirectly parallel the lives of the composer/director/actors (31.74; 35.72; 31.97). At the
beginning of *Le Mort en fuite* (36.85), the scene played out between Jules
Berry and Michel Simon turns out retrospectively to have been merely a
scene from a play in which they were acting. More commonly, the theme is
treated as if it were of the utmost importance. In the life of Beethoven, for
example, life is seen as the true source of inspiration for art, and art in its
turn is seen as the truest source of consolation for life's ills. Thus Beethoven

passes in the street a mother bewailing her dead daughter and goes home to compose the *Pathétique*. (He plays it to the mother, who is strangely reconciled.) When he goes deaf and a sympathetic Nature whips up a storm, we find him wildly composing the scherzo of the *Pastoral Symphony* and conducting the storm; when Juliette sacrifices her happiness and abandons Beethoven, he promptly sits down and composes the *Appassionata;* in the middle of her wedding to his rival, he suddenly blasts out the *Funeral March* on the church organ. Everything he composes is represented as a direct emotional response to his environment. The possibility that artistic creativity might be independent of any emotion directly generated by personal experience is the subject of frequent mockery (e.g., 35.98).

One of the principal thematic uses to which this affective interaction between life and theater was put was to debate the nature of sincerity—a theme which has been noted as being generated both by situations involving wealth and status and by situations involving lady-killers. In all such narratives, the central question is one of acting, yet acting can come to seem omnipresent. If role-playing is so central to everyone's life, could one ever be "sincere"? If one were sincere, how would that sincerity be distinguishable from a convincing act? This was a particularly contentious theme in the case of interpersonal relationships which had been represented over and over again in novels, plays, and films, such that the role of lover could easily seem pre-scripted to an unacceptable extent. Every word that might be uttered had already been used and reused to the point of exhaustion. The conventions of the sentimental drama had "infected" and "corrupted" real relationships, rendering suspect the passionate declarations of every lover. This situation acquires an added spice when it is represented in a fictional narrative, since the problem for the text is no longer simply to distinguish between acting and sincerity, but between actors *acting* acting, and actors *acting* sincerity.

These possibilities are to some extent explored in a scene in *Entrée des artistes,* but the more general question of the sincerity of a lover's declarations had long been explored through the lady-killer. The classic example of this figure in French cinema is Gérard Philipe's 1950s role in *Les Grandes Manœuvres,* but it had a long history in sound cinema. As early as 1931, a film had shown a variant of it, in the form of a woman who uses a dog trained to hop into expensive cars so that she can get acquainted with promising men. Unfortunately, she falls for one, who discovers her ploy and therefore doubts the sincerity of her affection (31.135). In another genre in the same year, an undercover policeman falls for a good-time girl and declares his love, but how can she ever believe him when she finds out about his deception (31.34)? More generally, once anyone's calculated routines for securing a romantic relationship have become known, how is the object of affection going to be able to distinguish whether the ploys are being used sincerely this time round? Ophüls's *Liebelei* (33.76) established the more common gender alignments for this situation, with a philandering young officer compromised in an affair with a baroness but experiencing true love for the first time with a young girl. Inevitably, he is apprehensive as to whether she will believe him if she learns that she is not the first. As in *Les Grandes Manœuvres*, the officer is taught a painful lesson: one must pay for emptying the words of love of meaning—in this case by his own and the girl's death. *The Merry Widow*, of which a French version was made, acts out a similar situation, but in a lighter genre, so with a happier outcome (34.111).

It is at least partly because she is an actress that the anarchist of *Le Bonheur* doubts the reality of the star's affection for him. Is she capable of feeling *anything* sincerely, or is everything merely an opportunity for a scene in which the "lover" is an audience to be won over? A more classic instance has Jules Berry seducing a girl on a mate's behalf, only to fall for her sincerely (36.13). She is, of course, outraged when she (inevitably) discovers the fraud and refuses to believe that despite his initial calculation he is now being sincere. Similarly, a cabaret dancer, paid to pretend a sudden passion, falls "sincerely" in love with her victim (37.23). And, as the title indicates, Gance's *Voleur de femmes* recycles this mythic situation in its entirety: Berry is again the seducer, but now of long standing, and he has become cynical. He falls sincerely for a young girl who learns of his past conquests and proceeds to marry another. Because this is a psychodrama, he must pay for his cynicism concerning love's conventions and routines (37.123).

The mix of cynicism and reflexivity concerning the "act" of courting took a number of forms toward the end of the decade. In *Le Dernier Tournant* (39.23), after so many murders and attempted murders disguised as accidents, Frank has accidentally killed Cora. His last soliloquy focuses on an imaginary reconciliation with Cora in the afterlife—"I'll take her in my arms and say it was an accident, and she'll believe me." This agony of the sincere assertion that is incredible precisely because it has been falsely asserted so often before is reversed in the melodrama *Le Mensonge de Nina Petrovna* (37.71), in which the problem is, rather, that the lover believes Nina's noble lies to the effect that she doesn't love him—he is just another of the many men she has strung along, including his commandant—but again, though the situation is reversed, the essence of the plot is the repetition of words, phrases, and situations which, previously acted out routinely and coldly, are suddenly meant sincerely. Nina, however, must twice deny her own sincerity, with fatal effects.

Le Mensonge takes place in a military setting, like *Liebelei*, *Gueule d'amour* (37.57), and later *Les Grandes Manœuvres*, since the uniformed ladykiller was a specialist in glamorous insincerity. In a sense, moving this theme to a group of aspiring actors in a realistic setting is a big jump for *Entrée des artistes* to make, but aside from foregrounding the theme of pretense, this film links with tradition in allocating one of the students (François) a part-time job with an escort agency, where his professional obligation to squire young women recapitulates (again in a more formally foregrounded manner) the role of lady-killer. François has, in fact, written to the girl whom we see him squiring a number of letters in which he has professed (insincerely) precisely the sentiments he is now professing sincerely to Isabelle, in precisely the same words. Isabelle, of course, learns of this—such plots always require that the woman should—and reiterates the old complaint—"That's what you say to all of them."

But while *Entrée des artistes* could be seen to that point to be engaging in the normal form of reflexivity expected of this theme of acting, it takes this reflexivity one step further by having the acting out of love scenes discussed in explicit relation to the cinema: François and Isabelle discuss how, in the cinema, the fact that they have just made love would be shown . . . thus; and, in the process, they both recapitulate the cinematic conventions and vary them, while in the epilogue, as they exit through the stage door, the students muse on the fact that their experiences could become the subject of a play . . . or even a film.

Apart from such pejorative uses of the notion of "acting," it is very rare for a thirties film to propose any sort of critique of art and the artist. Very occasionally, a film might gently mock the arrivisme and snobbism of artistic society (30.76), or an artist's success (achieved by pretending death), as he witnesses the statue which is being erected to his glory being peed on by a passing dog (32.113), but the great bulk of reflexive references are affectionate. Only twice in nearly three hundred films have I identified artists who are rejected as boring or inadequate, manifesting no more than a superficial glamour and romance (33.70; 36.121). If any form of art is mocked overtly, it is perhaps grand opera, seen as pompous in *Le Million* (31.84) where the grotesque declarations of the stage tenor are reproduced with sincerity and simplicity behind the décor by Michel and Béatrice— but Michel is, of course, himself an artist, as are most of the other main characters in the film, who are affectionately represented. In two films, novelists are seen as unworldly, needing to descend from their ivory tower to make contact with "real life," but then, the first of these is not only a novelist but a woman (32.127), and as we have seen thirties films did not take novelists as seriously as other artists, even when they were male. The other is *La Rosière des Halles* (35.98), in which the academic playwright who cannot compose a credible love scene has to be coached by his cook and her friends from the fruit-and-vegetable market. Even as he's being beaten up on suspicion of trifling with the cook's affections, he's delightedly making notes on the language and gestures of his assailants, and he subsequently mobilizes his newly acquired knowledge to see off his wife's lover. His "rehearsals" of his love scene offer further opportunity for playful confusion between life and art. And then, of course, there is *Drôle de drame* (37.37), which offers the public a serious writer who has become famous under a pseudonym, but has managed to achieve this status only by calling on the services of the milkman. Of all artists, it is only writers who suffer these inadequacies, and like the inadequacies of the middle class, whom they so resemble in this, they can only be made good by recourse to the innate creativity of the working class.

With these few exceptions, then, it is true to say that the great bulk of material involving art and artists that circulated in the French cinema of the thirties was intensely favorable, and constituted a form of self-glorification by the filmmaking community. This reflexivity, in which that community reflected on its own status and values, might have been expected to find its most explicit formulation in films made about filmmakers and filmmaking. This is for the most part not so. Some thirty films, apart from the asides in *Entrée des artistes,* deal with or comment directly on the cinema, but of these a significant majority are primarily preoccupied with the notion of "the star." The figure of the star as constructed/mobilized/recycled by these films is quite complex and not particularly attractive. Almost invariably female, the star is at once distant and familiar, desirable yet unlikable, often selfish, arrogant, and ruthless, yet an object of fascination. Basically, the star suffers from being seen as a figure of established power, and like all such figures is subject to mistrust and liable to subversion. Yet at the same time, for a population constantly prey to material anxieties and insufficiencies, the fantasy world of the screen was a form of fantasized escape, and the figures who embodied those fantasies attracted identification. So pretending to be a film star will guarantee any woman the admiration of the male she seeks to attract (38.109). In addition, on a pragmatic level, access to the glamorous world of the star, whether via screen tests, beauty pageants, or chance, could seem to solve all the financial problems that were at the origin of those material anxieties. Film magazines and daily papers constantly recycled anecdotes, biographies, and advice on how to become a star.

For the filmmakers themselves, however, and particularly for scriptwriters, the success of whose efforts were often dependent on a star's whims and talents, the star was, to say the least, a figure of ambivalent power. In films of the thirties, then, stars can be malicious and vengeful (31.44), temperamental and fractious (35.36), or flighty and selfish (39.77); in the latter film, she leaves her politician husband for another as he tries to negotiate peace for Europe. Their remoteness and indifference is tellingly evoked by the story of a young man who spends his days yearning over a star who lives in his neighborhood, spying on her through a telescope (36.94). Young women, once they have been tempted by the glamour of stardom, forget those who once meant a great deal to them, even if, as in Duvivier's

L'Homme du jour (36.55), they make initial attempts to show gratitude. They are thus worse than the stereotypical actress, and more malevolent than the dancer/singer. Not surprisingly, many other characters have good reason to hate them, so they constitute yet another potential murder victim in crime stories (32.143; 36.19).

Even in the early thirties, when escapist comedies abound, there are very few films in which the desire to become a star, made good by chance or by talent, proves to solve all problems. Three films have the rise to stardom leading to the resolution of a sentimental relationship (32.101; 35.63; 38.59), but two propose precisely the contrary—that the temptation to become a star is less important than personal relationships, and should be resisted (32.42) or is likely to lead to tragedy, so should be renounced (31.82). Perhaps the only film in the decade to successfully embody the myth of the star as romantic heroine and as worthy love object is *Trois Valses* (38.107). This episodic film covers three generations of actresses. In the first episode, a theatrical star is allied with a count, who stands up for her beauty and spirit in the face of family disapproval: beset by aristocratic pretensions and conventions, his family are, in his words, "prehistoric monsters"; but learning that the alliance might mean his being cashiered from the army, "which would kill him," the actress renounces happiness for his sake. In the second episode, her daughter, a star of operetta, meets the count's son, and again the potentially blessed union is undermined by anxiety about the proprieties—he finds her clothing indecent and tries to get her to abandon the theater. Instead, she abandons him, and he realizes "his place is not here" in the theater. The third episode brings together the granddaughter, this time a film star engaged to play the role of her grandmother in a filmed biography, with the grandson of the aristocratic family, now no longer an aristocrat. Her impresario acts as deus ex machina to get the young man the role of his grandfather in this drama, with inevitable romantic consequences. The cinema and the twentieth century are seen as more democratic environments, in which a love that has been thwarted for generations by class differences can at last be realized. In an epilogue, we find that she has bought his family home, complete with portraits of their predecessors, as a wedding present for him.

Although consecrating the notion of film star as modern goddess and identifying cinematic sentiments as the counterpart of real relationships, the film is gently satirical of the cinematic world, mocking affectionately the personnel, procedures, and mechanisms of the cinema as an institution. This attitude of self-mockery, usually stopping well short of real criticism, let alone satire, is a characteristic of most of the films in which the cinema as an institution, as opposed to simply the figure of the star, is represented. In Fernandel films, there is often a moment in which some sardonic in-joke is inserted, based on but also tending to refute negative stereotypes of the cinema. In *Le Rosier de Madame Husson* (31.118), the uptight matron seeking to promote chastity and propriety considers the cinema the hotbed of licentious behavior (not least because her long-suffering husband has finally left her for an attractive young film actress). At the end of the decade, drugged and waking up in an American jail, Fernandel is convinced by a guard who tells him that it is all part of a Hollywood movie of which he is the hero; his big scene, the electrocution, is next to be filmed. Fernandel becomes suspicious only because he finds the jail "sets" (notionally a real jail) unconvincing (39.16).

Such amiable reflexivities are given a little more satirical point in *Le Schpountz*, which is one of three films from the decade in which a gullible dupe ("schpountz") ends up acting in a film of which he believes he is the hero, only to be mocked by the filmmakers for his naivete and incompetence. In all three, the film in which the dupe acts turns out, to everyone's surprise, to be a great success (31.16; 37.104; 38.6). *Le Schpountz* is, in fact, Pagnol's attack on that other cinema of the early thirties, the American international multiple-version cinema, so is not as reflexive as it might seem. There are constant in-jokes relating to Paramount and its continental operations, summed up in the notorious phrase "He's a German or a Turk, he's learned Russian, which he speaks with an Italian accent; that's enough to qualify him as a great French director."

At the basis of all negative stereotypes of filmmakers voiced in this decade is an insistence on the heartless, merciless ruthlessness which they manifest as they use and exploit the naive and powerless. There is a constant nastiness about the filmmakers in *Le Schpountz,* only partially justified by the ridiculous pretensions of Fernandel's aspiring star. This nastiness is over-determined by being grafted onto the standard opposition between the provinces and the city, and notably between the expansive, warm-hearted Midi and the slick, knowing cynicism of Paris. So while the finale has Fernandel returning to his provincial town with all the appurtenances of a star, the thematics of the film as a whole undermine the myth of the film star and of the cinema itself. Yet at certain key moments, Pagnol inserts scenes which recapitulate the myth of the actor and the creative virtues of the director. Thinking he is acting a tragic role, the schpountz is distraught at everyone's laughter—the performance has, in fact, turned into a comic success, and his girl consoles him by reminding him that they are laughing not at the man but at the actor. He is thus in a position of superiority—indeed, the comic actor is the cure for the world's ills, a source of enjoyment, hope, and humanity in a difficult world. But the most painfully self-serving moment occurs when the entrepreneurial producer (à la Pagnol) takes his colleagues to task for mocking the schpountz, thus distancing the true French cinema (which is righteous, noble, and creative) from the American import (which is petty, malicious, and exploitative).

It is probable that a similar opposition between crass commercial film-making and creative artistic filmmaking was central to *Marchand d'amour* (35.72), a film which does not seem to have survived but in which the director of a series of wildly successful films that verge on the pornographic aspires to make one genuine, sincere film, based on his personal experiences, beliefs, and opinions. Needless to say, as the romantic myth requires, this auteurist autobiographical film is totally unappreciated by the movie-going public. Fortunately, the love of a good woman saves him from the slough of despond into which this blow to his professional self-esteem has cast him.

A more modern form of reflexivity turns up, a little surprisingly, in *Abus de confiance* (37.2) when the needy young girl has just succeeded in passing herself off as the (actually dead) daughter of a famous and wealthy writer. As she leaves and walks off through the night, her anguished state of mind is exteriorized in a distinctly Godardian manner in cinema billboards and posters that she passes, including one that proclaims the nature of her action and the film's title, "Abus de confiance." More conventionally, the next scene is set in a fairground, where the chaos of seething crowds, flashing lights, and half-naked women comments on her anguish in a way more traditional to the realistic/expressionistic tradition. This leads to a squalid attempted seduction in a sleazy hotel and a subjective montage of images from the past, accompanied by wild music. Altogether it must be considered one of the more aggressively Brechtian moments in thirties French cinema. Like *Le Crime de Monsieur Lange, Abus de confiance* engages in other Brechtian foregroundings of production, notably a violent series of punctuations resembling the tearing and burning away of one image as it is replaced by the next. Lange is particularly rich in such "virtuoso" effects, as are a surprising number of films from a period when pressures toward realism are generally considered to have hampered the poetical effects so beloved of artist filmmakers of the twenties. Such virtuosity might take the form of extravagant camera movements, rapid montage and superimposition effects, zip-pans, direct address to the camera, extreme camera angles, tilted frames, and aggressive focus changes. These have to some extent been catalogued in chapter 7 of *The Classic French Cinema*.[1] Their main formal justification was as expressive effects externalizing the subjectivity of the characters at a particular point in the narrative, but their implicit signification is the artistic standing of the filmmaker(s) whose mastery of expressive techniques the spectator is being called upon to admire. Yet it was not only directors and teams recognized, then or now, as artistically motivated who employed such foregrounded techniques. As I have noted elsewhere,

there is no watertight exclusion of such practices from films directed by Delannoy, Cloche, Clément and Autant-Lara . . . let alone Carné. It was not only magic, fantasy, horror, comedy, violence, chaos, or powerful subliminal forces that attracted these "aberrant" camera and lighting practices—not only, that is, criteria relating to expressionism, surrealism, the gothic, the baroque, or the allegorical. A perfectly realistic film might veer unpredictably toward them, because the site seemed compatible (a stairwell, a cliff-top, a fairground, or a forest) or for no perceptible diegetic motive. They formed, that is, part of an array of potential practices available to the industry, which might be mobilized according to genre, incident or personal preference. . . . Statistically, however, one or another of them was likely to occur in any given film, whatever the genre, narrative, or personnel. In these conditions they can scarcely be described as aberrant at all, but one more instance of the tension surrounding the production of a realist diegesis in the classic French cinema.[2]

It was not only by technical/stylistic means that the artistic claims of the filmmakers might be asserted; formal and structural patternings might achieve the same poetic effect—the same Brechtian distancing from the diegesis. This might take the relatively simple form of a narrative voice-over "presenting" the diegesis. Guitry's self-absorption and self-promotion often led him to employ this stratagem, usually to irritating effect (37.89; 38.87), though the extreme sophistication and infectious humor of its employment throughout *Le Roman d'un tricheur* (36.115) makes of that film a real gem. A number of other films were formally "presented" in their opening moments, especially those that had epic pretensions. The actors are thus presented in *Golgotha* (35.53), as is the whole film project in *L'Appel du silence* (36.7). In *Verdun* (31.147), a visitor to the front relates his experiences to his children, while at the end of the decade another reports his impressions of the Maginot Line (38s3). The latter is a documentary reportage, and one purpose of "presentation" in a fiction film was to authenticate the diegesis. Occasionally, this could be used in more purely fictional works, as when locals "recount" to a visiting reporter the reality of Marseille low-life (34.53). An interestingly ambivalent instance is the novelist character "Carco" in *Prisons de femmes* (38.83), played by the novelist Francis Carco, author of the film script, who introduces and comments on the action, including a number of flashbacks. But, of course, prison life was an element of "reality" that could be expected to attract authentication techniques when fictionalized. Perhaps the most charming of these presentations occur at the beginning of the decade, when they come across as an exuberant exploitation of the newfound possibilities of the talkies. In *Chacun sa chance* (30.18), the presenter says, in effect, "Since this is a talkie, we might as well talk," then proceeds to introduce the actors. A similar direct address to the audience takes place in the epilogue to the musical *Le Chemin du paradis* (30.21), in which the gratuitous big number of the finale is offered to us as a sort of extradiegetic bonus for having been a good audience. The opening of *La Crise est finie* (34.31) does something similar, as does that of *L'Opéra de quat'sous* (30.61), in which dummies, a mechanical clock, a presenter, and a song introducing the characters all conspire to distance the audience from the action. The use of dolls, dummies, puppets, or allegorical figures to introduce the themes and characters on a nonrealistic level can be found in a number of films early in the decade, the best known of which is *Boudu* (32.25; cf. 31.98; 31.109), while a trio of ghosts in effect narrate and comment on Ophüls's *La Tendre Ennemie* (35.109).

On a more comic level, Fernandel's character in *François 1ᵉʳ* (37.50), an understudy who is suddenly called on to act the role of the king, has himself hypnotized and is transported back in history to relive the life and times of François 1ᵉʳ. A more elaborate narrative frame is to be found in *Princesse Tam-Tam* (35.92), an otherwise quite unpretentious film, where it works to call into question retrospectively the status of much of what the audience had seen. Like many works developing ambivalence of this sort, it employs a writer figure, whose "book of the film" is mockingly presented at the end. The crucial events occur toward the end of what we might well to that point have taken as a unified diegesis, when the writer mentions that the previous scene constituted the last scene of his novel. If that was the last, which was the first? In effect, the viewer is being asked to reflect back on the film in order to identify the moment (if indeed there was an exact moment) when the represented events ceased being the filmic diegesis and became the film's visualization of the novel's diegesis. While all such narrative frames created a certain distance, the more aggressively Brechtian devices tend to occur in films with a programmatic purpose, such as the political propaganda work *La Vie est à nous* (36s2), which employs a brilliant array of techniques including maps, voice-over, a teacher/class situation, cartoons, choruses shouting slogans, satirical juxtapositions of rich and poor, inter-titles, extracts from Nazi and other documentaries, newspaper headlines, and direct address by political figures to frame three short fictional dramas, and also the more narrative *Le Temps des cerises* (37.109), which, despite its (unsuccessful) aspiration to enter the commercial circuits, employed titles, choruses, documents, caricatures, and satiric juxtapositions.

6.3 OTHER FORMS OF TRANSCENDENCE

It remains true, however, that the great bulk of foregrounding devices used in thirties films served primarily to signal the aesthetic status of the filmmaking team, and that the prime reason so many "artistic" figures appeared in thirties films was to promote the transcendental qualities of the artist as supreme humanist guide and mentor, which naturally rendered him or her superior to the rest of humankind—indeed, often made him or her a martyr in the cause of higher ideals. More traditional religious figures were rare. It is a commonplace to observe that the gradual decline of religious commitment over the last two hundred years has been paralleled by the progressive rise of the cult of art, in which the artist as demigod, creator of fictional worlds, displaces the supreme creator of religious belief. As a final comment on the thematic currents in thirties French films, then, this is a logical place to consider what forms of spiritual transcendence other than art these films proposed to their audiences. The briefest of surveys of those films would suffice to indicate that the place occupied by art and the artist is greater both in quantity and in mythic intensity than that occupied by more traditional forms of transcendence. Men of religion appear relatively rarely, even as secondary characters, in films of the decade, and when they do, it is less as guides and mentors than as figures of fun, or even of detestation.

Films which were calculated to appeal directly to the religious viewer by bringing to the screen the life of Christ and the saints invariably failed, often miserably. Despite intense publicity and a cast of stars (including Robert le Vigan as Christ, Harry Baur as Herod, and Jean Gabin as Pontius Pilate!), Duvivier's super-production *Golgotha* (35.53) was relatively unsuccessful at the box office in most regions; yet only a few months previously his *Maria Chapdelaine* had been one of the outstanding successes of the year, and a few months later his *La Bandera* was a stunning hit. One might find *Golgotha* a rather coldly "artificial" re-creation of the life of Christ, but one might find *La Bandera, La Belle Équipe,* and *La Fin du jour* equally stilted, and all attracted large audiences.

As further evidence, a film relating the miraculous cure of a lame boy by the Virgin at Lourdes (33.144) lasted only one week in exclusive release in Paris. The reception was so poor it could scarcely be said to have received a general release at all. In the same year, a film focusing on the original Lourdes story opened in a marginal theater and also experienced little, if any, general release (33.88). Yet these were precisely the years in which a concerted campaign was being waged by the Catholic church urging parishioners to bless such well-meaning films with their patronage (and to shun the more salacious). It was also when gross military vaudevilles were experiencing extraordinary popularity and when nightclub performances involving largely naked females were a commonplace in films. A film on Sister Theresa did a little better in the weeks immediately preceding the war, but then disappeared without trace (38.101). Another film which, in summary, sounds like the most pious of melodramas and in which St. Theresa's name is invoked to cure a seriously ill boy, had earlier faded with scarcely a trace (36.117). *Marie, légende hongroise* (32.81) did reasonably well at the box office, but primarily because of its melodramatic appeal, the Assumption to heaven being, as far as it is now possible to tell, no more than an epilogue.

I have identified only eight films out of thirteen hundred that propose a man of religion as the protagonist, and four of those are sentimental comedies in which the parish priest, either alone or with help, solves the romantic problems of a young couple. The most successful of these films, *Mon curé chez les riches* (38.64), was the third version of a popular novel (c.f. 32.91). Its representation of the parish priest is somewhat similar to that which was to find even greater popularity after the war, in the Don Camillo stories—the "humble village priest," vulgar, smoking and drinking and swearing, privy to all the secrets of his parishioners, a cherubic twinkle in his eye, and taking a malicious pleasure in doing down the malicious, yet ultimately an agent of harmony and reconciliation in the community. It is probable that the man of religion in *Mon oncle et mon curé* (38.65) served the same marginal role of facilitating the romance of the male and female leads. This was certainly the case in *L'Abbé Constantin* (33.1), which, despite its title, allows the amiable but rather bland priest to be manipulated by the local chatelaine for much of the film, and relegates him to a relatively minor role. His main claim to fame is that his adopted son (one of the young leads) is a marine aviator.

While this general tendency to minimize the role of men of religion can scarcely be said to hold true for *Drôle de drame* (37.37), the bishop played by Jouvet cannot have done much for the image of the spiritual life. His salacious taste for music-hall stars gets him into trouble, and he has to disguise himself as a grotesquely attired Scotsman in an attempt to recover the incriminating program. He is even accused of the murder of Madame Molyneux, and the people clamor for his lynching (or, indeed, for anyone's). It seems that a man of religion had to be marginalized or mocked, and when a film attempted something more serious, it failed. A single instance exists of the more heroic parish priest, solidly patriotic, hiding refugees and resistance fighters from the German army of occupation, himself a resistance leader, who outwits German spies, endures torture without speaking, and finally turns the tables on the enemy (39.27). Kneeling at the foot of a statue of Christ, he says that it is in prayer that he finds the courage to go on. Yet this heroic Christian is so anomalous that it is easier to see the success of the film late in 1939 and in 1940 (of course, only provisional, since its release was qualified by the conditions of the phony war, then the occupation) as being due to its place in the Deuxième Bureau tradition of spy thrillers, which invariably drew large audiences in those prewar years.

More typical of stories about men of religion were the three other parish-priest stories which told of anguished men torn between the flesh and the spirit, struggling to affirm their faith in the face of the temptations of this world. Such temptation might take the form of a young aristocratic woman whom he renounces, only to hear her dying confession years later

(33.72), or the widow whom his brother loves, but whom the man of religion hypocritically attempts to win over to a religious life (39.28); they will certainly be embodied in an attractive woman. In these stories, then, the priest is simply the archetypal instance of a slightly broader group of films in which disciplined men are sorely tempted by a seductive and often treacherous woman, but find solace in some ultimate redemption. The idea that the loss of virginity involves a loss of benign spiritual powers is a common theme (35.78), and it was played out in less immediately allegorical but more psychodramatic form in films such as *Le Puritain* (37.96), in which a rigid moralist assassinates a woman of loose morals only to realize that his act is motivated largely by love and jealousy, and even more so in the abominable *Les Musiciens du ciel,* in which a virtuous and idealistic young Salvation Army woman becomes fascinated by, and committed to saving, a sleazy but handsome villain (39.59). She becomes intensely jealous of the slut he has been living with, but resists the ultimate temptation and, by her selfless and tragic death, succeeds in passing on her spiritual vocation to the villain, who sees the light. In the same year, and released in the same week as *Les Musiciens du ciel, La Charrette fantôme* tells an analogous story, but drawing more obviously on melodramatic conventions, of a young Salvation Army woman who devotes herself to bringing back into the fold a lost soul in a handsome body. Again, triumphing over improbable odds, she ensures his salvation, but at the price of her own life (39.12). Earlier in the decade, another woman torn between the flesh and the spirit had renounced the veil in favor of her handsome singer; but then she was Spanish and living in a different set of genre conventions (30.20).

Les Musiciens du ciel is shot through with analogies from the martyrdom of Christ, as are numerous other films of the decade. They might find their way into the narrative of a humble schoolteacher (32.134), or of a Robin Hood figure (35.51), or of an artistic genius (36.135), but they find their most effective expression in a film which links them to the spiritual mission of French colonialism in Africa—*L'Appel du silence* (36.7). Immensely successful, this biography of Charles de Foucauld, a French officer in, then French missionary to, Africa, tells of his graduation from boisterous immoral youth, with a dancer as mistress, to his scandal and cashiering. He develops a fascination with the great spaces and silence of the desert, where he settles as a hermit. A peculiar intermediate episode has him disguised as a Jew, spying for France in Morocco, where he prepares for France's colonial expansion. Disenchanted by modern technological advances and the mastery of the material world that they offer, he asks for a sign and, with a clash of orchestral brass, Christ's face appears to him. He burns his past and abandons this world for the spiritual life. Called to Algeria, where his brothers are being martyred by the Tuaregs, he establishes a mission and befriends the natives so that the spiritual power of his ministry can reach them. This model spiritual biography is paralleled by the rise of his friend Laperrine in the army, and their twin civilizing mission takes them ever further into the desert. A series of biblical analogies involving desert locations, miracle cures, and ultimate betrayal by a Judas figure leads to his martyrdom by the Tuaregs, as he has foretold. He and his friend are buried together on a hill in the desert, symbols of France's military and spiritual grandeur in a bleakly beautiful world.

In thirties films, the desert provided a recurrent setting for the spiritual trials of noble visionaries. St Exupéry had used it thus, of course, and his *Courrier-Sud* was made into a film in 1936, and to some extent *L'Esclave blanc* (36.40) and *SOS Sahara* (38.95) exploited it similarly. Moreover, Charles de Foucauld was, in a sense, merely one among several of these historical figures carrying the torch of French civilization into benighted regions, and his martyrdom was, in a sense, merely recapitulating the self-sacrifice which formed the climactic gesture of any number of thirties films. His more thoroughly fictional predecessors in *L'Atlantide* (32.12) had known their own spiritual trial in the desert, where the drifting sands hid a matriarchal anti-civilization which called all their accepted values into question.

One of the most widely successful films to foreground a man of religion was *La Tragédie impériale* (37.113), in which the Russian peasant-Christ, Rasputin, takes the French village priest who smokes, drinks, and curses to typically Russian lengths. To the outrage of the formal church authorities, he preaches (and practices) enjoyment of the sensual life, engaging in orgiastic festivities, and "curing" the women of the parish in a less than spiritual way. Miracles seem to occur spontaneously in his vicinity, and seeing him as an instrument of God to be used to the church's advantage the bishops introduce him to the court. This provides an opportunity for even greater sensual excess. Blamed for the people's unrest under the czar, he is exiled to Siberia, but in time of crisis he is summoned back. His undue influence at court outrages the military, and they try to assassinate him. There is a truly wonderful scene in which a gun aimed at him misfires twice. His food is poisoned, to no effect; they shoot him again and again and again, only to see him recover and stagger out into the snow, singing. He has said he loves life as intensely as an animal, and he holds onto it no less tenaciously. As a portrait of a "people's saint" who might have saved the monarchy if they'd only listened, this is a splendid achievement, but it probably succeeded precisely because it was so remote from any normal representation of the spiritual. In fact, however broadly one defines the term "spiritual," it is an inescapable fact that representation of a spiritual vocation and the spiritual life are singularly rare in the films of the decade—almost as rare as the men of religion who notionally embody them. Salvation and redemption are much more likely to be found in and through other spheres of human experience, such as the nation, work, the land, and nature, not to mention love and even sensuality.

To invoke salvation and redemption through contact with the land, in the thirties, is to invoke Pagnol. While not every one of his thirties films deals with this sort of material, several do so, and it was a vein he continued to mine fruitfully through to the fifties. The three most striking instances from the thirties are all drawn from novels or short stories written by his Provençal compatriot, Jean Giono—*Jofroi* (33s5), *Regain* (37.100), and, to a lesser extent, *La Femme du boulanger* (38.34). In the first, a peasant, having sold his land, is nevertheless outraged when the purchaser, Fonse, proposes to rip up the old and fruitless orchard to plant wheat—the trees are part of his past, integral to his existence, and to rip them up is to kill him. He threatens suicide and pursues it in various quasi-comic fashions until the purchaser, thoroughly ashamed and guilty, takes to his couch and pines away, even though legally he has done nothing wrong. Finally, Jofroi dies naturally. The suddenly reinvigorated Fonse dashes out and rips up the orchard but leaves a few old trees in memory of Jofroi—"If he knows, he'll think that Fonse wasn't such a villain, after all."

This identification of peasant with land can't be taken further than the intensely moving *Regain,* in which the story of a dying village slowly regenerated by the last male inhabitant's passionate commitment to the land is paralleled by that man's acquisition of a wife and the formation of a family. In both cases, what had seemed barren and doomed proves fruitful, and the final images are of other families, attracted by the superior quality of the produce resulting from his old-fashioned labor-intensive farming methods, arriving to expand the new community. This "back to the land" theme is very close, of course, to Vichy's "Famille, travail, patrie." It is accompanied here by a powerful reaction against modernity in all its forms—specifically the mechanization of production, but also all forms of hierarchy and authority. Politics is rejected as divisive, as are all uniforms: "The clothes you wear for taking orders are no use for working in." Rather than a pre-Vichy ideology, this comes across as a profoundly anarchic and libertarian morale. In general, in both these and other Giono/Pagnol films, the basic essentials of an existence close to the land—the earth itself, water and springs, the baking of bread—are turned into sacraments that are explicitly opposed to the formal Christian sacraments proposed by the church, whose representatives are usually marginal or ridiculous.

Possibly the only other film of the decade to adopt this attitude is the early color film *La Terre qui meurt* (36.127). The countryside is dying, and the family farm is in hock to sinister, vulture-like lawyers from the city; the old mother is as dead as the earth itself, and the father is unable to manage. The two older children see the struggle to save the farm and the land as hopeless and are seduced by city life (which is far from glamorized by the film or by them but is, nevertheless, judged better than the death-in-life of rural existence); another seeks his fortune overseas; and the fourth, possessive and vindictive, is killed in a fire which he himself lights. The distrust of modernity is again present, with factories likened to prison, the power of money and the ideology of individual self-gratification seen as the prime threats, and rural regeneration is initiated by the young daughter and an "outsider" who loves her—they alone have that mystical union with the soil which will render it fruitful. A final title announces "Thus despite everything, the soil of France will become fertile again, through the love and work of its children." The disintegration of traditional structures is reversed, presumably including the restoration of the patriarchy (which has not, however, been represented in at all attractive a light in the film); and another generation of youngsters will engage in the twee folkloric rituals and round-dances that had opened the film.

In both *Regain* and *La Terre qui meurt,* salvation through identification with the land goes hand in hand with salvation through back-breaking manual labor in the fields. "Work" was not otherwise widely represented as an avenue to redemption, though *Vouloir* (31.148) which may in fact not have been a full talkie, if it was ever finished and released, was reputedly intended to glorify the work ethic of a northern weaver, and *Dans les rues* (33.41) has a worthy youth who has gone wrong saved from a life of crime by his industrious nature.

Films of the sort mentioned above are readily identified because of their programmatic nature. The plot is impossible to summarize without mention of the fertile earth, the sweat of one's brow, or the (attempted) renunciation of the flesh. If such forms of transcendence are relatively rare, two others are extremely common, but implicit rather than explicit, ideological rather than programmatic. Those two are love and nature. Both are seen as sources of inner harmony and of redemption, offering the characters moments or even (implicitly) a lifetime of transcendence. Because they are such an omnipresent ideological assumption, they are difficult to quantify. In general, of course, where love normally represents the narrative endpoint of a spiritual journey and comes as the resolution of a number of defeats, humiliations, and frustrations, nature offers momentary glimpses of that ultimate transcendence in the course of the plot, often in conjunction with love, and suffices to maintain the protagonist's spiritual drive, which is usually at a low ebb at that point.

In a sense, it is unnecessary to explicate these forms of transcendence since they are still so much with us. In particular, love, as a private form of transcendence bringing about the sentimental resolution of the narrative and involving the definitive formation of a heterosexual couple, has usually served to signal the resolution of some more public thematic conflict. So much a taken-for-granted of the times, it is rarely explicitly referred to, though regeneration through love is thematically central to the plot of *Les Frères Karamazoff* (31.60), and in a gentler vein love might bring about the salvation of a French underworld figure as well (33.127; 34.21), or, more improbably, a banker (32.141). Indeed, as a source of spiritual regeneration it was normal to oppose "true love" to some form of egotism or materialistic greed (e.g., 39.30) which was the initial cause of the spiritual fall from which the protagonist needed saving.

Nature as a source of salvation is a much more complex subject. It is clearly related to the back-to-the-earth-movement, but is lyrical rather than religious in kind. It could take various forms. Since at least 1926, German expressionism had established the mountain film as an explicit celebration of the literal and figurative transcendence of everyday mediocrity, and four early French sound films took up the theme (30.23; 33.7; 33.137; 34.88), including a Franco-German co-production directed by Fanck which in summary sounds, however, to have attempted to demystify the generic patterns, or at least to work against them. Later in the decade, with a renewed interest in mountain heights, alpine landscapes are used for both mythical and demystificatory purposes. Commonly the setting for romantic situations (39.41), snowy heights connote an implicit purity which can lend an ephemeral optimism to the most doomed relationship (37.71). They can even represent an ultimate escape from the mercenary machinations of contemporary society (38.71). As the *Carnet de bal* (37.117) episode shows, however, the mountaineer, disillusioned by women and returning to the mountains as one might previously have retired to a convent or hermitage, offers no more hope of redemption to Christine than had her other former dancing partners. And Epstein's *Altitude 3200* (38.5) does not allow the idealistic couples aiming to set up a less corrupt republic in the mountain heights any hope of fulfillment: they bring with them all the jealousies, distrusts, and resistances of the everyday world which they aspire to transcend.

This ambivalence between a straight mobilization of the myth of alpinism and the use of it as a logical aspiration which proves impotent in the face of everyday realities is typical of the more general myth of nature. In both cases, however, nature is basically being represented as a beneficent presence and an inevitable recourse in time of need. Only rarely is it represented as a fierce, jealous, or destructive antagonist and, when it is so, it is usually in the form of the sea (33.102; 39.79). In the occasional more explicit films in which nature represents a harmonious alternative to civilization, deprived urban dwellers are painfully but beneficially introduced to fresh air, exercise, and work in the fields (35.94), or the survivors of an airplane crash live harmoniously on a desert island but begin to squabble and bicker once "rescued" and returned to civilization. Needless to say, they decide to return to their island (35.56), as Princess Tam-Tam had decided to return to her North African village.

For the most part, however, nature (at least in the topographical sense) is not a fundamental structural element in the thematics of thirties films, but a digression, an episode, a momentary respite in the narrative trajectory which serves to revivify and relaunch the protagonists. Some such cases have been mentioned in chapters 2 and 3. Poil de Carotte, for instance, escapes from his awful family to his godfather and Mathilde in the countryside, where he swims naked in a stream and processes in a "marriage," accompanied by a barrel organ and farm animals. Throughout the decade, similar episodes offer urban dwellers momentary relief from their financial and sentimental stresses, even if only in a park where lovers can meet (36.63; 37.57). The alternative of a day in the country made famous in Renoir's film was equally common (e.g., 36s1; 37.109; 39.39). André begins to believe in Cœur de Lilas's innocence and to fall in love with her when he takes her boating in the Bois (31.34). When the wife of the engineer constructing the transatlantic tunnel becomes jealous, he takes her to the country, for only there can he hope to mend their relationship (33.134). Elsewhere, when a "criminal" boyfriend needs to distract the young lawyer's attention from her family's conspiracies, he takes her boating in a park and picnics in the hall of a nearby chateau, omitting to tell her it belongs to his family (36.136). When M. Poirier's son-in-law is beginning to fall in love with his own wife, he takes her for an idyllic trip into the countryside. (33.59). In all these instances, the resort to nature constitutes the single brief evasion from an otherwise totally urban setting. The contrast between elsewhere-prevalent urban and interior decors and this single brief excursion into genuine location shots is often quite startling (35.117). In *Le Temps des cerises*, of course, the attempt to make contact with these "natural" values through a fishing trip is frustrated by the wealthy landowners, who have appropriated nature for their own use (37.109). Similar, more ephemeral relief might be found in a *guingette* beside the Marne, a picnic, a fishing party, or a holiday on a farm. In *L'Alibi*, for instance, Hélène and André find a moment's respite from the mysterious murders committed by von Stroheim's sinister telepath and from the decadent nightclub ambience of the city in a swimming party at the river and a boating party with some amiable thugs (37.6). A similar idyll on a farm among sheep and chubby children offers respite to André and Françoise in *Orage* (37.87).

Indeed, any grim tale with an urban background could be expected to introduce a moment of euphoria amidst nature at about the halfway point. When the conspiratorial courtier Cercleux accords the errant prince a last moment to himself before assuming the duties of kingship, the prince takes Cercleux on a student camping trip to the countryside. Cercleux has never slept better, and is completely won over. He had only known nature at second hand before this; now, under its influence, he lightens up and decides to help the prince (38.29). In several films toward the end of the decade, a scouting trip, with its campfires and camaraderie, serves the same function, as in *La Fin du jour* (38.37) when Cabrissade accompanies his "son" the scout leader to an idyllic campsite by a stream (see also 38.117). Affections mature and are confirmed as true love in the context of trees and streams. In *Sans lendemain* (39.80) when Georges is trying to talk Babs into renouncing her Paris existence (and thus the job as chanteuse and good-time girl that he doesn't know about) and coming to live with him in Canada, he abducts her and takes her for a drive in the country. Their car breaks down and they take refuge in a deserted chateau, where momentarily it seems that she may be able to erase her past life and begin all over again from zero.

Within the general opposition of culture and nature, city and country, a more specific opposition often featured: that between night and day, night life and nightclub contrasting with an idyllic episode in the woods (36.62; 37.6). In certain Chaplinesque films, the open road and liberty are synonymous with nature, as in *Boudu, Les Bas-Fonds,* or *À nous la liberté,* in which nature is the ultimate narrative reward offered at the end to those who resolve or reject the tensions inherent in contemporary industrial society. In a less innocent version of this opposition, nature could also offer the opportunity to cast off the moral inhibitions of a repressive society. In this form, nature appears in a relatively few films as unbridled sensuality, sexual liberation. The allegorical desert island in *Les Aventures du roi Pausole,* where yet another aviator lands, provides such an opportunity, as does the shepherd, much more convincingly, in *La Femme du boulanger* (33.12; 38.34). As the old fisherman reports, in his wonderfully digressive account of coming upon the shepherd and the baker's wife in the woods, "There they were, stark naked, and *singing.*"

This all-too-brief indication of the presence and importance of nature in films of the thirties should be read in conjunction with the material in chapter 3 on workers, urbanism, *guinguettes,* days in the country, and working girls as flowers, and the material in chapter 2 on the role of the provinces in contrast with the representation of Paris, and on the role of barbarous lands and races with respect to European civilization. By itself, however, this discussion establishes nature as providing one of the most credible forms of transcendence available to the protagonists of this decade, second only to art. At a much less explicit level, however, the transcendence provided by romantic love is almost as omnipresent, if often less attainable. Compared to any of these three, the institutionalized transcendence offered by the church plays a very small role in the everyday life of the protagonists of these films.

In *La Règle du jeu,* of course, nature does not figure any euphoric transcendence of the constraints of an urban society, but a set of principles—animality and an anarchic disregard for all regulation—which are opposed to the rules and regulations of the civilized world but, at least in their pure form, are equally dangerous to any true humanity (39.78). The violence unleashed in the hunt scene, when civilized man systematically massacres the animal world, is matched soon after by that other, appropriately more chaotic, hunt scene in the chateau, as animality takes over the civilized world.

In fact, it is not to nature but to art as the preferred form of transcendence that this film ultimately reverts, since it places Renoir himself, as Octave, the unifier, at the formal center of the schematic set of relationships outlined by the film, alone capable of drawing together all the threads. The affectionate friend of all, with privileged access both above and below stairs, he has that more complete understanding of the human heart which the cinema of the time considered appropriate to the creator of the comédie dramatique. As the marquis says of him, he is a poet, and a dangerous poet; though here the term "dangerous" has connotations of reluctant admiration, used of a category of visionary who pushes situations and people to the limit and, in the process, reveals, both to them and to us, wry and uncomfortable truths. Admittedly, in *La Règle du jeu* the director as artist has his moment of self-doubt, of inadequacy. He is the disciple of that great conductor, Christine's father, who received him like a son, yet when he remembers that man's achievements in a supremely reflexive moment on the "podium" and makes as if to conduct the assembled forces, Octave/Renoir is forced to realize that the chaos which they have generated is by this stage beyond his or anyone's power to control. Yet it is, of course, not beyond his power to represent, and subsequent films directed by Renoir will not feel obliged to adopt even this modest degree of self-doubt, as socialist solidarity and even humanism begin to take second place to a transcendent belief in art such as had figured all too often in reflexive and rather complacent films of the thirties.

Part Two

GENRE, STAR, BOX OFFICE

[Genres are designed] to pander to the broadest, and basest, tastes
of the unconscious masses.
—Moussinac (1933)

[Because of the genre system] the true face of France is concealed
beneath a grotesque mask.
—Benoît-Lévy (1945)

Insofar as genres unify the tastes of the spectators . . . they prevent
the masses from becoming aware of themselves and contribute to
the reinforcement of the reigning ideology.
—Bächlin (transl. 1946)

All great films that delight us nowadays have only one thing in
common—precisely the fact that they escape from the framework
within which laws too hastily drawn up would confine the cinema.
—Spaak (1949)

I will go so far as to say that the generic system is the springboard
to creative freedom.
—Bazin (1957)

The American cinema is a classical art, so why not admire what is
most admirable in it—not just the talent of this or that filmmaker,
but the genius of the system.
—Bazin (1957)

There will never be any good European films unless we avoid genre
subjects, since every genre is essentially doomed.
—Rivette (1957)

SEVEN

Cinematic Genres in France:
"A grotesque mask" or "the genius of the system"?

7.1 CONTEMPORARY COMMENTARY ON
GENRE AND MYTH IN THE CINEMA 1930–60

7.1.1 Genre

As was noted in the introduction, neither the genre system nor the star system was as well developed in the classic French cinema as they were in Hollywood, so it is not surprising that genre was not a concept that figured prominently in the articles written by French critics and commentators of that period. Where they did find it useful as a critical concept was in the analysis of American films and, to a lesser extent, German films. Popular film magazines such as *Ciné Miroir* and *Ciné Magazine* regularly mentioned genres in the early thirties, though they gradually ceased to do so as it became apparent that they were not going to be central to the French cinema in quite the way they were to Hollywood, and that French audiences were giving their preference to French films. Thus *La Cinématographie Française* notes in 1930 that, after an interval due to the introduction of sound, adventure films have made a comeback in America, though not yet in France;[1] and *Ciné Miroir* in a discussion of the German expressionist tradition notes that the French cinema has not yet really explored the horror genre.[2] Similarly, J. P. Dreyfus, in *La Revue du Cinéma*,[3] notes that horror films are characteristic of the German and American cinemas, but not the French, while *Cinémonde* sees horror films and gangster films as typically American genres.[4]

The tendency for French film critics to reject genre as a useful tool for understanding the French cinema was to be taken up again after the war, and in order to provide a broader context for the views on genre and myth of thirties commentators in this section I survey all books and articles published on the topic of genre and myth during the period 1930–60. In the postwar years, *Positif* reiterated the view that genre and series were fundamentally un-French, seeing them as characteristic of the American cinema because of its industrial base,[5] and seldom mentioned them in its articles on the French cinema. Numerous accounts of the musical comedy in America in *Le Film Français* and *Image et Son* likewise wrote off French attempts at the genre, describing them as timid, tentative, and pitiful,[6] while *Cinéma 59* questioned whether there could ever be a non-American musical comedy.[7] Nevertheless, *Cinéma 54* (*55, 56*, etc.) and *Image et Son* were among the few French journals in the postwar years to deal seriously with genres, convention, and stereotype, devoting articles to the fantastic, to melodrama, and to science fiction, as well as to musical comedy.

The prevailing disregard for genre was apparent outside the confines of the film magazine. Most serious critics were committed to the notion of authorial creativity, which they saw as threatened, if not totally undermined, by the notion of convention, and they seldom referred positively to the concept of genre. Bazin's reflections on the Western are well known, but this, too, was an American genre. Although he sees such genres as having fueled the triumph of the American cinema throughout the world, he nevertheless usually speaks of European cinema in terms of the skills of individual directors (Bresson, de Sica, Eisenstein, Renoir, Cocteau, von Stroheim, but also Chaplin and Welles).[8] The same is true for most other serious critics. Ford refers briefly to "the genre question" in *On tourne lundi,* seeming in a curiously offhand remark to consider that there are really only two film genres that matter—the dynamic and the static, the action film and the psychological film.[9] Even Sadoul, who, as a Marxist talking of a popular medium, might have been expected to distance himself from the rampant individualism underlying auteurist criticism, constructs the entire history of the French cinema in terms of the rise and fall of individual directors, seldom even mentioning generic categories.[10] His 1948 book on world cinema does contain a chapter entitled "Film Genres," but after a very brief overview he digresses onto the documentary and the cartoon. Symptomatically, the running title at the head of these pages misspells the word "genre" as "génie," substituting cinematic geniuses for cinematic genres.[11] As he was to say in a later book. "In France, our vocabulary for designating film genres is poor."[12]

Moussinac, no less a Marxist, in his outline of the categories of books that would compose an ideal library on the film medium, does not once mention genre (except, again, in a chapter devoted to documentaries).[13] He lists history, aesthetics, technique, criticism, education, law, production and distribution, and the state, but throughout demonstrates an almost religious awe for the individual creative artist. In *L'Âge ingrat du cinéma,*[14] writing of the desperate measures being resorted to by the capitalist cinema, he describes genres as destined to flatter the basest tastes of the unconscious masses, and thus as a sign of the imminent death of the American cinema.

Among non-Marxist commentators, this scorn for generic formulas was, if possible, even more emphatic. There were generally considered to be two opposed and incompatible types of cinema—the popular, characterized by generic conventions, which was trivial and unworthy of serious comment, and the artistic, marked by directorial creativity, which alone was worthy of consideration. Jeanne and Ford in *Histoire du Cinéma*,[15] Charensol in *Renaissance du Cinéma Français*,[16] and Leprohon in *Présences contemporaines*[17] all assumed this position. Recapitulating it in 1950, Charensol was to confirm that in his view it was what distinguished the films of America and Europe, respectively. "Whereas in France a common drive to invent allows us to make films that break completely with formulaic productions, in Hollywood even the most famous directors ["metteurs en scène," not "réalisateurs" or "auteurs"] seem bogged down in formalism."[18]

Claude Mauriac, writing in 1954 specifically about ways of classifying films, notes the possibility of using the name of the director, the producer, the scriptwriter, or even the director of photography, as well as categories based on different ways of reading (psychoanalytic or Marxist), but never once contemplates the use of genres.[19] When he later mentions Westerns and gangster films, it is in the context of a discussion of the American cinema. Roger Régent's landmark book on the French wartime cinema, published in the late forties, deals exclusively with directors and individual films,[20] while Chauvet, writing in 1950 in auteurist terms, makes a plea for the cinema as art, but is happy to talk of the American cinema in terms of genre.[21] The same disregard is apparent in Jos Roger's book on film grammar: of the thirty-five questions that he considers a critic might ask of any film, not one relates to generic classification or inter-textual links.[22]

Denis Marion attributes this distrust of generic classification in France to the baleful influence of Brunetière, a late-nineteenth-century literary critic given to the "over-systematic classification" of literary texts. Reacting against this, "we have ceased to believe . . . in the existence of 'genres' that might possess their own autonomy and develop their own specific laws. When we divide up film production under different headings or discern different trends, we know very well that we are indulging a craving for a system which in the real world finds only the most superficial justification, and which is thereby at best artificial and arbitrary."[23]

The history of this long-standing dichotomy between convention and invention, the popular and the élite, money and art, the consumer-driven and the author-initiated has been adequately chronicled elsewhere, and it would be superfluous to rehearse it *ab initio* here. It is, however, worth noting the satiric glee with which the commentators who promoted this dichotomy listed the supposed excesses of filmmakers who worked within generic frameworks. Much of Charles Ford's *On tourne lundi* is organized around a pastiche of formulaic plots. Like many before him, he quotes the

notorious "thirty-six dramatic situations" which supposedly compose the
entire range of available plot lines (a disaster, a kidnapping, an enigma,
madness, remorse, etc).[24] In the same ironic tones, Sadoul, speaking to an
international conference in Basel, proposes such formulas as the arch-
enemy of the cinema. He reminds his audience of Elmer Rice's Purilia—
that fantasy-land in which all Hollywood films take place—a land from
which all nature and all humanity are excluded. It is a land "peopled with
operetta cowboys, femmes fatales, vamps, millionaires and their servants,
singers and dancers, where money appears miraculously, and where no one
works . . . where heroes always win out, and . . . those guilty of the mildest
of crimes against traditional morality are always punished. . . . Purilia is
that legendary world of modern times, where kings still marry shep-
herdesses, and millionaires their secretaries."[25]

Perhaps the best-known French put-down of generic conventions is
Charles Spaak's account of the script-writing machine that Feyder brought
back from America (of course) for him: "It was composed of three parts—
a notebook providing a sort of repertoire of possibilities, a needle mounted
on a pivot, revolving around a numbered clock-face, and a user's guide, of
the sort provided for pharmaceutical products." It provided lists of possible
male and female professions and occupations, places where a meeting
might take place, problems that might arise disrupting the resultant relationship, and mechanisms for reconciling the couple.

> The anonymous inventor of this singular instrument had . . . perfectly un-
> derstood that most films are produced according to the same formula: a man
> (handsome) and a woman (beautiful) meet, fall in love, but are thwarted in
> their desire by someone or something. Fortunately for the pleasure of the
> masses, a series of remarkable exploits allows them to triumph over these ob-
> stacles, and over all evildoers. A scenario, in its most basic sense, is just that.
> Apprentice scriptwriters, acquire such a machine, or fabricate one your-
> selves. It will provide you with as much imagination as many professional
> authors have.[26]

While not totally rejecting such a dependence on formulas, Spaak
claims that "all great films that delight us nowadays have only one thing in
common—precisely the fact that they escape from the [generic] framework
within which laws too hastily drawn up would confine the cinema."[27] For
him, scriptwriting is an art whose laws may be rigid but are unknowable;
creativity is and must remain a mystery. Attitudes such as this led to the
widespread denigration of any scriptwriter who explicitly exploited such
formulas, and who thus proved suspiciously prolific, such as Companeez,
who reputedly employed "a stable of hacks" to fill out the schematic plot
lines which he provided.

What is really interesting is that amidst all this denigration, there were some, though relatively few, critics of the opposite tendency, who recognized the importance of a generic or conventional base and saw the popular appeal of the cinema as central to its mythic status. Of about four hundred books on the cinema published in France between 1930 and 1960, about twenty-five relate explicitly to genres; when those specifically devoted to the cartoon, the documentary, and various American genres are subtracted, about twelve remain. Typical of these are Leprohon's *L'Exotisme au cinéma*[28] and Pornon's *Le Rêve et le fantastique.*[29] Both of these imply by their very existence that generic patterns are worthy of study, though neither attempts to provide a theoretical justification for that study, preferring to see genres as simply and self-evidently there. The former focuses primarily on documentaries, according only twelve pages to French fiction films, while the latter, with a foreword by Giraudoux, asserts the essentially oniric nature of the cinema in order to minimize the popular aspect of the fantastic genre and link it to the artistic afterglow of surrealism.

In addition to these books on specific genres, several books had arguments organized around the existence of genres or, in their single-minded determination to come to grips with the notion of contemporary myth in the cinema, foreshadowed much later work on the subject. Most authors who developed an argument about genre did so to some extent pejoratively. In *Ça c'est du cinéma,* Altman undertakes a left-wing ideological critique of genres in the context of the functions of a capitalist cinema;[30] in *Les Grandes Missions du cinéma,* Benoît-Lévy bases his critique on a realism which is seen as to some extent incompatible with all generic convention;[31] while in *Précis d'initiation au cinéma,* H. Agel and G. Agel manifest a right-wing distaste for genres, which they see as the opium of the people and a manifestation of collective infantilism.[32]

The only book published in France to come to grips with the economic and industrial base of genre production was Peter Bächlin's *Histoire économique du cinéma* (originally written in German and translated into French in 1946). In his Marxist analysis of capitalist production procedures as they affect the cinema, Bächlin notes the tendency of any system of mass production toward standardization because of pressures to reduce costs, and he likens the balance of difference and sameness within the genre system to the customization of car models. Bächlin sees the genres thus produced as having a basically conservative purpose: "Insofar as they unify the tastes of the spectators . . . they prevent the masses from becoming aware of themselves and contribute to reinforcing the reigning ideology."[33] He does accept, however, that the French production system, among others, is relatively free from genres because of its fragmented industrial structure. Faint echoes of Bächlin's arguments appear over the following decade in works by Bazin, by Morin, and by Agel and Agel, in the form of oblique references to the industrial and commercial origins of the generic system, though Morin is more inclined to focus on genres as an implicitly arbitrary set of rationalizations of the psychoanalytic work of the cinema.

For Benoît-Lévy, however, the existence of a multiplicity of genres is simply an unavoidable but inexplicable fact of filmmaking. It gives rise to one of his two fundamental "laws," allowing the filmmaker "*to classify an original idea within one of the genres.* [Thus the spectator] will learn to appreciate a film in terms of the genre to which it belongs."[34] This unusually forceful recognition of the importance of genre in both the production and the consumption of films is slightly qualified by the fact that his two main generic categories are (once again) the "documentary" and the "dramatic." Moreover, when he does begin to deal with specific dramatic genres, he is as inclined as other critics to mock stereotypes as simply false. "There are French films destined for the international market which show a France exclusively made up of the dancehalls and bars of Montmartre, and inhabited exclusively by models and toughs in berets and red scarves—a fantasy France conforming precisely to the ads put out by travel agencies: Paris by night, under reliable escort."[35] Thus "the true face of France is concealed beneath a grotesque mask." These anxieties about genres and formulas arise from the crucial place occupied in his ideological framework by the natural, the authentic, and the real. *Les Grandes Missions du cinéma* is thus a schizophrenic book, at once urging the centrality of genres to both production and consumption and bemoaning the "lies" which arise from the consequent presence of artifice and convention.

The systematic analysis of filmic conventions and of the ideology behind them which one might have expected from Sadoul or Moussinac is forcefully, and even viciously, expressed by Altman. Outlining in 1931 "the same script Hollywood has been serving up for fifteen years," and its French equivalents, Altman sees generic formulas as cumulatively embodying a "Paramount ideology" designed to reconcile the worker to his intolerable lot, and thus to defuse any revolutionary impulse.[36] Noting the typical settings, plot lines, and characters of romances, boulevard comedies, war films, adventure films, and crime movies, not to mention newsreels, he concludes that their formulaic patterns serve the interests of the forces of order—politics, religion, and the military—encouraging conformity and resignation. The various representations of the world which such conventions articulate are not just false, as Benoît-Lévy argued, but systematically false, leading the viewing public to suppose that the world need be neither explained nor transformed, but must simply be accepted. In this monstrous and quasi-conspiratorial cinema, all that Altman can find to defend are the relics of a Robin Hood pattern in Arsène Lupin, and the films of Charlie Chaplin, which might at least incite the viewer to reflect *"That too is what*

life is like. Is that just? Why should it be so? What should be done about it?"[37]
An art, in his view, can attain timelessness only when it calls everything into
question, when it refuses to accept the superficial laws of the genres which
underpin the conduct of contemporary life.[38]

A decade later, one of the commentators of the wartime period to acknowledge most forcefully the importance of the categorization of production into genres was Jean Keim. Writing in a prisoner-of-war camp, and
thus taking into account only prewar production, Keim devotes a hundred
pages of his *Un nouvel art: le cinéma sonore* to the problem of generic classification. As with other critics, documentaries and cartoons figure prominently in those hundred pages, but fifty of them are devoted to dramatic
genres, and Keim essays some general theoretical propositions to justify his
classificatory system. In this he is alone among commentators of the period
1930–60.

First, he recognizes the difficulties involved in any classificatory system—filmic output, as far as he can see, does not divide up into self-evident
categories, and no inherent distinguishing features suggest themselves. Unfortunately, he does not indicate why, in the face of these difficulties, he still
feels that the effort to develop such a system is so important. Indeed, his account of the formation of genres is as slighting as that of his contemporaries. When a film is successful, "a large number of similar films are made,
generally conceived in haste to profit from the fad, until the spectator, disgusted by these pale imitations, is repelled. It would be possible to follow
the periodic movements which lead to the production of these series; such
a history would be amusing from an anecdotal point of view, but from an
aesthetic point of view it would be deprived of all interest."[39]

Having got this off his chest and made a preliminary division into spectacle, documentary, and propaganda ("according to the purpose of the director"), Keim proceeds to outline a set of three intersecting criteria for
organizing a study of the first of these. It is here that his essay becomes interesting. The three criteria he will use are the character of the work, the
type of action, and the tendency of the plot. By the first, he means the degree of realism. His brief discussion of realism is fairly sophisticated, finally
defining it in terms of plausibility. Applying this, he distinguishes known
and unknown parts of the world, present and reconstructed past ages,
worlds that conform to known laws and worlds that do not. This leads to
identification of the fantastic and historical genres and the abstract film.

Under *type of action,* he distinguishes exterior and interior action, which
allows him to separate the psychological film from such action genres as the
Western, the epic, and the murder mystery. His preference for the former is
obvious, and he contrasts its exploration of the depths of the human soul
with the latter's emphasis on the body—"man can be seen, if not in all his

brutality, at best with a simple, direct mind that pays no attention to sub-
tleties. . . . The instincts gain the upper hand, and the veneer of civilization
is peeled away."[40]

Finally, in his section on *plot tendencies,* Keim surveys the range of production categories from the tragedy to the comedy, by way of the "comédie
dramatique," "without forgetting the adventure story, which constitutes
one of the most fertile areas," and which includes gangster films, crime stories, Westerns, war films, and exotic and colonial films. That he should have
felt it necessary to distinguish this category from the other, more conventional range of tragedy, comedy, and comédie dramatique may seem singular, yet will be seen to be characteristic of the day. His justification is that in
adventure films "tragedy and comedy exist only as secondary considerations. [What is central is] material struggle—struggle against men or against
the elements."[41]

While Keim's set of three intersecting criteria lead to a given genre, such
as the Western, appearing several times, in different sections, and while the
films that he uses to illustrate his categories and principles are very limited
in number, further contributing to a sense of repetitiousness, the very fact
that he attempted such an ambitious task as the systematic categorization of
international film production set him apart from all his contemporaries. It
is hard not to see his undertaking as related to the conditions under which
it was undertaken—a period of wartime imprisonment when he was forc-
ibly distanced from film viewing for a period of years, and able to reflect in
the abstract on the previous decade's production.

Toward the end of the thirty years under review, another book appeared
which used generic categories as a guiding principle—*Précis d'initiation au
cinéma* by H. Agel and G. Agel—but, like most others who accepted the
principle of genres, these authors were severely critical of the practice. Admittedly, this work was a textbook for college students, written in a carefully moral tone by authors accustomed to promoting a religious cinema,
but still the distrust of genres is almost pathological. Agel and Agel write of
a genre cinema as an escapist cinema, offering facile euphoria to the masses.
Certain time-worn stereotypes, especially romances organized around the
display of a star, are seen as covert eroticism, "appealing to the grossest instincts and the most deluded sentimentality."[42] Cumulatively, such generic
forms are acknowledged as having created "a cinematic mythology," but the
effects of that mythology are uniformly sinister.

Agel and Agel approvingly quote a pamphlet, *Éducation et cinéma no 1,*
put out by the Direction générale de la Jeunesse et des Sports, as saying that
genres deserve study "to see how they produce or encourage the process of
escape into a dream world which is the last, desperate resort of a collective
conscience incapable of accepting and coping with the real world. Tarzan
does not represent a nostalgic fantasy about far-off, sun-drenched land-

scapes so much as a rejection of slums, of dreary work in an office or factory, and of preparations for World War III; it is the negation of the here and now." Continuing this somewhat pessimistic explanation of genres, in their introduction to the major section of the textbook entitled *Les Genres au Cinéma*, Agel and Agel note that "it is most often the least successful films that . . . are easiest to catalogue and class by genre. . . . The great classics often belong to several genres . . . or transcend all aesthetic categories. . . . So it is with prudence that one should resort to this sort of categorization, which has above all a limitative and methodological value [*sic*]."[43]

As a consequence of their distrust, Agel and Agel decide not to use the normal (unjustifiable) generic categories, but a new range that they had devised on a more justifiable (though never actually justified) basis. These genres are based not on the story or the content, but on the implicit content and the style. Unfortunately, these terms, subsequently redefined as "the dominant" and "the line of force," are never rationally explained. They result, however, in the exclusion of historical and biographical films as "inauthentic," and of the politically committed film (*film à thèse*) as "opposed by definition to art because of its didactic purpose." Didacticism, they quote Bazin as saying, inevitably undermines psychological plausibility, complexity, and free will, and thus reduces the real to "an intelligible organization without mystery."[44]

The categories which do pass muster are the epic and its "regressive" forms—the crime story and the swashbuckler; the war film; the Western; the tragedy, drama, and melodrama; the comedy; the burlesque; the poem; the documentary; the short film; the cartoon; and the youth film. If there is a basis for accepting these and rejecting the others, it must be ideological; certainly, there is no logic to the internal ordering of their system, except a general tendency to move from the serious to the frivolous, then add on whatever is left over.

In the same year as the Agels' book appeared, *Cahiers du Cinéma* inadvertently conducted a debate on film genres. A discussion of authorship had led the magazine by negation to talk of convention. As is readily imaginable, the Young Turks of *Cahiers* were outspoken in their condemnation of genres. Rivette's comments summed up their attitude: asked by Bazin what he thought was at the origin of the mediocrity of the British cinema, he said simply that "the British cinema is a genre cinema," and later, "there can't be any good European films, far less great ones, unless one decides to avoid genre subjects, since every genre is essentially doomed."[45] In response to this, Bazin comes out with perhaps the only unequivocal defense of genres to have been published in the entire thirty years. He asserts that "the weakness of the European film industries is that they cannot rely on genres for their current production. . . . One of the main problems of the French cinema is its inability to sustain good basic genres that thrive as they do in

America."[46] This assertion can be taken in conjunction with his comments in the well-known article "De la politique des auteurs," which had appeared in the previous issue of *Cahiers,* where he had delicately kicked the stuffing out of his younger colleagues, "who look down on anything in a film that comes from a common stock of material, yet which can sometimes be entirely admirable." In his view, the popular American culture which lay behind the American comedy, the Western, and the gangster film was entirely beneficial,

> for that is what gives the cinematic genres their vigor and richness, resulting as they do from an artistic evolution which has always been in wonderfully close harmony with its public. Yet one can read a review in *Cahiers* of an Anthony Mann Western (and God knows I like Anthony Mann's Westerns) as if it were not, above all, a Western—that is, a whole collection of conventions in the script, the acting, and the direction. I know very well that in a film magazine one may be permitted to skip such details, but they should at least be implied, whereas what in fact happens is that their existence is glossed over rather sheepishly, as though they were a rather ridiculous imposition that it would have been inconvenient to mention.[47]

Bazin goes on to praise many "non-auteurist" Westerns, and concludes uncompromisingly that "the genre tradition is a springboard for creative freedom. The American cinema is a classical art, so why not admire in it what is most admirable, namely not just the talent of this or that filmmaker, but the genius of the system." The (re)allocation of the terms "talent" and "genius" to "filmmaker" and "system," respectively, is sufficient indication of the gulf between his thinking and that of his younger and more romantic colleagues.

7.1.2 Myth

As this review of comments on the principle of a genre cinema makes clear, there were few critics writing between 1930 and 1960 who took the principle seriously, and no one except Bazin—and he only at a very late date—who supported it. Certainly, none of the commentators indicated any appreciation that there might be a connection between generic categories and what might be termed a modern mythology, though such a connection might be considered implicit in Altman's discussion of the ideological significance of genres. Where a connection was sometimes explicitly made between a popular cinema and mythology, it was made not because of the existence of a genre system but rather on the basis of the cinema being a mass medium, or because of the existence of a star system. On the other hand, it was quite common for the connection between cinema and mythology to be made not because the cinema was a popular medium, but, on the contrary, because it could occasionally attain the status of a high art. For such commentators, the explicit assumption was that only great artists could aspire to be myth-makers.

Critics on the right, in particular, were inclined to see the highest artistic goal of filmmaking as the creation of a mythology of the modern age. At the same time as Altman was writing *Ça c'est du cinéma,* Abel Gance was asserting,

> All legends, all mythology and all myths, all founders of religions, and all religions themselves, all the great figures of history, all those millennia of objective reflections of the world of the imagination await their luminous re-creation [in the cinema], and heroes crowd at the door to enter. All our dream life, and all the dream that is our life, awaits its chance to register on our sensitized celluloid, and it is in no sense a grandiose overstatement to imagine that, given the chance, Homer would have filmed *The Iliad* or, better still, *The Odyssey.*
>
> The time of the image has arrived.
>
> We march forth, a select band, on wreaths of cloud, and when we engage in battle, it is with a reality that we strive to transform into dream.
>
> Each camera hides a secret divining rod, and its lens is a modern Merlin's eye.[48]

Both this exalted view of cinema as at its best aspiring to mythic status and the elitism implied in the term "a select band" were to be perpetuated in later books by Dekeukelaire and Duvillars, but as they were writing in the postwar period they were also building on the famous essay published by Malraux in 1941, which did to some extent explore a more popular origin for the concept of a cinematic mythology.[49] Malraux's fascination with myth had been apparent since his earliest writings, and he was arguably as much obsessed by myth as were his characters. For him, as for many others at the time, the cinema was a privileged site for the production of myth, not because of its aspiration to the status of high art, but precisely for the opposite reason—because of its mass audience. "The American cinema . . . attains willy-nilly that domain where art is never absent: myth. And the whole task of the cinema over at least the last decade has been to attempt to cope with myth. . . . The cinema addresses the masses, and the masses love myth, whether it be for good or for evil."[50] Again, establishing what was to become a commonplace among writers who succeeded him, he linked this mythic status of the cinema to the star system.

> A star is in no way simply an actress who makes films. A star is a person with that necessary minimum of talent whose face expresses, symbolizes, embodies a collective instinct. Marlene Dietrich is not an actress like Sarah Bernhardt, she's a myth like Phryné. The Greeks ascribed vague biographies to their in-

stincts, just as our contemporaries invent story after story for theirs, just as the creators of myths invented one after the other the Labors of Hercules. So true is this that stars recognize more or less vaguely the myths that they embody, and demand scenarios capable of perpetuating them. . . . A great actress is a woman capable of embodying a great number of different roles, whereas a star is a woman capable of bringing into being a large number of convergent scenarios.[51]

Published in the same year as Malraux's article, André Boll's rapid overview, *Le Cinéma et son histoire,* likewise sees the cinema as productive of myths, both in certain specific characters whom it elevates to mythic status (Zorro, Ben Hur) and in certain recurrent stereotypes (the swashbuckling hero, the vamp). Of the stars who embody these characters and character types, he says, "Their every gesture, their silhouette, gait, hairstyle and profile, their make-up and gaze, and the intonation of their voice . . . all serve instinctively as a model for the general public, which is drunk with the desire to imitate them."[52]

The notion of a model is a passive one. The phrasing of Malraux's statement might seem, on the contrary, to ascribe key agency to the star, who "brings into being" the myth. Dekeukelaire is clearer about the insignificance of the individual in the mythologizing process. "Myth does not arise . . . from the influence of a personality. It arises spontaneously, collectively. It is an ideal that the collectivity pursues all its life, and that corresponds to its true nature."[53] Recapitulating Dekeukelaire, Duvillars notes that once upon a time the theater embodied and exalted collective anxieties and needs, but now it is the cinema that does so: "It is the ideal vehicle for modern myths, because myth . . . is a collective fact, the sum total of the dreams aroused by a collective instinct and crystallized in a single man, the hero—even if that hero is of dubious morality. Incontestably, cinema alone has the necessary audience [to generate contemporary myths]."[54] For Duvillars,

the spectator seeks in the cinema the exteriorization of all his dreams and suppressed desires, and thus, favored by the surrounding darkness, liberates all his most profound anxieties. It is a sort of official . . . safety valve that allows the honest man to live out in an hour and a half all the adventures and experiences that he suppresses but secretly longs for. Safe in his comfortable theater seat, he avenges himself . . . on all that is above him in rank and wealth, and tramples underfoot the society that suffocates him, wielding his machine gun along with Scarface and Dillinger.[55]

Duvillars spends much of his book elaborating Malraux's comments by analyzing the images of stars of the day, notably Viviane Romance, Jean Gabin, Marlene Dietrich, Michèle Morgan, von Stroheim, and Chaplin.

At no stage does he extend this analysis to genres. Indeed, like Gance, he tends to see only "great filmmakers" (and he instances Eisenstein, Lang, Clair, Chaplin, and later Stiller, Carné, and Cocteau) as capable of recognizing and elaborating these mythic structures. That is, while myth is a collective fact, it is not directly the product of a collectivity, but relies on the mediation of a man of genius. Also, as the above implies and as Dekeukelaire makes clear, the task of reconciling the underprivileged to their lot and teaching them resignation is not an ignoble one. "[Our] civilization dreams of a reality that will make us forget weariness and work. It [achieves this in] myth, which condenses all desires in the hero." And if, at the end, "the last bullet fired, it returns [the spectator] to the street and to his daily responsibilities, his family, his office, restores to him his bourgeois soul and his habitual routines,"[56] this is seen as one of its strengths, one of its virtues—transcending commercial considerations rather than (as a leftist such as Altman would have claimed) serving them.

The rather unremarkable fact that the stars—as divinities, as (sex) goddesses—embodied mythic personae whose appeal to the people was of an exalting nature had become common currency by the mid-fifties. Henri Agel talks in 1953 of the obsessive faces of various stars (in France, Jean Marais and Viviane Romance), which "are not just human faces, but the disquieting faces of two idols all too ready to receive the suspect adoration of their faithful."[57] Likewise, the following year Claude Mauriac speaks of sex goddesses as allowing their worshipers to participate in the magic of myth. He entitles one of his essays "Mythology of the Cowboy," says of *Au-delà des grilles* that it represents "the death of the Jean Gabin myth," and speaks in general of the crowd's vague appreciation of the fact that "the least of films is a means of intercession by which it can make contact with that transcendent reality subtended by the world of appearances. It loves instinctively in the cinema what is dangerous and disturbing . . . contact with the sacred."[58] These and numerous similar observations speak of a general intellectual agreement in the mid- to late fifties about the mythic significance of the cinema, and specifically about the mythic stereotypes embodied by the stars.

At the same time, it is clear that the term "mythology" was being used with somewhat different connotations by different critics in different contexts. Was it acceptable to use the term, as Chauvet did, in a passing reference to the swashbuckling swordsman slaying modern "dragons" ("After all, haven't you heard of those legendary knights who overcame fabulous monsters with no more than a sword? The one myth is as valid as the other"[59]). Surely, a popular cinema as figured in the star and genre systems could not have the same status as the mythic aspirations of a high-art cinema in which intellectuals aspired to reproduce the timeless truths of ancient myths. This anxiety is captured in the otherwise excellent article by Raymond Barkan,

"Une mythologie du quotidien" (A mythology of everyday life), in which he feels it necessary to distinguish two types of cinematic mythology, the "noble" and the "humble": "While the frontiers between the commercial and the art cinema are not always easy to define, you could almost say that there are two categories of mythology in the cinema: an artificial mythology, fruit of the mercenary values of producers and of the need of the masses to contemplate up there on the screen the reflection of their most coarse and instinctual appetites, and that noble and authentic mythology of the work of art, which transposes life without betraying it and which endows our hopes and sufferings with grandeur."[60] In his view, it is clearly only from the latter, and not from the "inauthentic" and implicitly generic mythology, that anything of worth can emerge. Treading a difficult line, Barkan secures Gabin's heritage for the true (artistic) mythology, despite the fact that it is the masses who recognize themselves in the resultant "mythologization of the ordinary":

> There is no doubt that it was in the cinema that the masses first realized that their daily life, that monotonous daily struggle for existence . . . could aspire to as much tragic grandeur . . . as dramas portraying exceptional events and people. One's job, one's profession, the daily routine that one loves and that has a real social importance, have acquired, thanks to the screen, a prestige that they never had before. . . . Through this mythology of the real, the human masses have attained an almost physical, instinctive appreciation of the great truths of their lives, which would not have been possible before the cinema. . . . This spontaneous perception by the masses of the beauty of the true translates notably into the success of actors who are lacking in any physical attractiveness, but who identify totally with characters drawn from everyday life.[61]

This debate on the applicability of the term "myth" to popular culture provided some context for the development during the fifties by Roland Barthes of the notion of a contemporary mythology inhering in the rhetoric of contemporary culture as a whole. The ideas which he explored were quite common in critical debate of the day, but his conception of them was at once broader and less euphoric than was that of other commentators. Instead of seeing contemporary mythology as providing spectators with desirable glimpses of their own place in the transcendent scheme of things, Barthes saw the function of such a mythology as essentially conservative, naturalizing and depoliticizing the historical ascendancy of the bourgeoisie and thus working against the interests of a duped public. While the cinema was not central to his thought, his comments on Greta Garbo, on the Romans in historical films, and on the exotic locations in such films as *Lost Continent* serve to apply those general ideas to the filmic medium.[62] As a left-wing commentator picking up on but reworking a decade of commentary on the cinema, he can easily be read as continuing the work of Altman twenty years before, though in a more urbane tone and on a more solid theoretical base.

7.2 BROAD GENERIC CATEGORIES 1930–60

While the above discussion summarizes a not inconsiderable body of work on genre and myth in the years 1930–60, it is hard to avoid the conclusion that genres as a whole were disregarded or derided. When Richard Abel introduces a selection of critical essays from the period, he quite reasonably sees no need to mention genre at any stage.[63] Nevertheless, it was common practice for both the industry and the critical fraternity to use generic descriptors when classifying films. These commonly consisted of two sets of terms—a first, broader set, confined primarily but not exclusively to "drama" and comedy," and a second, narrower set of terms: "military" or "war" film, "poetic" or "fantastic" film, "musical," "psychological," "social," and "crime" film. Thus the annual lists would normally include such classifications as "crime drama," "musical comedy," or "psychological drama."

The primary division of all films into the categories of "drama" and "comedy" clearly corresponds to a gross distinction between serious and humorous films. It was the contemporary equivalent of the earlier theatrical practice of dividing productions into tragedies and comedies. The use of "drama" instead of "tragedy" is significant. In the early theater, both tragedies and comedies were "spectacles," presented to the public, but from about Shakespeare's time onward, and paralleling the development of humanism, the audience began to be invited to share the tragic protagonists' state of mind and emotional experiences, rather than simply "recognizing" them. The aim was to abolish any sense of distance between actors and audience. This dramatic involvement in the narrative through psychological identification with the characters led to serious productions being called "dramas" rather than "tragedies."

Along with the evolution of the tragedy into the drama went a devolution of agency from the gods to humanity. As Keim notes in his discussion of what he still calls "tragic" films, "the heroes are no longer princes but men marked by fate, burdened by exceptional circumstances, who pose often insoluble problems [and who] become representative types with a significance greater than their individual personalities."[64] Because he still saw them as tragedies, Keim was led to condemn any trace of optimism, let alone a happy end, in filmic "tragedies." Other commentators, using the term "drama," had no such difficulty, since the key consideration was the nature of the audience's experience resulting from specific techniques of audience involvement and identification, not the ultimate outcome of the narrative. Apart from Keim, very few contemporary film reviewers used the terms "tragedy" or "tragicomedy" in their categorizations , the term "drama" having almost entirely displaced them.

The distinction between "dramas" and "comedies" commonly employed by film reviewers, then, distinguished films that aimed to involve the spectator intensely in the action from those that aimed to provide a spectacle—in other words, it distinguished films that the audience was invited to feel along with from those that it was invited to be entertained by. To quote Keim on the comedy, "Real life is not represented here. . . . A world appears which, though it may not be deformed, sets aside all ugliness and grief. . . . Feelings are not profound; great sadness is rapidly dissipated; nothing seems really serious." Human beings and their relationships are merely the material for a textual game, executed for the delight of the spectator, and "joie de vivre carries the young and vital protagonists along apace, to a resolution which dissipates all misunderstandings and reunites all lovers."[65]

On the whole, comedies were not expected to deal with serious topics, though they might do so on occasion, and dramas were not expected to be wryly amusing, let alone hilarious; yet inevitably the two major categories were not watertight, and the industry acknowledged an intermediate genre, called the "comédie dramatique." Like the "true" drama, the comédie dramatique aimed to involve the spectator in the narrative action, but this action constituted a relatively gentle comment on human nature, in which affectionately drawn characters worked out problems of human relationships (but never social or political, let alone spiritual or transcendental relationships) in a basically optimistic way. Often, there was nothing comic in the English sense about these "comedies," since the French have always used that term more broadly, but even if the narrative ended badly, or ambiguously, the spectator came away from these films warmed and uplifted.

Over the years, commentators had difficulty clearly distinguishing comédies dramatiques from sentimental comedies and psychological dramas, but they felt that the effort to do so was justified because there was something peculiarly French (and therefore peculiarly valuable) about the production of comédies dramatiques. It was something that they felt they did better than any other nation, perhaps because it involved a profound understanding of the human heart. As Le Film Français was to say somewhat baldly, in 1947, "The comédie dramatique corresponds to the genius of our race, which is why there are so many of them in the year's production of sixty-five films."[66] Pagnol's films were regularly categorized as comédies dramatiques, as were Becker's postwar domestic comedies; one reason for the welcome extended to the New Wave was the perception that Truffaut, Chabrol, and Rohmer were renewing this typically French vein, then (correctly) considered to be in decline. Writing during the war, when the comédie dramatique was at its apogee, Keim was inclined to extend the category to include all contemporary realistic productions dealing with everyday situations. While no one else was as inclusive, Keim's definition is still useful: the comédie dramatique provides "a slice of life, with its joys and its difficulties, its grotesque incidents and its moving moments. . . . The common man is its protagonist, and he is motivated by feelings that the spectator also experiences in the course of his everyday existence."[67]

Likewise seeking to define the nature and the importance of the comédie dramatique, but in the context of a discussion of the importance for each film-producing nation to be true to its own national strengths, Benoît-Lévy sees the strength of French film as being neither in tears nor in laughter, but in

> that smile, half ironic, half affectionate, that has been seen by some as frivolous, but is really more philosophical. . . . You could say that elements of drama inflect all laughter in French films, which will never manifest the simple boisterousness of American laughter. The opposite is also true. An element of laughter inflects French drama, which can never achieve the harshness, often touched with grandeur, of certain foreign films. [This is due to] a profound understanding of human nature, made up as it is of both good and evil. The great wisdom [of French films] is to accept human beings as they are—with a smile. . . . Admittedly the French cinema has not produced exclusively comédies dramatiques. We must not forget robust dramas like Renoir's *La Bête humaine* or Duvivier's *Poil de Carotte*. . . . But especially since the advent of the talkie, the dominant tendency has been to infuse the living images with laughter and with tears, which melt into a smile of irony or of compassion.[68]

As a consequence of the prominence given to the intermediate category of the comédie dramatique, what resulted was not so much a binary system as a ternary system, though the third term was always in the minority. Indeed, as Keim's insertion of "adventure films" suggests, for some it was a quaternary system. The fourth term arose because "drama" was felt to be a very broad category—far broader than comedy, and far less homogeneous. It ranged from the "true" drama, moving for its representation of some somber and powerful aspect of the human condition, across the whole range of more "formulaic" dramas, which might be classified as historical or period dramas, murder mysteries, Westerns, horror, science fiction, and the fantasy. Throughout the classical period, there was some hesitation as to whether these latter works, which belonged to an already widely recognized genre and which unhesitatingly mobilized the relevant formula, should in fact be classified as dramas at all. Lacking any viable alternative term, many commentators simply labeled them crime "films" or war "films." By the war years, this division between true dramas and the more formulaic dramas simply called "films," while never clearly articulated except indirectly by Keim, had become almost routine. *Goupi Mains-Rouges* was labeled a "peasant film," *Pontcarral* a "period film," and *La Main du diable* a "poetic film." All of these more generic dramas were at one remove from contemporary reality, at least in their formal qualities, but usually also in their spatial or temporal remoteness. In their rule-governed, game-like way, they did not claim to reveal truths about contemporary social or psychological reality, but to set certain somber, dramatic, or poignant, but fairly stylized aspects of reality within known textual frameworks.

Since throughout the classic period industry journals routinely employed this ternary or quaternary system to describe the season's releases, it is possible to assess the proportion of each year's output which, in the eyes of the anonymous classifiers, fell into each of the broad generic categories. Figure 7.1, which accepts without question those anonymous categorizations, is based on a ternary division into dramas, comedies, and comédies dramatiques. It at once confirms certain widespread assumptions about the output of the classic French cinema and contains certain surprises. In general, it shows that, after an initial year in which dramas heavily outnumbered comedies, comedies prevailed throughout the 1930s, in a proportion of roughly fifty-five to thirty-five. During the war, however, the proportions abruptly reversed, and toward the war's end the proportion of dramas in the year's output hit an all-time high of about 60 percent. From 1946 onward, the proportions were about equal, though there were annual fluctuations which became more marked in the late fifties. Meanwhile, comédies dramatiques, which had been rising steadily in number throughout the thirties, reached a peak of 12 percent in 1947 and subsequently declined toward a low point of 5 percent in 1958.

The predominance of comedies in the early thirties is precisely what one would have expected on the basis of contemporary accounts. The great debate about filmed theater which raged throughout the thirties was triggered principally by the practice of filming theatrical comedies—vaudevilles, farces, operettas, and boulevard comedies. In September 1933, *La Cinématographie Française* listed 180 comedies filmed in the preceding two and a half years, and of these 121 were more or less direct transcriptions of theatrical comedies.[69] So it is not surprising that industry journals exclaimed over the increasing number of "frivolous comedies" in 1931 and over the excess of operettas in 1932. "Their time is past," wrote Lucie Derain, a little optimistically, in 1932, noting that of that year's production 60 films were either vaudevilles or operettas. "What can you hope for from a cinema like that?"[70] Yet in 1935, Charensol was still complaining about the number of operettas, vaudevilles, and music-hall productions transcribed for the cinema, protesting that "the cinema is basically a visual art. The

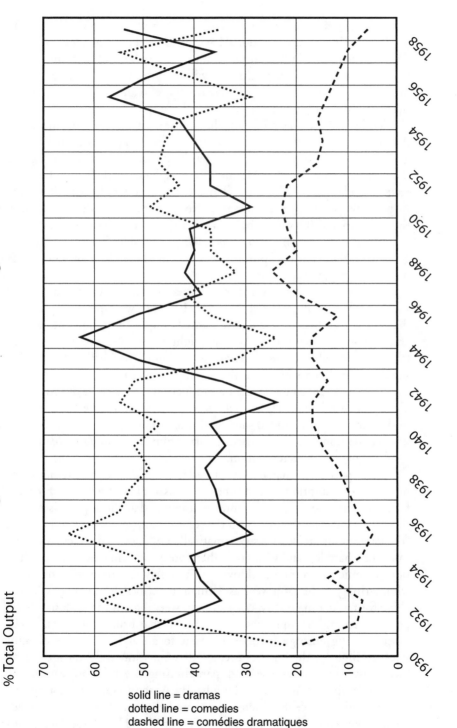

Figure 7.1. Main Generic Categories 1930–1958

% Total Output

solid line = dramas
dotted line = comedies
dashed line = comédies dramatiques

most obvious effect of the talkie has been to create two categories of film production: in one, the traditional laws [of the silent cinema] are respected, whereas the other confines itself to more or less faithful reproduction of theatrical works. Not surprisingly, I will tend to neglect the latter, not so much out of scorn as because I have no desire to analyze the repertory of the Comédie Française or the Palais Royal."[71]

While the production of comedies in the early thirties is unsurprising, their continuing predominance until the declaration of war is unexpected, given the wide reputation acquired by the poetic realist films of the late thirties. Commonly called "drames d'atmosphère" at the time, these can seem nowadays to have been the characteristic product of the period. That they seemed so even then is apparent from the role attributed to them in the early years of the war by both the French and the German authorities, as not just a prime symptom of France's prewar decadence, but a prime cause of it. Yet in terms of pure volume, the number of such productions at no time matched that of comedies.

Equally unexpected is the rapid disappearance of comedies once wartime production resumed. Not only is there a widespread assumption that wartime audiences would have wanted escapist entertainment, with an emphasis on comedy, but also we might expect Goebbels's notorious (though privately expressed, as far as we know) desire that the French should be provided with "films that are light, superficial, entertaining, but trivial" to have had some impact on production. Yet even the output of the German-controlled firm Continental, while it was dominated by comedies in the early stages, included more and more dramas after Goebbels's pronouncement, including Tourneur's horror film *La Main du diable* and *Le Corbeau*, of notorious reputation.

The expectations that are overturned by these data are based on a common-sense assumption that in times of crisis audiences will look for relief from their hard lot in escapist entertainment and artificial paradises. This theory is somewhat distinct from that of Altman, who saw what he called "the Paramount ideology" as systematically designed to distract audiences from their hard lot, and who saw it therefore as sinewing dramatic productions as much as comedies. However, it closely resembles that of Gorel who, writing in the same year as Altman, describes the cinema as "a machine for retouching reality, correcting it, weeding out the undesirable aspects, softening the asperities, the rocks, all that bruises or hurts."[72] His most startling analogy involves his visit to an asylum, whose director screened films for the inmates because they constituted the most effective mechanism for calming the mad: paraphrasing Brecht's observations, he sees it as leaving them exhausted but happy. As the asylum director memorably remarks, "Since the cinema came into being, sir, there are fewer madmen."[73] For Gorel, all that kept the soldiers of World War I at their stations was the American cinema. In the midst of chaos and suffering, "they would screen an American film and the soldiers would laugh like mad. This shook them up, purged them. And when the show was over, they would go off happily to die, thinking of Pearl White's long eyelashes."[74]

Even among those on the left, the conspiracy theory postulating an ideologically conservative purpose behind all capitalist film production was held to apply all the more strongly in the case of comedies, and their suspicions could only have been reinforced by prevailing commentary. In 1936, *La Cinématographie Française* protested, "We have quite enough opportunity to contemplate problems during the daytime, and thus we prefer that the cinema not confront us with yet more in the evening. If the entire French population were plunged into the direst pessimism, our line of conduct [i.e., in the film industry] would shine forth all the more clearly: our task would be to restore our spectators to a happy frame of mind. . . . A customer who enters a theater in a melancholy mood must leave it restored to tranquillity. If depressed, he must find in our theaters reason to be hopeful."[75] And two years later, speaking out against *La Marseillaise* as an instrument of propaganda, *Cinéopse* said, "The cinema has nothing to gain from intervening in politics, if only because it raises the anxiety level of so many citizens. . . . Its task is to give us shows that are entertaining, healthy, and reassuring, that will cause audiences to forget their excessive troubles, and that will maintain civil order and moral health."[76]

Essentially, this was the "theory" behind the celebrated musical comedy of 1934, *La Crise est finie*—an out-of-work theater group from the provinces decides that what Paris needs to drag it out of the depression is a rousing musical comedy. It's all a matter of attitude: sing along with the cast and all your troubles will disappear. And of course, in the film, their theory is validated: the troupe plays to packed houses and France is cured. Yet in practice the contrary was the case. Comedies dominated in the early thirties, even before the depression hit France, yet had no reported deterrent effect, while dramas dominated during the war, when conditions were at their most arduous for audiences. Indeed, as we will see in chapter 9, the same was true even in the second half of the thirties, when, in the face of prolonged economic and social disturbances, it was dramatic productions that were most popular, not the numerous comedies with which producers flooded the market. The more somber the experiences of the audience, the more they looked to somber representations of the world. The escapist theory seems not to hold, at least in any simple way.

Goebbels, then, in his celebrated and derided wartime statement was merely reproducing standard French industrial observations concerning the social function not only of comedy but of the cinema as a whole; *Ciné Miroir* is doing the same after the war when it publishes an article calling for more comedies: recognizing that "bad boys and bashings" had dominated production in recent years, it protests that, in view of the hard times and with daily life a constant struggle, producers should reorient their efforts toward comedies. "We see too many somber dramas, frightful tragedies, grim tales."[77] In fact, however, production of comedies and dramas was to equal out in the ensuing decade, which also saw the high point and gradual decline of the comédie dramatique. But this relative stability was disrupted in the late fifties by wild swings which suggest a rudderless production system desperately seeking a new formula to combat unpredictable, then dramatically declining, attendance.

While films formally classified as comedies were still numerous in the fifties, the conviction grew among commentators that the French cinema had lost its ability to produce amusing films, insofar as they believed it had ever had it. In 1953, reviewing the previous seven years' production, Doniol-Valcroze notes despairingly that the French comic film has been moribund for some time, and it is neither *Fanfan la Tulipe,* charming as it is, nor *Don Camillo* that will revive its fortunes.[78] In the same volume of essays, Tallenay entitles his contribution "Have the French Not Got a Sense of Humor?" "In the last seven years," he says, "successes can be counted on the fingers of one hand . . . in France we have neither a comic tradition nor a school of comedy."[79] The supposedly comic films that have been produced depend on the malicious observation of cowardice, human frailties, weakness, and baseness, which is "far from liberating as a form of comedy." Mauriac agrees about the absence of any true French comic tradition,[80] and in their chapter on comedy Agel and Agel also see the comic as depending on degradation and victimization. The only acceptable examples belong to the sentimental branch of the genre, close to the comédie dramatique.[81] Both Agel and Agel and Étienne Fuzellier distinguish two main sub-genres of comedy, the realist and the burlesque, but Fuzellier considers both of these to be destructive—indeed, he sees the intrinsic function of comedy as subversion, and rejoices in it.[82]

No one sees the comic genre as flourishing in the fifties, though all qualify their despair by mentioning Tati, whose work is seen as isolated and inimitable. It is not surprising, then, that in a survey conducted in 1959 by the Institut Dourdain, romances are the most popular genre, followed by crime stories, then historical and adventure films; "comedies received very few votes."[83]

7.3 NARROW GENERIC CATEGORIES 1929–39

Since the range of generic categories used by commentators of the day followed no system and evolved over time as the films themselves evolved, a large number of descriptive terms were used to identify specific genres.

Some of these were relatively stable throughout the thirty years of the classic cinema, while others appeared for a greater or lesser length of time, then disappeared. Some were closely related to one another, such as "fantasy" and "poetic film," or "burlesque" and "farce," or even "crime drama" and "drame d'atmosphère." The following discussion, which focuses on the ways in which films were commonly categorized by critics between 1929 and 1939, will adopt a modified version of the quadripartite division outlined earlier, beginning with the formulaic dramatic categories commonly termed simply "films," then proceeding from comedic sub-genres through to dramatic sub-genres by way of intermediate sub-genres which blended in different ways and to different degrees the comic and/or the escapist with the serious and/or the real.

7.3.1 Crime films, war films, period films

The genres which came to be known simply as "films" were seldom the subject of extended commentary. They were considered such a routine and quasi-permanent element of the cinematic environment that when they were mentioned in annual reviews or overviews, it was normally only to note unusually abundant or meager years. Nevertheless, cumulatively a view of their nature and function emerges from commentaries of the time. The most frequently mentioned was the **crime film**. Most of the articles devoted to this genre consist largely of historical lists of major films, though some testify to a belief that its popularity surged in the early thirties, remained high until the mid-fifties, then experienced a rapid decline marked by parodic mockery of the conventions. The high point of this trajectory was the war years, when the crime film was among the most prominent of genres.

The theme of many thirties articles on the crime film was that it was typically American rather than French, but that a number of fine examples were beginning to appear in France. In 1932–33, referring to such films as *Au nom de la loi, Cœur de Lilas,* and *La Nuit du carrefour,* commentators speak of "the rise of the crime film from its ashes" and "the renaissance of the crime film in France."[84] An article by Carné in 1932 giving a history of the genre[85] refers back to Fantômas, Judex, Mandrin, and the boy reporter Rouletabille, who had just been revived by L'Herbier in *Le Mystère de la chambre jaune* and *Le Parfum de la dame en noir.* A 1934 editorial in *Ciné Miroir* notes the anxiety expressed by police at the increasing popularity of the genre, but protests that there is no need to ban them, since, unlike their American counterparts, French crime films seldom involve the use of guns and always promote the agent of the law as having intelligence and flair. Indeed, "they have encouraged more young people to become police officers than to become criminals."[86]

It is precisely this exaltation of the forces of order that infuriates the irrepressible Georges Altman. Regretting the disappearance of the Robin Hood–type chivalrous outlaw of yesteryear, he sees only Arsène Lupin as still able "to turn the tables on the authorities, the police, and the courts. Everywhere else, force is on the side of the law." Police officers have become family men, without complexes, and with a single aim: "To defend, as good servants, the society that pays them." The moral of such films is that "it is useless to oppose the law, there is a world of middle-class values to be protected, consolidated, justified." More generally, the proliferation of such films suggests that, for contemporary society, "the only adventure worth undertaking, it seems, is the attack on or defense of Society's Moneybins. . . . It is money that orders life. It is for money that people become intoxicated, suffer, struggle."[87]

The genre's popularity fluctuated during the thirties, but within relatively narrow limits. *Cinéopse* saw 1937 as a particularly good year for the crime film and the spy film, while the following year *La Cinématographie Française* classed these two as "formulas particularly favored by the public."[88] Subsequently, *Ciné Mondial* was to note the regular success of crime films during the war, and critical interest was to increase in the postwar period as a series of pastiches of the genre, starring Eddie Constantine, regularly achieved box-office success.

The spy film was often associated with the crime film. It was common, and frequently if unhelpfully commented upon, in the immediate prewar years, when Edwige Feuillère figured as the seductive female spy. It was to experience a brief, unremarkable resurgence in the early fifties, when because of its technical coding it was generally grouped with the crime film as forming communally the *série noire,* but it was at no stage the subject of any serious analysis. In a sense, it was more closely related to the **war film**, which attracted slightly more extensive commentary from critics. This genre was recognized as having occupied a minor but constant place in European output consequent on World War I. The few articles published in *Cinémonde* and *Cinémagazine* are disparaging, implicitly contrasting the pretensions of these "celluloid heroics" with the mediocre quality of the resultant films. Moussinac sees it as primarily an American genre, and includes it in his remarks about these films being designed to flatter the basest tastes of the masses.[89] Most others, such as Keim and Arnoux, make an exception for three or four exemplary war films—usually *Quatre de l'infanterie, À l'ouest rien de nouveau, Croix de bois,* and less frequently *Westfront, No Man's Land,* or *Verdun, visions d'histoire.*[90]

Altman is, once again, the only critic of the thirties to attempt to discriminate in any detail between different types of war film, their different effects on the public, and their relationship to different national ideologies.[91] He identifies two main categories. On the one hand, standard war films attempt to glorify battle and conceal the reality of pain, suffering, and death. For them, the division of humanity into nations is taken as a fundamental fact of life, and the experience of these nations rising up in pride and anger against one another is cast as an exhilarating adventure. He comments in particular on the current vogue for films representing the war in the air, "in which war is reduced to a few stars heroically taking to the air, far from the immense anonymous mass of grubby foot-soldiers being sacrificed on the altar of nationalism, crawling on hands and knees amidst mud and blood. War, that great adventure that consists of massacring other human beings, has to be prettified to be bearable."[92]

As these comments imply, Altman's sympathies are internationalist and humanitarian. He praises films such as *Quatre de l'infanterie,* which show war as "a chaotic and incoherent bloodbath laced with mud and terror. . . . A deluge of steel, fire, earth, and passionately contorted faces," where even the hospitals provide "an appalling symphony of fear."[93] Another such film is *À l'ouest rien de nouveau,* through which "a grim wind of suffering blows, a violent wind bringing catastrophe, implacable and irreparable."[94] Ultimately, however, his fear is that even such "realistic" war films can be read against the grain by a generation trained in nationalistic reading practices, as he himself has witnessed with a group of children happily cheering along with the slaughter of *Quatre de l'infanterie.*

The **historical genre** (the historical film, the period film, the costume drama) was much more widely discussed during the thirties than either the spy film or the war film, and was seen as following the same general trajectory as the crime film. Well established since the period of the *film d'art,* it was widely recognized as a standard genre in the twenties and experienced a brief surge in popularity with the advent of sound. A 1930 article by Marcel Carné entitled "Les Œuvres romantiques au cinéma" in fact deals with such films as *Les Misérables, Le Collier de la reine,* and several Balzac transcriptions.[95] By 1932, the genre was felt to be so common that *Cinémonde* protested against its expansion. Why make *Les Deux Orphelines, Monsieur de Pourceaugnac, Les Trois Mousquetaires,* and *Violettes impériales*? "The cinema is a living art, not a history teacher. . . . What we would like to see on the screen is more images of contemporary life, not masquerades like these."[96] Less common for a few years, the historical film surged again in the late thirties. A review of 1938's films noted thirteen period films—over 10 percent of production—and the genre was noted as prominent in all reviews of the next decade. In 1946, *La Cinématographie Française* was to proclaim that "the world recognizes France as particularly strong at historical reconstructions,"[97] which by then constituted about 20 percent of the year's output. The genre continued to be seen as flourishing until 1954.

Two explanations for the genre's prominence were adduced by thirties commentators, one related to the needs of spectators and the other to industry conditions. Usually, the genre was dismissed as a nostalgic form of escape into a supposed golden age, whose romance and glamour contrast with the stress and squalor of the present. In 1934, *Cinémonde* criticizes the swashbuckler sub-genre, and notably *Le Bossu,* for its indefensible representation of the past. "Our tormented age is nostalgic for heroes like these, who track down the lost heirs of noble families, return daughters to grieving mothers, punish traitors with their vengeful swords, and console afflicted females (as long as they're attractive)."[98] The genre was not seen solely as escapist, however. Keim notes its potential for allegorical comment on the present, and later commentators were to interpret such wartime films as *Pontcarral* and *Les Visiteurs du soir* as providing just that distanced reference to the present. Leenhardt provides the standard comment on this aspect of wartime production when he asks what else filmmakers could do under the occupation, forbidden as they were to speak openly of current events. "They chose the most noble form of escapism—history."[99] In his view, all the best wartime productions were costume dramas. Less inclined toward such a political explanation and more toward the ideological, Altman had earlier seen danger in a genre of this sort, "which implies that everything of importance takes place among the great of the earth"[100]— and, of course, has already been settled, long ago.

Two commentators attempted to explain why certain historical figures rather than others were the focus of historical films. Arnoux notes the prominence of Napoleon (his wars did, after all, affect the greater part of Europe, he was a great self-publicist, and he left memorable images of himself for hagiographers to exploit), Catherine of Russia (democracies have always been fascinated by the imperial system they displaced, and there is an irresistible delight in contrasting her formal public face with her licentious private life), and Joan of Arc (the fascinating conjunction of the peasant and the divine, not to mention her patriotic significance). Finally, he proposes an implicitly mythic basis for the genre, which he sees as catering to "obscure lyric impulses, collective hallucinations . . . the demands of poetry."[101] Keim was also interested in identifying the reasons that certain figures and certain historical periods appealed to contemporary audiences, concluding that an age dominated by world war, the growth of nationalism, and the clash of political ideologies looked back to the past for a timeless justification of its problematic contemporary engagements.[102]

The main reason adduced for the fluctuating prominence of this particular genre related to its cost. This could explain its disappearance during the tough years of the mid-thirties and subsequent rise to prominence in the late thirties, when several production companies were flush with funds. Even more clearly, it could explain its prominence during the war. A cast of thousands and elaborate decors such as that required for *Les Enfants du paradis* would have been almost inconceivable previously. And we can be a little less astonished than Nino Frank that "there should have existed in France, at the very moment when a war-torn Europe was beginning to crack open [1944], a producer willing to undertake the preparation of a monumental *Louis XIV,* in two parts [which was to cost] 80 million francs, and for which it was planned to renovate the Grand Canal at Versailles, reconstruct the Escalier des Ambassadeurs, and create a hundred sets and a thousand costumes."[103]

7.3.2 Boulevard comedies, slapstick, military vaudevilles, musical comedies

While a large number of comedic sub-genres were recognized as existing, little significance was attached to the differences between them. Commentators routinely recognized "comédies gaies," "comédies sentimentales," "vaudevilles" (particularly "vaudevilles militaires"), "comédies boulevardières," comédies musicales" (including "operettas"), and even "comédies comiques." Less frequently they used the terms "farce," "burlesque," "comédie loufoque" or "comédie absurde," and "comédie régionale." But despite the proliferation of labels, comedies as a whole were most commonly seen as the classic instance of an escapist cinema aiming to distract spectators from everyday concerns and help them keep their sanity in the face of adversity.

The most aggressive case for comedy having the effect of a safety valve was made by Altman in his extraordinary tirade against the boulevard comedy (which he never explicitly names, however). The principal filmic genre espoused by the suaver set (Guitry, Mirande, Rivers), it provided a useful target for Altman because it treated the aristocracy and haute bourgeoisie as if they were the only categories of people worthy of attention. The elegant, often modernist, settings of such filmed theater are seen as substituting for any real humanity. In such plays and films,

> you find only people with titles and people with millions—that is, only the most restricted and least real portion of humanity—the falsest idea that could possibly be given of real life. . . . On these phantoms the cinema struggles in vain to bestow the gift of life. . . . Such films reproduce a milieu which the bulk of spectators can never know . . . an excellent stratagem for acknowledging and consolidating the barrier which must be erected between two social worlds, properly separated by both birth and standing— the life of the master race, presented by the masters themselves, condescendingly, to the slaves who gape glumly and accept. . . . Aside from these fixed settings, these milieus which establish the caste system of the cinema, you may also be introduced to that much-savored milieu called "Bohemia," the world of music-hall and stage, as a pretext for an affecting display of dancing girls' thighs.

And the People in all this?
The People?
They open doors
They carry baggage
They say, "Dinner is served, Madam."
They say "Thank you," when tipped.
They constitute the masses, and during newsreels they shout "Long live France."[104]

A large proportion of the vast literature directed against theatrical transcriptions in the early thirties was likewise aimed, explicitly or implicitly, at the boulevard comedy, though as much for its lack of congruity with cinematic technique and practice as for its ideological function. But if such "base idiocies" were often felt to be fundamentally conservative, nevertheless the potential for comedy to be subversive was occasionally acknowledged, though usually with the provision that such subversion seemed foreign to the French cinema. The labels applied to explicitly subversive forms of comedy were the **burlesque** and the **slapstick (comédie loufoque)**. Leenhardt speaks of the Prévert brothers' *L'Affaire est dans le sac* as a burlesque and notes that it has been banned by the censor. Most of his examples are American, and he regrets that "the French, who don't have the knack for the epic, don't seem to have the knack for the burlesque either."[105] It is interesting to find Bresson's earliest (and later disowned) film, *Les Affaires publiques*, being categorized thus, though condemned for its lack of pace. In 1937, *Drôle de drame* was greeted as an Anglo-Saxon transplant, and as the first French burlesque film. It is the sole French film that Keim can cite in his category of slapstick, where "the unexpected, the abnormal, and the incoherent have been pushed to the ultimate limits."[106]

The general tendency to be pessimistic about the subversive potential of such genres in France seems to have been related to a general agreement about the efficiency of the largely informal political censorship operating throughout the industry. If genres that were even implicitly subversive were suppressed, there was even less hope that **satire**, with its explicit critique of the status quo, could flourish. This view was expressed with considerable force by Lucie Derain as early as 1934, in an article called "Satire on the Screen": "[There must be] no disrespect for magistrates, or for the police, or for public servants, or for bankers, let alone for politicians or, of course, religion."[107] She can instance only three French films which might be considered satirical—Feyder's last silent film, *Les Nouveaux Messieurs;* Clair's *À nous la liberté;* and *Ces messieurs de la Santé,* which had to be reworked and toned down before it was granted a release. Twenty years later, presenting a retrospective called "The Comic in the French Cinema," *Image et Son* was still forced to acknowledge that "after an astonishing flowering in the silent

era, the comic genre faced a real crisis" in the sound era, when it was dominated by bland romantic comedies.[108]

In this generally pessimistic portrait of the comic genres, the **military
vaudeville** occupied an odd position. In its fragmentary and often parodic
representation of a key French institution, it clearly had explosive social potential, but even right-wing critics sensitive to that potential did not for the
most part see the genre as dangerous. As the threat of war increased, however, there were moves to suppress it, and the Renaitour inquiry heard of
the minister's attempts (unsuccessful, as it happens) to ban *Les Bleus de la
marine,* and of the Censorship Board's more effective pre-censorship of various "comic military and maritime films." The tone was still measured,
however—French spectators "can easily distinguish the element of fantasy"
in military vaudevilles, and thus "attach relatively little importance to the
matter." It was the ridiculing of the French military *abroad* that preoccupied the authorities, and the emphasis was on the need for a separate export
certificate to limit such negative propaganda.[109]

This is still the overt cause of the genre's banning on the outbreak of war,
though it now also begins to be seen as a potentially debilitating moral virus
sapping France's war efforts from within, as well. This is the official verdict
on the genre during the Vichy period, when it is one of the very few genres to
remain outlawed for the duration of the war. After the war, Charensol's claim
that censorship on the basis of quality would almost be justified if it hauled
the French cinema out of the mire of vaudeville was superfluous: the genre
made no substantial reappearance. "These days, no one dares make films like
La Margoton du bataillon, which only ten years ago broke upon us in wave
after wave."[110] Effectively, then, the military vaudeville was one of the distinctive genres of the thirties French cinema, though few then or later saw
this as a characteristic of which they could be proud.

The only other comic genre that was isolated for extended comment
was the **musical comedy**. Acknowledged as a significant category for the
classification of French production from the early sound years, when such
films as *Le Chemin du paradis* and *Le Congrès s'amuse* were among the most
popular hits, through the late thirties and the forties, when Tino Rossi
alone starred in some fifteen musicals, the genre was the subject of recurrent commentary in the postwar years and of an extensive ten-part retrospective in *Image et Son* between January 1959 and March 1960. The
parameters of the debate were double: was this so intrinsically an American
genre that the numerous French attempts at it would always have to be
viewed compassionately, and was it so intrinsically anti-realist that attempts
to integrate it into a realistic framework were doomed to aesthetic failure,
and were perhaps even heretical.

In 1945, referring to thirties examples, *L'Écran Français* proclaimed
musical comedies to be intrinsically American and difficult to transplant.

Identifying the genre with slick, highly choreographed, fast-moving, big-budget productions, *L'Écran Français* recognized that a French musical comedy was and had to be different, and less impressive. "We are at once the land of Montmartre, of sentiment, and of penny-pinching producers. The girls are rationed, the car hoods less long, the orchestras smaller."[111] This inferiority complex was to be most forcefully articulated in *Cinéma*, which devoted some 110 pages to the American musical comedy and questioned whether such a thing as the French musical comedy could even exist. Reviewing instances to date, the magazine condemned them as mere extensions of caf'conc, with occasional "items" for well-known singers. "The disaster has been total, and it has lasted for thirty years already."[112]

Most accounts of the genre were more affectionate. While the films were often seen as ineffectual in terms of narrative drive, the mere fact that they recorded the performances of such famous thirties music-hall artists as Chevalier, Mistinguett, Fréhel, and Josephine Baker (not to mention Gabin), and later Trénet, Piaf, Greco, Brassens, Montand, and Aznavour, was enough to justify the genre's existence; though, as René Gieure was to say in his retrospective, "It's still a painful sight to see famous music-hall singers collaborating only in the most execrable films."[113]

Most vitriol was reserved for clumsy attempts to play down the obvious artifice of the genre and render it more plausible. From his prisoner-of-war cell, Keim nostalgically recalled the gross trickery of the early French (and German) musical comedies, where "furniture moved about of its own accord in *Le Chemin du paradis*, rocking chairs swayed in time to the general rhythm in *Le Congrès s'amuse*, and cows wandered into houses and drank from goldfish bowls in *Les Joyeux Garçons*."[114] These fantasy worlds, with their own particular rules according to which people could intone their dialogue and suddenly break into a song or tap-dance, were what enchanted the critics. Attempts to incorporate the music-making into a realistic diegesis by organizing the narrative around a singer, a real or fictional composer, or the members of a band were almost universally derided as sentimental claptrap. As van Parys says sadly, "They felt the need to explain away the presence of any music. The cinema must on no account resemble the theater, where the actor could for no apparent reason abruptly burst into song. Nothing like that in the cinema, they said, where everything must ring true."[115]

Tino Rossi, Guétary, and Hirigoyan were the target of their most sarcastic remarks, and the conventions of the narratives constructed around them were frequently derided:

(1) A charming young man squanders his aunt's or uncle's money on the most typically Parisian of young women. Nightclubs, Pigalle, duets, French Cancan, Sacré Cœur, Champs Élysées, artists' studios, the roofs of Paris, unmade beds, and photogenic hangovers. In a word, Gay Paree. . . . Over the final kiss,

reprise of the film's theme song. Music by Misraki or van de Parys [*sic*].
(2) A sentimental story about a handsome Corsican/handsome Basque/
handsome Marseillais. Local color: the Island of Love, the Côte d'Argent,
the Old Port. The Big Smoke, the Evil Woman, the Broken Heart, the Return, the Fiancée-Who-Has-Waited, the Old Mother, Village Church Bells.
With or without regional accent. Guitars, aubade or serenade, floods of
tears, vats of rosewater. . . . Music by Vincent Scotto.[116]

7.3.3 The exotic and colonial genres

The exotic genres were also seen primarily as escapist. Quantitatively, the
exotic was long dominated by documentaries, often full-length, with such
titles as *La Croisière jaune, L'Afrique vous parle, Chez les mangeurs d'hommes,
Au pays des buveurs de sang, Symphonie exotique,* and *La Grande Caravane,*
but the exotic inflected a large number of fiction films as well. Moreover,
most accounts of it included documentaries and fiction films dealing with
the French empire. Occasionally the latter were distinguished as "the colonial genre," or (quite unabashedly) "national propaganda." The conventions
and social functions of these genres are all covered in Leprohon's 1945 review of the exotic, *L'Exotisme et le cinéma,* which inevitably deals primarily
with films made in the thirties.

Recognizing that the prime interest of the exotic was its sense of otherness, Leprohon deals with two parameters of the genre—first, as it represented the alien in factual and informative terms, or as myth; second as it
represented the alien as barbaric and archaic, or as impossibly paradisiacal.
Certain documentaries are identified as providing a new yet basically reliable understanding of the world. This informational function is seen as
being particularly attractive to the intelligentsia, whom it has been instrumental in bringing to the cinema. More often, however, whether documentary or fictional, the exotic is seen as poetic rather than prosaic, dealing in
dreams and fantasy rather than in reality.

But the nature of the dream varied. At times, Leprohon talks of the fascination of the genre as being the acquaintance it provides with the primitive, viewed as ugly and violent. "You feel, behind the images, the sinister
presence of a world alien to our understanding, our customs, our very
imagination," where "people with archaic ways live in the heart of a proliferating and unhealthy nature."[117] In such films, barbaric peoples practice
sorcery and ritual murder, while the ever-present threat that they may run
amok is a constant reminder of the frailty of social controls in the face of
instinctual violence.

At the other extreme, the primitive is often contrasted favorably with
more sophisticated European cultures, the genre setting up, as in *Nanook,*
"admirable models of primitive life for the instruction of our own civiliza-

tion, spoiled as it is by the comforts of life." *Moana* also exemplifies the natives' "happy existence in the midst of tropical nature, their tasks and games, the secular traditions of these purebred Polynesians."[118] The words "ease" and "serenity" recur to describe this "idyllic existence," this "terrestrial paradise." In its perfection, this alien civilization calls into question the notion of progress so dear to the Western mind, and the function of the genre is to reacquaint desiccated Westerners with something profound, something eternal, while recognizing that the very contact necessary to achieve their reacquaintance with it will irretrievably corrupt "these last refuges of felicity."[119]

The genre, then, is seen as engaging in the debate about the nature of Nature, and of human nature, of progress, and of civilization. But at times, in contrast to the twin poles of the barbaric and the paradisiacal, both of which underline the almost unimaginable gulf that separates "them" from "us," the genre is seen as working subtly to bridge that gulf. Over and above the otherness of these alien cultures, we experience a common bond with them. Leprohon quotes Ruttman, speaking of *La Mélodie du monde:* "What we had to show was the similarities as much as the differences between men, the relationship between man and animal, the bonds that tie men to the soil and the climate; we had to express those things which concern humanity across all ages and all frontiers: love, religion, arms, warfare; motherhood and children; the arts . . . nourishment, commerce, pleasures, sports."[120] And again, "beneath the surface we felt ourselves similar to Nanook, struggling to provide for his family's and his own existence." Here is something that speaks of a universal human condition, "close to our own, reduced to basic problems which, in our own civilization, we had grown unaccustomed to considering. . . . If it showed us what separated man from man, it also showed us what united them."[121]

Two summative statements by Leprohon point in different directions. At one point he speaks of the exotic as betraying a fascination with other times and places ("la nostalgie d'ailleurs et d'autrefois") and goes on to say that "we need to believe in Edens and El Dorados. Such an illusion sustains us."[122] Elsewhere, he points to the negative aspect of the exotic as "a contemporary manifestation of disquiet."[123] While he doesn't expand on that phrase, it is possible to read into it the confusions and uncertainties attendant on growing contact with cultures based on principles totally alien to those that one has long taken for granted as natural. In this reading, the exotic generates a form of national self-questioning and self-doubt, while a defensive reaction against this self-doubt produces the assertive nationalistic propaganda of the colonial genre.

Other accounts of the exotic genre in the years 1929–46 reproduced one or more of the above discourses. It was seen as one of the main generic groupings in the first two years of the sound cinema, with numerous films set in Oceania, India, and the Far East.[124] *Cinéopse* observed that with its picturesque images and mysterious ways, it proposed "a wider and more perfect view of the world. Places that we could not hope to see except by taking long and costly voyages, the screen brings to us with an intensity that leaves nothing to be desired. By way of the cinema the whole world is brought to us, and the most secretive tribes are no longer hidden from us."[125] Perhaps this early popularity was due to the Colonial Exhibition, since *Cinéopse* noted a diminution thereafter, though in 1933 *Ciné Miroir* could see the triumph of the exotic in the career of Reri, star of *Tabu*—symbolic of "that carefree island of eternal spring," even as she performed at the Gaumont Palace, fresh from the Ziegfried Follies.[126]

Perhaps the most passionate account of the genre comes from *Cinémonde*, which in 1932 published an article entitled "Mœurs cruelles et douces." Dealing mainly with documentaries, the article underlines the barbarous and repugnant aspect of the Other: "Man displays those core moments of his animal life—love, birth, death. . . . The screen projects an immense and monstrous human activity, an activity at once grimacing, vociferous, and demoniacal. Scenes of magic, sorcery, and incantations succeed tableaux of hunting and fishing. Death . . . death . . . life . . . life, in an unending alternation."[127] But *Cinémonde* also has something to say about the graceful Polynesian women and the exquisite naked breasts of their daughters, and in a balancing article, Lucie Derain welcomes the fact that such films had chased from French screens all the worldly dramas and facile comedies of recent years. By their power, "they make us regret that we're only petty shop assistants, lowly soldiers scrubbing out the barracks, businessmen tied to the telephone . . . unable to return to that slow, immutable vegetative life for which humanity is made."[128]

Thereafter, for over ten years, the exotic in its non-colonial form came primarily to signify a finer world "out there" which French citizens, for one reason or another, were prohibited from experiencing—it signified, that is, a fantasized escape from harsh realities. For this reason, the genre acquired a particular poignancy for wartime audiences. Writing (from Switzerland, admittedly) in 1943, Élie, in an otherwise forgettable book, notes, "For us, attached as we are to a town, a house, a job, the land that nourishes us, and without any real possibility of travelling, the cinema . . . carries us off to the most distant reaches of the world."[129] Writing five years later about the wartime cinema, Roger Régent notes, "Confined within restricted borders, our directors and producers strove to evoke distant lands, exotic customs. . . . We needed the feel of open spaces and the sight of distant horizons."[130] Certainly, during the war both *Le Film* and *Cinémonde* record the continuing success of the exotic, and in the immediate postwar years *Le Film*

Français could, in a retrospective on the genre, claim that it was still very popular.[131] But by the end of 1946, *La Cinématographie Française* was fore-telling its decline: "In the face of modernity, mechanization, and shrinking distances . . . exoticism is tending to disappear, both from reality and from our screens. For those who sought to flee the cares of everyday life by going to the movies, this type of film managed to create a sense of escape, as it re-vealed visions of the wider world for those haunted by the secret desire to set sail."[132]

Indeed, the exotic was thereafter to fade from critical view, except for a number of observations in the late fifties concerning exotic documentaries, which experienced a tentative revival with the advent of color and wide screens. So we can say that, like the military vaudeville, the exotic genre flourished primarily in the thirties and was one of the distinctive genres of that decade. However, the conventions which it mobilized seldom domi-nated an entire fiction film, but rather pointed to an idea of exotic other-ness which could be evoked briefly, usually as an idealized alternative to contemporary social reality.

The **colonial genre**, which had often been considered an integral part of the exotic because of its foreign locations, had a far shorter period of prominence than its parent genre. Not often recorded in the early thirties as an actualized genre, though often called for by nationalists, it was discussed more and more as a developing genre with the approach of war, but it dis-appears in 1940, never to re-emerge. In his review of the exotic in 1945, Leprohon accords an important place to the colonial propaganda film of the thirties, which he sees as having had the double function of bearing wit-ness to the civilizing mission and achievements of past heroes of the French nation, and of inspiring a younger generation to emulate those heroes. By recounting the work of Lyautey, de Foucauld, Brazza, and their like, such films had foregrounded "the prestige which France enjoys among its colo-nized peoples," and "shown the world what French civilization really means, and why the native peoples love France." "The public focuses its gaze above all on those sun-drenched lands where its ancestors courageously directed their steps. The immense empire conquered by our pioneers, our soldiers, and our missionaries represents in its eyes a form of exoticism with which it feels at one, to which it is attached by bonds more concrete than those of reverie or of poetry." Viewing such films cannot but "renew in French youth that love of courage, that active curiosity which inspired so many maritime and colonial vocations."[133]

This inspirational view of the colonial genre was to ring rather false in the France of 1946, but was common currency in the thirties. The fact that the French cinema was *not* exploiting the propaganda potential of film was a permanent source of astonishment and dismay to the more nationalistic commentators. From 1932 on, *Cinéopse*, in particular, calls repeatedly for the French cinema to emulate the Italian cinema, which under the guidance of Mussolini had become "a national force, applied to education, to training, to workers' use of leisure time, to tourism, and to propaganda."[134] It praises the Administrator of the Colonies, M. Chaumel, for his evening talks presenting propaganda documentaries, and welcomes all films which tend to demonstrate the civilizing effects of French colonization.[135] In the immediate prewar years, this journal's appeals for "films worthy of France" become more urgent, and it recommends ministerial coordination of propaganda via the cinema to eliminate unworthy films and promote those "glorifying the French spirit and supporting French honor."[136] It welcomes the initiative of M. Pietri, Minister for the Navy, when he permits the ships of the fleet to be used for a number of documentaries (*La Marine Française, La France est une île, Branlebas de combat*) and fiction films (*Veille d'armes, La Porte du large*). As the genre begins to succeed with the public, notably with *Alerte en Méditerranée, Légions d'honneur,* and *L'Appel du silence, Cinéopse* expresses its satisfaction: "Although the essential and principal aim of the cinema is entertainment, we have always maintained that it nonetheless had other tasks, and notably that of working for the grandeur and worldwide influence of our country. . . . It is toward our magnificent colonial empire that the cinema's activity is now [January 1939] turning. Yes, 'France is an empire,' as has often been said, and now is the time to demonstrate it." *Brazza, l'épopée du Congo, La Chevauchée héroïque, Lyautey l'Africain,* and *L'Homme du Niger* are "four important works, on which great hopes can be pinned."[137]

Other magazines, such as *Cinémonde* and *La Cinématographie Française,* were more preoccupied with the negative effects of films which presented France in a bad light. In the early thirties, the focus of these anxieties was the representation of the foreign legion. In 1931, Jean Dumas noted the proliferation of such films, with their tendency to represent legionnaires as reprobates and drunkards who were likely to lash out without reason and were tortured and tormented by officers, who acted more like prison guards. "It's time to redress this injustice toward men who have quite rightly been called knights-errant of the ideal. . . . Bound by their common commitment to the flag they serve, they harbor a real reverence for the honor of their military calling."[138] *Cinémonde* seems at times to see this "false image" of the legion as the product of an American conspiracy[139] and welcomes films, such as *Sergent X,* which call it into question by talking in terms of sacrifice, self-denial, and heroism. The growth of the colonial documentary is a cause for celebration. *La Symphonie malgache,* notes *Ciné Miroir,* reaffirms "our love and pride at the thought of our vast colonial empire," and "the freedom, tolerance, and justice that French colonialism has disseminated around the world. Everywhere before our arrival reigned . . . cruel superstitions, piracy, and slavery." Now, on the contrary, we find "a sentiment of equality and justice for the poor and humble. Everywhere we have elevated the condition of humanity."[140]

Moreover, from 1936 on, *La Cinématographie Française* joins *Cinéopse* in noting with satisfaction a parallel series of fiction films that are taking the French military as their subject. At last, "films which will exalt our country."[141] *Ciné Miroir,* which had also been regretting the fact that despite the centrality of maritime communications to the unity of the empire "we French seem to have lost our taste for the sea," welcomes the increasing presence and success of such films, though finds it not really surprising: "Films on the navy are always popular. Our lads in blue . . . always attract the admiration of the masses." Through such films as *Alerte en Méditerranée* and *Nord Atlantique* blow "the winds of adventure, great voyages, departures, and escape."[142]

In the mid- to late thirties, the focus of patriotic anxieties was not so much on foreign legion films as on the damaging effects of military vaudevilles (considered innocuous up to then), pacifist films such as *La Grande Illusion,* and poetic realist films. Hitler finds favor with *Cinémonde* for asserting that pacifist films fail to portray a sufficiently intransigent nationalism. Fortunately, by this time a large body of sufficiently intransigent nationalist productions existed to counter such debilitating films. In a series of African films, Charles Vanel embodied the noble man of action "who finds in himself the strength to struggle against the hostile elements" (*Légions d'honneur, L'Occident, Bar du sud, SOS Sahara*); while *Trois de St. Cyr*

> shows St. Cyriens to be motivated neither by ambition nor by self-interest; it is simply that they desire open spaces and movement and have a taste for action, and their souls are devoted to promoting the grandeur of their native land. St. Cyr is where those virtues of uprightness, courage, and honor, which have always typified the French officer, are formed. It is good that the cinema should exalt the highest qualities of our race. . . . The St. Cyr life, with its harsh discipline and its stoic young men, is a wonderful lesson in energy; it demonstrates to all those who believe us to be degenerate that our race has preserved the virtues that have made it great throughout history.[143]

By this time, the conventions of the developing genre could be readily recognized, and Leprohon lists them at length: "Here we find a sort of orientalized romanticism: young warriors with fierce eyes, tribal chieftains and their raiding parties, villages shrouded in the shadows of white-walled alleyways, caravans and palm trees, conflicts of race and religion, the Berber child raised among whites, the naval officers with their 'little wives,' the chant of the muezzin floating over the towns, and of prayers over the desert, burnooses and headdresses, displays of Arab horsemanship, the clash of arms, a highly colored world of violence, mystery and passion."[144]

There is "much simple-minded talk of honor, of duty and of heroism," but these are sentiments reserved for the whites, who as engineers, doctors, and missionaries, devote their lives to the civilizing mission of the empire, while the ungrateful natives do their treacherous best to undermine their every effort, and it all ends with a climactic attack by the rebellious natives. Leprohon sees the genre's main effect as confirming spectators' cliché-ridden views of empire. "All this is so insistent that the colonial cinema can seem . . . resolutely hostile to the very setting whose charms it claims to be promoting. It thus constitutes a sort of counter-propaganda, [giving] a distinctly odd idea of the civilizing mission of France."[145]

That conservatives cherished the postwar hope of resuscitating this genre, and the nationalist sentiments that went with it, is evidenced not just by the desires expressed in *L'Exotisme et le cinéma* but by a 1946 article in *La Cinématographie Française* regretting the disappearance of the exotic, and particularly the colonial, genre. "The French colonies are the order of the day. . . . Only the screen can illustrate the magnificent devotion that has been shown and is still being shown over there each day, often unrecognized or misunderstood, but which nevertheless places France in the front rank in terms of humanitarian achievement."[146] But any hope of regenerating the genre was necessarily to come into conflict with recent memories of defeat and occupation, and any belief in the natural affection of native peoples for France was soon to be undermined by a series of anti-colonial wars of liberation. A harsh censorship régime aimed specifically at suppressing any alternative views of these wars was to eliminate virtually any portrayal of these colonies from French screens during the fifties.

7.3.4 The realist drama, poetic realism, the youth film

As we have seen, dramas, while never produced in as great a number as comedies during the thirties, were nevertheless extremely popular with the public in the latter half of the decade. The form that attracted most critical commentary throughout the relevant period was the **realist drama**. There were four very general approaches to it: it was a fictional variant of the documentary, of which a central and essential element was the use of authentic locations, people, and events; it focused on certain contemporary social problems, regardless of whether these were filmed on location or in the studio; it might or should argue a case, leading to a debate as to whether propaganda was compatible with realism; it might or should threaten the existing order, leading to a debate as to the role of censorship.

The documentary approach early led to calls for the camera to descend into the street and to film what it saw there—predominantly the humble everyday existence of the "little people" of Paris, but also, by extension, the characteristic patterns of life in the various regions of France. Both of these were proposed as a reaction against the sophisticated frippery of boulevard comedies and motivated in part by the retreat from location shooting brought about by the introduction of sound. A number of articles in *Ciné-monde* in the years 1930–33 promoted the filming of "real life." A classic instance, "when the cinema descends into the streets of Paris," promoted the use of exteriors to bring to the screen the various districts of the capital.[147] It rapidly became normal for a significant proportion of each film's scenes to be shot on location, and a standard way of generating plots was for the scriptwriter and director to identify a regional setting with visual or dramatic potential and to settle into a local inn to develop a script based around that potential. As early as 1931, in an article on typical scenarios submitted to him at Pathé Natan, Franck Servais lists fictionalized documentaries focusing on workers and craftsmen and glorifying work in the factory, at the forge or the looms, or in the mines.[148] In a similarly euphoric mood, Arcy-Hennery in 1935 enjoins the apprentice scriptwriter to "take a lesson from the theater of the street—no spectacle is so rich; life seethes and refashions itself there; what a splendid study it can provide for you"—in, of course, "that noblest of tasks, discovering and glorifying the soul of our race."[149]

But if what the camera found in the streets represented the soul of France, that soul was far from healthy. More often than not, the term "realist drama" was applied to films that focused on the sordid aspects of everyday existence—poverty, slums, and the pressures that these exerted on the less fortunate to engage in a life of crime. It was not the everyday experiences of the workingman but the nighttime underworld of the milieu, with its apaches and its prostitutes—not the street but "the street"—that came to dominate the genre. French realism, that is, was heavily influenced by German expressionism, as the titles of films most commonly cited as early instances already indicated—*Une nuit à l'hôtel, Les Nuits de Port Saïd, Paris la nuit, Dans les rues, La Rue sans nom.* The startling success of *L'Opéra de quat'sous* was instrumental in this proliferation, and many of Gabin's early films were categorized in this genre—*Cœur de Lilas, Paris Béguin, Adieu les beaux jours, Du haut en bas,* even *Zouzou.*

Similar films had, of course, been made during the silent era, and it was to protest against their "false" realism that André Thérive published "Populism in the Cinema" in *Cinémonde,* calling for a more documentary and less mythologized view of social existence.[150] Certainly, he says, reality is often "grim, harsh, and vulgar," but the cinema should not ignore the humble everyday life of the healthy, vigorous, industrious French working class. The degenerate marginals on whom film and novel seem to be concentrating are not typical: "Alongside all these lay-abouts and perverts there are the people of the factories, the workshops, the offices." As examples of his preferred populist cinema he cites *En rade, La Tragédie de la mine, La Zone,* and *Ménilmontant.*

By 1933, however, it is the theme of youth that is being recognized as central to the realist drama. *Cinéopse* notes that *Dans les rues* is of burning importance "at a time when there is so much debate concerning the influence of the street on certain categories of young people who are thrown back on their own resources."[151] *La Maternelle, Jeunesse,* and *Maternité* generated further commentary concerning the problems facing young people during the crash, and particularly the problem of unmarried mothers, which attracted perhaps the only use of the term *film à thèse* in the thirties.[152] Commenting on *Jeunesse* and *Lac aux dames, Ciné Miroir* notes the difficult life of today's hard-working young people setting out idealistically on life's journey: "You hear everywhere the complaints of young people who have qualifications and have studied long and hard to get a job, but see doors shut in their face." The result is anguish, listlessness, and disaffection. Germany had produced stories like this in the 1920s, *Ciné Miroir* warns, and there is a risk of creating a similar pre-fascist situation in France.[153]

Pour Vous showed itself to be equally aware of the contemporary filmic preoccupation with young people, and between the end of 1933 and the end of 1935 published a number of (superficial) articles on this genre, which came to be called the "**youth film**" (*film de jeunes* and, much later, *film sur l'enfance*). These articles tended to focus on child and adolescent stars and on the social problems which they were being called upon to act out.[154] Seen as a whole, they are curiously ambivalent, unable to decide whether contemporary social conditions are such as to inevitably corrupt the innocence and purity of childhood, or rather such as to provide the young with opportunities that previous generations would have envied. In the former mode, which was the more common, it was normally males that were featured, whereas in the latter it was normally females. Thus the modern miss may come bursting into the room, brushing aside books, and throw herself down carelessly on the sofa to be interviewed. "Young girls have evolved terribly quickly," exclaims the interviewer. "See them on a surfboard, a defiant laugh on their lips, or driving a car, or astride a polo pony, as free as any boy. . . . How different from their predecessors."[155] Implicitly, this view of the young woman who is "liberated, independent, intending to live as she pleases" comes from America, whereas harassed, corrupted youths, beset by social problems not of their own making, are intrinsically European, and particularly German. Various commentators, however, note that in French films the representation of social pressures and institutions is less severe than that purveyed by German films.[156]

After a gap of three years, these concerns resurface in 1938 and 1939— not so much the promotion of a documentary realism, but, within a framework of social problematics, the "Germanic" focus on working-class marginals forced into a life of crime, and the "American" optimism about social progress. Summing up the production for 1938, one critic sees such youth films as providing "healthy and fresh scenarios," evoking the sentimental affairs of students, their hopes and fears, "all the exhuberance [*sic*] of that happy age."[157] But another reference to the genre recalls films that had focused on the hardships faced by the young—speaking of *films d'enfants*, Claude Bernier says, "For some years, reading newspaper articles on the martyrdom that so many kids endure these days, you might believe that in France we don't love our children, that we maltreat them, bring them up harshly, and deprive them of food and affection."[158] A number of more optimistic films are about to correct that impression—*Feu de paille, L'Enfer des anges,* and *Air pur* (the last of which never got made). "Let's hope that these works, full of compassion and suffering, will confound our misguided educators and put an end to ways of dealing with children which are a shame to humanity."[159]

The youth film was to become a characteristic genre of the mid- to late fifties, when the development of a "youth culture" ensured the success of films starring teenage actors such as Jean-Pierre Léaud. Critics of that time, such as Agel and Agel, readily acknowledged that the origins of the genre (and its various sub-genres) could be traced back to such films of the thirties as *Les Disparus de St. Agil, Jeunesse,* and *La Maternelle,* not to mention filmed versions of nineteenth-century melodramas. More generally, the role of a social cinema bearing on urgent contemporary problems was to be brought to the fore by postwar meditations on the occupation and the resistance, the decolonization process, the wars in Algeria and Vietnam, and the censorship debates consequent on them. Proportionately, it was to play a far greater role then than it had in the thirties, though it was never again to attain the mythic significance that it attained in that decade.

Another form of realist drama to gain critical attention was the "location film," which was considered to be proliferating in the thirties. An article in *La Cinématographie Française* in 1939 notes the recent success of the location film or "reportage," but lists under that heading everything from straight documentaries (*Neiges de France, La Croisière noire, La Grande Inconnue*) through fictionalized documentaries (Flaherty) and *Sommes-nous défendus?* to the Benoît-Lévy–Marie Epstein films (*La Mort du cygne, La Maternelle,* and *Altitude 3200*).[160] All of Jean Epstein's prewar writings, of course, testified to a passion for location shooting, for actors chosen from the local populace, and for scripts woven around local myth. Of *Finis terrae* he wrote, "I think that . . . there will be an ever greater demand for natural real-life actors, in all countries and all classes of society, and all occupations, and also for natural settings, true stories, and authentic atmosphere." And of *L'Or des mers,* he wrote, "I didn't want to ask actors to copy gestures, attitudes, characters, when there were people there who could live them."[161] Summing up his ideals, he said, "Each of [my] films is the savorous expression of one among millions of those little communities of which humanity is made up. . . . From a blacksmith we will learn about the life of his forge. An actor imitating a blacksmith won't give us reason even to suspect that there is anything to learn. . . . We must go out and uncover each of the thousands of varieties of humankind in its own environment, its own life."[162] Insofar as a genre of documentary realism existed in the thirties, it was largely a product of Epstein's theorizing, promotion, and practice.

As has been noted earlier, the underworld film, which had steadily moved up-market, was to become the poetic realist film, but considering its subsequent notoriety there was relatively little contemporary comment on it. Called **films d'atmosphère,** such films were regularly listed and noted as increasingly numerous, but it was the mythical character created in certain of them by Jean Gabin that attracted attention, rather than the genre as such, so they receive greater attention in the next chapter. Any contemporary mention of them tended to be in the condemnatory mode of the wartime and, particularly, Vichy régimes. Even before the war, *Cinéopse* could seldom resist this right-wing discourse, and one rather self-contradictory article reproached *Quai des brumes* for exploiting the baser tendencies of human nature: "Although such films . . . have sometimes proved profitable, they have always harmed the general interest of the cinema itself—all the more so when films of this type proliferate and drive from our theaters the family audience, the only audience big enough to enable us to recoup the cost of a film."[163] *Cinéopse* also raised the specter of a cinema of propaganda, reproaching *La Marseillaise* for being no more than a political tool.[164] The cinema had nothing to gain from such a course of action. *Cinéopse* felt, however, that the cinema had everything to gain by producing films that exalted the French soldier and sailor. Such films were not, of course, propaganda—they were not political, but national; not divisive, but unifying.

In the late forties, André Bazin was to mount a passionate defense of poetic realism, which he saw as metaphysical rather than social; a more balanced appreciation of the *drame d'atmosphère* as a coherent and significant body of films had to await the mid-fifties, when commentators such as Denis Marion and Pierre Leprohon were retrospectively to explore its conventions. Commenting on the Carné–Prévert films in *Présences contemporaines,* Leprohon lists as typical of the genre the themes of escape and of destiny, the aspiration of lost souls toward purity and happiness, a bitter vision of a doomed society, a romanticized view of the underworld, a fascination with the idea of departure, and a feel for the cyclical celebrations of the people. "Man is not at all inherently evil in these films; destiny has got him in its grip and traps him in a criminal act alien to both his nature and his intellect."[165]

One of the more remarkable observations to emerge from this survey of the generic categories most commonly used by contemporary French commentators is the extent to which the terms used to describe the national output of France are quite distinct from those used in other countries. Of course there is a degree of overlap, particularly among the "adventure" genres. The categories of musical comedy, period film, war film, and crime story or murder mystery were widely accepted elsewhere—but labels such as boulevard comedy, exotic film, military vaudeville, colonial film, poetic realist film, and youth film (not to mention poetic film and religious film, which were to become the subject of more critical comment than any other genre in the immediate postwar period) would have been less readily recognized. Yet it was precisely these latter categories of film which were the most widely recognized and discussed in France in the thirties. This distinctive array of genres points to a distinctive array of preoccupations in the French cinema and, in turn, a distinctive array of social problems exercising the minds of the film-going public.

Another observation to emerge is that most interest in generic classification was shown in the postwar years. No books on the topic were published in the years 1930–43; the first were *Le Cinéma et la Montagne* and *L'Exotisme et le Cinéma,* both by Leprohon and published, respectively, in 1944 and 1945. Of course, books on the cinema were not common in the thirties, and they were even less common in the years of the occupation, given the political constraints and paper shortages of that period. Yet a renaissance was evident at war's end, with IDHEC considering the topic of genre sufficiently central to warrant a course ("Literary and Cinematic Genres," given by Étienne Fuzellier), while several publishers now saw the cinema as a profitable field to exploit. From 1953 on, the contribution of Les Éditions du Cerf to this study of genres was very significant. This company published Bazin and Rieupeyrout's book on the Western, *Le Cinéma et le Sacré* by Agel, *Cinéma, Foi et Morale* by Ludmann, *Le Cinéma et l'Enfance* by Vandromme, *Le Film Criminel et le Policier* by Cauliez, *Miroirs de l'Insolite* by Agel, and *Images de la Science-Fiction* by Siclier. While this level of publication does indeed bear witness to a degree of interest in genres on the part of both commentators and readers, it has to be seen in the context of a level of production of books on films that averaged about twenty per year throughout the period 1945–60, in which books on genre were far outnumbered by books on film history, books on individual filmmakers, and even books on theory. Individual filmmakers were the subject, on average, of two books a year in the early fifties, rising to four, then six a year, to reach at least ten in 1960; the postwar years also saw the beginning of the long-term historical projects by René Jeanne and Charles Ford and by Georges Sadoul. When one adds to these the many books of memoirs, together with accounts of the industry and its processes, it becomes apparent how minimal was the interest in genres even in the postwar period.

Nevertheless, the fact that it existed at all must be due to some extent to the change in the nature of French film production under the wartime regime. The industrial anarchy of the prewar years had ensured that generic production could never dominate the French production system. Not only was it more possible during the war, because of the limited personnel available and the limited range of production firms, but the political constraints on production severely restricted the types of film that could be made. Under these conditions, it is not so surprising that commentators should have begun to find it easier to see patterns emerging from the rather limited annual production, and should have been encouraged to try to describe, name, and explain those patterns. In this sense, it is very likely that it was the sudden dominance of wartime production by such genres as the crime film, the poetic film, and the period film that triggered the (still relative) postwar resurgence of interest in genre as a way of discussing film. This is slightly ironic, since these genres themselves are seldom the focus of extended commentary, which is reserved for more novel categories of film such as the exotic, the fantastic, the religious, and even the youth film.

EIGHT

The Stars in Their (Dis)courses:
"Anemic dreams" and "poetry for pallid people"?

The worship of film stars will be the downfall of the cinema.
—Georges Altman (1932)

[These clapped-out hacks of surrealism] are all too anxious to
take us wandering along the banks of canals, and to evoke for
us the poignancy of bleak suburban wastelands, of rain-
drenched villages . . . and of piteous young girls caught up in
anemic dreams. . . . Never a true emotion, never a powerful
feeling. . . . What I hold against them is that they get lost in a
fog of literary allusions and of poetry for pallid people.
—Jean-Georges Auriol (1941), talking of the plots
and characters of poetic realism

8.1 CHARACTEROLOGICAL DISCOURSES 1930–39

Any attempt to come to grips with the range of mythic identities on
offer to audiences by the classic French cinema must deal sooner or
later with the ways in which the principal actors and actresses ("stars," for
simplicity, though they were not stellar in the Hollywood sense) of that cinema were represented to the public through the medium of fan magazines
of the period. The following analysis is based on a survey of several of the
most popular magazines published between 1930 and 1940: *Ciné Miroir,
Pour Vous,* and *Cinémonde.* In it, I attempt to identify the principal charac-
terological discourses that were woven around leading actors and actresses
from 1930 to 1940, and to chart the evolution of those discourses. It constitutes the initial section of a broader attempt to chart such discourses from
1930 to 1960, during which time some twenty major discourses were apparent. These are listed in table 8.1 in an order approximating the chronol-
ogy of their impact on the cinema and its public. The first ten of those
discourses are of particular interest to the thirties.

Each of the ten is here characterized by a single term (e.g., *nature, maturity, professionalism, the body*) and can be thought of as articulating a set of

interests, an implicit corpus of thematic material, or a distinctive view of human nature as manifested by the stars in their filmic roles and (supposedly) their private lives. The discourses crystallize into a set of normative questions asked of stars in interviews and of expectations concerning their replies, or into a normative account of their daily lives. When those discursive patterns recur insistently in issue after issue of a magazine, applied to star after star, then there is a case for claiming that they are "mythic"—that is, that they are closely related to fantasized identities that readers of the magazines were anxious to assume.

In chronological terms, the first discourses to occur were **popular vitality**, attached primarily to the male, and wide-eyed **childlike innocence**, attached almost exclusively to the female. Neither of them lasted for very long, particularly the latter, which is recognizably related to that well-known theatrical *emploi*, the ingénue. Commentators clearly expected that the cinema would have as great a need of such a supposedly basic character type as did the theater, and they consequently saw examples of it on all sides, but only for the first two years of the period. Pola Illery talks of having skipped barefoot through the fields in her childhood. "Ah, what youthful vitality she has," exclaims the interviewer, "like one of those bright, attentive young girls."[1] Lily Damita emerges from the shower, "her hair held back by a cute little pink clip that makes her look like a young girl, a delicious young girl," Dany Marèse is "a joyful, bubbly child," Danièle Darrieux "a graceful fresh-faced blonde . . . her limpid eyes wide open on the world," while Vera Sherbane is "disconcerting: this young thing, who behaves and moves like a child, nevertheless speaks with tranquil assurance of the most serious writers of the day, and of their work."[2] Indeed, it is common for this childlike freshness of face to be contrasted with an unexpected studiousness, or even wisdom. When not skipping through the fields, Pola Illery is surrounded by books on geography and engineering and is very excited by mathematics.[3]

Admittedly, many of these actresses were very young—no more than fifteen in many cases—so it is not unexpected that they should be so described, yet what is so interesting is that so many of them are described in these terms from 1930 to 1932. They dominate the pages of *Pour Vous,* in particular. The *benjamines* (that is, the latest cohort of starlets) of the French cinema are young, bright, fresh-faced, pure, overflowing with childish grace and vivacity, yet sure of themselves, well-read, and thoughtful. Simone Bourdet's eyes "gleam with intelligence, her alert air giving her the appearance of a *grande fillette* [girl on the verge of adulthood] who is just beginning to understand the world." Josseline Gaël has the face and figure of a child: "There is a freshness, an extraordinary naiveté, in her voice. Who would suspect that between takes she rushes back to her dressing room to do her homework."[4]

Table 8.1. List of Discourses 1930–1960

Note: The first ten of these discourses are of particular relevance to the thirties

1   **Childlike Innocence:** the ingenue, youthful, fresh-faced, gazing with wide-eyed wonder on the world that is opening up before her, but intelligent, wise beyond her years, modest, and self-effacing (1930–32, and occasionally to 1935)

2   **Popular Vitality:** a man of the people; joie de vivre; spontaneously bursting into song, so full is his heart (1930–1932 and occasionally thereafter). Momentary revival as a gruff sort of "mate" (1951–52)

3* **Sport, and the Sportsman:** dynamic, healthy, lover of all forms of outdoor activity, especially the more glamorous and expensive (1930–39 and occasionally during the war)

4* **The Sensitive Artist:** lover of all the arts; lets fingers drift over piano; a little unworldly; shrinks from the social scene; in the extreme, exhibits a world-weary lassitude (1932 on)

5* **Nature:** communicating with nature; wind in the hair; contemplation of sunsets; soaking up sun on the beach; retreating to the harmony and tranquillity of the countryside (mainly 1934–45)

6   **Patriotism:** worthy representative of empire; uniforms and military service; every Frenchman naturally a soldier (1933 on, but nowhere near as frequent as might be expected; more common in editorials). Features later as "war-work" (1940–42)

7   **Moral Regeneration:** rehabilitating a degenerate society by denunciation, and less often by example (occasional till 1936, peak years 1938–41; not commonly applied to stars; more frequent in editorials)

8   **Femininity:** delighting in frilly things or in elegant fashions; frivolity, gaiety; only a woman can understand (1936–44); women who are "all woman"

9   **Maturity:** solid, substantial, responsible men of authority; father figures (1937–39, and less frequently thereafter)

10* **Sensuality:** mysterious, seductive femmes fatales; passionate, mocking, treacherous; mostly of foreign extraction, as likely Nordic or East European as sultry Southern (1936–39)

---

11 **The Family:** proud fathers, loving mothers, many sons but few daughters; the humble pleasures of family life (1942–44)

12 **Internationalism:** international solidarity (but not with just anyone); cultural exchanges (1942–44)

13 **Anti-Fascism:** political correctness, or lack of it, during the occupation (1945–50)

14 **Realism:** ordinariness admired; the unglamorous; not stars but people off the streets (occasionally in the thirties, but peaking 1946–50)

15 **Professionalism:** craftsmanship, technique; acting as a craft; the construction of screen personae (1945–53)

16 **Existentialism:** ennui, and the craving to define oneself; alienated, insolent intellectuals, frequenting trendy bars; raging in St. Germain (1948–53)

17 **The Good Life:** middle-class comfort and affluence; the mansion in the country; the penthouse, tastefully arranged seventeenth- and eighteenth-century antiques (early to mid-fifties)

18* **The Cult of the Body:** at first through physical exercise, later more passive; most notable in its male version involving display of pectorals and biceps (1953 on)

19* **The Sex Kitten:** the female version of the carnal animal; a "healthy eroticism"; sulky, pouting, provocative, yet innocent (from 1952, but dominant from 1956)

20 **The Elfin Look:** androgynous, ethereal, diminutive; the startled wild creature; (1954–56)

* The dominant discourses of their time.

A key element of this discourse, and one which could be applied to both men and women, was their lack of pretension. Completely without any sense of self-importance, these bright-eyed young girls retreat modestly as soon as the spotlight is turned on them. In 1930, Marcelle Chantal and Suzy Vernon are the subject of full-page studies which focus primarily on their retiring nature and discretion, as well as their intelligence and thoughtfulness.[5] A year later, Madeleine Renaud murmurs to the interviewer about her distaste for the spotlight. "She is so young, so simple, so blonde, and yet so self-effacing," says the interviewer.[6]

In perhaps its last clear appearance, the discourse attempts to incorporate into its ranks the distinctly older Lilian Harvey, "so full of life, active, and changeable. From the gravest solemnity she can pass rapidly to a really childlike smile. . . . What is surprising about Lilian Harvey is her youth, accentuated, in moments when she is overtaken by some serious matter, by her habit of sticking her lower lip out, like a sulky child."[7] Rarer uses of the same discourse during 1932 and 1933 are applied to Rosine Deréan and Sylvia Sydney, and there is a late mention of Renée St. Cyr as "youthful, gay, carefree . . . with the most delicate and French of talents,"[8] but the intensity and frequency of its use has diminished markedly. A eulogy for the young girls of France late in 1935, intended (quite wrongly) as a foreshadowing of the tone of the coming year's output, constitutes instead a retrospective on the discourse, summarizing it most effectively. "This year's films will be youthful, fresh, direct. The cult of the *fille-fleur* [budding beauty] will be observed for our greater delight. . . . Youth is the meaning of life, the spice of love, the soul of the earth. . . . These figures of the dawning day bring to the cinema a sweet gentleness, a feeling of unfinishedness, a promise of love. . . . These young girls seem to figure again the creation of the world."[9]

Contrasting with this, but placing equal stress on the quality of vivacity, was the discourse of popular vitality. It tended to focus on male actors such as Lefèvre, Roanne, and Gravey, and particularly on male singers with a working-class background such as Préjean, Garat, and Trénet. Lefèvre, who knows what life is all about because he has had to take all sorts of menial jobs to keep body and soul together, never says "vous" to anyone, and probably wouldn't to the Pope himself.[10] Préjean summarizes his philosophy as "living in the sun, as close as possible to nature, with good mates, and not leaving your high spirits behind in the cloakroom." In the studio, "his good humor and high spirits are infectious. When Préjean is there you can be sure you won't be bored. He cheers up people with problems and brings a smile to the most stubborn face."[11]

This discourse was common in the early thirties, when the musical and operetta were omnipresent, and circulated in such enormously popular films as *Le Roi des resquilleurs* and *Théodore et Cie,* but it rapidly faded away, recurring fitfully in the late thirties. Charm, fantasy, and whimsicality are key characteristics, along with an amiable sentimentality and a fundamental good humor punctuated by outbursts of joie de vivre. The actor cannot repress the song that rises spontaneously to his lips. This discourse has a popular edge: the actor is a man of the people, and his irrepressible good humor and gaiety are a sign of their vitality. It also has an urban edge, applying as it does particularly to singers of Parisian industrial origin, or (with appropriate modifications) to singers from Marseille. This was perhaps the only discourse to be applied to comic actors, who were largely ignored by fan magazines in favor of dramatic actors, with whose personae spectators could more readily identify. For this purpose, actors such as Milton, Bach, and Rellys were readily confused with the (often recurrent) characters that they played. Milton—"a poor guy, making do and enjoying life, not complaining or whining about his lot, but staying honest and winning in love in the end"[12]—is praised affectionately for his gaiety and repartee, his sentimentality, and his sardonic, mocking spirit. He is "your typical Parisian . . . full of energy, warm-hearted, not rebellious, but not too patient either."[13]

Later in the thirties, Charles Trénet, emerging from music hall in 1938, is immediately categorized in terms of this sort of joie de vivre—"a lad bursting with exuberance and vitality, whose aim is to turn everything into a dance or a song."[14] In true populist mode, he is said to have spent his first earnings on a bicycle, that emblem of the thirties working class. The war puts an end to any residual traces of this discourse, though Maurice Chevalier (too old and a bit fat for the image, but at least a singer, exuberant, populist, superficial) appeals to it rather grotesquely on his arrival in Paris in 1941: France is basically unchanged, he says; the French should recapture their well-known gaiety, take heart in the new order, and sing along with Marshal Pétain.[15] It was for such rather unwise remarks that he was obliged to repent publicly in the immediate postwar years, yet he had only been picking up, in a politically tactless way, on the discourse that had been at the origins of his prewar prominence. A commentary on him in 1936 notes "the modest origins of this true Parisian, always joking and good-humored, with a mischievous twinkle in his eye. . . . In his kindly heart, his good humor, his subversive mocking attitude, and his inimitable whimsy, anyone can recognize a typical Parisian."[16] His early job as a mechanic in Ménilmontant is noted: "It's no doubt there that he picked up this spontaneous vitality." Among women, Paulette Dubost was one of the few actors to attract elements of this discourse, though Florelle, too, could be described as having "an exceptional and radiant joie de vivre . . . a spontaneity and whimsicality; all her life is an impromptu."[17]

The third and fourth discourses—of sport and of sensitivity, the extrovert and the introvert, the dynamic and the aesthetic—were by far the most common discourses to be applied to stars in the thirties, and were not limited to that decade. By the early thirties, it is already clear that the *sportif*— the sporty type whose leisure-time activities involve a healthy open-air lifestyle—is one of those ideal personae that interviewers expect any actor to assume. Favored sports are horseback riding, swimming (preferably in exotic locales), driving (fast cars), golf, yachting, tennis, skiing, and aviation. The emphasis is on expensive sports which readers/viewers could only fantasize about participating in. Encouraged by her friend Johnny Wiessmuller, Lily Damita can't wait to leave the suffocating atmosphere of the studio: "I leap into my car and head for the sea, where I relax in the broad swell of the Pacific. . . . Sport is one of my greatest joys."[18] Others head for the mountains to ski. Even Richard-Willm, in an atypical moment, is caught indulging in this activity. Alongside this rich man's sporting life, with its glamorous appeal, there is however room for the working-class *sportif*, who engages in cycling, boxing, and soccer. Gabin is frequently cited as the classic working-class *sportif*, with his love of these three sporting activities, but also of hunting. "Jean Gabin, a true son of Paris, is a *sportif*, and of the *sportif*—the true *sportif*—he has the openness, the simplicity, the healthy physique and the good humor."[19] Here the *sportif* myth partially overlaps with the myth of popular vitality.

Throughout the thirties, articles remark on the intimate and "natural" connection between sport and cinema: "All our stars love sport, because it's fashionable," says *Ciné Miroir* in 1931 in an article entitled "Stars on Horseback."[20] The practical aspect of this interest is recognized—they need to engage in these activities on screen, and prefer not to have to use a double—but there is also an element of moral strength to be gained through healthy physical activity: Murat "loves driving, swimming, sailing—everything that leads to healthy emotions and a balanced outlook."[21] Indeed, sport is "the natural proclivity of a virile race." "Long live sport," proclaim Meg Lemonnier, André Luguet, Jean Murat, Albert Préjean, and Jean Gabin in *Ciné Miroir*. "Not only does it transform the body . . . it revitalizes the spirit." "I have often pondered on the relation between sport and cinema," comments the interviewer; "certainly, it is undeniable that most of our stars are *sportifs.*"[22] In 1933, *Pour Vous* publishes a double-page spread on the connection between sport and cinema, noting that both are based on a certain dynamism. This article is in fact translated from English, and the commentary makes it clear that the French cinema's vogue for sports has been inherited from Hollywood, "the city which, more than any other, recognizes sporting prowess."[23]

This simple enthusiasm for the active life was at its apogee in the years 1929–34, and found its cinematic correlative in such films as *Hardi les gars* (Champreux, 1931), *Bidon d'or* (Christian-Jaque, 1931), *Toboggan* (Decoin, 1934), *Rivaux de la piste* (de Poligny, 1933), and later *La Grande Passion* (rugby, Kemin, 1937) and *Champions de France* (Rozier, 1938). To a large extent, they were building on the extraordinary popularity of *La Nuit est à nous* (Roussell, 1929), with its motif of automobile racing. Several articles regretted the tendency of early sound films to abandon location shooting, since they were thus sacrificing the expansive sense of liberty that went with open-air and sporting activities.

So dominant was the sporting personality in these years that any attempt by a star to disclaim sporting capacities was received with incredulity. When Marcelle Chantal proclaims herself "a swimmer of the fifty-sixth rank," the interviewer confides in an aside that she must of course be exaggerating out of modesty.[24] In the absence of any concrete information, commentators invent probable sporting scenarios for their stars. "I am certain," says a reviewer of Simone Genevois, "that racket in hand and hair flying in the wind she must enjoy hitting out on the tennis court. As for cars, well, of course! She probably roars down the highway all day long."[25] The public seems to have felt a particular affection for those who took the sporting life to death-defying extremes, involving acrobatics of a dangerous or eccentric kind. The *sportif* here approaches the "prankster" figure. José Noguero, an acrobatic *sportif,* bounds into the interview room, leaps onto the piano, and performs a tap dance. Roland Toutain and, later in the thirties, Maurice Baquet were particularly notable for the way they exploited this persona. Toutain, a champion acrobat, a member of the Club des Fous, and a notorious practical joker, kept himself in the limelight with his eccentric appurtenances and physical exploits—his eagle, his boa constrictor, his auto-giro races, and his aerial acrobatics.

Indeed, as was noted in the introduction, a special place is accorded the aviator in this sporting pantheon. Many stars in addition to Toutain were admired for their flying exploits—Marie Bell owns her own plane and attempts to set distance records in it; André Roanne is a "flying ace"; Jean Murat had been a pilot during the war. "The stars are not content with reigning on earth, they wish to reign in the heavens as well."[26] In 1936, *Ciné Miroir* runs a series of articles on stars who ascend into the heavens, and in 1938 it records the existence of an Aéroclub du Cinéma, so numerous are the stars with a passion for aviation. Of course, the aviator figure had long been established as a popular hero. World War I had seen him come to prominence for his reputed courage, gallantry, and daredevil aerobatics. The extension of this technology to civil aviation in the twenties had led both to a rage for setting long-distance and speed records across oceans and deserts—hitherto almost impenetrable barriers to communication—and to the gradual consolidation of regular mail and passenger routes, binding more tightly the far-flung colonies of empires.

By 1928, L'Herbier's silent film *L'Argent* had picked up on this romantic aviator figure, in the character of Jacques Hamelin, an aviator who undertakes a dangerous flight to French Guyana. In 1931, commenting on a Franco-American co-production (*L'Aviateur,* in its French release), a fan magazine identifies the aviator as the "supreme representative of the modern hero, the adventurer figure, who since the first exploits of World War I has caught the imagination of the whole world."[27] Early in 1939, another article, entitled "Knights of the Air," notes, "Aviation, by its sensational conquests, has conquered all humanity in the space of twenty years. . . . The human aspect [of this conquest] is as extraordinary as the mechanical aspect. Here, science is combined with human courage."[28] The article mentions St. Exupéry, Guillaumet, and Guynemer, "that knight of the skies, a veritable archangel of aerial combat. . . . His culture, his faith, and his heroism . . . have rendered his name immortal, not only in our land but throughout the whole universe [*sic*]. . . . Everything in Guynemer's brief life evokes irresistibly the stained-glass window—stained in the colors of the heavens, of blood, of fire, retracing the Stations of the Cross of a warrior archangel." Among the many films to pick up on this myth, *Courrier-Sud* (1936) was scripted by St. Exupéry himself, but Toutain's aviator figure in *La Règle du jeu* is probably the best known. The war years saw a renewal of interest in such heroic figures as Andrée Dupeyrou, the aviatrix on whose life *Le Ciel est à vous* is based, and Jean Mermoz, "paladin of the skies, guardian spirit of our childhood fantasies . . . may the young of France, uncertain of their future in this confusing age, depressed by the heritage of these recent years of chaos, find in your example the hope for a worthy and constructive life."[29] In the postwar years, however, the aviator lost his mythic status, becoming simply a pilot.

In 1933, a new myth—that of the actor as **sensitive artist**—partially eclipses the sporty figure of the earlier thirties. Actors such as Catelain and Préjean, hitherto figures of popular vitality and sporty types, are now discovered to have a passionate interest in all the arts. Marcelle Chantal is noted as having studied painting and being interested in dancing and singing. "She has a taste for what is restful and comfortable. A vast study lined with masses of curious objects. Many books on serious and deep subjects—poetry, history, foreign literature . . . but she remains primarily a musician, and not only on the piano."[30] "I've adored music for as long as I can remember. I was also devoted to dancing. What emotion I would feel when my mother, a very good musician, sat down to play! My heart quickened, and all a-tremble I would go and sit beside her, to listen with delight. Then I would get up and, inspired by that divinity, music, I would dance a few steps. Friends said, 'This child will be the next Isadora Duncan.'"[31] Clearly, the principal public function of this devotion to aesthetics is to lay claim to a sensitive, responsive nature.

On a slightly less exalted note, Simone Simon is noted as having studied singing, piano, and sculpture, and Marie Bell, now (1936) no longer a dashing aviatrix, sits in front of her piano letting her fingers drift over the keys, "evoking Chopin."[32] Late in the decade, Trénet is reworked as a serious artist, painter, and singer, with a certain weighty thoughtfulness about him. All the stars, even the working-class figures, profess a love for music. You could make up a decent orchestra out of our stars, exclaims *Pour Vous,* if you include the accordion (Claude Dauphin), the guitar (Toutain), and the ocarina (Gravey). And Baroux has always dreamed of being a conductor![33] Others appreciate painting more. Some, including, somewhat improbably, Gabrio, are represented as adept at it. The reporters exclaim that all the stars want to talk about is Liszt, Chopin, Debussy, Dante, Velasquez, and El Greco. Many of them, indeed, do not want to talk to reporters at all, but prefer the privacy of a life far from the public hurly-burly of the media. Especially after 1936, they flee publicity. Servais, Richard-Willm, Véra Korène, Jany Holt, Françoise Rosay, Lisette Lanvin, Henry Garat—all develop a reluctance to talk about themselves or allow the public gaze to intrude on their affairs. Pierre Fresnay becomes so shy of the media as to strike one over-insistent reporter.

An extreme version of this sensitive artistic soul was the tormented introvert, anguished, alienated, even suicidal in moments of despair. This persona tended to accrete around Pierre Blanchar, Jean-Louis Barrault, and Pierre Richard-Willm. It began as early as 1933 and provided the kick-start for the sensitive romantic myth, which can be seen as its paler echo. Richard-Willm is its most vocal (most taciturn?) representative, repeatedly informing interviewers that he does not find life very interesting and is merely trying to get through it with as little trouble as possible. In moments of lassitude and depression, he dreams of peace for the world and for himself, but the former is not possible, and the latter cannot exist without the former.[34] Playing the piano and a contemplative reclusive life are his techniques for enduring the pervasive ennui of contemporary existence. This modish angst is echoed by Marie Bell, who (as she evokes Chopin in the privacy of her study) groans, "I am so tired of it all."[35] Interviewing Dita Parlo, the critic mentions having seen her on the screen, her melancholy face lost in dreams, and insist that she's not like that in reality; yet he can't resist adding that "those eyes of hers, so reluctant to open, always reflect some indefinable nostalgia, some wistfulness in her soul."[36] Barrault, typically characterized as an alien, a creature from Mars, because of his gangling physique and contorted acting, is recognized as another such "soul in search of itself,[37] "destined by his physique to incarnate characters tested to the limit by life, suffering, with a tormented soul."[38] Pierre Blanchar is "typical of these cerebral heroes driven or haunted by a passion nobler than love, or a strange obsession baser and crueler than love; he is perfect for those disquieting heroes, fascinating and tormented, of Russian novels."[39]

Among female stars, this myth of the doomed aesthete appears most commonly as a limitless melancholy, a sensation of loss and of abandonment—an indefinable gravity which renders the actress unforgettable and her performances poignant in the extreme. This discourse engulfs Madeleine Robinson for some years,[40] but its field of delectation is Michèle Morgan, who in the years after 1938 triggered a reworking of the discourse peculiar to herself. An extended discussion of that persona can be found in the final section of this chapter.

These two discourses—the sporty type, which was present from the beginning of the thirties, and the melancholic aesthete, which appeared in 1933–34 to compete with it—seem irrevocably opposed, and an awareness of this opposition is apparent in certain articles appearing around the beginning of 1934. Mireille, who composes, has now become an enthusiastic skier. "Believe it or not, I almost prefer the ivory of the ski-slope to the ivory of my piano keys. Being creative with my hands was easy. . . . Now I have to learn to be creative with my feet, which is much harder."[41] Even more specifically, an article published a month earlier had asserted that women prefer *real* men, strong, silent, and self-contained. "That's why ambitious young men struggle to master themselves. They play sports not simply because they enjoy bashing balls about, or pulling on oars, but because they know that women love strong-willed, well-muscled men, with simple but strong souls—not the intellectuals and snobs who are always fawning on them."[42]

But if the two discourses were sometimes contrasted, they were also often applied to the same stars, and at the same time. Moreover, they found a common meeting ground in the discourse of **nature**, which gained prominence in commentaries from 1935 on. Essentially, this discourse was one of simplicity, of innocence, and of sincerity. One could retreat from the artifice, hypocrisy, and superficiality of contemporary life into a communion with nature, viewed as a source of harmony and tranquillity, and "be oneself." The sporty discourse was readily reconcilable with that of nature, since most of the relevant sports involved the open air and were presumed to produce a healthy mind in a healthy body. The romantic myth was equally reconcilable, since sensitive aesthetes could hope to find true happiness only far from the madding crowd, in the privacy and calm of a country retreat where they could be themselves.

Although there are sporadic appearances of a nature myth from 1930 on, it is pervasive by 1935. The evolution of the sporty discourse toward a nature myth is first evident with respect to Jean Murat, who is revealed in 1934 as enjoying various sports, primarily in pursuit of healthy emotions and a balanced life. "Between roles, he has only one desire: to immerse himself once more in nature, to experience the fresh mountain air and the warm sun of our flower-garlanded coasts."[43] This "one desire," to find a secluded country retreat where the cyclic rhythms of timeless nature take over from the relentless linearity of the contemporary urban world, is a constant theme thereafter. Growth, harvest-time, and the ephemeral sensual joys of sun, sea, and sand transformed the dynamism of the sporting myth into something more passive, more contemplative. All the stars suddenly discover that they have a fundamentally rustic soul. Mona Goya "loves the healthy freedom of country life, in the fields and woods."[44] Préjean knows no better way to relax after a tough day's work: "I plant, weed, dig, prune, water . . . it's so restful."[45] "Whenever possible I escape to the Marne to fish . . . or to the mountains."[46] "Fishing, but not catching anything, solely for the pleasure of hours passed on the water, with the smell of sea salt and the warmth of the sun's rays."[47]

Every summer thereafter, a routine special report in *Ciné Miroir* shows the stars getting away from it all: "What humanity loves most of all is liberty—losing oneself in the vastness of nature."[48] Marie Glory, like a young animal, values the freedom she finds in her country retreat—forests, fields, rivers, valleys, hills, pheasants, rabbits, hares. She hunts, but "walking in the open air, the wind in my hair, with the rustle of the trees and the grasses, is what attracts me, rather than killing animals."[49] Lilian Harvey has her farmhouse in Provence, Colette Darfeuil spends every weekend at her place in the country, Marie Glory lives there full time. At the other extreme, Jean Gabin finds true happiness in "my little property at Berchères sur Vesgue, hunting, fishing, just wandering about,"[50] as do, at their various country houses, Vanel, Bach, and Préjean.

In line with this modulation toward passivity and contemplation, the stars now have pets that they cuddle rather than horses to gallop about on—pets that they prefer to humans, because they are more faithful. They devote themselves to gardening, sunbathing, reading beside a lake, camping, and wandering through the fields, emoting as a hare starts up or a squirrel leaps from branch to branch. For Richard-Willm, lover of solitude, mountain and forest are friendly companions: "I need to be by myself, and I can only be so in the midst of nature."[51]

The move toward location shooting encouraged this discourse, and with her Provençal background, Orane Demazis was a particularly appropriate focus for it. In 1934, when she is interviewed about her role as Angèle, the interviewer knows to ask her if she feels at home in nature. "Infinitely," she replies. "It's only when you enter its embrace that you can really grow. All true artists draw on its wellsprings for the best part of their genius. For genius consists of simplicity, and what is simpler and truer than Nature? In life today, we have, alas, lost any real contact with it. We live in an artificial world."[52] Not long afterward, in an article inspired by the location shooting of *Angèle* and *Toni,* Altman (of all people) publishes an article in *Pour Vous* prefiguring Bazin and Rohmer's realist defense of the glories of nature:

> The greatest triumph of the cinema is not sound, not the talkie, nor color, nor eventually 3D, nor any other technical achievement, it's fresh air. . . . What a source of revitalization, of eternity is provided by a natural setting, by the open air. You soon get bored with [those all-too-conventional artificial sets], but it would be hard to get tired of the open sky, of fields, of the movement of clouds, of the tides, the river's flow, or the trembling of a tree's leaves, since they are there forever. . . . In such moments the cinema is practically a living thing, even more alive than living things, since it surprises nature in its own domain, as one captures a dream or a mystery and fixes it on a canvas.[53]

This adulation of the simplicity, purity, even divinity of nature persisted throughout the late thirties. An interesting description in 1939 of Henri Decoin and Danielle Darrieux swimming and lazing away their days at their cottage on the Côte d'Azur speaks of Danielle as "without a speck of powder on her shiny nose; her lips are naturally red; on her smooth forehead, a glint of reflected light plays; but her eyelashes, without cosmetics, have lost none of their length—they have become all blond, and give her face the look of a young girl; she places in her hair a big bunch of meadow flowers."[54]

In March 1940, apparently oblivious to the declaration of war, the annual report describes the stars as disporting themselves in nature, just as in preceding years. "After winter comes the hope of summer days, the irresistible call of the countryside . . . of wandering through woods and fields."[55] Even more incongruously, the following month, Gaby Morlay is portrayed in her country house overlooking the Seine, her garden "luminous with all the fairyland of spring. . . . 'Can you imagine! I lost fifteen hundred rosebushes to the frost this winter; and I was greatly saddened to see so many trees and plants dying, especially the flowers.'"[56] Not to mention human beings, one is tempted to say! This perpetuation of a discourse of nature and of the annual cycle of the stars' lives, as readers had been taught to know them, could, however, be read as an attempt to reassert a degree of normalcy during the "phony war."

In the period under discussion, there were two discourses that were omnipresent in French political and social commentary, as they were in the films of the day, but which are distinct from all others of the thirties in that they did not obtain as significant a purchase in the discourses surrounding stars as one might expect—the discourses of **patriotism** and of **moral regeneration**. The nationalist or colonial discourse was particularly strong in certain films, yet scarcely impinges on the persona even of those actors who most regularly played the role of soldier of empire (notably Victor Francen and Pierre Fresnay). Those who had served in the forces (Murat), been to naval school (Vanel), or done military service (Gabin) are occasionally recognized for this, while Garat's reluctance to serve is received with incredulity, as yet another reason to doubt his manhood. Murat, as a wartime aviator, bestrides several mythic roles and is often portrayed in uniform: "Every Frenchman is naturally a soldier, and the uniform is his most natural clothing."[57] And both Fernand Gravey and Pierre Blanchar are mentioned as having the souls of salt-sea sailors, the latter as a result of a spell in the École de Hydrographie. "He yearns for his boat and for those long sea voyages . . . the sea beckons to him."[58]

Aside from their relative lack of purchase on stars' images, these two basically right-wing discourses are distinguished by a second major factor: they emerge not from the general run of often anonymous and impressionistic articles that make up the bulk of the fan magazines, but rather from the editorial pages. That is, they are the most conscious and programmatic of the thirties discourses, foreshadowing those of the wartime and immediate postwar years. Perhaps it is not surprising, then, that they are the only ones that overflow into the "serious" press, emerging in editorials in *Cinéopse* and *La Cinématographie Française*, as well as in the more popular press.

There is a close connection between the two discourses, since the national civilizing mission of France, which is the central focus of the one, invariably leads to the invocation of the moral virtues inherent in the French character, which it is the duty of the armed forces, nurses, missionaries, and administrators to communicate to, if not impose on, other peoples. Where the nationalist discourse has no real negative, except divisive (because leftist, classist) representations of France, the moral discourse has an increasingly urgent negative as the thirties progress, in the debility which it sees Jews and other "degenerate subversives" as introducing into the very heart of French society.

In the early thirties, instances of either discourse were rare, and when they occurred they tended to focus on the representation of France overseas. "One could get the impression from our frivolous films," protests *Cinémonde* in 1930, "that France consists of two equally unlovely groups—the sophisticated and superficial wealthy, seen in comedies of manners, and the squalid perverts, lay-abouts, and degenerates of the underworld."[59] Moreover, the foreign legion was being slandered by (often foreign) films that represented legionnaires as the dregs of the gutters, hiding from a criminal past, maltreated and even tortured by vicious officers, when in truth they were knights-errant of idealism, united by their oath to the flag that they served in a devotion to military honor. Films must be made glorifying "the poetic force of these adventurers—their self-sacrifice, their self-denial, their heroism."[60] *Ciné Miroir* calls for a rectification of the too-prevalent view that the French are oppressing and enslaving the blacks of Africa; rather, the cinema should show "those strong young [doctors] who have abandoned our facile ways of life to undertake their campaign against death beneath a murderous sun. Dr. Jammot, that great man of learning who is at the head of our sublime teams of young white doctors and black aides, can best be seen as a saint."[61]

All publications agreed that what France needed was something closer to an authoritarian national cinema, like Hitler's vision of a German cinema or the USSR's effective propaganda machine. A particular admiration was frequently expressed in the later thirties for Mussolini's program for the Italian cinema. *La Cinématographie Française* quotes approvingly his view of the cinema as the strongest of a nation's weapons, and *Ciné Miroir* goes so far as to regret that France does not have a dictator as they do in Italy, who might introduce more fascist (i.e., "co-operative") methods. *Cinéopse* notes that the cinema is also a propaganda arm of the nation, and praises the progress of the Italian cinema under Mussolini: "Doubtless, Mr. Mussolini, as head of government, is himself primarily responsible for this, but he has managed to surround himself with competent collaborators . . . which is far from the case in France. This is where you must seek the reason for Italy's superiority among the Latin nations."[62]

As was noted in connection with the war genre, a corresponding enthusiasm was expressed on those occasions when French authorities moved in the same direction. In 1932, *Cinéopse* rejoices that M. Chaumet, Administrator of the Colonies, is devoting a series of evenings to talks, illustrated by documentaries, in the interests of "colonial propaganda."[63] In 1933, a Committee for Colonial Propaganda through the Cinema is set up, and *Cinémonde* hopes for fewer frivolous operettas and a greater place for the works of French engineers.[64] *Cinéopse* notes approvingly the efforts of the navy minister in support of such documentaries as *La Marine française, La France est une île, Branlebas de combat,* and such fiction films as *Veille d'armes, La Porte du large,* and later *Alerte en Méditerranée:* "All ministers should support such national propaganda." It also reports complacently on the introduction of censorship laws banning films that might bring ridicule on the military.[65]

As the war approaches the tone of these editorials becomes more strident and the moral outrage more explicit. *Quai des brumes* attracts general invective for "exploiting the lowest tendencies of human nature."[66] What is needed is "a colonial film that will prove to the adversaries of colonialism that the white—administrator, engineer, teacher, agronomist—has not proved unworthy of this great nation; that, quite the contrary, wherever he has passed, water, power, work, and wealth have burst forth."[67] "Wherever the Tricolor has fluttered, slavery has given way to liberty, ignorance to knowledge, barbarity to civilization. . . . Immense progress [has been] achieved by our administrators, our doctors, our teachers, our missionaries, and our soldiers."[68]

The end of 1938 saw a climax to this campaign for a cinema embodying "the French colonial spirit," when *La Cinématographie Française* published a manifesto drawn up by a number of cultural groups, including the Société des Gens de Lettres. Entitled "Le Redressement moral du pays,"[69] it evoked the spiritual strength of France and the true qualities of the race, "those which have made it great, strong, and respected in the world." It put forward a five-point program aimed at

(1) *Schools,* which should teach "the moral value of man, which has as its basis work, discipline, respect for the human individual, the cult of one's native land, and submission to the laws of the land."

(2) *Villages,* where folklore and local history should be cultivated, because "traditions which link the young to their ancestors create within them a love and pride for their native soil."

(3) *Political and social élites,* which have a duty to collaborate to create social harmony "so that a feeling of trust and friendship should reign between classes endowing the nation with a moral unity."

(4) *Radio and cinema,* because "the spirit of France must not be distorted or demeaned"; "serious problems of the day must be treated with that sincerity that is the due of a virile people."

(5) *Propaganda services abroad,* which must be organized "with the collaboration of spiritual and moral leaders whose only aim and reward must be the greatness of our country."

The editor associates himself with these sentiments, only advising that they be achieved by the carrot and not the stick. He reminds his readers of the French ambassador to Poland's recent embarrassment at certain French films screened in Poland—"what a strange atmosphere of vice they emanate, seen outside France. . . . I fear we have lost our sense of morality; while waiting to regain it, let's at least retain our sense of caution."[70]

Naturally, these anxieties proliferate during 1939, with articles rejoicing at the release of colonialist and triumphalist films and much talk of a new genre, the "national film."[71] For instance, the review of *Trois de St. Cyr* talks of the Military Academy as a place where one finds a total lack of self-interest or self-importance, because there is a thirst for open spaces and . . . a soul ready to devote itself to the greatness of our native land; St. Cyr forms those virtues of uprightness, courage, and honor which throughout history have been those of the French officer. It is good that the cinema should exalt the finest qualities of our race. . . . This St. Cyr way of life, with its harsh discipline and stoic young men, is a wonderful lesson in energy; it shows all those who see us as degenerate that our race retains the virtues which made it great throughout history.[72]

With the declaration of war, these national and moral discourses reached a climax and had practical consequences in the banning of many films. As Borel said, explaining the more aggressive censorship, "We wish to avoid, in those countries where we have numerous friends but where we also have to cope with the insinuations and distortions of the German propaganda machine, the screening of a representation of our country, our traditions and our race which is not just diluted but deceptive, distorted as it is through the prism of an artistic personality which may well be original but is not always healthy."[73]

Although these two related discourses from the late thirties did not become attached to specific actors, their more visible popular counterpart was the discourse of **maturity**, which certainly did. This was one of three gendered discourses to dominate the late thirties, and the only one of the three to apply to males. Essentially, it promoted as admirable the strong, silent patriarchal figure who imposed his will by sheer force of personality. Murat, Vanel, and Gabin, but also Baur, Raimu, and occasionally Jean Servais were its most common embodiments. Sober, dense, and substantial, they were seen as having the bulk that goes with moral authority, the forcefulness of a man of action, the solitude, austerity, and integrity that befitted an almost monklike commitment to a self-imposed mission. The link with the two previous discourses is apparent in the description of Vanel (on the basis of *Légions d'honneur, L'Occident, Bar du sud,* and *S.O.S. Sahara*) as having "that grim, clean-cut face of a man of action—a solitary man . . . who finds within himself the strength to outface the hostile, torrid, and featureless desert." He is one of that race of men who are forces of nature, "living in their remote outpost like men of religion in their monastery."[74]

Such a discourse of authority could accrete only around more mature actors, whose physique spoke of an ability to endure, to cope. These figures were the antithesis of the handsome but superficial young men who had competed with them for lead roles earlier in the decade. All referendums and surveys in the late thirties reflect this audience preference for unhandsome mature male actors who can serve as father figures. Gabin, Raimu, Baur, Jouvet, and Vanel figure alongside Fernandel at the top of the popularity tables. In the case of Gabin (and to a lesser extent Vanel), this discourse occasionally comes into embarrassing conflict with a series of roles in which he played the deserter, the *caïd*, the murderer—roles which, with the advent of war, were to see Gabin in particular identified as responsible for the degeneracy of the French populace and for France's humiliating defeat. During the thirties, however, they signify not degeneracy and failure, but a toughness and humanity that refuse to admit defeat. This image of the rough diamond, of the worthy individual alienated by the injustices of society, is most frequently associated with Gabin precisely because he selected (and, if necessary, modified) his films to conform to this mythic identity. Vanel, however, is almost as often characterized in similar terms. Indeed, the first occurrence of the discourse that I have identified relates to him:

> When you think of Vanel, two qualities inevitably come to mind—naturalness and simplicity. . . . Watch him approach, steadily, with a slowness that speaks of strength. His body solid, but not bulging with ostentatious muscle. His voice sober, steady, without any of those motile flourishes of intonation that even modest men might use. It is the voice of a man sure of himself, not given to bragging. It is a voice that never needs to be raised in order to be heard and obeyed. And don't forget his eyes . . .[75]

Subsequent articles emphasize his roles as a sailor, when his broad chest constitutes a sort of rampart thrust out against the fog, the tempest, the salt sea spray.[76] He is a figure of power, "a virile actor, who embodies on the screen a rugged type of man, masculine, commanding, reveling in action, but at the same time very human and compassionate."[77] So is Harry Baur, who has a " great, slow, but powerful body . . . that voice of rusted iron, marinated in alcohol, suffering, joy, and bitterness . . . and behind it all, a powerful life-force, multiple, secret, and terribly human."[78] In all descriptions of these sober, mature, and powerful figures there is the implication of a brutality that can easily veer toward the criminal.

Two female stereotypes developed in the later thirties which contrasted with this male stereotype and with each other: the flighty elegant and the sensual seductive. Earlier, female stars had tended to be described in somewhat varied terms, as delightful, gay, vivacious, or capricious, but by 1937 the adjectives have become more distinctive, and the interests, tastes, and appearance of the stars are described in ritualized terms. On the one hand are "feminine" stars, flighty, frivolous, and somewhat superficial, whose main interest is their self-presentation to the world; on the other hand are sensual, mysterious, somber, and potentially dangerous women, who had initially been termed "vamps," but who are soon refashioned as "femmes fatales."

It is the latter discourse—that of **sensuality**—that appears first, reaching a peak of intensity in 1937 and 1938. A number of stars are found, largely on the basis of the roles they play (spies, adventurers, two-timing vamps), and partly on the basis of their (reputed) private lives (possessions, clothing, behavior, relationships), to be vortexes of sensuality, wild and apparently uncontrollable, sulky, sultry, tempestuous, treacherous, but irresistibly fascinating. Simone Simon and Viviane Romance are represented as carrying this personality into their behavior on set, where their presence inevitably provokes passionate altercations. But it is Edwige Feui-llère's early performances that first seem to have foregrounded this discourse, in 1936.[79] Subsequently, Mireille Balin (interviewed in her home, amidst Oriental ivories and North African drapes), Suzy Prim (whose recurrent role "is that of the seductive woman, sensual, a little perverse"), and Viviane Romance are all enveloped in it. Romance "represents a sort of woman called 'fatale' because of her beauty, at once aggressive and mysterious, her somewhat ambiguous sex appeal, and her self-confidence, full of double meanings and suggestiveness."[80] She is attracted to the role of vamp, "which barely exists in the French cinema but is embodied in Marlene Dietrich."[81] Indeed, it had been applied to Dietrich as early as 1930, and not long afterward to Vanda Gréville, who evokes "poeticized desire, constructed of a mix of provocation and modesty, perversity and innocence, which arouses in us a higher form of sensuality."[82] Marlene herself is "a secretion, a concretization of sexual attraction, and acts like a sweet poison, penetrating and drugging, which spreads throughout the body and overcomes all one's resistance."[83] In the early thirties, however, the term is most often applied to foreign actresses, particularly blonde Nordic vamps. Only in the latter half of the decade are sultry French brunettes incorporated into the sisterhood of the vamp.

With the war and the occupation, femmes fatales became politically incorrect, and all references to them are historical, as when the term is referred to as a prewar character type or *emploi,* or when stars are seen as having been "trapped" in such roles, and are now trying to break out.[84] In this more distanced, reflective environment, *Ciné Mondial* can outline in some detail the nature and history of the femme fatale during the thirties. Complete with illustrations of Balin, Manès, Marchal, and Negri, it talks of the sort of woman who by her mere appearance on the screen disrupts the harmony of true love. "Better known for some years as the vamp . . . she is typically a beautiful brunette with green eyes . . . an imposing presence, perverse, cruel, provocative, without a trace of humanity in her." In the late thirties, "her malevolence was simply a form of revenge on life for its injustices, her indifference a sort of barrier that she erected to protect a too frail body." Now, however, "she often really loves the hero, and if at first she seems a flighty creature, she redeems herself at the end, and lays her fatal charms at the feet of the man of her life."[85]

While these accounts were in part motivated by the roles and private lives of the respective stars, they were also derived from certain racial stereotypes. Sensuality and passion were already well established as characteristic of the southern or Mediterranean stereotype, and a slightly different blonde voluptuousness was associated with the Eastern European seductress. Elvire Popescu's Romanian origins are considered relevant to the persona she projects, as is Véra Korène's Slavic birthplace to her recurrent role of seductive spy. Maria Casarès is Spanish, Marie Déa is Basque, Mireille Balin is half Italian, and "Edwige Feuillère has Italian blood, which explains many things."[86] In the absence of any such foreign origin, Viviane Romance nevertheless "gives the impression of being a mixture of races," because of her heavy, lush body.[87] So if the femme fatale enters French cinematic discourses rather earlier than is usually claimed, she is not seen as wholly French: it is partly her very foreignness which makes of her a mysterious creature, threatening to the status quo.

The other female discourse, that of frilly **femininity**, tends to be primarily oriented around fashion and the home. Women are seen as interested above all in talking about ornaments for the house, make-up, manicures, frocks, and all the little elegances that speak of feminine taste, "a woman's touch." Such women are "all woman." As early as 1935, female stars are interviewed at home and seen as surprisingly domestic in their tastes. They are homebodies, and their favorite activity is cooking up some tasty delight for their man, or rearranging the furniture.[88] Gradually, however, the emphasis turns to forms of dress—to appearance rather than activity. Although this discourse is applied to most female stars at one time or another, it gradually coalesces around Edwige Feuillère. Attempting, in early 1938, to escape the vamp/femme fatale image, both Feuillère and Mireille Balin tell interviewers about their love for dresses with trains, made with fourteen meters of muslin, and their preference for roles that allow them to wear thirty or more different costumes. A prime virtue becomes the ability to display these wardrobes to best account. A 1939 article spells out the contradictions involved in the Feuillère transformation. She is at once a femme fatale and a homebody—although she often plays vamp, adventurer, and diabolical spy, this has come about "inadvertently." "At heart she is all woman, loving pretty things—her house, her knick-knacks, her luxurious armchairs, her friends."[89] By 1939, this discourse of frilliness has largely displaced that of the sensual vamp. Such stars as Anne Vernay, Lisette Lanvin, and Yvette Lebon speak exclusively of their make-up, their dresses, their appearance, and their femininity.[90] Danielle Darrieux, interviewed at her dressmaker's, talks lovingly of *Battement de cœur*, "in which she wore a different dress for each sequence." Female stars have become primarily fashion models, and a principal function of their films is to display the fashion designers' latest collections.[91]

With the advent of war, this representation of women as pretty, charming creatures tied to the home was uncontroversial, and it survived. Even Arletty (!) is momentarily engulfed by it. Indeed, even in the climactic disruptions at war's end, with the world collapsing about their ears, *Ciné Mondial*'s reporters cling to this vacuous discourse, writing of such important matters as Micheline Presle's new flat and new frocks.[92] As in the case of earlier discourses, the perpetuation of such gossip can be seen as a way of maintaining one's bearings in a disintegrating world.

An overview of the thirties would see a distinct periodization emerging from the jostle of discourses, in which those involving forms of fantasized fulfillment gradually give way to those figuring forms of fantasized disruption and distress, accompanied by the desire for a strong leader.

Certain absences are striking. In a resolutely Catholic country, that not the faintest trace of an overtly religious discourse was mobilized around any of the actors or actresses of the decade is quite astonishing. While several of the films themselves, including some of the most popular, foregrounded star roles involving exemplary religious (and, even more often, exemplary moral) figures, and while religious organizations repeatedly called in their "house" journals for a more moral orientation of the industry, the calls for "moral regeneration" in editorials and elsewhere never resulted in overt religious propaganda in the popular magazines. Likewise, given the immense popularity of films involving martial figures or promoting France's civilizing mission in the colonies, it is remarkable how seldom the patriotic and martial discourses were attached to stars. In general, any discourse appealing to trans-individual allegiances or systems was weak, whereas discourses relating to personality were strong.

The main fields of predilection of such discourses were gender and class. In particular, as might be expected, several discourses dealt with gender. It was in the nature of woman to be "feminine," or to be dangerously seductive, or to bubble over with childlike gaiety. It was in the nature of man to be strong and responsible, or to live dangerously, or to prefer larks with his mates to life with a wife. Two of the discourses presented the working class in a particularly favorable light—most obviously that of popular vitality, but also that of the substantial mature male, often embodied in Gabin. The father figures of the thirties never embodied middle-class values and attitudes or bourgeois respectability; indeed, far more often than not they explicitly rejected such values as symptomatic of an unjust social system.

So the discourses dealt with a fairly narrow and changing set of personality orientations; nevertheless, they all proposed types of human being which they constructed as ideal and as timeless. Those who approximated these types in their stage roles or personal lives constituted an elite of exceptional human individuals who were beyond criticism. Incredulity was the only proper response to those who derided sport, or art, or nature; scorn the only proper response to those who, out of season, decried femininity, maturity, sensitivity, or childlike innocence. The myths underlying the discourses invariably made universalist claims, even when dealing with apparently local and ephemeral issues. And it was precisely because they situated these attributes confidently within a notionally permanent universe of unassailable values that they provided a solid framework for the fantasized identities which their readership craved in a turbulent political and economic age.

8.2 THE MOST POPULAR STARS

This set of mythic discourses was, of course, closely related to the mythic stereotypes repeatedly acted out by the various actors and actresses in the films of the period, and the global image of each actor and actress as registered by the French movie-going public consisted of an accumulation of knowledge about him or her acquired from these two principal sources (together with other lesser sources). As a result of this evolving knowledge, and in response to "referendums" organized by certain film magazines, French audiences felt able to rank those actors and actresses in order of popularity. Such polls of readers and/or industrial personnel provide a useful supplementary source of information as to the status of the different mythic stereotypes.

As in so many other spheres, the French cinema became much more systematic in chronicling the popularity of stars in the postwar years. From 1947 on, quasi-official referendums ("Les Victoires du Cinéma Français") were conducted by *Cinémonde* among its readers and by *Le Film Français* among theater managers (and later by *Le Figaro* among other prominent film personnel) to identify the most popular French stars, both male and female. These contests were clearly influenced from year to year by the release of specific films. For instance, Jouvet's popularity in 1949 resulted from a series of successful films over the previous eighteen months, including *Quai des Orfèvres* and *Les Amoureux sont seuls au monde,* and particularly *Entre 11h et minuit,* and Bardot's in 1957 was related to the success of three of her films in 1956—*Cette sacrée gamine, En effeuillant la marguerite,* and *Et Dieu créa . . . la femme.* The appearance of Blier on the list in 1950 was related specifically to the popular success of *L'École buissonnière* in 1949, and of Fernandel in 1953 to the popular success of *Don Camillo* in the previous year. Beyond that, however, the tables allow us to track certain stars who were consistently popular over a number of years, and who might therefore be assumed to correspond to certain mythic stereotypes. They also allow us to recognize differences of perspective between theater managers and spectators. For instance, Martine Carol was consistently appreciated by theater owners, but never achieved top placing with spectators, who always preferred Michèle Morgan.

For the years preceding inauguration of the "Victoires," the evidence concerning star popularity is more fragmentary. From 1936 to the outbreak of war and again after it, the industry journals conducted an annual poll of theater managers, which gives data of less certain reliability for the years 1936–38 and 1946–48; in 1945, an IFOP poll of the movie-going public provides equivalent information. Extended lists of runners-up in the "Victoires" give us further useful data. For the war years themselves, the only recorded data result from a referendum among film critics conducted by *Ciné Mondial* in 1942, which saw Raimu designated as best actor and Micheline Presle designated as best actress, followed by Michèle Morgan; Odette Joyeux and Bernard Blier designated as rising stars; and Blanchette Brunoy and Jean Tissier as "best loved." Table 8.3 indicates overall trends in star popularity between 1936 and 1948, leaving out these more enigmatic war years.

The least reliable data come from the early sound years, when fandom was as dominant as it ever was to be in the French cinema, and surveys were conducted by the popular magazines rather than by industry journals, and in terms which confuse rather than enlighten. Some surveys included males and females, others one or the other; some included both French and foreign stars, others exclusively French stars; most were designed to identify such factors as the best young lead, the best smile, the ideal couple, or the ideal husband/wife. Table 8.2 provides all the material that seems most useful, except for a 1930 poll of its readers by *Cinémonde* designed to identify three male and three female stars for inclusion in a foreshadowed Académie du Cinéma Français (the six stars designated were Dolly Davis, Gina Manès, and Louise Lagrange, Maurice Chevalier, Jean Angelo, and Jean Murat) and a 1931 poll of its readers by *Pour Vous* designed to identify the most photogenic stars (the five top stars were, in order, Suzy Vernon, Henri Garat, Lilian Harvey, Ramon Navarro, and Jeanette MacDonald).

While in many ways inadequate until 1947, the tables nevertheless outline a number of trends in star popularity in terms of nationality, gender, and age. First, they serve to remind us of the internationalism of the silent film, the subsequent rivalry with Hollywood, and the progressively greater dominance of the popular imagination by local stars. In 1929, all the favorite (male) stars are foreigners, with the leading French actors being Blanchar, the immigrant Mosjoukine, Angelo, Catelain, and Vanel. A poll concerning young leading men the same year confirms these rankings, though Ramon Navarro is still more popular than any French star and

Table 8.2. Popularity Polls 1929–35

Ciné Miroir Top Actors 1929	Cinémonde Best in World 1933	Ciné Miroir Prince Charming 1933	Ciné Miroir Nicest Smile 1935
Charlie Chaplin	Charlie Chaplin	Henri Garat	Jeanette McDonald
Ramon Navarro	Greta Garbo	Jean Murat	Annabella
Douglas Fairbanks	Marlene Dietrich	Charles Boyer	Gaby Morlay
Emil Jannings	Charles Boyer	Pierre Blanchar	Suzy Vernon
Adolphe Menjou	Ronald Colman	André Roanne	Marie Glory
Lon Chaney	Mae West	Jean Véber	Marlene Dietrich
Pierre Blanchar	Ramon Navarro	Fernand Gravey	Claudette Colbert
Ivan Mosjoukine	Annabella	Richard-Willm	Lilian Harvey
Jean Angelo	Pierre Blanchar	André Burgère	Edwige Feuillère
John Gilbert	Claire Brooks	Roland Toutain	Renée St Cyr
Harold Lloyd	Cohan		Norma Shearer
Jacque Catelain	Irene Dunne		Gina Manès
Charles Vanel	Fernandel		Colette Darfeuil
Ronald Colman	Florelle		Madge Evans
Conrad Veidt	Cary Grant		Gloria Swanson
André Roanne			
Buster Keaton			
Jean Murat			
Lucien Dalsace			
Léon Mathot			
Georges Biscot			
Ivan Petrovitch			
Antonio Moreno			
Ric Cortez			

Notes: The first column results from a poll to which 200,000 readers responded, covering French and foreign male actors; the second from a survey of readers to identify the best actors and actresses in the world; the third from a contest set up by the *Almanach Ciné Miroir* to identify the most loved French young leading men; the fourth from a poll in which 16,398 readers voted, nominally to identify the most beautiful smile, but effectively to rank French and foreign young leading ladies. Where both French and foreign stars are listed, the French stars are underlined.

Valentino, Petrovitch, and Charles Rogers outrank all except Catelain. The 1933 *Cinémonde* poll shows foreign stars still occupying ten of the top fifteen places and underlines the improvement of American rankings. Jennings, Veidt, and other Europeans have disappeared, and only Marlene Dietrich remains. Of French stars, only Pierre Blanchar has survived into the sound era, though Jean Murat and André Roanne continue to figure as "Prince Charmings."

Table 8.3. Most Popular Film Stars 1936–48

| La Cinématographie française | | | IFOP | Cinémonde | |
1936	1937	1938	1945	1947	1948
Male actors					
Boyer (1)	Fernandel (1)	Gabin (1)	Raimu (1)	Blanchar (3)	Fresnay (1)
R-Willm (2)	Gabin (3)	Fernandel (3)	Fernandel (2)	Marais (5)	Philipe (3)
Fernandel (3)	Raimu (4)	Jouvet (5)	Jouvet (3)	Jouvet (7)	*Blanchar* (6)
Baur (4)	Boyer (5)	Raimu (6)	Blanchar (4)	*Noël-Noël* (9)	Jouvet (11)
Baroux (5)	Rossi (6)	Fresnay (7)	Gabin (5)	Gabin (10)	Marais
France (6)	R-Willm (9)	Boyer (9)	Barrault (7)	Fresnay (12)	Meurisse
Rossi (8)	Guitry (10)	Guitry (12)	Chaplin (9)	Raimu	Bourvil
Berry (11)	Baur (11)	von Stroheim	Fresnay (11)	Boyer	Vanel
Chaplin (12)	Francen (12)	Rossi	R-Willm	R-Willm	Gravey
Raimu	Gable	M Simon	Boyer	Gravey	Ledoux
Gabin	Taylor	Berry		Vanel	Larquey
Blanchar	Berry	Vanel		Barrault	R Dary
Larquey	Larquey	Baroux		Coëdel	Dauphin
Bach	von Stroheim	Cooper		Ledoux	M Simon
Guitry	Blanchar	Blanchar		Rossi	Noël-Noël
Murat	Murat	Baur		Périer	Marchal
Gravey	Vanel	R-Willm			
Female actors					
Morlay (7)	Darrieux (2)	Romance (2)	Darrieux (6)	Feuillère (1)	Presle (2)
Darrieux (9)	Annabella (7)	Darrieux (4)	Morlay (8)	Morgan (2)	Feuillère (4)
Annabella (10)	Garbo (8)	Printemps (8)	Feuillère (10)	Romance (4)	Morgan (5)
Temple	Temple	Morgan (10)	Romance (12)	Darrieux (6)	Darrieux (6)
Garbo	Feuillère	Luchaire (11)	Presle	*St. Cyr* (8)	Morlay (8)
Popesco	Morlay	Annabella	Morgan	Sologne (11)	Robinson (9)
Dietrich	Dietrich	Popesco		Presle	Maffei (10)
Rosay	Popesco	Garbo		Ducaux	St. Cyr (12)
McDonald	Korène	Feuillère		Morlay	Casarès
Renaud	Rosay	Rosay		Rosay	Pascal
Chantal	Durbin	Ducaux		J Dary	Brunoy
Moréno	Colbert	S. Simon		Joyeux	Ducaux
Vernon	Romance	Temple		Renant	Romance
St. Cyr	Balin	Morlay			Joyeux
Feuillère	Crawford				Renant

Note: Underlined names were favored by fans rather than film directors; italicized names were favored by theater managers rather than fans. The *Cinémonde* referendums ("Victoires du Cinéma Français") relate exclusively to French stars; other columns include foreign stars.

As succeeding lists make clear, the tendency toward dominance of French stars continues throughout the thirties, more rapidly in the case of males, but steadily in the case of females, until only Greta Garbo, Shirley

Temple, and Gary Cooper can compete, and then only in lower rankings. Of course, the relative absence of American films from French screens during the war contributed to this progressive decline, with only Chaplin surviving the war. I know of no poll that measures the popularity of foreign actors alongside that of French actors after 1945, which in itself is interesting given their statistically equal presence on French screens throughout the period 1945–60. This was, of course, a period of intense international rivalry between the two cinemas, with the French filmmaking community fighting to preserve the government subsidies on which it had arguably come to depend, and the Americans bringing intense pressure for an open-door policy in which the two industries would compete for the French market on a (supposedly) equal footing. In these circumstances, it would have been surprising if industry journals had done anything at all to promote an awareness of Hollywood stars, but it is equally interesting that popular fan magazines avoided any explicit comparison.

In terms of gender, the deduction to be drawn from the available evidence is that French audiences preferred male actors to female actors for the greater part of the period, and certainly throughout the thirties, though a peak in the popularity of actresses was to occur just after the war. Early references to actor preferences seem to be related almost entirely to males. It is not that actresses are not mentioned as popular—quite the contrary, they are constantly referred to in those terms—but simply that their acting ability is not considered relevant. They are objects to be looked upon with delight, rather than professionals to be admired for their competence. From 1936 on, moreover, when the surveys of theater managers begin to allow direct comparisons between male and female actors, it is males who predominate. From 1936 to 1945, all polls show a higher regard for male actors, though the margin of preference is diminishing steadily in the immediate prewar years. This change in gender preference can be measured. In 1936, the men outscore the women by more votes than even the simple list order suggests, and in 1937, when Fernandel tops the poll with over 11,000 votes, Darrieux, who comes second, receives only 6,330. If one sums the votes for the male and female actors in the top twelve places, the proportion is 5:1 in favor of males in 1936, 3:1 in 1937, and less than 2:1 in 1938 (6,965:4,270). However, only in 1947, when Edwige Feuillère and Michèle Morgan outscore all males, and 1948, when, though not topping the poll, actresses occupy eight of the top twelve places, do females demonstrate a higher degree of popularity with spectators. In 1949, Michèle Morgan again tops the poll, but overall honors are about even, and from 1950 on there is no great discrepancy between the sexes, though the Stock Exchange of the Stars published annually by *Le Film Français* suggests that the presence of a male star was more likely to attract viewers to a film than was the presence of a female star, especially in the mid-fifties.

If there were identifiable box-office trends both in national popularity and in gender, there was an even stronger one in terms of age. In the early years of sound cinema it was clear from the terms in which the various magazines conducted their polls that they expected their readers to be interested primarily in younger stars. It is romantic leads who are the focus of the majority of polls, and *Ciné Miroir* had published a lengthy article in 1929 categorizing the types of young leading men—the sporty type (such as André Roanne), the whimsical (such as Albert Préjean), and the more mature [*sic*] leading man (such as Angelo, Mathot, and Murat). It had also run a competition to identify which of them was the most popular. It was not a French star, but Ramon Navarro, who came out on top, with over a third of the votes, followed by Jacque Catelain, Petrovich, Valentino, Charles Rogers, Jean Angelo, Pierre Blanchar, John Gilbert, Mosjoukine, and Pierre Batchef.[93] What the magazines do not seem to have noticed for some time is that it was already the more mature and solid leading men who had the highest ratings in polls. It is Chevalier, Murat, and Angelo who enter the Académie; it is Jean Murat who is recognized early in 1933 as "incontestably our best young lead";[94] it is Murat and Boyer who rate second and third in the *Almanach Ciné Miroir*'s poll later in the same year (topped by Garat, to the chagrin and bewilderment of *Ciné Miroir*);[95] it is Boyer who is the Toulouse favorite;[96] it is Murat, Boyer, and Chevalier (again with Garat) who are the male half of *Ciné Miroir* readers' ideal couple.[97]

In the latter half of the thirties, this preference for more mature, unhandsome male leads rather than young leading men becomes even more apparent. Baur, Gabin, Raimu, and Jouvet rise to dominance in the rankings, along with Baroux, Berry, Vanel, and Guitry. It is certainly not glamour and romance that is motivating people to vote for these actors in referendums, but something closer to the desire for a father figure, a responsible, confident, passionate, compassionate, and perhaps even ruthless male protector or role model. As we have seen, the discourse surrounding such stars in the fan magazines of the period represented them as solid, substantial men of authority—strong, silent, yet charismatic patriarchal figures, able to impose their will by sheer force of personality. They are not, of course, a homogeneous group. One of the few concrete indications of different audiences with differing tastes arises from the 1945 IFOP poll, in which Gabin and Fernandel are recorded as appealing particularly to the working class, whereas Barrault and Jouvet appeal more to the middle classes. At the level that concerns us here, however, it is their common characteristics which are striking.

The dominance of this mature masculine persona from 1937 to 1947 has as its correlative a tendency to see young leading men in much the same light as actresses were earlier seen—as depending on a gratuitous and transitory beauty, a superficial accident of fate that made them photogenic but had nothing to do with the art of acting or the ability to embody a mythic persona. It is perhaps significant that Marais, Barrault, and Philipe, who were to soar to the top of the charts in the postwar years, were all established theatrical actors before becoming film stars. Perhaps, also, we should recognize a relationship between the rise of the mature male persona and the parallel rise of the drama as a popular generic type. Both were more appropriate to the exploration of a range of situations extending beyond the sentimental and interpersonal, which constituted the normal sphere of action of the young leading man.

During the 1950s, it is still primarily mature male actors, such as Gabin, Boyer, Vanel, Fernandel, and now Eddie Constantine, who appear in the top ranks. Indeed, what strikes one most about the sequence of charts is the consistency of certain names over the years. Gabin, who enters them in 1936, is still near the top in the late fifties. Similar observations could be made regarding Boyer, Fernandel, and Vanel. Blanchar, who was already rated most popular French actor in 1929, is still at the top in the late forties, as were Baur and Raimu until their deaths in 1943 and 1946, respectively. Among females, Edwige Feuillère is progressively more popular from 1935 to 1947, when she tops the poll, and is still high on the lists in the late fifties. Michèle Morgan's popularity is even more amazing, given that she had long outlived her cult persona, and Danielle Darrieux rates not far behind in consistency. The French film-going public was far from fickle in its preferences.

This is most remarkable in the IFOP poll conducted in the immediate postwar period. Gabin, Boyer, Morgan, and Rosay all rate a mention, yet Gabin had been largely absent from French screens during the war, except in *Remorques* (though admittedly he benefited from his postwar aura as a conquering tank commander entering Paris with the Free French forces). Boyer had in fact lived in the U.S. since 1934, had become naturalized, and had acted in no French films since that time. Michèle Morgan had been scarcely more visible than Gabin over the preceding years, and Françoise Rosay had gone into exile during the occupation. Yet they still appear in the ratings lists in 1945 and after. So while to some extent the lists bear witness to the popularity of specific films, they also bear witness to the fact that French audiences remained faithful to their stars even when they seldom saw them in films. A measure of this loyalty in the fifties was the new rule that had to be introduced into the "Victoires": after three such "victories" a star became a permanent divinity and no longer needed to compete—indeed, was no longer allowed to compete. This rule was introduced to exclude Michèle Morgan, Jean Gabin, Gérard Philipe, Martine Carol, and later Danielle Darrieux, who otherwise seemed likely to dominate indefinitely.

8.3 TWO MYTHIC STEREOTYPES OF THE THIRTIES: "GABIN" AND "MORGAN"

Certain of these more popular stars exercised an obsessive fascination over audiences and critics alike, and thus became the object of endless commentary designed to identify the source of their fascination. Among these much-noted stars, three stand out—Jean Gabin and Michèle Morgan in the thirties, and Brigitte Bardot twenty years later. They are the clearest instances of actors or actresses who came to embody mythic stereotypes, which they subsequently brought ready-made to each new film. These were not, as we have seen, the only such stereotypes circulating within the French cinema, nor were they the only myths to attach themselves to these three actors over the years, but they are the only instances in which a stereotype came to be associated almost exclusively with a particular actor or actress.

As tables 8.2 and 8.3 show, other actors or actresses were as popular as these three in certain years, or even more so. Some were even as popular for almost as long as Gabin and Morgan—notably Jean Marais, Fernandel, Gérard Philipe, Danielle Darrieux, and Micheline Presle—yet their appeal was more transparent and less troubling. Other stars were recognized as better actors than these three, notably Barrault, Raimu, Blanchar, and Fresnay, but their acting ability was precisely the factor that allowed them to assume radically different roles from film to film. Yet others were as consistent in the persona that they projected from film to film, notably Tati, Fernandel, and Arletty. Yet neither professional competence nor consistent persona received the level of obsessive analysis which surrounded the performances of Gabin, Morgan, and Bardot. What follows is an attempt to summarize the commentary that surrounded Gabin and Morgan at the time, and to identify the source of the trouble they caused.

Of the two, Jean Gabin was the first to impose his cinematic persona on critics and the public. Commentators recognized this developing persona surprisingly early. Several discourses had played over him in the first half of the thirties, and certain phrases, such as "un rude gars" and "un chic type" were to recur for many years, as was mention of his love of boxing, hunting, fishing, football, and his place in the country. Yet from 1935 on, commentators feel these terms and phrases are inadequate to encapsulate a phenomenon which clearly has wider significance. It was *La Bandera,* released in September 1935, which triggered this awareness, reinforced in the following year by a series of prominent roles in *La Belle Équipe, Les Bas-Fonds, Pepe le Moko,* and *La Grande Illusion. Pour Vous* published a series of six articles in September–October 1935, in which Gabin is represented as reflecting on his life, and which serve to summarize the discourses that attached to him at that time.[98] They mention his working-class background, his distaste for school and tendency to play hooky, his laboring jobs, his love of earthy and violent sports, his entry into theater through the Folies Bergère, and the importance of friendship in his life.

But it is an article in *Ciné Miroir* that year which first begins to explore the complexities of the persona which Gabin was developing. It notes the diversity of roles that he has played up to and including the legionnaire's role in *La Bandera,* and asserts,

> No one is better fitted for this role of a black sheep who is transformed into a superbly courageous soldier. Indeed, Gabin has preserved from the company he kept as a young man and from his military service the impression of being a man of the people. He likes to assume the air of a freethinker, he speaks slang, he shrugs his shoulders, he's simple, frank, and open . . . and when the occasion calls for it, he knows how to send trouble-makers unceremoniously about their business. Jean Gabin could be said to have created on screen a character type that didn't exist before his arrival—the bad lad with the heart of gold, mocking, sardonic, sensitive, and generous, all of a piece, conscious of his strength but capable of putting it to use in the name of something higher.[99]

If there were relatively few references to this persona before the war, there were even fewer during it because of Gabin's physical and political distance, though Malraux in 1940–41 noted his persona as one of those mythic character-constructs, like "Marlene," "Garbo," and "Charlie Chaplin," that had evolved out of different but convergent scenarios.[100] But it was in the postwar years, between 1949 and 1957, when Gabin's persona was beginning to show its age, that commentators were most fascinated by it. In a review of *Au-delà des grilles, Écran Français* summarized the prewar archetype—fatalism, cages and grills, the glimpse of an impossible love, ports, departures, and the dream of a new life "over there"—only to point out that this latest film undermines that myth by humanizing and particularizing it, anchoring it too closely to a specific time and place.[101] The same film inspired Bazin to explore the fatality that seemed to grip the Gabin persona. Likening those outbreaks of rage that often seemed to seal his fate to the rage of Oedipus on the road to Thebes that led him to kill the charioteer who was his unrecognized father, Bazin talks of the now-conventionalized elements of the persona and of the modifications they were undergoing as the actor aged. While he refers to the possibility of a profound significance lying behind "Gabin," the nearest he comes to defining that significance is his parting reference to "a world without God."[102]

Some years earlier, Bazin had developed notes for use in a cine-club discussion of *Le Jour se lève* in which he explored the myth at greater length.

After an interrogation of the iconographic elements of the film, worthy, as he himself remarks, of Sherlock Holmes, he devotes three pages to summarizing the myth—essentially a malevolent fatality which hounds "Gabin," his stoic and solitary endurance of it, the glimpse of a possible salvation in the form of a woman, the disillusion caused by her impurity/betrayal, the outburst of anger that places him in thrall to a fatality he thought he had outdistanced, as personified in "that secular arm of contemporary destiny: the law, cops," and his final submission to that destiny. But here again, no clear interpretation of the myth is provided; the story and the persona caught up in it are seen as having "primarily metaphysical" significance, though Bazin does speak of the setting as a "suburban working-class Thebes where the role of the gods is displaced onto the blind but no less transcendental imperatives of society."[103]

For Duvillars, whose 1950 book is devoted exclusively to myth in the cinema, and specifically to those stars who in Malraux's formulation have given rise to convergent scenarios, "Gabin" is the principal mythic construct of contemporary French cinema. Recapitulating Bazin's error, Duvillars also is misled by the traditional connotations of the term "myth" to see in "Gabin" a trans-historical archetype, whose social and historical specifics are written off as "incidental." For him, as for Barkan a few years later, the greatness of the Gabin myth is to have endowed the everyday existence of the common man with a universal significance. No historical specificity is relevant in a myth.[104] Finally, although the title of Claude Mauriac's essay, "Jean Gabin, or the death of a myth," might suggest some awareness of the fact that myths are born and die for social and historical reasons, in fact the emphasis is on the aging of the Gabin persona itself and the failure of the central heterosexual relationship; henceforth, as in *Touchez pas au grisbi,* it is male friendships which will bear the weight of any external symbol of transcendence. Rather than having any wider meaning, the myth is seen as tied exclusively to the aging of the actor who embodies it.[105]

At least at first, the Michèle Morgan persona was dependent on the Gabin persona, but it acquired an autonomous fascination for some years. Remarked on briefly in the immediate prewar years, it experienced an even greater disruption on the advent of war, and was ultimately of briefer duration than "Gabin," partly (but only partly) because of reports incompatible with it concerning her private life which appeared in fan magazines in the fifties. *Ciné Miroir,* ever a useful source of commentary on the stars, begins to notice her in 1938. Her face is described as "young, yet it seems already touched by bitterness . . . she has a look about her that one does not easily forget . . . a shadow passes from time to time, then clears, and something almost childlike lights up her face, only to be rapidly replaced by an indefinable gravity."[106] The following year, an extended attempt to articulate her significance describes her as a mysterious artist, never completely fulfilled . . . despite her youth and beauty, she bears within her a secret melancholy . . . her climate is one of pervasive anguish, for as she says happiness is out of the question for her. . . . She seems to long for the inaccessible, the unattainable. [She has] a soul that is extremely sensitive, and little gestures that are most poignant. She has a child's face. She is frail, and scarcely uses make-up at all. And she has gray-green eyes that seem unreal. . . . She represents, in fact, that mystery which every woman bears within herself, every predestined creature; and this is what constitutes her charm, this is what troubles those who approach her. O mysterious feminine.[107]

Regretting her absence during the war, Roger Régent notes various roles that would have suited her, and expands on the narrative to which she is coming to be seen as central: "That character, always a little conventional, but which she renders not just convincing but overwhelming, of a woman about whom one knows nothing, who appears all of a sudden, and for whom you are willing to abandon everything, to risk everything. . . . She is the unknown, appearing out of the storm and leaving behind her an indelible image. Who could take the place in our cinematic mythology of that face, that look, that voice, so unforgettable that one can easily believe in their ability to utterly transform one's world."[108]

When he recapitulates these traits in 1950, Duvillars acknowledges in her persona something he had been unable or unwilling to recognize in other mythic types—its peculiar historicity. Reflecting on the lack of distinguishable character types in the young women of classical theater, he sees "the catastrophic young woman" whom Michèle Morgan in his view personifies as "a mythic being who is specifically modern," analogous to the young women of Anouilh's plays. He still speaks of the fatality that hounds her as "age-old," but notes that "there is something fresh, something specific to our century in her."[109]

Cinémonde's homage to her at the end of 1951 marks the end of the "Morgan" myth. More than any other commentary on her, it makes plain in a series of almost untranslatable phrases the tension between opposing principles which constituted much of her fascination. She is "a creature of extreme modesty, shy and distrustful, who tries at times to temper her dazzling physical presence by a distant reserve" ("pudeur ombrageuse . . . cette réserve hautaine . . . cet éclat qu'elle s'applique parfois à voiler").[110] Already, however, this report notes that she has had a son by a recently terminated marriage to an American, and in 1952, when she marries Henri Vidal, she becomes enmeshed in a quite banal discourse of the age, that of the happily married bourgeoise, with a much-loved family, a comfortably furnished flat, and ultimately an ivy-covered chateau overlooking the Seine (not to mention visits to Duvivier on the Riviera). The distinctive qualities which critics and spectators alike had once read into her performances are no longer evoked.

The early fifties saw, then, the termination or radical transformation of the only two truly mythic stereotypes which the thirties French cinema and its audiences had seen fit to embody in specific actors. A principal element in the fascination exercised by their personae, as later by that of Brigitte Bardot, is captured by the incessant oxymorons that appear in articles about them—each has a persona constituted of incompatible or even contradictory elements. "Gabin" is of humble origins yet inherently noble, guilty of more or less serious social misdemeanors yet intrinsically innocent, a rough diamond with a heart of gold. "Michèle Morgan" is at once familiar and inaccessible, dazzling and reserved, pure yet bearing some obscure guilt, dependent on a man to whom she is committed, yet apart, mysterious. These two figures seemed troublesome to contemporary commentators precisely because their personae were not readily definable in a simple term or phrase, as was the case with the discursive personae listed earlier. Their more complex images made them stand out from the more readily definable types that other actors assumed and discarded in the course of their careers. It was also this sense of internal complexity and contradictoriness which rendered them suitable for the task of representing some of the more problematic aspects of contemporary reality. Other actors might represent one aspect of a problematic, or even several in the course of successive roles, but these three embodied the problematic as a whole, allowing the spectator to recognize his or her own anguish, his or her own tension and indecision.

Whereas in general it is clear that for "Gabin" this ambiguity was played out at the level of class (and later for "Brigitte Bardot" at the level of intergenerational conflict), it is not quite so clear how to place "Michèle Morgan," though possibly she simply embodied a move to revise the stereotypes surrounding the term "woman." If so, we can say that, in a period of intense social and historical crisis, the three key mythic personae of the classic cinema worked to question and revise key assumptions about the three principal thematic fields of the time—class, gender, and age.

Finally, it is worth mentioning that Renoir used Gabin three times in the 1930s, and was in fact disposed to exploit the leading stars of the day in the normal course of his filmmaking. He had used in turn Michel Simon (three times), Fernandel, his brother Pierre Renoir (three times), Max Dearly, Larquey, Valentine Tessier, Jules Berry (twice), Florelle, René Lefèvre, Jouvet (twice), Pierre Fresnay, Simone Simon, and Suzy Prim, not to mention von Stroheim. All of these would have been well known to audiences of the day, highly rated by them in popularity polls, and a key attraction in the publicity campaigns. Yet of the seven leading roles in *La Règle du jeu*, not one was a "star" in the terms of the day. That Nora Grégor was an unknown is a widely recognized fact, and Renoir himself had only played minor roles in a few of his own films (plus one silent film and one German sound film). Of the other five actors, none had ever appeared in any of the popularity polls as an audience favorite except Toutain, who had been rated tenth as Prince Charming back in 1933! Of course, Carette, Gaston Modot, Dalio, and Paulette Dubost were well-known supporting actors, useful for character roles, comic off-siders and stooges, whose presence had invigorated many thirties films, including several of Renoir's own, but none was a lead actor of the sort to appear in large print on a playbill. Of the seven, only Toutain had ever figured so prominently in the popular imagination as to have a discourse woven about him: the slightly comic discourse of the acrobatic *sportif.* In its aviator form, that discourse is, of course, exploited by the film, but Toutain's presence was scarcely sufficient in itself to carry the film as Gabin, Jouvet, von Stroheim, and Fresnay had recently carried *Les Bas-Fonds, La Grande Illusion,* and *La Bête humaine.* In fact, the only other Renoir film of the thirties to resemble *La Règle du jeu* in its absence of "stars" is *Toni,* which takes this tendency to extremes. When one considers this fact in conjunction with the way Dalio is used against the grain and the volatile Toutain is killed off at the end, a degree of confusion in the reception of the film becomes more understandable.

NINE

Box-Office Success in the Thirties: Films "debased by popular taste"?

Future historians will only have to look through a group of box-office
successes and will need little critical judgment for their work. There
they will see our pitiful gestures, our current mannerisms, our false
sentiments—an unmistakable reflection of the poverty of the era.
                                    —Bardèche and Brasillach (1936)

The cinema is debased in its very essence, condemned irrevocably by
its dependence on popular taste.
                                    —Varlet

9.1 AUDIENCES AND EXHIBITION PRACTICES 1929–39

As another way of focusing attention on the films which spoke most intensely to French audiences of the thirties of matters central to their
identity, this chapter attempts to isolate those French films screened during
the thirties which attracted the largest audiences. While this might seem the
only logical way to deal with the problem, at least one alternative strategy
exists: to isolate films which returned the highest receipts.

The two measures could differ significantly, especially in the thirties,
when formal regulation of entry prices was minimal. There was always a
considerable difference in status and in entry price between different first-
release movie theaters, as there was between these theaters and the larger
array of local theaters, so a film which excelled in exclusive release could
earn far higher returns from the same number of entries. This was to be all
the more true in the late forties and the fifties, when prices were regulated
and certain films were accorded the right to charge a supplement on top of
the regular ticket price, primarily for reasons of production cost (color,
large casts, length, etc.). It was always the case, therefore, that the same
number of tickets sold for two different films could generate a markedly
higher or lower return, depending on the supplement charged and the release trajectories of the films. Table 9.1 provides a concrete illustration of
this problem from the fifties, when all the relevant data are available. When

Table 9.1 Top First-Release Films, Paris, 1954

In order of returns (millions of francs)		In order of entries (thousands)	
1. Si Versailles m'était conté (S)	274	1. Si Versailles m'était conté (L)	685
2. *Tant qu'il y aura des hommes* (S)	136	2. *Tant qu'il y aura des hommes* (L)	413
3. *Vacances romaines* (S)	107	3. *Vacances romaines* (L)	407
4. *Désert vivant**	98	4. Les Femmes s'en balancent	343
5. Touchez pas au grisbi (S)	96	5. Papa, maman, la bonne et moi	274
6. Les Femmes s'en balancent	91	6. *Désert vivant**	267
7. Papa, maman, la bonne et moi	89	7. *Les Temps modernes*	266
8. Monsieur Ripois	85	8. Touchez pas au grisbi	265
9. Le Rouge et le noir (S)*	85	9. *Pain, amour et fantaisie*	262
10. Le Blé en herbe	77	10. Escalier de service*	243
11. *Les Temps modernes*	76	11. *Un grain de folie*	241
12. *Pain, amour et fantaisie*	71	12. Le Blé en herbe	212

* First release not yet finished
(S) Price supplementation
(L) Longer than normal
Italics Foreign film
Source: *Le Film Français* (31 Dec. 1954)

box-office returns rather than entry numbers are the focus of attention, *Touchez pas au grisbi* and *Le Rouge et le noir* rise, respectively, from eighth to fifth and from off the table to ninth, largely on the basis of price supplements. Clearly, other price differentials were also operating to promote *Monsieur Ripois* from off the table to eighth, and to demote *Modern Times*.

There are different arguments for adopting entries and for adopting receipts as the measure of a film's mythic status. Possibly, within a capitalist society mythic status is most readily measured by the amount of money that the population as a whole is willing to spend in order to participate in the mythic experience. The alternative argument is that a myth is quantifiable in terms of the proportion of the social group affected. The more people drawn to a film, and the more often, the more significant is the myth. The latter viewpoint is the one on which the present calculations are based. Therefore, all figures given in this chapter are based on the number of entries for each film, and tend to measure the extent of reach of the myth through the population rather than the monetary value that those spectators implicitly assigned to it.

Whether the focus is on entries or returns, however, the task of ranking the films of the thirties in order of popularity can never be anything but controversial, because of the lack of reliable data. Audience numbers are, if anything, harder to ascertain than returns, since trade papers of the day, which constitute the primary source of information, were preoccupied

Figure 9.1. French Audiences 1930–60

Millions

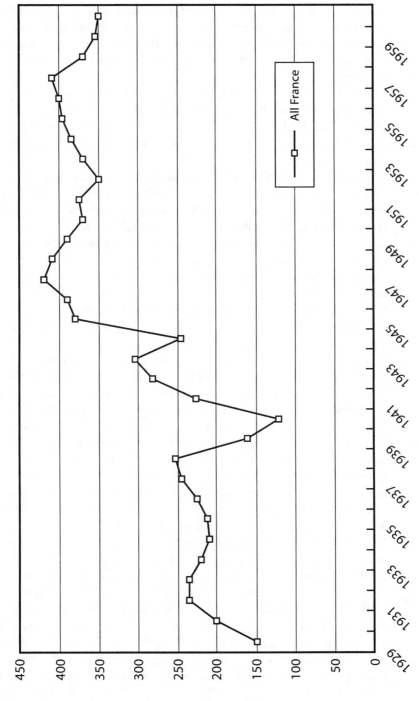

with profitability rather than with the procedures used by distributors and exhibitors to obtain those profits. Certain basic parameters are available, however, and they allow us to recognize the relative size of thirties audiences in the wider contexts both of the classic French cinema and of other national cinemas.

The size of the total French audience from 1930 to 1960 is known with some degree of reliability, and within that global total the size of the audience for French films has been fairly accurately documented. Figure 9.1 records the accepted figures. One unavoidable conclusion is that the cinema in France never achieved the levels of attendance achieved by the cinema in America, Britain, Italy, or even Germany. One cannot speak of it in quite the same confident way as a mass medium, a "people's cinema." Audiences of 220 million were regularly achieved in the thirties; the numbers surged briefly past 300 million in the "protected" environment of the war years, then rose again in the postwar years to their highest level ever—about 380 million. These figures represent about 5.8 entries per head in the thirties, and 9 entries per head in the fifties. Such figures pale beside 30 entries per head in Britain, and 40 per head in America. Even in 1957, half of the French population never went to the movies as much as once per year. Effectively, only 50 percent of the French population have ever been "moviegoers."

Several explanations have been proposed for these low attendance levels, not least the lack of penetration of the cinema into rural areas. As Ginette Vincendeau notes, if we can make any claim for the cinema in France as a popular medium, "we have to remember that we mean a popular *urban* (not to say metropolitan) spectacle, excluding an unusually large proportion of the population."[1] Among urban centers, Paris always recorded the highest attendance. At its peak, the city recorded twenty-eight entries per moviegoer per year, against twenty-one in larger provincial cities and ten in small towns.[2] Indeed, Paris always recorded about three times the national average of entries—at least 20 percent from about 6.3 percent of the population, and, if my calculations are correct, over 30 percent at times in the thirties—because of the more up-to-date equipment, the wider range of films on offer, and easy access to large numbers of movie theaters.

These variations need to be borne in mind since, as we will see, until the mid-fifties the preferences of Parisian and provincial audiences differed markedly, and the preferences differed from province to province. Discrepancies between Paris and the regions gradually became less important during the fifties, and it is reasonable to see this slow homogenization of French movie audiences as part of a wider homogenization of the nation, due partly to economic and political factors and partly to consequent social and cultural factors. Communications became more rapid, TV joined radio to provide a simultaneous cultural experience for the whole nation, rural areas were integrated into the road network, car ownership increased significantly, and tourism drew the population into a common experience of the different regions of "their" nation. In fact, by the end of the fifties, France was beginning for the first time to become a coherent cultural community.

But throughout the classic period 1930–60, audiences were differentiated almost as much by class as by region. The cinema was never predominantly a working-class medium in France, even in the urban environment where it was strongest. By the thirties, it was primarily the middle classes—or at least the lower-middle classes—who went to the movies, possibly in part because they took over so much of the theatrical repertoire which these audiences had patronized. Going to the movies, or at least to a certain sort of movie, could constitute a cultural experience which directly substituted for those "legitimate theater" experiences, which were rapidly becoming beyond the financial reach of even middle-class audiences. The industry journal *Cinéopse* returned to this topic several times in the early thirties,[3] and Durand reports a 1937 survey confirming that it is "the rising social class, working in the centers of big cities, and above all in Paris, [that] has become the prime target for the new theaters. Movie houses on the Champs Élysées and the boulevards, where the highest concentration of office workers is to be found, multiplied starting in the early thirties."[4] A series of studies by the Centre National de la Cinématographie (CNC) in the fifties produced similar results. Indeed, by 1957 and 1958, the CNC is contrasting England, where the working class go to the movies most often, with France, where it is the middle classes who do so, while the upper and upper-middle classes are less frequent movie-goers and the poor the least frequent of all.[5]

A series of surveys in the sixties and seventies related theater attendance directly to education level and found that the more highly educated went proportionately more frequently.[6] A significant proportion of these well-educated movie-goers were students. Indeed, at least as much as by region or by class, audiences for the classic French cinema can best be defined by age. In the fifties, a detailed survey noted that those aged fifteen to twenty-four went more often than anyone else—about thirty-two times per year, or twice as often as those aged twenty-five to forty-nine, and over four times as often as those aged fifty and above. The same survey noted in passing that the total number of English spectators under fifteen years of age was greater than that of all French spectators put together. It also began to break down audiences according to taste: up to the age of twelve, fantasy prevailed; from then on there was a greater demand for "realism," and the tastes of male and female audiences began to diversify according to traditional gender roles—male spectators (the majority) preferred sporting themes, fights, patriotic themes, Westerns, adventures, and exotic locations, whereas female spectators preferred artistic themes, luxurious settings, charm, love, and historical and social themes.[7] Courting couples significantly increased the numbers in the fifteen-to-twenty-four age group, though there is some suggestion that this category of spectator still "went to the movies" rather than going to see specific films. In sum, young, well-educated, middle-class spectators constituted a core of movie-goers on whom, according to Bonnell, the French cinema came to depend and still depends for its existence. He notes that at the beginning of the sixties about 42 percent of movie-goers (i.e., about 21 percent of the population) provided 80 percent of entries, with the rest recording irregular and fairly sparse attendance.[8] While a great number of these intensive movie-goers have always been students, they never constituted an absolute majority.

However rudimentary as sociological data, the above observations do serve to remind us that there was no single coherent audience for the classic French cinema; there were a number of different audiences, presumably with different ideological needs. Any attempt to identify mythic elements in the relevant films must take into account the difficulty of correlating a given mythic image or narrative with "its" audience. This problem is only exacerbated by the widely recognized tendency throughout most, if not all, of this period for some audiences to attend their local movie theater regardless of the film that was screening. Although the CNC survey in 1958 affirmed that this was still largely the case at that point, there is evidence to suggest that the progressively greater proportions of moderately wealthy and young spectators who made up audiences in the fifties were becoming more selective in their choice of film and ranging more widely in their search for a theater that screened the specific films and genres that suited them. Of course, if the tendency for audiences to attend local theaters regardless of what film was screening had been uniform, all films would have succeeded equally, and we know that this was not the case. The figures confirm that a high degree of choice was being exercised by a large proportion of spectators in all periods.

This choice did not always favor French films. Theater managers noted that in the prewar period such American super-productions as *Sign of the Cross, King Kong, Cleopatra,* and *Snow White* were more popular than most French releases of their year, along with Chaplin's *Modern Times* and Capra's *Mr. Deeds Goes to Town* and *Lost Horizons.* Similarly, in the postwar years, at or near the top of the (now more reliable) tables are such super-productions as *Gone with the Wind, Cinderella, Samson and Delilah, King Solomon's Mines, The Tunic, Quo Vadis, 20,000 Leagues under the Sea, The Ten Commandments,* and *Around the World in Eighty Days,* together with Hitchcock's *Rebecca, To Catch a Thief,* and *The Man who Knew Too Much.* Indeed, in terms of the number of films being screened, American films had a 50 percent share of the market in the thirties, whereas French films never had significantly more than a 30 percent share. On average, however, American films attracted fewer spectators than French films, so that both national cinemas attracted the same total audience.

During the occupation, of course, American films, and indeed those of most other countries, were banned from much or all of France, so French films enjoyed a significant advantage, and the proportion of spectators which they attracted grew from 50 percent to 75 percent and perhaps even 85 percent in a momentarily larger market. In terms of sheer profitability, the prospects for French producers during the war were even better than this suggests, since the number of films produced was limited by wartime shortages to between 30 and 75 per year, as opposed to about 120 to 160 per year before the war and 100 per year after it. The industry was well aware of the paradoxically beneficial effect of the war on profitability. "Commercially," *Ciné Mondial* noted at the end of 1941, "the cinema is becoming an excellent financial proposition, since covering the cost of a film is no longer, as it was only yesterday, a hypothetical possibility, but rather a certainty."[9] As always more than courteous toward the occupying forces, the magazine attributed this to the opportunity currently being provided to produce a truly original and national cinema, free at last of American influence.

It was not, of course, free of German influence, nor was it free of competition with German and Italian films. Several of these were extremely popular with French audiences. *Face au bolchevisme* played in thirty-eight theaters in the occupied zone in September 1941, and the long runs of *Hitlerjunge Quex* and *Le Juif Süss* are well known. In Paris, the latter played simultaneously in eight theaters in German and five in French, and it is mentioned as having been particularly successful in a wide range of provincial cities. To some extent, these long runs were due to the presence in France of occupation troops, viewing films in their own language, yet this cannot in itself explain the outstanding success of two German color spectaculars—*La Ville dorée* and *Baron Münchausen*—which were far more popular than most French productions in 1943 and 1944, respectively, the former playing continuously for forty weeks—not far short of *Les Enfants du paradis* at war's end.

After the war, with the return of American films, the share of audiences watching French films decreased again to 50 percent. Because of the postwar market boom, this proportion translated into numbers almost as high as the wartime 80 percent, though from twice the number of films. Taking all this into account, we can say that for French films, the audience stood at about 110 million in the thirties, then jumped briefly to about 240 million during the war, then stabilized at 200 million from 1947 until the final catastrophic years of the fifties. Moreover, if we allow for the considerable fluctuations in the number of French films released onto the market, we

Table 9.2. Changes in French Film Industry in the Thirties

	1930	1931	1932	1933	1934	1935	1936	1937	1938	1939[a]
Gross receipts (millions fr)										
All France	801	938	934	879	832	(840)	(875)	(1,045)	(1,205)	(995)
Paris	305	361	359	338	320	313	336	395	452	373
Gross audience (millions)[b]										
All France	(200)	234	233	219	208	(210)	(224)	(245)	(254)	(160)
Paris	(61)	72	72	68	64	63	67	(75)	78	48
Films produced	94	148	154	150	115	127	143	124	119	92
Films released	48	124	162	146	150	127	126	125	127	66
Spectators per film (thousands)										
All France	2,000	940	700	750	700	830	890	980	1,000	(1,200)
Paris	625	290	222	233	227	248	266	300	307	364
Sound theaters										
All France	(552)	1,215	1,797	2,537	3,228	3,450	3,650	3,979		
Paris	(100)	(160)	(190)	(220)	249	284	296	320	345	364
Weekly audience[c]										
All Paris	9,999	8,654	7,287	5,944	4,942	4,265	4,352	4,668	(4,559)	(4,348)
General release	7,000	5,219	4,312	3,377	2,845	2,413	2,467	2,550	2,508	2,380

a. Some parts of this column calculated for the eight months from January to August.
b. Gross audience for French films: approximately 50% of these figures.
c. Average weekly audience for each theater. French films averaged approximately 10% above, U.S. films 10% below.
Figures in parentheses, and for 1930 and 1939, contain some degree of uncertainty, for a variety of reasons.

can say that, in very general terms, wartime films were approximately twice as likely as postwar films and four times as likely as prewar films to be profitable. To put this more concretely, the average national audience for each French film was seven hundred thousand in the early thirties, rose to 1 million in the late thirties and to 4 million during the war, and settled at 2 million in the postwar period.

Though the overall figures suggest that both the thirties and the fifties were periods of relatively stable audience numbers, it did not seem so to the industry at the time, and for good reason. Contemporary accounts implied that there was a significant slump in 1933, which lasted until 1936, and a further slump in 1950, which produced a period of uncertainty lasting perhaps five years. It is possible to show that these periods when the market seemed depressed were periods of transition, when, although audience numbers were unchanged, tastes were changing, and filmmakers were struggling

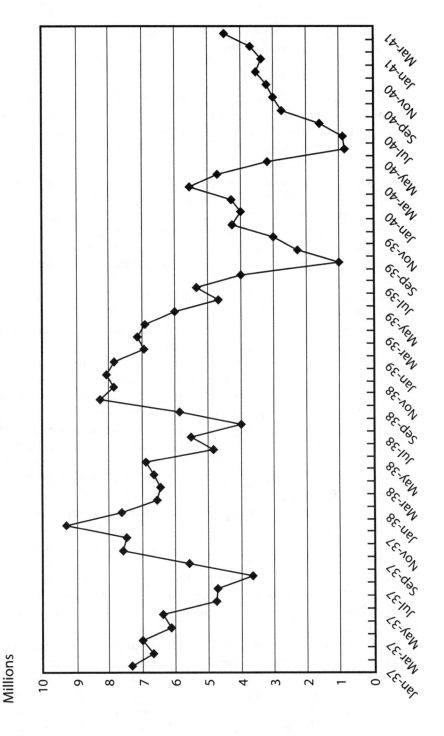

Figure 9.2. Monthly Entries 1937–41

to identify the direction in which they were turning. Consequently, during these periods there were relatively few really successful films and/or large numbers of unsuccessful films.

If we focus specifically on the thirties, we find that the overall French audience fluctuated more than is generally believed, the number of films coming onto the market fluctuated enormously, and the number of theaters equipped for sound increased throughout the decade, at first relatively rapidly, then more steadily. This affected the average audience available per French sound film released, and the average audience available per sound theater. It therefore affected both producers and exhibitors. Table 9.2 illustrates the extent of these fluctuations and of their effects on the industry.

The first thing to note is that after two years of relatively high audience numbers in 1931 and 1932, a steady decrease occurred, but that from 1936 on a quite rapid rise saw audiences at their highest for the decade. Detailed figures available from 1937 on (see figure 9.2) indicate that December 1937 was almost certainly the best month of the whole decade, and that during the period from August 1938 to April 1939, and perhaps even right through to August (except for December 1938, when many theaters were closed as a protest), Paris theaters, and no doubt those in the rest of France, experienced a boom unparalleled since 1930.

This fluctuation begins to explain the sense of crisis that seized the industry toward the middle of the decade, as the unimaginable wealth that the first sound film releases seemed to promise began to fade visibly before its eyes. Sound had abruptly generated increased audiences for entrepreneurs who had risked investing in the "new" technology, as autobiographies such as those by Richebé and Braunberger indicate.[10] Despite pressure not to mention box-office returns, Harlé, the editor of *La Cinématographie Française*, made an exception in 1930 because of the remarkable figures coming in for the first sound feature films.[11] In July of that year, reports from certain Paris theaters suggested that sound films were grossing between 30 percent and 130 percent more than silent productions had grossed the year before. Again in 1931 *La Cinématographie Française* exults in the profitability of the industry, despite the depression (which in fact did not hit France with full force until the following year).[12] The relatively cheap device of transferring to the screen a mass of successful theatrical comedies prolonged and broadened the euphoria. It was clear, however, to all observers that 1933 was a bad year. In January 1934, the returns for provincial towns for the previous year were noted as being down by 10 to 15 percent, and *La Cinématographie Française* (somewhat inaccurately) bemoaned the fact that even the big money-earners of that year had seldom passed two weeks in first release, whereas in the preceding years five weeks had not been uncommon.[13]Later in 1934, an 8.1 percent drop for Paris theaters was announced, and a further nationwide drop was predicted. The tone of alarm

sharpened in early 1935, when final figures for 1934 confirmed these apprehensions with a decrease of about 11 percent for both Paris and the
provinces.[14] The slump in confidence lasted for over two years, and was seen
by many as related not just to the depression but to general socio-political
disarray.[15]

In fact, the crisis in audience numbers had been exacerbated for producers by the dramatic increase in the number of films coming onto the
market, as more studios were equipped for sound production and more
producers sought to exploit the boom in profits generated by early sound
films. The number of films produced in France rose rapidly to a maximum
of about 150 in the years 1931 to 1933, and the subsequent release of these
films onto the market in 1932 to 1934 saw average audiences per sound
film fall from about 2 million in 1930 to seven hundred thousand in 1932.
It was in 1933 that this unexpectedly abrupt decline in receipts impacted
most forcefully on production companies, with the result that 1934 saw the
lowest production figures for the decade. This dramatic reduction constituted a form of involuntary self-regulation which was effective in stabiliz-
ing, then slowly improving, the average returns (i.e., the likelihood of
profit). Consequently, for producers the sense of crisis was already diminishing even as the 1934–35 season began. Tentative evaluations of the quality of the past year's output were positive, and producers seemed reassured
about the financial basis of the industry.[16] As a result of this restored confidence, producers again "over-produced" in 1936, though the number of
films actually released onto the market each season remained remarkably
stable up to the declaration of war.

During the slump in mid-decade, many of the less professional directors and production companies fell by the wayside, and the films that were
produced thereafter were perceived to be of noticeably higher quality.
Commentators speak of "the dramatic recovery of the French cinema" and
call 1935 "the year of fine films . . . with grand and sumptuous sets." In its
annual summary, *La Cinématographie Française* considers that the industry
can look forward to 1936 with confidence: "Never has the French cinema
been so able to rely on the beauty of its productions and its currently well-
deserved reputation."[17] A large proportion of the next two years' reduced
output was successful at the box office, and commentators attributed this in
large part to more lavish sets and costumes, and more generally to a greater
attention to the visual elegance of the image. The idea that quality was
preferable to, and incompatible with, quantity was beginning to take hold
of the industry's financiers, and the experience of the war years was only to
confirm their belief in this dictum.

By the end of 1937, several commentators in *Cinéopse* are expressing
the view that the current season's films are quite exceptional, and that the
French cinema is entering a period of glory. It is not just the new blood

(Marc Allégret, Carné, Chenal, etc.), whom Feyder talks of as bringing about "a renaissance of the French cinema," but international recognition in the form of awards and record-breaking runs in America. "There can be no doubt that the French cinema now takes pride of place in the international marketplace, after the American cinema."[18] This renewed confidence can be measured materially, both in the industry's willingness to undertake costly costume dramas and in its production of costly promotional brochures inserted in industry journals over the following years to promote those productions—in color, on glossy paper, and featuring elaborate fold-out sections. To judge by their continuing presence, the period of confidence lasted right through 1939 to the outbreak of war.

Interestingly, this resurgence of profitability and confidence took place in parallel with a number of political disturbances associated with the Popular Front which had potentially damaging effects on both production and exhibition. At the beginning of 1934, political disturbances had already cost the industry an estimated 7 million francs, and the industry's conservative journal expressed the hope that they would not further exacerbate what was then a worsening industrial situation.[19] Then, in June 1936, there was a series of strikes in all the studios, which *La Cinématographie Française* attempted to write off as of no importance. Further "social movements" in the second half of the year were again written off as "transient," barely deflecting "the common purpose of all sectors of the industry." Strikes, or threatened strikes, characterized as "useless" by the journal, also marred the first half of 1937, causing chaos and further losses.[20]

Yet the fact that the tone of the industry's organ remained so relatively benign in the face of such disruption is some indication of the fundamentally healthy state of the industry's economy in the years 1936–37. It is a little difficult to estimate exactly what proportion of production showed a profit in those expansive times, because no clear figures exist indicating either the true costs or the actual returns to French producers, and opinions differed as to what multiple of a film's cost had to be taken in at the box office before a producer cleared his expenses. Nevertheless, I would estimate, as did certain commentators at the time, that two thirds of the annual production in the late thirties cleared a profit, and only about five films failed catastrophically each year. A good dozen films each year, or about 10 percent of production, were outstandingly successful, both justifying their producers' policy of quality production and permitting its expansion. Most of the box-office successes were large-scale productions with elaborate sets, a technical finish rarely apparent earlier in the decade, and a narrative economy more typical of American films.

A producer's view of the thirties would therefore see the decade as neatly divided into two periods of profitability, interrupted by a crisis due almost exclusively to over-production of cheap, small-scale films. Once that error had been rectified, the industry looked set to satisfy all the expectations raised at the beginning of the decade. An exhibitor's view of the same decade would be less sanguine, seeing it as opening on a note of wild optimism to which events would subsequently give the lie. The principal source of their misfortune was a gradual increase in the number of theaters equipped for sound—or, rather, the source of their misplaced optimism in 1930 and 1931 was the relatively small number of theaters so equipped, such that the large sums generated by the first sound films released were channeled through the box offices of relatively few exhibitors. Their widely reported delight instantly encouraged others to attempt to participate in the bonanza. Although the rate of conversion of French theaters to sound was relatively slow by international standards, nevertheless an average of six hundred theaters was added to the total each year between 1930 and 1934. By that time, almost all the silent theaters that could justify the cost of equipment for sound had been so equipped, while many music halls and other public venues had also been converted and a large number of new theaters had been built.

This process was more rapid and extensive in Paris than in the rest of France. The number of theaters in the capital had been stable during the twenties, fluctuating between 185 and 190. On the introduction of sound, over 100 of them were equipped in the first year, and as well as equipping the rest over the next few years, the industry engaged in a hasty construction program. From 123 (out of 190) theaters equipped for sound by March 1931, the total rose to 364 by 1939. While various sources give slightly different figures, it is clear that an average of 20 new theaters were built each year in Paris, with peaks of 33 new and newly converted theaters in 1933, and 39 in 1935.

For exhibitors, in the context of relatively stable audience numbers, the consequences of this steady expansion in numbers of theaters were very serious. The exorbitant profits of 1930, when 800 million francs was shared between the (rather less than) 490 French sound theaters available in the course of that year, rapidly dropped as 900 million francs was shared in 1931 and 1932 between about 1,200, then 1,800, theaters. By 1934, the take had subsided to 832 million francs, now shared between about 3,200 theaters. Within four years the average annual take per theater had fallen from about 2 million francs to about 250,000 francs, and was to fall even further. These figures begin to explain the sensation of having hit the jackpot that the industry experienced in the first heady years of the thirties, with both producers and exhibitors sharing in the bonanza. But equally the rapid drop in receipts that occurred thereafter explains the progressive anxiety that overtook this side of the industry in 1933 and 1934. The drop was to some extent visible to exhibitors in falling attendance, as the average attendance per theater per week fell from well over ten thousand to under five thousand, and in suburban theaters to under twenty-five hundred. Under these circumstances, competition for customers became intense, commentators begin to emphasize the fragility of the exhibition sector, and a series of strategies was explored over the middle years of the decade to counter the deteriorating returns to exhibitors.

One such strategy was the double program. It is well known that certain theaters explored the possibility of offering not just two films for the price of one, but three, four, or six, together with the provision of food as an extra inducement. This strategy pitted exhibitors against distributors and producers, since in any multiple screening the same box-office take was divided among two or more films. A glance at weekly program guides for the time confirms the results of a survey of theater managers which, while identifying a wide range of variation, suggested that the normal length of a program was 150 to 170 minutes, and that many exceeded three hours. While a large number of those surveyed adopted the tactic of not responding to these questions, some 257 acknowledged that they regularly screened two full-length films, and another 287 that they screened a full-length and a mid-length film. The suspicion that this represented simply the tip of the iceberg was voiced by La Cinématographie Française in June 1933. "Will the somber effect of the double program darken our skies as it has darkened those of America, Germany, and England?" it asked. "Our films have difficulty covering costs as it is, and as receipts fall in all theaters, spreading the producers' share of those receipts over two or more feature films seems a dangerous experiment."[21] Yet by the end of 1934 the journal was forced to acknowledge that double programs were becoming the norm.[22]

Producers did not, however, stop campaigning for regulations to put an end to the practice. This was just one of several instances in which the entrepreneurial independence which the industry so valued, and defended so vociferously, came into conflict with the desire of one or another part of that industry to impose industry-wide norms and regulations that could only have been effected by government legislation of the sort imposed in Germany and later in occupied France. By September 1937, over two thirds of theaters were screening two or more films per program (67.43 percent, compared to 31.16 percent single features, the rest being programs of shorts or news[23]). Even second-run exclusive-release theaters were screening double programs. One incidental effect of this practice was to increase significantly the audience for many B-grade films which otherwise might not have recorded so many screenings. If Parisians recorded 78 million visits to the theater in 1938, they actually saw well over 100 million films, and perhaps even 150 million, many of which they were not really interested in seeing.

Another strategy that exhibitors explored to attract customers in an unregulated market was to undercut the entry price of competitors. This was

Table 9.3. Recommended Minimum Prices, 1936, 1938, 1939 (in francs)

	1936	1938	1939
First exclusive release	10, 8, 6	12, 10	12, 10
Second exclusive release	8, 6, 5	10, 8	10, 8
Third exclusive release		7, 6	8, 7
Pre-general release	6, 5	6, 5	7, 6
First general release	4, 3	5, 4	5, 4
Second general release		4, 3.50	4, 3
Suburban theaters	3, 2.50	3.50, 3	3.50, 3
News and documentary			4, 3

a potentially self-defeating measure, but the pressure to implement it was only exacerbated by the increasing penury of the potential clientele. Entry prices, which had been relatively stable in the early years of the decade, were in 1934–35 reduced (in some theaters) to two or three francs. Certain of them, even in Paris, advertised entry at one franc—indeed, one new theater even called itself the Ciné Un Franc. The undercutting of entry prices was not confined to local theaters. Reductions were bringing down the entry price even of first-run theaters on the Grands Boulevards and Champs-Élysées, normally between ten and twenty francs, to six or seven francs. The industry immediately instituted a campaign to establish minimum prices, resulting in a uniquely effective form of internal self-regulation. The Ciné Un Franc was induced to change its name to the Ciné Deux Francs, and others were likewise forced into line. For the rest of the decade, a table of (unofficial) minimum prices was published and widely observed. Table 9.3 provides an indication of these entry prices for the various categories of cinema in the latter half of the decade. The prices were minimums, and had to apply to not more than 30 percent of seats in a theater, the rest being at least 0.50 franc more expensive.

In fact, the average entry price for most of the decade was four francs nationwide, and five francs in Paris. The entry price seems to have increased by about 10 percent in the summer of 1937, so that in 1938 and early 1939 it was 5.80 francs in Paris,[24] with a further increase in March 1939 bringing the average Paris entry price to 6.8 francs. This still left the cinema a relatively cheaper form of entertainment than earlier in the decade, and it did little to placate exhibitors.

Given that the principal source of the exhibitors' problem was the expanding number of theaters, one logical strategy would have been to proceed as had producers in the face of an increase in films produced—to contract, or at least stabilize, the number of theaters which they themselves, after all, were building. From the middle of the decade on, a campaign to this effect was waged by spokesmen for some exhibitors, with little or no success. Even in 1934, commentators were noting that the 262 Paris theaters then equipped for sound already provided 3.7 million seats for 2.8 million Parisians.[25] Surely, a saturation point had been reached; yet by 1938 an article in an otherwise upbeat review of the industry, entitled "Danger: Too Many Theaters," noted that the proportion had now increased to two seats per inhabitant per week, when each inhabitant attended only eighteen times a year.[26] "The construction of new theaters is an aberration," proclaimed the industry journal, "especially when so many of those that already exist are experiencing such difficult times."[27] Yet the previous year had seen another 24 theaters opened in Paris alone, and the same was to occur in 1938, with a further 20 opened before the outbreak of war. "Should we have a statute limiting the construction of theaters?" asked the journal,[28] conveniently forgetting that the industry's principal anxiety for some years had been the fear of government intervention in the industry's affairs. The threat then, however, had been of nationalization by a left-wing government. Now the industry could hope for more "constructive" intervention.

Throughout the last year before the war, the industry continued its campaign for the licensing of theater ownership and construction, without any effect. It is noticeable that these preoccupations of the exhibition sector ran parallel to and were in marked contrast to the renewed vigor and optimism of the rest of the industry. As one set of headlines proclaimed the vitality and drive of the French cinema, another set of headlines reported that the general assembly of the industry was anxiously calling for a formal maximum to be set on theater numbers and a six- to twelve-month moratorium on all construction. Ironically, it called at the same time for the governmental regulation of entry prices and receipts, which it had so long resisted.[29]

It may seem hard to understand why a sector of the industry should be so unable to control a process for which it was itself responsible. The main reason is that the exhibition sector was far from coherent as a body. It consisted, at one extreme, of a few large corporations which dabbled in production and/or distribution, and which had a number of exclusive-release theaters in all the main cities, and at the other end of a multitude of owners of local suburban, provincial, and rural theaters whose organizational base was weak. Not all suffered equally, because the relationship between exclusive-release and general-release theaters was unequal and constantly evolving throughout the decade.

Because this set of relationships affects our ability to recognize which were the most popular films of the decade, it is worth outlining the changes in institutional practices that took place in the course of the decade. In the late twenties, there had been few exclusive-release theaters (*salles d'exclusivité*), and those that existed were all on the Grands Boulevards—the Gaumont Palace, of course, and the Madeleine, but also the Cameo, the Marivaux, the Aubert Palace, and the Max Linder. Several of these were independent (for instance, the Marivaux, the Cameo, and the Max Linder), and it was not the case that all films were released through them. They did, however, have the pick of the more prestigious films, which commonly ran for several months each, while the rest of the available films were released directly into suburban theaters (*salles de quartier*), some of which belonged to the big firms but most of which were independent.[30] There was therefore effectively a grading of output into A films, which had exclusive release, and B films, which went straight into the suburban theaters. Only the A films received the extensive publicity that went with exclusive release.

By contrast, the first sound films all qualified as "cinematic events," so they received exclusive releases whether their quality justified it or not. Perhaps because of this, but also because the paucity of sound films on the market in those early months gave the prestige theaters no choice—they had to take whatever sound film was on offer, whether good or bad—it subsequently became normal for all sound films to be released into one or more exclusive theaters, before general release into suburban theaters. Although not necessarily advantageous to the exhibitors in the long run, this system benefited the producers and distributors, since it tended to maximize profits for all films. All their films had the high visibility that went with exclusive-release publicity, and the exclusive-release audiences paid more per seat. But one consequence was that exclusive release no longer carried with it the expectation of a run of several months; it quickly became common for films to last no more than a week or two in exclusive release. Exhibitors were not pleased at committing funds to an advertising campaign for a film which lasted only a week in their theater.

This problem was exacerbated by the boom in theater construction that took place in the years 1930–32, when new first-release theaters were constructed on the Champs Élysées and in the Clichy-Barbès area. But within a two-year period the problem was reversed: the number of French films being released increased from about a dozen in the first season to about a hundred in the second and a 150 in the third, while the rate of conversion of theaters to sound was relatively slow. Consequently, by 1932 almost any Parisian theater equipped for sound might be called on to act as a first-release theater. A short list of about fifteen were regularly used in this way (notably the Paramount, Marivaux, Colisée, Aubert Palace, Impérial, Caméo, Olympia, Madeleine, Capucines, and later the Rex and the Gaumont Palace), but at least fifteen others were commonly used, and another forty on occasion. Commentators began to express doubts about the financial sanity of this "system," asserting that "exclusive release" needed restricting to fewer films, and that the number of first-release theaters needed to be reduced correspondingly.

During the 1932–33 season, there were signs that this was happening. Some of the first-release theaters, such as the Caméo, were used as second-run theaters, taking films over from the Gaumont Palace or the newly constructed Rex, which were too large to maintain a film for more than two weeks. The Artistic, Victor Hugo, Lutetia, Royal, Impérial, Gaumont Théâtre, Carillon, Max Linder, Moulin Rouge, and Folies Dramatiques all began to assume this character of second-run theaters, ensuring successful films a longer run in exclusive release, at a price between that of first run and general release. The hierarchy never became total, with second-run theaters occasionally being used for first release, and the Gaumont Palace and the Rex being used more and more often not so much for first runs but rather to give a final week of high-profile first release to a film whose successful run was nearing its end.

This system survived throughout the decade, modified by a tendency to release films not into a single theater but into a cluster of two or more, followed by progressively larger and larger clusters. Under this system, a film might be released simultaneously into several smaller first-run theaters, such as the Agriculteurs, Biarritz, Bonaparte, César, and CinéOpéra, disappearing from one after the other as first-run audiences for the film decreased, whereupon it would be released into seven to ten second-run theaters. The theaters in these clusters tended to be all owned by one chain, and some of them, such as the Demours, the Sélect, and some twenty others, came to be used regularly as third-run theaters. The first formal mention that I have found of this latter category occurs in 1936. In addition, when, for some reason, such as a summer break, a long gap arose between this first series of releases and a film's general release, one of the lower-ranked exclusive-release theaters might feature it again, and thus serve to remind the public of its successful earlier runs just before it entered general release ("pre-general release"). A break of at least a few weeks between exclusive and general release was thought desirable in principle by the industry, since it signaled a clear separation in status between exclusive release and general release, and also made customers feel that it was worth spending the extra money to see a film in exclusive release rather than wait up to several months for general release.

Several instances can serve to illustrate the way this system worked. *Accord final,* a moderately successful film, was released in the Colisée, and after five weeks it was given a final high-profile week, first in the Rex, then in the Gaumont Palace. Subsequently it went to the Ermitage and the St. Didier (second-run), then the Vivienne-LaScala-Panthéon-Régent (third-run), before its general release into thirteen suburban theaters. *L'Affaire Lafarge,* released in the Aubert Palace, was given a final boost in the Rex, then the Gaumont Palace, before going to the Gaumont Théâtre and the Victor Hugo for a second run. The summer dead season intervened, so it resumed eight weeks later in the Pagoda and the Panthéon before its general release. *Claudine à l'école* was released into four small first-run theaters, disappearing from one of them in the sixth week and from two others the following week. After two weeks' complete absence, it reappeared in three second-run theaters for a single week, then went into general release in week 13.

To complicate these release patterns even further, in 1938 general-release theaters also began to be formally sub-categorized as first- and second-screening theaters, both of which were superior to the uncategorized suburban theaters. The evolution of these patterns of exclusive and general release can be glimpsed in table 9.3, where "third-run" and "second-screening" theaters appeared between 1936 and 1938. In general, of course, the reason that this elaborate hierarchy of theaters developed was to maximize the number of weeks in exclusive release, and thus to maximize returns. It was flexible enough to adapt to evolving audience response to any given film, and contained a series of graduated entry prices in order to tempt interested spectators to pay the maximum they could afford to pay for entry to each film. One consequence of the system was, however, that the graduated hierarchy of more and more numerous exclusive-release theaters tended to merge almost imperceptibly into general release, which itself assumed a lesser role as the decade progressed. This tendency, together with the fact that from second release onward a film might be teamed up in a double or multiple program with one or more films at a quite different stage of release, made the division of a film's release into "exclusive" and "general" less and less clear-cut. While the global figures given in the tables later in this chapter for each film are reasonably reliable, the distinction between exclusive and general-release figures is not always as certain as it may seem.

9.2 CALCULATING BOX-OFFICE SUCCESS

It would be useful to be able to supplement this knowledge of global attendance figures, release practices, and average audience sizes with detailed data on the relative box-office success of specific films, and thus also of the various genres. Unfortunately, very little work has been done on this aspect of the classic French cinema. There is a very good reason for this: the lack of readily available and reliable data. From late 1948 onward, the CNC published some details of film entries and earnings in Paris and key provincial cities in first-run theaters, and also the accumulated attendances over the first three to four years for leading films (by the end of which time a film's returns to its producers were largely complete). Using these data, it is possible to identify with some degree of accuracy what postwar audiences wanted to watch. For the years preceding the war, however, the researcher is faced with a total lack of reliable information, since no official data on attendance were ever collected, let alone published. One reason that they were never collected is that producers, distributors, and exhibitors were always adamantly opposed to their publication. During the silent period, *La Cinématographie Française* had provided some data of this sort, but noted that it had not been able to do so for 1928–29 because of express prohibition by the Service des Finances.[31] The early figures for the talkies were so astounding that Harlé risked the wrath of the authorities to publish them and in the face of industry opposition fought a running battle over several years to see how much data he could publish without being prosecuted. In 1933, when the magazine published a particularly interesting, though still largely subjective, set of figures based on a survey of theater managers, one owner brought a case against it which prevented even such impressionistic data from being published again. The matter was finally settled, on appeal, in the magazine's favor, in 1936.[32] From then until the war, and again after it, a somewhat chastened *La Cinématographie Française* conducted annual surveys of theater managers to identify and rank each year's most successful films, though the resultant tables have no claims to be authoritative and contain patent inconsistencies.

However, even had the industry been willing to release, or allow the release of, the data available to it, the evidence given to the Renaitour inquiry in 1936 suggests that at least for the prewar period they would have been totally unreliable. The representative of "intellectual workers" at that inquiry complained that the producers, and thus the filmmakers, never actually knew how well their films did and never received the returns due to them, because it was the distributor, not the producer, who monitored the returns on each film and who passed this information on to the producer. "But it seems that these operations were often conducted according to a somewhat whimsical method of accounting, or at least one difficult to verify, so that in general producers had a genuine reason to complain that even they had no way of knowing what their film had returned."[33] Only the distributors could know with any degree of certainty, and many of them saw good reason to keep everyone else in the dark. To further complicate matters, Jarville claimed to the inquiry that even these distributors were kept in the dark by the theater managers, who were striving to keep returns secret not just from the rest of the industry but, primarily, from the taxation office.[34] It is not surprising, then, to find *Ciné Mondial* at its conspiratorial best explaining in 1942 why theater managers were fighting the monitoring of ticket sales proposed by the occupiers: "The truth is that more than one of them enjoyed playing the petty tyrant, and used to tell the tax collector whatever suited them—that is, the least possible."[35]

If this explains the absence of data for the thirties, entry numbers should in principle be known for all wartime audiences, since after much procrastination a prewar decree designed to institute detailed documentation of entries and returns was drawn up. It was to enter into effect on 16 August 1939; unfortunately, it got lost in the turmoil of the times. A year later, one of the first acts of the occupying forces was to implement a system for monitoring and documenting all entries and receipts. Although these data were definitely collected, as an article in *Ciné Mondial* on the activities of COIC made clear, they were never published, and they no longer seem to exist in any of the likely archives. Recent research suggests that they were destroyed at war's end, perhaps once again by interested parties. Certainly, contemporary commentators were unaware of them, since the CNC's initiative in 1948 was greeted enthusiastically by *La Cinématographie Française*, which expressed the hope that at last some light would be shed on "the almost total obscurity prevailing since 1940" (much longer, in fact, but the journal wished to imply that the Germans were at fault) about box-office receipts.[36] While some light was indeed shed, there remained isolated areas of darkness due to industry pressure. Even in 1956, the official data collected by the CNC could not be published in full, because that bureau was considered bound to secrecy by professional obligations.[37]

Indeed, as soon as detailed data concerning box-office receipts began to appear in the postwar years, theater managers again tried to have them suppressed. They had always claimed that the figures were unreliable and misleading, and their anxieties were most clearly expressed in a letter to the editor of *La Cinématographie Française* in 1952,[38] concerning the publication of Parisian first-release figures, which were described as inaccurate, short term, and local, and thus giving no indication of long-term national success or profitability; they were also said to be of a private nature and protected by professional agreements. Indeed, one of the more defensible arguments for suppression was that the progressive publication of such data would detrimentally affect the career of a film which began its run badly, for whatever reason. Harlé published a long reply, defending publication of the data and pointing out that they should be reliable, since they were provided by the theater managers and producers themselves. Yet there was some justification for theater owners' anxiety: at least until the fifties, as various surveys show, there were enormous local and regional differences in profitability and success, especially between Paris and the provinces, and (to some degree related to this) there were also enormous differences between the short-term and long-term success of different genres. First-run Paris audiences were indeed not a totally reliable guide to the long-term overall success of a film.

As a result, and whatever the justification, one element or another of the industry succeeded in suppressing all or much of the necessary information for a third of the thirty-year period under discussion, records for a further eight years were lost or destroyed, and data available for the remainder are

Table 9.4. Best Box Office according to Theater Managers, 1932, 1936–38

1932		1936		1937		1938	
239	La Ronde des	3,020	César	12,500	La Grande		*Snow White*
	heures	2,718	L'Appel du si-		Illusion	3,750	Quai des
235	Le Roi des		lence	9,810	Ignace	2,498	brumes
	resquilleurs	2,200	Le Roi	7,125	Un carnet de	2,050	Katia
217	Marius	2,009	Mayerling		bal	1,927	La Femme du
194	En bordée	1,695	Veille d'armes	2,970	Les Perles de la		boulanger
151	La Bande à	1,665	*Modern Times*		couronne	1,900	Alerte en
	Bouboule	1,504	Marinella	2,340	Abus de		Méditerranée
129	Croix de bois	1,474	Les Bas-Fonds		confiance		*Robin Hood*
128	Mam'zelle	1,470	La Porte du	2,280	Double Crime	1,700	Barnabé
	Nitouche		large		sur la LM	1,670	La Maison du
121	Le Congrès	1,319	Un de la légion	1,870	Pepe le Moko	1,260	Maltais
	s'amuse	1,197	L'Équipage	1,840	Naples au		Trois Valses*
120	Il est charmant	1,170	Mioche		baiser du feu	1,160	Prison sans
119	La Petite	1,023	Kœnigsmark	1,540	Trois Artilleurs	1,060	barreaux
	Chocolatière	1,000	Baccara		en vad..		Prison de
113	Accusée, levez-		Au son des gui-	1,020	Les Rois du	970	femmes
	vous		tares		sport		Entrée des
106	Le Chemin du		Messieurs les	858	*Le Roman de*		artistes*
	paradis		Ronds de Cuir		*Marguerite*		L'Étrange M.
104	L'Aiglon		Les Deux		*Gautier*		Victor
101	Un soir de rafle		Gosses		Marthe		Le Schpountz
97	*Trader Horn*		Le Roman		Richard, au		Gibraltar
91	Le Roi du		d'un tricheur		service de la		Mon curé chez
	cirage		*La Fille du bois*		France		les riches*
88	Le Chanteur		*maudit*		Ces dames au		Légions
	inconnu		Michel Stro-		chapeau vert		d'honneur
87	Après l'amour		goff		Nitchevo		Adrienne
84	Princesse à vos		Jim la Houlette		Regain*		Lecouvreur
	ordres		Bichon		La Mort du		Marie
77	Capitaine		Samson		cygne*		Walewska
	Craddock		*Mutiny on the*		L'Homme à		Orage
76	L'Atlantide		*Bounty*		abattre		Éducation de
70	*All Quiet on the*		Les Loups		L'Alibi		prince
	Western Front		entre eux		L'Habit vert		Le Révolté
69	Les Gaietés de		*Charge of the*		Le Messager		*Toura*
	l'escadron		*Light Brigade*		La Dame de		Ramuntcho
64	L'Affaire		Les Hommes		Malacca		Un de la
	Blaireau		nouveaux#		Gribouille		Canebière
62	Sergent X		L'Amant de		Le Coupable		Lumières de
59	*Quatre de*		Mme Vidal#		Gueule		Paris
	l'infanterie		Port Arthur#		d'amour		Belle Étoile*
58	*City Lights*		Jenny		Courrier Sud		Quadrille
49	Le Champion		(Etc.: total 75 films)		La Citadelle du		Ultimatum
	du régiment				silence		Conflit*
41	Le Chant du				Les Hommes		(Etc.: total 55 films)
	marin				nouveaux#		
39	Atlantis				*Ramona*		
					Hula		
					Le Fauteuil 47		
					(Etc.: total 64 films)		

\# Listed in two different years.

* Still on first release at time of survey.

Italics: non-French films

Sources: *La Cinématographie Française,* no. 760 (27 May 1933) (column 1); no. 960 (26 Mar. 1937) (column 2); no. 1012 (25 Mar. 1938) (column 3); no. 1065 (31 Mar. 1939) (column 4).

Table 9.5. Best Films according to Readers of *Pour Vous,* 1932–34

1932		1933	1934	
1,227	Fanny	Il était une fois	679	Le Grand Jeu
932	Croix de bois	La Maternelle	311	La Bataille
644	L'Atlantide	Un soir de réveillon	290	Les Misérables
342	Poil de Carotte*	L'Épervier	281	Angèle
310	Ariane	Théodore et Cie	207	Maria Chapdelaine
201	Il est charmant	14 juillet	178	Lac aux Dames
180	Gaietés de	Le Maître de forges	150	La Maison dans les
	l'escadron	La Robe rouge		dunes
113	Tumultes	L'Agonie des aigles	131	Les Nuits
	Belle Marinière	L'Ordonnance		moscovites
	La Femme nue	Simone est comme ça	54	Jeanne
	Mélo		43	Toboggan
	Le Fils d'Amérique	Plus (alphabetically):	40	Liliom
	Allô Berlin, ici	Les Ailes brisées	40	La Dame aux
	Paris	La Bataille		camélias
	La Petite	Cette vielle canaille		Scandale
	Chocolatière	Colomba		Si j'étais le patron
	Hôtel des Étudi-	Les Deux Orphelines		La Flambée
	ants	Une femme au volant		Sidonie Panache
	Paris-Méditerranée	L'Héritier du Bal		Madame Bovary
	Un rêve blond	Tabarin		Zouzou
		Mater Dolorosa		Adémaï aviateur
		Roger la Honte		Rapt
		Une vie perdue		Ces messieurs de la
				santé
				La Banque Nemo

* Paris only

Sources: *Pour Vous,* No. 219 (26 Jan. 1933) (column 1); No. 276 (1 Mar. 1934) (column 2); No. 326 (14 Feb. 1935) (column 3).

selective. The nearest that journals of the thirties came to publishing lists ranking the decade's films according to popularity was the occasional survey of theater managers undertaken by *La Cinématographie Française* relating to 1932, then 1936 to 1938, and the surveys of their readers undertaken by *Pour Vous* relating to 1932 to 1934, and *La Dépêche de Toulouse* relating to 1933 to 1935 (see tables 9.4, 9.5, and 9.6). The numbers of votes for each year varied widely because different voting systems were in use, but they have been retained because they indicate relative success within a given year.

As with any poll, however, there are numerous potential flaws in such tables. Aside from the built-in subjectivity, the date of the polls was usually aimed at surveying the previous calendar year, but the release of films was based on a quite different annual cycle. Moreover, release in Paris and

Table 9.6. Best Films according to Readers of *La Dépêche de Toulouse*, 1933–38

1933		1934		1935		1938	
1,826	Fanny	10,673	Lac aux	14,477	La Kermesse	11,832	Quai des
1,771	*The Sign of*		Dames		héroïque		brumes
	the Cross	10,431	Les	13,392	La Bandera	11,475	Les Trois
1,650	Marius		Misérables	9,437	Deuxième		Valses
1,562	L'Atlantide	9,782	*Caravan*		Bureau	10,693	*Snow White*
1,397	La Mater-	8,484	Angèle	8,289	Pension	9,299	La Bête
	nelle	6,922	La Bataille		Mimosas		humaine
1,232	Le Chanteur	4,084	Le Maître de	7,461	Maria	9,197	Alerte en
	inconnu		forges		Chapdelaine		Méditer-
1,210	Croix de	3,875	Le Grand	7,449	Les Nuits		ranée
	bois		Jeu		moscovites	7,582	Hôtel du
1,122	*All for Love*	3,270	*Cleopatra*	7,038	Crime et		Nord
1,023	Les Deux	2,137	L'Or		châtiment	7,429	Entrée des
	Orphelines	1,928	IF 1 ne	6,875	La Dame		artistes
990	La Petite		répond plus		aux camélias	7,225	Katia
	Chocolatière			6,721	*The Bengal*	7,055	Lumières de
968	Jocelyn				*Lancers*		Paris
924	Il est			5,797	Les Yeux	6,562	La Maison
	charmant				noirs		du Maltais
891	L'Agonie des						
	aigles						
858	Violettes						
	impériales						
847	La Nuit est à						
	nous						
803	Poil de						
	Carotte						
715	Topaze						
660	Atlantis						
660	Maurin des						
	Maures						
649	L'Homme à						
	l'Hispano						
616	Mam'zelle						
	Nitouche						
605	Sergent X						
605	Les Trois						
	Mousque-						
	taires						
500	La Chanson						
	d'une nuit						

Italics: non-French films.
Sources: *La Cinématographie Française*, no. 795 (27 Jan. 1934); no. 847 (26 Jan. 1935); no. 901 (8 Feb. 1936); no. 1074 (2 June 1939). 1933: 5,205 votes cast; 1935: 24,784 votes cast; 1938: 22,821 votes cast.

leading provincial cities quite commonly occurred in a different year or season from release in provincial towns, and a fortiori from provincial general release. Consequently, several films reappeared in successive polls (should totals be summed?), or did not appear in the poll for either year, or were "still in release," so the estimates are unreliable. Moreover, the opinions of viewers and theater managers, where they can be compared, were by no means identical, partly because they were answering slightly different questions. Yet given that these inadequate tables are the best information available in published sources of the day, when later commentators on the thirties remark on the relative popularity of specific films it is normally on the basis of this sort of unsystematic, subjective material, or on the promotional claims of producers—which, as Jeancolas observes, were no more than the product of fantasy, publicity, and drunken guesses.[39]

It would obviously be desirable to begin to build a more reliable basis for estimates of relative popularity, especially when, as here, those estimates are going to lead to the attribution of a quasi-mythic status to the most popular among them. The only surviving source for such work is the weekly theater programs of the day, as published in *La Semaine de Paris* and various dailies or weeklies. From such programs it is possible to identify, first, how many weeks each film ran in exclusive release and in which theater(s), and second, how many local theaters subsequently screened it during its general release.

Once this is known, the problems posed by exclusive release and by general release are somewhat different. In the latter case, since average general-release audiences are known for each year, all that is necessary to estimate the total general-release audience for a film is the normal range of variation in audience size for successful and unsuccessful films, as measured by the number of local theaters in which they were screened. The average number of general-release theaters in which any given French film would be screened in Paris rose steadily throughout the decade, from about twenty-eight in 1931 through about thirty-seven in 1937, as more theaters were built in each neighbourhood, and films had to be screened in more theaters to have a hope of reaching the total Parisian audience. To some extent, this steady increase in general-release screenings compensated for the gradual decrease in audiences per screening, though it remains the case that general release dropped in significance in Paris with respect to exclusive release as the decade progressed.

The problems posed by attempting to calculate audience size in exclusive release are of a different order of complexity because of the enormous range of variation in the size of exclusive-release theaters. At one extreme, the 6,000-seat Gaumont Palace might attract from 50,000 to 60,000 spectators in a single week, while the Paramount (1,903 seats) quite commonly attracted even more, and the Rex (3,500 seats) 40,000 to 50,000. In most weeks it was in fact the Paramount that recorded the highest figures. Other large theaters, such as the Alhambra and the Moulin Rouge (2,000 seats), the Marignan (1,800), and the Marivaux (1,250), might attract from 15,000 to 25,000 per week, while mid-sized theaters such as the Colisée (650 seats), the Aubert Palace (750), and the Madeleine (800) might attract from 8,000 or 10,000 to 12,000 or 15,000. At the other extreme, art theaters such as the Pigalle, the Panthéon, the Ursulines, and the Vieux Colombier, with about 250 to 400 seats and less regular screenings, might attract from 1,000 to 5,000. In general, first-run theaters attracted more than second-run, and all exclusive-release theaters tended to attract more than general-release theaters because nearly all of the former ran continuous screenings every day, while the latter would normally have a maximum of one screening a day and a weekend matinée. Fortunately, all the necessary data concerning the capacity of the various theaters in Paris and the normal range of audience size can be assembled or calculated from a disparate set of sources published at the time. Consequently, the exclusive-release audience for any given film can be estimated, based on the theaters in which it ran and the number of weeks in which it ran in each of them. Occasional specific figures for specific films mentioned in trade journals allow for cross-checking, though their reliability is always questionable.

9.3 ANNUAL TABLES OF FILMS ATTRACTING OVER THREE HUNDRED THOUSAND SPECTATORS

It is on the basis of such calculations that the tables of top box-office films below are based. They include every film of the decade which, by my calculations, attracted over three hundred thousand spectators in Paris within two years of its release. The task of compiling the tables was an arduous one, since it involved following the release patterns of over thirteen hundred films for a period of some twelve years in some 150 to 350 theaters, while allowing for the differences in capacity between different theaters and for the different average size of audience in each of these theaters for good, average, and bad runs. Inevitably, some errors will have crept into calculations of this magnitude, but I have tried to keep them to a minimum. Fortunately the results can be, and have been, globally cross-checked by verifying that the accumulated attendance figures calculated for all the films of a given year correspond to the known figures for French films released in Paris in the respective year. In fact, the figures given turn out to be about 7 percent below this, possibly because of a tail of unnoticed screenings in suburban cinemas that most films experienced outside the first period of release and any subsequent major re-release.

The tables are organized not according to calendar year but according to the industry's seasonal cycle. Tables published in French journals have al-

Table 9.7. The 1929–30 season by order of release (week/year)
9 out of 12 (75%)

La Nuit est à nous (3/30)	350	162	512 (3)
La Route est belle (4/30)	285	150	435 (4)
Le Mystère de la Villa Rosa (14/30)	130	174	304
Sous les toits de Paris (17/30)	232	318	550 (2)
Mon gosse de père (18/30)	172	186	358
Le Spectre vert (18/30)	255	156	411 (5)
La Tendresse (20/30)	116	186	302
Un trou dans le mur (23/30)	144	210	354
La Grande Mare (29/30)	503	390	893 (1)

Numbers listed in Tables 9.7 through 9.16 are for exclusive release (1st column), general release (2nd column), and total Paris audience (final column).

ways hesitated between these two procedures, but the seasonal pattern seems most desirable not just because it corresponds to the industry's own screening practices but also for the practical reason that it better allows for the release of the first talkies in late 1929 and for the last prewar films in 1939. The seasonal low point in the annual cycle was summer, when Parisian audiences left the city en masse, and its high points were the feast days, such as Mardi Gras and Easter, and the holiday period at Christmas and New Year. These seasonal patterns are very apparent in figure 9.2, which charts the fluctuations in attendance over the yearly cycle, and are even more vividly illustrated in figure 9.3, which charts the response to these fluctuations by the industry, since it indicates the total number of films released each week of the annual cycle over a six-year period. Producers were very reluctant to see their films released during or just before the summer break and tried to have them released either in the new season, to returning audiences, on saints' days (holidays) or at a high point in the season such as late December or early January. Each film in the following annual tables (9.7 to 9.16) is dated by week of release, with calendar week 30 corresponding to the low point in early August. Exclusive release figures are given first, then general release, and finally the total Paris audience. The top forty films of the decade are listed in the final table of the chapter (table 9.17).

Finally, in the annual tables the rankings of the leading ten films of each season (only five in the first season, because so few were released) have been indicated in parentheses. This has been done because it might be argued that there is no direct comparability of films across years in which viewing conditions, industrial practices, and audience numbers varied so much. According to this line of thinking, a film which scored an audience of 350,000 in the 1933–34 season had demonstrated an appeal comparable to that of a film which scored 450,000 in the 1931–32 season or 550,000 at the end of the decade, since it had won that smaller audience under more trying institutional conditions.

Figure 9.3. Seasonal Releases, August to July
(new year = week 24)

Number of Films

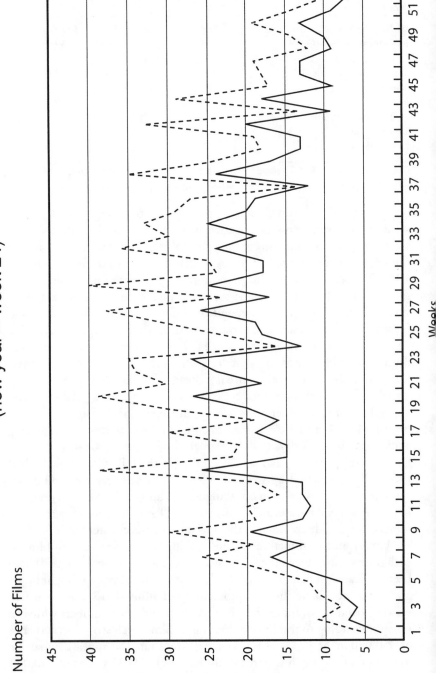

Weeks

While all the figures in these tables are less precise than they seem, I have included many of the assumptions on which they are based so that other researchers, interested perhaps in a particular film, director, year, or genre and inclined to check that specific film or group of films in greater detail, may be able to identify invalid assumptions or figures, and thus improve on them.

During this first season of sound film releases (see table 9.7), the figures given for both exclusive and general release are a little more uncertain than for subsequent years. A number of factors make it difficult to estimate normal audience sizes. On the one hand, the total audience for sound films (as opposed to the residue of silent films that continued to be screened, though in diminishing numbers) can only be conjectured, since I have not seen any reliable figures for it. This problem rapidly decreases in importance, and by the 1932–33 season it has largely disappeared. On the other hand, Paris theaters were being equipped for sound at a relatively rapid rate, so the number of theaters available for general release was escalating rapidly throughout the season. It is therefore difficult to know by what figure to divide that total audience in order to get the average audience size in local theaters, which in turn is needed to calculate general-release figures for each film.

The first feature-length 100 percent talkies that can justifiably be called French are *La Nuit est à nous* and *La Route est belle.* The two that preceded them do not technically qualify because the first, *Le Collier de la reine,* was produced as a silent film then partially sonorized with music and some dialogue, while the second, *Les Trois Masques,* was under an hour in length. Both were successful, especially *Le Collier de la reine,* which benefited from being the first (partially) French-speaking film to be released. In this it resembles *The Jazz Singer,* which likewise was not 100 percent dialogued, but became notorious primarily because it was the first to be released. *La Route est belle,* filmed in Britain, was released next, but only in Marseille; in Paris, it was preceded by a week by *La Nuit est à nous.* While both were enormously successful at the time, they clearly benefited in the same way as did *Le Collier de la reine* from the timing of their release, since neither of them experienced the repeated revivals over the following years that went with deep popular affection for a specific film. The only film in the first season to experience such a revival was *Sous les toits de Paris,* which, like *Le Million,* was to keep René Clair's name alive in France long after he departed for England in 1934. Yet, on its initial general release *Sous les toits de Paris* registered relatively low figures, appearing in a desultory way in only a few of the theaters equipped for sound. The same low-key general release was to befall *L'Opéra de quat'sous* two years later, though in that case it was more clearly due to the fact that audiences had already seen it in a cheap first-release art theater.

Of the twelve films released in this first season, only one failed catastrophically—*Quand nous étions deux.* Several other shorter sound films, forty to sixty minutes in length, were released. Some of them did very well, and perhaps because of their prominence in reviews and advertisements of the day they have found their way into filmographies. *Chiqué,* which is often so listed, was only about half an hour long, and *Une femme a menti* seems to have been substantially less than an hour long. The demand for sound films was so great, and French facilities still so inadequate, that several films had to be made in Britain (*La Route est belle*), the U.S. (*Le Spectre vert*), or Germany. In the meantime, and indeed for some years to come, producers tried to generate pseudo-sound films by dubbing silent films. Several films were progressively upgraded over the following years until they could be presented to the trade as 100 percent sound films. *Le Requin* was noted even by contemporaries as being primarily a silent film, sonorized and at best partially dialogued. Chomette withdrew his name as director because the producer had totally re-edited the silent film he had made, and he felt that only the final dialogued scene was at all true to his intentions. The status of *La Bodega* as a 100 percent talkie is in doubt, and the mid-length *Trois Masques* largely avoided the synchronization of voices by having immobile masks "speak." *Les Saltimbanques,* screened near the end of the season, was also categorized at the time as not a true sound film.

Finally, the demand for product was so great in this first season that *La Grande Mare* was released right at the end of the season (as was *L'Enfant de l'amour* soon afterward), when potential audiences might be expected to be departing on holiday. It justified its producers' faith by running right through the summer months in the Paramount theater, going into general release during the Christmas/New Year high season.

During the 1930–31 season (see table 9.8), 101 feature films were released, together with a very large number of mid-length films which the industry did not at the time distinguish from feature films. A number of the "true" feature films experienced a high degree of success, not solely, as had been the case in the preceding year, because of their novelty value but because of a genuine popular appeal which was to see them prove enduringly popular throughout the decade. In order of release, the most popular were *Accusée, levez-vous, Le Roi des resquilleurs, Le Chemin du paradis, La Ronde des heures, Jean de la lune, Le Million,* and *Un soir de rafle.* Of these, *Le Roi des resquilleurs* was the most startling box-office success of the decade. It opened in November 1930 at the Moulin Rouge, a two-thousand-seat music hall/theater, and ran for thirty-four weeks uninterrupted in exclusive release. It then moved, under the "second-run" system which was just developing, to the five-hundred-seat Impérial, where it ran for a further twenty-six weeks. Exclusive release had lasted for sixty weeks and attracted, by my estimate, nearly nine hundred thousand spectators, many of them

Table 9.8. The 1930–31 season by order of release (week/year)
25 out of 101 (25%)

L'Enfant de l'amour (32/30)	236	(102)	(338)
Accusée, levez-vous (37/30)	268	273	541 (4)
Atlantis (39/30)	210	210	420
Lévy et Compagnie (43/30)	81	325	406
Le Roi des resquilleurs (46/30)	888	299	1,187 (1)
Le Chemin du paradis (46/30)	113	342	455 (8)
Cendrillon de Paris (47/30)	110	273	383
Arthur (1/31)	82	231	313
Le Chanteur de Séville (7/31)	167	176	343
La Ronde des heures (7/31)	90	318	408
Jean de la Lune (9/31)	324	445	769 (2)
David Golder (10/31)	108	202	310
Le Tampon du capiston (12/31)	161	180	341
Le Million (14/31)	202	270	472 (7)
Le Dactylo (14/31)	148	274	422
Ma cousine de Varsovie (15/31)	65	245	310
Princesse, à vos ordres (15/31)	73	352	425
Le Petit Café (19/31)	246	234	480 (6)
Le Rêve (19/31)	190	202	392
Grock (19/31)	124	(192)	(316)
Big House (20/31)	298	148	446 (10)
Autour d'une enquête (23/31)	128	176	304
Un homme en habit (27/31)	260	191	451 (9)
Un soir de rafle (28/31)	217	349	566 (3)
En bordée (29/31)	178	305	483 (5)

no doubt second- and third-time viewers. Yet there was still a large public for the film: on general release in February 1932, it screened in about forty-one theaters in suburban Paris. Moreover, it became one of the standard "revival" films, to be reintroduced several times in brief exclusive releases and further general releases in later years, whenever films were lacking or audiences falling off. Its title inspired a host of imitations hoping to capitalize on the original's popularity—*Le Roi, Le Roi des palaces, Le Roi des facteurs, Le Roi des galéjeurs, Les Rois de la flotte, Les Rois du sport,* and many other shorter films, not to mention a 1945 remake with the same title. It launched the comedian Milton in his role as Bouboule on a series of comic adventures in *Le Roi du cirage, La Bande à Bouboule, Bouboule 1er, roi nègre* (notorious for representing France at the 1934 Venice film festival), and finally *Prince Bouboule.* In addition, it was influential in determining a swing away from dramas, which had dominated the first season of French production, and toward the comedy genre. In this it was aided by the parallel success of the romantic comedy *Jean de la Lune,* which stayed in exclusive release less long but reached many more spectators in general release, and which was, if anything, re-released even more often than *Le Roi des res-quilleurs*. The preference for comedy was no less underlined by the extraordinary (indeed, incomprehensible by modern lights) success of the military vaudeville, instanced here by two films starring Bach—*Le Tampon du capiston* and *En bordée*. These launched Bach's sound career, generating fifteen more comic films in which he starred during the decade, six of them military vaudevilles, and twelve of them (like *En bordée*) directed by Wulschleger, who "managed" Bach's films much as Colombier managed several of Milton's. At least three more of Bach's films were among the big successes of the decade—*Bach millionnaire, Le Train de 8h47,* and *Mon curé chez les riches,* finally resulting in a 1939 compilation called *Bach en correctionnelle* which organized the highlights of his previous films within a perfunctory frame.

This outline of the comic successes of the 1930–31 season has not even mentioned René Clair's *Le Million,* which, after a substantial success at the Olympia, was used to open the Ambassadeurs, or the musicals *Le Chemin du paradis* and *Princesse, à vos ordres,* whose immense popularity established Henri Garat and Lilian Harvey as the heartthrobs of the early thirties and generated further successes in *Le Congrès s'amuse, La Fille et le garçon, Une heure près de toi, Un rêve blond,* and *Les Gais Lurons.* Add to these Maurice Chevalier's *Le Petit Café* and it is easy to see how lighthearted films featuring Milton, Bach, Michel Simon, René Lefèvre, Maurice Chevalier, and the Henri Garat–Lilian Harvey couple could come to seem the route to effortless profitability for the French cinema.

These comic successes should not, however, overshadow the two dramas—one a crime story, *Accusée, levez-vous,* and the other recounting the fall and rise of a sporting hero, *Un soir de rafle*—not to mention *La Ronde des heures,* which the survey of theater managers in May 1933 reported (and the general-release audience figures go some way to confirm) as the most profitable film they had screened in 1932. Altogether, given that 1929–30 had been a foreshortened year with few sound film releases, the 1930–31 season can be considered the first, and arguably the greatest, year of French thirties cinema, heralding a renaissance of the national cinema, establishing certain patterns for at least the first half of the decade, and promising producers limitless profits from a delighted public. If this picture needs qualifying, it might be by recognizing that a disproportionate number of these successful productions were, in some commentators' eyes, not French at all, in that they were "merely" French versions of foreign films shot in Germany and America. This was not true of *Le Roi des resquilleurs, La Ronde des heures,* or *Jean de la lune,* but *Atlantis, Le Chemin du paradis, Princesse, à vos ordres,* and *Salto mortale* (just off the chart) were originally German films by Dupont, Thiele, and Schwarz reshot in Germany by French (sub)directors using a cast consisting predominantly of French

Table 9.9. The 1931–32 season by order of release (week/year)
40 out of 148 (27%)

Azaïs (32/31)	186	230	416
Rive gauche (34/31)	172	160	332
L'Aiglon (35/31)	122	335	457 (7)
Le Bal (37/31)	140	165	305
Rien que la vérité (37/31)	201	175	376
Atout-cœur (38/31)	112	205	317
Faubourg Montmartre (38/31)	93	230	323
Le Juif polonais (38/31)	90	225	315
Pas sur la bouche (39/31)	128	180	308
Gagne ta vie (41/31)	210	160	370
Marius (41/31)	428	226	654 (1)
L'Opéra de quat'sous (45/31)	192	115	307
Le Parfum de la dame en noir (45/31)	160	230	390
Le Roi du cirage (46/31)	272	180	452 (8)
La Chienne (47/31)	168	260	428 (10)
Le Chanteur inconnu (49/31)	150	160	310
Après l'amour (49/31)	118	270	388
Le Capitaine Craddock (49/31)	130	290	420
Mam'zelle Nitouche (49/31)	150	255	405
Mistigri (49/31)	149	165	314
À nous la liberté (51/31)	117	185	302
La Bande à Bouboule (51/31)	348	245	593 (2)
Le Rosier de Madame Husson (5/32)	146	188	334
La Tragédie de la mine (5/32)	145	155	300
La Petite Chocolatière (7/32)	220	230	450 (9)
Cœur de Lilas (7/32)	94	206	300
Paris-Méditerranée (8/32)	268	210	478 (4)
Il est charmant (9/32)	202	208	410
Ariane, jeune fille russe (9/32)	180	184	364
Sergent X (11/32)	81	235	316
La Femme en homme (11/32)	203	112	315
Monsieur, Madame et Bibi (11/32)	88	220	308
L'Affaire Blaireau (11/32)	176	172	348
Croix de bois (12/32)	356	196	552 (3)
Le Vainqueur (13/32)	112	215	327
Au nom de la loi (16/32)	223	114	337
Tumultes (17/32)	194	276	470 (5)
Un fils d'Amérique (23/32)	112	192	304
Une heure près de toi (23/32)	183	124	307
L'Atlantide (24/32)	262	196	458 (6)

actors, while *Le Chanteur de Séville, Le Petit Café,* and *Big House* (like *La Grande Mare* before them) were French versions of films shot in America for MGM and Paramount.

312 | GENRE, STAR, BOX OFFICE

The 1931–32 season was clearly another highly profitable season for the French cinema as a whole (see table 9.9). Although there were no outstandingly profitable films in the category of *Le Roi des resquilleurs,* there were a greater number of well-made films scattered throughout the year, which must have returned significant profits within their first year of release—*Marius, Croix de bois, Paris-Méditerranée, Au nom de la loi, Tumultes,* and the fascinating, though rather clumsy, *L'Atlantide.* But then, it was not only good films that succeeded. Several films which now register as clumsy to the point of incompetence attracted large audiences. *L'Opéra de quat'sous* is a case in point. It ran almost continuously at the Ursulines or the Pagode for the next few years, though because these were small art theaters and were not screening continuously (*en permanence*) (and, indeed, alternate screenings were in German), the global audience figures are not enormous. Four weeks at one of the larger theaters would have generated the same audience. Nevertheless, this film's continuous presence in the weekly programs made it an inescapable element of the Parisian cultural scene during these years, and the degree of its success seems to have taken everyone by surprise. Another clumsy film, *Le Rosier de Madame Husson,* benefited from the fury of local censorship, which provided excellent publicity, but it is hard to see how technical or narrative competence (let alone Fernandel's acting) could have been relevant to its popularity. Even more remarkable was the relative success of *Un chien qui rapporte.* Like *Le Rosier de Madame Husson,* this is a one-joke comedy offering slightly scabrous titillation, but it is so incompetently assembled as to be largely incomprehensible at times. Thus, if Renoir's *La nuit du carrefour* and Prévert's *L'Affaire est dans le sac* failed in this same year, it was not solely because of their undoubted narrative and technical incompetence, since many worse-made films did much better. The same was to be true for the next several seasons, as films like *L'Escale, La Rue sans joie, Les Bas-Fonds,* and even *La Bandera* succeeded apparently on the basis of the inherent interest of their stereotypes and situations rather than efficient story-telling. They corresponded, that is, to certain contemporary French preoccupations—the needs, desires, anguishes, and aspirations of the audiences of the day.

On the other hand, a large number of films did fail quite badly. This was the first season in which more French feature films arrived on the market than were needed to satisfy demand, and, while there can be no doubt that the top quarter (those listed in table 9.9) would have readily returned a profit, some seventeen films made only the most marginal appearance on the market before disappearing from sight. Some of these, indeed, though formally presented to the trade, may never have been accepted by a distributor for release, since I have been unable to find any record of them in theaters, in this or any subsequent season. Another twenty-five failed so badly in their Paris release, whether exclusive, general, or both, that it is impossible that the producer could have recouped his investment, even in the long run. Since most of these forty to fifty flops were produced by the smallest of the production companies, it is easy to see why so many companies went bankrupt in this and succeeding years. It is less easy to see why certain directors who already in this year were establishing a reputation for catastrophic losses should have been able to continue making films for the rest of the decade. Some didn't, of course—Dini, Boudrioz, Daumary, Mourre, Jean Godard, Torre, Perojo, and Reichmann either gave up or were unable to find further funding after early flops, and the same is true of one of the few female directors of the decade, Solange Terac/Bussi. Vernay's career was arrested for five years by a series of flops. Jaeger-Schmidt ran a remarkably unsuccessful production company from Lille for some years, which his own repeated lack of success as a director helped bring to ruin. A few directors, however, having almost inexplicably managed to find further funding, went on to justify this faith—Forrester, Mittler, and Guarino, all of whom made at least one successful film, and, more dramatically, Joannon, Choux, and Vernay.

Yet a surprising number, having failed initially, persisted, only to fail repeatedly throughout inexplicably long careers. Pierre Weill's *Mardi gras* flopped, his *Cure sentimental* disappeared without a trace, and even his military vaudeville was unsuccessful, yet he was able to find funding for four more films in 1935 and 1936, all of which bombed. Astonishment is equally appropriate at the persistent career of Sévérac and Pallu, despite repeated losses. Sévérac's one late success, *Les Réprouvés,* can scarcely have been sufficient to counter the catastrophic career of *Sirocco* (except perhaps for Arab audiences), *Razzia, Le Crime du chemin rouge, Colomba, Le Mystère Imberger, La Boutique aux illusions,* and *Adieu Vienne,* yet he was still making films in 1960. Such a record speaks of the chaotic financial situation of the industry at the time, which so many commentators have mentioned— the wild hopes of unlimited gain aroused by certain early sound successes, the lack of alternative investment in a period of depression, and the unregulated nature of the industry. It also raises interesting questions about the career of better-known directors. Of course, Renoir was fortunate in having a large inheritance, much of which he "squandered" on a series of films that failed—*On purge bébé, Boudu sauvé des eaux, Chotard et Cie,* and *La Nuit du carrefour*—and while the last three were not total catastrophes at the box office, and while we may well find it difficult to understand why *Boudu* and *Chotard* were not better received, it is still interesting to speculate what might have happened to Renoir's career without the inheritance and his one unqualified success in these years, *La Chienne,* to bolster his standing, his finances, and his self-esteem.

It is not easy to generalize about the films of the successful 1931–32 season. They ranged from a film evoking the experienced chaos of combat

Table 9.10. The 1932–33 season by order of release (week/year)
24 out of 150 (17%)

Quick (35/32)	108	220	328
Les Vignes du Seigneur (38/32)	143	184	327
Les Gaietés de l'escadron (38/32)	250	320	570 (4)
Une petite dame dans le train (39/32)	159	148	307
Le Congrès s'amuse (43/32)	240	365	605 (3)
Embrassez-moi (43/32)	191	220	411 (9)
La Femme nue (43/32)	102	220	322
Fanny (44/32)	454	210	664 (2)
Maurin des Maures (49/32)	178	240	418 (7)
Sa meilleure cliente (51/32)	135	220	355
Topaze (2/33)	140	270	410 (10)
Quatorze juillet (3/33)	136	210	346
La Chanson d'une nuit (6/33)	92	330	422 (6)
La Tête d'un homme (6/33)	118	189	307
IF 1 ne répond plus (9/33)	220	260	480 (5)
Le Chasseur de chez Maxim's (10/33)	158	185	343
Les Deux Orphelines (10/32)	138	167	305
Le Martyre de l'obèse (13/33)	200	159	359
La Dame de chez Maxim's (14/32)	149	202	351
Théodore et Cie (15/33)	539	291	830 (1)
Mademoiselle Josette, ma femme (15/33)	87	260	347
Nu comme un vers (19/33)	210	114	324
Moi et l'impératrice (20/33)	131	189	320
Le Margoton du bataillon (24/33)	148	270	418 (7)

(*Croix de bois*) to a historical melodrama (*L'Aiglon*), a comédie dramatique (*Marius*), a romantic comedy done as a musical (*Paris-Méditerranée*), and a riotous comedy acting as a sequel to *Le Roi des resquilleurs* (*La Bande à Bouboule*). On the whole, the number of dramas and comedies at the top of the table was more nearly balanced than in previous years. In the 1932–33 season, however, comedies were again to dominate (see table 9.10). *Théodore et Cie* is in a direct line with the riotous prankster comedies mentioned above, and *Le Congrès s'amuse* is another romantic comedy done as a musical and featuring the Henri Garat–Lilian Harvey couple. *La Margoton du bataillon* is another military vaudeville, as is *Les Gaietés de l'escadron,* its success triggering a string of films with analogous titles—*Les Gaietés de la finance, du palace, de l'exposition,* and the mid-length *de l'escouade.*

The list of the top ten films of the season contains only two dramas—*IF 1 ne répond plus* and the comédie dramatique *Fanny.* This became more and more a matter of critical debate as the season progressed, and commentators remarked on the number of theatrical comedies of a more or less vulgar sort that were being transcribed into film form (successfully, alas).

The titles of many of these were clearly intended to tease and titillate—*La Femme nue, Nu comme un ver* (and later *On a trouvé une femme nue*), *Embrassez-moi, Les Surprises du divorce, Mademoiselle Josette, ma femme, Le Mari garçon, Le Fils improvisé, Madame ne veut pas d'enfant, Je te confie ma femme,* and *Le Coucher de la mariée.* Given the profitability of many of these films, it was natural that producers should have been willing to cater to a taste that was clearly widespread, though widely considered blameworthy. Toward the end of this season, the French version of the Czech film *Exstase,* featuring Hedy Lamarr in fairly explicit scenes as an unfulfilled wife but a fulfilled lover, had an extended run at the Théâtre Pigalle, then the Studio Diamant. Twenty-two weeks in small theaters did not generate an enormous audience, and the nature of the film seems to have precluded widespread general release, but like *L'Opéra de quat'sous,* if to a lesser extent, it was highly visible on the cultural scene for a long time. It is not hard to see why serious filmmakers (and, a fortiori, moralists) might view with dismay an industry apparently overtaken by frivolity and licentiousness.

To some extent, these anxieties about the nature of the industry's output were related to the first signs of a downturn in demand. After the expansionary optimism of the three preceding seasons, this was disconcerting. Aside from industry statistics, the evidence is visible in table 9.10, where a smaller proportion of the year's output appears than in preceding years. This was the moment when commentators began to emphasize the fragility of the exhibition sector, in which over one third of French theaters were still not equipped for sound (and most of those never would be), and two thirds of those equipped held no more than four screenings a week. Urban first-run theaters, with their *permanence* of up to thirty-six screenings a week, were wildly untypical, and it is easy to see how the nineteen first-run theaters in Paris could generate one tenth of the whole country's receipts.

The crisis of confidence within the industry was exacerbated during the 1933–34 season (see table 9.11). The film list is shorter than for previous years and contains the smallest proportion of the year's releases. It is tempting to correlate this with the marked change in direction that is apparent in the output. The list of most successful films was dominated by social and psychological dramas—*La Maternelle, La Bataille, L'Épervier, Le Scandale, Le Grand Jeu, Le Maître de forges,* and *Lac aux Dames.* There are few comic successes—the vaudevilles *Tire-au-flanc* and *Le Train de 8h47*—and most are less successful than their counterparts of previous years had been. The latest Bouboule film, which represented France at Venice, doesn't come near to making the table. It is perhaps in this context that we should view the relative failure of *Le Dernier Milliardaire* in the following season—a failure which, after a run of extremely popular comic films, was reputedly crucial in Clair's decision to move to England for the rest of the decade.

Table 9.11. The 1933–34 season by order of release (week/year)
19 out of 160 (12%)

La Maternelle (36/33)	276	230	506 (4)
Tire au flanc (40/33)	179	314	493 (5)
L'Abbé Constantin (43/33)	212	180	392 (9)
L'Épervier (47/33)	89	348	437 (7)
L'Agonie des aigles (48/33)	208	135	343
Le Maître de forges (49/33)	150	281	431 (8)
Paprika (49/33)	68	238	306
Bach millionnaire (52/33)	98	221	319
La Bataille (1/34)	230	366	596 (2)
Au bout du monde (5/34)	186	135	321
Trois pour cent (5/34)	101	272	373
Les Misérables I, II and III (from 6/34), each	140	230	370
Ces messieurs de la Santé (12/34)	157	173	330
La Garnison amoureuse (12/34)	156	188	344
Le Grand Jeu (17/34)	197	400	597 (1)
Lac aux Dames (20/34)	247	231	478 (6)
Le Train de 8h47 (21/34)	245	273	518 (3)
L'Or (22/34)	124	130	354
Le Scandale (26/34)	226	149	375 (10)

However, a number of the directors later to be thought of as auteurs filmed dramas this year, in all cases with mediocre success. Renoir's *Madame Bovary* did better than is generally thought, at least in exclusive release, and might possibly have broken even. And after *Poil de Carotte,* which was a critical success but did no more than reasonably well in general release, Duvivier's *Le Petit Roi* (again with Robert Lynen) and *Le Paquebot Tenacity* also figured in the middle range of popularity. Fritz Lang's somewhat hastily made dramatic fantasy, *Liliom,* received surprisingly favorable reviews and did well in exclusive release, but faded in general release. Pabst and Ophüls had no more than middling success with *Du haut en bas* and *On a volé un homme,* respectively, though the latter's *Liebelei* did remarkably well on its initial release in German, and if one cumulates audiences for both versions it did better than average. Even Pagnol, directing his first films, *Le Gendre de Monsieur Poirier* and the mid-length *Jofroi,* must have been disappointed with the results after the success of his plays in film versions directed by others.

Some directors of an earlier (silent-film) wave were beginning to look fragile in the context of sound cinema, too: Baroncelli directed a series of unsuccessful films, culminating this season with *L'Ami Fritz* and *Crainquebille* (though the films he directed later in the decade were to be very popular), while Cavalcanti added yet another poorly received film (*Coralie et Cie*)

Table 9.12. The 1934–35 season by order of release (week/year)
30 out of 120 (25%)

La Maison dans la dune (31/34)	119	191	310
Mon cœur t'appelle (37/34)	148	187	335
Trois de la marine (39/34)	144	169	313
Minuit, place Pigalle (40/34)	190	128	318
Adémaï aviateur (41/34)	449	293	742 (1)
Sidonie Panache (42/34)	55	306	361
Angèle (43/34)	256	408	664 (2)
La Chanson de l'adieu (44/34)	150	278	428
La Dame aux camélias (44/34)	206	269	475 (8)
L'École des contribuables (44/34)	55	283	338
Un homme en or (45/34)	139	234	373
Les Nuits moscovites (46/34)	287	302	589 (4)
Maria Chapdelaine (50/34)	305	307	612 (3)
Dédé (51/34)	151	211	362
Zouzou (51/34)	132	298	430 (10)
Sans famille (52/340	184	180	364
Le Billet de mille (2/35)	97	273	370
Pension Mimosas (3/35)	255	256	511 (7)
La Veuve joyeuse (4/35)	252	120	372
Compartiment de dames seules (5/35)	154	228	382
Le Bonheur (6/35)	198	241	439 (9)
Itto (12/35)	212	108	320
Justin de Marseille (14/35)	192	173	365
Nous ne sommes plus des enfants (15/35)	138	194	332
Tovaritch (18/35)	122	205	327
Folies-Bergère (19/35)	242	281	523 (5)
Quelle drôle de gosse! (20/35)	144	180	324
Crime et châtiment (20/35)	297	220	517 (6)
Un oiseau rare (22/35)	120	302	422
La Mascotte (30/35)	192	187	379

to a list of seven French sound films that included only one moderate success, *Le Mari garçon*. Jean Epstein and the Benoît-Lévy–Marie Epstein team were, however, at the peak of their popularity with *La Châtelaine du Liban* and *La Maternelle*, respectively. For Jean Epstein, it was to be a brief flirtation with popularity, but Benoît-Lévy and Marie Epstein were to continue with a series of amazing successes—*Itto, Hélène, La Mort du cygne,* and *Altitude 3200*. The Tourneurs father and son seemed equally unable to put a foot wrong, especially the latter. Even those of their films which have not survived and which seem to have been based on less than inspiring material were at least reasonably well received. At this crisis point in the decade, such an ability to put together a string of successful productions was of inestimable value.

The 1934–35 season has already been remarked upon as witnessing the beginnings of a renewal of confidence, based on a reduction of output and an improvement in quality (see table 9.12). Very soon, increased audiences were to bolster that optimism. The major prestige films of the season were *Angèle, Les Nuits muscovites, Maria Chapdelaine, Pension Mimosas, Le Bonheur, Itto,* and *Crime et châtiment.* All were dramas, once again, though there was one remarkable comic success in *Adémaï aviateur,* which established Noël-Noël with the public and led to other Adémaï films. I have not included Gance's *Napoléon Bonaparte* in the year's releases, since it was largely a sonorized version of the silent film, and despite further critical acclaim in exclusive release it could not have a general release because of its need for specialized projection equipment. Nor have I included *Zéro de conduite,* because of its relative brevity. *L'Atalante* was released early in the season, and was about tenth from bottom in the audience it received. Pagnol's *Angèle* was his first personal success as a director. It would join *Marius* and *Fanny,* and the later *César* among the elite of films repeatedly revived in the course of the remainder of the decade, such that (as in their case) the estimated audience given here is probably somewhat short of the actual number of spectators who would ultimately have paid to see it by the time war was declared.

Three more directors could be said with confidence to be establishing a reputation in the trade as competent and reliable at this stage in the decade: Feyder, L'Herbier, and Marc Allégret. Feyder had directed a string of popular sound films, beginning with the French version of *Le Spectre vert,* and continuing with *Le Grand Jeu* and *Pension Mimosas.* This record was to reach its apogee with *La Kermesse héroïque* in the following season. L'Herbier's record was, if anything, even more remarkable. His amiable but clumsy thrillers in the early years had been surprisingly popular, though not as much as *L'Épervier, Le Scandale,* and *Le Bonheur;* and while *L'Aventurier* and *Forfaiture* did nothing to harm his reputation, *La Route impériale, Veille d'armes, Les Hommes nouveaux, La Porte du large, La Citadelle du silence, Nuits de feu, La Tragédie impériale, Adrienne Lecouvreur,* and especially *Entente cordiale,* all of which figured among the most successful films of their respective years, did everything to confirm it. Like others, but more successfully, in the second half of the decade he consistently exploited a nationalist sentiment fostered by the approach of war, and he must rank high among directors who attracted the most spectators to their films in the thirties.

In this he would be closely contested by Marc Allégret, however. If *Lac aux Dames* in the 1933–34 season was perhaps his most noted film, as much for what it said about the state of the national cinema as for what it said about the director, it must nevertheless take its place in a string of well-received films interspersed with two more moderate successes. As well as

Table 9.13. The 1935–36 season by order of release (week/year)
32 out of 132 (24%)

Les Yeux noirs (35/35)	196	224	420
La Bandera (38/35)	366	450	816 (2)
Deuxième Bureau (38/35)	185	405	590 (7)
Les Mystères de Paris (38/35)	102	220	322
Pasteur (38/35)	181	156	337
L'École des cocottes (39/35)	148	177	325
La Route impériale (41/35)	111	324	435
L'Équipage (43/35)	226	396	622 (6)
J'aime toutes les femmes (43/35)	134	174	308
Les Beaux Jours (45/35)	191	132	323
Fanfare d'amour (46/35)	152	174	326
La Kermesse héroïque (49/35)	264	238	502 (10)
Kœnigsmark (49/35)	180	255	435
Veille d'armes (50/35)	270	427	697 (4)
Baccara (51/35)	234	279	513 (9)
La Marraine de Charley (3/36)	97	245	342
Mayerling (5/36)	292	380	672 (5)
Le Secret de Polichinelle (6/36)	237	105	342
Roses noires (7/36)	74	234	308
Le Nouveau Testament (7/36)	178	284	462
Les Mutinés de l'Elsinore (9/36)	221	103	324
La Garçonne (9/36)	204	156	360
Bichon (10/36)	192	328	520 (8)
Samson (10/36)	266	445	711 (3)
Tarass Bulba (11/36)	225	165	390
Les Petites Alliées (13/36)	164	180	344
Marinella (13/36)	300	192	492
La Peur (15/36)	122	264	386
L'Appel du silence (18/36)	660	227	887 (1)
Club des femmes (21/36)	277	138	415
Une gueule en or (24/36)	159	201	360
Moutonnet (28/36)	134	174	308

Lac aux Dames, all the following registered among the top films of their respective years: *Mam'zelle Nitouche, La Petite Chocolatière, Les Beaux Jours, Les Amants terribles, Zouzou, Sous les yeux d'Occident, Gribouille, La Dame de Malacca, Orage,* and *Entrée des artistes.*

Finally, it is worth mentioning two directors of comedies who would also rank high in such a list of the consistently popular: Colombier and Wulschleger. Although Colombier never again obtained quite the comic success of *Le Roi des resquilleurs* and *Théodore et Cie,* neither did anyone else; he and Wulschleger directed a very large number of films in the course of the decade, with Bach, Milton, and later Fernandel, and only one of those seems to have totally failed at the box office (*Le Dompteur*). Their contributions to this and later seasons helped to stem the swing against comedy, particularly Colombier's, with *L'École des cocottes, La Marraine de Charley, Le Roi, Une gueule en or, Ignace,* and *Les Rois du sport,* among others.

The success of *La Bandera,* coming at the beginning of the new season, was seen as a highly significant event (see table 9.13). Though not as popular, the other film of the season noted by critics as significant was *La Kermesse héroïque. La Bandera* was followed by *L'Équipage, Veille d'armes, Mayerling,* and *L'Appel du silence*—these five social, psychological, or metaphysical dramas, most with nationalist sentiments, confirmed for critics the preeminent place of the dramatic genres in the late years of the decade. Although *Samson, Baccara, Bichon,* and *Marinella* were as popular, they received relatively little critical attention. The dramas struck commentators as cumulatively significant in defining a new direction in generic patterns— the moment when military and nationalistic films appealed to the popular imagination. *Deuxième Bureau* can be added to this list, though it was more a spy story, establishing the fictional Capitaine Benoît as a figure comparable to James Bond in the sixties. He was to reappear in *L'Homme à abattre* and *Capitaine Benoît,* both of which (particularly the former) were immensely popular, as was *Deuxième Bureau contre Kommandantur* in the months immediately preceding and following the declaration of war (though *Nadia, femme traquée,* also involving the Deuxième Bureau, was less so). Murat, who played the captain/spy in this series, had played the spy previously in *La Châtelaine du Liban,* not to mention numerous captains, but this series systematically promoted such figures as national heroes. From this point until the war, French military officers and colonial agents, engaging, as the genre required, in heroic feats of prowess against indigenous rebels or enemy aggressors, were to be a standard resource of the French cinema.

La Kermesse héroïque was singled out by critics as indicative of the move toward quality production, with elaborate and highly aesthetic sets and sophisticated camerawork. These characteristics tended to go hand in hand with the rise of the historical genre, the costume film. *Kœnigsmark, Mayerling,* and the slightly less successful *Lucrèce Borgia* confirmed this hypothesis. Prior to this, only Meerson's work for René Clair had attracted the critics' eye to sets, but from now on Trauner and Wahkevitch were much sought after, and their visual style helped to define the output of the last years of the decade, and indeed the next decade.

The 1936–37 season produced the rewards consequent on the developing multiple-exclusivity strategy (see table 9.14). The numbers of spectators attending one form or another of exclusive release, with their higher entry prices, to see such films as (in order) *Pepe le Moko, César, La Grande*

Table 9.14. The 1936–37 season by order of release (week/year)
38 out of 133 (29%)

Les Loups entre eux (35/36)	175	372	547 (8)
Sept hommes...une femme (35/36)	160	147	307
La Belle Équipe (38/36)	161	232	393
Jenny (38/36)	219	138	357
Le Roman d'un tricheur (38/36)	205	198	403
Un de la légion (38/36)	91	273	364
L'Amant de Mme Vidal (40/36)	209	277	486
Les Grands (40/36)	120	213	333
Rigolboche (40/36)	140	162	302
Hélène (42/36)	222	168	390
La Porte du large (43/36)	149	195	344
Au son des guitares (43/36)	161	165	326
Le Roi (44/36)	367	201	568 (6)
Le Mioche (45/36)	91	234	325
Au service du Tsar (46/36)	151	156	307
César (46/36)	550	174	724 (3)
Les Bas-Fonds (50/36)	242	171	413
Port-Arthur (50/36)	176	177	353
Les Hommes nouveaux (51/36)	179	266	445
Nitchevo (51/36)	257	348	605 (5)
Faisons un rêve (1/37)	168	132	300
Le Coupable (3/37)	129	388	517
Courrier-Sud (4/37)	163	238	401
Pepe le Moko (5/37)	562	259	821 (2)
Le Chemin de Rio (6/37)	136	217	353
Messieurs les Ronds de Cuir (6/37)	148	344	492
L'Homme à abattre (9/37)	255	266	521 (10)
Vous n'avez rien à déclarer (9/37)	184	150	334
Les Dégourdis de la 11e (11/37)	260	(150)	(410)
Mademoiselle Docteur (16/37)	211	105	316
Marthe Richard (16/37)	249	273	522 (9)
Nuits de feu (16/37)	241	125	366
Ignace (18/37)	302	266	568 (6)
Les Perles de la couronne (20/37)	431	259	690 (4)
La Danseuse rouge (21/37)	239	95	334
La Grande Illusion (23/37)	522	530	1,052 (1)
Troïka sur la piste blanche (25/37)	252	95	347
La Dame de pique (27/37)	255	135	390

Illusion, Les Perles de la couronne, and *Le Roi* was far higher than anything seen since the 1930–32 period, when *Le Roi des resquilleurs, Théodore et Cie, Marius,* and *Fanny* had recorded similar figures. If this was sometimes at the expense of general release, producers were not likely to be disturbed (though suburban theater owners were). Moreover, *La Grande Illusion* followed up this impressive performance by general release into more than a hundred Parisian theaters in the course of the next year, while both *Pepe* and *Perles* also did extremely well.

In generic terms, however, this season confirmed the rise of war and spy stories already noted in 1935–36. *Les Loups entre eux* was followed later in the year by *Marthe Richard,* which, together with *Mademoiselle Docteur,* shifted the emphasis away from fearless heroes such as Capitaine Benoît in *L'Homme à abattre* and toward the sultry female spy. At least four other popular films had military or marine settings. Several of these were Russian. Clearly, the importance of Russia in French films of the thirties was not dependent solely on the existence of Albatros Films and Russian emigrants. For the French, Russia seems to have been a vicarious France through which they could experience their own preoccupations, very slightly distanced. *Les Bas-Fonds* is only the best known of a series that in this season included *Au service du Tsar, Port-Arthur,* and *Nuits de feu,* as well as *Troïka sur la piste blanche,* set in Poland.

The other most popular films in general release were, on the one hand, *Ignace* and *Un de la légion,* which, along with *Les Dégourdis de la 11e,* confirmed Fernandel's place as the leading comic actor; and, on the other, *Le Coupable,* which joined *Nuits de feu* in presenting a magistrate forced to come to terms with his own complicity in the situation he is judging. Altogether, the proportion of films attracting 250,000 or more spectators approached half the year's releases for the first time ever. As table 9.14 shows, nearly 30 percent exceeded 300,000, and the extent of some of these successes, as reflected in regular surveys, justified the industry's optimism.

This confidence came despite the tense political situation relating to the Popular Front and its disintegration. The only film in table 9.14 which indirectly captures something of the political aspirations of the time is *La Belle Équipe,* which was perhaps successful not for this reason but rather because it was based on a number of extremely conventional and proven narrative strategies. *Le Crime de Monsieur Lange* had not made the previous year's table, though it had had an honorable career, and *La Vie est à nous* was never intended as a commercial proposition and never released in theaters. Nor, despite its slightly more conventional form, was *Le Temps des cerises.* When it was presented somewhat hopefully to the trade late in 1937, the trade journal commented acidly that it was a harsh and simplistic film which did not appear to have any prospect of normal (i.e., commercial) release.[40]

In view of the understandable antagonism which faced Sacha Guitry as a result of his support for recorded theater, it is worth remembering how popular his films were. This had become apparent in the 1935–36 season, when all three of his films proved attractive to spectators, but it was even more apparent in 1936–37, when the remarkable performance of *Les Perles de la couronne* was backed up by another three successes and by that of the mid-length film *Le Mot de Cambronne*. *Perles,* with its overview of four hundred years of French history, was to lead in later years to a number of other equally atrocious overviews, based on similar narrative pretexts (*Remontons les Champs-Élysées, Si Versailles m'était conté, Si Paris nous était conté*). Pagnol, who occasionally sounded as if he intended to implement a similar principle, was not proving so consistently successful. *César* benefited from its position as the final episode in a trilogy of which all France had seen the first two, now re-screened in parallel with it, but *Cigalon, Merlusse,* and even *Topaze* had not done very well during the preceding season.

Among other well-known directors, Ophüls had little success in these years. *Divine* was not a hit, while *La Tendre Ennemie* and *Yoshiwara,* if a little more popular, attracted less than the average number of spectators in Paris. None equaled the greater, though still modest, achievement of *Liebelei,* which had attracted more than this number in German, even before its French version appeared. Only in the "phony war" period did Ophüls come into his own, with the success of *Sans lendemain* and *De Mayerling à Sarajevo*. In contrast, it is worth restating the degree of success enjoyed by L'Herbier's films throughout the decade. Whatever the genre, his films seldom attracted fewer than 300,000 spectators in Paris, and sometimes twice that figure. In the 1936–37 season, *La Porte du large, Les Hommes nouveaux,* and *Nuits de feu* all had audiences exceeding 300,000. A similarly successful run was, as is well known, experienced by Carné's first film, *Jenny,* which appeared in the 1936–37 season. If *Drôle de drame* was just short, with about 247,000 spectators, the figures for his five succeeding films constituted a record the equal of any other director. Even Duvivier, often mentioned deprecatingly by critics in the same breath as Carné—the two meticulous craftsmen of their age—could not quite equal Carné's achievement despite the striking success of *La Belle Équipe* and *Pepe le Moko* this season and of *La Bandera, Maria Chapdelaine,* and *Un carnet de bal* before and after. Duvivier's career was, after all, studded with failures, even ambitious failures, and with modest successes that were sometimes ambitious, sometimes not. The reception of *Le Golem* and *Golgotha* must have given his producers cause for anxiety.

Finally, among successful directors who have received little recognition, Litvak and Mirande deserve, in their different ways, our attention. *Mayerling* and *L'Équipage* had followed *Cette vieille canaille* (and the earlier *Cœur de Lilas*) as successful films for the former, while the latter, aside from his scriptwriter's role in numerous boulevard comedies which were brought to the screen, directed four successful films in the 1936–37 season, including *Messieurs les Ronds de Cuir,* following *Baccara* in the previous season and leading to three further successes, the most significant of which was *Derrière la façade*.

Table 9.15. The 1937–38 season by order of release (week/year)
42 out of 122 (39%)

Mademoiselle ma mère (32/37)	189	178	367
Le Messager (36/37)	150	217	367
Un carnet de bal (37/37)	422	446	868 (1)
Gribouille (37/37)	214	190	404
Gueule d'amour (38/37)	312	260	572 (5)
Les Rois du sport (38/37)	168	160	328
La Citadelle du silence (39/37)	198	170	368
Double Crime sur la Ligne Maginot (39/37)	188	229	417
Fauteuil 47 (39/37)	218	153	371
La Dame de Malacca (40/37)	136	185	321
Feu (43/37)	201	150	351
L'Habit vert (45/37)	299	196	495 (9)
Le Mensonge de Nina Petrovna (45/37)	236	113	349
L'Affaire du courrier de Lyon (46/37)	174	155	329
Abus de confiance (49/37)	240	404	644 (3)
Désiré (49/37)	208	159	367
Sœurs d'armes (50/37)	209	93	302
Claudine à l'école (51/37)	186	135	321
Naples au baiser du feu (51/37)	283	289	572 (6)
L'Alibi (52/37)	291	296	587 (4)
Ces dames au chapeau vert (52/37)	234	172	406
Orage (2/38)	188	283	471
Le Puritain (2/38)	168	245	413
Mollenard (4/38)	226	89	315
Quadrille (4/38)	266	223	489 (10)
L'Innocent (6/38)	140	171	311
La Marseillaise (6/38)	248	127	375
Prison sans barreaux (7/38)	255	328	583 (5)
Légions d'honneur (7/38)	298	174	472
L'Occident (7/38)	199	138	337
Ramuntcho (8/38)	189	336	525 (8)
Hercule (9/38)	304	132	436
L'Affaire Lafarge (10/38)	260	165	425
La Tragédie impériale (13/38)	289	165	454
Le Schpountz (15/38)	274	150	424
Les Disparus de St Agil (15/38)	224	110	334
L'Étrange Monsieur Victor (18/38)	289	110	399
Barnabé (19/38)	276	144	420
Quai des brumes (20/38)	554	300	854 (2)
La Présidente (21/38)	199	138	337
Le Petit Chose (22/38)	195	138	333
Altitude 3200 (29/38)	253	75	328

The 1937–38 season must have been even more satisfying for the industry than the previous one had been (see table 9.15). It contained only two outstandingly popular films—*Un carnet de bal* and *Quai des brumes*—but by my calculations nearly 40 percent of the year's films attracted over 300,000 spectators in Paris. Audiences were spread more generally across the year's output. Only about thirty of the 122 films looked, on the basis of their Paris performance, as if they might lose money, and only about five failed badly. These figures had been steadily improving over the years, since 1930–31, when, despite immense audiences for some films, at least twenty failed badly. *Quai des brumes,* released late in the season, ran all through summer, with secondary and tertiary exclusive runs taking it up to week 47 of 1938, and immediate general release into thirty-four first-screening theaters in week 48. Its general release lasted until about week 10 of 1939, and it was just being re-released in a further exclusivity as the war began. At first banned, it experienced another successful re-release in 1941. It was therefore the first film whose long-term career was significantly disturbed by the outbreak of war, and the figures given for its total audience might well have been greater had its career not been interrupted.

In this season, for the first time, a significant number of successes on the home market began to translate into festival prizes and export earnings. Festival recognition came, of course, from the only film festival then functioning, the Venice Biennale (which had first included film in 1932). It began in 1935 and 1936, with Pierre Blanchar and Annabella winning the Coupe Volpi for best actor and best actress, and Feyder winning best director for *La Kermesse héroïque.* But in 1937, *Un carnet de bal* was designated best foreign film, *La Grande Illusion* won the jury prize, and *Les Perles de la couronne* won the prize for best scenario. Export recognition was most valued when it came from the industry's great rival, America. Now, for the first time since before World War I, producers could hope to see most of their locally successful films exported to the United States. In 1936, the U.S. National Board of Review designated five French films among the "ten best foreign films of the past year"—*Crime et châtiment,* which came out on top, *La Maternelle, La Bandera, Maria Chapdelaine* and *Le Dernier Milliardaire.* In that same year, *La Kermesse héroïque* ran for fifteen weeks in New York and was designated best film of the year—the first foreign film ever to be so designated—while *La Croisière jaune* and *Les Misérables* made the top-ten list. In 1937, *Les Bas-Fonds* and *Mayerling* also earned high recognition: the former was ranked second among foreign films, the latter fourth, and *Golgotha* came sixth. *Mayerling* ran for twenty-four weeks in New York, and made $300,000 there alone, which provoked endless analyses in French trade journals. Again in 1938 the National Board of Review designated a French film—*La Grande Illusion*—the best foreign film of the year, with three other French films following it. Forty copies of *La Grande Illusion* circulated simultaneously in the United States. And in 1939 *Quai des brumes* was designated joint best film of the year with *Confessions of a Nazi Spy.* In that year, *Regain* received the American Press Prize, having initially been banned there then released uncut.

La Bandera, Veille d'armes, Pepe le Moko, and a dozen other French films were soon routinely being screened in America, which had previously been so resistant to foreign-language films. *Un carnet de bal* ran for thirteen weeks, and *Un grand amour de Beethoven* for twelve weeks. The same thing happened in other countries, which were more open to foreign-language films. England gave a good reception to all of the above, together with *La Belle Équipe,* while *Un carnet de bal* ran for eighteen weeks and *Le Roman d'un tricheur* fourteen weeks, the latter screening in a dubbed version in four hundred British theaters. In Japan, the 1937 list of ten best films included *Pension Mimosas* (1), *Maria Chapdelaine* (4), *La Bandera* (5), *Crime et châtiment* (6), and *Du haut en bas* (8), while in Sweden the 1938 list of the top ten films also included five from France—*Le Roman d'un tricheur, Les Perles de la couronne, Les Bas-Fonds, La Grande Illusion,* and *Prison sans barreaux.* Further triumphs followed throughout Europe and in the Americas. In March 1938, a quarterly review laid particular emphasis on these export successes, noting that "France incontestably took second place in the international marketplace in 1937," after the United States.[41] By August 1938, the industry could boast that in the previous year it had astounded the world: "For the first time, hundreds of American theaters have been screening French movies."[42] At the Venice Festival that year, France was awarded the Coupe du Jury for its entire national offering, including a retrospective mounted by the Cinémathèque Française.

This degree of foreign recognition contrasts starkly with the lack of export success experienced by French producers between 1930 and 1935, when only René Clair's films, and perhaps *Poil de Carotte,* were known abroad. Other than these, any export success won by production companies had related primarily to Greece or to Egypt, Palestine, and Syria.[43]

Another measure of the increasing prestige that was beginning to accrue to French production in Anglo-Saxon countries is the large number of remakes of French films that were produced in these years. After the famous instance of *Pepe le Moko,* remade as *Algiers* (and later as *Casbah*), came English-language versions of *Prison sans barreaux, J'étais une aventurière, Café de Paris, Adémaï aviateur, Les Yeux noirs, La Bataille silencieuse, Alerte en Méditerranée, Carrefour,* and *La Chienne.* Not coincidentally, it was also at this time that large numbers of French film personnel began to be honored by the nation for services to their country: René Clair and Renoir received the Légion d'Honneur in 1937; Léon Mathot, Duvivier, Chevalier, and Raimu in 1938; and Louis Lumière himself in 1939. Previously, only Raymond Bernard had, to my knowledge, received such recognition, and that due principally to *Croix de bois.*

**Table 9.16. The 1938–39 season by order of release (week/year)
38 out of 123 (31%)**

Alerte en Méditerranée (35/38)	300	162	462
La Femme du boulanger (36/38)	315	232	547
Le Joueur (36/38)	165	234	399
Le Train pour Venise (37/38)	258	75	333
La Maison du Maltais (38/38)	194	262	456
Adrienne Lecouvreur (39/38)	211	177	388
Éducation de prince (40/38)	333	72	405
Entrée des artistes (40/38)	364	165	529
Lumières de Paris (40/38)	195	156	351
Prisons de femmes (41/38)	254	227	481
Katia (42/38)	263	279	542
Le Révolté (43/38)	231	171	402
Retour à l'aube (46/38)	210	174	384
Gibraltar (48/38)	272	276	548
Remontons les Champs-Élysées (48/38)	338	177	515
Hôtel du Nord (50/38)	375	320	695
Trois Valses (50/38)	472	420	892
La Bête humaine (51/38)	514	(400)	(914)
Conflit (51/38)	129	245	374
J'étais une aventurière (51/38)	345	165	510
Mon curé chez les riches (51/38)	127	262	389
Le Capitaine Benoît (1/39)	192	248	440
Trois de St. Cyr (5/39)	259	319	578
Raphaël le tatoué (6/39)	150 (180)	—	[360]
L'Esclave blanche (7/39)	238	211	449
Le Récif de corail (9/39)	261	—	[480]
Les Cinq Sous de Lavarède (10/39)	221	211	432
Derrière la façade (11/39)	262 (290)	—	[530]
Le Déserteur (11/39)	166 (201)	—	[360]
La Fin du jour (12/39)	205 (321)	—	[580]
Entente cordiale (16/39)	168	—	[750]
Le Dernier Tournant (20/39)	148 (184)	—	[310]
Le Jour se lève (23/39)	195 (475)	—	[850]
Fric-Frac (24/39)	238 (350)	—	[700]
Deuxième Bureau contre Kommandantur (25/39)	65 (200)	—	[340]
La Règle du jeu (27/39)	138 (244)	—	[420]
Circonstances atténuantes (30/39)	120 (238)	—	[470]
Louise (34/39)	80 (230)	—	[320]

In these circumstances, it was inevitable that producers should begin to link large-scale quality productions and a technical finish that registered as aesthetic sophistication with festival acclaim and export success. Tentative comments to this effect in the 1935–36 season were consolidated into accepted wisdom during 1937–38. Interviewed at the end of 1937, a number of industry executives independently expressed a view that shorter and more modest productions were becoming commercially nonviable: "It is less risky to spend three or four million francs to make an ambitious film than to film small-scale projects on the cheap." In their view, "too many smaller films are cluttering up the market."[44] Succeeding quarterly reviews showed them becoming confirmed in their view that lavish financing of sumptuous sets and costumes was giving the French cinema success at home and a reputation abroad, and that in general quality should prevail over quantity.[45] Clearly the "cinéma de qualité" which Truffaut was to attack in the fifties was not, or not solely, a fifties phenomenon, or even a wartime phenomenon, but was a direct outcome of the economic conditions of the industry in the mid- to late thirties, furthered by the peculiar conditions of wartime production and profitability.

As indicated above in the case of *Quai des brumes*, estimates of the degree of popularity that films released in the 1938–39 season enjoyed, or would have enjoyed, are difficult to make because the war cast its shadow back on that season's releases (see table 9.16). Week 35 of 1939 was the last week in which anything approaching normal programming could take place. After that point, the chaos attendant on mobilization and the regulations which greatly reduced audience sizes for fear of air raids affected the performance of films released and discouraged the release of further films for some months. Perhaps foreseeing these disruptions, and anxious to get in if possible before they occurred, the industry had continued to release promising films through the normally bleak period of late July and early August. Consequently, at the outbreak of war about a dozen promising films were still in the middle of (or in some cases had just begun) their exclusive release, and estimates of their audience are necessarily more tentative than in earlier cases. Among these were *Deuxième Bureau, Fric-Frac, Entente cordiale, Le Jour se lève, Circonstances atténuantes,* and *La Tradition de minuit,* not to mention *La Règle du jeu,* which had, like some of the others, just ended its (reportedly tumultuous) first run but had not yet opened in second-run or later exclusive-release theaters. It might have been expected to attract another hundred thousand spectators before its exclusive release ended.

Some of the films whose release was interrupted resumed their run, though in dramatically different circumstances, during the following season (when some runs were again cut short by the German occupation of Paris) or in later years. A number were banned by one regime or another, and resumed their runs only much later, if they still existed. This makes reliable estimates of audience numbers for exclusive release well-nigh impossible, and at least partially invalidates any direct comparison with earlier seasons.

The actual entry figures obtained by each film before the war began are given in table 9.16; the figures in parentheses constitute estimates of their final exclusive-release figure if circumstances had been normal. The general-release figures for many of these films once war was declared are for the most part nonexistent or so distorted by prevailing conditions as to be unreliable, since there was a disruption in both the printing and the archiving of sources on which such estimates might be based. As mentioned, the fear of air raids brought radical limitations to the maximum audience size permitted in all theaters. These maximums were initially so low—some large theaters were only permitted forty or fifty, and the absolute maximum was three hundred—that many theaters couldn't afford to open, despite the authorities' pleas for them to do so as a public service. By mid-October of 1939, however, half of the Paris theaters had reopened, and by early November, 243 out of 350 were open. By then, in fact, the requests by theater managers for a relaxation of the regulations had begun to have effect, and, as figure 9.2 shows, audiences had crept up toward 50 percent of those experienced in recent years. In early December, a further relaxation saw several theater managers for the first time expressing some degree of satisfaction with receipts and declaring that "the stagnation is at an end."[46] By April of 1940, indeed, receipts were back to normal (though not entries, because there had been a significant price rise); but almost immediately the threat of occupation began to drive Parisians out of Paris, and the exodus which accompanied the actual invasion in June took attendance to an all-time low from which it did not recover for years. Even in 1941, the population of Paris was lower by 400,000 than in 1938, and theater attendance was only two thirds that of 1938.

Surviving data therefore do not permit accurate estimates for the period of September to December 1939 (and indeed later, though with decreasing indeterminacy). What I have done is to apply probabilities based on previous releases by the same director and/or in the same genre to get a hypothetical figure for total audience, and to base my calculations on the known proportion of normal audience size, as indicated in figure 9.2, that was applicable in each of these contentious months. The result is given in brackets, to indicate an even higher degree of uncertainty than is indicated by parentheses.

Inevitably, these uncertainties affect most profoundly the films released toward the end of the season. The first of this season's releases to be directly affected was *La Bête humaine,* which was released at Christmas 1938, and which, after thirteen weeks at the Madeleine, enjoyed a varied second and third run in nine different theaters, including the two largest, the Rex and the Gaumont Palace. This was probably about to end when war broke out. When it reappeared in week 6 of 1940, it was treated as if it were resuming after a summer break, with a "reminder" release, then a truncated general release, which offers little guidance as to what would have happened in normal times.

Any film which was released from February on and which experienced any degree of success met problems of a similar nature. *La Femme du boulanger, Entrée des artistes,* and *Katia,* however, which had been released in the first weeks of the 1938–39 season, experienced something resembling a normal successful career. A number of promising films were released around the end of 1938 to capitalize on the seasonal cycle—*Gibraltar, Remontons les Champs-Élysées, Hôtel du Nord, Trois Valses,* and *La Bête humaine.* Though only the last of these was still in release at the outbreak of war, nearly all the others, along with those which were at all successful thereafter, were cut short in ways that require the application of calculations such as those I have outlined above. In fact, attendance figures were not as high as they might normally have been at the end of 1938 because of a protest by prominent theater managers which involved some closures, but counterbalancing this, attendance in March and April was anomalously high, and audiences were large right up to the outbreak of war. Ignoring for the moment the catastrophe that followed, the industry would have had every reason to be as satisfied with this season as with the two that had preceded it. Only in June 1939 does a note of pessimism begin to intrude on contemporary accounts of record attendance and export successes, as Germany and Italy become difficult to deal with commercially, and a number of countries which had welcomed French films cease to exist.[47]

Up to that point, the popularity of films such as *Les Trois Valses, Katia, Remontons les Champs-Élysées, Hôtel du Nord, Entente cordiale,* and *Le Jour se lève* can only have confirmed the industry's belief in large-scale productions, technical finish, and elaborate sets, which, when not elegant, at least aestheticized the squalor they represented. The continuing success of costly war and spy stories (admittedly subsidized by the Defense Forces) pointed in the same direction, most notably *Alerte en Méditerranée, Gibraltar, Le Capitaine Benoît, Trois de St. Cyr,* and *Deuxième Bureau contre Kommandantur.* Yet there were two more intimate small-scale, bleaker productions which experienced an unexpected degree of success—*Entrée des artistes* and *La Fin du jour.* Indeed, the surprise expressed by the industry at their success was directly related to its growing conviction that such films were no longer viable. Only two comedies made a real impact this season, both starring Michel Simon and both released just before the outbreak of war—*Fric-Frac* and *Circonstances atténuantes.* If one also takes into account the two Renoir films and another Jean Gabin–Michèle Morgan film, *Récif de corail,* which has apparently been lost, together with Pagnol's *La Femme du boulanger,* it becomes apparent what a rich and varied season the French cinema experienced just before the catastrophe.

The contrast with the 1939–40 season could not be greater. Politically, the latter belongs to the forties rather than the thirties, but since the careers of films made in the thirties were centrally affected by it a few comments are justified. Records do not allow any statements about this period to be made with confidence; I have been able to trace only thirty-nine films released between September 1939 and June 1940. Of those released before the end of 1939, only *Ils étaient neuf célibataires, Le Bois sacré,* and *Pièges* looked set for reasonable runs. Many films made in 1939, such as *L'Enfer des anges, La Nuit de décembre,* and Rozier's *Espoirs* (not to mention *Remorques,* though for quite other reasons) were not released until 1941, while *Macao, l'enfer du jeu* and *La Piste du nord* appeared only in 1942. Malraux's *Espoir,* known then as *Sierra de Teruel,* and not strictly a French film, as well as a few lesser-known films, did not appear until 1945. Only six of the films produced during the phony war found their way onto the market before the end of the 1939–40 season, including *Paris-New York, Miquette,* and *La Fille du puisatier* (though the latter not in Paris). Outstanding among releases in the latter half of this confused season was *Battement de cœur,* which was in exclusive release at the Madeleine from week 6 of 1940 on, and resumed its exclusive release early in 1941. With its general release starting in week 40 of 1941, it ran in at least seventy-seven Paris theaters before the end of the year, accumulating a total of about 900,000 spectators by that time. It thus ranks as one of the most popular of the films produced in the thirties.

9.4 REGIONAL AND NATIONAL AUDIENCES

These seasonal tables call for several comments, some of which are relevant to any attempt to extend them to their logical end, which is obtaining a long-term and nationwide list of the most popular films of the decade. First, if the tables for Paris are anywhere near accurate, then it is apparent that there are gross disparities between the performance of films in exclusive release and in general release. This should not be surprising, since, as indicated above, the relationship between exclusive and general release was always unequal, and was constantly evolving over the decade. Even more important, the performance of a film in these two categories depended entirely on the release strategy adopted by the producer and distributor. In the extreme, several dozen films had no exclusive release at all, yet some of these did quite well in general release. Finally, the two categories of release attracted statistically different audiences with significantly different tastes and preoccupations. Cumulatively, this could mean that success in exclusive release was not a reliable predictor of success in general release. As table 9.17 shows, a list of the top films in exclusive release does not correlate at all closely with a list of top films after general release. It compares the forty films which by my calculations achieved the greatest number of spectators in exclusive release in Paris with the forty films that achieved the greatest number of spectators after their general release in Paris.

Foreign films have not been included in either of the columns, though if they had been there would be about fifteen foreign and twenty-five French in each list. In the fifties, when *Le Film Français* conducted a detailed analysis, twenty-five out of the sixty films which attracted over 300,000 viewers in exclusive release were foreign, and thirty-five were French. Among the former, *Bridge on the River Kwai* rated highest, at second, with 643,000 viewers, and the only other foreign film in the top ten was *Ben Hur*, at fifth with 570,000. In the thirties, a roughly similar proportion would have achieved that level of popularity, nearly all of them American.

What the tables make immediately apparent is that some thirties films rose markedly in rank after general release, while others fell. Among the former are *Jean de la Lune*, *Trois Valses*, and *Mayerling*, while another eight do not even appear among the top forty in exclusive release yet figure quite highly after general release. Notable among these "sleepers" are *Le Grand Jeu*, *Nitchevo*, *Angèle*, *Abus de confiance*, *L'Équipage*, and *Le Congrès s'amuse*, and above all *Deuxième Bureau*, which achieved only 185,000 in exclusive release. Among those that fall after general release are *Pepe le Moko*, *César*, and *Les Perles de la couronne*, while several disappear completely from the second list. Among these are *Le Roi*, *Entrée des artistes*, *Croix de bois*, *La Nuit est à nous*, *J'étais une aventurière*, *Remontons les Champs-Élysées*, and *Éducation de prince*.

If these dramatic changes in ranking seem dubious, the analogy of the fifties can again be cited. At that time, the audiences for all films at all stages of their career were meticulously tracked and monitored, not just for Paris but nationwide, and precisely the same sort of disjunction is apparent. Neither *Le Roi Pandore* nor *Prélude à la gloire* would have rated a mention on the basis of their 1950 exclusive-release figures, yet ultimately they provided the fourth and tenth best returns for films produced in 1949. The same is true of *Alerte au sud* in 1953, a year in which *La Belle de Cadix* and *Les Enfants de l'amour* also improved their ratings dramatically once out of first release. In 1956, *Don Juan*, *Sans famille*, and *Christine* rose from anonymity only when out of exclusive release. And these are just the most marked of a large number of such films identified by CNC long-term data. It is equally true that a number of films which promised well in that decade subsequently slumped in the ratings. Perhaps the most dramatic instances were *La Ronde* and *Monsieur Ripois* in 1954, but the tables document many others.

These more reliable figures from the fifties can reassure us that the disparities noted for the thirties are not unreasonable. Again on analogy with

Table 9.17. A comparison of exclusive and general-release figures for Paris

After exclusive release		After general release	
Le Roi des resquilleurs	888	Le Roi des resquilleurs	1,187
L'Appel du silence	660	La Grande Illusion	1,052
Pepe le Moko	562	La Bête humaine	(914)
Quai des brumes	554	La Grande Mare	893
César	550	Trois Valses	892
Théodore et Cie	539	L'Appel du silence	887
La Grande Illusion	522	Un carnet de bal	868
La Bête humaine	514	Quai des brumes	854
La Grande Mare	503	Le Jour se lève	(850)
Le Jour se lève	(475)	Théodore et Cie	830
Trois Valses	472	Pepe le Moko	821
Fanny	454	La Bandera	816
Adémaï aviateur	449	Jean de la Lune	769
Les Perles de la couronne	431	Adémaï aviateur	742
Marius	428	César	724
Un carnet de bal	422	Samson	711
Hôtel du Nord	375	Entente cordiale	(700)
Entente cordiale	368	Fric-Frac	(700)
Le Roi	367	Veille d'armes	697
La Bandera	366	Hôtel du Nord	695
Entrée des artistes	364	Les Perles de la couronne	690
Croix de bois	356	Mayerling	672
La Nuit est à nous	350	Angèle	664
Fric-Frac	(350)	Fanny	664
La Bande à Bouboule	348	Marius	654
J'étais une aventurière	345	Abus de confiance	644
Remontons les Champs-Élysées	338	L'Équipage	622
Éducation de prince	333	Maria Chapdelaine	612
Jean de la Lune	324	Le Grand Jeu	608
La Fin du jour	(321)	Nitchevo	605
La Femme du boulanger	315	Le Congrès s'amuse	605
Gueule d'amour	312	La Bande à Bouboule	593
La Maternelle	308	Deuxième Bureau	590
Maria Chapdelaine	305	Les Nuits moscovites	589
Hercule	304	L'Alibi	587
Ignace	302	Prison sans barreaux	583
Marinella	300	La Fin du jour	(580)
Alerte en Méditerranée	300	Trois de St. Cyr	578
L'Habit vert	299	Naples au baiser du feu	572
Mayerling	292	Gueule d'amour	572

the fifties we might expect to be able to make certain generalizations about the long-term popularity of certain genres and actors. In that decade, for instance, general-release audiences favored actors who embodied the current image of "the common man," such as Bourvil (*Le Cœur sur la main*, 1949; *Le Roi Pandore*, 1950) and Blier (*Sans famille*, 1958), as they favored the comic blundering of Fernandel (particularly in *Don Juan*, 1956; *Le Chômeur de Clochemerle*, 1957; and *La Loi, c'est la loi*, 1958). The same seems to be true of the thirties, when general-release audiences showed strong support for the "man of the people"—Milton, Bach, and Fernandel, not to mention Michel Simon and René Lefèvre. Thus a check of the annual lists of top films which were "sleepers," in the sense that they showed little promise in exclusive release but far greater popularity on general release, turns up films starring Gabin (*Cœur de Lilas*), Boyer (*L'Épervier*), Bach (*Sidonie Panache, Bach millionnaire*), Fernandel (*Un de la légion*), and Lefèvre (*Paprika*).

Another predictable tendency was for more intellectual films to do better in exclusive release, often to crash on general release (*L'Opéra de quat'sous, Itto, Altitude 3200*, even *L'Étrange Monsieur Victor*), while those which aimed for emotional intensity moved in the other direction. Moreover, general-release audiences preferred certain specific genres, such as the melodrama, whether classic (*Les Mystères de Paris, Le Mioche*), realist (*Faubourg Montmartre*), or relating to artists' lives (*La Ronde des heures, Louise*), and romantic comedy (*Atout cœur, Trois pour cent*, and *Princesse à vos ordres*, and succeeding Garat–Harvey romances). Again, as *Louise* and *La Ronde des heures* suggest, anything dealing with the trials of an artist was likely to do better in general release than its exclusive release would have led one to expect. *La Chanson d'une nuit* was a sleeper of this sort, foreshadowing *Entrée des artistes* and *La Fin du jour*, both of which astounded the industry later in the decade. Another thematic field, that of suppressed guilt and the resurgence of the past, struck a chord with the general public which it had failed to awaken in the exclusive-release public, as *Le Coupable* and *Le Juif polonais* indicate. *Sergent X* experienced the same sort of success, working with an analogous theme. Finally, the farce and the military vaudeville often scored more favor with the general public, as did anything featuring the military. Films as different as *Sergent X, Un de la légion*, and *Sidonie Panache*, all foreign legion films set in North Africa, proved more popular with the general-release public than they had with the exclusive-release public.

On the other hand, from 1937 on, any tale of spies, smugglers, or gunrunners proved disappointing on general release, for instance *Mademoiselle Docteur, La Danseuse rouge, Troika sur la piste blanche, Sœurs d'armes*, and even *Mollenard*. This may have been partly due to an evolving disaffection for East European, particularly Russian, settings, which had been a mainstay for some production companies before that point. Certainly, these films constituted the bulk of the productions that succeeded in exclusive release but failed in general release in the later years of the decade, as opposed to melodramas, sentimental comedies, and farces, of which the reverse was true.

While it is interesting to note these actual or possible differences between exclusive-release and general-release audiences, a more serious qualification that needs to be introduced to any discussion of the seasonal tables is the extent to which they provide us with an accurate evaluation of the long-term *nationwide* success of the listed films. To what extent, that is, did regional audiences echo Parisian preferences? If they did so with any accuracy, then since Paris audiences constituted about 30 percent of the national audience all that would be needed to obtain the total national audience for the films listed in the tables is to multiply by 3.33. Yet clearly this procedure would not be valid in all cases. The more reliable data available from 1948 on, supplemented by the less reliable but still significant figures available for the period 1930–47, suggest that there were indeed, as the industry claimed, important differences between Parisian and provincial preferences, between urban and rural preferences, and thus between early predictions concerning a film's success based on its Parisian record and its actual long-term nationwide popularity. For instance, from the early thirties on, it is clear that a number of more ambitious films, notably those directed by individuals now recognized as auteurs, failed outside Paris, just as they failed with general-release audiences inside Paris. On the available evidence, in contrast with their (sometimes only relative) Parisian success, several of Feyder's films flopped in the provinces (*Le Spectre vert, Si l'empereur savait ça,* and *La Piste du nord*), as did *Caïn, L'Opéra de quat'sous, Entrée des artistes,* and several of Duvivier's more ambitious films (*Golgotha, Le Golem,* and *David Golder*). Two of Grémillon's wartime films, *Remorques* and *Lumière d'été,* failed outside Paris, as did *Les Parents terribles* (*Orphée* failed everywhere).

Generally, provincial audiences were more likely to favor films and genres favored by the general-release audience in Paris. This had the effect of reinforcing the sleeper effect of such films and genres over time. The one exception is historical romances, which were widely popular with Parisians, even or especially on general release, but not with provincial audiences. L'Herbier's historical romances, such as *L'Épervier* and *La Route impériale,* had demonstrated this sleeper effect in Parisian general release, while *Entente cordiale* was popular with all Paris audiences. But if provincial audiences did not agree about historical romances, they did support the Paris general-release audiences in their taste for melodrama and farce. Two of the outstanding wartime successes, *Le Voile bleu* (a melodrama with Gaby Morlay) and *Fièvres* (a musical drama with Tino Rossi), were to prove successful almost solely because of provincial support. The fifties provide many instances of another provincial predilection—that for musicals. In 1951, *Andalousie, Chacun son tour, Musique en tête,* and *Boîte de nuit* all did dis-

proportionately well outside Paris. Those featuring Luis Mariano were particularly popular in the provinces (*Quatre jours à Paris, Le Chanteur de
Mexico,* and *Violettes impériales*). What now can seem rather vacuous postwar musicals organized around the singularly undramatic activity of some
band popular at the time—Jacques Hélian's in *Paris-St Germain des Prés*
and *Musique en tête,* Ray Ventura's in *Mademoiselle s'amuse, Nous irons à
Paris,* and *Nous irons à Monte Carlo*—were (even) more successful in the
provinces than in Paris. While musicals rated highly everywhere in the early
thirties, there is some evidence to suggest that they were even more popular outside of Paris than in the city.

The provinces cannot, however, be treated as a coherent bloc, whose
"backward" or "rural" attitudes might be globally opposed to those of a
more sophisticated Paris. A detailed study of regional variations still needs
to be undertaken, but certain generalizations can safely be made. Toulouse
audiences, for instance, were notorious for replicating the more sophisticated taste of Paris. The ranking given French films screened in Toulouse in
1933 was remarkably consistent with the ranking given those same films by
Paris audiences. Both groups ranked highly *L'Atlantide, La Maternelle,* and
Les Deux Orphelines, as well as *Fanny* and *Marius, Les Croix de bois, La Petite
Chocolatière,* and *Il est charmant.* Toulouse placed *Le Chanteur inconnu* and
Jocelyn higher, but the differences are minimal. Lille, as befits the image of
an austere and pragmatic northern town, was sometimes more favorably
disposed toward serious and even somber films than was Paris. Duvivier's
Golgotha, which did not do very well in Paris and appeared on no other poll,
topped the Lille poll for 1934–35.[48] At the other end of the country,
Provence, with its own production system and actors, tended to favor films
with a local setting and accent. Films starring Fernandel were widely appreciated throughout France, but nowhere so intensely as in Provence. The
most impressive instances were to be *Uniformes et grandes manœuvres* and *Le
Boulanger de Valorgues,* in a later decade, but that similar preferences were already operative in the thirties is apparent from the 1933 returns from Marseille's four principal theaters, which show Colombier's *Charlemagne* as far
and away the most profitable and his *Sa meilleure cliente* in fifth place. Neither rated as highly elsewhere.[49] The same is true of *Il était une fois,* a curious
film about an operation that transforms a woman morally as well as aesthetically: low on Paris lists, it came fourth in Marseille. Even more dramatic
was the success of *L'Ordonnance,* a military melodrama, and *Une femme au
volant,* both of which failed in Paris but scored second and seventh, respectively, in Marseille. Although there were common favorites in all years,
Provençal audiences nevertheless differed measurably in their appreciation
of certain films and certain genres. They did not take to René Clair's films
as Paris audiences did, showing no interest at all in *Quatorze juillet.* Like

most regions, they were equally uninterested in *Tumultes* and the science-fiction film *IF 1 ne répond plus.*

Finally, for obvious reasons, the German-speaking areas, for as long as their linguistic culture remained distinctive, recorded anomalous returns. In fact, the Alsace population didn't much like any French films in the thirties and forties, and those that it did favor were totally unpredictable and unrelated to the lists from other regions. In Strasbourg, even in the early fifties, a mediocre German film could expect to draw three times the audience of a good French film.[50] In sum, for much of the classic period, France was effectively a patchwork of regional audiences with notable differences in their preferences relating to regional identities, and in order to obtain any definitive figures for the total national audience for a given film these regional and rural preferences would have to be addressed. To do so would involve accessing numerous regional theater programs covering the whole decade, and would involve lengthy calculations.

TEN

Conclusion

The data so far accumulated concerning the films of the thirties and the discourses that surrounded them allow us to explore the ways in which the French cinema of the thirties might be defined, both from within and from without. To do this, we need to be able to answer two questions: first, what are the terms, elements, motifs, and figures which best characterize this cinema, what are the relations between them, and what is the nature of the macrotext which they serve to construct; second, what are the characteristics which distinguish this cinema both from other national cinemas of the period and from the French cinema of the decades that preceded and followed it. The comments that follow should be considered no more than preliminary indications of the direction which such an exploration might take.

First, it is apparent that the French cinema of the thirties did not deal equally with all aspects of human experience. No national cinema, of course, ever does, and the fields which it deals with most intensively are those which pose the most important questions concerning identity for the audiences of the day. French films of the thirties showed a marked predilection for the fields of class and of gender, and for the notions of art and of nature as forms of transcendence. They avoided almost entirely, however, those binaries more typical of the horror and science-fiction genres which call into question what it means to be human, and which, in the case of the German and American cinemas, characterized periods of national crisis. On the evidence of this cinema, "knowledge," whether scientific or arcane, was not a preoccupation of the decade, and the various social crises did not trigger any form of national paranoia. Very few of the decade's films deal in any way at all with the "ultimate purposes of existence," whether by way of opposition between the human and the animal or between the human and the divine, nor do they appeal to supernatural forces. Certainly, there were categories of film which saw "the human" as divided between the instinctual and the spiritual, the barbaric and the civilized, but in such cases civilization itself is defined in social terms rather than in religious or even simply political terms. The possibility that established religion might constitute a valid form of transcendence is seldom broached in the course of the decade, and never, when it is, to popular acclaim.

Nor, until fairly late in the decade, are broadly "international" considerations given any significant weight in popular mythology. Large numbers of foreigners appear in the films of the decade, but the great majority of them are based on stereotypical national representations mobilized for perfunctory comic or dramatic effect. That other peoples are different, and that their differences are innate and known once and for all, is a fact that can be largely taken for granted. Only when war threatens do a number of still fairly conventional spy stories involving external relations displace the military vaudevilles so common earlier in the decade, and these are successful mainly with urban audiences. French engagement with the outside world is largely confined to specific overseas territories in which France has a colonial interest, and that engagement is pursued primarily by legionnaires, with a supporting cast of engineers and administrators.

These absences ensure that the focus of the decade's cinema will be primarily internal and social. Yet even within the social, in a cinema which provided its citizens with numerous myths concerning society, class, and gender as key categories for understanding their place in the world, it is surprising how little attention is paid to children, to education, and to the media. Early in the thirties, a series of conventional melodramas, dating for the most part from an earlier age, exploit the innocence and vulnerability of children to sentimental effect, and a few late films foreshadow the attention to be paid during the war years to the future generation ("youth," though seldom "children"), who risk being corrupted by the sins of their elders. But statistically they are absent from the cinema of this decade. As a generic category, the youth film was mentioned occasionally in the thirties, but nowhere near as often as in the following twenty years, when it was to become better known as the *film sur l'enfance*. The religious film was also to become a much more widely recognized generic category in the postwar period, though the number of films to be so categorized would never be great; rather, a relatively few religious films were to have a relatively large impact on audiences, and critics with a Catholic orientation were to seize on this (wrongly, as it turned out) as a sign of things to come.

There are, then, significant absences from the mythology constructed by the cinema of the thirties, and these allow us to better circumscribe the fields on which it concentrates with some intensity. These fields can best be described, at least initially, by compiling a list of the objects, settings, figures, and events which constitute the repertoire of recurrent textual elements underlying this cinema's representation of reality. These objects, settings, figures, and events can be thought of as the nodes of the textual web, each one caught up and articulated with a number of others in a series of intersecting narratives. Each of them, through intensive use and reuse, acquired metaphoric and/or metonymic associations which allow us to recognize its significance in the mythology of the day.

To list these recurrent textual elements is to bring together sections of the various chapters of both Part 1 and Part 2. Among objects and settings are the accordion, the *guinguette*, the bar-restaurant, the nightclub, and the music hall; the dockside with its ships and its grills; flowers, bicycles, and taxis; racecourses and boxing rings; circuses and fairgrounds; Montmartre, the Vieux Port, la place Blanche, and the urban slums of Belleville. Among the figures are orphans, twins, and doubles; amnesiacs, athletes, engineers, and aviators; good-time girls, seductive vamps, and spies; tramps and bankers; gullible provincials; artists, actresses, stars, and singers; stereotypical foreigners; the "little people" of Paris together with the crooks and police with whom their lives intersect; shrews and bigots; powerful aging males and vulnerable waifs; florists and laundresses, reporters, and Salvation Army girls. Among the events which mark the lives of such figures are gambling scenes, lottery wins, and problematic inheritances; exchanged babies and arranged and unconsummated marriages; joining the legion to expiate one's guilt in a climactic Arab attack; the ship that sails without one, and the woman who betrays one's trust and destroys male solidarity; the day in the country, the revelation of artistic talent or of male magnificence, and the rejection of wealth as one hits the road.

While this list may, despite its incompleteness, seem long, the exclusions that preceded it allow us rather to see it as a dense concentration of elements that are closely related to one another in multiple ways via more or less conventional narrative sequences, and that articulate a relatively small number of intensely experienced anxieties relating to gender and sexuality, particularly masculinity and forbidden desires; to nature and nurture, the city and the country, and the cost of progress; to human fallibility and the possible forms of expiation; to sincerity, money, and worth; and to the various forms of corruption, inequality, and injustice dominating social existence, together with a number of fantasized forms of escape from that existence. Very generally, that is, they articulate questions concerning social and sexual identity, establishing a mythical framework which allowed audiences to understand obliquely who they were, whether this identity was predestined or escapable, and if the latter who they might become, and why, and how.

Certain of the textual elements constituting this mythical web of meaning were over-determined, in the sense that at different times and in different films, or even in a single film, they could fulfill multiple functions. If orphans were so common, it was because their status as "floating" social elements could serve to articulate general statements about the lack of a well-anchored social identity and about disenfranchisement, but also because they could be used to evoke dysfunctional families and misunderstood children, because the vulnerability of the orphan could be used to evoke social injustice and iniquitous power relations—because it could, in fact, stand for a number of oppressed social groups. If lottery wins and their analogues were so common, it was because they could figure a form of fantasized escape from these social injustices and deprivations, but also because, by shifting status and class, the recipient could become someone else, and thus demonstrate in much the same way as identity shifts triggered by exchanges of clothing that social identity was not in fact predestined, but rather socially, and even arbitrarily, imposed. This new status opened up the theme of sincerity, as did all forms of wealth, with their concomitant anxieties about "true" friendship and "true" love. Finally, the sudden acquisition of wealth was represented as incompatible with art and with creativity—indeed, was inherently corrupting, and thus to be rejected in favor of, say, mateship and the open road.

The actor figure was similarly over-determined, serving, most obviously, to promote art and, reflexively, the status of the filmmaker as artist—the high road to spiritual salvation and transcendence in a degraded world. In addition, acting went to the heart of identity, proposing social personae as roles that the performer could assume or shuck off at will, and this in turn might be represented as an entertaining game or as a source of existential terror, opening up the possibility of an absolute lack of any inherent identity. The actor figure also could be used to evoke the question of sincerity, which constituted one of the fundamental themes of the decade. In fact, the actor could fluctuate from being one of the falsest and most suspect of figures to being the truest and most authentic of figures, alone able to get in touch with some fundamental reality and to transmute a degraded reality into something purer and finer.

As a final instance, it was inevitable that the financier should be a central element of the textual web of this cinema, since quite aside from his demonization as the figure principally responsible for the social collapse and consequent injustices of the day, he stood metonymically for the prevailing economic system; while this was seldom mentioned directly, it was (again metonymically) present in the form of "money" as discussed above. Whence the constant oppositions between financier and artist, financier and worker, financier and provincial, and financier and tramp—oppositions in which the financier was doomed to defeat by the superior values of art, of nature, of love, of sincerity, or of freedom. Finally, as powerful male authority figures, financiers could feature in patriarchal narratives problematizing masculinity and dysfunctional families, in which they might take up with or take over much younger females in quasi-paternal relationships which both caricature the unequal power relationships between male and female and raise questions of forbidden sexuality.

More generally, not just the over-determined elements of the web but all of its nodes served cumulatively to articulate a set of opposed values relating to having or not having secure identities—relating to exile and belonging, solidarity and divisiveness, sincerity and falseness, oppression and escape. A large number of the key nodes figure various forms of prison, both actual and metaphorical, in which the protagonist finds himself or herself trapped—penal colonies, reformatories, boarding schools, unhappy families, slums, rigid social and gender roles, conventional moral codes—something so huge and multiform that it sometimes seems to equate with life itself, with "reality." The governors and warders of this system come in for consistent and implacable abuse, though a number of films recognize that these figures too are prisoners of the system, as in favorable circumstances they may themselves come to realize. All the inmates of this system are in some sense in exile, disenfranchised, if only because they are not in control of their own destiny. Iniquitously put in the wrong, they acquire the status of criminals, as do in their eyes, those who betrayed and enslaved them, whence the omnipresence of a metaphorical criminality.

The forms of fantasized escape from this prison are on occasion celebrated, but more often they are discredited as impossible of achievement or as ineffectual. The implacability of the destiny which has condemned them is apparent in the almost complete absence from the web of any form of social or political action that might transform the conditions of their existence. Part of the problem is the fact that the very articulateness which might allow them to conceptualize such transformations has been appropriated by their jailers, whose glib line of talk and whose sleight of hand leaves those imprisoned with an inarticulate desire for freedom which, unspoken, can find expression only in a series of visual metaphors. Toward the end of the decade, a few films begin to represent the conditions of imprisonment as something short of definitive, as the new "humanizing" paradigm begins to recognize the inmates no longer as "criminals" but as "unfortunates," in need of compassion rather than of punishment.

This mention of a late evolution of the textual web brings up the question of its stability in the course of the decade. A number of industrial factors would suggest that in economic terms a periodization involving a paradigm shift took place toward the middle of the decade. This can already be seen in table 9.2, in which some of the crucial factors are listed. These have been charted in figure 10.1 in such a way as to make their correlation clearer. The two lowest graphs indicate the number of films produced and released each year. These indicate that something significant happened in 1934–35, since the graphs dip significantly for those years. An initial explanation for this dip is provided by the two roughly parallel graphs above them: the number of spectators in millions per year and the gross receipts in millions of francs per year which these audiences produced

Figure 10.1. Industry Changes 1930–39

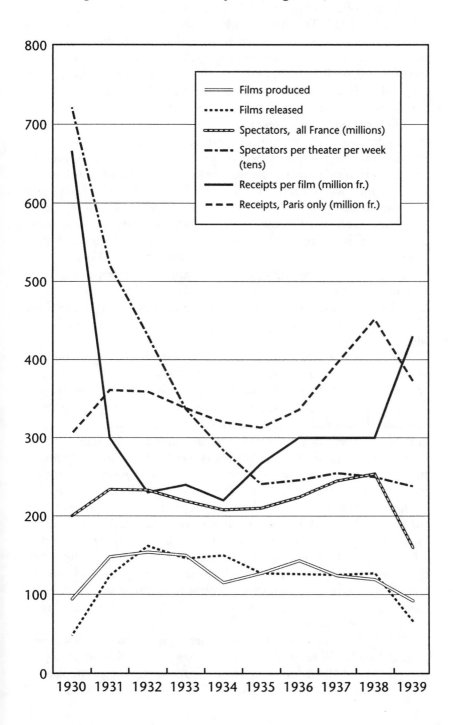

Legend:
- Films produced
- Films released
- Spectators, all France (millions)
- Spectators per theater per week (tens)
- Receipts per film (million fr.)
- Receipts, Paris only (million fr.)

(given for Paris, which equaled approximately 30 percent of the French totals): both peaked in 1931 and 1932 and declined steadily thereafter to a low point in 1935. This corresponds to the impact of the depression in 1932 and the worst period of social and economic tension in the following three years. However, the number of spectators rose again thereafter until 1938 (indeed, until August 1939), and when one factors in the increases in entry price that took place over those same years, the result is a quite startling increase in receipts from 1937 to August 1939.

While these factors suggest that a difficult few years in the middle of the decade separated two periods of relative prosperity, the industry was not affected uniformly: the distinctive impact of the depression on the production and exhibition sectors can best be seen in the two more dramatic graphs beginning at the top left. The top graph, which (multiplied by ten) gives the average weekly audience per theater in Paris general release for French sound films, reveals the extent to which the exhibition sector benefited from the introduction of sound. As more and more theaters were converted for sound and more and more sound films became available to the market, however, the weekly audience per sound theater dropped abruptly from over seven thousand to about twenty-four hundred in 1935. Thereafter, the stabilization of production and release, together with the recovery of audience numbers, brought about a stabilization of weekly audiences which lasted until the war.

The remaining graph indicates the even more startling turnaround in the fortunes of producers that occurred in 1934–35. The average returns per French sound feature film had been astronomical in the first years of the decade, but had plummeted to under half their 1930 level by 1932. This caused numerous bankruptcies and the sudden decrease in production in 1934. But thereafter, the conjunction of a number of favorable circumstances—stable production, increasing audiences, increased entry prices, and no doubt also the developing mythology outlined above—saw the average returns per French feature film improve markedly in 1936 and, indeed, generate something of a bonanza for producers in the period from late 1938 to August 1939. This stabilization of industrial conditions in the last years of the decade, and most notably the relative prosperity of the production sector, doubtless explains why the sense of crisis so loudly voiced by the industry in 1934 and 1935 dissipated fairly rapidly, and why the public inquiries resulting from it never came to anything. Government inaction between 1935 and 1939, so often criticized, was probably due in fact to decreased pressure from the industry for the government to act.

The industry's economics would therefore suggest that the introduction of sound saw a few years of prosperity followed by a crisis occurring between 1933 and 1935, during which significant, though largely unplanned and involuntary, changes took place, and these ensured that stability, and even a return to prosperity, characterized the period from 1936 until the declaration of war. The comments in industry journals quoted in chapter 9 bear out this periodization, but also indicate the industry's belief that it was primarily the high quality of technical finish with which the films of the late thirties were endowed that made them a success on both the national and international markets. The reverse could as easily be argued—namely, that the high technical finish was a consequence of greater availability of funds to producers after 1936.

The question that arises is whether this "industrial" division of the 1930s into two periods of approximately the same length (1930–34, 1935–39) corresponds in any way to a periodization of filmic content. A number of references to such a periodization have been made in earlier chapters, and certain of these are worth recalling. As a first observation, although the first year of the decade saw a larger number of dramas than of comedies, the gross production level of comedies was thereafter far higher than that of dramas. The popularity of these comedies with spectators, however, showed a dramatic decline in the 1933–34 season, when they were displaced in terms of popularity by social and psychological dramas. The 1930–31 and 1931–32 seasons had both been dominated by comedies which ran in exclusive release for years, notably *Le Roi des resquilleurs* and its immediate successors, together with *Jean de la lune* and *Théodore et Cie,* and the host of sentimental comedies and musical comedies starring Maurice Chevalier and the Henri Garat–Lilian Harvey couple, the military vaudevilles which acquired a surprising following, and the "vulgar" theatrical comedies which attracted such condemnation from moralists and movie lovers alike. Recognition of the dominance of comedies was widespread among industry personnel, not least theater managers, and *La Cinématographie Française* commented on its survey of their views on 1932 releases to the effect that "light-hearted and inoffensive films hold top spot."[1] It is not surprising, therefore, that the discourse of "popular vitality" promoting the hoodlum, the working-class "wise guy" with a dynamic personality and a boisterous comic edge, should have been so prominent in fan magazines of this period, nor that it should have been attached not just to René Lefèvre and Albert Préjean but also to comedians such as Bach, Rellys, and Milton. It was the only discourse to embrace such comic actors. Again, it was only in this early period—say, 1930 to 1933—that lists of popular stars focused primarily on young leading men and women who starred in romantic comedies—"Prince Charming" and "The Nicest Smile"—or that the ingénue discourse had any currency in fan magazines.

Even then, as we have seen, audience interest in young romantic stars was ambivalent, but it is incontrovertible that older men with a more somber and substantial persona came to the fore from 1935 on, as the preference for social and psychological dramas began to become apparent.

Thereafter, Fernandel was the only comic actor to feature among the twenty most popular stars, though Bach made a final appearance in twentieth place in 1936. The associated discourse of maturity that circulated in fan magazines promoted men of authority, father figures who bore the weight of the world on their shoulders. From 1933 on, these masculine personae were required in films of the day either to uphold and extend French social, cultural, and spiritual authority in military and, occasionally, religious roles or to embody a higher moral authority that contested the values and attitudes currently prevailing in society on behalf of some marginalized group. Or, at least, their ability so to do was postulated and questioned. National films, military films, and particularly spy films began to figure prominently in annual box-office statistics, and the seductive foreign vamp or her sensual French counterpart became a recognized *emploi*; as well, the outsider figure, most memorably embodied in Gabin, came to the fore. Boulevard comedies, with their casts consisting of the upper bourgeoisie and its camp followers involved in farcical narratives and superficial problems, lost their appeal, giving way to questions of guilt and expiation.

These diverse trends do not lend themselves easily to summary, but it is true to say that the main nodes of the textual web and the main connections between them are much more characteristic of the second half of the decade. Undoubtedly, most of them can be traced back to the first half of the decade, if not always in a clearly identifiable form. There, however, they do not constitute the bulk of the strands of the web, nor even the most prominent strands. It is more accurate to see the French cinema of the early sound years as primarily working with myths and stereotypes inherited from previous decades and preexisting media, while "coasting" on the novelty of the new sound technology and assuming (wrongly as it turned out) that this strategy would be sufficient to ensure box-office profitability.

It is hard to avoid a correlation between the economic ebullience of the early sound cinema, the prominence of comic successes, and the widespread assumption that France had been spared and would continue, miraculously, to be spared the effects of the depression. This optimism was, of course, to be proved wrong by the downturn of 1933–34. After this point, the elements of the web related to the mythic identities outlined above better answered the needs of audiences, and adventitious matter tended to fall away. This explanation would relate the web described above most specifically to the effects of the depression, while recognizing that most of its elements had been present in one form or another in the first half of the decade, and even earlier. At first sight, it would seem that a cinema deriving its principal constituent elements from a social crisis that struck most other European countries at approximately the same time was not going to be wildly unlike the cinema of those other countries. What is surprising is that the web as it developed in France did arguably contain certain strands that were peculiar to France alone. The section of the web related to what is now called "poetic realism" was one such. It was, however, only one small section of a larger thematic cluster relating to powerful masculine figures, unequal gender relations, dysfunctional families, and disturbed sexual patterns, which cumulatively constitute a distinctive core peculiar to the French cinema of this decade. To this block can be added the intense focus on art, the artist, and the actor/actress, which seems to me to be carried further here than in other national cinemas.

One final way to get at the characteristic patterns of the thirties is to isolate those few elements of the web which were considered characteristic of contemporary life, distinguishing it from the past and foreshadowing the future. The films sometimes help us in this task by themselves reflecting on the contemporaneity of certain textual elements. As has already been mentioned, technology and technicians are clearly represented in them as "newly mythic." From the lowest to the highest, anyone associated with technology is endowed with an aura. The taxi driver or mechanic, the race-car driver, the engineer, and the aviator are all felt to be, in their different ways and to different degrees, contemporary heroes. Indeed, the engineer (and sometimes the doctor, though not the scientist) speaks of a society newly confident of its ability to transform the physical world, as it was so clearly unconfident of its ability to transform the social world. In the cultural arena, the equivalent "contemporary" occupations are jazz musician and bandleader, two roles that are already beginning to displace the established roles of street singer and realist singer. Negroes are beginning to make their presence felt on the cultural scene, and after the war they and the big bands were to dominate the popular musical scene. Films of the late thirties clearly indicate that a new spirit is abroad related to the lifestyle of the young and of students, and that this lifestyle revolved around music. The films of the next decade would confirm this trend.

Partaking of both technological advances and contemporary cultural popularity, the cinema itself constitutes one of the "progressive" elements of the thirties mythology, and anyone associated with it—but particularly the star—is assured of a place in the forefront of the age. *La Boutique aux illusions* (39s3) is already reflecting on the importance of cinema in a modern mythology. This technological prominence of the media extended to the radio and to television, which figure in several aggressively contemporary narratives, and to all forms of advertising, which repeatedly appear in critiques or parodies of modern life.

For the most part, however, the decade's films were too preoccupied with the problems facing them in the present to reflect on the forms that "progress" might be taking at that time, and too preoccupied with the possibility of war to look to the future with anything but apprehension. The world was closing in around the "little people" of Europe, and the only categories of peculiarly contemporary people who attract admiration are those who seem to escape the prison walls—notably the reporters, whose job may take them to the most exotic regions of the world, and the aviators, whose freedom to escape the earthbound problems of contemporary society attracted unreserved envy. When Noël-Noël wins a plane it is the archetypal updating of the lottery win, which even his boss envies.

Indeed, as we saw at the beginning, an aviator made the perfect romantic hero for Renoir's last prewar film, though to kill him off at the end was certainly an unusual move. Apart from this move, however, and in the same way that the opening of *La Règle du jeu* can be shown to draw on a number of elements from the repertoire made available by the textual web of the cinema and of adjacent media, so the final scenes can be shown to do the same. A brief reference to those final scenes will serve to round off the indications given so far of the ways in which this film draws on the thirties macrotext. The following points are by no means exhaustive:

1. The mechanism used to trigger the tragic denouement, **the exchange of clothing which leads to a case of mistaken identity**, was, as we have seen, a commonplace of the day, and indeed has a long history. It is mobilized twice here—first, Lisette lends her cloak to Christine, which leads Schumacher to believe that he is seeing Octave embracing his wife; second, Octave, in an impulsive gesture, lends his overcoat to Jurieux, leading Schumacher to believe that he is seeing Octave returning to the scene of his "crime," when in fact it is Jurieux. In sum, Schumacher successively mistakes Christine for Lisette and Jurieux for Octave, with deadly consequences. As we saw in chapter 1, the well-known "borrowed plumage" narrative which leads to mistaken identity was a stock in trade of scriptwriters of the thirties, though it was usually introduced in order to foreground a class theme or to associate the wealthy with the criminal underclass. Often the mistake in identity was made more understandable by basing it on a widely recognized uniform. The equivalent effect is achieved in Renoir's film by having Schumacher's purchase of the cloak for Lisette and her rejection of it foregrounded in an earlier scene.

2. Nevertheless, although the killing of Jurieux is the result of a mistaken identity, the film represents it as **the working out of a predestined pattern**. Some of the mechanisms by which 1930s films represented (or, rather, constructed) this sense of destiny were also noted in chapter 1. Common among them were premonitions and metaphorical foreshadowings of the sort used in *La Règle du jeu*. Fortune-tellers, sorcerers, destiny figures, or simple apprehensions might all serve to predict the outcome of the narrative, as here more overtly the dance of death and the slaughter of the rabbits serve to introduce audience expectations of

a violent end. Indeed, given that Jurieux is early established as the chief "rabbit" in the film, unable or unwilling to control his animal passions, it is far from the case that his death is due to mistaken identity—he was destiny's intended victim from the start, and Schumacher the game-keeper was his intended executioner. This too was a commonplace of the period—for the "unforeseeable eventuality" to prove, on reflection, to have been extraordinarily appropriate.

3. At a more trivial level, even the phrase "**a deplorable accident**" by which the marquis attempts to gloss over the tragedy might have been recognized by audiences of the day as a typically understated and ironic response to events of this nature. In *Les Disparus de Saint-Agil* (38.25), for instance, when Lemel accuses Walter of being a spy and a brawl erupts, the lights fail and Lemel tumbles from the balcony to his death. "A terrible accident" is the official pronouncement, though it is clearly far from accidental. A similar phrase occurs at the end of *Le Dernier Tournant* (39.23) as the protagonist fantasizes about a reconciliation in the afterlife with his mistress, for whose death he is responsible—he'll take her in his arms and explain that it was "all just an accident," and she'll believe him. In the war years, the same sort of reaction was to turn up in *Lumière d'été*, in which the lord of the manor and his mistress reminisce about "the tragic hunting accident" that conveniently disposed of his first wife, and in *Un Seul Amour*, where the vengeful husband who has bricked up his wife's lover in a wardrobe and left him to die goes off hunting and, unable to live with the knowledge of his wife's and his own actions, dies in what is reported as "a terrible accident." Filmic murders and suicides were regularly presented in such euphemistic terms within the textual world, in the expectation that spectators would see through the hypocrisy. This is a minor point, but it makes clear that, in little as in big things, a recognizable stock of situations, events, gestures, and phrases found its way into scenario after scenario.

4. Finally, placing the film once again in the context of its day can help us to understand the reception that awaited it at the box office. Essentially, the ending involves the tragic death of a principal character occurring immediately after a hilariously riotous and even farcical chase through the chateau, in which Schumacher flourishes his hunting gun and looses shots at all and sundry, and in which more or less guilty adulterers take shelter wherever they can find it, including under fat ladies' skirts; meanwhile, a deliberately amateurish series of theatrical performances, at once humorous and intensely ominous, provides entertainment for the guests and for us. The **contrast in tone** evident in this description of the final scenes, which is indeed characteristic of the film as a whole, has often been blamed for the film's (purely relative) lack of success. The mechanism noted above as at the origin of the narrative denouement—

an exchange of clothing leading to mistaken identity—was far more typical of farce than of tragedy, and retains a certain tonal ambivalence in this film. Neither clearly drama nor clearly comedy, the film is best categorized as a comédie dramatique, and these were not nearly as common in the thirties as they were to be in the forties and fifties, nor were they anywhere near as successful at the box office as they were later to be. Pagnol was the only director consistently to produce plays and films that could be classified thus and that were popular with audiences of the day. In *Marius* (31.81), he even managed to achieve this while providing an anti-romantic ending, though there was no death involved. By far the greater number of his films end on the humane, wry, and gentle note more typical of the genre. Attempts to end a comédie dramatique in an anti-romantic way, or a fortiori in a grim way, were usually unsuccessful even when undertaken by skilled scriptwriters and directors. *L'Homme à l'Hispano* (33.65) is a case in point.

Replacing *La Règle du jeu* in the context of the textual web from which so many (indeed, arguably all) of its elements were drawn can thus serve to extend our understanding of both its construction and its reception. In combination with an awareness of the social and industrial context within which it arose, such an understanding can lead to an appreciation of the reasons why that particular arrangement of textual elements might have originated then and there, and been acceptable or not to the "gatekeepers" who determined whether it would be made and screened or not, and been enjoyable or not to the spectators who saw it. If this sort of conclusion is possible in the case of such a film as *La Règle du jeu,* it will certainly be possible in the case of any other and lesser film we might care to analyze.

A VIEWER'S GUIDE

The two hundred films listed here are all available commercially or through film institutes. They have been listed alphabetically by year, and graded as follows:

1 = Watchable only by the committed
3 = Watchable
5 = Good
7 = Very good
9 = Excellent

The grade accorded each film appears in parentheses after the title. The number preceding each title refers to the film's position in the filmography.

1930

30.13 *Le Blanc et le noir* (2)
Learning that her husband is unfaithful, she swears to offer herself to the first comer. He is a Negro, but in the dark she doesn't notice! There is a baby, of course, which must hastily be swapped. A casually racist and trivial film from a Guitry play.

30.18 *Chacun sa chance* (4)
A musical in which Gabin as a shop-window dresser swaps roles with a baron, with "amusing" consequences.

30.21 *Le Chemin du paradis* (4)
An early musical comedy that established Garat and Harvey as the leading romantic couple of the early thirties. Mild satire of big business, perhaps with some influence from the Marx brothers.

30.59 *Le Mystère de la chambre jaune* (3)
An expressionist-influenced murder mystery solved by an ebullient reporter. The police inspector is in fact an international bandit (and the heroine's first husband) in disguise.

30.61 *L'Opéra de quat'sous* (3)
The Beggar's Opera. A Brechtian "presentation" of the rise and rise of a criminal, in cahoots with the chief of police, as a parody of capitalist enterprise. Negligible narrative drive and coherence. Notable for the revolt of the underclass—the army of the poor. Tableaux and songs.

30.66 *La Petite Lise* (5)
A melodrama concerning an honorable ex-prisoner who rescues his undeserving daughter and her man at the cost of returning to prison. The first fifteen-minute sequence set in Guyana is amazingly good (8/10), especially as far as sound is concerned.

30.69 *Prix de beauté* (7)
An at times powerful critique of the destructive effect of the press/beauty contests/stardom. The first half and the end have a fascinating soundtrack with some splendid documentary and montage segments. A magnificently ironic finale.

30.78 *Le Roi des resquilleurs* (6)
(1945 version viewed) Immensely popular in its year. A tale of an amiable working-class rogue out to con his way into money and the affection of attractive women. Mythic locations—horse racing, boxing matches, cycling, football, a beauty parlor, Montmartre and street singer, and so on.

30.79 *La Ronde des heures* (3)
(1949 version viewed) Poignant and very popular drama about a singer married "above his station" who is despised by his father-in-law, loses his voice and is unable to support the family, and so disappears to a job in a circus. There he makes good again, and finally recovers voice, wife, and daughter.

30.84 *Sous les toits de Paris* (6)
René Clair's first sound film, exploring sound/silence techniques. A cold and unsentimental play with myths of "the little people of Paris"—apaches, a blonde vamp, a street singer, mateship, casual sexuality.

1931

31.1 *À nous la liberté* (6)
An effective satire of capitalism as hard labor and bosses as greedy crooks, the deadening effect of clocks, routines, and assembly lines. Some wonderful moments, but a bit heavy-handed. Celebrates mateship and the open road, yet it is machines that finally free the mates to hit that road.

31.11 *Au nom de la loi* (7)
A grim, well-told realist crime story involving murder, drug smuggling, and a seductive female who is behind it all. Her line about criminality being

synonymous with adventure and freedom and about living for the moment wins over the young cop planted in her gang. The climax resembles the situation in *Le Jour se lève*.

31.18 *Baroud* (3)
French civilizing mission and inter-religious tension. A French soldier in Africa and his Arab mate, united in a struggle against rebellious Arab tribes but divided by the Frenchman's love for the Arab's sister.

31.34 *Cœur de Lilas* (7)
A moving murder mystery. A policeman goes on leave to investigate privately the murder of an industrialist, and gradually becomes involved with the chief suspect, only to have her confess her guilt at the end. His growing affection for her and her gradual realization of the new life opening up before her are well done. Songs by Fréhel, and by Gabin in an unusually unsympathetic role.

31.38 *Le Congrès s'amuse* (3)
A Garat–Harvey vehicle: a romantic costume drama involving a relationship between the czar and a serving wench, in which the demands of public life destroy a private idyll.

31.45 *Croix de bois* (9)
A very powerful reconstruction of trench warfare in World War I, organized around the experiences of a small group of enlisted men. Little narrative drive, just endurance; little sense of hatred, more of futility.

31.55 *Faubourg Montmartre* (4)
A blend of melodrama and social realism typical of the time. Paris, drugs, thugs, poverty, prostitution, the poor but honest shop-girl and her fallen sister, and their old dad from the provinces. Worth watching for an extraordinary peasant exorcism. Songs by Fréhel and Florelle.

31.68 *Il est charmant* (5)
A musical comedy with Garat as a feckless law student who turns the provincial law practice which his uncle buys him into a cross between a night-club and a brothel. Various ingenious (for the time) special effects.

31.74 *Ma cousine de Varsovie* (4)
Typical boulevard comedy. Country house, nonchalant adultery, everyone trying to deceive and cuckold everyone else; entries and exits, concealments and revelations. Popescu in one of her better roles as the Polish cousin who stirs the pot.

31.77 *Mam'zelle Nitouche* (5)
A vaudeville in which everyone seems to have two identities—a daytime one in the convent and a nighttime one in the nightclub. This, together

with a dashing lieutenant and a plot that requires everyone including the heroine to disguise themselves as soldiers in his regiment, makes for good fun.

31.81 *Marius* (8)
The first installment in Pagnol's trilogy involving Marius, his "typically Provençal" father César, and Fanny, to whom Marius is engaged. But Marius dreams of the South Seas and of adventure. . . . Wonderfully constructed meridional characters, with quaint charm, volatility, and an amiable indolence.

31.84 *Le Million* (5)
The little people of Paris, a lottery win, a lost ticket, a balletic chase, a night at the opera. Trivial material, well orchestrated.

31.97 *Paris-Béguin* (2)
Mixture of musical (rehearsal and staging of a production) and low-life/gangster genres. Gabin, as a seductive thug, is shot and dies in the star's arms, but she goes on stage and sings her little heart out. Hokum.

31.98 *Paris-Méditerranée* (5)
Romantic musical comedy involving mistaken identities, in which a salesgirl accidentally comes to travel to the Riviera with an English lord, with predictable consequences. A good role for Arabella.

31.107 *Pour un sou d'amour* (5)
An odd mixture of melodrama and romantic comedy, in which a millionaire swaps roles with his secretary in a search for true affection. Visually and technically interesting, with music/songs that have structural significance. Grotesque African flashbacks!

31.118 *Le Rosier de Madame Husson* (2)
Clumsy filmmaking, and awful acting from Fernandel, but worth seeing for its notoriety. It satirized provincial authorities, moral and otherwise, and was widely banned. It's hard to see why, now, given what other films got away with.

31.134 *Tumultes* (6)
A low-life drama focusing on an ex-con played by Boyer. Released from prison, he reasserts himself in the milieu, but is betrayed by his girl (and his mate!).

31.135 *Un chien qui rapporte* (1)
An amazingly discontinuous one-joke film about a dog trained to jump into rich men's cars. Grossly over-acted, but with a few technically interesting sequences.

31.146   *Vampyr* (4)
Expressionist film with perfunctory sound and painfully detailed generic motifs and themes. The effect is not so much sinister as slightly grotesque.

1932

32s1   *L'Affaire est dans le sac* (2)
A clumsy attempt at Marx Brothers humor and at surrealist atmosphere. An incompetent student-prank film that has been retrospectively (over)mythologized.

32.12   *L'Atlantide* (6)
A fantasy about a lost civilization in the desert ("Atlantis") ruled over by a fascinating but ruthless goddess/queen, who destroys all men lured to her domain. Of two French explorers, one resists out of fidelity to his mate; the other cedes and, in a drug-induced madness, kills his mate.

32.25   *Boudu sauvé des eaux* (7)
A hilarious performance from Michel Simon as a tramp who is rescued from drowning by a bourgeois book-seller and proceeds to seduce both his maid and his wife, and dismantle the respectable facade of the household. Momentarily tempted by respectability, he finally returns to the open road.

32.33   *Le Chien jaune* (4)
A standard Simenon/Maigret crime story, efficiently told. Brittany, drug smuggling, and a seedy Le Vigan.

32.24   *Chotard et Cie* (7)
An entertaining tale of a bourgeois family's scorn for their poet son-in-law, and his ultimate triumph over and reconciliation with them. Typically fascinating camera work, sound bridges, depth of field, optical effects— Renoir having fun.

32.50   *Les Deux Orphelines* (2)
A classic maudlin melodrama about piteous defenseless orphan girls, one of them blind, abandoned in a big city, prey to fiendish exploiters of female flesh. Slums, mistaken identities, coincidences, an illegitimate child, madness.

32.58   *Fanny* (7)
The second panel of Pagnol's trilogy. A family melodrama softened by comic meridional dialogues and by-play. A typical example of a comédie dramatique. Some impressive documentary filming in Marseille.

32.59   *Fantômas* (3)
An episode in Inspector Juve's endless quest to foil and capture the master criminal Fantômas. Gothic atmosphere and an attempt to evoke pervasive evil.

32.67   *Les Gaietés de l'escadron* (2)
A typical military vaudeville, episodic to the point of incoherence. Sides with the men to ridicule most officers. Clumsy efforts at comedy by Gabin, Fernandel, and Raimu.

32.97   *La Nuit du carrefour* (2)
Bleak version of Simenon crime story directed by Renoir. Often incomprehensible, but creating a certain atmosphere—night, misty drizzle, dreary flat terrain.

32.109   *Poil de Carotte* (7)
A young boy's experience of growing up in a dysfunctional family, with a malevolent mother and a withdrawn, apparently indifferent father. Moments of idyllic happiness, moments of (special effects) terror, final understanding with father.

32.116   *Quatorze juillet* (8)
An extraordinary experiment in narrative technique. A sardonic look at the "little people" of Paris over twenty-four hours, held together by the patterning of objects—hats, wallets, coats, umbrellas, taxis, flowers, and people treated as objects. As usual with Clair, a fascinating soundtrack.

32.130   *Stupéfiants* (3)
Peter Lorre as a sinister drug dealer in a drug-smuggling racket run by big business. The trail leads from the theater world to Portugal and South America.

32.134   *Topaze* (6)
An unworldly schoolteacher, used as a front by a crooked financier and set up to take the rap, ends up turning the tables. A wonderful role for Jouvet.

1933

33.1   *L'Abbé Constantin* (3)
A romantic comedy in which an amiable village curate and his godson get involved in a struggle between a local countess and two American women for control of the local chateau.

33.12   *Les Aventures du roi Pausole* (2)
Intended as an amiable erotic comedy, but put together too incompetently to be either erotic or comic.

33.23   *Ces messieurs de la Santé* (7)
A fascinatingly ambivalent film, at once distrusting businessmen as confidence tricksters and yet expressing a guilty delight in the machinations of one of them. The vacuous poor need money-making machines like him to take their money and multiply it, no holds barred. A great comic role for Raimu.

33.26 *Cette vieille canaille* (7)
Harry Baur as a respectable doctor who becomes involved with a fairground girl, whom, Pygmalion-like, he sets about "educating." At times almost her suitor, he is at times almost her jailer. She "escapes" with a circus performer, whom the doctor is required to operate upon in a well-calculated finale. An unusually subtle and complex relationship. A three-minute montage sequence in the middle.

33.41 *Dans les rues* (4)
A realist "street" film—slums, a poor family, a good and a bad brother, thugs, thieves, and a gang fight. Respectability is mocked, but family affection and an honest job ultimately win out over the lure of the street and of quick money.

33.59 *Le Gendre de Monsieur Poirier* (4)
Pagnol's filmed version of his comedy about a nouveau riche who marries his daughter to a ne'er-do-well aristocrat. The son-in-law finally comes to appreciate the daughter's simple goodness, and he reforms.

33.62 *Le Grand Jeu* (8)
Feyder's famous foreign legion film turning on an ambiguity about the identity of the wan young woman whom he finds in the North African garrison town. She has amnesia and has lost her past, but he too is anxious to recapture his past through her.

33.65 *L'Homme à l'Hispano* (5)
Begins as a bouncy romantic comedy—appearing rich and suave in a borrowed car, the impoverished Georges lives out a brief romance with a titled Englishwoman, until his deceit catches up with him and tragedy supervenes. An extraordinary virtuoso technical sequence in the middle.

33s5 *Jofroi* (6)
Pagnol's short film about a peasant who sells his orchard but can't stand the idea of the buyer cutting down "his" trees. Comic attempts to do away with himself in more and more exotic ways, to bring pressure on the new owner.

33.76 *Liebelei* (3)
A banal costume drama about an officer who is a bit of a rake with the girls, and who is called to account just when he has found true love. Vienna, military settings, the aristocracy, balls, duels, points of honor, noble gestures.

33.80 *Le Maître de forges* (7)
A fine film, though the subject can seem dated—a nouveau-riche entrepreneur and his stolid devotion to an aristocratic young woman, who finally comes to appreciate his qualities. Interesting technical effects, superimpositions, and montages.

33.92   Les Misérables (6)
Well-told transcription of Hugo's melodrama about the rehabilitation of a former convict.

33.114   La Rue sans nom (6)
A street film that doesn't try to aestheticize the squalor—slums, raw poverty, desperation, violence, and nastiness, with typical melodramatic plot incidents. The arrival of an old mate and fellow criminal with his attractive daughter evokes a past better suppressed, but ultimately mateship proves stronger than poverty, lust, selfishness, and so on.

33.124   Théodore et Cie (7)
An enjoyable and very popular comedy involving working-class mates on the make, conning a wealthy uncle and his wife's lover out of vast amounts of money by means of various deceits and disguises.

33.134   Le Tunnel (4)
(English version viewed) Science fiction. Having built the Channel Tunnel in 1940, our hero, an engineer, is funded to build a transatlantic tunnel. His trials, both technical and financial, but also of course sentimental, and his ultimate success.

1934

34.1   Angèle (7)
Pagnol's Provençal melodrama of seduction, illegitimacy, sequestration, and reconciliation. Good acting, even from Fernandel, and much location work.

34.9   L'Atalante (5)
A routine story of a newly married canal-boat master, his young wife tempted by the bright lights, and their final reconciliation. Saved by some wonderfully surreal images and Michel Simon's baroque persona.

34.17   Le Bossu (2)
A stagy costume drama: an evil prince assassinates an aristocrat to marry his widow, and a hero who swears to avenge the foul deed and save the aristocrat's daughter. Returning seventeen years later disguised as a hunchback, he rights all wrongs and marries the daughter.

34.30   Le Comte Obligado (4)
An elevator attendant inherits, and decides to blow it all in three days of high life. He becomes a "count," with much opportunity for (rather crass) class satire. One of Milton's surviving comedies, with a standard morality play about the heart and sincerity being more important than money or position.

34.31   *La Crise est finie* (6)
The joys and disappointments of stage life. Provincials mount a show in Paris that single-handedly banishes the gloom of the depression. Narrative drive and technical competence.

34. 34   *Dédé* (5)
A musical comedy in which Dédé and his mate, an indolent millionaire, con a bourgeois and seduce his wife. The film purveys a bland optimism— "Dans la vie, faut pas s'en faire."

34.35   *Le Dernier Milliardaire* (4)
A quaint fantasy set in Casinario/Monte Carlo. The princess, her suitor the banker (called Banco), who alone can save Casinario's economy, and the orchestra conductor she really loves. This film's failure at the box office prompted Clair to leave France.

34.47   *Hôtel du Libre Échange* (4)
A Feydeau farce about the discontents and dissatisfactions of respectable married life. Attempts to realize libidinous desires, entries and exits, deceits and revelations, mistaken identity. All make fools of themselves in one way or another.

34.52   *Jeunesse* (4)
A street film: an abandoned girl, an unwanted pregnancy, an attempted suicide. Various young men try unsuccessfully to tempt her into narratives of desire. A curiously glum and inconsequential film, with no point of identification, yet impressive as a downbeat, unheroic look at "today's youth."

34.53   *Justin de Marseille* (5)
A tough gang boss in Marseille, a criminal and enforcer but with a sense of honor and responsibility, and loved by the people. Similar in some respects to Pepe le Moko, but Justin has an understanding with the police.

34.54   *Lac aux Dames* (5)
Rohmeresque character drama set in a spa resort. An impoverished swimming instructor and his involvement with a number of women, notably Puck (Simone Simon), an elfin creature in complicity with nature.

34.55   *Liliom* (3)
Charles Boyer as a charismatic brute loved by a pallid but good girl. Killed in a failed hold-up, he is given a second chance on earth by the heavenly bureaucracy in order to see his girl and their child. Grotesque heavenly sequences.

34.70   *Les Nuits moscovites* (6)
Well-told "Russian" drama, with soldiers, honor, spies, gambling debts, and noble gestures of renunciation. Harry Baur has the best role as a massively

forbidding merchant, rival of the hero. Some montages of war documents, and fine sets.

34.76 *Pension Mimosas* (5)
On the margins of the gambling industry, a passionate relationship between a godmother and her ne'er-do-well "son." Slow at first (and the copy viewed was not very good until halfway through), but obsessive toward the end.

34.92 *Sans famille* (3)
A genuine melodrama: an English aristocrat's baby son is stolen and abducted to France. Brought up in poverty, he escapes with a troupe of traveling players. Pickpockets, inheritances, and slow poison, and finally a family reunited.

34.97 *Si j'étais le patron* (6)
A comedy/fantasy in which the French car industry is saved by an inventive worker, an eccentric investor, and the mateship of the employees, who take over the firm and introduce a more labor-friendly environment.

34.115 *Zouzou* (4)
A fairground: Gabin and Josephine Baker as white brother and adopted black sister. She loves him, but he follows the call of the sea and finally prefers her friend. But she makes good on the stage, and sings on through her tears. The last thirty minutes are taken up mostly by the show she sings in.

1935

35.1 *Adémaï au moyen âge* (1)
Clumsy and slack comedy set in the Middle Ages (the war between the French and the English), intended to capitalize on Noël-Noël's success as Adémaï in a previous film. Desperate but unsuccessful attempts at humor.

35.5 *Baccara* (6)
A well-told "marriage of convenience" romantic comedy featuring a returned war hero (improbably played by Jules Berry) and a kept woman in danger of expulsion from France. In the trial scene, society itself is on trial, as is her protector, a corrupt banker.

35.6 *La Bandera* (6)
Gabin as a character forced to flee Paris and joining the Spanish foreign legion. A classic of the genre: hounded by a bounty hunter, he rehabilitates himself by the heroic defense of an outpost and dies "a worthy death."

35.12 *Le Bonheur* (7)
Boyer as an anarchist cartoonist who develops a love-hate relationship with a film star. Attempting to assassinate her because of the vacuous escapist optimism she peddles, he comes to love her, and she comes to incorporate the assassination into her next film. Finally he departs, and she is seen on

stage acting that departure. The sardonic anarchist is more appealing than the lover.

35.13 *Bonne Chance* (4)
Another gentle play on the idea of incest, as Guitry and Delubac set off on a trip as "brother and sister," then "father and daughter," but end up husband and wife. Gambling and a lottery win foreground the "luck" of the title.

35.20 *Cigalon* (4)
A slight Pagnol comedy about a (typically Provençal) master chef so refined that he can never bring himself actually to prepare a meal for anyone, but is outraged when a rival establishment opens in "his" village.

35.27 *Le Crime de Monsieur Lange* (9)
One of the greatest of films. Renoir's splendid Popular Front tale of a corrupt publishing house taken over by the workers, who succeed with the help of Lange the dreamer and his Arizona Jim fantasies.

35.28 *Crime et châtiment* (5)
A reasonable attempt at transcribing the Dostoevsky novel in which Raskolnikov plays cat and mouse with the judge and with God, and is finally saved by the love of a good woman.

35.42 *L'Équipage* (7)
Aerial warfare: the young pilot discovers, to his horror, that the woman he loves is in fact his admired squadron leader's wife. "But your husband and I are more than brothers, we're a team!" The only solution, of course, is death. Mythologization of war, of proving oneself a man, of the aviator figure, and of male camaraderie.

35.43 *Escale* (3)
A wily smuggler and an honorable merchant-marine lieutenant vie for Eva's favors, the latter not realizing her murky involvement with the former. Idyll and tragedy. A curiously dated film.

35.52 *Le Golem* (2)
Straight from the German expressionist tradition, a tale of the Jewish ghetto in Prague and a clay monster infused with life by the rabbi's secret rituals, which ultimately breaks loose to destroy their persecutors.

35.53 *Golgotha* (3)
Duvivier's heavy-handed retelling of the Christ story, with Le Vigan as Christ (!) and Gabin as Pontius Pilate (!).

35.62 *Jim la Houlette* (4)
A Fernandel comedy in which he plays a novelist's secretary but is in fact the author of the romances, which are aimed at his boss's wife. He is in-

duced to write a crime story about the bandit Jim la Houlette, whereupon the real Jim appears. Great ideas, but weak implementation.

35.67   *La Kermesse héroïque* (3)
Slow and painfully unfunny tale of cowardly greedy Dutch burghers and their more generous wives, who deal very effectively with their Spanish ruler and his army. Splendid sets, and immensely popular in its day, but vastly overrated.

35.92   *Princesse Tam-Tam* (4)
Josephine Baker as a lowly North African shepherdess full of vitality. She is taken up by a novelist and presented in France as a princess. Orientalism and Pygmalion scenes. Much of the film turns out to have been the novel he was writing about her. A great final scene.

35.93   *Quelle drôle de gosse* (7)
Screwball comedy, fast-paced, with Darrieux in a Katherine Hepburn role as an outrageous female. "You're exploiting the fact that I'm just a feeble woman" is, in context, a hilarious line.

35.98   *La Rosière des Halles* (4)
A country girl comes to town as cook for a playwright who is having trouble getting the feel for the way the "people" talk. She and her market mates unwittingly provide the necessary inspiration. A mildly amusing play on art and life.

35.109   *La Tendre Ennemie* (6)
Ghosts of three people involved in a girl's past offer a delightfully distancing commentary on and intervention in her sentimental affairs. Flashbacks, multiple narrators, drifting transitions, and a nicely structured finale.

35.110   *Toni* (7)
A wonderful documentary quality to this tale of passion, jealousy, and murder among immigrant workers in the south of France.

35.117   *Un soir de bombe* (7)
A very amusing comedy in which a banker under pressure absconds and is replaced by his double, a tramp suffering from amnesia. Larquey is good in the double role, being clapped in the loony bin as a banker and hitting the road again with his mate as a tramp.

1936

36s1   *Une partie de campagne* (9)
A wonderfully evocative fragment of a never-completed film. The possibilities opened up by a day in the country are stifled by bourgeois marriage, leaving unspoken regrets.

36s2   *La Vie est à nous* (9)
A bewilderingly inventive film using an astonishing range of techniques (many taken up later by Godard) to promote the Communist Party and ridicule the fascists. Absolutely brilliant.

36.7   *L'Appel du silence* (7)
A mythologized biography of Charles de Foucauld, soldier and missionary, fascinated by the solitude and the silence of the African desert. France's civilizing mission.

36.11   *Au son des guitares* (5)
A Tino Rossi musical based in Corsica: tempted away by the wiles of a woman, he can be happy only when he returns. The best sequence is when he joins tramps under the bridges of Paris. Unlike some French singers, this lad had a voice.

36.13   *Aventure à Paris* (4)
Jules Berry as an impoverished but bumptious con man preying on a biscuit manufacturer. Trivial but watchable, with a nice mockery of advertising at one point.

36.15   *Les Bas-Fonds* (3)
Renoir's very popular transposition to France of the Gorky novel. A confused narrative and stagy sets, but some nice moments, including the final images.

36.17   *La Belle Équipe* (6)
A famous Popular Front film, full of the motifs of working-class life. Worth seeing for that alone. Usually shown with the replacement happy ending.

36.21   *César* (6)
The last part of Pagnol's trilogy, in which Césariot finally gets to know and respect his father, and Marius and Fanny finally get together.

36.27   *Le Coupable* (5)
A melodrama about a man torn between his family's legal traditions and his own love of music, finally called on to pass judgment, unawares, on his own illegitimate son.

36.42   *Faisons un rêve* (3)
A classic boulevard comedy and a trivial vehicle for a self-satisfied Guitry. A recorded play.

36.54   *L'Homme de nulle part* (7)
Pirandello's splendid story of a man who escapes a bleak family situation when he is believed dead. He constructs a second identity and relationship, despite the threatened return of the old one. A satire on greed, self-interest, and calculation.

36.62   *Jenny* (5)
Jenny runs a nightclub/casino, which is going downhill because she's obsessed by young Lucien, but Lucien falls for her prudish daughter, who is shocked to discover the details of her mother's life. Carné's first film, therefore worth seeing.

36.69   *Mademoiselle Docteur,* or *Salonique, nid d'espions* (4)
A daring German female spy, an atmosphere of intrigue, confusion, and deception; she is, of course, torn between her duty to her country and her love for a French counterspy.

36.75   *Marinella* (5)
A Tino Rossi musical organized around the opening of a nightclub and the star's love for the director's humble secretary, who turns out to be the notorious "masked singer." As usual, the choreography is awful.

36.77   *Mayerling* (6)
The emperor disapproves of his son, Archduke Rudolph, who mixes incognito with the hoi polloi, has reprehensibly democratic ideas, and is dallying with the "unworthy" Marie. A tragic end. High production values.

36.78   *Ménilmontant* (6)
Slum kids and the building of a facility for them. Class enmity is represented as primordial—the rich are selfish and inhumane, and the authorities pompous and overbearing.

36.80   *Messieurs les Ronds de Cuir* (5)
This surprisingly effective "farce" opposes civil servants and red tape to a riotous night life and the Folies-Bergère. Typical episodic vaudeville structure.

36.83   *Mon père avait raison* (4)
Guitry boulevard comedy. Misogyny and unhappy families. One is always basically alone, except for male friends. Yet, the tentative and rather hypocritical moral conclusion proposes the need to break the cycle of mistrust between male and female.

36.85   *Le Mort en fuite* (3)
Two disconsolate actors (Berry and Simon) conceive a kidnapping plan to promote themselves, but nobody notices. A strained and somewhat vacuous comedy.

36.91   *Le Nouveau Testament* (4)
Another Guitry comedy with an interesting but tenuous plot, witty (or "witty") dialogue, much flirtation and adultery, and a condescending role for the master. The implications of incest are even more overt than usual.

36.95   *Paris* (1)
Cross-class love story—the characters are trivial and the situations sentimentalized. A cliché-ridden tourist's view of Paris.

36.99   *Pepe le Moko* (8)
The Kasbah as both refuge and trap for rough diamond Pepe; his dreams of Paris, his betrayal by Gaby, the steamer that sails without him, the grill, the cops, the suicide. Essential viewing.

36.112   *Rigolboche* (3)
Mistinguett, on the run from a supposed crime in Dakar, makes good in the nightclubs of Paris. A cliché-ridden plot and a slack copy of American choreography.

36.115   *Le Roman d'un tricheur* (9)
Guitry's one uncontestable cinematic masterpiece. A splendidly picaresque tale with sardonic commentary. A wonderfully immoral tale.

36.121   *Sept hommes . . . une femme* (5)
A surprisingly amusing boulevard comedy in which an attractive widow tests her seven suitors. The central section in particular has a number of close similarities with *La Règle du jeu*.

36.123   *Sous les yeux d'Occident* (4)
A "Russian" tale of a student caught up in political events that don't really interest him; he betrays revolutionary friends, yet is thought a hero by them. Much anguish and the usual implacable fatality.

36.127   *La Terre qui meurt* (3)
An early color film about "the land," tradition and ritual versus the city and its real, if qualified, opportunities. The country is in hock to the city and its vulture-like lawyers, but it can still be productive in the hands of someone who loves it.

36.135   *Un grand amour de Beethoven* (1)
Pretentious nonsense from Gance about the grandeur and tragedy of artistic genius; but at least there is some good music in this one. Stilted acting, poor continuity, all done in tableaux and grandiloquent gestures. Unintentionally comic.

36.136   *Un mauvais garçon* (5)
A young female law student, too independent for her own good, is brought into line by her family when she is conned into falling for the man they had chosen for her in the guise of a criminal she has to defend. Darrieux here replaces Lilian Harvey opposite Garat in an amusing, if anti-feminist, romantic comedy.

1937

37.2   *Abus de confiance* (6)
Guilt toward the young: a penniless law student cons a worthy middle-class family into believing she is their long-lost daughter, and in her first legal cases finds herself pleading for other young people in her situation. Vanel is excellent, as usual.

37.3   *L'Affaire du courier de Lyon* (2)
An atrocious costume drama and eighteenth-century crime story based on doubles, coincidences, and mistaken identity. But some fine landscapes.

37.6   *L'Alibi* (7)
A "fantastic" murder mystery, in which von Stroheim plays a sinister criminal cum fairground magician and man of many disguises. Bizarre sets and weird relationships.

37.11   *Arsène Lupin, detective* (3)
A clumsy comedy and knowing pastiche, as the notorious gentleman crook sets up a detective agency run by his gang as a front for his next master stroke.

37.22   *Chéri-Bibi* (7)
The tough but basically decent criminal, exiled to a penal colony in Guyana: a grim life, despair, but camaraderie between the inmates. The love of a good woman, and an escape in which he dies; but his inherent nobility is acknowledged by the guards.

37.30   *La Dame de Malacca* (5)
The fascination of the exotic for an English girl caught in a loveless marriage in Malaya. Stuffy European conventions contrast with the excitement and sensuality, but also the dangers, of the Orient.

37.34   *Désiré* (6)
One of Guitry's better comedies, which sides with the servants in mocking and conning the usual upper-bourgeois family. An upstairs-downstairs plot is unusual in its use of dreams and of Freud to establish the butler's erotic relationship with the mistress.

37.37   *Drôle de drame* (7)
Very English goonish humor in a parody of a detective story, with police dressed as old ladies, Jouvet as a salacious bishop in a very becoming kilt, and Barrault as a crazed cyclist who kills butchers, and so on. Not terribly well received in its day, and a bit slow-paced, but it has become a cult classic.

37.40   *L'Étrange Monsieur Victor* (5)
M. Victor runs a business as a front for criminal activities. Barrault as an innocent man whom he has caused to be wrongfully imprisoned for seven

years, but who escapes and unmasks him. A typical example of the "facade of respectability" films which were so common.

37.42 *Fauteuil 47* (2)
A boulevard comedy focusing on an actress and her relations with various men, notably Paul, author of a mutist [*sic*] play. The usual casual adultery and marginally incestuous relationships.

37.48 *Forfaiture* (7)
The Orient as the dark Freudian underside of white society. Mongolia, the staunch European engineer with his development projects, and his wife led astray by curiosity and desire, and finally branded by the fierce and lustful prince.

37.53 *Les Gens du voyage* (6)
A circus story in which the resurgence of the past in the form of an escaped convict father complicates then resolves a romance between his son and the boss's daughter. Simmering sexuality and a fine climactic chase.

37.54 *La Grande Illusion* (7)
An immensely popular film playing on the notions of nation, race, and class during World War I. A rather slack narrative, but with some unforgettable moments, and ultimately a pacifist message.

37.55 *Gribouille* (5)
Michèle Morgan as an immigrant cleared of murder, and Raimu as one of the jurors instrumental in clearing her. He takes responsibility for her, but his family is disrupted by her disturbing presence. A fascinating set of ambivalent relationships.

37.57 *Gueule d'amour* (7)
Gabin and Balin, as lady-killer and heartless vamp, play another variation on male camaraderie and female sexuality, love and money, affection and calculation.

37.58 *L'Habit vert* (3)
A trivial farce mobilizing clichés about stuffy aristocracy, the extravagances of artists, the Folies-Bergère etc. Mildly amusing.

37.67 *Mademoiselle ma mère* (4)
A romantic comedy in which a bumptious young thing marries to escape parental pressure and falls for her husband's son. Obvious (and explicit) Oedipal implications.

37.69 *La Marseillaise* (3)
A curiously distanced and dispassionate version of the French revolution, made by Renoir on subscription. Disorganized storytelling, stagy sets and acting.

37.70   *Marthe Richard, au service de la France* (4)
A spy story set during World War I: simplistic nationalistic triumphalism, partially subverted by von Stroheim's powerful presence as the German commander who is the spy's lover; her betrayal of him, and his dignified suicide.

37.71   *Le Mensonge de Nina Petrovna* (5)
A tragic Russian tale of a high-class tart who comes to believe for a moment that she might be able to transcend the past through her relationship with young Franz who loves her, but who is finally forced to sacrifice her chance of happiness for his sake. Another very Oedipal story.

37.75   *Mollenard* (7)
A piratical merchant captain and arms smuggler, loved by his crew but stifled by hypocritical bureaucrats and crapulous company officials. And his wife. Weakened, he is "kidnapped" and humiliated by his wife, then re-kidnapped by his crew for a final voyage.

37.80   *Naples au baiser du feu* (5)
A musical drama of temptation, repentance and forgiveness. A singer is seduced by a mysterious young woman who compulsively fictionalizes her life in order to exercise power over every man. But male friendship and the homely girl win out.

37.87   *Orage* (5)
Michèle Morgan here softens the traditional representation of the femme fatale toward that mysterious but fascinating "other woman" with unplumbed potential for commitment whom she was often to play.

37.89   *Les Perles de la couronne* (1)
Slow, stagy tale tracing through the ages the events surrounding the pearls in the crown. Strained humor, self-satisfied commentary, reverence for tradition and position, together with total reliance on cliché and stereotype.

37.95   *Prison sans barreaux* (5)
A conflict of philosophy in the running of reform institutions (here, for adolescent girls): in one corner, a belief that wickedness is innate, requiring hierarchy and discipline, and in the other the enlightened new director who blames sociological factors and promotes compassion and understanding.

37.100   *Regain* (6)
A splendid Pagnol film about the rebirth of a dying village in Haute Provence. A mythic play with the notions of family, soil, plow, and grain, and a profound scorn for civil service and progress. Right-wing anarchism, but powerful.

37.103   *Sarati le terrible* (7)
Another film overtly fascinated by incest: Harry Baur as a tyrannical Algerian dock boss overly attracted by his niece Rose. She, alas, falls for a French

aristocrat who (incognito) is trying to redeem himself in the colonies. One genuinely erotic moment.

37.104 *Le Schpountz* (4)
Fernandel as a gullible provincial dreaming of movie stardom, and finally winning out over the snide mockery of the industry. The comedian as a cure for all the world's ills, and a nice satire on Paramount's European operations.

37.109 *Le Temps des cerises* (3)
An episodic narrative, with inter-titles, caricatures, and documents, devised as propaganda for the Communist Party's policies toward the aged. The working class as a group hero, iniquitously treated.

37.113 *La Tragédie impériale* (7)
Baur in a lovely role as Rasputin, presented as an outrageously vulgar Russian peasant version of Christ. The climax, where he is unsuccessfully assassinated again and again, is wonderful.

37.117 *Un carnet de bal* (7)
A quality production: a widow revisits dancing partners from a ball held in her youth, providing an opportunity for eight brief genre tales. Nostalgia for youthful aspirations, regret for lost illusions, age and its disappointments. Finally, the good son.

37.124 *Yoshiwara* (4)
A Japanese geisha, a Russian officer, a secret mission, spies and counterspies. High emotion, self-sacrifice, and a double death. One sequence uses anti-realistic cross-dissolves of painted backdrops and props that points forward to Ophüls's postwar films.

1938

38.2 *L'Accroche-Cœur* (4)
Guitry boulevard comedy with an atypical and very effective downbeat ending. A gentleman thief has a brief romance with a society woman, but his money runs out and he admits defeat.

38.4 *Alerte en Méditerranée* (3)
International collaboration between rival European navies staves off disaster when a pirate ship threatens the known world with a cloud of poison gas. Very popular in its time, though it now seems clumsy and incompetently narrated. The noble German captain gives his life to save French passengers.

38.12 *La Bête humaine* (8)
A great film right from the opening "documentary" railway images. Zola's story of a man doomed by his genetic inheritance to kill the woman he

desires. Gabin was never better, and Renoir himself appears in a small role. Immensely popular.

38.14   *Café de Paris* (3)
A murder mystery in which an eminently killable press baron is duly killed, and all suspects are revealed to have their darker side, which usually finds expression in the Café de Paris's private rooms.

38.16   *Carrefour* (8)
A fascinating tale of a wealthy bourgeois who has suffered amnesia in the war, and is obliged to explore his own past self to discover a possible criminal persona. Does it matter, if he has now redeemed himself? Vanel very fine again.

38.18   *La Chaleur du sein* (5)
Gilbert has a surfeit of mothers, and his father (Michel Simon) is intent on adding further to the collection; but all prefer the son to the husband. A comedy about the difficulties besetting "the modern family," ending with a reconciliation between father and son, which turns out to be what really matters after all.

38.25   *Les Disparus de St Agil* (6)
A murder mystery in a boy's school, with those elements of the fantastic and the bizarre for which Véry was renowned. The headmaster turns out to be the boss of a gang of relatively amiable forgers. Mildly reflexive, notably when discussing the relative political utility of Art and a box of matches.

38.27   *Le Drame de Shanghaï* (7)
A dense and rich evocation of Russian refugees caught up in Chinese politics and civil war, and a sympathetic portrait of a young communist party activist. Reminiscent of *La Condition humaine* in its ambition and in its political stance.

38.29   *Éducation de prince* (4)
A mildly amusing fantasy about the oil-rich country Sylvestrie, whose prince is being educated in democratic values and in gaiety by his French fellow students. Space for mild satire on royalty, business, and politics.

38.31   *Entrée des artistes* (4)
Drama students being educated into their high calling by Jouvet. Pretentious waffle about life and art, acting and truth; rather boring, but a surprise success with the public.

38. 32   *Ernest le rebelle* (2)
A grotesque tale in which Fernandel gets washed up penniless in the banana republic of Cucaracha and ends up leading a peasants' revolt. Incompetent storytelling.

38.34   *La Femme du boulanger* (7)

Pagnol's well-known Provençal community; the baker's young and sexy wife (and his inspiration) is seduced away by a shepherd, and he won't bake till she returns. Its charm depends on its quaint characters and its digressive narrative. More simmering sexuality.

38.37   *La Fin du jour* (4)

A desultory story about aging actors, their desperate dignity, and their self-delusions. Jouvet, Simon, and Francen, all poorly used. Myths of the actor, of art and life. A surprise success.

38.50   *Hôtel du Nord* (8)

A little community in a Paris rooming-house. Fine roles for Arletty and Jouvet, but a painful pair of young lovers. Orphans, immigrant refugees, and homosexuals are all treated sympathetically, as are all marginals who dream of a way out, or in. Carné and Jeanson (not Prévert) and classic set design.

38.52   *Je chante* (4)

Trénet in a musical about the rise of a young singer, whose verve and bonhomie saves the girls' hostel run by his uncle, which he then turns into a music school. Some good songs.

38.54   *Le Joueur d'échecs* (8)

A wonderful film set in the time of Polish revolt against Russian domination. The Baron's workshop for constructing automata is a delight, and the mechanized chess pieces which he constructs there serve multiple metaphoric purposes.

38.56   *Katia* (2)

The love affair between Czar Alexander and Katia Dolgorouki. A Russian period piece which like most of its kind involves a sentimental trivializing of history. If only they'd listened to Katia, the Russian Revolution need never have happened.

38.60   *La Maison du Maltais* (5)

An unusually interesting role for Dalio as a feckless North African poet cum smuggler involved in an interracial love affair which is doomed by poverty, parental malice, and fatal delays and misunderstandings.

38.63   *Métropolitain* (4)

An unusual and intriguing poetic realist film with Préjean and Ginette Leclerc in the lead roles of worker and vamp. As in *Le Jour se lève*, a crapulous stage magician slyly manipulates their lives. A nice circularity sees the initial staged murder repeated for real at the end.

38.64   *Mon curé chez les riches* (5)

A village priest who smokes, swears, sings, and extorts money for "his poor" is caught up in local politics when a nouveau riche tries to buy his way to power. The priest organizes a coalition against politicians and for France. Poor continuity and riddled with clichés.

38.66 *Monsieur Coccinelle* (8)
One of the great unknown films of the decade. Astonishingly inventive and constantly amusing tale of a bureaucrat whose dead aunt proves to be irrepressibly alive.

38.69 *Noix de coco* (3)
A boulevard comedy in which the respectable pater familias comes to realize that he had once had an affair with his own wife when she was a good-time girl in Saigon. More multiple adultery and quasi-incestuous relationships. Marie Bell in another double role.

38.83 *Prisons de femmes* (3)
A contorted narrative with tense changes and a diegetic novelist/narrator who investigates the social pressures that drive women into unsavory company. An oddly incompetent film, but worth viewing for its ambition.

38.84 *Quai des brumes* (9)
One of the greatest films of the decade. This Carné/Prévert world is a bleak foggy dockside which drives the deserter figure played by Gabin into impossible dreams of escape. To be on one's own is to be free, but first the spotty dog then Nelly undermine his independence. Typically weird roles for Michel Simon and Le Vigan.

38.85 *Raphaël le tatoué* (4)
Fernandel as a humble night-watchman who invents a dashing twin brother, Raphaël ("Je suis mon frère"), and gets to become him. A clumsy pastiche of motor racing, with futuristic cars.

38.87 *Remontons les Champs-Élysées* (1)
Guitry as a teacher instructing us in French history as seen from the conservative right. He gives himself all the best roles and lines. Painfully redundant, gross overacting, simpering anecdotes about royalty; but very popular in its day.

38.92 *La Route enchantée* (5)
A whimsical Trénet musical which strains after Marx Bros humor. A young singer dreams of then follows the enchanted road which leads to adventure, romance, and success, and to a chateau with ghosts, baroque sets, and a lovely daughter. Several of his best songs.

38.93 *La Rue sans joie* (4)
A well-worn combination of melodrama and squalid realism (poverty and female invulnerability) modulating into a murder mystery with Préjean as reporter/investigator bursting into court at the last moment with evidence

to save our heroine—and to condemn the social conditions which breed such injustice.

38.103 *Tricoche et Cacolet* (6)
A riotous farce in which a fine cast of actors runs through all the tricks of the trade—disguises, deceptions, manipulations. And songs. And all at a hectic pace.

38.107 *Trois Valses* (4)
A musical in three episodes opposing bourgeois rectitude and wealth to Bohemian gaiety through three generations. A quality production, gently reflexive.

38.109 *Un de la Canebière* (3)
A sentimental musical comedy about three Marseille fishermen who want to set up a sardine factory to impress their girlfriends, who in turn are pretending to be movie stars. The Aunt Clarisse sub-plot is reminiscent of Charley's aunt, and Rellys makes a wonderfully repugnant transvestite.

1939

39.2 *Battement de cœur* (6)
A very popular romantic comedy. Impoverished, and forced to choose between a reformatory, a pseudo-marriage, and a school for pickpockets, Arlette chooses the latter and is caught up in political maneuvers which lead to adoption by an aristocrat and a real marriage.

39.4 *Berlingot et Cie* (3)
A farce set in a fairground: two mates, a little girl they look after, a madman on the loose, and a crazy manager. Momentarily heroes for catching some thugs, the two mates nevertheless hit the road again at the end. A Fréhel song.

39.11 *Cavalcade d'amour* (4)
Three parallel tales in different ages, in which cross-class romances are thwarted twice and finally accepted. As usual, financiers have an image problem, but artists don't. A fairytale-like structure.

39.12 *La Charrette fantôme* (3)
Duvivier again explores timeless legends in an expressionist, or at least poetic, style. The Salvation Army officer and her quest to save the soul of David Holmes from the Grim Reaper in his insufficiently eerie chariot.

39.16 *Les Cinq Sous de Lavarède* (4)
Fernandel as a braggart who is trapped into a round-the-world race against the clock in order to gain a fortune. Jailed in New York, smuggled out of San Francisco in a coffin, a maharaja in a harem in Calcutta (etc.); and accidentally winning the Tour de France.

39.17   *Circonstances atténuantes* (7)
Michel Simon as a dried-up old judge stranded with his family in a dive where he and his wife are revitalized by the humanity and camaraderie of a class of people they would once have despised. They in their turn come to admire his criminal skills.

39.21   *De Mayerling à Sarajevo* (3)
The Austro-Hungarian empire and the Archduke Ferdinand, felt by his father to be too liberal in his leanings, not to mention too popular, and to have chosen unwisely in falling for Countess Chotek. Standard hokum. Several interesting series of cross-dissolves.

39.23   *Dernier Tournant* (6)
An effective telling of *The Postman Always Rings Twice:* the footloose vagabond, the naive husband and his sexy wife, the faked accidents and the real one; tension between independence and commitment.

39.25   *Derrière la façade* (4)
A typical Mirande script—an episodic narrative in which each of the suspects in a murder mystery is revealed, in his or her separate genre tale, to be hiding guilty secrets. A cynical view of society as corrupt from top to bottom. A compendium of genre conventions.

39.27   *Deuxième Bureau contre Kommandantur* (3)
A World War I spy story involving identical twins—a resistance leader and a man of the cloth. The triumphalist finale is undercut by the spectator's identification with the German investigating officer, whose merits even the French acknowledge.

39.33   *Entente cordiale* (5)
Rehearses the English–French political entente in the years 1898–1918 with an eye to the approach of World War II, but with a pacifist dedication. Incidental glorification of French culture, military feats, and values.

39s6   *L'Espoir* (4)
The Spanish civil war: internationalist allies struggle against Franco's superior forces, undertaking a mission to bomb a key bridge. Some striking images at the end. In Spanish.

39.37   *La Famille Duraton* (2)
A media producer on holiday discovers a "hilarious" provincial family who stand for the real France, and develops a radio program around them without their knowledge. It is, of course, very successful, revealing the French to be joyous, amusing, outspoken, and fundamentally likable.

39.39   *Fric-Frac* (5)
Fernandel as a gullible jeweler's assistant, caught up in and quite exhilarated by an amiable criminal plot to rob his boss. "There are no honest people;

everyone's a thief, we just do it openly." Again the discovery that humanity lies with the people, however criminal, especially when embodied in Michel Simon and Arletty.

39.45 *Ils étaient neuf célibataires* (2)
Labored play on the idea of foreigners in France anxious to marry absolutely anyone in order to get French citizenship, but the down-and-out bachelors exploited for this purpose revolt. Hammy acting, classist and chauvinist values.

39.48 *Le Jour se lève* (8)
Gabin as the worker holed up in an apartment building recalling the sequence of events that led to him murdering the fast-talking showman. A wonderful role for Jules Berry. A famous Carné–Prévert film that is obligatory viewing.

39.49 *Louise* (1)
Yet another mythologization of the artist from Gance, as crassly conventional as ever. Every move signaled well in advance, and a grossly melodramatic plot with the worst sort of cultural chauvinism. Oedipal rivalry between the composer and Louise's jealous father.

39.51 *Macao, l'enfer du jeu* (6)
An actress on tour gets caught up in strife in Canton, and thence in Macao with an adventurer/gunrunner. Also a sinister Oriental banker/gambler and his daughter who doesn't realize what he does. Also an eager young French reporter, who saves her. Exotic adventure, Balin and von Stroheim as soldiers of fortune, and a curiously effective evocation of turbulent South China.

39.54 *Menaces* (5)
A fascinating film, made during and about the political events leading up to the declaration of war and the occupation, seen through the eyes of a little community in a hotel. Clumsy, but important. An awkward upbeat end was added after the liberation.

39.59 *Les Musiciens du ciel* (3)
A hymn to the altruism of the Salvation Army—a noble female officer is committed to saving the soul of a handsome wastrel. She saves him as she has saved others, but at a dreadful price. . . . Ho hum.

39.69 *Paradis perdu* (1)
Gance and the glory of the artist's creative powers, again. Heavy-handed comedy and painfully ironic tragedy (war declared on their marriage day, for instance). The painter wants to marry a young woman suspiciously resembling his daughter, but dies of some unnamable disease too soon (or perhaps not soon enough).

39.71   *Pièges* (5)

A murder mystery in which a young girl whose friend has been one of the victims is used as bait. An excuse for several sketches involving von Stroheim, Maurice Chevalier, and Pierre Renoir, some of a mildly perverse nature.

39.78   *La Règle du jeu* (10)

One of the greatest films ever made, to be seen again and again. A formally exquisite play on questions of rules and passion, civilization and nature, inside and outside, upstairs and down. Rich in metaphors of poachers, and rabbits, and mechanical men.

39.79   *Remorques* (9)

One of the great Gabin–Morgan films, obligatory viewing. The tugboat captain and the mysterious woman who appears out of the storm, to disrupt his life. A Prévert script, full of wonderful metaphors—the towline, the starfish, the lost fingers, etc.

39.80   *Sans lendemain* (6)

A sophisticated contemporary melodrama about a good-time girl whose past love appears; she has to try to keep him in the dark about the present, just as before she had to keep him in the dark about her past. Directed by Ophüls.

39.85   *Sur le plancher des vaches* (4)

Winner of an airplane in a lottery, an ordinary Frenchman (Jean Durand!) proves surprisingly adept and wins the heart of his flying instructress by a (failed) attempt to rescue her. Low-key precursor of *Le Ciel est à vous.*

39.87   *Tourbillon de Paris* (3)

A celebration of the swing band and its popularity with modern young things, which allows frequent opportunities for mockery of classical music, opera, etc. Provincial musicians who make the big time in Paris.

39.88   *La Tradition de minuit* (5)

A murder mystery in which two of the tight group of suspects are drawn together and marry . . . but his past catches up with him and a squalid police agent further dooms his hope of ever redeeming himself.

And, made after war was declared, but still in 1939:

39.95   *L'Homme qui cherche la vérité* (3)

Suspecting that he is unloved, cheated by everyone, and cuckolded by his son, a banker simulates deafness and thus induces everyone to betray their real feelings for him. Bloody bourgeois, they even want to be loved sincerely.

PRIZES AND FESTIVAL ENTRIES

As an indication of the films which were regarded at the time as the most prestigious among each year's production, I list below those films entered in international competitions, and those films awarded prizes by various industrial authorities.

Venice Biennale

1932   French entries: *Au nom de la loi, Azaïs, À nous la liberté, Un coup de téléphone, David Golder, Hôtel des étudiants, La Bande à Bouboule.*

1934   French entry: reputedly *Bouboule 1er, roi nègre.*

1935   French entries: *Crime et châtiment, Marie des Angoisses, Maria Chapdelaine, Le Voyage imprévu.*
        Coupe Volpi: Pierre Blanchar for his role in *Crime et châtiment.*
        Best colonial film: *Itto*

1936   French entries: *L'Appel du silence, Veille d'armes, Anne Marie, Mayerling, Le Grand Refrain, La Tendre Ennemie.* Later *Le Roman d'un tricheur* was added, while *La Kermesse héroïque,* which had been deliberately omitted by the French government, was screened at the express wish of the jury.
        Coupe Volpi: Annabella, for her role in *Veille d'armes.*
        Coupe Alfieri: Feyder, for *La Kermesse héroïque.*

1937   French entries: *La Grande Illusion, Les Perles de la couronne, Un carnet de bal, Hélène. Le Messager* was added later.
        Coupe Mussolini (best foreign film): *Un carnet de bal.*
        Coupe du jury international: *La Grande Illusion.*
        Coupe de la Direction Générale de la Cinématographie: (best scenario): *Les Perles de la couronne.*

1938   French entries: *Paix sur le Rhin, Le Joueur d'échecs, L'Innocent, Quai des brumes, Altitude 3200, La Mort du cygne, Ramuntcho, Abus de confiance, L'Affaire Lafarge.* The British and American jury members resigned because of the awarding of best film to *Triumph of the Will* and the Coupe Mussolini to Vittorio Mussolini's film *Luciano Serra, pilote.*

1939   French entries: *Derrière la façade, La Fin du jour, Le Jour se lève, Jeunes Filles en détresse, La Bête humaine, Le Grand Élan.* No prizes were awarded, but *La Fin du jour* reputedly received exceptional applause.

Festival International du Cinéma, Exposition de Bruxelles

1935   French entries: *La Bandera, L'Équipage, Les Mystères de Paris, Variétés.*
        Best music track: *L'Équipage.*
        Medals: *La Bandera, Variétés.*

Cannes Festival

1939   The Cannes festival was due to be held in September, but due to the declaration of war it was deferred, initially until January 1940. It was finally held in 1946.

French entries: *La Loi du Nord, La Charrette fantôme, L'Homme du Niger, La France est un empire, L'Enfer des anges.*

Grand Prix du Cinéma Français

This prize was intended to identify the best French film of the year, but a strict (and evolving) definition of "French" served to exclude such films as *Jenny, Les Bas-Fonds, Mayerling, Le Crime de Monsieur Lange,* and many others.

1934   *Maria Chapdelaine.*
1935   *La Kermesse héroïque* (over *Veille d'armes, Crime et châtiment, Deuxième Bureau*).
1936   *L'Appel du silence* (over *Un amour de Beethoven, Courrier-Sud, Hélène*).
1937   *Légions d'honneur* (over *Ces dames aux chapeaux verts, J'accuse, L'Affaire du courrier de Lyon*).
1938   *Alerte en Méditerranée* (over *Les Filles du Rhône, Entrée des artistes, Trois de St-Cyr, Fort Dolorès*).
1939   *Quai des brumes* (over *Feu de paille, La Fin du jour*).

An additional prize was awarded in 1937 to mark the great exhibition of that year. It went to *La Mort du cygne* (over *Abus de confiance,* which received the jury's compliments, *Les Hommes sans nom, Les Perles de la couronne, La Bataille silencieuse,* and *Gribouille*).

Prix Louis Delluc

This prize was created by a group of independent critics under forty years of age, including Achard, Altman, Bessy, Bost, Charensol, Franck, Gilson, Jeanson, and Régent, as a radical alternative to the official Grand Prix. It was awarded in December each year.

1936   *Les Bas-Fonds* (over *Sous les yeux d'Occident, La Belle Équipe, Le Roman d'un tricheur, César, Jenny,* and *Le Crime de Monsieur Lange*).
1937   *Le Puritain.*
1938   *Quai des brumes* (over *Les Disparus de St-Agil, La Femme du boulanger,* and *Entrée des artistes*).

Prix Méliès

Awarded for overall quality by the Académie du Film (150 elected film-makers) which was formed in 1939.

1939   *La Bête humaine* and *Quai des brumes* jointly.

Prix Jean Vigo

Awarded by the Académie du Film for a courageous work.

1939   *Les Disparus de St-Agil*

Prix Janie Marèse

Awarded by the Académie du Film for the best actress/most original performance.

1939   Arletty, for her role in *Hôtel du Nord.*

Prix Pierre Batcheff

Awarded by the Académie du Film for best actor/most original performance.

1939   Michel Simon, for his role in *Les Disparus de St-Agil.*

FILMOGRAPHY

This filmography attempts to list all French sound feature films produced between the introduction of sound in 1929 and the declaration of war in 1939—roughly, that is, the decade of the thirties. Especially for the earlier part of the decade, this is no easy task. There are a number of reasons for this. First, the sonorization of French studios and movie theaters was a long-drawn-out process, and many films designed as silent films were hastily and often only partially sonorized, either during production or some time afterward. It is difficult to know whether to include films with no more than a recorded music-track or, at best, a few scenes of added dialogue. Second, the existence of multiple language productions, both inside and outside France, makes it difficult to define what is to constitute "a French film." Third, the concept of "a feature film" was not clearly defined anywhere in the world at the time, and most especially in France, where fiction films of different lengths, from 20 minutes to 120 minutes, had been made during the twenties, and continued to be made after the introduction of sound. Fourth, many films more or less episodic, didactic, or documentary in nature, and structured by a more or less recognizably narrative form, were sometimes distributed and exhibited in the same way as more conventional feature films. Finally, many films promoted to the trade as available to the market at the time were never in fact made, or if made were very possibly never released.

The establishment of a definitive filmography is therefore impossible, even without the endless uncertainties created by the absence of surviving copies and the fragmentary or contradictory nature of surviving documents. Anyone working in the field must take as a starting point the two most reliable sources of information concerning film production of this period—Vincent Pinel's *Filmographie des longs métrages sonores du cinéma français*[1] and the *Catalogue des films français de long métrage: films sonores de fiction 1929–1939* produced under the supervision of Raymond Chirat.[2] These two filmographies overlap substantially, but do not entirely coincide precisely because they take different positions on some of these questions. Yet even within their different terms of reference the two filmographies are, as their authors acknowledge, not entirely reliable. Both contain many films far shorter than an hour in length, and Pinel knowingly includes certain mid-length films of the period which were relatively unknown at the time but which have since become well known—*L'Affaire est dans le sac* (32s1), *Zéro de conduite* (33s8), *Jofroi* (33s5), *Une partie de campagne* (36s1), and so on—but does not mention hundreds of other mid-length films that were produced and widely screened in the same years, often to far greater acclaim. Despite its title, Chirat's catalogue includes films that are not fiction, as does Pinel's, though in the latter case it is deliberate. Moreover, both filmographies contain numerous problematic entries due to the accidental or deliberate inclusion of some (but by no means all) films which were either silent or only partially sonorized. Both contain a number of films which were never released, if they were ever made, and avoid taking a position on the necessity of release as a criterion of inclusion. Finally, Chirat includes films, such as *Sirocco* (30s16) and *Espoir* (39s6), which are not in French and thus scarcely conform to his own precondition for inclusion.

While recognizing that there is still a lot of work to do, the present filmography attempts to rectify the bulk of these errors and inconsistencies, and to supplement the existing filmographies by including a small number of films that seem to have been overlooked by their compilers. As a necessary step toward achieving these aims, an explicit stand should be taken on each of the problems outlined above—what constitutes a sound film, what constitutes a French film, and what constitutes a feature film.

SOUND FILM

Few of the early films commonly listed as "the first French sound films" were in fact 100 percent talkies. They may have had a music-track and/or a noise-track, but (particularly in the case of the many sound-on-disk films) the dialogue was often restricted to specific scenes or to occasional songs. *Le Collier de la reine* (29s1) was "merely" sonorized, not dialogued, and only the final trial scene of *Le Requin* (29s2) was dialogued. *La Cinématographie Française* at first attempted to categorize the films that it reviewed for the trade in terms of the degree of sonorization, so that exhibitors would know the status of the films on the market, which it was for the most part in the interests of the producers and distributors to conceal. Indeed, many advertisements in trade journals were drastically misleading, claiming for the films a far higher degree of sonorization than they in fact manifested. Some that were ultimately never made at all were nevertheless advertised as already available and fully dialogued.

To confuse matters even more, silent or partially sonorized films might later, as the market and technology developed, be "upgraded" to a more nearly fully dialogued form, though they might not find a distributor even then. In the years of greatest confusion (1930–33), reviewers developed systems of categories to identify the degree of sonorization, though they were never entirely consistent or reliable. One of these was as follows: (1) "films with sound and dialogue," or "films with 100 percent French dialogue"; (2) "sonorized films, with [some] French dialogue"; (3) "sonorized films with sounds, music, and songs." The latter description might sound like a full talkie, but was in fact far from it. In the first season of sound production, very few films qualified as "with 100 percent French dialogue." By May 1930, only about a dozen of these had been released, and many films normally included in filmographies such as this one are to be found in the second category—*Le Collier de la reine* (29s1) and *Mon béguin* (29.1), for instance. Some were even in the third category, where they were listed alongside *The Jazz Singer* and other early Warner Brothers and MGM productions. A year later, lists of films previewed by the film censors still distinguished "sonorized films," "sonorized films with dialogue," and "films with dialogue."

In this filmography, I have included only those films which the surviving evidence suggests were indeed fully talking films, though I have left in films such as *Caïn* (30.15) and *L'Or des mers* (32.99), which, in one way or another, while not fully dialogued, exploited or seem to have exploited the experimental nature of sound recording by designing largely undialogued scenes, or which, as in the case of Clair's films, constituted a systematic protest against the very nature of sound film. All sonorized or partially dialogued films excluded from the present filmography but included by Pinel or Chirat are found in a supplementary list at the end, with explanations for their exclusion. Where the evidence for exclusion has not been conclusive, the films have been provisionally left in, and a second supplementary list designates such "suspect" films.

FRENCH FILMS

Pinel adopts a restrictive definition of what constitutes "a French film," based on the source of funding and the nationality of the director, whereas Chirat includes all those, together with many more co-productions, notably all those "made with French-speaking actors, and by a team which includes people of French nationality." In general, I follow Chirat in this matter, defining Frenchness in very broad terms. A key criterion for inclusion in the present filmography is the film's reception by the public, and in particular the language spoken by the actors, whereas the make-up of the production team and the nationality of the director are irrelevant. Ideally, then, this filmography aspires to include every film that would have seemed French to the French audience of the day. In pursuit of this aim, and with the help of Sadoul,[3] I have included several French versions of multilingual productions which Chirat overlooked, though there is still work to do here. A particular problem is posed by French-speaking films from Belgium, Switzer-

land, and Canada. Certainly, nationals of these countries would be outraged to see "their" films included here as French, yet in some cases a French
audience might not at the time have registered their foreignness. Several
Belgian films by Schoukens and *Le Carillon de la liberté* (32s4) by Roudès
were advertised as Belgian, and have been included in the secondary filmography, as have foreign-language films such as *Espoir* (39s6) and *Sirocco*
(30s16).

FEATURE FILMS—LENGTH

In the late twenties, there was no institutional standard for "a feature film."
The term did not exist in French, and in English it is an institutional term
describing films that "feature" as the principal attraction in a program. The
French term *long métrage* was never closely defined, but Pinel and Chirat
are in agreement that a line has to be drawn somewhere, and that the term
should be reserved for films over 1,650 meters—that is, over one hour—in
length. I have gone along with this, while recognizing that it excludes a
large number of films—perhaps hundreds—of between forty and sixty minutes which did in fact constitute the principal feature in programs of the
early years of the decade. Nevertheless, there is some evidence that the industry itself accepted, or very soon came to accept, a distinction of this
sort. Films under 1,650 meters in length are several times in key film lists of
the decade categorized as *films de première partie*, while those longer than
1,650 meters are called *grands films*.

Film length is not always easy to ascertain in the absence of the film itself. The only attempt at a catalogue of French films less than sixty minutes
long is patently incomplete and often inaccurate, and surviving evidence is
particularly contradictory in this area. Nevertheless, I have been able to exclude from Pinel's and Chirat's lists a large number of films which certainly
or almost certainly were under one hour in length. *Les Trois Masques* (29s3),
for instance, usually listed as the first French sound feature film, was less
than an hour long. So, according to contemporary censorship lists, were
Chiqué (30s5), *Le Roi du camembert* (31s7), *Je t'adore mais pourquoi* (30s9),
Y'en a pas deux comme Angélique (31s8), *La Fille du Bouif* (31s5), *Brumes de
Paris* (32s3), *L'Indésirable* (33s3), and many others which Pinel and/or Chirat include. On the other hand, contemporary evidence suggests that
Jimmy (30.45) may have been 1,666 meters long (i.e., just over sixty minutes), so it is included. It is, moreover, listed by GFFA among its *grands
films* rather than its *films de première partie*.

Many other films in the filmography are only just over sixty minutes—
L'Âge d'or (30s2, 62 minutes), *Prix de beauté* (30.69, 65 minutes), *Ah!
Quelle gare* (32.3, 65 minutes), *Mon ami Tim* (30.89, 66 minutes), *La Perle*
(32.105, 63 minutes), *Un peu d'amour* (32.141, 65 minutes), *La Tendre*

Ennemie (35.109, 64 minutes), and others—but this would be the case wherever the line was drawn. A number are of unknown length, since the evidence is either absent or radically contradictory. A simple typographical error may give the length as 1,450 meters in one document and 2,450 meters in another. Where real doubt persists, the film is included, but noted in the "suspect" list. A typically problematic case is *La Maison jaune de Rio,* which Chirat includes despite acknowledging that it was cut to 38 minutes (!) "for reasons of exhibition," and was totally incomprehensible. The trade review at the time of release gave its length as 2,500 meters (i.e., 92 minutes), though the censorship list in early 1931 records it as having been only 1,300 meters (i.e., 48 minutes) when passed for release. At least everyone agrees that it was never screened in anything approaching feature-length form, so it should not figure in the filmography.

FEATURE FILMS—NARRATIVE

Certain films listed in standard filmographies are not, or may not have been, primarily narrative in nature. In general, the prime criterion for inclusion in the present filmography has been the existence of a fictional narrative diegesis as the dominant structure of the film. Thus, where the function of the film is primarily descriptive or didactic and any narrative structure is secondary, the film has been excluded from this filmography. Several propaganda films, such as *La Vie est à nous* (36s2) and *Le Monde en armes* (29s9), are primarily didactic in this way. *Sommes-nous défendus?* (38s3) was exhibited as the principal feature in a program and has a perfunctory narrative frame in which a reporter describes to a Parisian audience his experiences when invited to view the fortifications on the northern frontier, but it is nevertheless primarily directive and descriptive. The descriptive element is also predominant in long documentaries such as *La Croisière jaune* (31s4) and *La Croisière noire* (1926), and such films have been excluded. *L'Amour qu'il faut aux femmes* (33s1) seems to have been primarily didactic, consisting of an instructional medical frame explicating in a condescending way the emotional needs of women, treated in brief fictional sections. *Courrier d'Asie* (39s5) seems to have combined propaganda, travelogue, and advertising, and had, at best, a perfunctory narrative frame. Pinel and Chirat include most or all of these, since the former at least aims to list all feature-length sound films, regardless of function or structure. Here, they can be found in the supplementary filmography.

In all these matters, the decision as to where to draw the line was difficult. An easier decision was the relegation of such films as *Paramount en parade* (30s12), which was no more than a series of sketches, few of which were even in French. Likewise, *Voilà Montmartre* (34s3), *La Boutique aux illusions* (39s3), and others of the same sort have been eliminated, since they were no more than a record of a series of music-hall sketches or silent shorts, sometimes in a perfunctory narrative framework. A slightly more difficult case is *Méphisto* (30s11), which consisted of a series of four forty-minute episodes designed as a serial to accompany the feature films in four successive programs. It seems to have been included in other filmographies simply because it was the first serial of the sound era, and was thus reviewed extensively, but there is no real justification for including it if all the others that succeeded it are not included. A slightly different situation arises when two or more full-length films are produced as a coherent whole, but screened separately. Such was the case with *Sidonie Panache* and *Chabichou* (34.98), the three parts of *Les Misérables* (33.92), and possibly *Le Tigre du Bengale* and *Le Tombeau hindou* (37.110). These have been listed under the first title, as parts 1, 2, 3, and so on.

PUBLICATION

Many novels have been written but never published, and they cannot be said to be part of the corpus of their national literature. Similarly, a film that was never released publicly cannot be said to form a part of the cinematic corpus of the nation. The simplest case is provided by films that were destroyed in a fire in 1940 before being released, and were never remade. More generally, any film that did not achieve public release, commercial or otherwise, has been excluded from the present filmography, but noted for interest's sake in the supplement. It is, of course, not always easy to identify which films were not released. Many films of the thirties can be traced through conception, production, and post-production to presentation to the trade and review. They were thus "available to the market," yet there is no clear evidence that a distributor ever took them up and released them.

As usual, *La Cinématographie Française* is invaluable in listing films released onto the market, but it was far from comprehensive in reviewing such films, and when it did so it was sometimes unclear as to whether the film was simply "finished," or approved for release by the censors, or actually screened. It listed most films going into first-release theaters, though not all (since it wasn't, alas, aiming to cater to future researchers), and not all films went into first-release theaters. A number of less prestigious films slipped onto the suburban market unpublicized and unrecorded. Even the alphabetical lists in *La Semaine à Paris*, giving the week's film programs for all Paris theaters together with films currently on exclusive release, are of uncertain reliability in some years, and it is not possible to say for certain that a film was never released without surveying the individual programs of all suburban theaters (and, in theory, all provincial theaters) over the probable period of release. Even so, some films surfaced only long after their nominal release date. *L'Ensorcellement de Séville* (31.54), shot from August to October 1930, edited in January 1931, "available" for many months thereafter, and approved by the censor in the course of 1931 was reputedly not screened till 1936, and I have not been able to trace even that screening. *Pour un soir* (31.106), filmed as *Sancta Maria* in April 1931 and as *Stella Maris* in May, edited in June, publicized to the trade for months thereafter, and approved by the censor by August 1932 was actually presented to the trade only in August 1933, when it was condemned as impossible to screen in its existing form. Nevertheless, it was screened publicly in Paris for one week at the end of 1933, before disappearing "forever." (In fact, paradoxically, it is one of the relatively few films from that year of which a copy is commercially available.)

Certain production companies can be identified as particularly problematic in their release practices. Nord Films, based in Lille, consistently advertised a bracket of films (*Fumées* [30s8], *Vouloir* [31.148], *Virages* [30.94], *La Chanson du lin* [31s2], *L'Équipe*) as if they were finished and 100% talkies, but it only gradually produced some of them, and then, as far as can be ascertained, usually in lesser degrees of sonorization. None, except very briefly *Virages* and, less certainly, *Vouloir* seems ever to have been released in Paris, though others may have been released in Lille. Likewise, a number of directors' names can be associated with such problematic films: Jaeger-Schmidt of Nord Films, of course, together with Monca, Pallu, Perojo, Sévérac, Mittler, Weill, Pujol, Roudès, Marca-Rosa, Rosca, Rozier, Guarino, and Péguy, for instance. Some occasionally made successful films, but it is hard to see how their track record could have justified continued funding. Certainly, the near invisibility of much of their production in the journals and programs of the day renders the compilation of a definitive filmography close to impossible.

To summarize the above observations, the following filmography attempts to list all French feature films of the thirties which were or probably were 100 percent talkies, which were or probably were over one hour in length, which were probably received by French audiences as French, and which constructed as their primary effect a fictional diegesis structured by narrative. Many will feel, with some justification, that certain films here relegated to the supplementary list should be included in the main filmography, and notably those which at some stage had sound, and on occasion some dialogue, added after production. The date under which the films are listed is the date when production began. I have taken these from Chirat and Pinel, except where the release date suggested that the year of production proposed in those filmographies was impossible—either the film had already been released in the previous year, or it was released before week 5 of the proposed year of production. The Paris release date is given after the director's name, to the nearest week. Thus 18/30 after the director's name signifies that the film was released in week 18 of 1930. I have not bothered to record the precise release date, even where it is known, since the place of the films in the annual seasonal programming, together with the number of weeks of screening, was of primary concern here. Where I am unsure if the film was ever in fact released, I have simply put a question mark. Where I suspect an earlier untraced release, I have followed the release date that I give with a question mark.

Underlined films are those which Pinel, with his more restrictive definition of Frenchness, does not include in his filmography. Films which figure in the annual tables of most popular films are printed in boldface type. The films which I have viewed in preparing this book have been indicated in the filmography by an asterisk. Those which are commercially available, or which other commentators report having viewed, but which I have not myself viewed, are marked with a hash mark. With contributions from other researchers, this should ultimately lead to a knowledge of the total corpus of films which have survived into the twenty-first century. Each year's output is numbered, and all in-text references in part 1 give the film's year of production and its position on the annual list. Thus 32.18 refers the reader to the 18th film on the 1932 list (*Le Béguin de la garnison,* Vernay and Weill, released in week 15 of 1933). This has been done to avoid cluttering the text with lengthy references or thousands of footnotes. Alternative titles have been given only when the film was released or sometimes screened under an alternate title.

1929

1 <u>*Mon béguin*</u>, Behrendt, 50/30
2 *Mystère de la Villa Rose, Le,* Hervil & Mercanton, 4/30
3 *Nuit est à nous, La,* Roussell, 3/30
4 *Quand nous étions deux,* Perret, 18/30
5 *Route est belle, La,* Florey, 4/30

1930

1 *À mi-chemin du ciel,* Cavalcanti, 23/31
2 **Accusée, levez-vous!,** Tourneur, 37/30
3 *Amour chante, L',* Florey, 47/30
4 *Amours de minuit, Les,* Genina & M. Allégret, 3/31
5 <u>*Amours viennoises,*</u> Choux & Land, 1/31
6 *Anglais tel qu'on le parle, L',* Boudrioz, 24/31
7 *Anny je t'aime,* Lamac, 44/33?
8 *Arlésienne, L',* Baroncelli, 38/30
9 **Arthur,** Perret, 1/31
10 <u>**Atlantis,**</u> Dupont & Kemm, 39/30
11 *Barcarolle d'amour,* Roussell, 41/30
12 <u>**Big House,**</u> Fejos & Hill, 20/31
13 *Blanc et le noir, Le,* M. Allégret & Florey, 21/31*
14 *Bodega, La,* Perojo, 26/30
15 *Caïn, aventure des mers exotiques,* Poirier, 48/30
16 *Capitaine jaune, Le,* Sandberg, 51/30
17 **Cendrillon de Paris,** Hémard, 47/30
18 <u>*Chacun sa chance,*</u> Steinhoff & Pujol, 51/30*
19 <u>*Chanson des nations, La,*</u> Meinert & Gleize, 26/31
20 <u>**Chanteur de Séville, Le,**</u> Noé & Navarro, 7/31
21 <u>**Chemin du paradis, Le,**</u> Thiele & de Vaucorbeil, 46/30*
22 *Chérie,* Mercanton, 51/30
23 <u>*Chevaliers de la montagne, Les,*</u> Bonnard, 13/31
24 <u>*Chute dans le bonheur, La,*</u> Pujol & Steinhoff
25 <u>*Contre-enquête,*</u> Daumery, 49/30
26 *Dans une île perdue,* Cavalcanti, 4/31
27 **David Golder,** Duvivier, 10/31 #
28 *Défenseur, Le,* Ryder, 22/30
29 <u>*Dernière Berceuse, La,*</u> Righelli & Cassagne, 23/31
30 *Deux fois vingt ans,* Tavano, 11/31
31 <u>*Deux Mondes, Les,*</u> Dupont, 37/30
32 *Douceur d'aimer, La,* Hervil, 42/30
33 **Enfant de l'amour, L',** L'Herbier, 32/30
34 *Énigmatique Mr. Parkes, L',* Gasnier, 41/30
35 *Étrangère, L',* Ravel, 6/31
36 *Femme d'une nuit, La* (L'Herbier), 18/32

37 *Femme et le rossignol, La,* Hugon, 11/31
38 *Fin du monde, La,* Gance, 4/31
39 <u>*Flagrant Délit,*</u> Schwarz & Tréville, 10/31
40 *Folle Aventure, La,* Froelich and Antoine, 11/31
41 *Fra Diavolo,* Bonnard, 16/31
42 **<u>*Grande Mare, La,*</u> Henley & Bataille-Henri, 29/30**
43 <u>*Haï-Tang,*</u> Eichberg & Kemm, 38/30
44 <u>*Homme qui assassina, L'*</u>, Bernhardt & Tarride, 3/31
45 *Jimmy,* Epstein, 1931?
46 <u>*Joker, Le,*</u> Waschneck, 46/30
47 *Lettre, La,* Mercanton, 47/30
48 **<u>*Lévy et Cie,*</u> Hugon, 43/30**
49 <u>*Lopez, le bandit,*</u> Daumery, 6/31
50 *Maison de danses,* Tourneur, 9/31
51 *Maison de la flèche, La,* Fescourt, 50/30
52 *Marius à Paris,* Lion, 46/30
53 *Miracle des loups, Le,* Bernard, 29/31
54 *Mon ami Victor!,* Berthomieu, 52/30
55 <u>*Mon cœur incognito,*</u> Noé & Antoine, 3/31
56 **<u>*Mon gosse de père,*</u> Limur, 18/30 #**
57 *Monsieur le Duc,* Limur, 9/31
58 <u>*Monsieur Le Fox,*</u> Roach, 3/31
59 *Mystère de la chambre jaune, Le,* L'Herbier, 6/31*
60 *Nos maîtres, les domestiques,* Grantham-Hayes, 45/30
61 **<u>*Opéra de quat'sous, L',*</u> Pabst, 45/31***
62 **<u>*Parfum de la dame en noir, Le,*</u> L'Herbier, 45/31***
63 *Paris la nuit,* Diamant-Berger, 52/30
64 <u>*Père célibataire, Le,*</u> Robison, 49/32
65 **<u>*Petit Café, Le*</u> , Berger, 19/31**
66 *Petite Lise, La,* Grémillon, 49/30*
67 *Princes de la cravache, Les,* Wion (?)
68 *Prison en folie, La,* Wulschleger, 4/31
69 *Prix de beauté,* Genina, 19/31*
70 *Procureur Hallers, Le,* Wiene, 46/30
71 *Razzia,* Sévérac, 47/31
72 *Rebelle, Le,* Millar, 41/31
73 *Refuge, Le,* Mathot, 2/31
74 <u>*Réquisitoire, Le,*</u> Buchowetzki, 9/31
75 **<u>*Rêve, Le,*</u> Baroncelli, 19/31**
76 *Roi de Paris, Le,* Mittler, 36/30
77 *Roi des aulnes, Le,* Iribe, 9/31
78 **<u>*Roi des resquilleurs, Le,*</u> Colombier, 46/30**
79 *Romance à l'inconnue,* Barberis, 8/31
80 **<u>*Ronde des heures, La,*</u> Ryder, 7/31**
81 *Roumanie, terre d'amour,* Morlhon, 36/31

82   *Secret du docteur, Le*, Rochefort, 39/30
83   *Si l'empereur savait ça*, Feyder, 44/30
84   **Sous les toits de Paris**, Clair, 17/30*
85   *Spectre vert, Le*, Feyder & Barrymore, 18/30
86   **Tampon du capiston, Le**, Francis & Toulot, 12/31
87   **Tendresse, La**, Hugon, 20/30
88   *Toute sa vie*, Cavalcanti, 45/30
89   *Tu m'oublieras*, Diamant-Berger, 52/30
90   *Un caprice de la Pompadour*, Wolff & Hamman, 18/31
91   **Un trou dans le mur**, Barberis, 23/30
92   *Une belle garce*, Gastyne, 51/30
93   *Vacances du diable, Les*, Cavalcanti, 12/31
94   *Virages*, Jaeger-Schmitt, 16/31

1931

1   *À nous la liberté*, Clair, 51/31*
2   *Affaire Blaireau, L'*, Robert, 11/32
3   *Aiglon, L'*, Tourjansky, 35/31
4   *Allô Berlin, ici Paris*, Duvivier, 47/32
5   *Amour à l'américaine, L'*, Heymann, 52/31
6   *Amour et discipline*, Kemm, 6/32
7   *Amoureuse aventure, L'*, Thiele, 4/32
8   **Après l'amour**, Perret, 49/31
9   *Ariane, jeune fille russe*, Czinner, 9/32 (in Fr)
10   *Atout-cœur*, Roussell, 38/31
11   **Au nom de la loi**, Tourneur, 16/32*
12   *Autour d'une enquête*, Siodmak & Chomette, 23/31
13   *Aviateur, L'*, Selter, 11/31
14   **Azaïs**, Hervil, 32/31
15   **Bal, Le**, Thiele, 37/31
16   *Baleydier*, Mamy, 3/32
17   **Bande à Bouboule, La**, Mathot, 51/31
18   *Baroud*, Ingram, 45/32* (in Eng)
19   *Bête errante, La*, Gastyne, 4/32
20   *Blanc comme neige*, Ellias, 31/31
21   *Buster se marie*, Brothy & Autant-Lara, 2/32
22   *Calais-Douvres*, Litvak & Boyer, 39/31
23   *Camp volant*, Reichmann, 37/32
24   *Cap perdu, Le*, Dupont, 14/31
25   *Capitaine Craddock, Le*, Schwarz & de Vaucorbeil, 49/31 #
26   *Ceux du "Viking,"* Ginet (& Frissell), 9/32
27   *Chance, La*, Guissart, 52/31
28   *Chant du marin, Le*, Gallone, 4/32
29   **Chanteur inconnu, Le**, Tourjansky, 49/31

30   <u>*Chauve-Souris, La*</u>, Lamac & Billon, 13/32
31   **<u>*Chienne, La*</u>, Renoir, 47/31***
32   *Cinq gentlemen maudits, Les,* Duvivier, 7/32 #
33   *Circulez!,* Limur, 47/31
34   **<u>*Cœur de Lilas,*</u> Litvak, 7/32***
35   *Cœur de Paris, Le,* Benoît-Lévy & M. Epstein, 19/32
36   <u>*Cœurs joyeux,*</u> Schwarz & de Vaucorbeil, 49/32
37   *Coiffeur pour dames,* Guissart, 21/32
38   **<u>*Congrès s'amuse, Le*</u>, Charell & Boyer, 43/32***
39   *Coquecigrole,* Berthomieu, 51/31
40   *Cordon-Bleu,* Anton, 2/32
41   *Costaud des P.T.T., Le,* or *Le Roi des facteurs,* Bertin & Maté, 50/31
42   *Côte d'Azur,* Capellani, 28/32
43   *Coups de roulis,* La Cour, 21/32
44   *Couturière de Luneville, La,* Lachmann, 16/32
45   **<u>*Croix de bois, Les*</u>, Bernard, 12/32***
46   *Croix du sud, La,* Hugon, 20/32
47   **<u>*Dactylo,*</u> Thiele, 14/31**
48   *Delphine,* Campellani & Marguenat, 47/31
49   *Disparu de l'ascenseur, Le,* Torre, 4/32
50   <u>*Durand contre Durand*</u>, Thiele & Joannon, 48/31
51   <u>*Échec au roi*</u>, d'Usseau & de la Falaise, 36/31
52   *Échec et mat,* Goupillières, 36/31
53   **<u>*En bordée,*</u> Francis & Wulschleger, 29/31**
54   *Ensorcellement de Séville, L',* Perojo, 1936?
55   **<u>*Faubourg-Montmartre,*</u> Bernard, 38/31***
56   <u>*Femme de mes rêves, La*</u>, Bertin, 7/32
57   *Fille et le Garçon, La,* Thiele, 10/32
58   <u>*Fils de l'autre, Le*</u>, de la Falaise, 10/32
59   *Fortune, La,* Hémard, 4/32
60   <u>*Frères Karamazoff, Les*</u>, Ozep, 4/32
61   *Fuite à l'anglaise,* Kemm
62   **<u>*Gagne ta vie,*</u> Berthomieu, 41/31**
63   *Galeries Lévy et Cie, Les,* Hugon, 5/32
64   <u>*Gloria,*</u> Behrend & Noé, 44/31
65   *Grains de beauté,* Caron, 11/32
66   **<u>*Grock,*</u> Boese & Hamman, 19/31**
67   *Hardi les gars!,* Champreux, 43/31
68   **<u>*Il est charmant,*</u> Mercanton, 9/32***
69   <u>*Inconstante, L',*</u> Behrend & Noé, 25/31
70   **<u>*Jean de la Lune,*</u> Choux, 9/31**
71   <u>*Jenny Lind*</u>, Robison, 7/32
72   **<u>*Juif polonais, Le*</u>, Kemm, 38/31**
73   *Laurette ou le cachet rouge,* Casembroot, 14/31

74 *Ma cousine de Varsovie*, **Gallone, 15/31***
75 *Ma tante d'Honfleur*, Maurice, 11/32
76 *Magie moderne*, Buchowetzki, 41/31
77 *Mam'zelle Nitouche*, **M. Allégret, 49/31***
78 *Marchand de sable, Le*, Hugon, 4/32
79 *Mardi gras*, Weill, 18/33
80 *Marions-nous*, Mercanton, 10/31
81 **Marius, Korda, 41/31***
82 *Masque d'Hollywood, Le*, Badger & Daumery, 17/31
83 *Miche*, Marguenat, 18/32
84 **Million, Le, Clair, 14/31***
85 **Mistigri, Lachmann, 49/31**
86 *Mon amant l'assassin*, Bussi, 24/32
87 *Mon cœur et ses millions*, Berthomieu, 45/31
88 *Monsieur de minuit, Le*, Lachmann, 33/31
89 *Monsieur le Maréchal*, Lamac, 44/31
90 *Monts en flammes, Les*, Trenker & Hamman, 46/31
91 *Nicole et sa vertu*, Hervil, 1/32
92 *Nuit d'Espagne*, de la Falaise, 14/32
93 *Nuits de Port-Saïd, Les*, Mittler, 41/33
94 *Nuits de Venise*, Billon & Wiene, 9/31
95 *On purge bébé*, Renoir, 26/31 #
96 *Papa sans le savoir*, Wyler, 15/32
97 *Paris-Béguin*, Genina, 41/31*
98 **Paris-Méditerranée, May, 8/32***
99 *Partir*, Tourneur, 35/31
100 ⁄ **Pas sur la bouche, Evreïnoff, 39/31**
101 *Passeport 13.444*, Mathot, 27/31
102 *Petit Écart, Le*, Schünzel & Chomette, 43/31
103 **Petite Chocolatière, La, M. Allégret, 7/32*??**
104 *Petite de Montparnasse, La*, Schwarz & de Vaucorbeil, 13/32
105 *Piste des géants, La*, Walsh & Couderc, 12/31
106 *Pour un soir*, or *Stella maris*, Godard, 52/33 #
107 *Pour un sou d'amour*, Grémillon, 9/32*
108 **Princesse, à vos ordres, Schwarz & de Vaucorbeil, 15/31**
109 *Prisonnier de mon cœur*, Tarride, 17/32
110 *Procès de Mary Dugan, Le*, de Sano, 46/31
111 *Quand on est belle*, Robison, 12/32
112 *Quand te tues-tu ?*, Capellani, 47/31
113 *Quatre vagabonds, Les*, Lupu-Pick, 15/31
114 **Rien que la vérité, Guissart, 37/31**
115 **Rive gauche, Korda, 34/31**
116 **Roi du cirage, Le, Colombier, 46/31**

117 *Ronny*, Schünzel & Le Bon, 4/32
118 *Rosier de Madame Husson, Le*, Bernard-Deschamps, 5/32*
119 *Salto mortale*, Dupont, 22/31
120 *Sergent X, Le*, Strijewski, 14/32 #
121 *Serments*, Fescourt, 43/31
122 *Service de nuit*, Fescourt, 15/32
123 *Soixante-dix-sept rue Chagrin*, de Courville, 46/31
124 *Sola*, Diamant-Berger, 7/31
125 *Son Altesse l'Amour*, Schmidt & Péguy, 40/31
126 *Sous le casque de cuir*, de Courville, 17/32
127 *Soyons gais*, Robison, 16/31
128 *Sur la voie du bonheur*, Joannon (?)
129 *Tout ça ne vaut pas l'amour*, or *Un vieux garçon*, J. Tourneur, 42/31
130 *Tout s'arrange*, Diamant-Berger, 30/31
131 *Tragédie de la mine, La*, Pabst, 5/32
132 *Train des suicidés, Le*, Gréville, 33/31
133 *Tu seras duchesse*, Guissart, 8/32
134 *Tumultes*, Siodmak, 17/32*
135 *Un chien qui rapporte*, Choux, 1/32*
136 *Un coup de téléphone*, Lacombe, 13/32
137 *Un homme en habit*, Bossis & Guissart, 27/31
138 *Un soir au front*, Ryder, 12/31
139 *Un soir de rafle*, Gallone, 28/31
140 *Une histoire entre mille*, Rieux, 1936?
141 *Une nuit à l'hôtel*, Mittler, 18/32
142 *Une nuit au Paradis*, Lamac & Billon, 19/32
143 *Vacances*, Boudrioz, 2/32
144 *Vagabonde, La*, Bussi, 37/31
145 *Vagabonds magnifiques, Les*, Dini, 34/31
146 *Vampyr*, Dreyer, 40/32*
147 *Verdun, souvenirs d'histoire*, Poirier, 45/31
148 *Vouloir*, Jaeger-Schmidt (?)

1932

1 *À moi le jour, à toi la nuit*, Berger, 52/32
2 *Adhémar Lampiot*, Christian-Jaque, (?)
3 *Ah! Quelle gare!*, Guissart, 36/33
4 *Allo, Mademoiselle!*, Champreux, 50/32
5 *Amour en vitesse, L'*, Guter & Heymann, 33/32
6 *Amour et la veine, L'*, Banks, 52/32
7 *Amour . . . amour*, Bibal, 39/32
8 *Amours de Pergolèse, Les*, Brignone, 14/33
9 *Âne de Buridan, L'*, Ryder, 52/32

55 *Enfant du miracle, L',* M. Diamant-Berger, 23/32
56 *Enlevez-moi,* Perret, 44/32
57 <u>*Extase,*</u> Machaty, 11/33
58 *Fanny,* M. Allégret, 44/32*
59 *Fantômas,* Fejos, 21/32*
60 <u>*Faut-il les marier?,*</u> Lamac & Billon, 27/32
61 *Femme en homme, La,* Genina, 11/32
62 *Femme nue, La,* Paulin, 43/32
63 *Fils improvisé, Le,* Guissart, 47/32
64 *Fleur d'oranger, La,* Roussell, 42/32
65 *Folle Nuit, La,* Bibal & Poirier, 15/32
66 <u>*Foule hurle, La,*</u> Hawks & Daumery, 41/32
67 *Gaietés de l'escadron, Les,* Tourneur, 38/32*
68 *Gamin de Paris, Le,* Roudes, 35/32
69 *Gitanes,* Baroncelli, 10/33
70 <u>*Homme qui ne sait pas dire non, L',*</u> Hilpert, 11/33
71 *Hôtel des étudiants,* Tourjansky, 39/32
72 *IF1 ne répond plus,* Hartl, 9/33
73 *Il a été perdu une mariée,* Joannon, 52/32
74 <u>*Je vous aimerai toujours,*</u> Camerini, 23/33
75 *Jugement de minuit, Le,* Esway, 11/33
76 <u>*Kiki,*</u> Lamac & Billon, 4/33
77 *Ma femme . . . homme d'affaires,* Vaucorbeil, 36/32
78 <u>*Madame ne veut pas d'enfants,*</u> Steinhoff & Landau, 15/33
79 *Maquillage,* or *Je t'attendrai,* Anton, 19/33
80 *Mariage de Mlle Beulemans, Le,* Choux, 1932
81 *Marie, légende hongroise,* or *Une histoire d'amour,* Fejos, 52/32
82 *Martyre de l'obèse, Le,* Chenal, 13/33 #
83 *Mater dolorosa,* Gance, 2/33
84 *Maurin des Maures,* Hugon, 49/32
85 *Mélo,* Czinner, 43/32
86 *Merveilleuse Journée, La,* Mirande & Wyler, 47/32
87 *Mirages de Paris,* Ozep, 3/33
88 <u>*Moi et l'impératrice,*</u> Hollaender & Martin, 20/33
89 <u>*Mon ami Tim,*</u> Forrester, 26/32
90 *Mon cœur balance,* Guissart, 44/32
91 *Mon curé chez les riches,* Couzinet, 18/32
92 *Monsieur Albert,* Anton, 26/32
93 *Monsieur de Pourceaugnac,* Lekain & Ravel, 42/32
94 *Monsieur, Madame et Bibi,* Boyer (& Neufeld), 11/32
95 *Moune et son notaire,* Bourlon, 34/33
96 *Ne sois pas jalouse,* Genina, 5/33
97 *Nuit du carrefour, La,* Renoir, 16/32*
98 <u>*Occupe-toi d'Amélie,*</u> Viel & Weisbach, 52/32
99 *Or des mers, L',* Epstein, 20/33

100   *Panurge,* Bernheim, 49/32
101   *Paris-Soleil,* Hémard, 6/33
102   *Pas de femmes,* or *Pas besoin de femmes,* Bonnard, 28/32
103   *Passionnément,* Guissart & Mercanton, 38/32
104   *Pax,* Elias, 26/33
105   *Perle, La,* Guissart, 31/32
106   *Picador, Le,* Jaquelux, 47/32
107   *Plaisirs de Paris,* Gréville, 2/34
108   <u>*Plombier amoureux, Le,*</u> Autant-Lara, 52/32
109   *Poil de Carotte,* Duvivier, 45/32*
110   *Pomme d'Amour,* Dréville, 51/32
111   *Poule, La,* Guissart, 21/33
112   *Pouponnière, La,* Boyer, 6/33
113   *Pour vivre heureux,* Torre, 51/32
114   *Premier mot d'amour, Le,* Guarino, 4/34
115   *Prenez garde à la peinture,* Chomette, 22/32
116   *Quatorze juillet,* Clair, 3/33*
117   <u>*Quick,*</u> Siodmak, 35/32
118   *Rien que des mensonges,* Anton, 32/52
119   <u>*Rivaux de la piste,*</u> de Poligny, 8/33
120   *Rocambole,* Rosca, 50/32
121   *Roche aux mouettes, La,* Monca, 24/33
122   *Roger la Honte,* Roudès, 11/33
123   <u>*Roi bis, Le,*</u> Beaudoin, 52/32
124   *Roi des palaces, Le,* Gallone, 51/32
125   *Rouletabille aviateur,* Szekely, 2/33
126   *Sa meilleure cliente,* Colombier, 51/32
127   *Si tu veux,* Hugon, 38/32
128   *Simone est comme ça,* Anton, 53/33
129   <u>*Soir des rois, Le,*</u> Daumery, 2/33
130   <u>*Stupéfiants,*</u> Gerron & Le Bon, 52/32*
131   *Suzanne,* Joannon & Rouleau, 44/32
132   *Tête d'un homme, La,* Duvivier, 6/33
133   *Toine,* Gaveau, 13/33
134   *Topaze,* Gasnier, 2/33*
135   *Triangle de feu, Le,* Gréville, 48/32
136   *Trois mousquetaires, Les,* Parts 1 and 2 (*Milady*), Diamant-Berger, 51/32
       and 8/33
137   *Truc du Brésilien, Le,* Cavalcanti, 50/32
138   <u>*Un fils d'Amérique,*</u> Gallone, 23/32
139   *Un homme heureux,* Bideau, 8/33
140   <u>*Un homme sans nom,*</u> Ucicky & Le Bon, 39/32
141   <u>*Un peu d'amour,*</u> Steinhoff, 47/32
142   <u>*Un rêve blond,*</u> Martin, 43/32
143   *Une étoile disparaît,* Villers, 34/32

144   *Une faible femme*, Vaucorbeil, 12/33
145   *Une heure près de toi*, **Lubitsch, 23/32**
146   *Une idée folle*, Vaucorbeil, 18/33
147   *Une jeune fille et un million*, Neufeld & Ellis, 41/32
148   **Une petite femme dans le train, Anton, 39/32**
149   *Vainqueur, Le*, **Heinrich & Martin, 13/32**
150   *Vignes du Seigneur, Les*, **Hervil, 38/32**
151   *Violettes impériales*, Roussell, 51/32
152   *Voix qui meurt, La*, Dini, 8/33
153   *Vous serez ma femme*, de Poligny, 21/32
154   *Voyage de noces*, Schmidt & Fried, 2/33

1933

1   *Abbé Constantin, L'*, **Paulin, 43/33***
2   *Adieu les beaux jours*, Meyer & Beucler, 45/33
3   *Agonie des Aigles, L'*, **Richebé, 48/33 #**
4   *Ailes brisées, Les*, Berthomieu, 25/33
5   *Âme de clown*, or *Teddy et partner*, Didier & Noé, 42/33
6   *Ami Fritz, L'*, Baroncelli, 46/33
7   *Amour guide, L'*, Taurog & Boyer, 4/34
8   *Ange gardien, L'*, Choux, 8/34
9   *Assommoir, L'*, Roudès, 26/33
10   *Au bout du monde*, **Ucicky & Chomette, 5/34**
11   *Au pays du soleil*, Péguy, 5/34 #
12   *Aventures du roi Pausole, Les*, Granowsky, 51/33*
13   *Bach millionnaire*, **Wulschleger, 52/33**
14   *Bagnes d'enfants*, or *Gosses de misère*, Gauthier, 31/33
15   *Barbier de Séville, Le*, Bourlon & Kemm, 52/33
16   *Bataille, La*, **Farkas, 1/34 #**
17   *Belle de nuit*, Valray, 9/34
18   *Bleus du ciel, Les*, or *L'Avion blanc*, Decoin, 48/33
19   *Bouboule 1er, roi nègre*, Mathot, 16/34
20   *Caprice de princesse*, Hartl & Clouzot, 3/34
21   *Casanova*, Barberis, 15/34
22   *Cent mille francs pour un baiser*, Bourlon & Delance, 32/33
23   *Ces messieurs de la Santé*, **Colombier, 12/34***
24   *C'était un musicien*, Zelnik & Gleize, 17/34
25   *Cette nuit-là*, Sorkin, 53/33
26   *Cette vieille canaille*, Litvak, 46/33*
27   *Champignol malgré lui*, Ellis, 43/33
28   *Chant du destin, Le*, Legrand, 41/35
29   *Charlemagne*, Colombier, 52/33
30   *Château de rêve*, von Bolvary & Clouzot, 45/33
31   *Châtelaine du Liban, La*, Epstein, J., 6/34

32   *Chemin du bonheur, Le,* Mamy, 1/34

33   *Chourinette,* Hugon, 9/34

34   *Ciboulette,* Autant-Lara, 46/33

35   *Colomba,* Couzinet, 47/33

36   *Coq du régiment, Le,* Cammage, 52/33

37   *Coralie et Cie,* Cavalcanti, 23/34

38   *Coucher de la mariée, Le,* Lion, 21/33

39   *Crainquebille,* Baroncelli, 11/34

40   *D'amour et d'eau fraîche,* Gandera, 49/33

41   *Dans les rues,* Trivas, 45/33*

42   *Dernière Nuit, La,* Cassembroot, 16/34

43   *Deux Canards, Les,* Schmidt, 16/34

44   *Deux 'Monsieur' de Madame, Les,* Jacquin & Pallu, 16/33

45   *Du haut en bas,* Pabst, 51/33

46   *Épervier, L',* **L'Herbier, 47/33**

47   *Étienne,* Tarride, 51/33

48   <u>*Étoile de Valencia, L',*</u> de Poligny, 25/33

49   <u>*Ève cherche un père,*</u> Bonnard, 53/33

50   *Fakir du Grand Hôtel, Le,* Billon, 1/34

51   *Faut réparer Sophie,* Ryder, 49/33

52   *Femme idéale, La,* Berthomieu, 4/34

53   *Femme invisible, La,* Lacombe, 23/33

54   *Feu Toupinel,* Capellani, 10/34

55   <u>*Fille du régiment, La,*</u> Lamac & Billon, 24/33

56   *Fusée, La,* Natanson, 19/33

57   *Gardez le sourire,* Fejos, 14/34

58   **Garnison amoureuse, La, Vaucorbeil, 12/34 #**

59   *Gendre de Monsieur Poirier, Le,* Pagnol, 51/33*

60   <u>*Georges et Georgette,*</u> Schünzel & Le Bon, 5/34

61   *Grand Bluff, Le,* Champreux, 36/33

62   **Grand Jeu, Le, Feyder, 17/34***

63   <u>*Guerre des valses, La,*</u> Berger & Ploquin, 50/33

64   *Héritier du Bal Tabarin, L',* Kemm, 43/33

65   *Homme à l'Hispano, L',* J. Epstein, 13/33*

66   <u>*Idylle au Caire,*</u> Schünzel & Heymann, 27/33

67   *Il était une fois,* Perret, 41/33

68   *Illustre Maurin, L',* Hugon, 51/33

69   *Incognito,* Gerron, 11/34

70   *Iris perdue et retrouvée,* Gasnier, 52/33

71   *Je te confie ma femme,* Guissart, 16/33

72   *Jocelyn,* Guerlais, 35/33

73   *Judex 34,* Champreux, 18/34

74   *Knock, ou le triomphe de la médecine,* Goupillières & Jouvet, 45/33

75   *Léopold le bien aimé,* Brun, 7/34

76   <u>*Liebelei,*</u> or <u>*Une histoire d'amour,*</u> Ophüls, 11/34 (in Fr)*

122   *Tambour battant*, Robison & Beucler, 9/34
123   *Testament du docteur Mabuse, Le*, Lang & Sti, 17/33
124   **Théodore et Cie, Colombier, 15/33***
125   **Tire au flanc, Wulschleger, 40/33**
126   *Toi que j'adore*, von Bolvary & Valentin, 10/34
127   *Toto*, J. Tourneur, 36/33
128   *Touchons du bois*, Champreux, 14/33
129   *Tout pour l'amour*, May & Clouzot, 38/33
130   *Tout pour rien*, Pujol, 38/33
131   *Trois balles dans la peau*, Lion, 24/34
132   *Trois hommes en habit*, Bonnard, 27/33
133   **Trois pour cent, Dréville, 5/34**
134   *Tunnel, Le*, Bernhardt, 51/33* (in Eng)
135   *Un certain M. Grant*, Lamprecht & Le Bon, 43/33
136   *Un coup de mistral*, Roudès, 6/34
137   *Un de la montagne*, Le Henaff & Poligny, 26/35
138   *Un fil à la patte*, Anton, 12/34
139   *Un jour viendra*, Lamprecht & Veber, 13/34
140   *Un soir de réveillon*, Anton, 42/33 #
141   *Une femme au volant*, Gerron, 38/33
142   *Une fois dans la vie*, Vaucorbeil, 6/34
143   *Une vie perdue*, Rouleau & Esway, 37/33
144   *Vierge du rocher, La*, or *Le Drame de Lourdes*, Pallu, 32/34
145   *Vingt-huit jours de Clairette, Les*, Hugon, 13/33
146   *Vive la compagnie*, Moulins, 11/34
147   *Voie sans disque, La*, Poirier, 20/33
148   *Voix du métale, La*, or *L'Appel de la nuit*, Marca-Rosa, 25/34
149   *Voix sans visage, La*, Mittler, 48/33
150   *Volga en flammes*, Tourjansky, 15/34

1934

1   **Adémaï aviateur, Tarride, 41/34**
2   *Affaire Coquelet, L'*, Gourguet, 42/35
3   *Amok*, Ozep, 37/34
4   *Amour en cage, L'*, Lamac & de Limur, 26/34
5   **Angèle, Pagnol, 43/34***
6   *Antonia, romance hongroise*, Boyer & Neufeld, 2/35
7   *Aristo, L'*, Berthomieu, 36/34
8   *Arlette et ses papas*, Roussell, 37/34
9   *Atalante, L'*, or *Le Chaland qui passe*, Vigo, 37/34*
10 *Auberge du Petit Dragon, L'*, Limur, 50/34
11 *Aux portes de Paris*, Baroncelli & Barrois, 12/35
12 *Aventurier, L'*, L'Herbier, 52/34 #
13 *Banque Némo, La*, Viel, 30/34

14 *Bibi la Purée,* Joannon, 8/35
15 **Billet de mille, Le, Didier, 2/35**
16 *Bleus de la marine, Les,* Cammage, 39/34
17 *Bossu, Le,* Sti, 52/34*
18 *Brevet 95–75,* Lequim, 34/34
19 *Calvaire de Cimiez, Le,* Baroncelli & Dallière, 18/34
20 <u>*Caravane,*</u> Charell, 43/34
21 *Cartouche,* Daroy, 43/34
22 *Caserne en folie, La,* Cammage, 13/35
23 *Cavalier Lafleur, Le,* Ducis, 50/34 #
24 *Cessez le feu,* or *Amis comme autrefois,* Baroncelli, 22/34
25 <u>**Chanson de l'adieu, La,**</u> **von Bolvary & Valentin, 44/34**
26 *Chansons de Paris,* Baroncelli, 24/34
27 *Chéri de sa concierge, Le,* Guarino, 34/34
28 *Cinquième Empreinte, La,* Anton, 27/34
29 **Compartiment de dames seules, Christian-Jaque, 5/35**
30 *Comte Obligado, Le,* Mathot, 5/35*
31 *Crise est finie, La,* Siodmak, 40/34*
32 *Dactylo se marie,* May, 20/34
33 **Dame aux camélias, La, Gance & Rivers, 44/34**
34 **Dédé, Guissart, 51/34***
35 *Dernier Milliardaire, Le,* Clair, 41/34*
36 *Dernière Heure,* Bernard-Derosne, 39/34
37 **École des contribuables, L', Guissart, 44/34**
38 *Enfant du carnaval, L',* Volkoff, 17/34
39 *Famille nombreuse,* Hugon, 43/34
40 *Fanatisme,* Lekain & Ravel, 17/34
41 *Fédora,* Gasnier, 12/34
42 *Filles de la concierge, Les,* or *Mes filles,* J. Tourneur, 22/34
43 *Flambée, La,* Marguenat, 46/34
44 *Flofloche,* Roudès, 30/34
45 *Greluchon délicat, Le,* Choux, 39/34
46 *Homme à l'oreille cassée, L',* Boudrioz, 13/35
47 *Hôtel du Libre Échange, L',* M. Allégret, 45/34*
48 **Itto, Benoît-Lévy & M. Epstein, 12/35 #**
49 *J'ai une idée,* Richebé, 50/34
50 *Jeanne,* Marret, 48/34
51 <u>*Jeune fille d'une nuit, La,*</u> Schünzel & le Bon, 20/34
52 *Jeunesse,* Lacombe, 21/34*
53 **Justin de Marseille, Tourneur, 14/35***
54 **Lac aux Dames, M. Allégret, 20/34***
55 *Liliom,* Lang, 17/34*
56 **Maison dans la dune, La, Lampin, 31/34**
57 *Maître Bolbec et son mari,* Natanson, 48/34
58 *Mam'zelle Spahi,* Vaucorbeil, 44/34

104   <u>*Turandot, princesse de Chine*</u>, Lamprecht & Veber, 7/35
105   ***Un homme en or,*** **Dréville, 45/34***
106   *Un tour de cochon,* Tzipine, 26/34
107   *Un train dans la nuit,* Hervil, 39/34
108   *Une femme chipée,* Colombier, 41/34
109   *Une nuit de folie,* Cammage, 17/34 #
110   <u>*Vers l'abîme*</u>, Steinhoff & Veber, 35/34
111   <u>***Veuve joyeuse, La***</u>, **Lubitsch, 4/35**
112   *Votre sourire,* Banks & Caron, 49/34
113   *Voyage de Monsieur Perrichon, Le,* Tarride, 19/34
114   *Voyage imprévu, Le,* Limur, 52/34
115   ***Zouzou,*** **M. Allégret, 51/34***

1935

1   *Adémaï au Moyen-Age,* Marguenat, 43/35*
2   *Amants et voleurs,* Bernard, 46/35
3   *Arènes joyeuses,* Anton, 51/35
4   *Aux jardins de Murcie,* Gras & Joly, 48/36
5   ***Baccara,*** **Mirande & Moguy, 51/35***
6   ***Bandera, La,*** **Duvivier, 38/35***
7   <u>*Barcarolle*</u>, Lamprecht & Lebon, 13/35
8   <u>*Baron Tzigane, Le*</u>, Hartl & Chomette, 27/35
9   ***Beaux jours, Les,*** **M. Allégret, 45/35**
10   *Bébé de l'escadron, Le,* Sti, 48/35
11   ***Bichon,*** **Rivers, 10/36**
12   ***Bonheur, Le,*** **L'Herbier, 6/35***
13   *Bonne Chance,* Guitry & Rivers, 38/35*
14   *Bourrachon,* Guissart, 47/35
15   *Bourrasque,* Billon, 25/35 #
16   *Bout de chou,* Wulschleger, 34/35
17   <u>*Cavalerie légère*</u>, Hochbaum & Vitrac, 50/35
18   *Chant de l'amour, Le,* Roudès, 27/35
19   *Chemineau, Le,* Rivers, 46/35 #
20   *Cigalon,* Pagnol, 49/35*
21   *Clown Bux, Le,* Natanson, 20/35
22   <u>*Contrôleur des wagons-lits, Le*</u>, Eichberg, 7/35
23   *Coqueluche de ces dames, La,* Rosca (?)
24   *Coup de trois, Le,* Limur, 16/36
25   *Coup de vent,* Dréville, 15/36
26   *Couturier de mon cœur,* or *Le Roi de la couture,* Cesse & Jayet, 45/35
27   *Crime de Monsieur Lange, Le,* Renoir, 4/36*
28   ***Crime et châtiment,*** **Chenal, 20/35***
29   *Debout là-dedans,* Wulschleger, 51/35
30   *Dernière Valse, La,* Mittler, 34/35

31   *Deuxième Bureau*, **Billon, 38/35**
32   *Diable en bouteille, Le*, Hilpert & Steinbicker, 14/35
33   *Dieux s'amusent, Les*, Schünzel & Valentin, 37/35
34   *Divine*, Ophüls, 46/35 #
35   *Domino vert, Le*, Selpin & Decoin, 2/36
36   *Dora Nelson*, Guissart, 45/35
37   *École des cocottes, L'*, **Colombier, 39/35**
38   *École des vierges, L'*, Weill, 44/35
39   *Enfant du Danube, L'*, Derlé & Alexandre, 5/36
40   *Époux célibataires, Les*, Boyer, 29/35
41   *Époux scandaleux, Les*, Lacombe, 28/35
42   *Équipage, L'*, **Litvak, 43/35***
43   *Escale*, Valray, 21/35*
44   *Famille Pont-Biquet, La*, Christian-Jaque, 38/35
45   *Fanfare d'amour*, **Pottier, 46/35**
46   *Ferdinand le noceur*, Sti, 8/35
47   *Fille de Madame Agnot, La*, Bernard-Derosne, 41/35
48   *Folies-Bergère*, **Achard, 19/35**
49   *Gaietés de la finance, Les*, Forrester, 6/36
50   *Gangster malgré lui*, Hugon, 18/35
51   *Gaspard de Besse*, Hugon, 51/35
52   *Golem, Le*, Duvivier, 6/36*
53   *Golgotha*, Duvivier, 15/35*
54   *Gondole aux chimères, La*, Genina, 15/36
55   *Haut comme trois pommes*, Ramelot & Vajda, 10/36
56   *Heureuse Aventure, L'*, Georgesco, 21/35
57   *Impossible Aveu, L'*, Guarino, 22/35
58   *J'aime toutes les femmes*, **Lamac, 43/35**
59   *Jérome Perreau*, Gance, 47/35
60   *Jeunes Filles à marier*, Vallée, 27/35
61   *Jeunesse d'abord*, Stelli, 22/36
62   *Jim la Houlette*, Berthomieu, 44/35*
63   *Joli monde*, Le Henaff, 31/36
64   *Jonny, haute-couture*, Poligny, 15/35
65   *J'te dis qu'elle t'a fait de l'œil*, Forrester, 36/35
66   *Juanita*, Caron, 39/35
67   *Kermesse héroïque, La*, **Feyder, 49/35***
68   *Kœnigsmark*, **Tourneur, 48/35**
69   *Lucrèce Borgia*, Gance, 51/35 #
70   *Lune de miel*, Ducis, 50/35
71   *Mademoiselle Mozart*, Noé, 4/36
72   *Marchand d'amour*, Gréville, 25/35
73   *Marie des Angoisses*, Bernheim, 30/35
74   *Mariée du régiment, La*, Cammage, 45/35
75   *Marmaille, La*, Bernard-Deschamps, 52/35

76 *Marraine de Charley, La,* **Colombier, 3/36**
77 *Martha,* Anton, 3/36
78 ***Mascotte, La,* Mathot, 30/35**
79 *Merlusse,* Pagnol, 49/35 #
80 *Michel Strogoff,* Baroncelli, 10/36
81 *Moïse et Salomon parfumeurs,* Hugon, 50/35
82 *Monsieur Sans-Gêne,* Anton, 12/35
83 *Mystère Imberger, Le,* Sévérac, 15/35
84 ***Mystères de Paris, Les,* Gandera, 38/35**
85 *Odette,* Houssin (& Zambon), 25/35
86 *Paris, mes amours,* Blondeau, 23/35
87 *Paris-Camargue,* Forrestier, 35/35
88 *Parlez-moi d'amour,* Guissart, 40/35
89 ***Pasteur,* Guitry & Rivers, 38/35 #**
90 *Petite Sauvage, La,* Limur, 1/36
91 *Pluie d'or,* Rozier (9/41?)
92 *Princesse Tam-Tam,* Gréville, 43/35*
93 ***Quelle drôle de gosse!,* Joannon, 20/35***
94 *Retour au paradis,* Poligny, 46/35
95 *Roman d'un jeune homme pauvre, Le,* Gance, 8/36
96 *Rose,* Rouleau, 8/36
97 ***Roses noires,* Boyer (& Martin), 7/36**
98 *Rosière des halles, La,* Limur, 41/35*
99 *Route heureuse, La,* Lacombe, 7/36
100 ***Route impériale, La,* L'Herbier, 41/35**
101 *Sacré Léonce,* Christian-Jaque, 3/36
102 *Sœurs Hortensias, Les,* Guissart, 52/35
103 *Son Excellence Antonin,* Tavano, 23/35
104 *Sonnette d'alarme, La,* Christian-Jaque, 23/35
105 *Sous la griffe,* Christian-Jaque, 46/35
106 <u>*Sous la Terreur,*</u> Forzano & Cohen, 4/36
107 <u>*Stradivarius,*</u> von Bolvary & Valentin, 42/35
108 *Tampon du colonel, Le,* Pallu & Lerel (?)
109 *Tendre Ennemie, La,* Ophüls, 43/36*
110 *Toni,* Renoir, 8/35*
111 *Touche-à-Tout,* Dréville, 44/35
112 ***Tovaritch,* Deval, Tarride, & Trivas, 18/35**
113 *Train d'amour, Le,* Weill, 44/35
114 *Train de plaisir,* Joannon, 10/36
115 <u>*Un homme de trop à bord,*</u> Lamprecht & Le Bon, 49/35
116 ***Un oiseau rare,* Pottier, 22/35 #**
117 *Un soir de bombe,* Cammage, 49/35*
118 *Une fille à papa,* Guissart, 16/36 #
119 <u>*Une nuit de noces,*</u> Monca & Kéroul, 34/35
120 <u>*Valse royale,*</u> Grémillon, 1/36

121   *Variétés,* Farkas, 40/35
122   Veille d'armes, L'Herbier, 50/35
123   *Vertige, Le,* Schiller, 8/35
124   *Vie parisienne, La,* Siodmak, 6/36
125   *Vogue mon cœur,* Daroy, 48/35
126   *Voyage d'agrément,* Christian-Jaque, 28/35
127   Yeux noirs, Les, Tourjansky, 35/35

1936

1   *À minuit le 7,* Canonge, 3/37
2   *À nous deux, Madame la vie,* Mirande, 13/37
3   Amant de Madame Vidal, L', Berthomieu, 40/36
4   *Amants terribles, Les,* M. Allégret, 34/36
5   *Ange du foyer, L',* Mathot, 9/37
6   *Anne-Marie,* Bernard, 10/36
7   Appel du silence, L', Poirier, 18/36*
8   *Argent, L',* Billon, 21/36
9   *Assaut, L',* Ducis, 52/36
10   Au service du Tsar, Billon, 46/36
11   Au son des guitares, Ducis, 43/36*
12   *Avec le sourire,* Tourneur, 49/36 #
13   *Aventure à Paris,* M. Allégret, 48/36*
14   *Bach détective,* Pujol, 43/36
15   Bas-Fonds, Les, Renoir, 50/36*
16   *Bateliers de la Volga, Les,* Strijewsky, 6/36
17   Belle Équipe, La, Duvivier, 38/36*
18   *Bête aux sept manteaux, La,* Limur, 9/37
19   *Blanchette,* Caron, 11/37
20   *Brigade en jupons, La,* Limur, 28/36
21   César, Pagnol, 46/36*
22   *Chanson du souvenir, La,* Poligny, 21/37
23   Chemin de Rio, Le, or Cargaison blanche, Siodmak, 3/37
24   Club de femmes, Deval, 21/36
25   *Cœur de gueux,* J. Epstein, 15/37
26   *Cœur dispose, Le,* Lacombe, 19/36
27   Coupable, Le, Bernard, 3/37*
28   Courrier-Sud, Billon, 4/37
29   *Course à la vertu, La,* Gleize, (?)
30   *Dame de Vittel, La,* Goupillières, 6/37
31   *Demi-Vierges, Les,* Caron, 50/36
32   <u>*Deux Favoris, Les,*</u> Jacoby & Hornez, 19/36
33   *Deux Gamines, Les,* Champreux & Hervil, 15/36
34   *Deux Gosses, Les,* Rivers, 37/36
35   *Disque 413, Le,* Pottier, 30/36

36   <u>Donogoo</u>, Schünzel & Chomette, 28/36
37   *École des journalistes, L'*, Christian-Jaque, 22/36
38   *Empreinte rouge, L'*, Canonge, 26/37(?)
39   *Enfants de Paris*, Roudès, 50/40(?)
40   *Esclave blanc, L'*, Paulin, 40/36
41   *Faiseur, Le*, Hugon, 32/36
42   **Faisons un rêve, Guitry, 1/37***
43   <u>Femmes</u>, Gardan & Bernard-Roland, (?)
44   *Flamme, La*, Berthomieu, 19/36
45   *Gaietés du palace, Les*, Kapps, 50/36
46   <u>Gais Lurons, Les</u>, Martin & Natanson, 41/36
47   **Garçonne, La, Limur, 9/36**
48   *Gigolette*, Noé, 8/37
49   *Grand Refrain, Le*, Mirande, 38/36
50   **Grands, Les, Bibal & Gandera, 40/36**
51   *Guerre des gosses, La*, Daroy & Deslaw, 43/36
52   **Hélène, Benoît-Lévy & M. Epstein, 42/36**
53   **Homme à abattre, L', Mathot, 9/37**
54   *Homme de nulle part, L'*, Chenal, 8/37*
55   *Homme du jour, L'*, Duvivier, 9/37 #
56   *Homme sans cœur, L'*, Joannon, 10/37
57   **Hommes nouveaux, Les, L'Herbier, 51/36 #**
58   *Île des Veuves, L'*, Heymann, 18/37
59   *Inspecteur Grey*, Canonge, 21/36
60   *Jacques et Jacotte*, Péguy, 28/36
61   *J'arrose mes galons*, Darmont & Pujol, 52/36
62   **Jenny, Carné, 38/36***
63   *Jeunes Filles de Paris*, or *La Vie n'est pas un roman*, Vermorel, 6/37
64   *Josette*, Christian-Jaque, 4/37 #
65   *Joueuse d'orgue, La*, Roudès, 46/36
66   *Jumeaux de Brighton, Les*, Heymann, 44/36
67   *Loupiote, La*, Bouquet & Kemm, 4/37
68   **Loups entre eux, Les, Mathot, 35/36**
69   **Mademoiselle Docteur or *Salonique, nid d'espions*, Pabst, 16/37***
70   *Madone de l'Atlantique, La*, Weill, (?)
71   *Maison d'en face, La*, Christian-Jaque, 5/37
72   *Mari rêvé, Le*, Capellani, 2/37
73   *Maria de la nuit*, or *Nuit d'Espagne*, Rozier, 27/36
74   *Mariages de Mlle Lévy, Les*, Hugon, 42/36
75   **Marinella, Caron, 13/36***
76   *Maris de ma femme, Les*, Cammage, 10/37 (?)
77   **Mayerling, Litvak, 5/36***
78   *Ménilmontant*, Guissart, 4/37*
79   *Mes tantes et moi*, Noé, 6/37

80 *Messieurs les Ronds de Cuir,* **Mirande, 6/37***
81 *Mioche, Le,* **Moguy, 45/36**
82 *Mister Flow,* Siodmak, 44/36
83 *Mon père avait raison,* Guitry, 48/36*
84 *Monsieur Personne,* Christian-Jaque, 49/36
85 *Mort en fuite, Le,* Berthomieu, 47/36*
86 *Moutonnet,* **Sti, 28/36**
87 *Mutinés de l'Elseneur, Les,* **Chenal, 9/36**
88 *Mystérieuse Lady, La,* Péguy, (?)
89 *Nitchevo,* **Baroncelli, 51/36**
90 *Notre-Dame d'Amour,* Caron, 46/36
91 *Nouveau Testament, Le,* **Guitry & Ryder, 7/36***
92 *Œil de Lynx, détective,* Ducis, 35/36
93 *On ne roule pas Antoinette,* Madeux, 21/36
94 *Pantins d'amour,* Kapps, 17/37(?)
95 *Paris,* Choux, 3/37*
96 *Passé à vendre,* Pujol, 10/37
97 *Pattes de mouche, Les,* Grémillon, 21/36
98 *Peau d'un autre, La,* Pujol, 3/37
99 *Pepe le Moko,* **Duvivier, 5/37***
100 *Petite Dame du wagon-lit, La,* Cammage, 19/36 #
101 *Petites Alliées, Les,* **Dréville, 13/36**
102 *Peur, La,* or *Vertige d'un soir,* **Tourjansky, 15/36**
103 *Pocharde, La,* or *Le Crime de la Pocharde,* Bouquet & Kemm, 9/37
104 *Port-Arthur,* **Farkas, 50/36 #**
105 *Porte du large, La,* **L'Herbier, 43/36**
106 *Prends la route,* Boyer, 6/37 #
107 *Prête-moi ta femme,* Cammage, 39/36
108 *Puits en flammes,* Tourjansky, 12/37
109 *Quand minuit sonnera,* Joannon, 48/36
110 *Reine des resquilleuses, La,* Gastyne & Glass, 11/37
111 *Réprouvés, Les,* Sévérac, 8/37 #
112 *Rigolboche,* **Christian-Jaque, 40/36***
113 *Roi, Le,* **Colombier, 44/36 #**
114 *Roman d'un spahi, Le,* Bernheim, 13/36 #
115 *Roman d'un tricheur, Le,* **Guitry, 38/36***
116 *Romarin,* Hugon, 1/37
117 *Rose effeuillée, La,* or *La Vie de Sainte Thérèse de Lisieux,* Pallu, 25/37
118 *Samson,* **Tourneur, 10/36**
119 *Secret de l'émeraude, Le,* Canonge, 33/36
120 *Secret de Polichinelle, Le,* **Berthomieu, 6/36**
121 *Sept hommes . . . une femme,* **Mirande, 35/36***
122 *Souris bleue, La,* Ducis, 24/36
123 *Sous les yeux d'Occident,* M. Allégret, 12/36*

124 *Symphonie des brigands, La,* Feher, 21/37
125 *Tarass Boulba,* Granowsky, 11/36
126 *Tentation, La,* Caron, 34/36
127 *Terre qui meurt, La,* Vallée, 17/36*
128 *Toi c'est moi,* Guissart, 49/36 #
129 *Topaze,* Pagnol, 22/36 #
130 *Tout va très bien Madame la Marquise,* Wulschleger, 48/36 #
131 *Trois dans un moulin,* Weill, (?)
132 *Trois jours de perm',* Kéroul & Monca, (?)
133 *Trois . . . six . . . neuf,* Rouleau, 3/37
134 *Un de la légion,* Christian-Jaque, 38/36 #
135 *Un grand amour de Beethoven,* Gance, 3/37*
136 *Un mauvais garçon,* Boyer, 50/36*
137 *Une femme qui se partage,* Cammage, 8/37
138 *Une gueule en or,* Colombier, 24/36
139 *Une poule sur un mur,* Gleize, 21/36
140 *Vagabond bien aimé, Le,* Bernhardt, 19/36
141 *Valse éternelle,* Neufeld, 14/36
142 *Vingt-sept rue de la Paix,* Pottier, 46/36
143 *Vous n'avez rien à déclarer?,* Joannon, 9/37 #

1937

1 *À Venise une nuit,* Christian-Jaque, 46/37
2 *Abus de confiance,* Decoin, 49/37*
3 *Affaire du courrier de Lyon, L',* Autant-Lara & Lehmann, 46/37*
4 *Affaire Lafarge, L',* Chenal, 10/38
5 *Alexis, gentleman-chauffeur,* Vaucorbeil, 29/38
6 *Alibi, L',* Chenal, 52/37*
7 *Aloha, le chant des îles,* Mathot, 51/37
8 *Amour veille, L',* Roussell, 15/37
9 *Anges noirs, Les,* Rozier, 44/37
10 *Appel de la vie, L',* Neveux, 21/37
11 *Arsène Lupin, détective,* Diamant-Berger, 18/37*
12 *Au soleil de Marseille,* Ducis, 22/38 #
13 *Balthazar,* Colombier, 5/38
14 *Bataille silencieuse, La,* Billon, 37/37
15 *Belle de Montparnasse, La,* Cammage, 24/37 #
16 *Boissière,* Rivers, 22/37
17 *Boulot aviateur,* Canonge, 26/37
18 *Cantinier de la coloniale, La,* Wulschleger, 28/37
19 *Ces dames aux chapeaux verts,* Cloche, 52/37
20 *Chanteur de minuit, Le,* Joannon, 50/37
21 *Chaste Suzanne, La,* Berthomieu, 22/37
22 *Chéri-Bibi,* Mathot, 4/38*

23 *Chipée,* Goupillières, 6/38
24 *Choc en retour,* Kéroul & Monca, 15/37 #
25 *Cinderella,* Caron, 27/37
26 **Citadelle du silence, La,** L'Herbier, 39/37
27 **Claudine à l'école,** Poligny, 51/37 #
28 *Club des aristocrates, Le,* Colombier, 36/37
29 *Concierge revient de suite, Le,* Rives, (?)
30 **Dame de Malacca, La,** M Allégret, 40/37*
31 **Dame de pique, La,** Ozep, 27/37
32 **Danseuse rouge, La,** Paulin, 21/37
33 **Dégourdis de la 11e, Les,** Christian-Jaque, 11/37*
34 **Désiré,** Guitry, 49/37*
35 *Deux combinards, Les,* Houssin, 8/38
36 **Double Crime sur la ligne Maginot,** Gandera, 39/37 #
37 *Drôle de drame,* Carné, 43/37*
38 *Escadrille de la chance, L',* Vaucorbeil, 26/38
39 *Êtes-vous jalouse?,* Chomette, 2/38
40 **Étrange M. Victor, L',** Grémillon, 18/38*
41 *Euskadi,* Le Henaff, 24/37
42 **Fauteuil 47, Le,** Rivers, 39/37*
43 *Femme du bout du monde, La,* J. Epstein, 3/38
44 *Fessée, La,* Caron, 46/37
45 **Feu!,** Baroncelli, 43/37
46 *Fille de la Madelon, La,* Mugeli & Pallu, 42/37
47 *Filles du Rhône, Les,* Paulin, 16/38
48 *Forfaiture,* L'Herbier, 49/37*
49 *Franco de port,* Kirsanoff, 20/37
50 *François Ier,* Christian-Jaque, 7/37 #
51 *Fraudeur, Le,* or *Ceux de la douane,* Simons, (?)
52 <u>*Gangsters de l'exposition, Les,*</u> de Meyst, 19/39(?)
53 *Gens du voyage, Les,* Feyder, 9/38*
54 **Grande Illusion, La,** Renoir, 23/37*
55 **Gribouille,** M. Allégret, 37/37*
56 *Griffe du hasard, La,* Pujol, 13/37
57 **Gueule d'amour,** Grémillon, 38/37*
58 **Habit vert, L',** Richebé, 45/37*
59 **Hercule,** Esway, 9/38 #
60 *Hommes de proie, Les,* Rozier, 27/37
61 *Hommes sans nom, Les,* Vallée, 49/37
62 **Ignace,** Colombier, 18/37
63 **Innocent, L',** Cammage, 6/38
64 *J'accuse,* Gance, 3/38
65 *Liberté,* Kemm, 15/38
66 *Ma petite marquise,* Péguy, 49/37
67 **Mademoiselle ma mère,** Decoin, 32/37*

68 *Maman Colibri*, Dréville, 49/37
69 ***Marseillaise, La*, Renoir, 6/38***
70 ***Marthe Richard au service de la France*, Bernard, 16/37***
71 ***Mensonge de Nina Petrovna, Le*, Tourjansky, 45/37***
72 ***Messager, Le*, Rouleau, 36/37 #**
73 *Miarka, la fille à l'ourse*, Choux, 52/37
74 *Mirages*, Ryder, 4/38
75 ***Mollenard*, Siodmak, 4/38***
76 *Mon député et sa femme*, Cammage, 31/37
77 *Monsieur Bégonia*, Hugon, 52/37
78 *Monsieur Breloque a disparu*, Péguy, 13/38 #
79 *Mort du cygne, La*, Benoît-Lévy & M. Epstein, 48/37
80 ***Naples au baiser de feu*, Genina, 51/37***
81 *Neuf de trèfle*, Mayrargue, 52/37
82 *Nostalgie*, Tourjansky, 9/38
83 *Nuits blanches de Saint-Pétersbourg, Les*, Dréville, 11/38
84 ***Nuits de feu*, L'Herbier, 16/37**
85 *Nuits de prince*, Strijewski, 4/38
86 ***Occident, L'*, Fescourt, 7/38**
87 ***Orage*, M. Allégret, 2/38***
88 *Passeurs d'hommes*, Jayet, 49/37
89 ***Perles de la couronne, Les*, Christian-Jaque & Guitry, 20/37***
90 *Pirates du rail, Les*, Christian-Jaque, 3/38 #
91 *Plus Beau Gosse de France, Le*, or *Le Mari de la reine*, Pujol, 43/37
92 *Plus Belle Fille du monde, La*, Kirsanov, 31/38
93 *Police mondaine*, Bernheim & Chamborant, 15/37
94 *Porte-Veine, Le*, Berthomieu, 43/37
95 ***Prison sans barreaux*, Moguy, 7/38***
96 ***Puritain, Le*, Musso, 2/38 #**
97 ***Quadrille*, Guitry, 4/38 #**
98 *Quatre heures du matin*, Rivers, 4/38
99 ***Ramuntcho*, Barberis, 8/38**
100 *Regain*, Pagnol, 44/37*
101 *Rendez-vous Champs-Élysées*, Houssin, 17/37 #
102 ***Rois du sport, Les*, Colombier, 38/37 #**
103 *Sarati le terrible*, Hugon, 31/37*
104 ***Schpountz, Le*, Pagnol, 15/38***
105 *Secrets de la Mer Rouge, Les*, Pottier, 36/37
106 *Si tu reviens*, Daniel-Norman, 8/38
107 ***Sœurs d'armes*, Poirier, 45/37**
108 *Tamara la complaisante*, Gandera, 7/38
109 *Temps des cerises, Le*, Le Chanois, (?)*
110 <u>*Tigre du Bengale, Le*</u>, Parts 1 and 2 (*Le Tombeau hindou*), Eichberg, 11/38 and 12/38
111 *Titin des Martigues*, Pujol, 6/38#

112   *Tour de Nesle, La,* Roudès, 31/37
113   *Tragédie impériale, La,* L'Herbier, 13/38*
114   *Treizième Enquête de Grey, La,* Maudru, 26/37
115   *Troïka sur la piste blanche,* Dréville, 25/37
116   *Trois artilleurs au pensionnat,* Pujol, 11/37
117   *Un carnet de bal,* Duvivier, 37/37*
118   *Un déjeuner de soleil,* Cravenne, 50/37
119   *Un meurtre a été commis,* Orval, 15/38
120   *Un scandale aux galeries,* Sti, 46/37
121   *Un soir à Marseille,* Canonge, 12/38
122   *Une femme sans importance,* Choux, 10/37
123   *Voleur de femmes, Le,* Gance, 10/38
124   *Yoshiwara,* Ophüls, 33/37*

1938

1   *Accord final,* Rosenkranz & Sierck, 6/39
2   *Accroche-Cœur, L',* Caron, 35/38*
3   *Adrienne Lecouvreur,* L'Herbier, 39/38
4   *Alerte en Méditerranée,* Joannon, 35/38*
5   *Altitude 3200,* Benoît-Lévy & M. Epstein, 29/38
6   *Ange que j'ai vendu, L',* Bernheim, 23/38
7   *Avion de minuit, L',* Kirsanoff, 31/38
8   *Bar du sud,* Fescourt, 12/38
9   *Barnabé,* Esway, 19/38
10   *Belle Étoile,* Baroncelli, 47/38
11   *Belle Revanche, La,* Mesnier, 19/39
12   *Bête humaine, La,* Renoir, 51/38*
13   *Ça, c'est du sport,* Pujol, 34/38 #
14   *Café de Paris,* Lacombe, Mirande, & Vernay, 38/38*
15   *Capitaine Benoît, Le,* Canonge, 52/38
16   *Carrefour,* Bernhardt, 43/38*
17   *Ceux de demain,* or *L'Enfant de la troupe,* Millar & Pallu, (34/38)
18   *Chaleur du sein, La,* Boyer, 44/38*
19   *Champions de France,* Rozier, 51/38
20   *Cité des lumières, La,* Limur, 49/38
21   *Clodoche,* or *Sous les ponts de Paris,* Lamy & Orval, 29/38
22   *Cœur ébloui, Le,* Vallée, 22/38
23   *Conflit,* Moguy, 51/38
24   *Deux de la réserve,* Pujol, 15/39
25   *Disparus de Saint-Agil, Les,* Christian-Jaque, 15/38*
26   *Dompteur, Le,* Colombier, 50/38
27   *Drame de Shanghaï, Le,* Pabst, 43/38*
28   *Durand bijoutier,* Stelli, 27/38
29   *Éducation de prince,* Esway, 40/38*

30   *Entraîneuse, L',* Valentin, 2/40 #
31   **Entrée des artistes, M. Allégret, 40/38***
32   *Ernest le rebelle,* Christian-Jaque, 45/38*
33   *Eusèbe, député,* Berthomieu, 10/39
34   **Femme du boulanger, La, Pagnol, 36/38***
35   *Femmes collantes, Les,* Caron, 17/38
36   *Feux de joie,* Houssin, 5/39 #
37   **Fin du jour, La, Duvivier, 12/39***
38   *Firmin, le muet de Saint-Pataclet,* Sévérac, 36/38
39   *Fort-Dolorès,* Le Henaff, 10/39
40   *Frères corses,* Kelber, 18/39
41   *Gaietés de l'exposition, Les,* Hajos, 20/38
42   *Gargousse,* Wulschleger, 30/38
43   **Gibraltar, Ozep, 48/38**
44   *Glu, La,* Choux, 18/38
45   *Gosse de riche,* Canonge, 23/38
46   *Goualeuse, La,* Rivers, 42/38 #
47   *Grand-Père,* Péguy, 17/39
48   *Grisou,* or *Les Hommes sans soleil,* Canonge, 19/38
49   *Héros de la Marne, Le,* Hugon, 48/38
50   **Hôtel du Nord, Carné, 50/38***
51   *Inconnue de Monte Carlo, L',* Berthomieu, 4/39
52   *Je chante,* Stengel, 48/38*
53   **J'étais une aventurière, Bernard, 51/38 #**
54   *Joueur d'échecs, Le,* Dréville, 48/38*
55   **Joueur, Le, Lamprecht & Daquin, 36/38**
56   **Katia, Tourneur, 42/38***
57   **Légions d'honneur, Gleize, 7/38 #**
58   **Lumières de Paris, Pottier, 40/38 #**
59   *Ma sœur de lait,* Boyer, 19/38
60   **Maison du Maltais, La, Chenal, 38/38***
61   *Mariage de Véréna, Le,* or *La Bâtarde,* Daroy, (22/39)
62   *Marraine du régiment, La,* Rosca, (19/39)
63   *Métropolitain,* Cam, 6/39*
64   **Mon curé chez les riches, Boyer, 51/38***
65   *Mon oncle et mon curé,* Caron, 10/39
66   *Monsieur Coccinelle,* Bernard-Deschamps, 44/38*
67   *Monsieur de cinq heures, Le,* Caron, 11/38
68   *Moulin dans le soleil, Le,* Didier, 13/39
69   *Noix de coco,* Boyer, 6/39*
70   *Nouveaux Riches, Les,* Berthomieu, 24/38 #
71   <u>*Or dans la montagne, L',*</u> Haufleur, 19/39
72   *Paix sur le Rhin,* Choux, 45/38
73   *Paradis de Satan, Le,* Gandera, 36/38
74   *Patriote, Le,* Tourneur, 24/38

75   *Père Lebonnard, Le,* Limur, 25/39
76   *Petit Chose, Le,* Cloche, 22/38 #
77   *Petite Peste,* Limur, 8/39
78   *Piste du Sud, La,* Billon, 36/38
79   *Place de la Concorde,* Lamac, 1/39
80   *Présidente, La,* Rivers, 21/38 #
81   *Prince Bouboule,* Houssin, 2/39
82   *Prince de mon cœur,* Daniel-Norman, 46/38 #
83   *Prisons de femmes,* Richebé, 41/38*
84   *Quai des brumes,* Carné, 20/38*
85   *Raphaël le tatoué,* Christian-Jaque, 6/39*
86   *Récif de corail, Le,* Gleize, 9/39
87   *Remontons les Champs-Élysées,* Bibal & Guitry, 48/38*
88   *Retour à l'aube,* Decoin, 46/38
89   *Révolté, Le,* Mathot, 43/38
90   *Rois de la flotte, Les,* Pujol, 42/38
91   *Roman de Werther, Le,* Ophüls, 49/38 #
92   *Route enchantée, La,* Caron, 48/38*
93   *Rue sans joie, La,* Hugon, 16/38*
94   *Ruisseau, Le,* Autant-Lara & Léhman, 43/38 #
95   *S. O. S. Sahara,* Baroncelli, 33/38
96   *Serge Panine,* Méré & Schiller, 3/39
97   *Son oncle de Normandie,* Dréville, 23/39
98   *Tarakanowa,* Ozep, 12/38
99   *Tempête sur l'Asie,* Oswald, 16/38
100   *Terre de feu,* L'Herbier, 39/42
101   *Thérèse Martin,* Canonge, 23/39
102   *Train pour Venise, Le,* Berthomieu, 37/38
103   *Tricoche et Cacolet,* Colombier, 36/38*
104   *Trois artilleurs à l'opéra,* Chotin, 19/39
105   *Trois artilleurs en vadrouille,* Pujol, 27/38
106   *Trois de Saint-Cyr,* Paulin, 5/39 #
107   *Trois valses,* Berger, 50/38*
108   *Ultimatum,* Siodmak & Wiene, 43/38 #
109   *Un de la Canebière,* Pujol, 38/38*
110   *Un fichu métier,* Ducis, 41/38
111   *Un gosse en or,* or *Cœur de gosse,* Pallu, 4/39
112   *Une de la cavalerie,* Cammage, 16/38
113   *Une java,* Orval, 3/39
114   *Vacances payées,* Cammage, 50/38
115   *Vénus de l'or, La,* Delannoy & Méré, 19/38
116   *Vidocq,* Daroy, 12/39 #
117   *Vie est magnifique, La,* Cloche, 9/39
118   *Vierge folle, La,* Diamant-Berger, 47/38
119   *Visages de femmes,* Guissart, 10/39

1939 (Jan.–Aug.)

1   *Angélica,* Choux, 39/40
2   *Battement de cœur,* Decoin, 6/40*
3   *Bécassine,* Caron, 51/40 #
4   *Berlingot et Cie,* Rivers, 17/39*
5   *Bois sacré, Le,* Mathot, 48/39
6   *Brazza ou l'épopée du Congo,* Poirier, 5/40
7   *Brigade sauvage, La,* Dréville & L'Herbier, 17/39
8   *Café du Port, Le,* Choux, 19/40
9   *Campement 13,* Constant, 50/40
10 *Cas de conscience,* Kapps, 20/39
11 *Cavalcade d'amour,* Bernard, 3/40*
12 *Charrette fantôme, La,* Duvivier, 7/40*
13 *Chasseur de chez Maxim's, Le,* Cammage, 45/39
14 *Château des quatre obèses, Le,* Noé, 21/39
15 *Chemin de l'honneur, Le,* Paulin, (1940?)
16 *Cinq Sous de Lavarède, Les,* Cammage, 10/39*
17 *Circonstances atténuantes,* Boyer, 30/39*
18 *Club des fadas, Le,* Couzinet, 31/39
19 *Coups de feu,* Barberis, 16/39
20 *Danube bleu, Le,* Reinert & Rodé, 12/40
21 *De Mayerling à Sarajevo,* Ophüls, 18/40*
22 *Dédé la Musique,* Berthomieu, 9/42
23 *Dernier Tournant, Le,* Chenal, 20/39*
24 *Dernière Jeunesse,* Musso, 35/39 #
25 *Derrière la façade,* Lacombe & Mirande, 11/39*
26 *Déserteur, Le,* or *Je t'attendrai,* Moguy, 11/39
27 *Deuxième Bureau contre Kommandantur,* or *Terre d'angoisse,* Bibal & Jayet, 25/39*
28 *Duel, Le,* Fresnay, 28/41
29 *Embuscade, L',* Rivers, 12/41 #
30 *Émigrante, L',* Joannon, 11/40 #
31 *Empreinte du dieu, L',* or *L'Empreinte de Dieu,* Moguy 20/41*
32 *Enfer des anges, L',* Christian-Jaque, 7/41
33 *Entente cordiale,* L'Herbier, 16/39*
34 *Esclave blanche, L',* Sorkin, 7/39
35 *Étrange Nuit de Noël, L',* Noé, 33/39
36 *Face au destin,* Fescourt, 18/40
37 *Famille Duraton, La,* Stengel, 10/40*
38 *Feu de paille, Le,* Benoît-Lévy, 13/40
39 *Fric-Frac,* Autant-Lara & Lehmann, 24/39*
40 *Gangsters du Château d'If, Les,* Pujol, 7/39 #
41 *Grand Élan, Le,* Christian-Jaque, 50/40
42 *Grey contre X,* Gragnon & Maudru, 4/41(?)

43   *Héritier des Mondésir, L',* Valentin, 19/40 #
44   *Homme du Niger, L',* Baroncelli, 4/40 #
45   *Ils étaient neuf célibataires,* Guitry, 43/39*
46   *Intrigante, L',* Couzinet, 38/40
47   *Jeunes Filles en détresse,* Pabst, 34/39
48   *Jour se lève, Le,* Carné, 23/39*
49   *Louise,* Gance, 34/39*
50   *Ma tante dictateur,* Pujol, 28/39
51   *Macao, l'enfer du jeu,* Delannoy, 49/42*
52   *Mahlia la métisse,* Kapps, 20/42
53   *Marseille mes amours,* Daniel-Norman, 18/40
54   *Menaces,* Gréville, 2/40*
55   *Monde tremblera, Le,* or *La Révolte des vivants,* Pottier, 5/45 (1941?)
56   *Monsieur Brotonneau,* Esway, 31/39
57   *Monsieur le Maire,* or *Dr Herr Maire,* Sévérac, (?)
58   *Moulin Rouge,* Hugon, 3/41
59   *Musiciens du ciel, Les,* Lacombe, 7/40*
60   *Nadia, la femme traquée,* Orval, 24/41
61   *Narcisse,* d'Aguiar, 13/40
62   *Nord Atlantique,* Cloche, 15/39
63   *Notre Dame de la Mouise,* Péguy, 15/41 #
64   *Nuit de décembre,* Bernhardt, 9/41
65   *Nuits de bal,* Litvak, (1939?)
66   *Or du Cristobal, L',* Becker & Stelli, 15/40
67   *Ôtages, Les,* Bernard, 12/39
68   *Paradis des voleurs, Le,* Marsoudet, 24/39
69   *Paradis perdu,* Gance, 50/40*
70   *Paris–New York,* Mirande, 14/40
71   *Pièges,* Siodmak, 50/39*
72   *Piste du Nord, La,* Feyder, 9/42
73   *Pour le maillot jaune,* Stelli, 43/40
74   *Président Haudecœur, Le,* Dréville, 15/40
75   *Quartier Latin,* Chamborant, Colombier, & Esway, 34/39 #
76   *Quartier sans soleil,* Kirsanoff, (1945?)
77   *Rappel immédiat,* Mathot, 24/39
78   *Règle du jeu, La,* Renoir, 27/39*
79   *Remorques,* Grémillon, 48/41*
80   *Sans lendemain,* Ophüls, 12/40*
81   *Saturnin,* or *Saturnin de Marseille,* Noé, 2/41
82   *Sérénade,* Boyer, 9/40
83   *Sidi-Brahim,* Didier, (1945?)
84   *Sixième Étage,* Cloche, 22/41
85   *Sur le plancher des vaches,* or *Le Plancher des vaches,* Ducis, 7/40*
86   *Tempête,* Bernard-Deschamps, 14/40 #

87   *Tourbillon de Paris,* Diamant-Berger, 49/39*
88   *Tradition de minuit, La,* Richebé, 16/39*
89   *Trois tambours, Les,* or *Vive la nation,* Canonge, 51/39
90   *Une main a frappé,* Roudès, 30/39
91   *Veau gras, Le,* Poligny, 15/39 #
92   *Vous seule que j'aime,* Fescourt, 26/39
93   *Yamilé sous les cèdres,* Espinay, 22/39

Note: After the declaration of war, the production of a further three feature films was begun before the end of 1939:

94   *Après Mein Kampf, mes crimes,* Ryder, 10/40
95   *Homme qui cherche la vérité, L',* Esway, 12/40*
96   *Roi des galéjeurs, Le,* Rivers, 17/40

SUPPLEMENTARY LIST OF RELEGATED FILMS

29s1	***Collier de la reine, Le,* Lekain & Ravel,**	
	42/29	**Sonore**
29s2	*Requin, Le,* Chomette, 11/30	Mostly sonore
29s3	*Trois Masques, Les,* Hugon, 42/29	Under 1 hour
30s1	*Adieu les copains,* Joannon	Silent, later dubbed; unpub?
30s2	*Âge d'or, L',* Buñuel, 49/30*	Silent, later partly sonore
30s3	*Au pays des basques,* Champreux	Doc, not narrative
30s4	*Au pays des buveurs de sang,* Gourgaud	Doc, not narrative
30s5	*Chiqué,* Colombier, 14/30	Under 1 hour
30s6	*Crime de Sylvestre Bonnard, Le,*	
	Berthomieu, 31/5	Silent, later partly sonore?
30s7	*Étrange Fiancée, L',* Pallu	Sonore, later dubbed; unpub?
30s8	*Fumées,* Benoît & Jaeger-Schmidt, 13/32	Silent, later dubbed; unpub?
30s9	*Je t'adore, mais pourquoi?,* Colombier, 4/31	Under 1 hour
30s10	*Maison jaune de Rio, La,*	
	Grüne & Péguy, 12/31	Under 1 hour
30s11	*Méphisto,* Debain & Winter, 29/31	Serial in 4 episodes
30s12	*Paramount en parade,* de Rochefort	Compilation
30s13	*Poignard malais, Le,* Goupillières, 5/31	Under 1 hour
30s14	*Saltimbanques, Les,* Jaquelux & Land, 29/30	Sonore only
30s15	*Servante, La,* Choux, 17/31	Silent, later sonorized
30s16	*Sirocco,* Sévérac, 51/31	Arabic, with titles
30s17	*Une femme a menti,* Rochefort, 27/30	Under 1 hour?
31s1	*Boudoir diplomatique, Le,* de Sano	No trace
31s2	*Chanson du lin, La,* Monca	Under 1 hour?
31s3	*Chant du Hoggar, Le,* Ichac	Primarily documentary

31s4	*Croisière jaune, La,* Poirier & Sauvage	Documentary
31s5	*Fille du Bouif, La,* Bussi	Under 1 hour?
31s6	*Je serai seule après minuit,* Baroncelli	Under 1 hour
31s7	*Roi du camembert, Le,* Mourre	Under 1 hour
31s8	*Y'en a pas deux comme Angélique,* Lion	Under 1 hour?
32s1	*Affaire est dans le sac, L',* Prévert*	Under 1 hour
32s2	*Bidon d'or, Le,* Christian-Jaque	Under 1 hour
32s3	*Brumes de Paris,* Sollin	Under 1 hour
32s4	*Carillon de la liberté, Le,* Roudès	Belgian
32s5	*Colette et son mari,* Pellenc	Under 1 hour
32s6	*Cure sentimentale, La,* Dianville & Weill	No trace
32s7	*Daïnah la métisse,* Grémillon, 34/32	Under 1 hour
32s8	*Léon . . . tout court,* Francis, 13/33	Under 1 hour
33s1	<u>*Amour qu'il faut aux femmes, L',*</u> Trotz, 9/34	Didactic, not narrative
33s2	*Grillon du foyer, Le,* Boudrioz	Never rev or released?
33s3	*Indésirable, L',* Ruelle	Under 1 hour
33s4	*Indiens nos frères, Les,* Tatayna	Doc, not narrative
33s5	*Jofroi,* Pagnol, 3/34*	Under 1 hour
33s6	*Nous les mères,* del Torres, 41/33	Dubbed
33s7	*Voleur, Le,* Tourneur, 49/33	1 hour or less
33s8	*Zéro de conduite,* Vigo, 44/34*	Under 1 hour
34s1	*Hommes de la côte, Les,* Pellenc	Never made?
34s2	*Malade imaginaire, Le,* Jaquelux	Under 1 hour
34s3	*Voilà Montmartre,* Capellani, 19/34	Revue, not narrative
35s1	*Promesses,* Delacroix	Never made?
35s2	*Marius et Olive à Paris,* J. Epstein	Under 1 hour (Le Film #5)
35s3	*Napoléon Bonaparte,* Gance, 19/35	Silent; later part dialogue
36s1	*Une partie de campagne,* Renoir*	Under 1 hour
36s2	*Vie est à nous, La,* Renoir*	Didactic, not narrative
37s1	*Arabie interdite,* Clément	Doc, not narrative
37s2	*Mystère du 421, Le,* Simons	Belgian
37s3	*Un coup de rouge,* Roudès, 47/37	Music-hall sketches
38s1	*Jeannette Bourgogne,* Gourguet	Didactic; never released?
38s2	*Mon père et mon papa,* Schoukens	Belgian
38s3	*Sommes-nous défendus?,* Loubignac, 45/38	Documentary/propaganda
38s4	*Vie des artistes, La,* Bernard-Roland, 36/38	Under 1 hour, biog sketches
39s1	*Adieu Vienne,* Sévérac	Never reviewed or released?
39s2	*Bach en correctionnelle,* Wulschleger, 50/40?	Compilation. Prod Dec 1939
39s3	*Boutique aux illusions, La,* Sévérac, 16/39	Compilation of silents
39s4	*Chantons quand même,* Caron, 9/40	Under 1 hour. Prod Nov 1939

39s5	*Courrier d'Asie,* Gilbert & Marcilly, 10/41	Documentary/propaganda
39s6	*Espoir,* Malraux, 25/45*	Spanish dialogue
39s7	*France est un empire, La,* Barrois et al.	Primarily propaganda
39s8	*Gardons notre sourire,* Schoukens	Belgian
39s9	*Monde en armes, Le,* Oser, 23/39	Propaganda montage
39s10	*Monsieur Bossemans,* Schoukens, 20/39	Belgian

SECTION THREE:
FILMS GIVEN THE BENEFIT OF THE DOUBT

The following films have been left in the main filmography because the evidence against them was not conclusive, or was conflicting. All were completed and either reviewed by the trade or passed by the censor.

29/1	*Mon béguin*	Possibly only sonorized
30/14	*Bodega, La*	Possibly only or mainly sonorized, later full sound
30/15	*Caïn*	Little dialogue, but deliberately so?
30/16	*Capitaine jaune, Le*	Possibly only or primarily sonorized
30/45	*Jimmy*	Different sources give 58 and 61 minutes
30/53	*Miracle des loups, Le,*	Possibly shot silent, later (partly?) sonorized
30/54	*Mon ami Victor*	Possibly only sonorized. Possibly under 1 hour
30/67	*Princes de la cravache, Les*	Never released?
30/71	*Razzia*	Not 100% talkie?
31/22	*Calais-Douvres*	Either 1,360 or 2,360 m.
31/54	*Ensorcellement de Séville, L'*	Pinel claims 1936 release, unconfirmed
31/64	*Gloria*	Early record says 800m, Chirat says 85 min
31/76	*Magie moderne*	Just over one hour?
31/106	*Pour un soir*	Just over one hour?
31/128	*Sur la voie du bonheur*	No recorded screening
31/140	*Une histoire entre mille*	Possibly released 1936. Just one hour?
31/147	*Verdun, souvenirs d'histoire*	Silent film with voice over?
31/148	*Vouloir*	No recorded screening. Only sonorized?
32/2	*Adhémar Lampiot,*	No recorded screening
32/99	*Or des mers, L',*	Either 1,400 or 2,500 m. Mainly sonorized?
33/24	*C'était un musicien*	Under one hour?
33/76	*Liebelei*	Partially dubbed
35/23	*Coqueluche de ces dames, La*	No recorded screening, but in a 1940 catalogue
35/108	*Tampon du colonel, Le,*	Just over one hour?
36/29	*Course à la vertu, La,*	No recorded screening

36/41	*Faiseur, Le*	Just over one hour?
36/43	*Femmes*	No recorded screening, but in a 1945 catalogue. At base a Polish film
36/70	*Madone de l'Atlantique, La*	60 or 85 min; no recorded screening, but in a 1941 catalogue
36/88	*Mystérieuse Lady, La*	No recorded screening
36/131	*Trois dans un moulin*	No recorded screening
37/51	*Fraudeur, Le*	No recorded screening
37/109	*Temps des cerises, Le*	No commercial screening (in the thirties)?
39/31	*Empreinte du dieu, L',*	Completed with modifications in 1940
39/15	*Chemin de l'honneur, Le*	No recorded screening
39/52	*Mahlia la métisse*	Only exteriors shot in 1939; completed 1942
39/56	*Monsieur le Maire*	Alsace dialect; no recorded screening (in Paris)
39/70	*Paris–New York*	Completed with modifications in 1940

NOTES

INTRODUCTION

1. J.-P. Jeancolas, *15 ans d'années trente* (Paris: Stock, 1983).
2. F. Garçon, *De Blum à Pétain: cinéma et société française, 1936–1944* (Paris: Les Éditions du Cerf, 1984).
3. Geneviève Sellier, "Les non moins fantastiques années 30," in "Théories du cinéma aujourd'hui," *CinémAction* (1988): 109.
4. Colin Crisp, *The Classic French Cinema, 1930–1960* (Bloomington and Indianapolis: Indiana University Press, 1993).
5. For figures cited in this paragraph, see J.-P. Jeancolas, "French Cinema of the 1930s and Its Sociological Handicaps," in Ginette Vincendeau and Keith Reader (eds.), *La Vie est à nous!*, NFT Dossier no. 3 (London: BFI, 1986), p. 69. See also R. Borde, *Positif,* no. 296 (1985), where the survey results were reported.
6. Crisp, *The Classic French Cinema,* pp. 224–226.
7. Ibid., pp. 359–366.
8. Will Wright, *Sixguns and Society* (Berkeley, Los Angeles, and London: University of California Press, 1975), pp. 14–15.
9. Vladimir Propp, *Morphology of the Folktale* (Austin and London: University of Texas Press, 1968).
10. *La Cinématographie Française,* no. 616 (23 Aug. 1930).
11. *Ciné Miroir* (1929): 291.
12. *Ciné Miroir* (1929): 563.
13. *Cinémonde* (1931): 595.
14. Garçon, *De Blum à Pétain,* pp. 121–122.
15. Aspects of this analysis of the opening scenes of *La Règle du jeu* were first presented in a paper that I gave at the conference "A Century of Cinema" at Melbourne University, April 1995.
16. Ginette Vincendeau, "The Popular Cinema of the Popular Front," in Vincendeau and Reader, *La Vie est à nous!*
17. Michèle Lagny et al., *Générique des années 30* (Vincennes: Presses Universitaires de Vincennes, 1986).
18. Noël Burch and Geneviève Sellier, *La Drôle de guerre des sexes du cinéma français: 1930–1956* (Paris: Nathan, 1996).
19. Jeancolas, *15 ans d'années trente.*
20. Marc Ferro, "Introduction," in Garçon, *De Blum à Pétain,* p. 10.
21. Geneviève Guillaume-Grimaud, *Le Cinéma du Front Populaire* (Paris: Lherminier, 1986).
22. Raymond Chirat, *Cinéma des années 30* (Paris: Hatier, 1983).

6. ART AND TRANSCENDENCE

1. Colin Crisp, *The Classic French Cinema, 1930–1960* (Bloomington and Indianapolis: Indiana University Press, 1993).

2. Ibid., p. 400.

7. CINEMATIC GENRES IN FRANCE

1. *La Cinématographie Française,* no. 620 (20 Sept. 1930).

2. *Ciné Miroir* (1929): 171.

3. *Revue du Cinéma,* no. 10 (1930).

4. *Cinémonde* (1932): 125.

5. *Positif,* no. 12.

6. *Le Film Français,* no. 14 (9 Mar. 1945); *Image et Son,* no. 108 (Jan. 1958).

7. *Cinéma 59,* no. 39 (Aug.–Sept. 1959).

8. See, for instance, Hugh Gray (ed. and transl.), *What Is Cinema?* (Berkeley, Los Angeles, and London: University of California Press, 1974), vol. 1, p. 29.

9. Charles Ford, *On tourne lundi* (Paris: Jean Vigneau, 1947), p. 71.

10. See, for instance, Georges Sadoul, *Le Cinéma français* (1890–1962) (Paris: Flammarion, 1962).

11. Georges Sadoul, *Le Cinéma* (Paris: La Bibliothèque Française, 1948).

12. Georges Sadoul, *Les Merveilles du cinéma* (Paris: Les Éditeurs Français Réunis, 1957), p. 168.

13. Léon Moussinac, *Panoramique du cinéma* (Paris: Sans Pareil, 1929; reprint, 1946).

14. Léon Moussinac, *L'Âge Ingrat du Cinéma* (Paris: Sagittaire, 1946).

15. René Jeanne and Charles Ford, *Histoire encyclopédique du cinéma* (Paris: Robert Laffont, 1958), pp. 381–412.

16. Georges Charensol, *Renaissance du Cinéma Français* (Paris: Sagittaire, 1946).

17. Pierre Leprohon, *Présences contemporaines* (Paris: Debresse, 1957).

18. Georges Charensol, "Le Film parlant (1930–1948)," in Denis Marion (ed.), *Le Cinéma par ceux qui le font* (Paris: Arthème Fayard, 1949), p. 65.

19. Claude Mauriac, *Amour du cinéma* (Paris: Albin Michel, 1954).

20. Roger Régent, *Cinéma de France* (Paris: Bellefaye, 1948).

21. Louis Chauvet, *Le Porte-Plume et la caméra* (Paris: Flammarion, 1950), pp. 5 and 98.

22. Jos Roger, *Grammaire du cinéma* (Bruxelles et Paris: EUF, 1956), pp. 147–149.

23. In Henri Agel et al., *Sept ans de cinéma français* (Paris: Cerf, 1953), p. 38.

24. Ford, *On tourne lundi.*

25. Georges Sadoul, "Les Ennemis du cinéma," in *Cinéma d'aujourd'hui* (Paris and Geneva: Trois Collines, 1945), p. 42.

26. Charles Spaak, "Le Scénario" in Marion, *Le Cinéma par ceux qui le font,* p. 113.

27. Ibid., p. 115.

28. P. Leprohon, *L'Exotisme et le cinéma* (Paris: Les Éditions J. Susse, 1945).

29. C. Pornon, *Le Rêve et le fantastique* (Paris: La Nef de Paris, 1959).

30. Georges Altman, *Ça, c'est du cinéma* (Paris: Les Revues, 1931).

31. J. Benoît-Lévy, *Les Grandes Missions du cinéma* (Montréal: Pariseau, 1945).

32. H. Agel and G. Agel, *Précis d'initiation au cinéma* (Paris: L'École, 1957).

33. Peter Bächlin, *Histoire économique du cinéma* (Paris: La Nouvelle Édition, 1947), p. 180.

34. Benoît-Lévy, *Les Grandes Missions,* p. 26. Emphasis in original.

35. Ibid., p. 326.

36. Altman, *Ça, c'est du cinéma.* See chapter 3, "La vie au cinéma."

37. Ibid., p. 263. Emphasis in original.

38. Ibid., p. 85.

39. Jean Keim, *Un nouvel art: le cinéma sonore* (Paris: Albin Michel, 1947), p. 159.

40. Ibid., p. 178.

41. Ibid., p. 186.

42. Agel and Agel, *Précis d'initiation au cinéma,* pp. 18–20.

43. Ibid., p.167.

44. Ibid., pp. 168–170.

45. J. Rivette, "Six Characters in Search of Auteurs: A Discussion about the French Cinema," *Cahiers du Cinéma* 71 (May 1957), reprinted in Jim Hillier (ed.), *Cahiers du Cinéma: The 1950s* (Cambridge, Mass.: Harvard University Press, 1985), p. 32.

46. A. Bazin, "De la politique des auteurs," *Cahiers du Cinéma* 70 (Apr. 1957), reprinted in Hillier, *Cahiers du Cinéma,* p. 257.

47. Ibid.

48. Quoted in P. Duvillars, *Cinéma: mythologie du XXe siècle* (Paris: l'Hermite, 1950), p. 117.

49. André Malraux, *Esquisse d'une psychologie du cinéma.* Originally in *Verve* (1941), reprinted in Marcel L'Herbier (ed.), *Intelligence du Cinématographe* (Paris: Corréa, 1946).

50. Ibid., p. 383.

51. Ibid., p. 382

52. André Boll, *Le Cinéma et son histoire* (Paris: Sequana 1941), p. 95.

53. Quoted in Duvillars, *Cinéma,* p. 109.

54. Duvillars, *Cinéma,* p. 30.

55. Ibid., p. 49.

56. Ibid., p. 29.

57. Henri Agel, "Activité et passivité du spectateur," in É. Souriau (ed.), *L'Univers filmique* (Paris: Flammarion, 1953) p. 49.

58. Mauriac, *Amour du cinéma,* pp. 229 and 237.

59. Chauvet, *Porte-Plume,* p. 98.

60. Raymond Barkan, "Une mythologie du quotidien," *L'Âge Nouveau,* no. 93 (July 1955): 28.

61. Ibid., p. 34.

62. Roland Barthes, *Mythologies* (Paris: Seuil, 1957); originally published 1954–56 in the monthly *Les Lettres Nouvelles.*

63. Richard Abel (ed.), *French Film Theory and Criticism,* vol. 1: *1907–1939,* vol. 2: *1929–1939* (Princeton: Princeton University Press, 1988).

64. Keim, *Un nouvel art,* p. 190.

65. Ibid., p. 199.

66. *Le Film Français,* no. 159, special issue, Overview of 1947 (1947): 75.

67. Keim, *Un nouvel art,* p. 194.

68. Benoît-Lévy, *Les Grandes Missions,* pp. 329–331.

69. *La Cinématographie Française,* no. 778 (30 Sept. 1933).

70. *La Cinématographie Française,* no. 725 (1932).

71. Georges Charensol, *Quarante ans de cinéma* (Paris: Sagittaire, 1935), p. 197.

72. Michel Gorel, *Le Monde truqué* (Paris: Nilsson, 1931), p. 179.

73. Ibid., p. 28.

74. Ibid., pp. 94–96.

75. *La Cinématographie Française*, no. 945 (12 Dec. 1936).

76. *Cinéopse*, no. 223 (Mar. 1938), p. 59.

77. *Ciné Miroir*, no. 863 (4 Nov. 1947).

78. J. Doniol-Valcroze, "De l'avant-garde," in Agel et al., *Sept ans*, pp. 7–25.

79. J.-L. Tallenay, "Les Français n'ont-ils pas la tête comique?" in Agel et al., *Sept ans*, pp. 51–52.

80. Mauriac, *Amour du cinéma*, p. 158.

81. Agel and Agel, *Précis d'initiation au cinéma*, pp. 189 et seq.

82. Étienne Fuzellier, "Le Comique cinématographique," *Âge Nouveau*, no. 93 (July 1955).

83. Quoted in Jacques Chabannes, *Les Coulisses du cinéma* (Paris: Hachette, 1959), p. 150.

84. *La Cinématographie Française*, no. 705 (1932); *Cinémonde* (1933): 359.

85. Marcel Carné, "Vingt ans de films policiers," *Cinémonde* (1932): 443.

86. *Ciné Miroir* (1934): 146.

87. Altman, *Ça, c'est du cinéma*, pp. 143 et seq.

88. *Cinéopse*, no. 221 (Jan. 1938); *La Cinématographie Française*, no. 1039 (Sept. 1938).

89. Léon Moussinac, "État du cinéma international," reprinted in Moussinac, *L'Âge Ingrat du Cinéma*, pp. 165–166.

90. *Cinémonde*, no. 74 (1930); *Cinémonde* (1931): 551; *Cinémagazine* (Mar. 1930); Alexandre Arnoux, *Du muet au parlant* (Paris: La Nouvelle Édition, 1946), p. 106; Keim, *Un nouvel art*, p. 188.

91. Altman, *Ça, c'est du cinéma*, pp. 115–143.

92. Ibid., pp. 130–131.

93. Ibid., p. 116.

94. Ibid., p. 119.

95. *Cinémonde*, no. 83 (1930).

96. *Cinémonde* (1932): 772.

97. *La Cinématographie Française*, no. 1188 (28 Dec. 1946): 75.

98. *Cinémonde* (1934): 890.

99. Roger Leenhardt, *Chroniques de cinéma* (Paris: Étoile, 1986), p. 135.

100. See Altman, *Ça, c'est du cinéma*, pp. 44–47.

101. Alexandre Arnoux, "Films historiques" (1938), reprinted in Arnoux, *Du muet au parlant*.

102. Keim, *Un nouvel art*, pp. 163–168.

103. Nino Frank, *Petit Cinéma sentimental* (Paris: La Nouvelle Édition, 1950), p. 180.

104. Altman, *Ça, c'est du cinéma*, pp. 43–48.

105. Leenhardt, *Chroniques de cinéma*, p. 24; originally in Esprit (Dec. 1934).

106. Keim, *Un nouvel art*, p. 200.

107. Lucie Derain, "La Satire à l'écran," *Cinémonde* (1934): 421.

108. *Image et son*, no. 106 (Nov. 1957): 17.

109. *Où va le cinéma français?* (Paris: Éditions Baudinières, n.d. [1937]), pp. 213, 358, 362.

110. Charensol, *Renaissance du cinéma français*, p. 205.

111. *L'Écran français*, no. 14 (3 Oct. 1945).

112. *Cinéma 59* (Aug.–Sept. 1959).

113. *Image et son*, no. 129 (Mar. 1960), p. 12.

114. Keim, *Un nouvel art*, pp. 139–140.

115. G. van Parys, "Le Musicien," in Marion, *Le Cinéma par ceux qui le font*, pp. 265–266.

116. *L'Écran français,* no. 14 (3 Oct. 1945).
117. Leprohon, *L'Exotisme et le cinéma,* p. 80.
118. Ibid., pp. 135–137.
119. Ibid., p. 144.
120. Ibid., p. 196.
121. Ibid., pp. 296–297.
122. Ibid., pp. 297–298.
123. Ibid., p. 13.
124. See *Ciné Miroir* (Jan. and Feb. 1929); *Revue du Cinéma,* no. 7 (1929); *Cinémonde* (1931): 595, 725.
125. *Cinéopse,* no. 149 (Jan. 1932), editorial.
126. *Cinémonde* (1933): 138.
127. *Cinémonde* (1932): 612.
128. Ibid.
129. Eva Elie, *Puissance du cinéma* (La Chaux-de-fonds: Aux Éditions des Nouveaux Cahiers, 1942).
130. Régent, *Cinéma de France,* p. 171.
131. *Le Film,* no. 35 (28 Feb. 1942), no. 56 (Jan. 1943); *Le Film Français,* no. 84 (9 June 1948).
132. *La Cinématographie Française,* no. 1188 (28 Dec. 1946): 113.
133. See Leprohon, *L'Exotisme et le cinéma,* chapter 5, especially pp. 100, 199, 209–214.
134. *Cinéopse,* no. 201 (May 1936): 89–91; cf. *Ciné Miroir* (1935): 82.
135. *Cinéopse,* no. 149 (Jan. 1932), no. 160 (Dec. 1932), no. 165 (May 1933).
136. *Cinéopse,* no. 210 (Feb. 1937), no. 213 (May 1937).
137. *Cinéopse,* no. 233 (Jan. 1939).
138. *Cinémonde* (1931): 40–41.
139. *Cinémonde* (1933): 142.
140. *Ciné Miroir* (1934): 102 (1936): 77 (1939): 3.
141. *La Cinématographie Française,* no. 912 (25 Apr. 1936), no. 946 (19 Dec. 1936).
142. *Ciné Miroir* (1935): 277 (1939): 243.
143. *Cinémonde* (1939): 147.
144. Leprohon, *L'Exotisme et le cinéma,* p. 204.
145. Ibid., p. 208.
146. *La Cinématographie Française,* no. 1188 (28 Dec. 1946): 113.
147. *Cinémonde,* no. 85 (1930).
148. *Cinémonde* (1931): 595.
149. Arcy-Hennery, *Destin du cinéma français* (Paris: Société Française d'Éditions Littéraires et Techniques, 1935), p. 135.
150. André Thérive, "Le populisme au cinéma," *Cinémonde* (1930): 203.
151. *Cinéopse,* no. 172 (Nov. 1933).
152. Franck Servais in *Cinémonde* (1931), p. 595.
153. *Ciné Miroir,* no. 457 (5 Jan. 1934).
154. *Pour Vous,* no. 248 (17 Aug 1933), no. 276 (1 Mar. 1934), no. 303 (6 Sept 1934), no. 342 (6 June 1934), no. 347 (11 July 1935), no. 370 (Christmas 1935).
155. *Pour Vous,* no. 342 (6 June 1935).
156. See, for instance, *Pour Vous,* no. 347 (11 July 1935).
157. *La Cinématographie Française,* no. 1039 (Sept 1938): 88–89.
158. Claude Bernier in *Ciné Miroir* (1939): 323.
159. Ibid.

160. *La Cinématographie Française,* no. 1066 (7 Apr. 1939).

161. Jean Epstein, *Écrits sur le cinéma* (Paris: Cinéma Club/Seghers, 1974), vol. 1, pp. 196, 223 (1929 and 1930 interviews).

162. Ibid., p. 237; originally published in *Pour Vous* (Apr.–May 1933).

163. *Cinéopse,* no. 233 (Jan. 1939): 20.

164. *Cinéopse,* no. 223 (Mar. 1938).

165. Leprohon, *Présences contemporaines,* pp. 231–237.

8. THE STARS IN THEIR (DIS)COURSES

Note: While every attempt has been made to refer the reader to relevant sources for the statements made in this chapter, many of those statements do not relate to single sources but to commonly repeated terms and phrases occurring in a number of different sources. In general, the most useful sources were *Ciné Miroir* (1929–1940, but not postwar), *Pour Vous, Ciné Mondial* (1940–44), *L'Écran Français* (1944–51), and *Cinémonde* (1951–1959, but not prewar).

1. *Pour Vous,* no. 59 (2 Jan. 1930).

2. *Pour Vous,* no. 89 (31 July 1930), no. 135 (18 June 1931), no. 150 (1 Oct. 1931), 77 (8 May 1930).

3. *Pour Vous,* no. 208 (10 Nov. 1932).

4. *Pour Vous,* no. 106 (27 Nov. 1930).

5. *Pour Vous,* no. 82 (12 June 1930).

6. *Pour Vous,* no. 121 (12 Mar. 1931).

7. *Pour Vous,* no. 169 (11 Feb. 1932).

8. *Ciné Miroir* (1935): 707.

9. *Pour Vous,* no. 370 (Christmas 1935).

10. *Pour Vous,* no. 78 (15 May 1930), no. 214 (22 Dec. 1932).

11. *Pour Vous,* no. 230 (13 Apr. 1933).

12. *Cinémonde,* no. 135 (1931): 135.

13. *Pour Vous,* no. 172 (3 Mar. 1932).

14. *Ciné Miroir* (1939): 19.

15. *Ciné Mondial,* no. 8 (26 Sept. 1941).

16. *Ciné Miroir* (1936): 35.

17. *Pour Vous,* no. 286 (10 May 1934).

18. *Pour Vous,* no. 89 (31 July 1930).

19. *Pour Vous,* no. 214 (22 Dec. 1932); see also no. 296 (19 June 1934).

20. *Ciné Miroir* (1931): 412; see also *Pour Vous,* no. 160 (10 Dec. 1931) on Pierre Ney.

21. *Ciné Miroir* (1934): 67; see also *Pour Vous,* no. 173 (10 Mar. 1932).

22. *Ciné Miroir* (1939): 387.

23. *Pour Vous,* no. 260 (9 Nov. 1933).

24. *Ciné Miroir* (1934): 134.

25. *Pour Vous,* no. 157 (19 Nov. 1931).

26. *Ciné Miroir* (1931): 395.

27. *Ciné Miroir,* no. 306 (12 Feb. 1931).

28. *Ciné Miroir* (1939): 163.

29. *Ciné Mondial,* no. 82 (1943).

30. *Ciné Miroir* (1936): 67.

31. *Pour Vous,* no. 180 (28 Apr. 1932).

32. *Ciné Miroir* (1936): 6.

33. *Pour Vous,* no. 329 (7 Mar. 1935).

34. *Ciné Miroir* (1938): 478.

35. *Ciné Miroir* (1936): 6.

36. *Pour Vous,* no. 213 (15 Dec. 1932).

37. *Ciné Miroir* (1937): 299.

38. *Ciné Miroir* (1938): 443.

39. *Ciné Miroir* (1937): 635.

40. See *Ciné Miroir* (1938): 443.

41. *Pour Vous,* no. 275 (22 Feb. 1934).

42. *Pour Vous,* no. 271 (25 Jan. 1934).

43. *Ciné Miroir* (1934): 67.

44. *Ciné Miroir* (1936): 534.

45. *Ciné Miroir* (1935): 251.

46. *Ciné Miroir* (1935): 611.

47. *Ciné Miroir* (1936): 374.

48. *Ciné Miroir* (1936): 451.

49. *Ciné Miroir* (1936): 646.

50. *Ciné Miroir* (1936): 654

51. *Ciné Miroir* (1937): 587.

52. *Pour Vous,* no. 311 (1 Nov. 1934).

53. *Pour Vous,* no. 340 (23 May 1935).

54. *Ciné Miroir*—in August 1939 (!).

55. *Ciné Miroir* (22 Mar. 1940).

56. *Ciné Miroir* (Apr. 1940).

57. *Ciné Miroir* (1934): 67.

58. *Ciné Miroir* (1934): 19 (1935): 62.

59. *Cinémonde* (1930): 203.

60. *Cinémonde* (1931): 40–41; see also *Cinémonde* (1933): 170–172.

61. *Ciné Miroir* (1931): 123.

62. *Cinéopse,* no. 201 (May 1936): 89–91; see also *Ciné Miroir* (1932): 827 (1933): 170; *La Cinématographie Française,* no. 1020 (1938).

63. *Cinéopse,* no. 160 (Dec. 1932).

64. *Cinémonde* (1933): 172.

65. *Cinéopse,* no. 210 (Feb. 1937).

66. *Cinéopse,* no. 233 (Jan. 1939): 20.

67. *Ciné Miroir* (1936): 770.

68. *Ciné Miroir,* no. 769 (29 Dec. 1939): 834.

69. "Le Redressement moral du pays," *La Cinématographie Française,* no. 1043 (28 Oct. 1938).

70. Ibid.

71. See *Ciné Miroir* (1939): 3, 66, 147, 163, 243, 354, 834.

72. *Ciné Miroir* (1939): 147.

73. *La Cinématographie Française,* no. 1093–94 (14–21 Oct. 1939).

74. *Ciné Miroir* (1938): 195.

75. *Pour Vous,* no. 97 (25 Sept. 1930).

76. *Pour Vous,* no. 157 (19 Nov. 1931).

77. *Ciné Miroir* (1938): 411.

78. *Pour Vous,* no. 217 (12 Jan. 1933).

79. *Ciné Miroir* (1936): 614 (1937): 283.

80. *Ciné Miroir* (1938): 52.

81. *Ciné Miroir* (1939): 675.

82. *Pour Vous,* no. 125 (9 Apr. 1931); see also *Pour Vous,* no. 70 (20 Mar. 1930).
83. *Pour Vous,* no. 145 (27 Aug. 1931).
84. *Ciné Mondial,* no. 58 (2 Oct. 1942), no. 64 (13 Nov. 1942).
85. *Ciné Mondial,* no. 86 (23 Apr. 1943).
86. *Ciné Miroir* (1939): 115.
87. *Ciné Miroir* (1939): 675.
88. See, for instance, *Pour Vous,* no. 306 (27 Sept. 1934), on Françoise Rosay.
89. *Ciné Miroir* (1939): 115.
90. *Ciné Miroir* (1939): 226–227.
91. *Ciné Miroir* (1939): 579.
92. See, for instance, *Ciné Mondial,* no. 3 (22 Aug. 1941), on Ducaux; *Ciné Mondial,* no. 16 (21 Nov. 1941), on Arletty; *Ciné Mondial,* no. 59 (9 Oct. 1941), on Morlay and Darrieux; *Ciné Mondial,* nos. 135–136 (14–21 Apr. 1944), on Presle.
93. *Ciné Miroir* (1929): 691 ("Quel est le jeune premier que vous préférez, et pour quelles raisons?"), 724 (results).
94. *Ciné Miroir* (1933): 195.
95. *Ciné Miroir* (1933): 802.
96. *La Cinématographie Française,* no. 847 (26 Jan. 1935), reporting on a *Dépêche de Toulouse* survey.
97. *Ciné Miroir* (1934): 802.
98. *Pour Vous,* Nos. 355–360 (5 Sept. to 10 Oct. 1935).
99. *Ciné Miroir* (1935): 630; see also *Ciné Miroir* (1937): 115.
100. André Malraux, "Esquisse d'une psychologie du cinéma," in Marcel L'Herbier (ed.), *Intelligence du Cinématographe* (Paris: Corréa, 1946), pp. 382 et seq.
101. *L'Écran Français,* no. 223 (17 Oct. 1949).
102. *Radio-Cinéma-Télévision* (1 Oct. 1950).
103. André Bazin, "Le Jour se lève," in Jacques Chevallier and Max Egly (eds.), *Regards neufs sur le cinéma* (Paris: Seuil, 1956) (originally written 1947), p. 162.
104. P. Duvillars, *Cinéma: mythologie du XXᵉ siècle* (Paris: l'Hermite, 1950), pp. 31–39 and 67–75. See also Raymond Barkan, "Une mythologie du quotidien," *L'Âge Nouveau,* no. 93 (July 1955): 29.
105. Claude Mauriac, "Jean Gabin, ou la mort d'un mythe," in Claude Mauriac, *Amour du cinéma* (Paris: Albin Michel, 1954), pp. 229 et seq.
106. *Ciné Miroir* (1938): 283.
107. *Ciné Miroir* (1939): 403.
108. Régent, *Cinéma de France,* p. 36.
109. Duvillars, *Cinéma mythologie du XXᵉ siècle,* pp. 52–53.
110. *Cinémonde* (24 Nov. 1951).

9. BOX OFFICE SUCCESS IN THE THIRTIES

1. Ginette Vincendeau, "The Popular Cinema of the Popular Front," in Ginette Vincendeau and Keith Reader (eds.), *La Vie est à nous,* NFT Dossier no. 3 (London: BFI, 1986), p. 75.
2. René Bonnell, *Le Cinéma exploité* (Paris: Éditions du Seuil, 1978), p. 32.
3. *Cinéopse,* no. 149 (Jan. 1932), no. 155 (July 1932), no. 161 (Jan. 1933).
4. Vincendeau and Reader, *La Vie est à nous,* p. 75.
5. See reports in *La Cinématographie Française* (Dec. 1957 special issue), *La Cinématographie Française,* no. 1768 (Festival Special 1958), and *Cinéma 58,* no. 31 (Nov. 1958).

6. Bonnell, *Le Cinéma exploité*, p. 52. The surveys assume that it was more of a working-class entertainment before this.

7. *Cinéma 58*, no. 31 (Nov. 1958).

8. Bonnell, *Le Cinéma exploité*, p. 47.

9. *Ciné Mondial*, no. 15 (14 Nov. 1941).

10. Roger Richebé, *Au-delà de l'écran* (Monaco: Pastorelly, 1977); P. Braunberger, *Cinémamémoires* (Paris: Centre G. Pompidou, 1987).

11. See *La Cinématographie Française*, no. 622 (4 Oct. 1930); no. 623 (11 Oct. 1930), no. 632 (13 Dec. 1930).

12. *La Cinématographie Française*, no. 642 (21 Feb. 1931).

13. *La Cinématographie Française*, no. 794 (20 Jan. 1934).

14. *La Cinématographie Française*, no. 869 (29 June 1935).

15. See, for instance, *Cinéopse*, no. 205 (Sept. 1936): 171–172.

16. See, for instance, *La Cinématographie Française*, no. 817 (30 June 1934), no. 830 (20 Sept. 1934), and particularly no. 842/43 (22–29 Dec. 1934).

17. *La Cinématographie Française*, no. 895 (28 Dec. 1935), editorial. See also *La Cinématographie Française*, no. 882 (29 Sept. 1935).

18. See *Cinéopse*, no. 219 (Nov. 1937); *La Cinématographie Française*, no. 973 (25 June 1937), editorial, no. 1012 (25 Mar. 1938), editorial.

19. *La Cinématographie Française*, no. 836 (10 Nov. 1934).

20. *La Cinématographie Française*, no. 947 (20 Dec. 1936), no. 964 (23 Apr. 1937).

21. *La Cinématographie Française* (June 1933).

22. *La Cinématographie Française*, no. 842/843 (22–29 Dec. 1934).

23. *La Cinématographie Française*, no. 985 (17 Sept. 1937).

24. *Le Film*, no. 16 (24 May 1941).

25. *La Cinématographie Française*, no. 798 (17 Feb. 1934).

26. *La Cinématographie Française*, no. 1039 (30 Sept. 1938).

27. "La Construction des salles devient une dangereuse aberration," *La Cinématographie Française*, no. 1000 (31 Dec. 1937).

28. *La Cinématographie Française*, no. 1040 (7 Oct. 1938).

29. See *La Cinématographie Française*, no. 1048 (2 Dec. 1938) and no. 1075 (10 June 1939).

30. *See La Cinématographie Française*, no. 699 (26 Mar. 1932) for an account of these processes.

31. *La Cinématographie Française*, no. 575 (9 Nov. 1929).

32. See *Cinéopse*, no. 200 (Apr. 1936); *La Cinématographie Française*, no. 907 (21 Mar. 1936), for an account of the case.

33. *Où va le cinéma français?* (Paris: Éditions Baudinières, n.d. [1937]), p. 306.

34. Ibid., p. 393.

35. *Ciné Mondial*, no. 43 (19 June 1942).

36. See *Ciné Mondial*, nos. 151–153 (4–11 Aug. 1944).

37. See *La Cinématographie Française*, no. 1677 (7 July 1956).

38. *La Cinématographie Française*, no. 1459 (15 Mar. 1952).

39. J.-P. Jeancolas, *15 ans d'années trente* (Paris: Stock 1983), p. 13.

40. *La Cinématographie Française*, no. 996 (3 Dec. 1937).

41. *La Cinématographie Française*, no. 1012 (25 Mar. 1938).

42. *La Cinématographie Française*, no. 1032 (12 Aug. 1938).

43. *La Cinématographie Française*, no. 842/843 (22–29 Dec. 1934).

44. "L'Avenir appartient aux grands films," *La Cinématographie Française*, no. 1000 (31 Dec. 1937).

45. *La Cinématographie Française,* no. 1012 (25 Mar. 1938), no. 1039 (30 Sept. 1938).

46. See *La Cinématographie Française,* no. 1089 (23 Sept. 1939), no. 1090/92 (6 Oct. 1939), nos. 1093–94 (14–21 Oct. 1939), no. 1095–96 (28 Oct.–3 Nov. 1939), no. 1099 (25 Nov. 1939), no. 1101 (9 Dec. 1939), no. 1103 (23 Dec. 1939).

47. *La Cinématographie Française,* no. 1077 (24 June 1939).

48. Reported in *La Cinématographie Française,* no. 884 (12 Oct. 1935).

49. Tables reprinted from *Cinéma-Spectacle* in *La Cinématographie Française,* no. 795 (27 Jan. 1934).

50. *La Cinématographie Française,* no. 1449 (5 Jan. 1952).

10. CONCLUSION

1. *La Cinématographie Française,* no. 760 (27 May 1933).

FILMOGRAPHY

1. Vincent Pinel, *Filmographie des longs métrages sonores du cinéma français* (Paris: La Cinémathèque Française, 1985).

2. Raymond Chirat, *Catalogue des films français de long métrage: films sonores de fiction 1929–1939* (Brussels: Cinémathèque Royale de Belgique, 1975).

3. G. Sadoul, *Le Cinéma français, 1890–1962* (Paris: Flammarion, 1962).

BIBLIOGRAPHY

The aim of this bibliography is to begin to develop a list of all books on the cinema published in France and French-speaking countries between the years 1929 and 1939. It has not always been possible to discover all the bibliographic details.

1929

Arnoux, Alexandre. *Le Cinéma*. Paris: Crés, 1929.

Charensol, Georges. *Panorama du cinéma*. Paris: Sans-Pareil, 1929.

Coissac, Georges-Michel. *Les Coulisses du cinéma*. Paris: Paul Duval, 1929.

Florey, Robert. *Histoire du cinéma américain*. Paris, 1929.

Leloir, Maurice. *Cinq mois à Hollywood avec Douglas Fairbanks*. Paris: J. Peyronnet et cie, 1929.

Moussinac, Léon. *Panoramique du cinéma*. Paris: Sans-Pareil, 1929.

Prévost, Jean. *Polymnie*. Paris: É. Hazan, 1929.

Schwob, René. *Une mélodie silencieuse*. Paris: Grasset, 1929.

1930

Billecoque, G. *Régime fiscal du cinéma en France*. Montpellier: Canne, 1930.

Coissac, Georges-Michel. *Le Cinéma dans l'enseignement et l'éducation en France*. Paris: Le Tout-Cinéma, 1930.

(Collectif). *L'Art cinématographique*. Paris: Alcan, 1930.

Ducom, Jacques. *Le Cinématographe muet, sonore, parlant*. Paris: A. Michel, 1930.

Gance, Abel. *Prisme*. Paris: Gallimard, 1930.

Henri-Robert, J. *De la prise de vues à la projection*. Paris: Paul Montel, 1930.

Jeanne, René. *Tu seras star*. Paris: Nouvelle Société d'Éditions, 1930.

Marotte, P. *L'Application des droits d'auteurs et d'artistes aux œuvres cinématographiques et cinéphoniques*. Paris: Recueil Sirey, 1930.

Moris, R. *Le Cinéma: étude économique*. Montpellier: Canne, 1930.

1931

Altman, Georges. *Ça, c'est du cinéma*. Paris: Les Revues, 1931.

Coissac, Georges-Michel. *L'Évolution du cinématographe et la réalisation de quelques grands films*. Paris: Le Tout-Cinéma, 1931.

Falco, A. *Les Droits d'auteur et le film sonore dans la législation française.* Paris: Joute et Cie, 1931.

Gorel, Michel. *Le Monde truqué.* Paris: Nilsson, 1931.

Hemardinquer, Pierre. *Le Cinématographe sonore.* Paris: Librairie d'Enseignement Technique, 1931.

Jeanne, René. *Le Cinéma allemand.* Paris: Alcan, 1931.

Mathos, P. *Décors: du studio au plateau.* Paris, 1931.

Soupault, Philippe. *Charlot.* Paris: Plon, 1931.

1932

Coissac, Georges-Michel. *Le Cinéma au service de la civilisation et de la propagande.* Paris: Le Tout-Cinéma, 1932.

Fescourt, Henri (ed.). *Histoire des spectacles II: Cinéma.* Paris: Cygne, 1932 (sometimes given as 1934).

Fescourt, Henri (ed.). *Le Cinéma des origines à nos jours.* Paris: Cygne, 1932.

Jeanne, René. *Le Cinéma français.* Paris: Cygne, 1932.

Lapierre, Marcel. *Le Cinéma et la paix.* Paris: Valois, 1932.

Salmon, André. *Marlène Dietrich.* Paris: La Nouvelle Librairie Française, 1932.

1933

Chevanne, A. *L'Industrie du cinéma: le cinéma sonore.* Bordeaux: Delmas, 1933.

Mesguich, Félix. *Tours de manivelle.* Paris: Grasset, 1933.

Noë, Yvan. *L'Épicerie des rêves.* Paris: Baudinière, 1933.

Vellard, R. *Le Cinéma sonore et sa technique.* Paris: Étienne Chiron, 1933.

1934

Bancal, Jean. *La Censure cinématographique.* Paris: José Corti, 1934.

Berthomé, J. *Des droits d'auteur en matière de reproduction phonographique, cinématographique et radiophonique.* Nantes: Imprimeries des Presses de l'Ouest, 1934.

Félix, Jean. *Le Chemin du cinéma.* Paris: Édition film et technique, 1934.

Kossowski, A. *L'ABC de la technique du cinéma.* Paris: Chiron, 1934.

Lobel, Léopold et Dubois, M. *La Technique cinématographique.* Paris: E Dunod, 1934.

1935

Arcy-Hennery. *Destin du cinéma français.* Paris: Société Française d'Éditions Littéraires et Techniques, 1935.

Bardèche, Maurice et Brasillach, Robert. *Histoire du cinéma.* Paris: Denoël et Steele, 1935.

Charensol, Georges. *Quarante ans de cinéma.* Paris: Sagittaire, 1935.

Epstein, Jean. *Photogénie de l'impondérable.* Paris: Corymbe, 1935 (brief essays).

Lang, André. *Tiers de siècle.* Paris: Plon, 1935.

Leprohon, Pierre. *Charlot, ou la naissance d'un mythe.* Paris: Corymbe, 1935.

Mayer, C. *Aspects du droit d'auteur en matière cinématographique.* Paris: Librairie Technique et Économique, 1935.

1936

Cendrars, Blaise. *Hollywood, La Mecque du cinéma.* Paris: B. Grasset, 1936.

De Carmoy, Guy. *L'Industrie cinématographique en France.* 1936.

Ehrenbourg, Ilya. *Usines de rêves.* Paris: Gallimard, 1936.

Jamelot, Y. *La Censure des spectacles.* Paris: Éditions Jel, 1936.

Petsche, Maurice. *L'Industrie cinématographique.* 1936.

Ruskowski, A. *L'Oeuvre cinématographique et les droits d'auteur.* Paris: Recueil Sirey, 1936.

Vellard, R. *Le Cinéma sonore: théorie et pratique.* Paris: Dunod, 1936.

1937

Kessel, J. *Hollywood, ville mirage.* Paris: Gallimard, 1937.

Où va le cinéma français? (Report of the Renaitour enquiry). Paris: Baudinière, 1937.

Le Rôle intellectuel du cinéma. Paris: Cahiers de la Société des Nations, IICI, 1937.

1938

Braun-Larrieu. *Le Rôle social du cinéma.* Paris: Éditions du Cinéopse et de Ciné-France, 1938.

Naumberg, Nancy (ed.). *Silence, on tourne!* Paris: Payot, 1938.

De Rothschild, P. *Le Cinéma: les techniques au service de la pensée.* Paris: F. Alcan, 1938.

Vivié, Jean. *Le Cinéma d'amateur.* Paris: Cinéma Pour Tous, 1938.

1939

Arroy, J., and Reynaud, J-C. *Attention, on tourne.* Paris: Tallandier, 1939.

Jeannot, Fred. *Le Film de cinéma.* Paris: Étienne Chiron, 1939.

Lhermitte. *L'Image de notre corps.* Paris: Nouvelle Revue Critique, 1939.

Vincent, Carl. *Histoire de l'art cinématographique.* Bruxelles: Trident, 1939.

Watts, Stephen (ed.). *La Technique du film.* Paris: Payot, 1939.

INDEX

Page numbers in italics refer to tables or figures. All references to specific films are found in the separate Film Index.

Mongolia. *See* Asian characters and settings

Montage sequences, 152

Montand, Yves, 232

Montesquieu, C.-L. de Secondat, baron de, xxiv

Montherlant, H.-M.-J. Millon de, xxi

Montmartre/Pigalle (Paris), 36, 58, 65–66, 98, 340

Moral regeneration (character type), *248,* 258–61, 265, 346

Morand, Paul, xxiv

Moreno, Marguerite, 112

Morgan, Michèle: character type discourses and, 255; films of, 96, 117, 119, 127, 330; as mythic stereotype, 273–78; popularity of, 267, 270, 272

Morin, Edgar, 207–208

Morlay, Gaby, 257, 335

Morocco. *See* North African characters and settings

Mosjoukine, Ivan, 267, 271

Mother-son relationships, 19, 127–29

Mountain films, 197

Mourre, Antoine, 313

Moussinac, Léon, 204, 226

Murat, Jean: character type discourses and, xxii, 251–52, 256, 258, 261; films of, 126, 141, 152, 320; popularity of, 267–68, 271

Murder mysteries, 5, 35, 111, 140, 152, 209, 219, 244. *See also* Crime films; Detective films

Music and musicians: as artists, 166–67; background, xiii, 176; big bands and, 175–76, 336, 347; destiny represented by, 27–28, 30; identity and, 10–11; Negro, 175, 347; oppositions and, 77–78, 133, 176; singers and, xiii, 77–78, 90–91, 170–73, 340, 347

Musical comedies, 170, 204, 217, 223, 229, 231–33, 244, 335–36

Musset, Alfred de, xviii–xix

Mussolini, Benito, 237, 259

Mythology, modern. *See* French cinema, textual system of

National stereotypes, 31–71, 339–40; artistic culture and, 40, 44; erotic desire and, 39, 42–44; French civilization expansion and, 40, 45–51; functions of, 39–57; international conflict and, 51–57; nostalgia and, 50–51; Paris and the provinces as, 51, 57–68; political criticism and, 40–42

Nationalism, 51, *248,* 258–61, 265, 320

Nature: artists and, 133; character type discourse and, *248,* 255–57; exoticism and, 234; tramps and, 76; transcendence of, 196–200, 338; urban-rural conflicts and, 63, 67–68; working class and, 91–93. *See also* Open road settings

Navarro, Ramon, 267, 271

Negroes, 175, 347

Nightclubs, xiii, 64, 85, 101, 191, 340

Nobility, 10, 17, 22, 33–34, 72–74, 120

Noël-Noël, xxiii, 318, 348

Noguero, José, 252

Nord Films, 386

North African characters and settings, 33, 45, 48–51, 63, 98–99, 148

Nostalgia, 39, 50–51, 98–99, 159, 227

Ocean liners, 24

Oceania. *See* Asian characters and settings

Oedipal relationships, 19, 49, 113, 123–25, 127

Older man/woman–younger woman/man relationships, 113, 119–29, 154, 340–41

Open-air restaurants *(guinguette),* xiii, 67, 92–93, 199, 340

Open road settings, 12, 76–77, 103, 199, 340–41

Operettas, xiii, 170, 220

Ophüls, Max, 28, 183, 190, 316, 323

Oppositions, 342; of city/country, 62–68, 161, 173, 187, 199; of gender, 20, 45, 94–95, 171–73; of identity, 9; of masculinity, 132–35, 341; musical, 77–78, 133, 176; of nature/society, 199; of night/day, 199; of public celebration/private despair, xix, 73; of the real and the recorded, 181; of sincerity and glamour/money, 78–79, 101, 110–11, 341–42; of technical practices, xxiii; of true love, 136, 197

Orientals. *See* Asian characters and settings

Orphans or abandoned children, xiii, 5, 87–88, 131–32, 157, 340–41

Otherness, 34, 115, 117, 233–36

Outsiders, xxiv, 71, 141, 168, 346

Pabst, George, 42, 56, 85, 316

Pacific area characters and settings, 33–34, 79, 103, 148

FILM INDEX

The index includes films mentioned in the text regardless of country or date of production. The numbers in parentheses refer to the chronological Filmography.